PENG

THE LOS'

Brian Hanley is the author of *A*

IRA 1926–1936. Scott Millar is a journalist with the

The Lost Revolution

The Story of the Official IRA and the Workers' Party

BRIAN HANLEY
and **SCOTT MILLAR**

PENGUIN BOOKS

PENGUIN BOOKS

Published by the Penguin Group
Penguin Books Ltd, 80 Strand, London WC2R ORL, England
Penguin Group (USA) Inc., 375 Hudson Street, New York, New York 10014, USA
Penguin Group (Canada), 90 Eglinton Avenue East, Suite 700, Toronto, Ontario, Canada M4P 2Y3
(a division of Pearson Penguin Canada Inc.)
Penguin Ireland, 25 St Stephen's Green, Dublin 2, Ireland (a division of Penguin Books Ltd)
Penguin Group (Australia), 250 Camberwell Road, Camberwell, Victoria 3124, Australia
(a division of Pearson Australia Group Pty Ltd)
Penguin Books India Pvt Ltd, 11 Community Centre, Panchsheel Park, New Delhi – 110 017, India
Penguin Group (NZ), 67 Apollo Drive, Rosedale, North Shore 0632, New Zealand
(a division of Pearson New Zealand Ltd)
Penguin Books (South Africa) (Pty) Ltd, 24 Sturdee Avenue, Rosebank, Johannesburg 2196, South Africa

Penguin Books Ltd, Registered Offices: 80 Strand, London WC2R ORL, England

www.penguin.com

First published by Penguin Ireland 2009
Published in Penguin Books 2010

005

Copyright © Brian Hanley and Scott Millar, 2009
All rights reserved

The moral right of the authors has been asserted

Printed in England by Clays Ltd, St Ives plc

ISBN: 978-0-141-02845-3

www.greenpenguin.co.uk

In memory of Una Hanley 1944–1989

and

in memory of Diarmuid O'Leary 1976–1998

Contents

Contents

Prologue

The clapping and cheering died down and the throng around the bar went quiet as the stocky 71-year-old man mounted the stage. Restrained emotion was evident on his face as he gripped a handful of notes and prepared to begin his speech. Approximately 150 people had gathered in the basement hall of the Teachers' Club in Dublin's Parnell Square. Outside sleet fell on a cold November night. Inside the atmosphere was more akin to a family reunion than a political meeting. The mainly middle-aged audience warmly greeted performances of ballads that celebrated the struggle for Irish independence and international socialism.

Sean Garland, the president of the Workers' Party of Ireland, began his address. His speech was delivered without formality, in an unmistakably Dublin accent. Garland condemned his arrest, seven weeks previously in Belfast, on foot of a United States warrant accusing him of aiding the North Korean government of Kim Jong-il in an international multi-million 'super-dollar' counterfeiting scam. He praised the efforts of those gathered to bring attention to the arrest, which occurred on the eve of his party's annual conference. He berated the Police Service of Northern Ireland for doing the 'dirty work' of the United States Secret Service and the 'so-called neo-cons' who ruled that country. Warming to his theme, he denounced Tony Blair and Silvio Berlusconi as 'the willing lackeys' of George Bush's regime, which was set upon the domination of the world. He reminded the audience, who greeted his more intemperate remarks with claps and cheers, of the anti-imperialist struggles of the last 50 years that had pitted revolutionaries against the agents of the United States across the globe. In the process he dismissed the 'so-called new democracies' of the former Eastern Bloc for their subservience to the US and their complicity in the secret torture prisons of the CIA.

Closing his speech, Garland outlined the career of late US civil rights lawyer Arthur Kinoy, who had defended those accused of communist sympathies in the 1950s, including Ethel and Julius Rosenberg, executed in 1953 for passing US nuclear secrets to the USSR. Garland quoted from a speech of Kinoy's: 'I will never quit. I am old and small, but I will not stop because I know what I am doing and the others do not. And I believe in what I am doing and the others believe in nothing and fear everything.' Garland added that 'this statement stands as testimony to all those who have gone before us throughout the world who have lived their lives by the principles of Arthur Kinoy and to those who continue his and our struggle today. We can do no better than to follow the example of our fellow comrade US citizen Arthur Kinoy.' Garland then left the stage to cheers and clenched-fist salutes.

Initially organized as a folk concert to raise funds for the Stop the Extradition of Sean Garland campaign, the event had taken on a more celebratory air since Garland had travelled south of the border on the grounds that he required medical tests, and then announced that he would not be returning to Belfast for an extradition hearing, claiming that he would not receive a fair trial. Instead he declared that he would place himself 'under the protection of my own government and my country's constitution which will guarantee me basic human rights and freedoms'. In the process he forfeited £30,000 in bail.

The US indictment outlined a case officially titled 'The United States of America v Sean Garland, aka The Man With The Hat'. US agencies claimed that they had evidence of the central role the elderly Irishman played in an attempt to undermine the US economy. The indictment also identified Garland as Chief of Staff of the Official Irish Republican Army. It alleged a conspiracy involving former KGB agents, the North Korean secret service, British criminals and members of the Official IRA. Garland's network was said to have distributed $29 million worth of high-quality forged $100 bills that had been printed in a secret location in North Korea. According to the indictment, the US authorities had first become aware of a possible Irish connection in the early 1990s, when Irish banks had stopped handling over-the-counter transactions of $100 bills because of the number of forged notes in circulation.

The people among whom Garland circulated following his speech were not concerned by these accusations. They were in the main the loyal remnants of a party that had once aspired to political power in Ireland. These men and women, unlike many in a country struggling to come to terms with the aspirations brought about by a dramatic economic boom, took pride in the designation 'working class'. No matter how small and politically obsolete the Workers' Party of 2005 appeared, for the faithful few gathered in this hall they were the true inheritors of the Irish revolutionary tradition stretching back to the United Irishmen in 1798 and continuing on through the IRA that fought against British rule after 1916.

Like a number of his comrades gathered in Parnell Square that night, Sean Garland was a child of north Dublin. Born in 1934, he was raised in one room of a run-down tenement at 7 Belvedere Place as one of nine children, some of whom died in childhood. He was educated by the Christian Brothers, then worked as a messenger boy and a bar help. He joined the IRA in June 1953 after making contact with them through the *United Irishman* newspaper. Like most of his comrades, Garland had joined the republican movement driven by a belief that Ireland's greatest ill was partition. Stencilled slogans on the dilapidated walls of Dublin declared 'Freedom calls: join the IRA', while songs recounting the glories of the patriot dead were sung in pubs and learned by children. To 'remove the border and unite the country' was, Garland recalls, the only aim.

Between 1956 and 1962 Garland and his IRA comrades had attempted to achieve this aim, in the so-called Border Campaign, which ended with an order to dump arms in February 1962. That order was to be the starting point of a political odyssey for Garland

and for Tomás Mac Giolla, who became president of Sinn Féin in that year. Mac Giolla would serve on the IRA Army Council with Garland during the 1960s, and side with him in 1969 when the republican movement split into Official and Provisional wings. As Garland sat beside the 81-year-old Mac Giolla in the Teachers' Club, they may have dwelt on memories of comrades from times past as the band struck up 'Sean South'. Garland sat quietly as many in the crowd joined in with the chorus of the song that recalled that day in January 1957 when an IRA column of fourteen men under Garland's command attacked an RUC barracks in Brookeborough, County Fermanagh. The raid left Sean South and Fergal O'Hanlon dead, and Garland, among others, badly injured. From the jaws of this defeat the republican movement, as it had done many times before, drew a moral victory. Outpourings of nationalist sentiment at the young men's deaths resulted in thousands of people lining the streets for South's funeral cortège and for a time restored the IRA's position as idealistic heroes in the eyes of many. The raid also consolidated Garland's position as a man of action within the IRA.

In June 1989, when the Workers' Party had won seven Dáil seats and its president Proinsias De Rossa had topped the poll for the European Parliament in Dublin, Garland had been the party's general secretary. But within three years the party had torn itself apart in a bitter split. Hence many of Garland's former party colleagues were not present that November night. These included the then Labour Party leader Pat Rabbitte and his colleagues Liz McManus, Joe Sherlock, Eamon Gilmore and Kathleen Lynch as well as MEP Proinsias De Rossa. Also absent were the numerous former members of the party in senior positions in the trade unions, the media, academe, the judiciary and the state sector on both sides of the border.

Of the TDs who had once represented the Workers' Party only Mac Giolla was present, accompanied by his wife May, herself a republican activist since the 1940s. They sat beside Garland and his wife Mary, as the night's entertainment neared its end with 'The Red Flag'. The juxtaposition of the socialist anthem with a final rendition of 'Amhrán na bhFiann', the Irish national anthem, may have caused Garland and Mac Giolla to ponder the political journey they and their colleagues had made over the decades. The story of that journey is told in this book for the first time. It encompasses armed insurrection, several bitter splits, and the development of the most successful radical political grouping in the Republic of Ireland in recent decades – a party that would play a large part in the death of irredentist ideology in the South and stand for unity between Catholics and Protestants in Northern Ireland's working class as they teetered on the brink of civil war. The movement served as the training ground for much of the leadership of the present-day Labour Party and trade unions in the South. The revolution it struggled for, through violence and political activism, never took place; but the struggle helped shape modern Ireland.

1. The Patriot Game

'I was taught all my life cruel England to blame,
And so I'm a part of the patriot game.'

Dominic Behan, 'The Patriot Game'

In early September 1962, six months on from the cessation of the Border Campaign, Cathal Goulding was appointed Chief of Staff of the IRA. Born in December 1922 in Dublin's East Arran Street, close to the River Liffey, Goulding had the perfect pedigree to assume the highest rank within the movement. His grandfather had been a member of the Invincibles, the offshoot of the Fenian movement that had assassinated British ministers in the 1880s. His father Charles and uncle James had been members of both the secret Irish Republican Brotherhood and the Gaelic League. In 1913 Charles joined the Irish Volunteers, and in 1916 both Goulding brothers took part in the Easter Rising as part of the Jacob's factory garrison. Both were deported and interned in the rebellion's aftermath. Charles became a member of the Dublin Active Service Unit of the IRA during the War of Independence and took the Anti-Treaty side in the Civil War. A house painter, like many other republicans he found it difficult to gain employment in the post-Civil War period. He became a self-employed 'jobbing contractor', finding intermittent work during the hungry 1920s.

Cathal Goulding attended national school in Strand Street, and then St Joseph's Christian Brothers school when the family moved to Ballybough. He left school in his early teens and became a house painter, his father's trade. He was a neighbour of the Behan family in Russell Street, with whom his father worked. He and Brendan Behan were 'like brothers', and both joined the republican boy scouts, Na Fianna Éireann, in 1931. In 1939 Goulding joined the IRA itself and in December of that year took part in the organization's successful raid on the Irish Army's ammunition stores in the Phoenix Park. But the IRA was entering a grim period, having launched a disastrous bombing campaign in England the previous January. The beginning of the Second World War and the potential threat the IRA posed to the Irish state's neutrality saw Éamon de Valera's government clamp down hard on their former comrades. Hundreds of IRA members were jailed or interned without trial, while several were executed or died on hunger strike. In November 1941 Goulding was jailed for a year in Mountjoy prison for membership of an 'unlawful organization' and possession of IRA documents. On his release in 1942 he was immediately interned in the Curragh Camp in Kildare, where he remained until late 1944. The Curragh saw numerous splits and schisms, as comrades became enemies overnight. But the young Goulding was a conventional IRA man and stayed loyal to what was seen as the hard-line faction led by Liam Leddy.

Goulding and most of his fellow republican prisoners emerged from internment and prison during 1945 to find the IRA shattered. It had lost several leading members during the war years, among them Chief of Staff Sean Russell, who had died on a German U-boat en route to Ireland. The leadership's tactical alliance with the Nazis had proved contentious while its involvement in gun battles that left several Gardaí dead had shocked public opinion. So complete was the organization's defeat that the Fianna Fáil Minister for Justice Gerald Boland reputedly boasted the IRA was dead and that he had killed it.

But among some republicans there was a determination to carry on, and in 1945 Kerryman Paddy Fleming was appointed as the IRA's new Chief of Staff. The 22-year-old Goulding was among a minority of former internees who returned to activity and was sent to help reorganize local units. In early 1946 representatives of the IRA from across the country met in the Ardee Bar in Dublin, only to be arrested by waiting Garda Special Branch officers. Several, including Goulding, again received prison sentences.

By 1947 Goulding was out of prison and involved in running training camps in the Wicklow Mountains. In September 1948 the IRA held an important army convention, bringing together delegates from across the country to discuss the organization's future. This meeting saw a new leadership trio, who would dominate the IRA for over a decade, come to prominence. The 'three Macs', as they came to be known, were led by Tony Magan, a farmer from Co. Meath who had spent five years interned in the Curragh and was now Chief of Staff. Magan had a reputation for single-mindedness and discipline and was set on ridding the IRA of the gangsterish image it had picked up during the war years. Sean Garland, who would later work closely with Magan, recalled him as 'a very decent individual and a very generous man' and as having 'no left or right [political] vision, just straight ahead'. The second of the Macs was Padraig McLogan, a native of Armagh, who had previously been a member of the IRA's seven-man Army Council during the 1930s but was now a publican in Portlaoise. Within the organization McLogan was viewed by many as cold and autocratic. Completing the trio was Cork's Tomás Mac Curtain, who was released from Portlaoise jail in 1948. Sentenced to death for the murder of a Garda in 1940, Mac Curtain had been granted clemency, partly because his father, the Mayor of Cork, had been murdered by British forces during the War of Independence. While imprisoned Mac Curtain had refused to wear prison uniform or conform to regulations. He was recalled as a 'great mixer' and the most sociable of the new leaders.

The three Macs believed that a degree of political mobilization was necessary to help rebuild the IRA, and towards this end a monthly republican newspaper – the *United Irishman* – was launched in May 1948. During 1949 IRA volunteers were ordered to join the moribund Sinn Féin party. Sinn Féin recognized that supreme authority rested with the IRA Army Council and maintained a strict adherence to the policy of abstentionism – refusal to take seats in either the Southern or Northern parliaments. Republicans regarded both institutions as puppet creations of British imperialism. For the same reason, arrested IRA volunteers refused to recognize the courts, North or South, a stance that usually guaranteed a conviction. Non-recognition and abstentionism were seen as key principles that marked republicans out from corrupt, compromising politicians.

The year 1948 had seen the election of a new inter-party government in the South, which included the recently formed Clann na Poblachta. This party was dominated by former senior IRA figures, including Seán MacBride, who had been Chief of Staff in the late 1930s. Despite the larger coalition party being the pro-Treaty Fine Gael, the new government had within a few months of taking office withdrawn the state from the British Commonwealth and declared it a republic. While the IRA denounced the actions of its former comrades in entering the Dáil and still refused to recognize that the southern state was *the* Republic, they were forced to acknowledge that a new situation existed. Due in part to the changed political atmosphere and in part to lingering public revulsion at the deaths of several Gardaí and republicans during violent clashes between 1939 and 1945, the IRA leadership decided it would now avoid 'any type of aggressive military action' in the South. Instead all energies would be focused on a campaign in the North. In 1950 McLogan became Sinn Féin president and Magan also took a place on the organization's ruling executive, the Ard Chomhairle, ensuring that the party was 'in every sense IRA controlled'. In May 1951 a Military Council was formed within the IRA leadership to plan 'a successful military campaign against the British Army of occupation in Ireland'.

The 1950s might have offered fertile ground for Irish revolutionaries. The Republic was desperately poor at the start of the decade, and real national income stagnated between 1950 and 1958. The 1956 census revealed that the state's population was 2,894,822, the lowest ever, and net emigration was higher than in any period since 1881. Seventy per cent of emigrants were under 30 years of age. Economic distress led to some protest by the unemployed, but Ireland remained notably conservative, and the lack of a vibrant left did not preclude the existence of an intensely anti-communist right. In 1949 150,000 people, including many trade union leaders, had taken to the streets in Dublin to protest at communism in Eastern Europe. Collections were taken up at church gates to aid the Italian Christian Democrats in their struggle with Italy's 'reds' in 1948. The powerful Archbishop of Dublin, John Charles McQuaid, sponsored private clerical investigations into left-wingers, augmenting those of the Special Branch. Catholic papers such as the *Standard* hounded unemployed activists, and groups like Maria Duce warned Irish cinema-goers of the influence of communists in Hollywood. The deference shown by government ministers to the Catholic hierarchy during the thwarted attempt by Clann na Poblachta health minister Noel Browne to introduce free health care for women and children in 1951 was a potent illustration of Church power. Away from public view unmarried mothers, their children and working-class young offenders were subjected to often horrific abuse in Church-run institutions, details of which would only emerge in later decades. Emigration helped siphon off what anger there was.

Meanwhile, a great deal of emotion was expended on the question of partition. During 1949 an all-party campaign had organized a nationwide church-gate collection, rallies and public meetings in support of Irish reunification. For many people, the claim by the *Irish Press* in the midst of the Second World War that 'there was no kind of oppression visited on any minority in Europe that the Six County nationalists have not also endured' was not an exaggeration. Hence there were solid reasons behind the IRA's belief that if it avoided confrontation with the authorities in the South, a campaign in the North might be tolerated. The republican movement also benefited from public disillusionment over the lack of progress of state-endorsed anti-partitionism. Tomás Mac Giolla, who would become chairman of the IRA Army Council and president of Sinn Féin, was one of a number of people who left mainstream anti-partition groups, including Clann na Poblachta, to join the IRA in this period.

The IRA did not challenge the ethos of the 1950s southern state; in fact, in many ways they promoted a more extreme version of it. Republicans blamed the state's poor economic conditions on the legacy of British rule and argued that once the British were ousted from the North, the island would flourish. Republicans bemoaned the loss of 'the nation's life blood' through emigration and promised that a free Ireland would stop it. But the *United Irishman* also felt that one of the evils of emigration was that it exposed Irish youth to the 'irreligious completely materialistic atmosphere of England'. That paper celebrated the 'intertwining of Catholic and separatist thought' and cranky notions about Judeo-Masonic conspiracies found their way into its pages. In 1952, in a state in which cultural censorship was already pervasive, Sinn Féin launched a 'Stop Foreign Publications' campaign that aimed to prevent the circulation of material that was 'not merely anti-Catholic or anti-Christian but definitely and deliberately Pagan'.

The politics of the IRA reflected the ethos of the southern state in other ways. Dublin Fianna boys on their weekend hikes in the Wicklow Mountains were always marched into Enniskerry for Sunday mass. In 1951 the IRA made clear that it had 'no link' with communism, an 'ideology repugnant to the overwhelming majority' of Irish people. Army Order No. 4, forbidding membership of the IRA to communists, had been in force since 1933. Despite the paranoia, the actual number of communists in Ireland was minuscule. In the South most were organized in the Irish Workers' League, which had 79 members in 1953. Several of this group's activists were ex-IRA members who attended the Wolfe Tone commemoration at Bodenstown every June. Their presence provoked warnings from the speaker's platform to ignore them; but some would go on to play important roles within the republican movement. Among the communists attending the 1953 Bodenstown commemoration were former Curragh internees Ned Stapleton and Joe O'Connor, along with Eamon Smullen, who, as a 19-year-old IRA volunteer ten years previously, had been convicted of shooting and badly wounding an informer. In Portlaoise Smullen had followed Mac Curtain's example and refused to wear prison uniform, instead fashioning a smock from blankets; this disobedience earned him extensive periods in solitary confinement. On release Smullen had drifted out of the IRA and into communist politics. In 1954 the communist contingent at Bodenstown was joined by Trinity College Dublin graduate Roy Johnston.

According to Sean Garland, issues such as unemployment 'didn't impinge or in any way disturb' the 1950s IRA, which remained focused on partition. Yet many young men did join the movement out of unease at the economic situation, believing, however vaguely, that the IRA's campaign to unite Ireland would also improve living standards. Mick Ryan, from Dublin's East Wall, vividly recalled the poignant scenes as emigrant ships left Dublin port, those on board waving handkerchiefs to family left behind. Articles in the *United Irishman* on the need to stop emigration sparked his interest in republicanism. Mac Giolla remembered seeing the 'people heading for the boat' at Westland Row station 'with [their] big cardboard cases . . . it would really shatter you'.

But the ultimate aim of the IRA was a campaign against the Northern Ireland state. The prevailing belief in the nobility and heroism of the War of Independence, reinforced by numerous romantic accounts published during the 1950s, contributed to a sincere conviction that a guerrilla struggle could be successfully waged against British occupation. Mac Giolla remembered people 'saying things like "We were able to keep Munster with one flying column", [and] that was only 30 years before'. The Southern-based leadership of the IRA wishfully believed that Northern unionists would accept republican appeals to 'refuse to become embroiled in the conflict between the foreign forces of oppression and the volunteer soldiers of the IRA'. They even asked that the locally recruited (and mainly Protestant) RUC and B-Specials 'stand aside' and allow the IRA to fight it out with the British Army.

But in the early 1950s it looked unlikely that such a fight would occur any time soon. In 1951 the Garda Special Branch calculated that the IRA had 'no real organization in most areas' and did not 'want trouble with the authorities'. By the summer of 1952 police estimates of membership were about 200 in Dublin and 50 in Cork. Around 750 people attended Bodenstown that year. But there was evidence of arms training and an effort to revive interest through Sinn Féin and the *United Irishman*. Private houses were used for smaller weapons classes. Mac Giolla remembered one of his first classes in the Crumlin area of Dublin: 'I was led up the stairs in darkness . . . a man lit a candle and I could see other people in the room and we crowded around as we were shown basically how to use a rifle and assemble it and clean it. You had a real feeling of a very secret conspiracy.' It was only after he left the meeting that Mac Giolla found out that the session took place in darkness because the old woman who let the IRA use her house could not afford her electricity bill; the IRA men then held a collection for her. Some impetus also came from an arms raid on Ebrington Barracks in Derry, in June 1951.

Cathal Goulding was increasingly prominent in the organization, taking charge of the Dublin Brigade at the unveiling of a statue of Sean Russell in September 1951. Tony Magan had high regard for Goulding and entrusted him with organizing a raid on an Officer Training Corps base at Felsted in Essex. In June 1953 an IRA gang succeeded in stealing a substantial amount of weapons from the base, only to be captured when their overloaded van attracted police attention on the way to London. Goulding was arrested along with Derry man Manus Canning and Sean Stephenson from Essex. During their trial Goulding informed the court that he and his fellow defendants were:

. . . soldiers of the Irish Republican Army who believe that the only way to drive the British army of occupation out of Ireland is by force of arms. We make no excuse or apology for capturing arms from the enemy for that purpose and our one regret is that, in this instance, we were not successful in placing them in the hands of our comrades at home for use against the British forces in Ireland.

The three received eight-year jail sentences; Goulding would spend much of his in Pentonville, Wakefield and Stafford prisons.

The IRA had more success with a raid on Gough Barracks in Armagh, in June 1954. The raid was the brainchild of Leo McCormack, a former British Commando and Dublin IRA training officer. He had noticed the lax security at the base and, aware of the success the Fenians had had in infiltrating the British Army during the 1860s, considered that establishing a contact inside might be the best method of operating. Young IRA recruit Sean Garland agreed to go to Armagh in March and enlist in the Royal Irish Fusiliers. Garland was then able to supply maps, documents and photographs of the base to the IRA in Dublin. In a final preparation for the raid, Dublin IRA officers Charlie Murphy and Eamonn Boyce visited the base for a dance along with a member of the republican women's organization Cumann na mBan. Under cover of an amorous encounter Garland took her on a detailed inspection of the entire barracks. On a Saturday afternoon in June a stolen truck arrived in the barracks yard and the sentries were held up; within 20 minutes the weapons – including 250 rifles, 37 Sten guns and 7 Bren guns – were spirited away. Garland, still undercover, remained behind, to be told by one of his sergeants that the IRA were 'terrible bad men'. Public interest in the raid saw sales of the *United Irishman* reach 39,000. In Tralee republicans took over a cinema and interrupted a movie entitled *The Raiders* by displaying a slide proclaiming 'Join the IRA: we have the guns now'. Several county councils expressed support for the Armagh raid and extended congratulations to the IRA.

Garland's regiment was due to depart for Kenya that winter but he had 'no intention' of going to 'fight the Mau Mau'. Instead he deserted in October, having first helped reconnoitre Omagh barracks for another IRA raid. The Omagh operation, in October, was unsuccessful, ending in a shoot-out with several IRA men wounded and others captured; but the fact that they had engaged in a gun battle with British troops, for the first time since the 1920s, further boosted confidence. The Gardaí were forced to reassess the level of threat from the IRA, describing it that month as 'a problem of considerable and growing importance'. It was felt within the IRA that the organization had 'gained immeasurably in prestige' by the success of the Armagh raid, as well as increasing 'the striking power of the army'. At Bodenstown a week after the Armagh raid there were shouts of, 'Give us the arms,' while the speakers emphasized that the weapons were for 'use against the

British occupation forces' and that there was 'no fear' of civil war
in the South. The Gardaí feared that the IRA would 'receive the
sympathy, if not the actual support, of increasing numbers of the
general public', and noted that the organization was carrying out
training on a more extensive basis as those seeking to join increased.
The Armagh raid was the deciding factor in 18-year-old Mick
Ryan finally joining the IRA, and Omagh was the 'clincher' for
Jim Lane in Cork, as several of those captured were local men.
The raids inspired Seamus Collins, then a teenager in Limerick, to
want to 'be in something like that'. During the same year 16-year-
old Máirín de Burca joined Sinn Féin in Newbridge, Co. Kildare.

In August 1955 the IRA attempted another arms raid in Britain,
at Arborfield in Berkshire. Despite making off with a major haul
the raiders were caught and Seamus Murphy, Joe Doyle and Donal
Murphy sentenced to life in prison. The three men joined
Goulding in Wakefield. Among those imprisoned with the IRA
men were several members of the Greek Cypriot group EOKA,
then waging a bloody campaign against the British, and Klaus
Fuchs, the German-born spy who had worked on the development
of nuclear weapons in the US and then passed on vital information
to the Soviets. The IRA men had plenty of time for discussion
with fellow prisoners and access to a wide variety of reading
material. Goulding and Seamus Murphy developed an interest in
the Russian Revolution, and their reading of Fitzroy MacLean's
biography of Marshal Tito resulted in the Yugoslav communist
leader becoming something of a hero to the Irishmen.

The IRA made two attempts to free Goulding. On the first
occasion he almost made it over the wall before being captured.
The near success resulted in Goulding receiving a long period of
solitary confinement, and patches marking him out as an attempted
escapee were sewn on to his prison uniform. On the second
occasion it was decided that the IRA would, if necessary, shoot
their way into Wakefield Prison and rescue both Irish and EOKA
prisoners. IRA volunteers practised scaling walls with extension
rods at Croke Park before Garland travelled to England to reconnoitre the rescue mission. Judging it a possibility, he returned with

fifteen other volunteers, including five women posing as an acting troupe, in a plane chartered from Aer Lingus. Weapons were concealed under the women's clothing and Garland carried a Thompson gun strapped to his body. The 'troupe' arrived safely but the escape attempt had to be aborted and the weapons dumped in England.

The IRA revival of the mid-1950s came against the backdrop of the emergence of rival armed groups. The most significant of these was Saor Uladh, formed by Liam Kelly from Pomeroy, Co. Tyrone. In October 1951, after Kelly was dismissed by the IRA for carrying out an unauthorized raid in Derry, he took a large part of the local organization with him. To the disgust of the IRA, Kelly's group carried out armed robberies and also formed a political party, Fianna Uladh, in 1954. Fianna Uladh had 'no quarrel with the constitutional position' of the 26 counties, and called on republicans to take part in politics there, including taking seats in the Dáil. In Northern Ireland it continued to support abstentionism. This was not an abstract position, as in 1953 Kelly was actually elected to Stormont for Mid-Tyrone. He was jailed for a year for making a seditious speech and during this period was nominated to the Southern Senate by Seán MacBride. The IRA considered this treachery and poured a regular stream of invective on Kelly and his 'partitionist organization'. But Kelly's popularity in his native area, where he was greeted by a crowd of 10,000 on his release, meant that there was nothing they could do about him. In November 1955 Saor Uladh attacked Roslea RUC Barracks in Fermanagh and one of Kelly's key men, Connie Green, a former Royal Marine, was killed. Saor Uladh's activities had the potential to win over impatient recruits from the IRA. In Belfast a number of republicans, including Billy McMillen, who been jailed for IRA activity during 1953, were attracted to it.

The introduction of IRA General Order No. 8 after the Omagh raid, expressly forbidding any conflict with the Gardaí or the Irish Army, caused some resentment among militants. The discontented rallied around Joe Christle, a law student and charismatic orator who had taken part in both the Armagh and Omagh raids. While

Christle attracted some support, Garland and others resented what they saw as the 'elitism' of his faction. During 1956 Christle and a number of his supporters were expelled or left the Dublin IRA. As far as the IRA was concerned, both Kelly's Roslea raid and Christle's group might draw unwelcome attention to their military plans. A great deal of effort was put into building up intelligence on the splinter groups, with Mick Ryan assigned to shadow Christle himself. Unfortunately for Ryan, Christle was a champion cyclist, one of the founders of the Rás Tailteann, and he regularly sped away from him on his modern racing bike.

Despite the criticism of the splinter groups over the lack of urgency in IRA military preparations, increased training *was* taking place, with weekend camps and forced marches in the Dublin and Wicklow Mountains and west Cork. The Lee-Enfield Mark IV rifle, the Sten and Thompson sub-machine guns and the Bren light machine gun were the standard equipment. Political circumstances were aiding preparations. From 1954 a new inter-party coalition was in government and many felt that Garda attention was notably more relaxed than it had been during Fianna Fáil administrations. New recruits continued to come in. Dublin Fianna boy Frank Ross (later Proinsias De Rossa) joined the IRA within a few weeks of his sixteenth birthday in May 1956, one of '40 or 50' youngsters who took the pledge of loyalty to the Irish Republic in front of Tomás Mac Giolla. Earlier that year IRA members in Dublin had been told that serious operations were in the offing and only those ready to take part in them should stay in the organization.

During 1955 Sean Cronin, a journalist and former Irish Army officer, had arrived back in Dublin from the United States. Despite being a new recruit to republicanism Cronin brought a dynamism to preparations, partly because, as Garland recalls, he seemed to know 'a lot more than many of us about military matters'. He was quickly promoted to taking charge of training. Outlining his ideas in a booklet, *Notes on Guerrilla Warfare*, Cronin argued that no nation had a greater tradition of guerrilla fighting than Ireland and that there was no other means by which 'a small nation fighting for freedom' could defeat its oppressor. He was influenced by the guerrilla campaigns then taking place against the British in Cyprus and the French in Algeria. According to Cronin's thesis, guerrilla strategy should be to 'cut all communications, telephone, road and rail; destroy all petrol stations and enemy vehicles; hit enemy strategic strong points [and] strike at their supplies and their administration'. In time, centres of resistance established by guerrilla units would be knitted together into one 'liberated area . . . where the enemy's writ no longer runs'. Cronin became the chief strategist behind the IRA's planned campaign in the North, 'Operation Harvest'. Flying columns from the South would launch attacks on RUC barracks, destroy communications and link up with the local IRA in the border region, eventually creating 'liberated areas' where nationalist alienation would guarantee popular support. Volunteers would wear battledress with tricolour insignia in order to comply with the Geneva Convention.

On 11 November 1956 an alliance of Saor Uladh and the Christle group destroyed six customs huts along the border. Whether or not the IRA's hand was forced by the activities of these groups, as the Gardaí contended, is a matter of dispute. Garland contends that Mac Curtain argued that the campaign should not be attempted without building a stronger organization within Northern Ireland. But the IRA were optimistic, in part because there had been political returns in the North from the Omagh raid. In May 1955 two of the Omagh prisoners, Tom Mitchell and Phil Clarke, won seats in the Westminster elections for Mid-Ulster and Fermanagh-South Tyrone respectively. Even more encouragingly, when Mitchell was disqualified he held his seat in the resulting by-election. Altogether Sinn Féin, running men held as prisoners in England and Northern Ireland as candidates, won 152,310 votes. The results came mainly in rural areas, where mainstream nationalists were not contesting the poll. In the Belfast constituencies Labour candidates polled more than double Sinn Féin's vote. Nevertheless, the elections added impetus to the belief that Northern nationalists would respond positively to an armed campaign.

In December 1956, with the world's attention focused on the aftermath of the Soviet invasion of Hungary and the Suez crisis, about 150 men were moved from various points in Southern Ireland to a farm at Athboy, Co. Meath. Here Jim Lane met Sean South from Limerick, who greeted him with a question: 'An e seo rud atha meid ath feitheamh le fada?' (Is this the thing we have been waiting for, for so long?) South, a clerk, always began conversations in Irish. A former member of Maria Duce, he was a devout Catholic and conservative even by the standards of the day. Yet Garland, who had decided early on that he 'had no time for religion or God or anything else', found South 'very kind . . . gentle' and '[the] kind of person you would have as a friend'.

Four fighting columns named after republican heroes – Pearse, Clarke, Teeling and Lynch – were created at Athboy. To Mick Ryan's dismay, when Cronin read out a list of the column personnel the Dublin volunteers who had trained together were split up into units with men from other parts of the country. His humour was not improved when he discovered he was to join a group far from the border, in north Antrim. Garland was made Officer Commanding (O/C) of the Pearse Column, with Cork man David O'Connell second in command. South, who had been in the Irish Army Reserve, was given the job of setting compass and directing the column. Equipped with nothing heavier than Bren guns and some mines, grenades and Molotov cocktails, the columns set off.

Operation Harvest began in the early hours of 12 December 1956. There was an abortive attack by Garland's column on his old regiment's base at Gough Barracks. Bridges were blown in Fermanagh, and a Territorial Army barracks attacked in Enniskillen. In Magherafelt, Co. Derry, a unit led by Seamus Costello, an 18-year-old from Bray, destroyed the local courthouse. A special republican bulletin announced that 'organized resistance to British rule' had begun and that 'many clashes with British military, armed B-Specials and police' had taken place. (While the B-Specials were not explicitly targeted, units had permission to engage them if confronted.) Despite formal condemnation of the IRA by the

Catholic hierarchy, many units were given absolution before going out on operations.

Some veterans claim there were orders that 'not a shot was to be fired in Belfast' because of the combustible nature of that city's sectarian make-up; in reality, moves to create an Active Service Unit in the city were abandoned because of fears that informers had access to the IRA's plans. The Belfast question became academic as the Northern government rapidly rounded up and interned republican suspects, including Sinn Féin, IRA and Saor Uladh members. Over 100 men, including the majority of Belfast activists, were arrested on 12 January 1957.

On New Year's Eve 1956 Garland's column, after spending their Christmas in Dublin, attacked Brookeborough RUC Barracks in Fermanagh in what became the iconic encounter of the campaign. The barracks was a symbolic target: Lord Brookeborough was prime minister of Northern Ireland – or, as republicans saw it, 'Stormont's puppet premier'. The plan was for the Bedford truck carrying the fourteen IRA volunteers to pull up opposite the barracks and cover the placing of a mine at the barracks door. However, the truck pulled up under the gable end of the barracks, directly underneath a window, and after the attack began police were able to open fire on the lorry from the window overlooking it: 'Yer man did tremendous damage with the range and angle,' Garland recalls. South was unable to return fire from the IRA's Bren because of the lorry's positioning. Both he and 18-year-old Fergal O'Hanlon were fatally wounded; Garland was hit in the left thigh and three other volunteers were also injured.

Garland gave the order to withdraw and, despite the lorry stalling and its tail tipping and almost spilling the men on to the road, they made it out of the town. They regrouped at a farmhouse, knowing that RUC patrols were in pursuit. It was decided to leave the bodies of South and O'Hanlon in a cow-byre. Garland argued that if he and another wounded man, Paddy O'Regan, were a burden then they should be left to 'stand our ground and give the others their opportunity to get away'; O'Regan remembers being some-what dismayed when Garland asked if he would take a Thompson

and 'fight a rearguard action' with him. In the end it was decided
the two men would be carried by their comrades into the mountains and across the border. The escape took them over harsh
terrain, with Garland in pain and 'fucking everything from Jack to
Jill' – so much so that one of his comrades admonished him to
stop cursing lest he 'bring bad luck'. In Monaghan the injured
were taken to hospital and the others arrested.

With the deaths of South and O'Hanlon the raid quickly passed
into mythology. IRA men had been killed in gun battles with the
Gardaí during the 1940s, but *these* men had died fighting to free
the North. The words of a new rebel song, 'Sean South from
Garryowen', were published in the *Irish Catholic* within a week.
Thousands lined the route of South's funeral as it passed through
Monaghan and then on to Dublin, where Proinsias De Rossa was
part of the Fianna guard of honour, and to Limerick. *They Kept
Faith*, a pamphlet recounting the story of the raid, sold 10,000
copies in the space of a month. For a brief period it looked as if
the IRA had indeed unleashed the latent irredentist soul of the
South. Garda reports confirmed that IRA membership reached its
highest level since 1945, numbering almost 1,000.

There was also an electoral pay-off for Sinn Féin. In March the
inter-party government fell over disagreements on what measures
were needed to deal with the IRA. Fianna Fáil won the ensuing
general election but Sinn Féin polled a healthy 5 per cent of the
vote, with its sixteen candidates winning four seats. All the victories
were in rural areas: Sligo-Leitrim, South Kerry, Monaghan, and
Longford-Westmeath, where Ruairí Ó Brádaigh, whose column
had killed a policeman at Derrylin just before the Brookeborough
raid, took a seat. In Dublin, Sinn Féin stood three candidates who
won 7,522 votes between them but did not come close to taking
a seat. Increasing anger over unemployment was reflected in the
election of a Dublin TD on an Unemployed Protest Association
ticket. While Sinn Féin had avoided engagement in unemployment agitation, some of Christle's group had become involved. As
protest spread to Waterford and Cork, the IRA remained aloof.
Cork Sinn Féin members were threatened with expulsion if they

became involved and use of the movement's Thomas Ashe Hall was denied to the unemployed protesters.

The new government at first adopted a wait-and-see attitude towards the IRA's campaign, but the killing of an RUC constable in July 1957 provided the impetus for Fianna Fáil to act decisively. Internment without trial was introduced and 63 republicans were arrested within two days, including Mac Curtain, McLogan and Mac Giolla. Soon over 100 men were held in the Curragh Camp. Having absconded from his hospital bed in January, Garland was captured training in Glencree along with 37 others, including De Rossa, in May 1957. After serving several months in Mountjoy, all of the IRA prisoners were transferred to the Curragh. There they would be joined by several volunteers captured in the South, among them Malachy McGurran, an 18-year-old from Lurgan, Seamus Costello and Mick Ryan.

The Saor Uladh–Christle alliance meanwhile continued their activities North and South. They blew up the locks on Newry Canal in May 1957, and during the same month their robbery of gelignite from a quarry in Co. Laois was denounced by the IRA. When internment was introduced twelve of the group's members were rounded up and placed in the Curragh, where they were ostracized by the IRA prisoners; some in the IRA blamed Christle's activities for giving Fianna Fáil an excuse to introduce internment in the first place.

The impetus of the IRA campaign dissipated within a year. The emotional response to the deaths of South and O'Hanlon was not replicated on the same scale after other republican casualties, such as at Edentubber where five men died when a mine exploded prematurely. Indeed certain IRA actions produced hostility. Seamus Collins remembered getting 'terrible stick around Dublin' after the killing of a policeman in a booby-trap explosion. People asked him, 'Ah Jaysus, what did ye do to that poor RUC sergeant?' By 1958 there were already many in favour of calling the campaign off, and the Cork IRA had already effectively withdrawn. In 1959 there were just 27 IRA operations, compared with 341 two years earlier. Morale was not helped by a bitter and debilitating dispute in the Curragh. A large number of internees became extremely hostile to Tomás Mac Curtain, the camp O/C. As far as Garland was concerned the split was 'all centred on personalities and not on politics'. He felt closer to Mac Curtain and Magan than to their critics, who had 'no discipline or structure'. A breakout took place without permission from the camp's IRA leadership, and some prisoners refused to join official escape attempts.

By mid-1958, 500 republicans were in jail or interned North and South. Sean Cronin joined them later that year after being arrested with a number of other senior IRA men. But the decline in activity meant Fianna Fáil felt confident enough to end internment in March 1959. After their release Garland, Ryan and McGurran met Cronin at a farmhouse in Laois. Despite their disenchantment, Cronin, 'a persuasive individual', was able to convince them to continue the campaign. His view was that it was keeping 'the flame alive' and that events might yet turn in the IRA's favour. But arms and ammunition were now in short supply. In late 1959 Garland was sent to reorganize in Belfast, which he already knew a little from nights out while in the British Army. Cronin had authorized IRA operations in the city, but a shipment of explosives from Glasgow had been discovered by the RUC and surveillance was stepped up. Garland was arrested at Great Victoria Street Station, despite having dyed his hair black and claiming to be a Glasgow University student called John S. Hamilton. In November 1959 he was sentenced to four years in jail. He eventually became IRA O/C in Crumlin Road Jail, where quite a few of the prisoners were worried that they would never be released while the campaign stuttered on. A number took the opportunity to 'sign out', pledging to give up IRA activity. But most internees refused the opportunity and remained in jail. In Crumlin Road there was some discussion on the future of republicanism. Belfast volunteer Art McMillen remembered these debates amounting to 'the same old doldrums, 1798, 1803, 1848, 1867, 1916, 1921 and all, you were running it off like a rigmarole and they were still talking the same auld bullshit'. But Leo McCormack stirred things up with a lecture on the socialist ideas of James Connolly; some prisoners walked out and others almost came to blows.

Hopes that Northern nationalists would respond positively to the armed campaign had been misplaced. In the Westminster elections of October 1959 Sinn Féin's vote slumped to half that of 1955, despite several internees and prisoners being put forward as candidates. Teenage Fianna boy Brendan Mackin collected for the prisoners in bars along the Falls Road in Belfast, finding some 'sympathy and respect' but no real support. The Unionist government seemed unmovable and 'even the most optimistic of people could see it [the campaign] was not going to succeed'.

In the South many people were as moved by the death of Dubliner and Manchester United football player Liam Whelan in the Munich air crash of February 1958 as they were by fatalities north of the border. About 3,400 people attended Bodenstown in 1959; the Special Branch counted 79 members of the Dublin IRA, including Mac Giolla, De Rossa and Cathal Goulding, who commanded the parade. Goulding had been released from prison that April and on returning to Dublin was appointed IRA Quartermaster General. With Mick Ryan he took charge of a shipment of bazookas from the United States. The weapons were tested on St Stephen's night 1959 in the Dublin Mountains, and were found to be duds. When news of this anticlimax was eventually conveyed to volunteers it created an even greater sense of demoralization. Internment had ended but republicans were still being jailed. De Rossa, Peter Pringle and Tony Hayde were among those arrested during 1960, as was Joe Sherlock from Mallow, caught with a rifle. In local elections that year Sinn Féin stood 134 candidates but polled badly, winning only 2,000 votes in Dublin. A year later the general election saw Sinn Féin lose its four seats. The Gardaí estimated that only one-sixth of the IRA's membership was still active. Fianna Fáil were returned to power and an up-and-coming TD named Charles Haughey was appointed Minister for Justice. He promised that he would 'use every means ... including the army if necessary' to bring the IRA's 'futile, evil campaign of violence to an end'.

The campaign continued without any great strategy except the hope that a 'spark would ignite' popular feeling. During 1961 two RUC men were killed and the Southern government was put under pressure to crack down on the IRA again. In November the Military Tribunals, used against the IRA during the war years, were revived by Haughey. By the end of 1961, 25 men – including Cronin, Goulding and Mac Giolla – were imprisoned under their auspices. Mac Giolla recalled being 'pulled out of bed at six in the morning' and jailed for 'refusing to account for my movements before three colonels in Collins Barracks'. Sentences of up to eight years were doled out. There were also major arms finds in Dublin and Monaghan in early 1962. The Department of Justice was in no doubt that Haughey's move to establish the Military Tribunals played a major role in forcing the IRA to end the campaign. The RUC concurred, noting that the 'fear' the sentences produced had the 'greatest possible effect' on republicans, North and South.

The decision to end the campaign was made in early February 1962, and it was enacted on the 26th with an order to dump arms. In Crumlin Road a sarcastic warder, an Orangeman, called to Garland's cell to inform him that 'the war's over'. It had not been an easy decision. Considerable sacrifice and emotion had been invested in the struggle, particularly among those who had opened up their homes to men on the run. Mick Ryan, who was Director of Operations, received a 'cold reception' at one billet when he supported the ceasefire statement. These reactions were felt across the movement. Máirín de Burca recalls crying herself to sleep the night the end of the campaign was announced.

What became known as the Border Campaign cost the lives of 18 people, including 11 republicans (5 in combat), and singularly failed to achieve its objective. Although the IRA had not killed any civilians nor undertaken any aggressive action in the South, it had attracted repression there. Fianna Fáil had once again delivered a crushing blow to the organization. The electoral support won in 1957 had drained away and the movement had not been rewarded for its adherence to abstentionist principles. The statement announcing the end of the campaign lamented that the public's mind had been 'distracted' by 'secondary issues'. The hoped-for uprising of Northern nationalists had also failed to materialize. Some Southern republicans had come to realize how little they actually knew about the North and unionism; Garland recognized that it 'was a much deeper problem than we envisaged'. The failure of the campaign was a formative experience for the core group who would lead the IRA for the next decade, causing them to rethink many of the certainties that had inspired it. During the 1960s they would embrace the revolutionary tradition of the eighteenth-century United Irishmen, rediscover the socialist republicanism of the 1930s, and finally seek inspiration from, and hope to emulate, left-wing national liberation movements from Cuba to Vietnam.

2. Army of the People: 1962–1968

'The fight for freedom is a class struggle . . . The Republican army, North and South, must become the Army of the People in fact as well as name.'

Sean Garland, Bodenstown, 1968

The IRA had been defeated in 1962, though it would be some time before it would publicly acknowledge that fact. Their ceasefire statement emphasized the brave fight they had waged against unequal odds and struck a defiant note. The 'Irish Resistance Movement' pledged 'eternal hostility' to British rule and looked forward to a 'period of consolidation, expansion and perfection for the final victorious phase of the struggle for the full freedom of Ireland'.

In reality the IRA was in a bad way and their opponents knew it. Such was the government's confidence that it began to release IRA prisoners, including those jailed by the military courts. During April those let go included Goulding, Mac Giolla and Cronin. Minister for Justice Charles Haughey, with more than a hint of condescension, argued that there was 'no particular reason to fear' the 'organizing ability' of these men of 'limited education and poor personality'. Recommending a general amnesty, he speculated that:

It is probably true to say that at no time in the past forty years has the IRA had less hope of being backed by public opinion. They publicly admit it. A resort to arms in present circumstances and for some considerable time to come appears to be out of the question . . . they have no funds: their external sources have dried up . . . it is likely that quite a number will avail of the present situation to ease themselves out of the organization.

The Northern authorities were more cautious. Garland was not released until August 1962, and the other four IRA prisoners in their custody remained until December 1963. Joe Doyle, the last IRA prisoner held in Britain, had been released in July that year.

The Ireland they emerged into was changing rapidly. Sean Lemass, who had succeeded Éamon de Valera as Taoiseach in 1959, had made clear his intention to abandon protectionism and open up the Southern economy to international investment. These moves, coinciding with the boom in US multinational investment in Europe, had a dramatic effect. Unemployment was lower by a fifth in late 1960 than it had been a year earlier, and the numbers emigrating dropped from 212,000 between 1956 and 1961 to just 80,000 over the next five years, while some of those who had left during the 1950s returned. For the first time in generations Ireland experienced a feeling that things were getting better. The rigidness of traditional Irish Catholic thinking and practice was being questioned, in part due to the influence of the Second Vatican Council, which sat from 1962 to 1965. There was a slow liberalization of the censorship laws. Radio Telefís Éireann made its first television broadcast on New Year's Eve 1961, dramatically expanding horizons in a variety of ways. When RTÉ was launched there were 93,000 licensed TVs in the Republic (mostly on the east coast, where British channels were also available); by 1968 there were 377,000. All of these developments contributed to a sense that old-style Irish nationalism was finished. Under Lemass and Northern premier Terence O'Neill the governments of the two states were enjoying a rapprochement, discussing trade and peaceful relations. Charles Haughey, now Minister for Agriculture, entertained his Northern counterpart Harry West at his home in Dublin during 1965, something unthinkable a decade earlier. Commentators in Northern Ireland remarked on how sectarian tensions seemed to be easing and how many of the young were mixing without concern for religion.

For the IRA, much of 1962 was taken up with dealing with the fallout from the campaign's failure. The ceasefire was not universally accepted; Magan and McLogan, still smarting from the

Curragh disputes, demanded that a statement be issued absolving them of responsibility for the end of the campaign. Mac Curtain, who had been largely marginalized since his release in 1959, also associated himself with the two men. The critics toured Sinn Féin cumainn pushing their view, and the new IRA leadership eventually had them expelled from the party, a small number of other members resigning in solidarity. In many ways the row was a culmination of the disputes that had begun in the Curragh, representing more a generational divide than a political one. After years working with them Garland respected the 'three Macs', Magan in particular, as 'honourable people', but he felt they were 'too honourable to be revolutionaries. You can't fight an enemy with your hands tied behind your back or [with] some kind of principles, where you say I won't do this, I won't go into parliament and tell lies, I won't recognize courts and this kind of thing. You have to have your hands free to do what's possible or what you want to do.'

Another dispute arose when some Irish republicans in America accused Sean Cronin of being a communist and of having been responsible in some way for the execution of IRA leader Charlie Kerins in 1944. The first accusation centred on Cronin's 'progressive' American wife Terry Millen and on positive articles in the *United Irishman* regarding Castro and Cuba. The claim about Kerins related to Cronin having once been an officer in the Irish Army. An IRA Army Council investigation into the allegations cleared Cronin but he left the IRA anyway, though remaining sympathetic. That an inquiry was held at all disgusted Garland, who felt that it was 'McCarthyism'. It was also an indication of how powerful anti-communist sentiment remained. The *United Irishman* of July 1962 re-emphasized that the republican movement had no connection with 'atheistic communism'. This statement reflected the views of many, if not most, within the IRA, and even those sympathetic to radicalism were very wary of the communist label.

The IRA constitution specified that in peacetime the General Army Convention should meet every two years. Units from around the country sent delegates who elected an Army Executive of twelve, who in turn elected a seven-member Army Council, the supreme leadership body, which met once a month. The organization's Chief of Staff was then selected from among these seven. By all accounts Goulding, then aged 40, was reluctant to take up the position of Chief of Staff when his colleagues offered it to him in September 1962. His view later was that not many others wanted to do the job and that he represented 'the shakings of the bag'. But after a week's consideration Goulding accepted the position, succeeding Ruairí Ó Brádaigh, who had held the post since 1960. Ó Brádaigh returned to Roscommon, a teaching post and his young family, though he remained on the Army Council.

The five other men on the Army Council were all well known to one another. Seamus Costello, then 24 and working as a car salesman in Dublin, was nicknamed the 'boy general' because he had led a flying column during the Border Campaign while still a teenager. Costello exuded charisma. Many were struck by his dark good looks and a tendency to slowly draw upon a cigarette in a manner which drew attention to a missing finger, a battle scar from his recent military activity. Costello's job gave him access to high-powered cars, which he drove 'like a madman'. An exasperated passenger once complained that taking a lift from him was like travelling in a spaceship; Costello's curt response was, 'Were you ever in a spaceship?' Some of his senior colleagues found Costello arrogant and abrasive, but volunteers liked the fact that he wasn't afraid of 'getting his hands dirty ... He led from the front.' Mac Giolla was both chairman of the Army Council and president of Sinn Féin. Mick Ryan kept in close contact with the grassroots of the organization nationwide. At 26, he was regarded as very much a military figure and only 'reluctantly' began to pay attention to political developments during the 1960s. Completing the 1962 Army Council were two volunteers based outside Dublin. Paddy Mulcahy, aged 45, was a Limerick insurance agent and Sinn Féin councillor who had joined the IRA in the 1930s. His wife Susan was a senior figure in Cumann na mBan. Finally there was Clare IRA leader Dennis McInerney, in his mid-twenties and a printer by trade. Of these seven only Ó Brádaigh and Mac Giolla had received third-level education, both at University College Dublin. Goulding appointed Costello to the post of Adjutant General, which was arguably the most important position after the Chief of Staff, while Ryan was now Quartermaster General.

Members of the Dublin-based General Headquarters staff oversaw the day-to-day running of the IRA and other branches of the movement, including the *United Irishman*. Each of the IRA divisional areas had its own local command staff, largely replicating the roles of the Army Council and headed up by an Officer Commanding (O/C). These local commanders were appointed by the Chief of Staff but in practice had to be popular locally if good order was to be maintained.

With the decline of active involvement after the order to dump arms, it was a very junior volunteer indeed who did not have some rank within the organization. Those leading volunteers who made up the GHQ staff, army executive and local commands were a mixed group – a coalition of men with differing political views and backgrounds united only in the desire to use physical force to end partition. Garland, then 30, was typical only in his belief that there could be no question of walking away after the ceasefire: for him 'the IRA existed', there were comrades in prison whose release had to be campaigned for, and Ireland's revolution was still unfinished. He operated full-time for the IRA after 1962, following a short period working in a dairy. Garland's military record gave him tremendous authority and he was highly respected, if not liked, by all. Many saw him as a dour figure, though those who knew him well felt this arose from shyness. He maintained his low public profile during the early 1960s.

After his return from prison in England Goulding resumed running his family's small painting and decorating firm. He had moved to Rathfarnham on Dublin's south side, and often met Garland and Ryan at the weekend in local pubs such as The Yellow House or Slattery's. Malachy McGurran, a native of Lurgan who had come to prominence during the recent campaign, and Tom Mitchell, the Omagh prisoner who had won a Westminster seat in 1955, were also occasional members of this social group. Costello was living with his wife Maelíosa and their children in Cornels-court, a south-side suburb of Dublin. He didn't socialize much with his fellow IRA leaders, although Goulding had been the best man at his wedding.

The Gardaí estimated that the IRA had 657 volunteers in the South at the end of 1962. The question for those still involved was, 'What next?' To many, including members of the leadership such as Mick Ryan, simply preparing for a 'new and better campaign' was the answer. Clandestine recruiting, training and rearming were resumed. Weapons instruction and drilling took place with small groups in private houses, including Costello's own home. Emphasis was placed on teaching recruits how to care for and dismantle small arms. Weekend or week-long camps were organized intermittently in secluded districts such as the Slieve Bloom Mountains or the Glen of Imaal, where firing practice, explosives training and instruction in battle techniques took place. Often the volunteers would have little idea where they were, having been transported at night in the back of a van to an isolated farm or woodland. Becoming accustomed to living and sleeping in rough conditions was an important part of the training, and for the physically unfit the regime could be quite a shock to the system. The weapons used were often old. These included Lee-Enfield rifles dating back to the Civil War, Thompson guns, and a variety of revolvers and automatic pistols. Sometimes Goulding or another senior figure would attend and give a lecture outlining the organization's aims. The wider public was made aware of ongoing IRA activity in July 1963 when Gardaí raided a camp in the Knockmealdown Mountains. Four men were arrested and eight weapons, including a Bren gun, seized. Charged in relation to this incident, Belfast man Bobby McKnight told the court that the weapons were 'to be used against the British forces of occupation in the six counties'. He and his colleagues were sentenced to two months in jail.

One source of IRA recruits was the Fianna Éireann, which was reorganized in the post-1962 period by a new 'Chief Scout', Seán Ó Cionnaith. Born Sean Kenny in Ballinasloe, Co. Galway,

Ó Cionnaith had been active in Sinn Féin in London in the late 1950s. Fianna branches were established or revived in Belfast, Castlebar, Ennis, Limerick, Cork, Galway and several parts of Dublin. Groups were also established in England and the United States. Much Fianna activity was similar to that of ordinary scouts, and its summer camps were advertised openly. Other activities were less public. In Belfast, Fianna members were employed in intelligence gathering and surveillance; one task was to watch for patrols on the Falls Road by RUC Special Branch detectives Harry Taylor and Davy Armstrong. Many Fianna progressed to arms training classes, at which IRA officers would start by instructing the boys in the use of handguns before moving on to the Thompson and finally to explosives. Girls still joined Cumann na gCáilíní, the female version of the Fianna, which placed less emphasis on military training.

The failure of the Border Campaign had illustrated, to Goulding at least, the inability of the IRA to achieve its aims solely through force of arms. He had come to feel that in the past the IRA had been elitist, its attitude towards the mass of people being that 'we didn't care what these bastards want, we know what is good for them'. But now he felt that the 'demand for revolution should come from the people, not from a number of people sitting in a back room'. As a youth Goulding had witnessed the radicalization of the 1930s, when a number of socialist-leaning IRA officers broke away to form the Republican Congress. The group split after only five months over the question of whether or not to become an openly socialist party; some of its leading figures later departed to fight for the Republicans in the Spanish Civil War. Despite its short existence the Republican Congress had left an indelible mark on left-wing republican thinking, not least due to its ability, however fleetingly, to overcome the Northern sectarian divide: Congress supporters from Belfast's Protestant Shankill Road famously carried a banner inscribed 'Break the connection with capitalism' at the 1934 commemoration at Bodenstown. In 1963 awareness of these aspects of republican history was becoming more widespread. Desmond Greaves' biography of James

Connolly, which made clear the influence of Marxism on the 1916 martyr, was published in 1961, and in 1963 Republican Congress veteran Peadar O'Donnell's memoir *There Will Be Another Day* brought the left-wing republican analysis of the Civil War to a new generation. George Gilmore, a Republican Congress founder from a Protestant background, would advise Goulding and other members of the IRA leadership on the lessons of this failed left-wing venture. Goulding concluded that the great mistake of O'Donnell and his comrades had been to leave the movement. If the socialists had stayed inside the organization, he believed, they could have eventually won over the majority of the 1930s IRA.

Goulding hoped to use the bicentenary of the birth of Theobald Wolfe Tone, in 1963, to bring people together for a re-examination of republican strategy. Following discussions with Sean Cronin and others he started to assemble like-minded thinkers into the Wolfe Tone Directories. Initially these groups were focused on attempting to reawaken interest in Tone's widely misunderstood legacy. Regarded by many as the 'father of Irish republicanism', Tone, a young Dublin Protestant lawyer, had been a leading figure in the clandestine Society of United Irishmen of the 1790s. This organization, dominated by Northern Presbyterians, had attempted to introduce the ideas of the French Revolution to Ireland, eventually leading the ill-fated rebellion of 1798. To republicans, Tone's most profound statements were his wish 'to substitute the common name of Irishmen in place of the denominations of Protestant, Catholic and Dissenter' and to 'break the connection with England' – ideas that seemed to offer the possibility of an Ireland free from British rule and sectarian division. Dismayed at the failure of many of his own propertied class to support the United Irishmen, Tone had written: 'Our independence must be had at all hazards, if the men of property will not support us, they must fall: we can support ourselves by the aid of that numerous and respectable class of the community, the men of no property.'

Goulding hoped that the discussion groups would decide upon appropriate events to commemorate the bicentenary 'as a launching point from which the doctrine of Republicanism could be taught anew'. Although many of those involved in the Wolfe Tone Directories were serving or former members of the IRA, non-IRA members were also included in an attempt to broaden the ideological pool from which republicans could draw inspiration. Among the plans drawn up were ceremonies at the graves of the leading United Irishmen Thomas Russell, William Orr and Jemmy Hope. There was also a commemorative event on Cave Hill, overlooking Belfast, which marked a 1795 gathering there by United Irish leaders. The highlight of the year's commemorations was a series of lectures in Dublin's Mansion House in September. By this stage the number and range of people contributing to the Wolfe Tone Directories had grown. The openness and success of the lectures was surprising, considering the concept had emerged from the clandestine world of the IRA. Roger McHugh, head of English at University College Dublin, was director of the event and delivered a paper, as did the Protestant essayist Hubert Butler. Discussions within the movement increasingly focused on the egalitarian aspects of the United Irishmen. Tomás Mac Giolla and others were enthused by reading about the life of Jemmy Hope, a Downpatrick Presbyterian weaver whose political struggle had continued for decades after 1798 and whose writings seemed to provide a working-class analysis of the rebellion. In 1964 Sean Cronin published a pamphlet on Hope that was promoted as recommended reading for IRA volunteers by the organization's clandestine journal *An t-Oglac.*

Goulding's increasing embrace of left-wing concepts shocked many who knew him as an orthodox IRA man. Some began to suggest that he had been converted to Marxism by the spy Klaus Fuchs in Wakefield. However, his fellow prisoner Seamus Murphy contends that Goulding 'turned to the left on his own steam' through reading and discussions with other republicans and that 'Fuchs never tried to turn anyone – it was hard to get a word out of him!' A cursory glance at contemporary developments in Asia, the Caribbean and Africa might also have pointed Goulding towards socialism as a model that offered his revolutionary organiz-ation the best chance of success. A quarter of the world's population lived in societies that defined themselves as communist: the USSR, China, Eastern Europe, North Vietnam, North Korea and Cuba. The age of European empire was over. France had been humiliated in Vietnam and at Suez and was on its way out of Algeria. Its partner in the 1956 Middle Eastern debacle, Britain, had seen repression fail to halt independence in Kenya and was giving up its colonies in Africa in rapid succession. By the mid-1960s Portuguese colonial rule in Africa, along with the last bastions of white supremacy on that continent, Rhodesia and South Africa, were being challenged by guerrilla movements. The Cuban experience struck a particular chord with some Irish republicans. As Mac Giolla reflected, 'All our heroes were losers . . . Che and Fidel were the first winners.' It was easy to conclude that socialism in some form would ultimately be victorious over capitalism. The Soviets themselves, through the KGB, decided in 1961 to utilize national liberation movements in order to 'create circumstances . . . which would assist in diverting the attention and forces of the United States and its allies' and destabilize western capitalism.

Despite the economic advances of the early 1960s, poverty and inequality remained a part of Irish life. Emigrants returned to a housing crisis in Dublin, where four people died when tenements collapsed in 1963. Thousands of families lived in dilapidated flats while awaiting an affordable home. The west of Ireland continued to decline, as small farms vanished. Fianna Fáil ministers such as Charles Haughey and Brian Lenihan cultivated relationships with property developers and the 'mohair suit brigade' who frequented the Shelbourne Hotel's Horseshoe Bar and had none of the old Fianna Fáil reticence about ostentatious wealth. Meanwhile, liberalization went only so far. In 1965 author John McGahern was sacked from his job as a teacher after the Catholic Church objected to his book *The Dark*, which was itself banned in the Republic.

But there were stirrings of opposition. Cooperatives were set up in the hope of reversing rural decline, and Fr. James McDyer's 'Glencolmkille experiment' of cooperative farming in Donegal and the 'Save the West' campaign attracted wide interest. Liberal clergymen emerged demanding action on problems such as housing. The changing political climate even saw the Irish Labour Party begin to talk cautiously about socialism. Workers were unwilling to wait until gifted their share of the economic boom: strikes, official and unofficial, became commonplace. In Northern Ireland, Catholics were still deprived of equal access to jobs in many areas, and the linkage between local voting rights and home ownership disenfranchised the poorest, disproportionately Catholic. Ulster's heavy industries were in decline and uncertainty about the future seeped into the Protestant working class. The dynamics of Northern Irish society were also affected by Catholics taking advantage of free third-level education and entering Queen's University Belfast in ever greater numbers; 22 per cent of Queen's students were Catholic by 1961. This generation would be more ready than their parents to question both the Northern establishment and their own community's structures.

The idea that the Protestant working class's changing relationship with the establishment might lead that community to re-appraise republican politics was the basis of much discussion among radicals. For some Southern Border Campaign veterans, their first experience of the reality of Northern Protestant identity had come in jail. Garland broke up the monotony of prison routine by attending Sunday hymn recitals given by Protestant church choirs in Crumlin Road:

It struck me at the time . . . how determined and sincere they were in proclaiming [their] beliefs. The mixture of the religious and the political was so dominant, you could see that these were people who were not engaged in some frivolous thing; for them it was deadly serious . . . By the end of the time I was in the jail I had a different view of the make-up of the society.

In 1965 *An t-Oglac* argued that 'the successful completion of the Irish national revolution [is] going to depend on the movement building good relations with disaffected elements among the present supporters of unionism. This means basically the Belfast working class, many of whom support Labour.'

In Belfast, internees released during 1961 found that there were only about 24 IRA volunteers in the city, with access to a minuscule quantity of weapons. Billy McKee, a 1940s veteran and devout Catholic, took over as the local O/C. The first task was to convince former prisoners to 'report back', but the results were disappointing. Several men had left for Britain to find work. A number of others, like Joe Cahill, declined to re-involve themselves. But reorganization was aided by the fact that the Saor Uladh schism had been healed in Belfast; after returning from a spell working in England, Billy McMillen became McKee's adjutant.

The two men were central to a row that would shape the Belfast organization for a generation. The confrontation developed around a Wolfe Tone commemorative parade from Beechmount to Casement Park in June 1963. Just a few hours before the parade, the RUC demanded that the event proceed without the tricolour, the display of which was illegal in Northern Ireland. The organizers, including McKee, reluctantly agreed, but many other IRA men were disgusted. They claimed a failure to show defiance had made the IRA a laughing stock. While spectators were watching entertainments in Casement Park, a furious row erupted in the Belfast republican movement's HQ in Cyprus Street. McKee was severely criticized and left in a fury, resigning as O/C and eventually leaving the IRA altogether. At the age of 35, Billy McMillen became the new Belfast commander. A scaffolder by trade, he was stocky and short, a fluent Irish-speaker who was active in the Gaelic League (where he was generally referred to as Liam). McMillen's elder brother Bob had served several years in jail during the Second World War, having been wounded in Belfast in 1942, in an incident believed to have been the inspiration for F. L. Green's novel *Odd Man Out*. His brother Art was also a member of the IRA's D Company, having joined the Fianna in 1945. McMillen's command staff included Bobby McKnight, Jim Sullivan, Denis Toner and Leo Martin, all of whom had been imprisoned during the Border Campaign. Unlike some of his contemporaries, 'the wee man', as McMillen was known, was comfortable in non-republican company.

The Falls Road was the spine of nationalist Belfast, stretching from Divis Street out to the new housing estates of Andersonstown. The heart of Belfast republicanism was the area of narrow terraced housing bordered by the Grosvenor Road, Cullingtree Road, Albert Street and the Falls Road near the city centre. This was the home of Belfast Brigade's First Battalion, D Company, a designation that harked back to the days when the city's IRA structure contained hundreds rather than dozens of volunteers. Men were sworn into the IRA in an upstairs room adjacent to the Long Bar in Leeson Street, so called because its entrance was in Leeson Street and the exit in Cyprus Street. It was owned by Paddy Leneghan, 'a gentleman' who was on friendly terms with his republican customers. Family background was very important in Belfast republicanism and most of the IRA's recruits in the 1960s were already connected with the movement. Sean Curry from Abercorn Street grew up playing hurling and going to Irish dancing classes. Curry joined the Fianna in January 1965 because he 'knew a lot of people in it', and it was some time before he realized it was actually illegal. Many of those who joined the IRA had no great expectations; it was 'just something you done . . . you never thought anything would come of it'.

There were active republicans in other areas of the city such as the Markets, New Lodge and Ardoyne, but in much smaller numbers. Seamus Lynch, a docker from Moffat Street in 'Sailortown', joined the IRA in 1965 when a monthly sale of 25 *United Irishman* was considered good in north Belfast. Republicans formed a subculture within broader nationalist society and had never been a majority among Catholics in the city. Attitudes towards them ranged from passive respect to bemusement and at times hostility. 'Catch yourself on' was a common refrain when young Fianna members collected for the prisoners in bars along the Falls right up to the late 1960s. One republican remembered an occasion when he and a comrade were carrying rifles and desperately trying to evade capture by the RUC; they entered what they thought was a supportive house, but the occupants 'tried to push us back into the street'.

Republicans generally socialized in their own pubs and clubs, and many of the senior figures did not drink or socialize with non-republicans at all. A few of them cultivated an aloofness that sometimes annoyed their younger comrades. At one Easter commemoration men wearing Glasgow Celtic scarves were told to leave the parade, with some regarding Celtic fans as 'cornerboys', not real republicans. Gaelic games and Irish dancing were encouraged, with Dwyer's GAC on the Falls the club most associated with the movement.

Public attention was drawn to the movement in 1964 when Sinn Féin contested the Westminster elections as 'Republicans', in order to circumvent Northern Ireland's ban on the party. In Belfast there were four candidates in the IRA-run campaign – McMillen, McKnight, Frank McGlade and David McConnell. In late September rioting broke out after the RUC smashed into McMillen's election headquarters in Divis Street and confiscated a tricolour from the office's window. A Free Presbyterian minister called Ian Paisley, who was making a name for himself as a demagogic preacher, had threatened to march on Divis Street if the flag was not removed. When the tricolour was displayed again the next day, the police returned in riot gear but were met by bottles, stones and petrol bombs. Over the next three days up to 2,000 people were involved in fighting on the Falls with the RUC. McMillen and McKnight symbolically hung out another tricolour and led crowds in 'Amhrán na bhFiann'. Support of the candidates also came from James Connolly's youngest daughter Ina, who claimed that 'your cause is my father's cause'. Later that week 5,000 people marched behind the tricolour on the Falls, escorted by Fianna boys carrying hurleys. Meanwhile 2,000 Paisley supporters rallied at the Ulster Hall. Speaking to the Falls Road crowd, McMillen made it clear that it was not the intention of republicans to provoke unionists, with the tricolour only being displayed in a completely nationalist area. But it was clear that communal loyalties were a powerful mobilizing force. Smaller-scale trouble broke out elsewhere during the election, with loyalists attacking republicans campaigning in several rural towns. According to McMillen, the IRA in Belfast gained a 'couple of dozen new recruits' after the riots, but local rivalries were apparent too. The Republican Labour Party accused the Unionists of trying to boost Sinn Féin by giving them publicity in order to split the nationalist vote. (A Unionist actually won the seat.)

Away from the sectarian tensions of Northern Ireland, the maintenance of Ireland's distinct cultural identity was a major concern for the IRA leadership. The IRA's 1963 Easter statement had asserted that 'the continued existence of the Irish people as a distinct national entity is endangered as never before by the proposed immersion of a weak, anglicised and foreign-occupied Ireland' into a 'Western European Superstate'. Agitation against the European Common Market would become a major facet of republican activity over the next few years. Much of the rhetoric was explicitly traditionalist. In 1964 the IRA stressed that 'our native language and culture are being systematically obliterated . . . our finance is being controlled by the Bank of England . . . our land is being grabbed at an alarming rate [and] our industry and commerce is controlled by foreigners'.

There was little there for republicans of the 1950s to disagree with, but the involvement of Roy Johnston and Anthony Coughlan in discussions within the Wolfe Tone Directories – which were reconfigured as the Wolfe Tone Society in 1964 – was leading to increasing internal unease. Both were seen as outsiders and, worse, as communists. Johnston, now 34, had emigrated with his young family to London in 1960. While there he joined the Communist Party and both he and Coughlan were members of the Connolly Association. Coughlan was a graduate of Cork University and had been a member of the Irish Labour Party before he emigrated in 1958. He had been secretary of the West London branch of the Connolly Association. He returned to Ireland in 1961 to take up a post at Trinity College, and now rented a downstairs flat in Johnston's home in Ranelagh.

The origins of the Connolly Association lay in the remnants of the Republican Congress in Britain during the 1940s. Its leading figure was the historian Desmond Greaves, who also edited its paper the *Irish Democrat*. Outsiders often saw it as the British communists' bridge into the Irish community, but the Communist Party was not very enthusiastic about work among Irish emigrants and the Connolly Association generally ploughed its own furrow. Greaves' ambition was to make Irish unification the policy of the British labour movement. He believed that activists should not criticize the southern Irish state, which he once described as 'the most progressive state in western Europe', but rather concentrate on exposing injustice in Northern Ireland. Greaves suggested that 'both pro-communists and anti-communists [should] forget that little quarrel until we get Ireland free', but this did not stop priests warning their congregations in Kilburn and elsewhere against buying the *Irish Democrat*. In addition to its directly political content, the paper also provided a forum for Irish workers to highlight health and safety issues, particularly in the building industry, and brought progressive opinions into Irish communities on issues such as apartheid and Vietnam. Greaves' most important idea was to launch a civil rights campaign to discredit Ulster unionism in Britain by exposing its discrimination towards Catholics. He believed that this would lead to sympathy for Irish unity. This strategy had been the policy of the Connolly Association since 1955.

The relationship between the Irish communists and the association was not straightforward. For a start there were two Irish parties: the Communist Party of Northern Ireland and the Irish Workers' Party. The parties took subtly different positions on partition and discrimination in the North. The CPNI had a significant membership among trade unionists from Protestant backgrounds in Belfast while the IWP had a small but important base in Dublin trade unionism. The chairman of the IWP was Mick O'Riordan, a bus conductor and veteran of the Spanish Civil War. He won 183 votes in the 1965 general election, which was an accurate reflection of the party's popular appeal. Blessed with plenty of personal courage and routinely denounced from the pulpit for many years, O'Riordan was single-mindedly loyal to Moscow, as was his party. After 1965 the IWP's youth wing, the Connolly Youth Movement, a more flexible and popular body, began to recruit among Dublin working-class youngsters.

Johnston and Coughlan were seen by some IRA leaders as agents of Desmond Greaves, and hence of the British Communist Party. Although Johnston and Coughlan were close socially and shared similar views, both believing that Lemass's economic policies were increasing the dependence of the South on British capital, facilitating a master plan to reintegrate the Republic into the 'British Imperial system', the pair had differences in their political approach. Johnston was not a doctrinaire communist thinker. His personal experience had led him to conclude that the Irish communists were so entranced by Russia that they ignored the Irish historical tradition: 'Moscow was Rome to them.' Johnston was attracted by the idea of civil rights but he thought that Greaves was too dismissive of the potential of republicanism. For Johnston it was 'a matter of attempting to influence the radical tradition in a national context, as distinct from the radical tradition in an alien context'. By 1964 he was impressed by the example of Cuba, where a broad-based movement, rural as well as urban, had 'upstaged' a narrow Moscow-line Communist party and carried through a popular revolution. He also departed from orthodoxy by stressing that, in Ireland as in Algeria, 'resistance to imperial domination was more likely to be rural-based than urban-based'. A lecture by Johnston on economic resistance was published in the *United Irishman* of October 1964 under the byline Ríogh MacEoin. In the following month's paper he put forward a suggestion that Ulster unionism could be divided by a campaign for democratic rights that highlighted the issue of discrimination against Catholics.

Coughlan was much closer to Greaves in his thinking. His aim was 'real' Irish independence – defending Irish economic sovereignty against Britain and the EEC – rather than any form of socialism, which for him was not on the agenda. Neither Johnston nor Coughlan had any of the traditional republican worries about entering parliament. Johnston built a close relationship with Goulding, who invited him into the IRA during the summer of 1964, creating more unease in the ranks. Apart from their communist connections, there were several other reasons why Johnston and Coughlan were regarded with suspicion. They had never been militarily active in a movement that above all valued such experience, preferably with some jail time included. Johnston had a bad stammer that made listening to him frustrating; some found him arrogant; and his background as a Protestant Trinity graduate counted against him in some circles. Coughlan's status as a key adviser to the IRA leadership, even though he had not actually joined the organization, was also resented. In British Intelligence reports he was referred to as an IRA 'travelling lecturer'.

Suspicion among some IRA members about the leadership's direction was intensified by the untimely death of one of the 'three Macs' in July 1964. Padraig McLogan, who collected handguns, was found in his Blanchardstown home with a bullet wound to the head, and a Walther 9mm pistol was found beside his body along with a spent cartridge. An inquest ruled that his death was accidental, resulting from a fall while carrying a loaded weapon, but among republicans there were rumours McLogan had been murdered because of his opposition to the Goulding leadership. Eventually Garland was identified in these conspiracy theories as the main suspect. The murder allegation had little basis in reality but it gained adherents as the years went on. Another republican who died during 1964 was Goulding's friend Brendan Behan, whose alcoholism led to his death at the age of 41. Despite his wayward relationship with the movement Behan was given an IRA funeral complete with colour party. Goulding, who was the first person to reach Behan's deathbed, soon began a relationship with Beatrice Behan, the writer's widow, despite being married himself; the couple eventually had a son, Paudge.

Goulding's plans for republican revitalization involved convincing IRA members of the importance of social agitation. An IRA Department of Political Education was set up in early 1965 and began organizing educational sessions for volunteers. All units were ordered to appoint an education officer, *An t-Oglac* explaining that 'the idea is that each area shall have one specialist who understands the nature of British rule in Ireland in *all* its aspects'. It was emphasized that to 'fight the chequebook is going to require a high order of skill. The enemy is not going to be so obliging as to make it easy for us to shoot at him with a gun.' Therefore all units needed to appoint someone who understood the importance of 'economic intelligence . . . where is land being sold up to foreigners [and] what is the likely effect of a proposed new factory on the economy of the area?' One of the first education meetings took place in March at the La Cabena Ballroom in Howth, where about 20 IRA members heard Johnston and others present lectures on the importance of political education, economic resistance, co-operatives and trade unions. At a later conference Northern speakers introduced a session on 'Local democracy as a threat to Unionist rule'. Units were asked for details of their volunteers' occupations and whether or not they were active in trade unions or cooperatives. This information was used to help education officers formulate plans for 'economic resistance'. The department's work was bolstered by Bobby McKnight's transfer from his duties as a training officer to work countrywide on education.

The IRA's 1965 Easter statement mentioned a major 'internal examination' taking place within the army. This was a reference to a 'special conference of Republicans' which had been proposed at the 1964 General Army Convention to 'discuss political tactics, policy and internal organization and make recommendations'. Mac Giolla recalls this period as consisting of 'meeting after meeting after meeting' in rooms 'absolutely chock-full of smoke'. The discussions resulted in ten recommendations being put forward for debate at an extraordinary General Army Convention held on 5 June 1965. Delegates from across the country gathered to take part in the first major discussion of the movement's future direction since 1962. Among the recommendations up for debate was that elected republicans take their seats in Leinster House. This was guaranteed to produce dissension, and Goulding, who had concluded that abstentionism would have to go if serious political advances were to be made, addressed a special pre-convention message to all IRA volunteers, urging them to study the recommendations 'without emotion or prejudice'. He was aware that 'some of our finest' were in favour of taking seats in the Dáil just as 'some of our finest' were opposed. He asked that they all give it their 'maturest thought [and] give a reasoned and fair reply'. In particular Goulding urged:

Should it happen that you are against the recommendation you must not regard those who favour it as traitors; should it happen that you favour the recommendation you must not regard your opponents in the matter as either stupid or traditionalist. You will debate this question, as all others, with comrades and friends, not with enemies.

The proposal to drop abstentionism was defeated by a large majority, despite the support of Goulding and Costello. Even so, the debate over the future direction of the movement had moved from the drawing-room discussions of the Wolfe Tone Society to the floor of an army convention. The convention had also renewed calls for preparations to be made for a new campaign, and a 'military council' that included Garland (now an Army Council member) and Mac Stíofáin was given the job of formulating a plan of action.

Among the prominent opponents of the proposal to drop abstentionism was Seán Mac Stíofáin, O/C of the Cork/South Kerry area, who was elected to the Army Council at the convention. Born in London in 1928 as John Stephenson and of only distant Irish extraction on his mother's side, Mac Stíofáin had done national service in the Royal Air Force but became involved with Sinn Féin and the IRA in the late 1940s. Imprisoned for his part in the Felsted raid in 1953, he moved to Ireland with his wife upon his release in 1959. His status as a convert to Irish republicanism made him quite zealous, even by the IRA's standards. Goulding considered Mac Stíofáin a 'courageous' person, but would later suggest the Londoner was 'continually trying to prove that he [was] as much an Irishman as anyone else'.

At his first Army Council meeting Mac Stíofáin argued that Johnston's IRA membership was in contravention of the organization's standing order against communists being volunteers. Goulding refused to countenance this argument, warning that if Johnston was forced out then he would resign as well. Meanwhile Johnston attempted to encourage Mac Stíofáin to support the new political direction, introducing him to the work of Italian communist Pier Paolo Pasolini, who had made a film based on the Gospel according to Saint Matthew. In Johnston's view the work portrayed 'Jesus Christ as a revolutionary in the Roman environment', which he hoped would appeal to the strongly Catholic Mac Stíofáin; but there was to be no meeting of minds.

The question of political development was not the only source of strains. The IRA was in no state to reopen military hostilities and there were disagreements as to how seriously the organization was taking this task. New weapons would obviously be required, as much of the IRA's arsenal had been lost during the previous campaign. Mick Ryan as Quartermaster General on occasion had to move a single .303 rifle from one end of the country to the other for training purposes. He proposed a plan whereby two volunteers, unknown to the Gardaí, would join the British Army in England and prepare the ground for an arms raid there. Goulding disagreed, arguing that it was not the priority at that time. Frustrated by the unwillingness to take rearming seriously, Ryan resigned from his position in October 1965 and decided to concentrate on his day job. But he remained on friendly terms with his IRA comrades, continuing to drive Garland around the country on organizing trips.

While these debates were going on the IRA had become more intensely involved in social agitation. In December 1964 the organization issued a statement condemning the exploitation of Irish fishermen by foreign competition – in the opinion of the *Irish Democrat* this amounted to the organization's first 'independent political statement' since the 1930s. During February the IRA became embroiled in a struggle over evictions in Midleton, Co. Cork. The town, with a population of 2,700, was owned by the Earl of Midleton, who had announced his intention of selling up. The IRA, with local O/C Mac Stíofáin to the fore, began a protest campaign demanding that the government acquire the land by compulsory purchase and give the local tenants and leaseholders the option of purchasing their property at a minimal sum. Volunteers distributed a leaflet arguing that 'every town in Ireland should be the property of the people who live in it. No town should be condemned to live or die in the manner ordained by any outside body, whether in London or Dublin.' They called for locals to consider the possibility of cooperative ownership and promised to 'take the necessary steps to prevent any evictions'. The campaign built up momentum, with 2,000 people marching in Cork city and boycotts of property sales taking place.

IRA volunteers were finding social issues to become involved with in other places as well. In Dublin the growing housing crisis escalated in August 1965 when homeless families barricaded themselves into Griffith Barracks. A total of 18 families, 87 people in all, were being housed in old army quarters while awaiting accommodation. The barracks were overcrowded and unsanitary, and men and women were segregated after 10 p.m. There was barbed wire on the walls and soldiers on guard duty. Gardaí eventually moved in to remove the barricades and evict the homeless families – who then marched across the city to Mountjoy Square, where they set up home in wooden shacks and tents on a derelict site. The encampment was adjacent to the *United Irishman* offices at Sinn Féin headquarters in 30 Gardiner Place, which became the centre of much of the agitation.

During the same summer a two-month strike took place at Dundalk Engineering Works. Local IRA volunteers were involved in support work for the strikers and the *United Irishman* gave the issue extensive coverage. The IRA was also involved in mobilizing opposition to redundancies at the Castlecomer mines in Kilkenny, holding local meetings to rouse support and calling for cooperative ownership of the industry. Most controversially in October 1965 the organization backed striking telephonists, who were demanding recognition for their union, the Irish Telephonists' Association. Clashes on picket lines led to arrests and the government using the Offences Against the State Act to jail several strikers. A hunger strike followed. In December, the strike went down to what an IRA statement termed 'shameful defeat' due to the lack of support from the other trade unions.

Some republicans feared that such social interventions meant the military role of the IRA was being downgraded. Mindful of this view, Goulding continued to stress that 'the only way to rid this country of an armed British force is to confront them with an armed force of Irishmen backed by a united Irish people. The British forces in the six counties will be confronted by such a force.' However, the IRA leadership was also intent on social agitation in Northern Ireland. Addressing the Easter 1965 commemoration in Belfast, Mac Giolla outlined the importance of a new campaign for 'one man, one vote'. He stated that until recently republicans had not understood the importance of the restrictions on local government voting in the North. Now, however, the movement was preparing a national and international campaign to highlight this discrimination. He assured his 3,000 listeners that this was not a 'distraction' from the goal of a united Ireland.

Eagerness for armed activity meant that some activists were continuing to be attracted to splinter groups. One such group was the Dublin-based 'Invincibles', led by 'Ructions' Doyle. Numbering around a dozen, they undertook rifle practice on Dollymount Strand. One former IRA member recalls leaving this group after six months when he realized that Doyle was 'a headbanger, even by our standards'. In Cork, internal dissatisfaction found violent expression during 1963. President de Valera had been invited to unveil a memorial at the city's republican plot, in St Finbarr's Cemetery, on St Patrick's Day. The plot included the grave of John Joe Kavanagh, who had been killed by the Gardaí in 1940. Some IRA members demanded that action be taken, but they were refused permission by Mac Stíofáin. The night before the unveiling, two Border Campaign veterans, Desmond Swanton and Gerry Madden, attempted to blow up the new memorial. The mine they had constructed exploded prematurely, killing Swanton and maiming Madden. The IRA made it clear that they were 'not responsible' for the explosion, but admitted that Swanton and Madden had been members.

Several of Swanton's comrades found their efforts to give him a full IRA funeral blocked by the local leadership and were dismissed from the organization. They published leaflets announcing the formation of a new group; MacStíofáin and one of his adjutants, Gerry McCarthy, responded by raiding the group's premises. The dissidents retaliated by seizing copies of the *United Irishman* meant for sale in Cork and arriving armed at the Thomas Ashe Hall. A stand-off ensued when Goulding came to Cork to adjudicate, and negotiations to ensure a compromise broke down. Republicans in Cork were informed that Swanton's comrades were now 'enemies' of the IRA. By 1964 the breakaway group, which included Jim Lane, was using the name Irish Revolutionary Forces and a year later publishing a journal entitled *An Phoblacht*. The IRF retained access to arms and made clear that they would not be 'stood down' by the IRA. Politically they declared themselves 'Marxist-Leninists' of the Chinese variety.

Similar dissent over the lack of armed action was causing rumblings in Dublin. In early 1965 a local IRA officer, Frank Keane, was court-martialled and dismissed for organizing units without Army Council authorization. Keane recalls being tired of training with weapons that were 'out of date for Jesse James's time'. Some volunteers were also unhappy about being ordered to sell the *United Irishman* and partake in open political work, which they felt was beneath their status as members of a 'secret army'. Such attitudes contributed to a decision by a group of Dublin IRA men to carry out a robbery of a rent office, without Army Council authorization, in December 1965. One of the raiders, Joe Dillon, was sentenced to five years in jail for the robbery.

A visit by Princess Margaret to Birr and Abbeyleix in January 1965 sparked off a round of conflict between local IRA volunteers and Gardaí. Prominent graffiti appeared, bearing slogans such as 'British Royalty get out!' and trees were felled across roads leading into Birr. Clashes erupted with Gardaí during protests against the visit and several people were injured. Ten republicans were arrested and more scuffles broke out when they appeared in court. Eventually a crowd of 200 people tried to storm Mountmellick courthouse and were repelled by baton charges. In September of that year the IRA attacked the British torpedo boat HMS *Brave Borderer* during a visit to Waterford. The boat was hit by fire from an anti-tank rifle; three volunteers were later arrested and jailed for the attack. Another vessel, HMS *Lofoten*, was due to visit Cork in October and Garland was sent to the city to work with MacStíofáin on planning an attack. The Gardaí received information that machine guns and a bazooka were to be used on the control room of the vessel, with a view to causing casualties. The visit was cancelled, and the IRA claimed this was due to their threat of action against the ship. In October the Special Branch placed a British Hydrographic Service naval team working in Glencolmkille under armed guard after they discovered IRA plans to blow up the group's equipment. The same month volunteers raided Belfast's St Gabriel's Secondary School, where a British army recruiting film was being shown. Ten masked men armed with hurleys destroyed the film projector and injured the projectionist and an army youth liaison officer. In a statement the IRA warned that such 'immoral proselytism' of Irish youths would not be tolerated. In November five young Belfast IRA men were arrested and charged with unlawful possession of bayonets and documents dealing with RUC movements. None of the men spoke or gave evidence during their trial and all were sentenced to twelve months in jail. The 'five silent men' included Joe McCann from Turf Lodge, whom the RUC described as the leader of the group. McCann, an 18-year-old bricklayer who had joined the movement in 1963, was tall and lean with gangly arms, which no coat sleeves ever seemed to cover. He was already marked out by his peers as a leader, one recalling: 'He could read a situation very, very quickly . . . he had the run of everybody.'

The Garda Special Branch estimated that there were 48 IRA training camps in the South between February 1965 and October 1966. The camps had begun to reflect the new political priorities, incorporating lectures on history and social agitation. The shortage of weapons remained a problem. The Gardaí captured 40 IRA weapons, including 7 machine guns and 1 anti-tank rifle, plus 6,000 rounds of ammunition and 344 sticks of gelignite, in the 1965–6 period. *An t-Óglac* warned that 'the Army cannot afford the loss of a single weapon, nor can it afford the loss in morale and prestige consequent on a successful police search'. One of the weapons captured, a Belgian Vigneron sub-machine gun, signalled that the IRA was trying to procure new equipment. IRA members in Britain were instructed to survey Territorial Army bases and their weapons stocks. One base in the West Midlands looked like a good bet for a raid, but plans were cancelled when it was decided that the local IRA did not have the capacity to store the arms. Small amounts of weaponry continued to arrive from the United States. But short of a successful raid or a substantial donation the only way to acquire arms was to buy them.

This pointed to a further pressing problem: the movement had hardly any cash. The *United Irishman* often teetered on the edge of bankruptcy as local units and Sinn Féin cumainn used monies owed to the paper to pay other debts. Producing posters, leaflets, election deposits and running the Gardiner Place office were all a drain on resources. The families of prisoners also had to be looked after. Then there was the cost of the army itself. Mick Ryan recalls on occasion being reduced to 'begging your way around the country' in order to gain much-needed funds. Collections, fund-raising dances and donations from abroad made only a small dent. Ryan and Garland on occasion were forced to ask Moss Twomey, the 1930s IRA leader and shopkeeper, for a loan of £100, and then ask republican supporter Donal O'Connor, of the Castle Hotel in Gardiner Row, for £100 to pay Twomey back.

Irish America had traditionally provided support, but the later stages of the Border Campaign had seen tensions emerge within Clan na Gael, the IRA's main US support network. There were vocal complaints about the perceived lack of militancy among the IRA leadership and suggestions that they were willing to compromise with the 'Free State'. Goulding travelled to Philadelphia in November 1963 and attended the Clan convention and its Battle of Gettysburg commemoration. But the Clan was no longer a powerful or wealthy organization. While it claimed members in most of the large US cities, only five supporters picketed a visit by Sean Lemass to Philadelphia during 1963 and just fifteen took part in a protest at UN headquarters in New York a year later. By the early 1960s the FBI had decided to scale down its surveillance due to the Clan's 'lack of activity'. The vast majority of Irish Americans had no interest in the IRA, and without an armed campaign even those who had were reluctant to devote much time or money to it. The political direction in which Goulding was taking the movement was also not to the liking of many American supporters. Senior Clan figures such as Tom McGuigan would complain of the appearance of 'anti-American' views in the *United Irishman*. Nevertheless, Goulding cultivated the movement's American contacts, such as Manus Canning, his co-defendant from the Felsted raid, and the IRA leadership received a 'steady though not great' flow of finance from America as a result. Ryan recalls feeling that if 'gear and money' were no longer forthcoming from America then it was time to 'look somewhere else'. Feelers were put out to the Algerian revolutionary government but came to nothing. Despite the growing interest in socialism among some in the leadership, Garland recalls that the IRA were still 'innocents abroad in terms of the international communist movement'. During the 1920s the IRA had received funding and sought arms from the Soviet Union, but establishing ties with the Soviets was still too politically contentious in 1965.

There was another option. Ryan and Garland heard from a sympathetic railwayman that large sums of money were being transported, unguarded, on the Dublin–Cork train. They travelled on the train and came to the conclusion that robbing it was a real possibility. During the 1940s the IRA had robbed banks and post offices, but it was felt that they had 'lost a tremendous amount of popular support' as a result, and such activity was now forbidden in the South under Army Order No. 8. When Garland suggested the plan to the Army Council it faced furious objections; Ryan recalls that Ó Brádaigh feared such an operation would bring the IRA into 'disrepute'. The idea was dropped for the time being and the funding problem remained unresolved. The IRA leadership had decided to prioritize political campaigning, and the weapons it held were just about adequate for training purposes and the type of low-level armed activities it was carrying out. The strategy was re-emphasized to volunteers: 'It will be necessary to widen the basis of support for the national revolutionary movement before thinking in terms of armed action again.'

Political developments in Britain during the 1960s had an impact in Ireland. In 1964 the republican movement set up Clann na hÉireann as a support group in Britain in place of a staid Sinn Féin organization. Former Fianna chief scout Seán Ó Cionnaith returned to England to become Clann organizer. One of the major tasks of the new organization was to provide funding for the movement in Ireland. Clann organized weekly club nights where céilí and 'old-time' music was played. Birmingham and Glasgow were the two busiest areas of Clann activity; in contrast London is recalled as 'a morass of warring factions' which 'never realized its potential'. Birmingham Clann leader Seamus Collins, who had emigrated to England in 1963, felt that one of his teenage recruits, Padraig Yeates, brought 'a political brain' to the fledgling organization in the English Midlands. Yeates, the English-born son of Dublin parents, suggested a campaign for emigrants' rights in early 1965, noting that only the Legion of Mary was concerned with the conditions of Irish people living in England. However, the major organizations in the Irish community tended to be the Counties Associations, which Yeates recalls as 'dominated by people who craved acceptance and middle-class respectability, and very Catholic'. The Church itself remained a force, and Clann sold papers and distributed leaflets outside mass on Sundays.

The IRA recruited from Clann's membership and maintained its own structure in Britain. Volunteers travelled to Ireland for training, usually in Wexford or Wicklow, which were convenient to the ferry. At the time many republicans were interested in the idea of pan-Celtic unity between Welsh, Irish, Scots and Breton groups, and Ó Cionnaith was very much in favour of establishing contacts with groups like the Free Wales Army. Members of the Welsh group would eventually travel to Dublin for Easter commemorations and train in Ireland with the IRA. In return the IRA leadership hoped to obtain gelignite from the FWA, whose members claimed to have access to it from the mines in South

Wales. A number of joint operations were planned, including an arms raid in Chester. The FWA were to claim the raid and the IRA would take the bulk of the arms. The link with the FWA proved to be more trouble than it was worth, however, especially after it started to become public knowledge. On one occasion the FWA requested that a large store of gelignite the IRA were holding for them be moved from Glasgow to Salford. The IRA feared that the explosives were becoming unstable and were forced to dump them in a canal, drawing the attention of the police.

Clann attempted to tread a careful line between the various left-wing organizations and the Irish community. It disassociated itself from leftists who became involved in a clash outside the Irish Embassy in April 1965. Much of Clann's campaigning was along traditional lines, the 'Buy Irish' campaign of 1964–5, where efforts were made to enlist support from mainstream Irish organizations, being a case in point. The IRA felt that the campaign had given Clann 'a certain amount of respect heretofore missing'. During 1965 and 1966 efforts were made to get Clann members to Donegal to work on Fr. McDyer's cooperative project. Clann also picketed the Irish Embassy in support of strikers in Ireland and occupied it in protest at the jailing of republicans in July 1966. Some Clann members were sympathetic to the Connolly Association, though relations between the two bodies could be fraught. Some younger Clann members saw the association as too conservative, while older republicans distrusted it because of its communist links.

Other sections of the British left also had their attractions for republicans. After emigrating from Belfast Brendan Mackin, who had been a Fianna boy, became an active trade unionist in the building industry and joined the Labour Party. Others joined the Communist Party, while Yeates would join the International Socialists, who were very active in Birmingham. Some were drawn into campaigns against racism, in which republican building workers, armed with lengths of heavy cable up their sleeves, helped steward meetings against attack by far-right groups. On another occasion during a strike in the Midlands a gang of bikers had assaulted pickets before Clann members armed with pickaxe handles saw them off.

The IRA saw major opportunities in the fiftieth anniversary of the Easter Rising, in 1966. Northern members reported to the Army Council that 'every' commemoration committee in Northern Ireland was under republican control and 'widespread publicity' was being planned. In Belfast the 'whole resources' of the movement were put into organizing a major commemoration in the city, which Billy McMillen hoped would 'drive a coach and four' through the laws that banned display of the tricolour. In the South, the early months of 1966 were dominated by the state-endorsed commemorations. RTÉ ran numerous programmes on the Easter Rising and the local and national press contained hundreds of articles and memoirs. Popular nationalism was reflected in the pop charts. The Beatles, the Small Faces and the Rolling Stones all had hits in Ireland that year, but it was Dermot O'Brien's version of Dominic Behan's 'The Merry Ploughboy' that spent six weeks at number one with its cheery if anachronistic chorus:

> And we're all off to Dublin in the green, in the green
> Where the helmets glisten in the sun,
> Where the bayonets flash and the rifles crash
> To the echo of a Thompson Gun.

But the IRA was not going to have 1966 all to themselves. The issue of 'communist infiltration' in the movement became a matter for public discussion early in the year. First the Fianna Fáil Minister for Justice Brian Lenihan warned of a 'definite policy' of intervention by 'anti-state' groups in the telephonists' dispute. Then the *Evening Herald* reported on how 'Reds' were becoming involved with republicans. In January 1966 the *Sunday Independent* exposed the 'communists' quiet revolution' within the IRA. The article, which clearly drew from Special Branch sources, noted how 'sinister' intellectuals had assumed positions of influence within the organization, committing it to a policy of encouraging social disorder. The paper stated that what was happening was an 'exact repeat' of the Republican Congress of 1934 except that, whereas the congress had been a schism, now the mainstream IRA itself had been converted to communism. Intervention in Midleton and the telephonists' strike had been the result. Significantly, the article noted that some IRA leaders were 'uneasy' with this trend and many of the rank and file were 'unaware' of the communist influence on their leadership.

The Special Branch had collected a significant amount of internal IRA correspondence and first-hand reports on discussions at conventions through at least one senior IRA informer – George Poyntz, the Monaghan O/C. In a February 1966 *Belfast Telegraph* interview, Tony Meade admitted that allegations of a person holding communist sympathies being in a leadership position were current but denied there was any truth in them. Communist influence in the IRA was also the subject of discussion among British intelligence officers in Whitehall during April, though they identified the IRA Director of Education as a Trinity professor, whereas Johnston, who had been appointed to that position, worked for Aer Lingus; it is possible that they had Johnston confused with Coughlan.

In February an RUC vehicle and the Unionist Party HQ in Belfast were petrol-bombed, though the IRA denied any connection with these incidents. Two Catholic schools were firebombed during the same month. In March Billy McMillen and Denis Toner were arrested and held over the Easter period. More critically, in February Goulding was stopped by Gardaí while driving through Portlaoise. Asked what was in the sacks weighing down his large Consul car, he replied 'potatoes, carrots and parsnips', which was true, though he also had 3,000 rounds of ammunition and a Luger pistol. Goulding was held until June. In an April court appearance he stated, 'If you find me guilty of this charge, you are finding every Irishman of every generation from Tone to the men of 1916 guilty of the same thing.' He was eventually convicted but released after the Army Council broke with normal policy and paid a fine.

The increased Garda attention was intended to prevent the IRA from capitalizing on the 1916 anniversary with a show of arms, but this was exactly what the republican leadership intended in Newry that spring. A raid on a Territorial Army lock-up was planned, involving Garland, McGurran and selected volunteers. Some of the raiders were to pose as RUC men and hold up a car outside Warrenpoint before entering Newry. IRA intelligence indicated that every Sunday arms were delivered to the local Territorial Army unit in two RUC Land Rovers. The IRA raiders planned to take over the lightly guarded lock-up, hold up the RUC and drive the Land Rovers and their cargo across the border to Dundalk. However, on the night before the planned raid a local guide, a smuggler, 'bottled it' after McGurran teased him about the likelihood of a long jail sentence if he was caught, and the operation was called off at the last minute. The following day scouts spotted a heavy RUC presence in the area of the TA lock-up. George Poyntz was one of those supposed to take part in the raid, and those involved came to suspect that they were being led into a trap.

In May Garland was arrested in Co. Laois. On his person were copies of plans drawn up by the special Military Council. He was convicted of IRA membership and jailed for two months. In contrast to Goulding, Garland remained silent during his trial, sitting with his arms folded and refusing to answer questions from the judge. Brian Lenihan read out selected passages of the captured plans in the Dáil, drawing attention to the IRA's strategy for 'infiltration' of trade unions and social agitation. The quoted documents actually drew praise from *TCD*, a Trinity student magazine, which welcomed them as representing a 'well-thought-out plan of social reform and democratic ideals'. The IRA claimed that the plan was for discussion purposes only but Tony Meade took the opportunity in the *United Irishman* to laud the plan. He argued that republicans had to face up to what had been their 'conspicuous failure' from 1922 onwards. The captured plan had contained 'no romanticism . . . no escapism, no attempt to find a miracle cure for the evils which afflict the Republic we cherish'. Instead it had offered practical steps to attain popular support.

Meanwhile, republicans continued to carry out armed actions.

Richard Behal, who had been jailed for the *Brave Borderer* attack, escaped from Limerick Prison in February without consulting the leadership and then appeared at several social events in his native Kilkenny. During March and April Behal and his allies blew up a telephone exchange, felled trees and tore up railway sleepers in the south-east. In the same period several attacks were carried out in Dublin, with an attempt to blow up a telephone exchange, the firebombing of the residence of the British Military Attaché and a petrol bomb thrown into the gym in Cathal Brugha Barracks. Most dramatically, former members of Joe Christle's group blew up the 134-foot Nelson's Pillar in O'Connell Street on 8 March. The IRA stated that it had nothing to do with these attacks and claimed not to be concerned in the 'slightest way with the destruction of monuments of foreign origin'. It reiterated that its policy since 1954 had been to avoid armed action in the South, the one exception being the *Brave Borderer* attack. It warned that the 'recent senseless attacks' could give the authorities 'an excuse to reintroduce internment without trial'. Behal issued his own statement, claiming that the actions in the south-east had 'achieved their purpose' by focusing attention on the continuing detention of republicans. He denied any connection with the Dublin attacks, though he later claimed that they were carried out in support of him. Behind the scenes patience had run out. Behal was court-martialled and sentenced to death, the Army Council dividing 4–3 on the issue. Costello, who was acting Chief of Staff while Goulding was in jail, wanted Behal shot, but it was decided instead to exile him, on the grounds that killing him would be unpopular with rank-and-file republicans. He was dismissed from the IRA and emigrated to New York.

Easter brought more incidents. There were two republican parades in Belfast on successive Sundays, despite loyalists planting a bomb at Milltown Cemetery. Clashes also took place after a Paisleyite rally in the city centre. The Northern government had banned railway travel between Belfast and Dublin in the run-up to the Easter holiday to prevent republicans travelling north. But in Belfast itself 20,000 people took part in the republican parade, while the Falls was festooned with tricolours. Betty Sinclair, president of Belfast Trades Council and a leading member of the Communist Party, had been due to speak but agreed to stand down due to pressure from the GAA, which threatened to withdraw the use of Casement Park if she did so. Costello delivered the main oration, welcoming the participation of trade unionists in the parade and explicitly blaming 'capitalism' for dividing the working class in the North. The numbers attending commemorations in Northern Ireland reflected the occasion: 7,000 in Coalisland, 1,000 in Derry city and the 'biggest parade since the 1930s' in Newry. The authorities banned the commemoration in south Derry, deploying 200 police to ensure there was no parade. Instead 700 people visited republican graves. The turnouts reflected different traditions from area to area. The previous year only 150 had attended the commemoration in Derry city, where there were only about six active IRA members in early 1966. In contrast there were several Republican Clubs active in Tyrone, with particular strength in the east of the county. The commemorations drew new recruits for the IRA and the Fianna in Derry and Belfast.

In Dublin, about 5,000 people set out on the parade from St Stephen's Green to Glasnevin Cemetery on 24 April. At their head the colour party unfurled the blue Óglaigh na hÉireann flag of the IRA's Dublin Brigade. Detectives tried to seize it but were repelled in a series of scuffles. There were further clashes outside Trinity College, and at the Parnell Monument in O'Connell Street fierce fighting broke out, with batons, fists and boots used freely. The Gardaí were still unable to capture the flag, and later that evening 400 republicans paraded with it from Parnell Square. Gardaí tried to seize it again and during the fighting Bobby McKnight 'walloped' a Superintendent. Under cover of darkness Gardaí attempted to take revenge for their earlier loss of face and a number of marchers were badly beaten. Several arrests took place and a number of IRA members received prison sentences including McKnight, Leo Steenson and Lar Malone. McKnight expected a beating after his arrest but recalls being surprised to find Gardaí whispering 'good man yourself' to him; it transpired that the officer he had hit was rather unpopular with his men. Seventeen-year-old Tony Heffernan had gone to both the government and republican parades. During the disturbances he was struck by a Garda and afterwards became interested in republican politics – 'which probably proves that there is nothing that will politicize you as quickly as a whack of a baton'.

The post-Easter period brought grim reminders of the reality of politics north of the border. Early June saw serious trouble in the Markets area of Belfast when Ian Paisley led a protest march through Cromac Square against the supposed 'Romanizing tendencies' within the Presbyterian Church. Local people gathered to oppose him and violent clashes took place. After the RUC attempted to disperse crowds in the area there were dozens of injuries. The following night a large force of police again moved in and the IRA responded by attacking RUC vehicles with hand grenades and petrol bombs. Tensions were high because the revived Ulster Volunteer Force had publicly stated that it was declaring war against the IRA and had launched a campaign of violence. On 27 May a UVF gang had shot a Catholic man, John Scullion, on the Falls Road. He died on 11 June. They had planned to kill IRA officers Leo Martin and Jim Sullivan; on 26 June UVF members had been watching Martin's home before they killed another Catholic, Peter Ward, instead. A Protestant woman, Matilda Gould, died of burns received when her home was mistakenly firebombed by the group.

The emergence of the UVF reflected increased unease among working-class Protestants, unease encouraged by Paisley and others. Billy Mitchell, a future member of the UVF leadership, remembered hearing rumours that the IRA were going to take over City Hall in Belfast or seize Newry and 'make a stand like they did in 1916'. Gusty Spence, jailed for the 1966 killings, later claimed that members of the Unionist Party establishment had helped set up his organization to undermine Premier Terence O'Neill. The IRA believed that prominent RUC detectives had provided information on Sullivan and Martin to the UVF. These developments indicated that it was going to be difficult for

Goulding and his allies to 'get through to the Protestant working class', though they remained optimistic. During 1965 *An t-Oglac* had claimed that 'the crumbling of Unionist support is only beginning, *but it has in fact begun*', and the 1966 IRA Convention passed a motion 'that the Army do everything possible to widen the rift between the UVF and the Unionist Party'.

In June Johnston wrote a letter to the *United Irishman* criticizing the saying of the rosary at republican commemorations. There was an immediate backlash and Mac Stíofáin refused to have the paper sold in his command area, an action that resulted in him being suspended from the IRA for a short period. More opposition to the IRA leadership was expressed during the Republic's June presidential election. De Valera was the Fianna Fáil candidate, opposed by T. F. O'Higgins of Fine Gael. Among the IRA documents captured on Garland when he was arrested in May were draft leaflets for surreptitious distribution by republicans urging voters to 'reject de Valera'. One leaflet stated that 'de Valera has led us to the generation of Lemass, Haughey and Lenihan . . . they have sold everything in sight and will sell more given encouragement'. The proposal caused problems in North Kerry, where trouble had been simmering since Easter when the local organization had rejected Denis Foley as a speaker for their commemoration because he was associated with moves to abandon abstentionism. Now they refused to distribute a leaflet they claimed 'would have us supporting a candidate in a 26-county "presidential" election', something that would 'have made a mockery of our dead'. During the autumn three IRA members from North Kerry were court-martialled and dismissed by the Dublin leadership.

At Bodenstown in June the Dublin IRA flag again led the parade, which included a delegation from the Belfast Trades Council. In his oration Costello emphasized that the policy of the movement was that key industries be nationalized, with the eventual aim of cooperative ownership by the workers, and that the large estates owned by absentee landlords be compulsorily purchased and worked on a cooperative basis. To imagine that this could be

achieved by constitutional means, Costello said, '[was] utter folly
. . . in the final analysis the robber baron must be disestablished by
the same methods he used to enrich himself and retain his ill-gotten
gains, namely, force of arms'.

Another opportunity for the IRA to utilize force during 1966
concerned the Irish language. During the autumn Máirtín
Ó Cadhain, Professor of Irish at Trinity College, approached Mick
Ryan, the ex-Quartermaster General who had resigned as QMG
but was now back as Dublin O/C, with a request. Ó Cadhain, a
former IRA officer who was interned during the 1940s, wanted
the IRA to disrupt a public meeting of the Language Freedom
Movement in Jurys Hotel. The LFM, of which the playwright
John B. Keane was a prominent supporter, was campaigning for
Irish to be non-compulsory in schools. The Dublin IRA acted on
Ó Cadhain's request, with volunteers turning the meeting into a
shambles. Republicans also helped disrupt a much larger LFM
meeting in the Mansion House in September. In early 1967 the
LFM leader Christopher Morris publicly highlighted the role he
felt Tomás Mac Giolla had played in the Mansion House disturb-
ance, adding that he had knowledge of a plan by the IRA to
attempt the kidnap of the chair of the second meeting, broadcaster
Gay Byrne. He also blamed republicans for a break-in at his home.

The Military Council's plans captured with Garland, which supported Costello's assurances to volunteers that force was still an
essential component in the republican strategy, also contained
more radical suggestions. The section dealing with 'political action'
contained a list of six key strategic programmes. Topping the list,
and of 'fundamental importance', was that 'the movement assume
an organizational form that will attract back people of national
outlook in the Trade Union Movement so that their efforts can
be co-coordinated'. A group under the control of the Chief of
Staff would organize union activity. This body would act to make
the unions 'more revolutionary' and also to educate IRA volunteers on labour agitation. Committees to oversee intervention in
housing and other campaigns would also be set up. Another crucial

proposal was that no longer would men be recruited on the basis of an 'emotional appeal to arms': in future recruit training would emphasize 'social and economic objectives' ahead of 'arms and battle tactics'. It had to be understood that 'boring' and 'unromantic' work would have to be done in order to build republican influence.

The document also called for the empowering of Sinn Féin, hitherto a 'rubber stamp' for IRA decisions. The new aim was to have a 'political, national and social revolutionary organization with an open membership and legal existence'. The IRA would develop revolutionary action legally and seek to develop political action as openly as possible. The IRA would be able to choose its recruits from the 'best and most conscious' members of Sinn Féin. The problem was still that 'not enough' republicans had experience or links to social agitation. Only a few had any experience of trade unions or co-ops. Local cumainn needed to set up 'specialized groups' for work in tenants' associations, youth groups, credit union groups and cooperatives. Special importance was placed on the formation of factory cumainn in workplaces. These groups would be the 'dynamos generating local and specialized republican leadership in all areas of the people's needs'. They would also be the 'basic channel' for recruitment into the movement and serve as a training ground for revolutionary government. In theory the use of social and economic agitation along with growing electoral strength might see a 'dual power' situation emerge, with the 'Army, trade unions and co-ops as the new organs of state power'. This would be the 'signal for the completion of the job by military action'.

The section of the document dealing with military strategy was similarly ambitious, stressing the need to 'learn from the Cypriots and engage in terror tactics only'. It stated that 'our campaign will be fought in the six-county area' but recognized that the IRA was as yet unprepared for such a campaign. Due to the hostility of the unionist majority and the strength of the RUC and B-Specials, 'classic guerrilla-type operations cannot be successful'. A five-stage plan involving 'large stunt-type operations', 'agricultural and industrial sabotage' and assassinations was outlined. It was made explicit that 'the idea is to prepare the way for a campaign . . . to get our people psychologically prepared for future killing'. Suggested tactics included 'open assassinations' of police, using silencers and even 'poison darts'. Meeting the needs of the plan would require a dramatic upping of the IRA's military capacity: the document enumerated a wish list including '10 tons plastic explosive . . . 5,000 grenades, 1,000 short arms . . . 200 Automatic Rifles . . . 300 Bazookas and 3,000 shells'. The possibility of a 'coup d'état' in the South was also discussed. The groundwork for a coup would have to include 'proper infiltration of the police and military' as well as 'propaganda aimed at undermining the loyalty to the state'.

Newer political strategies were also being attempted. On 13–14 August a Wolfe Tone Society convention took place at the home of republican Kevin Agnew in Maghera, Co. Derry. Johnston attended along with a number of society members from across Northern Ireland, including Fred Heatley and the journalist Jack Bennett. Goulding was also present with a number of IRA officers. Eoghan Harris, a 23-year-old recalled by Johnston as a 'fringe member' of the Dublin Wolfe Tone Society, read out a strategy document written by Coughlan, who was unable to attend. The young Corkman's eloquence was preferred to Johnston's stammer. Coughlan's document addressed the task of how to win an 'all-Ireland Republic . . . politically and economically in control of its own destiny' where the 'exploitation of man by man would be abolished'. Looking at the situation in Northern Ireland, he argued that the moves towards reform by Terence O'Neill were having the effect of 'unfreezing' political life. The Unionist government was being forced to modernize against its wishes, but this was creating resistance on its right wing. The Unionists should now be 'squeezed' from the left by demands from the 'disenfranchised, oppressed Catholic and nationalist minority'. Republicans 'must be to the fore' in demanding 'civil rights [and] electoral reform'. The task was to 'force O'Neill to concede more than he wants to do or thinks he can give without risking overthrow by the more reactionary elements among the Unionists'. Such a movement, it was believed, had the potential to win support from progressive Protestants provided it 'completely divorced itself from any elements of Catholic sectarianism'. The temptation to engage in provocative actions that would allow the Unionists to portray the movement as subversive should also be resisted. The meeting decided to develop the idea of a 'civil rights charter' and involve groups already working on related issues. These included the communists and the Campaign for Social Justice, a pressure group that had been founded in Dungannon in 1964 by Dr Conn McCluskey and his wife Patricia. Since the early 1960s the couple had been collecting data and attempting to publicize cases of discrimination against Catholics in housing and jobs. While the IRA's attempts to form 'one man, one vote' committees in 1965 had failed, it was hoped that this new initiative might provide a springboard to a wider audience.

The IRA Convention of October 1966 passed a motion that an 'Economic Resistance Campaign' be developed. The 55 delegates also endorsed the emphasis on internal education, but demanded that all these politically centred programmes have the caveat that they 'will not replace but supplement ordinary unit activities and training programmes'. It was decided to order volunteers to join Sinn Féin; if there was no cumann locally they would establish one themselves. (Goulding himself finally joined the party.) Volunteers were also ordered to join trade unions. According to Garda surveillance Brian Quinn from Tyrone replaced Paddy Mulcahy on the Army Council at this convention. In November a meeting of the Army Council affirmed the need to bring Sinn Féin policy in line with that of the IRA, with one member even suggesting that if it did not, a new party should be formed, possibly based on the Wolfe Tone Society. It was also decided that GHQ was to 'make every effort to obtain modern weapons'.

Gardaí estimated in December 1966 that there were now 1,039 IRA members in the Republic, of whom only 251 were Border Campaign veterans, suggesting many new recruits. They also speculated, however, that only 312 of the IRA's volunteers would engage in armed action if ordered to do so. Dublin Brigade strength was estimated to be 306, with 80 likely to involve themselves in military activity. The Gardaí considered that the IRA had 'not been very successful in securing financial support or amassing any significant amount of arms or explosives'. Hence they might leave armed force 'in abeyance' for a period in order to build public support for Sinn Féin. Army Council members of the period suggest that while the organization was growing, the police figures were overestimates.

Even as the IRA leadership moved leftwards, they were also subject to criticism from the left. During 1966 the dissident Irish Revolutionary Forces in Cork opened a bookshop in Tower Street. They continued to criticize the republican movement for having, in their view, neither a military strategy nor clear revolutionary politics. Ó Brádaigh was deemed 'a petty bourgeois reactionary' and Mac Giolla came in for particular abuse. Criticism also came from émigré sources. In London during 1965 Gery Lawless, a leftist agitator who had been part of Joe Christle's group before emigrating, had helped establish the Irish Communist Group, whose publications celebrated the memory of Saor Uladh. Ex-IRA and Sinn Féin members such as Liam Walsh, Phil Flynn and Frank Keane became involved in the group, as did other young emigrants without republican backgrounds, such as Eamonn McCann, Michael Farrell and Brendan Clifford. The group soon divided into Maoist and Trotskyist factions, with the Maoists, led by Clifford, eventually breaking away to form the Irish Communist Organisation. Lawless and his Trotskyist comrades, meanwhile, formed the Irish Workers' Group. Lawless was dubious about the supposed leftward turn of the IRA leadership; he reserved particular ire for Mac Giolla, whom he claimed had been 'hounding socialists out of the republican movement' in the early 1960s and yet now called himself one. The Irish Workers' Group's *Irish Militant* also adopted a hysterical tone towards Johnston, referring to him as 'a Stalinist hack and long-time servant of the Russian bureaucracy'. The IWG made contact with a Dublin-based IRA splinter group in 1966, seeing them as a left-wing opposition to the IRA leadership. They were inclined to view even right-wing republican opponents of Goulding as anti-Stalinists rather than conservatives, and the *Irish Militant* gave positive coverage to attacks on the IRA leadership by one such conservative, Cork's Gerry McCarthy.

Beyond the political debate, there was continued dissension over the lack of immediate armed action. In January 1967 a group of former Dublin Brigade members robbed the home of a licensed arms dealer and stole 26 old but serviceable handguns and 5 rifles. They then took £3,500 in a raid on the Royal Bank in Drumcondra that February. This was the first bank robbery in the South for decades and caused a major stir. In October the group carried out a firebomb attack on Fianna Fáil headquarters, issuing a statement claiming the action was taken to highlight the cases of republican prisoners. At the 1966 IRA Convention it had been agreed to take action to 'stamp out' such splinter groups, and in November 1967 the IRA abducted a man in Bray and held him overnight in the Dublin Mountains, where he was assaulted and questioned about splinter-group activity. But it was understood that such measures might well be counterproductive, and no general action was taken. During April and June 1968 members of the Dublin splinter group robbed three banks of a total of £8,300. There were no more public statements of intent, but the suggestion in republican circles was that the group's members, fed up with IRA inactivity, were setting about collecting the means necessary to fund an armed campaign. The fact that this type of activity was rare created an aura of mystique around the group and some admired their audacity. However, IRA members suspected that much of the money was being spent in 'Doheny & Nesbitt's, Toner's, Grogan's and the International Bar' rather than on arms.

Some military actions were sanctioned. In May 1967 the IRA bombed Territorial Army centres in Belfast and in Lisburn. The explosions took place simultaneously at night, leaving the Belfast centre 'wrecked'. The IRA leadership ordered the operations in response to increased British Army recruiting publicity. But the focus for the organization that year was primarily political. A major effort was made to get volunteers from the country involved in the widespread campaign of marches and pickets being waged by the National Farmers' Association. In Derry IRA members were to the fore in a number of confrontations with bailiffs during evictions. *An t-Oglac* explained how 'an Army section actually helped the occupants of houses threatened with eviction to barricade their homes, and actually stayed with the family for a week to help them resist eviction'. At Bodenstown in June Goulding drove home the importance of political agitation when he attacked 'dream-filled romantics' who hankered for 'glory-full military victory' but did not want the 'painful, slow gruelling work' necessary to bring that victory about. He complained that even though the movement had decided to involve itself in social struggles, 'we have done almost nothing'. He warned that the demands of the people for their rights would 'come into physical conflict with the forces of the Gombeen establishment'. Belfast's Joe McCann was one of those 'quite taken' by Goulding's speech, according to his comrade Gerry Adams.

During the summer of 1967 Garland asked Mick Ryan to undertake a tour around the country to assess the state of the movement at local level. Taking his two weeks' annual holiday from his job as an insurance salesman, Ryan set off in his Austin Mini. At the end of the tour Ryan concluded in his report to the Army Council that there was 'no movement'. He recalls his analysis provoking an angry retort from Goulding: 'There *is* a fucking movement!' But Ryan had provoked an honest debate, and the result was an important decision made at a meeting of the 'most active' officers held over a weekend at Andy McDonnell's farm in Pallas, Co. Tipperary, in August 1967. The meeting heard that just 212 of the IRA's 614 volunteers were active in Sinn Féin and that the 'Army has enough ammo for one good job [and] a very limited amount of arms and explosives'. Nevertheless there was a consensus that, in Ryan's words, 'no social revolution was possible without the use of arms' and that IRA units should be 'trained in the use of assault weapons'. It was agreed that there had to be a major reorganization effort and that the army's energies were to be put fully behind political agitation. The *United Irishman*, which was deep in debt and losing circulation, had to be stabilized and used as the basis for expansion. The IRA would openly declare itself to be working for a 'Democratic Socialist Republic'.

Following the Pallas meeting four organizers were appointed to oversee IRA activities across Ireland: Malachy McGurran in Ulster, Ryan in Leinster and Waterford, Seán Ó Cionnaith in Connacht and Barty Madden in Munster. IRA volunteers were to throw themselves into selling the *United Irishman*, organizing pickets and protests, and stewarding demonstrations. They would assist in Sinn Féin election campaigns and stand for election themselves. Most of their work would be completely open and much of it would be legal. But if necessary they were to provide the 'back-up' for illegal activity, to 'do things ordinary Sinn Féin members wouldn't do'. *An t-Oglac* stressed in December that the IRA 'must have men that are capable of leading the people in an armed struggle. For of this last let there be no doubt, there will be an armed struggle against the forces who are at present in control of this country.' The IRA's journal also serialized Che Guevara's writings on guerrilla warfare and continued to issue instructions on arms and explosives.

In Dublin Ryan had established an Active Service Unit (ASU) of seven trusted volunteers, most of whom were unknown to the Gardaí. Jim Monaghan, a Donegal man who had moved to Dublin as a youth and joined the IRA in 1964, was in charge of organizing most ASU activities. Lar Malone, a dynamic if quick-tempered union activist from Donnycarney, was another key member of the unit. One IRA recruit who was assigned to the ASU recalled seeking information on joining the movement from a man selling the *United Irishman* at the GPO in 1967. He was summoned to a meeting in the Clarence Hotel on a Sunday morning. Entering a boardroom, which had been hired under the auspices of 'the Irish Workers' Cultural Society, or something to that effect', he was questioned as to his motives by several men sitting behind a table, headed by Malone. The prospective recruit had heard about the leftward direction of the IRA and was interested in it but was confused by the questions. He was asked if he knew what the

IRA's policy was, but because the answer seemed so obvious he thought it was some sort of test and was hesitant in responding. Eventually he convinced them he was genuine and was accepted into the organization's recruitment process. Training camps in Glendalough followed. Due to his lack of a republican record, he was asked to join the ASU but not to attend republican functions or join Sinn Féin; as he recalls, 'they were keeping me very quiet'.

Despite having only a tiny arsenal of weaponry, and a perception that training was being downgraded, the IRA carried on with what McMillen called a 'happy blend of political agitation and military activity'. In January 1968 the IRA bombed Tyrone House, the Royal Ulster Rifles Territorial HQ on Belfast's Malone Road. The organization claimed that the action was taken in protest at the recruiting of Irishmen as 'Black and Tans' in Britain's 'occupied territories'. They warned that responsibility for any civilian injuries rested with the British.

Armed involvement in social agitation was increasing. In Shannon, Co. Clare, there was a strike at the US-owned EI plant, a subsidiary of General Electric. The company was refusing to recognize the ITGWU. On the night of 29 May, IRA units destroyed buses and cars being used to ferry strikebreakers to Shannon, and in Limerick a Garda was held up while six buses and a car were burnt out. Buses were also burnt in Louth and Meath and unsuccessful attacks took place in Clare and Dublin. At Bodenstown a few weeks later Garland made clear that the EI actions were 'no isolated incident . . . the day is past when the homeless, the worker or the landless . . . will be left unprotected'. Now physical force would be employed where necessary to 'defend people who are agitating for their rights'. The criticisms of 'mealy-mouthed sentimentalists' would not be allowed to stop the IRA becoming the 'Army of the People'.

In July the Belfast IRA carried out a grenade attack on an RUC patrol in Cyprus Street after luring the police by a false 999 call. The attack was in retaliation for Special Branch raids and led to the RUC nicknaming the area 'Nogoland' and patrolling it only in strength. On 1 August a US-owned lobster trawler, the *Mary*

Catherine, was destroyed by the IRA at Rossaveal, Co. Galway. An IRA statement explained the action was a protest against 'exploitation by foreign interest' of Irish natural resources. Gardaí noted that the 'expert' bombers had not damaged any of the other boats docked at the same pier. In September a man was injured during an IRA arms raid in Belfast. In October IRA volunteers in Portmagee, Co. Kerry, burnt out a bus in connection with a local school dispute. The same month saw IRA members place a bomb under the car of a landlord in Dalkey, Co. Dublin, who had been targeted because of clashes with republican housing campaigners. The device did not explode and the IRA did not claim the action; one volunteer recalls Goulding stressing to Dublin activists that such actions shouldn't 'look like it's organized by us . . . it should look as if it's spontaneous'. In November the Gardaí intercepted a group of IRA members on their way to burn a German-owned farmhouse in Meath.

Meanwhile the role of women in the movement was beginning to change, following a decision that they could now join the IRA proper rather than remain in the traditionally subordinate Cumann na mBan. Women were recruited directly into the IRA in Belfast, Dublin and Cork. Some but by no means all of these women were related to men already in the movement. Joint training sessions were organized for the first time, and not everyone involved enjoyed the experience. During a training session in the mud and rain at Belcamp in Dublin, one female recruit stormed off after being ordered to crawl along the ground by her training officer. Others, such as the woman who was given command of the women's section in Dublin, were enthusiastic, recalling that 'we saw ourselves as the first women in the IRA who weren't Cumann na mBan, [who] were full members of the IRA' though she recognized in retrospect that 'we were in our arse full members of the IRA'. There were also moves to make the Fianna open to girls as well as boys, though their camps would remain separate.

Resentment at the rise of women came from both male and female republicans. Cumann na mBan saw its role being superseded while some men believed that women had no place in the IRA.

Tensions had come to a head at Bodenstown in June, when Cumann na mBan members objected to the presence of communists in the parade. Their contingent split over the issue, with the majority refusing to join the march. The organization was then stood down by the IRA leadership and refused use of republican premises. But local groups remained in existence led by those, like Maire Drumm in Belfast, who were politically alienated from the IRA leadership. Younger women, such as Margaret O'Leary in Dublin, had been highly unimpressed by the old Cumann na mBan in the first place and were happy to be integrated into all aspects of the movement.

The stressing of radical non-sectarian politics had seen a number of Southern Protestants joining the IRA. Stephen Hilliard, an Irish-language enthusiast and member of the Church of Ireland, whose uncle Robert had been killed fighting with the International Brigades in Spain, became an IRA training officer in Dublin. A young Kerry Protestant was also a key activist in the Dublin ASU. Volunteers recall discussing the prospect that 'Southern people . . . would have to fight the revolution in the 26 counties, fighting moves to European union, fighting multinationals, seeing these as the key problems'. The North, in other words, would not necessarily be the first battleground.

By the September 1968 Army Convention Goulding's supporters had decided a fundamental restructuring of the IRA was needed. Once again a motion to end abstention from Leinster House was defeated, but another proposal was passed that increased the size of the Army Council from seven to twenty members. The new structure brought Johnston and McGurran on to the highest executive of the organization, along with a number of local commanding officers and organizers, such as Ó Cionnaith, McMillen and Cork's Eddie Williams. This had the intended effect of giving Goulding's supporters a secure majority on the council. It caused consternation for Mac Stíofáin, who later deplored having been left 'in a minority' to people who were 'obsessed with parliamentary politics and Marxist debates'.

The convention had also decided to launch the long-planned

'nationwide Economic Resistance campaign' with special emphasis on 'all lands held by foreigners and large estates held by natives'. Action was to be taken against both land agents and property. Efforts were also to be made to win the support of 'dissident' Catholic and Protestant clergy in order to 'weaken the authority' of both the Catholic hierarchy and the Orange Order. A resolution was adopted to seek the financial and military support of inter-national revolutionary groups and socialist governments, and again it was decided to make 'maximum effort' to secure modern arms and equipment.

The implications of the IRA's new direction and energy were being recognized. The *Irish Times* speculated on how the 'chance that a bomb' might be used in labour disputes could have adverse effects on foreign investment in Ireland. In a feature forwarded to Dublin by Irish diplomats in the US, the *Washington Post* noted the EI attacks and described how the IRA had decided to 'soft-pedal its old demands for unification . . . in favour of agitating, via trade unions . . . for a socialist workers' republic'. The internal machina-tions of the IRA were also having an impact on Irish politics and society North and South – through the movement's political manifestations, Sinn Féin and the Republican Clubs, and increas-ingly through the issue of civil rights.

3. A New Revolution

Sinn Féin and the Republican Clubs 1962–1968

'The Republican Socialist ideology is the only one which can unite the
mass of the Irish people both Catholic and Protestant. If we are to
create such unity we cannot remain in isolation. We must be prepared
to ally ourselves with other radical forces . . . A new generation of
Irishmen are creating a new revolution in Ireland and this time they
will not be satisfied with half measures.'

Tomás Mac Giolla, Sinn Féin Ard Fheis, 7 December 1968

The Sinn Féin party of which Tomás Mac Giolla took leadership
in September 1962 was a largely moribund organization. The
Gardaí estimated that membership of the party stood at 5,000 in
November 1961. Cumainn had little existence outside periods of
electioneering, campaigning for prisoner releases, selling the *United
Irishman* each month and lilies at Easter. They sent delegates to an
annual Ard Fheis in Dublin, where they rubber-stamped decisions
that had already been taken by the IRA and elected officer boards
that needed the approval of the army. In the North, where the
party and *United Irishman* were illegal, Sinn Féin was only a slightly
more public manifestation of pockets of the IRA and its supporters.
Proinsias De Rossa, co-opted on to the party Ard Chomhairle in
1962, recalls only two really active branches in Dublin, with little
more than a dozen members in each. Many members of the IRA
were not even nominal members of Sinn Féin.

The tall, slender, pipe-smoking Mac Giolla, with his gentle-
manly demeanour, had already at the age of 38 taken on an appearance reminiscent to some of de Valera. His first presidential Ard

Fheis speech addressed the need to combat 'materialism of every brand'. He argued that if 'the Communist menace is a battle for men's minds' then republicans 'should undoubtedly be playing a leading part in the fight against it'. He also stated that 'the spirit in the Irish people is being slowly asphyxiated by American and British materialism and it is now to be finally extinguished in the new materialist Europe on the specious plea that we are aiding in the fight against Communism'. These sentiments were reassuring to the membership, as was Mac Giolla's position within the leadership of the IRA.

Mac Giolla came from a 'pro-Free State family' in rural Tipperary; an uncle had been a Home Rule MP. He had come to Dublin to study accountancy after a short period in a seminary and had been drawn to republicanism through the anti-partition campaign of the late 1940s. After attending UCD he became an ESB clerk. He was 'an enormous reader' not just of the republican staples but also of fiction, particularly the works of John Steinbeck. He was a practising Catholic and a Pioneer. He first met Goulding in 1959, and Goulding introduced him to the radical ideas of George Plant, 'the pride of Tipperary' – a Protestant IRA man executed by the Fianna Fáil government in 1942. Goulding also spoke of his first-hand experience of the Republican Congress of the 1930s and told Mac Giolla that his objective was 'to take the whole movement in that [radical] direction, not to break away, to stick with it and to take all the movement'.

In 1961 Mac Giolla had married May McLaughlin. Her father Larry had been a member of James Connolly's Citizen Army and her brother Paddy an IRA training officer. She had been sent to America during the Border Campaign to organize for the republican prisoner support group An Cumann Cabhrach. Active in Cumann na mBan and (along with Tomás) in the Sean Russell cumann in north-inner-city Dublin, May Mac Giolla was seen by younger republicans as a traditionalist.

Whereas after 1962 the IRA was led by a close-knit group based largely in Dublin, Sinn Féin support was drawn mainly from rural Ireland. In the 1961 general election Sinn Féin received a combined first-preference vote of only 2,619 in the three Dublin constituencies it contested, coming bottom of the poll in two. In rural constituencies it fared slightly better, contesting 16 seats and gaining 30,517 first preferences. What these voters were supporting, beyond a defiant attachment to militarist nationalism, was ill defined. Sinn Féin economic policy harked back to the protectionism of Arthur Griffith that had been put into practice by the first de Valera administrations. It included rudimentary concepts of national rendition of capital and profits alongside support for cooperative development. But there was little evidence of commitment to practical economic redistribution beyond calls to 'give the land to the people' and support for the Glencolmkille cooperative venture of Fr. McDyer. Breaking the Irish punt's link with sterling was seen as key to separatist economic development. Complete opposition to Irish entry into free-trade agreements with the UK and the European Economic Community was the logical extension of this.

Irish-Ireland concerns were also to the fore. The Irish census of 1961 found that three-quarters of the population of 2.8 million said they had little knowledge of the Irish language; and only a very small faction of those who had some knowledge used it as their first language. Sinn Féin policy was to 'restore Irish to the vernacular'. In March 1965 the *United Irishman*'s front page had been devoted to outrage over the introduction of the English language into the Catholic mass rather than Irish. This wish to stand against a turning tide on cultural issues was also evident in the party's total support for the GAA's ban on the playing of 'foreign games'. The *United Irishman* advertised the anti-Semitic works of Fr. Denis Fahey such as *Money, Manipulation and the Social Order* into late 1965. Sinn Féin's *Nation or Province*, published in 1963, warned that Masonic influences lay behind the EEC.

The party's ruling executive, the Ard Chomhairle, continued to be dominated by conservatives. The new strategies being hotly debated by the IRA and the Wolfe Tone Directories made little impact at its meetings during the first months of Mac Giolla's tenure. This lack of debate was due both to the subservient role the party played within the movement and the fact that the IRA men who dominated the party's upper echelons were already well briefed on developments. Sinn Féin did call for action in the wake of the collapse of dilapidated buildings in Dublin's Bolton Street and Fenian Street, which cost four lives, including those of two young girls, in early 1963. A speaker was provided for a protest on the issue in October, and the same month's edition of the *United Irishman* carried a statement from the Sinn Féin Ard Chomhairle calling for government investment in housing stock.

In August 1963 the party announced the launch of its Buy Irish campaign, which included postering and pickets of foreign enterprises in addition to opposing attempts by the Industrial Development Authority to encourage foreign companies to invest in Ireland. The campaign's economic impact was negligible in the context of the governmental abandonment of protectionism, but it gave activists a new focus. By the December 1963 Ard Fheis the republican leadership was clear enough on the need to modernize party policy to propose the drawing up of a new economic programme in time for the following year's Ard Fheis.

The movement's struggle to define its political objectives in the early 1960s was mirrored in its slowly changing international perspective. Coverage of international issues in the *United Irishman* was eclectic. There was support for the right-wing General Grivas in Cyprus, while articles denouncing Portuguese rule in Africa and Franco's repression of the Basques were accompanied by explanations that they were not the *United Irishman*'s official viewpoint. In 1964 the Ard Chomhairle vetoed a motion calling for support for Nelson Mandela, who had recently been jailed by the South African government, and although by December of that year the party had decided to affiliate to the Anti-Apartheid Movement, letters defending apartheid, Portuguese colonialism and Franco's Spain still occasionally appeared in the paper. A series on the Cuban revolution was accompanied by the caveat that support for Castro was not party policy. Hope was expressed that Cuba could find some way of becoming independent of both the US and Soviet blocs, and the Catholic make-up of the Cuban population was seen as a cause for optimism.

During 1964 it started to become clear to the Sinn Féin membership that the radical reappraisal of policy by Goulding and his allies would challenge some long-established principles. Some may have been reassured by the 'economic resistance' paper, penned by Johnston, which was distributed to Sinn Féin cumainn for discussion that summer. This paper, which was reprinted in the October issue of the *United Irishman*, focused on themes long associated with Sinn Féin economics, such as the need to break totally from the 'imperialist' economic system once more entangling Ireland through trade agreements with Britain and the EEC. Republican concerns were to the fore in Johnston's call to replace 'gombeen capitalism' with community enterprise in the form of the cooperative movement and credit unions.

Sinn Féin contested every Northern seat in the Westminster election of October 1964, under the label 'Republican' as the party was illegal north of the border. The twelve candidates included Tom Mitchell, Billy McMillen and Bobby McKnight, all IRA members. They did not win any seats but took a substantial overall vote of 101,628, largely in rural areas, with Mitchell gaining 22,810 votes in Mid-Ulster. McMillen's poll of 3,256 was the highest republican vote in Belfast, though he came behind the Unionist, Northern Ireland Labour Party and Republican Labour candidates. Unionists won all 12 constituencies while the NILP's 102,759 votes, though derided by republicans as votes for 'British Labour', seemed to point to the possibilities in urban areas offered by the adoption of left-wing policies. The NILP took 54,482 votes in Belfast compared to 8,985 for the republicans.

At the December 1964 Ard Fheis, held in Dublin's Bricklayers' Union Hall, a motion from the Newry cumann calling for the formation of Republican Clubs in the North was carried. This, it was hoped, would allow the movement to circumvent the Sinn Féin ban and organize openly in Northern Ireland. Republican Clubs were organized in each of the four Belfast constituencies in January 1965, with a Directorate chaired by Frank McGlade overseeing their activities. Also passed was a motion from a Wicklow cumann calling for a national scheme of resistance to foreign takeover of land and industry. In his presidential address, Mac Giolla sought to drive home the message that more than the removal of the border was now required by republicans in their struggle against 'the British Imperial system'; 'we are therefore seeking four freedoms: political, economic, social and cultural – not any one or two but all four'. In this struggle the labour movement was to be a key ally: 'the Republican Movement and the Trade Union Movement must be made to realise their common objective – to restore to the people of Ireland control over all the resources of their country'.

With the movement undergoing reorganization Sinn Féin did not contest the April 1965 general election in the South, which saw Fianna Fáil win a majority of just one seat. The *Irish Times* political correspondent argued that the election had heralded the 'birth of a new Irish social democracy'. His view reflected policy shifts by both major opposition parties. In 1963 the Labour Party had absorbed the small National Progressive Democrat Party, whose two TDs included Noel Browne, and in June 1964 Labour leader Brendan Corish described the party as 'socialist'. Fine Gael was also embracing change. The party's 1965 general election manifesto 'Towards a Just Society' included plans for bank credit controls and greater central planning. This was a dramatic turnaround for what had been Ireland's most conservative party, led until that year by James Dillon, president of the Ancient Order of Hibernians and an outspoken anti-communist. In response Fianna Fáil's rhetoric became more noticeably right wing as it took the lead in attacking Labour as 'red'.

The first signal that the summer of 1965 would see a growing rift on the issue of abstentionism was the March issue of the *United Irishman*. The editor, Denis Foley, was closely allied with Goulding, Garland and Costello, and his editorial condemned abstentionism as being tantamount to fear of real political involvement. Foley argued that it was time for republicans to re-examine their policies in the light of high emigration, high unemployment and the unavailability of higher education to people of modest means. He asked, 'Do the Irish people have to wait indefinitely for the miracle which the Republicans promise in the "free Ireland"?' Instead of clinging to outdated shibboleths, 'every avenue should . . . be explored, every shackle cast off, every forum used'. The message was rammed home with an ironic cartoon of a ghostly spectre beckoning fearful Sinn Féin TDs into Leinster House, one TD saying to the other, 'No, no, don't go in, you'll be corrupted.' Over the next couple of months correspondence condemning the editorial dominated the *United Irishman*'s letters page, with few supporting Foley's anti-abstentionist stance. Seán Ó Brádaigh and others refused to sell the issue in protest.

By June's special conference both the pro- and anti-abstentionist arguments had been well rehearsed. The IRA, with its majority on the Sinn Féin Ard Chomhairle, set an agenda which it hoped would see the party brought in line. One motion included a clause that would allow republicans to grant de facto recognition to the Irish courts, thereby allowing them to offer a legal defence. The delegates voted against this, and against motions that would have enabled the party executive to allow members to accept a bond of good behaviour or fines imposed by the courts, or allow organizers to notify authorities in either jurisdiction about proposed collections or parades. Motions were passed calling for greater cooperation between the IRA and Sinn Féin at local level. A motion that placed 'infiltration and direction of other organisations' as the 'essential work of the republican movement' was watered down. The amended text called for cooperation with other organizations on 'limited objectives as preparation for an ultimate confrontation with the British Government on the national issue'.

All the key motions that sought to lay the groundwork for ending abstentionism were defeated. A similar fate befell a clause that sought to bring the executive of the IRA and Sinn Féin into a single body that would control the entire movement. Supporters of abstentionism had won the day against Goulding and his supporters. In a conciliatory move Goulding had given the duties of chair at the event to Ruairí Ó Brádaigh, and this allowed those who were against the new direction to make their voices heard. Gerry McCarthy was to the fore, deriding the entire process as 'something very old and very dirty'. The failure of the conference to even consider a re-examination of abstentionism was too much for Belfast's Sean Caughey, a Sinn Féin vice-president, who resigned from the party.

Some within Sinn Féin were responsive to the IRA leadership's agenda. A disillusioned Máirín de Burca had left Sinn Féin during 1962, but the party's support for striking telephonists in late 1965 encouraged her to rejoin. She felt 'a total sea change' was taking place and was rapidly given an official position in the organization. Proinsias De Rossa, enthusiastic and 'reasonably good at organiz-ation', stood out among the mostly older members of the Russell cumann. Having been interned and jailed twice during the Border Campaign, De Rossa had become weary of military activity. When in late 1960 he was ordered by Seamus Costello to go on active service in the North, he refused, was dismissed from the IRA and remained in Sinn Féin only at the insistence of Mac Giolla. Adjacent to the Ross family's vegetable wholesale business was Stafford Street, where anyone entering faced being 'bate, ate and thrown up again', and the poverty he saw made an impact on the young De Rossa. His experiences during the 1957 election in Dublin North-East, 'knocking on doors' and finding that 'people didn't know who we were', had illustrated to him how remote Sinn Féin's agenda was to many. After reading an article on the activities of Britain's Citizens' Advice Bureaux, he approached the party about establishing its own version. The November 1965 issue of the *United Irishman* carried its first advertisement for the Russell cumann's Citizens' Grievance Bureau. In a city where social ser-vices largely depended on the Catholic Church or clientelistic politicians, the office was soon inundated with letters requesting assistance, overwhelmingly on the issue of housing.

By the October 1965 Ard Fheis, Mac Giolla was clearly aligning himself with Goulding's project for the movement, albeit in his customarily cautious manner. In his presidential address he stated that the choice was not between 'an un-Christian capitalist and individualist system' and 'an anti-religious, materialist and com-munist' one. There was a republican alternative: 'cooperativism

as preached by James Connolly, that is cooperative control of
the means of production, distribution and exchange'. Quoting
Connolly's observation that only the working class were the 'incorruptible inheritors' of the struggle for Irish freedom, Mac Giolla
presented the left's case without once mentioning socialism. He
was also careful to emphasize that Sinn Féin's idea of economic
resistance did not include opposition to free enterprise per se and
was not linked to 'foreign communism'.

Those opposed to Goulding's direction were equally intent on
pushing their own agenda. In January 1966 a Sinn Féin 'reorganization' plan was announced. This plan was to be overseen by Walter
Lynch, Tony Ruane and Seán Ó Brádaigh, three figures who
strongly supported the retention of abstentionism. Their aim was
to prepare the party for elections with the eventual aim of winning
a majority of TDs and establishing a rival republican Dáil.

In April 1966 five republican candidates were fielded in another
Westminster general election. The movement claimed that it had
decided not to stand candidates in Belfast for fear of adding to
growing sectarian tension. In the five constituencies republicans
saw their combined vote decline from 83,534 in 1964 to 62,782.
The results were particularly disappointing given that two of the
candidates, Charles McGleenan in Armagh and Tom Mitchell in
Mid-Ulster, were former MPs.

The election resulted in a large Labour majority at Westminster,
cementing Harold Wilson's position as Prime Minister. The
Unionist monopoly on Northern Ireland seats had meanwhile
been broken, with Gerry Fitt of Republican Labour taking West
Belfast. Fitt quickly became a spokesman for Catholic grievance at
Westminster. A master of the black arts of Belfast electioneering,
including use of the 'graveyard vote', he promoted himself as a
working-class socialist in Britain while proving adept at appealing
to communal support in Belfast. A notable star turn was his appearance on a platform on the Falls with former Glasgow Celtic hero
Charlie Tully in a celebration of the club's European Cup win
in May 1967. Members of the Republican Clubs reported that

abstentionism, highly unpopular among the electorate, had cost the party votes. Some felt that politicians like Fitt would monopolize support unless challenged by non-abstentionist republican candidates.

By the Ard Fheis of November 1966, held in Moran's Hotel, friction between those supporting the IRA agenda of ending abstentionism and those ranged against was to the fore. In his presidential address, which preceded most of the debate, Mac Giolla reprised his role of mediator between factions – a role that he also fulfilled on the Army Council. He asked members to focus on combating the 'integration' with the British economy, which all in the party saw as embodied in the British-Irish Free Trade Agreement of 1965 and which was 'disastrous to the economy [and] national culture'. He made clear that 'the question of becoming another Free State political party was discussed openly and at length by our organisation last year and there was an overwhelming decision against it'. But there were motions from Dungarvan, Dunamore and Armagh calling for the end of abstentionism. Dublin's John Mitchel cumann, based in Ringsend, countered with a motion that 'any members of Sinn Féin who advocate entry into Leinster House be expelled'.

Tensions over policy were not confined to abstentionism. A motion from North Kerry attempting to ensure 'that no member of the Army Council be a member of the Ard Chomhairle of Sinn Féin' most clearly illustrated the fissure between the IRA leadership and much of the Sinn Féin membership. With a two-thirds vote needed to change party policy, such divisive motions were unsuccessful. Seán Ó Brádaigh complained about the movement's continuing failure to publish the new Social and Economic Programme: as far as he was concerned the document was the party's 'major contribution to the commemoration of the men of Easter Week 1916' and was ready to be released shortly to the public. In fact Goulding and his allies had already shelved the programme, which sought to totally remake the Irish economy on a cooperative model, seeing it as unrealistic.

The Ard Chomhairle elected at the Ard Fheis reflected the

growing emphasis placed on developments in the party by the IRA leadership. Mac Giolla maintained his position as president with Larry Grogan and Joe Clarke, the 76-year-old Dublin bookshop owner and 1916 veteran, elected as vice-presidents. Éamonn Mac Thomáis and Máirín de Burca were elected party secretaries. The rest of the Ard Chomhairle comprised Niall Fagan, Tony Ruane, Seán Ó Brádaigh, Tom Mitchell, Frank Driver, Frank McGlade, Seamus Costello and, for the first time, senior IRA figures Cathal Goulding, Seán Mac Stíofáin and Roy Johnston. Of these Goulding, Johnston, Costello and de Burca were strongly identified with the new agenda while Mac Stíofáin, Ó Brádaigh and Ruane were traditionalists. The position of the others was less clearly defined. Beyond the disquiet of North Kerry and general support shown by Northern members for ending abstention, distrust of Goulding's agenda of change had no clear geographical basis.

From late 1966 the IRA decision to exert greater control over Sinn Féin began to change the nature of the party. Key army figures were placed in positions of influence at all levels. A steering committee met weekly to decide on business between Ard Chomhairle meetings. This group initially included Ruane, Mac Stíofáin and Seán Ó Brádaigh but was dominated by Costello, Goulding, de Burca, Mac Giolla, Johnston and others associated with the left. A Republican Education Department was also established with Johnston for the IRA, Coughlan for the Wolfe Tone Society and Seán Ó Brádaigh for Sinn Féin. Its programme was heavily based on Johnston's ideas of 'economic resistance'. The adoption of the radical agenda was also facilitated by an influx of young members attracted by the commemorations of 1966. The Jubilee year's rehabilitation of Connolly to a central role in the development of republican politics had also accentuated the left-wing aspect of the movement's history. Many of these new members had a perception of the movement shifting rapidly to the left. This said more about the Dublin-based IRA leadership's aspirations for Sinn Féin than its reality, as Sean Dunne, a working-class teenager from a non-republican background in Dublin, found out when he joined the party in the summer of 1966. His reading of Connolly and 'some Soviet history' had not prepared him for the reality of the Russell cumann. There was:

A woman knitting in the corner, someone . . . talking about the abstentionist policy, I didn't know what the abstentionist policy was, I thought it was to do with drink . . . I really took it on board, you can't drink . . . which was grand, it suited me fine, especially when they said we won't enter Leinster House . . . I thought it was a pub. So I made up my mind not to drink. I didn't find out for about a year what they were actually arguing about . . . I realized [then] that the politics I was reading about in the *United Irishman*, which was left-leaning . . . wasn't in the cumann I was in, or [in] anyone I met . . . but that it was coming from the IRA. So I decided to join that.

Other cumainn revitalized or newly established by the influx of IRA volunteers and new members were freer of the traditionalist element. When Tony Heffernan, now aged 19, joined the Pearse cumann in Rathmines during 1968 he found its membership a 'fairly middle-class' group of 'interesting people'. These included Roy Johnston, Seamus Brogan and the Flemish architect and Waffen-SS veteran Staf van Velthoven. Younger members included Dubliner Gerry Parker and Nuala Nolan. Nolan joined the movement in 1965, aged 19, and was a Fianna training officer. She married Jim Monaghan, O/C of the Dublin Active Service Unit, during 1968. Other new branches – such as the Jackie Griffith cumann, established in 1968 in the Donnycarney/Coolock area of Dublin's north side – were set up and dominated by left-wing IRA members. Lar Malone, of the Griffith cumann, was emerging as an important figure within the organization. A clerk with the B&I ferry company and a union activist, Malone was 20 when he joined the IRA in 1963. As the son of a Garda Superintendent he was an unlikely recruit. Andy Smith, a docker from Ringsend, was another activist pushing his local cumann towards social agitation. The Anne Devlin cumann in Rathfarnham was even more closely tied to the leadership's agenda, with its meetings held in Goulding's home. By 1968, eleven cumainn were operating in Dublin, though the leadership regarded only seven as active.

One marker of the shifting political and cultural climate within which the movement found itself evolving was the growing popularity of folk music, in which nationalist and radical sentiments were often fused. Some of this enthusiasm was brought back to Ireland from the clubs of Britain by returning emigrants, including Johnston's wife Máirín and Dominic Behan, an IRA supporter who was close to Goulding and Garland and who had worked closely with the British folk revival's most influential figure, Ewan MacColl. Behan's song 'The Patriot Game' was a scathing critique of the simplistic politics of the 1950s IRA (and, he claimed, the inspiration for Bob Dylan's 'With God On Our Side'). The ethos of the folk revival was seen by many in the republican movement as complementing the politics of Goulding and his supporters, and the *United Irishman* strongly promoted the music. Republicans frequented Dublin venues such as O'Donoghue's Pub on Merrion Row, Slattery's of Capel Street, the Embankment in Tallaght and Ned Stapleton's Piper's Club in Thomas Street. Fleadhs attracted thousands of young people to country towns for weekend-long concerts; Lar Malone and a group of young IRA men often performed at these events.

The decade's atmosphere of cultural change was evident, too, in Trinity College Dublin, where the 1916 commemoration had a striking impact. Trinity was described by *Hibernia* magazine in 1966 as the 'last bastion of the English establishment and Protestant Ascendancy' in Ireland. Until 1970 Catholics had to get their bishop's dispensation before enrolling in the college. But by 1966 growing numbers of Catholic middle-class students were entering the university, and enrolment of UK grant-aided working-class students from Northern Ireland and Britain complemented the trend. Among the founders of the Trinity Republican Club, Eoin Ó Murchú from London and Kevin McCorry from west Belfast were both on UK grants. They were joined in an initial core group by Des White, a student from Cavan, and law student Ronnie Lindsey. The endeavour also had a degree of support from

Trinity academics, with Máirtín Ó Cadhain and the Reverend Terence McCaughey being early patrons. The Club's inaugural event was a speech by Professor Theo Moody on 'Wolfe Tone and the Republican Protestant Tradition'. The Republican Club quickly became one of the college's largest student groups.

Due to university rules the Club was not officially linked to Sinn Féin, but members sold the *United Irishman*, promoted the movement's policies and hosted meetings addressed by IRA leaders. Early members recall a mainly middle-class Catholic membership with a more working-class core. The Republican Club was closely linked to the university's An Cumann Gaelach, an association of students interested in the Irish language and music. Although IRA membership was not a prerequisite of Club membership, and many Club members were not in the 'Army', Dermot Nolan, who joined in 1967, remembered that 'people that wanted to get on in the movement felt they should join the IRA'. This undercurrent was evident at the funeral of Des White, who died in a car accident in the summer of 1968. An IRA member, his hearse was accompanied by a colour party of Republican Club members who had drilled for the occasion in the university gym.

The leading members of the Republican Club were strongly committed to Goulding's agenda, and in Nolan's view they were also seen as important to its success: 'The movement saw it as a possible source of intellectuals.' Sean Dunne later had the role of liaising between the Club and the Dublin IRA leadership. Their independence from Sinn Féin allowed the Club's leadership to express freer opinions on major issues, including abstentionism. Initially these were carried in a monthly Republican Club column in the *United Irishman*, until the Club launched its own publication, *Republican News*, in April 1968. This was edited by Dalton Kelly and Terry Murphy, Ó Murchú's brother. Many of the student republicans used New Books, the Communist bookshop on Pearse Street, as a source of reading material. During 1966 Maoism had arrived in Trinity with the setting up of the Internationalists, a group whose members carried portraits of Mao and brandished copies of his 'little red book'; and the Young Socialists also established a presence in the college. Their often uneasy interaction with these other left-wing groups gave Republican Club members access to arguments not heard elsewhere in the movement. When J. B. O'Hagan called into Ó Murchú's Trinity rooms, after driving the student back from a commemoration in Lurgan, he was surprised to be confronted by posters declaring 'solidarity with [North] Korea'.

Whereas the Trinity Republican Club was partially funded by the college, attempts to form similar Clubs in University College Dublin and University College Galway met with disapproval from the National University of Ireland. With assistance and advice from members of the Trinity Club a small group of UCD students, among them Dubliners Tony Gregory and Jim Sherry, began campaigning for recognition of their Club in 1967. It would take another year before the UCD branch of the Labour Party allowed the Club to become affiliated to it and so gain de facto official recognition by the college administration. The UCD Club claimed 64 members by November 1968.

Dwyer's pub on Merrion Row was a 'mixing pot' for the left and the Connolly Youth ran a venue on Pembroke Lane close to Gaj's restaurant. This restaurant was run by Scotswoman Margaret Gaj, herself a left-wing activist, and was promoted as the place where 'all the best spies drink their Russian tea'. In Gaj's and the nearby bars activists could be found 'huggermuggering in the back . . . very cloak and dagger', imagining 'we were a threat to the world'.

Increased republican activity during and after 1966 was evident in the areas of natural resources, housing and civil rights. The National Waters Restoration League had been formally launched during March 1966 at a meeting in Galway, though the initial planning took place in IRA man 'Paddy Kilcullen's back kitchen in Ballina'. The campaign had begun as a localized dispute by Galway fishermen, involving protests and illegal fishing, over their right to fish in Galway Bay outside the so-called 'king's mile' beyond the mouth of the river Corrib. The legal rights to fish this area were owned by members of the British gentry, whose families had been granted them during the Cromwellian settlement, and similar situations existed on many of Ireland's other rivers. The league was intent on highlighting and if possible reversing this state of affairs. Republicans in Westmeath were also involved in establishing a Land League on the 1,100-acre Knockdrin Estate, owned by the Duke of Mecklenburg, and called for foreign-owned property to be divided among small farmers.

A Wolfe Tone Society seminar on civil rights, featuring Kadar Asmal, a South African exile lecturing in law at Trinity College, was held in Belfast on 28 November 1966. Those in attendance included members of the Communist Party, Northern Ireland Labour Party and republicans, with most of the city's IRA members ordered to attend. At a second Belfast meeting on 29 January 1967, an organizing committee was elected to establish a new civil rights body. IRA members, once more ordered to attend, were also told whom to vote for, to ensure a republican and Communist presence on it. The committee included Billy McMillen representing the Republican Clubs, Paddy Devlin of the NILP, Betty Sinclair of the Communist Party and Fred Heatley of the Wolfe Tone Society. It also co-opted a Young Unionist, Robin Cole. Two members of the British National Council for Civil Liberties attended the event and the new body's constitution was consciously modelled on that of the NCCL, with a broad remit on the promotion of civil rights. McMillen was one of a three-person subcommittee that drew up a proposed constitution for the new body. The Northern Ireland Civil Rights Association (NICRA) was then formally launched at a conference on 9 April. McMillen, whose IRA position would have drawn hostile attention very quickly, stood down from the committee that month and was replaced by Kevin Agnew. NICRA's early tactics were confined to lobbying and its first year was relatively quiet, but republicans pushed from an early stage for the adoption of protest marches as a tactic. The involvement of republicans gave NICRA a potential activist base, particularly in rural Ulster, that none of the other organizations possessed.

Paddy Devlin's involvement was considered significant by republicans. Devlin had been an IRA volunteer until 1951. Republicans had an uneasy relationship with his party in Belfast and McMillen blamed the NILP for sabotaging attempts to launch 'one-man-one-vote' committees during 1965. Most NILP members were committed to social reform within the United Kingdom and highly suspicious of republicans; the party also included a strong evangelical Protestant current, and some in the party saw the issue of civil rights as a 'republican conspiracy'. However, the party's Young Socialist group, which included Harry McKeown from west Belfast and Queen's student Michael Farrell, were influenced by more radical views. When republican Brendan Mackin returned to Belfast from Britain, McMillen advised him to remain active in the NILP and push for support for NICRA.

In early 1967 Northern Ireland Minister for Home Affairs William Craig used the Special Powers Act to declare the Republican Clubs an illegal organization. Craig claimed fears of disorder associated with plans to hold commemorations of the 1867 Fenian Rising lay behind the move. The ban did not prevent the Clubs from holding an illegal convention in March 1967. Much of NICRA's early activity was centred on campaigning against the Republican Club ban. Another response was that students at Queen's University, drawn in the main from the growing number of Catholic students now attending the former unionist bastion, established their own Republican Club. One such, Mary McMahon from Armagh, 'thought it would be a good idea to join an organization which Bill Craig banned'. In November 1967, 1,000 people joined a protest at Craig's home against the ban. The march passed off peacefully despite a counter-demonstration led by Ian Paisley in Belfast city centre.

Another issue that mobilized republicans at this time was housing. In Derry IRA activists began housing agitation under the banner of Young Republicans. During October 1966 a group of republicans aided the McDonnell family in Harvey Street in forcibly resisting eviction by council bailiffs. Those involved included Johnnie White, then a shop steward at the BSR factory in Creggan, and Finbar O'Doherty, who had been drawn to the republican movement by its newly radicalized image. Derry, with its Catholic majority but Unionist-dominated council, was a potent symbol of Stormont misrule. It was also a 'one-industry city' with a mostly female workforce employed in its shirt factories. There was high male unemployment and poor housing. Even though the city displayed blatant manifestations of sectarian discrimination it had little tradition of republicanism beyond a handful of families and core activists. Eamon Melaugh had dropped out of Sinn Féin in the city during 1963 because of the lack of republican interest in social problems. He became interested again when the *United Irishman* began to cover the living conditions in Springtown Camp on the edge of the city. Though Catholic Derry was dominated politically by the Nationalist Party there was also an active NILP branch in the town. Although it was an essentially moderate body it was subjected to periodic denunciation as communist and to openly sectarian attacks from the Nationalists who would claim that 'the Protestants' were voting NILP. But radicals Dermie McClenaghan and Eamonn McCann were a vocal element in the local party. An active party youth wing, eventually the Young Socialists, numerically larger than the local republicans, became an important source of agitation in the city.

White and the other republicans pushed forward activity on housing and unemployment. Melaugh and White set about a survey of the condition of local housing, finding homes there with 'bugs falling from the ceilings . . . children with bug bites on their arms and legs'. The Derry Housing Action Committee embarked on a campaign that was to involve squatting and occupation of the city's Guildhall. Agitation on unemployment also continued. In the eyes of the younger activists, Sean Keenan and other traditionalist republicans in the city 'didn't accept housing and unemployment as relevant'. Activities were not confined to the Catholic Bogside and Creggan. White, who had worked alongside B-Specials in BSR, had no problem with the movement's aim of influencing Protestant workers; but it was not always possible to put this into practice. The group was approached by a man from the Protestant

Fountain estate who asked them to advise locals on housing issues; after a visit to the area by republican activists the man's windows were smashed and his family was forced to move. The Derry campaigners received effusive praise in the *United Irishman*, which claimed that their housing efforts would 'eclipse all the similar committees in the country'.

Housing was also an issue in the South. In February 1967 Tony Meade, who had replaced Denis Foley as editor of the *United Irishman*, highlighted a United Nations report that indicated that Ireland had the lowest per capita production of housing in the western world. Dublin's population had grown from 1961 to 1965 by a greater amount than in any five years since at least 1900. In human terms this meant 6,000 families in the Dublin area alone living in overcrowded conditions, with many others living in condemned buildings. Dramatic cases such as the tenement collapses of 1963 and the Griffith Barracks protests had led to short-lived housing campaigns. The most visible sign of the government and Dublin Corporation's response to the housing shortage was seven fifteen-storey high-rises named after the seven signatories of the 1916 proclamation and built in Ballymun, on the northern edge of the city. The first tenants moved into Ballymun in 1966 and when the scheme was completed in 1969 it housed nearly 20,000 people. The development was separated from areas of non-public housing by a twelve-foot concrete wall. Dublin Corporation was meanwhile facing mass protest over the introduction of a differential rent system that would see corporation tenants' rents rise beyond the levels agreed in their contracts. Meade lamented that while the Labour Party was 'unwilling' to begin a campaign, Sinn Féin was 'too weak' to lead the necessary 'housing revolution'. However, the party intended to do just that.

In May 1967 the Dublin Housing Action Campaign was launched. Arising from the work of the citizens' advice bureaux and the IRA's general strategy, the DHAC sought to bring together republican activists and other radicals in a campaign involving the homeless themselves. All families living in inadequate accommodation were defined by the campaign as 'homeless'.

These included people living in severe overcrowding and families forced to live with in-laws, paying excessive rent or squatting. At the same time the operations of the advice bureaux were to be extended to every area of the capital. Each Sinn Féin cumann was now to have the responsibility of appointing a member to run an advice office. The operations of this network were overseen by a central office run out of Sinn Féin headquarters in 30 Gardiner Place, with Sean Dunne appointed its first chairman.

As with the creation of the advice bureaux, De Rossa was the 'prime mover' in initially establishing the DHAC. Paddy Stanley, a returned emigrant living in a caravan in Portmarnock, was elected chairman and Denis and Mary Dennehy, a couple also living in roadside accommodation, became key activists from an early stage. Most DHAC committee positions rotated among republican activists already involved in the advice bureaux, most prominently Sean Dunne, Seán Ó Cionnaith, Seamus Rattigan and Máirín de Burca. From an early stage the Irish Workers' Party and the Irish Communist Organisation were also involved, and another important non-republican ally was Fr. Michael Sweetman, a Jesuit priest and one of a small number of radicals emerging from the Catholic Church at the time. Sweetman's involvement was seen as a useful deterrent to allegations of communist manipulation. The DHAC highlighted the housing crisis in a campaign that began with pickets on landlords' homes, demonstrations at Dublin City Council meetings demanding 'build houses not office blocks', and eventually occupations of vacant property. Initially activists restricted the use of force to halting evictions from premises in which families already lived, but by the first half of 1968 activists were breaking into unused properties to allow families to squat. These properties were then physically protected by DHAC activists. As Sean Dunne saw it 'the main thing was to get the homeless involved. They did get involved [and] some . . . joined the movement as well, or joined the IRA. So in all the committees we had a majority. It wasn't organized that way but that's the way it went.'

The increase in republican activity in the South encouraged a belief within Sinn Féin that there would be a political pay-off in the June 1967 local elections. But despite the new energy and a panel of 110 candidates, Sinn Féin polled badly. There were a few notable successes. Costello and Joe Doyle were elected in Bray, Francie O'Donoghue in Carrickmacross, Paddy O'Callaghan in Killorglin, Redmond O'Sullivan in Killarney, Jim McElwaine in Monaghan, Peter Duffy in Dundalk and Joe Sherlock in Mallow. Seamus Rodgers held his seat in Glenties, as did a number of other rural Sinn Féin councillors including Norbert Ferguson, who became mayor of Sligo. But the party clearly lacked an urban base: no candidate in Dublin or Cork city had come close to a seat, and Sinn Féin did not even stand in Waterford city. The real story of the election in Dublin was that the Labour Party had replaced Fine Gael as the second party in the city. Labour's rhetoric had been getting consistently more left wing and its election literature had spoken freely of socialism. Goulding and his supporters worried that Labour would benefit from further radicalization while republicans fretted over abstentionism. Republicans did not contest May's municipal elections in Northern Ireland, and a variety of Labour candidates were successful in both Catholic and Protestant working-class areas.

If Goulding's radical agenda was to be successful, members needed to believe in the new strategy. The Republican Education Department's role was to instil such confidence while reassuring the maintenance of republican principles. By March 1967 conferences had been held in Belfast, Dungannon, Ballina, Cork, New Ross, Wexford, Waterford, Gorey and Dublin. Meanwhile the IRA continued their own education meetings, with experts from outside the movement often giving the lectures. Johnston was aware of the 'pretty uneven' progress of movement education. At one IRA meeting addressed by Kadar Asmal, a volunteer declared within earshot of the speaker: 'I see you have coons involved here.' Many activists had little formal education and had to struggle to keep up with the new concepts. Desmond Greaves met McMillen in Belfast during 1967 and found him studying an exercise book in which he had transcribed some of the new ideas. He told Greaves that the IRA would 'like to cooperate with everybody, including the communists' but there was a 'strong group of old-fashioned Sinn Féin in the way'. By early 1968 McMillen would be among those meeting delegations from the Communist Party in Belfast.

In October 1967 an educational manual written by Johnston was distributed throughout the movement. In it he tried to place the movement's leftism within the Irish radical tradition of Tone, Mellows and Connolly while also introducing republicans to Stalinism and Trotskyism. Johnston argued republicans could no longer 'insulate' themselves from international politics and theoretical debates. Explanations of terms like 'progressive', 'reactionary' and 'capitalism' followed. He argued that the 'negative tradition of Stalinism' had been a major flaw of the Communist movement, particularly with reference to its dependence on Moscow. However, the 'wealth of trade union experience' of the Irish communists could not be ignored by republicans. Johnston hoped that the initiation of dialogue between the Vatican and the USSR had ended the 'state of cold war' between the two and made it possible for Catholic radicals to find common ground with Marxists.

The document outlined a strategy of forming a 'progressive' alliance, which would include 'pragmatic' groups such as members of the Labour Party, nationalists, and social and cultural organizations. Republicans and communists would lead this alliance. Campaigns could be begun on housing, control of resources, rural depopulation, and wages and conditions. There was even an outline of a strategy to aid the 'survival of small shopkeepers' – not an orthodox Marxist concern but one very much shared by Sinn Féin, who vocally defended Irish shopkeepers against the threat of foreign supermarkets.

Republicans had to recognize that the two major forces of the establishment in Ireland, Fianna Fáil in the South and the Unionists in the North, were disillusioning their traditional support base. The 'bright young men of Fianna Fáil' were seen as intent on bringing Ireland into greater integration with foreign capital, all the better to maintain neo-colonial control. Unionism, the 'most reactionary' force in Ireland, was divided and an opportunity existed to undermine it by a campaign for civil liberties. This would concentrate on the discrimination against Catholics in housing and employment and seek to build on the work that had been done by groups like the Campaign for Social Justice. However, no long-term change was possible without the support of Protestant workers, and Johnston argued that they could be won to the campaign by a focus on how local government property qualifications disqualified poor Protestants from voting. The perceived influence of communists within the Northern trade unions was seen as key to introducing these ideas to Protestant workers. Optimistically Johnston argued that insofar as support for Ian Paisley weakened the Unionist government, Paisley was an 'ally', and it would be 'wrong to class Paisley's rank-and-file supporters as the enemy'. Two new political threats to the republican project were highlighted. One was the Trotskyists, who were essentially 'anti-national' because they were unconcerned with defending Irish sovereignty from bodies like the EEC. The other was the 'extreme republican' position that upheld physical force and non-participation in Leinster House as principles rather than tactics. There were possibilities for republicans to make gains through cultural and language groups and it was important to try to 'make it fashionable to speak Irish in urban working-class circles'. It was also necessary for republicans to make clear their identification with left-wing struggles in places such as Vietnam or Cuba, partly in order to 'build for the movement funds of goodwill for the future'.

The November 1967 Sinn Féin Ard Fheis was held in Liberty Hall. The main thrust of Mac Giolla's presidential address was the perceived 'change among the Protestant community'. He suggested that 'they are beginning to think for themselves. Once they open their minds to new ideas no one will be more receptive than them to republican principles. They were the founders and leaders of the first republican movement in Ireland – the United Irishmen ... the Protestant Industrial workers in the North could today capture the leadership of radical republican thought, if they would only admit they are Irish and have an obligation to their fellow

Irishmen.' He made clear that the republican movement was not waiting for events to happen but was becoming a catalyst for change: 'it is not enough for a man to say he is a socialist, that he is for a Workers Republic and against Capitalism . . . revolutionary ideas must be followed by revolutionary action'. The Ard Fheis left no doubt that the republican movement had embraced the rhetoric of socialism. Goulding moved an amendment to the party's constitution, which declared it in favour of a 'Democratic Socialist Republic'.

Costello had attempted to use the election of a new Ard Chomhairle to bring about the end of abstentionism. His motion seeking the abandonment of abstentionism as a principle was watered down by a compromise leadership motion seeking to allow the incoming Ard Chomhairle to examine the matter over the coming year. Costello had been appointed by the Army Council to oversee the IRA's block voting for Ard Chomhairle positions. This was done by the distribution of a secret written order to volunteers who were Ard Fheis delegates listing who they should vote for. Costello substituted the agreed army list with a list of his own, which was heavily skewed in favour of his supporters and anti-abstentionists. The switch became known to other members of the leadership prior to Costello's list being put into circulation. For his attempt to usurp the Army Council Costello was court-martialled and suspended from the leadership for a short period. The Ard Chomhairle that emerged from the Ard Fheis had a majority who were supportive of Goulding's direction. Among them were Mick Ryan, his mother Monica, Mitchell, Costello and de Burca. Among those opposed were Mac Thomáis, Seán Ó Brádaigh and the two vice-presidents Grogan and Clarke. Garland was co-opted on to the Ard Chomhairle along with two regional IRA officers, Eddie Williams from Cork and Paddy Kilcullen from Mayo, both advocates of the new policies.

Not everyone shared the enthusiasm for the emphasis on economic rather than nationalist issues. De Rossa was shocked when Paddy McGlynn confronted him about the housing campaigns and argued that landlords had every right to do as they wished with their own property. McGlynn was far from alone in Sinn Féin in being opposed to the move to the left. During early 1968 Gerry McCarthy savagely attacked Johnston's role at a commemoration in Cork. He compared Johnston to Mrs Lindsay, a Protestant informer killed by the IRA in Cork during 1921, and urged that he and his supporters be 'kicked out . . . lock, stock and barrel'. Another dissident remembered 'lots of clandestine activity going on inside the movement' in opposition to the leadership. Dissension was concentrated most intensely in North Kerry. Sinn Féin there had refused to contest the local elections in June and had even expelled two members who had helped the party's campaign in South Kerry. The three local IRA members who had been dismissed by the Army Council in late 1966 had also remained active in the party. Eventually the Sinn Féin leadership, on the proposal of Seán Mac Stíofáin, agreed to disband six North Kerry cumainn. A small number of those loyal to Dublin remained active while a large group of former members in the region now operated independently.

Despite the internal problems and the disappointment at the local elections Sinn Féin's increasing activity began to pay off during 1968 with new recruits and national attention being drawn to its campaigns. It was aided by tumultuous events around the world. The left gained a new martyr when Che Guevara was killed fighting in the Bolivian jungle in October 1967, Garland writing an obituary in *An t-Oglac*. Fidel Castro criticized the Soviet Union and China for not devoting all their resources to support for armed struggle in Vietnam and South America and seemed to offer an alternative vision of Third World socialism. The January 1968 Tet offensive by the National Liberation Front inflicted a fatal blow to America's claims to be winning in Vietnam. During March huge anti-war demonstrations took place across Europe and the United States and in London marchers battled police at the US Embassy. The assassination of Martin Luther King Jr. in April saw over a hundred of America's cities burn in rage. Later that year mass demonstrations occurred at the Democratic Party convention in Chicago. During May, protests by students in Paris led to a week of street fighting followed by a general strike by ten million French workers. The Olympic Games in Mexico were marked by Black Power protests by American athletes and a massacre of student protesters by Mexican troops. The Czech communists' experiment in 'socialism with a human face' was ended by Soviet tanks in August. Student riots took place in Germany and Italy.

The question of social transformation in the West was no longer abstract. Young republicans like Tony Heffernan were caught up in the mood: 'There was a real sense . . . that we were on the verge of a sort of very profound change all over the world. With the arrogance and confidence that only 18-year-olds can have, we were sure we were on the verge of revolution.' In the *United Irishman* Alan Matthews described the events in France and Germany as an 'inspiration' to Irish students. During 1967 the *United Irishman* had begun to take a more upfront line on the Vietnam War, having previously cautiously called for negotiations. Sinn Féin called on Irish emigrants not to become 'tools of the imperialists' after four Irishmen had died in combat in early 1967, three in the British Army in Aden and one in Vietnam. Apartheid was also on the agenda: Trinity republicans held meetings addressed by Thabo Mbeki of the African National Congress, and the *United Irishman* interviewed ANC leader Oliver Tambo on a visit to Dublin that summer. Ideologically the republican movement weathered the Soviet invasion of Czechoslovakia well. While the Irish communists suffered internal upheaval, Sinn Féin issued a statement condemning the invasion, arguing that 'socialism . . . can only flourish under conditions of national independence'. Some republican students joined marches protesting at the Soviet action. Among the leadership opinion was mixed. Desmond Greaves, who strongly supported the invasion, recorded that Johnston 'was not persuaded that the Russians might have a case in Czechoslovakia'. Goulding was increasingly close to Mick O'Riordan, who had supported the Moscow line on the crisis. In fact a 'secret mechanism' for contact between Goulding and his allies on the Army Council and the Irish Communist leadership had already been established.

There was some criticism of the *United Irishman*'s international coverage, particularly from American republicans. Jerry Boyle in San Francisco complained that the articles were 'doing grave harm' to the movement in the US, which was 'green . . . not red'. Some republicans were also less than enthusiastic about what they saw as the permissive nature of the new left. One reviewer in the *United Irishman* criticized both American Black Power advocates and comedian Lenny Bruce as 'degenerate'. Many of the newer recruits to the movement would not have agreed. They brought a different cultural ethos as well as new ideas. Some new members thought there was 'nothing incompatible' between being in Sinn Féin and listening to rock music and following soccer. Jer O'Leary, a 22-year-old who joined the movement during 1967, was a supporter of both Drumcondra and Glasgow Celtic. He delighted in reminding GAA devotees that the Dublin IRA's commander in 1921, Oscar Traynor, had been a soccer player. Younger republicans dressed differently, with both men and women wearing combat jackets, and often seemed irreverent to their older peers. One woman felt that some veteran female members were 'mad resentful of young flirtatious women' in make-up and miniskirts, some of whom procured the illegal contraceptive pill from a premises in Mountjoy Square.

Sinn Féin's activities were given a major boost by the appointment of a new editor of the *United Irishman* in November 1967. Séamus Ó Tuathail was a young teacher at Belvedere College, a cycling enthusiast and a former chairman of Misneach, an Irish-language activist group. He was not a member of Sinn Féin or the IRA and his appointment gave the paper an editorial independence it did not have under Foley or Meade. This coincided with the decision by the leadership to place a new emphasis on the *United Irishman* as 'the basis of the beginning of the rebuilding of the organisation'. Ó Tuathail found the paper in a precarious situation, with circulation down to around 14,000 a month and in massive debt to its printer. Controversies over the paper's editorial line had damaged its distribution in many areas and apart from a handful of shops it was dependent upon pub rounds and a pitch outside the

GPO in Dublin for most of its sales. With Ó Tuathail at a remove from the internal debates of the movement, and with an eye on greater sales, he turned the *United Irishman* into a campaigning paper; 'he made policy'. He gave greater coverage to the activities of the Dublin Housing Action Campaign, and his articles in the 'Poacher's Guide to Ireland's Waterways' series rejuvenated the campaign to nationalize fishing rights. A regular column, 'Who Owns Ireland?', outlined the men behind the major banks, companies and multinationals. Ó Tuathail highlighted the fact that members of the British aristocracy were still being paid ground rent for property in Ireland. Jim Fitzpatrick, a young artist who had designed an iconic poster of Che Guevara during 1968, also produced several images for the *United Irishman*. Paper sales reinforced a sense of equality of membership, with everyone from the Sinn Féin president down helping out. Often after he finished editing an issue Ó Tuathail would be found selling it outside the GPO. It was claimed that sales had increased to 24,000 a month during 1968.

By January 1968, when the DHAC picketed the home of the Minister for Local Government Kevin Boland, and participated in the 'battle of Sarah Place' in Inchicore, the organization had gained considerable notoriety by its actions and innovative publicity. In Inchicore, activists were aiding residents who had barricaded themselves inside their cottages rather than be relocated to Ballymun. Council bailiffs and 30 Gardaí attempted to break the barricades and evict the families. As word spread, more activists arrived. Mick Ryan, driving out of Dublin on IRA business, happened to be passing the area and became involved. By the end of the incident 24 people, including Dunne, De Rossa, Jim Monaghan, Lar Malone and Mick O'Riordan had been arrested. Only 23 would be charged as Ryan made good his escape from the back of a Garda van as it was entering the Bridewell.

At Easter the DHAC 'commandeered' a number of four-storey Georgian houses on Mount Street that were due to be developed into office blocks by their London-based owners. The Starry Plough and tricolour flags were flown from the buildings and

homeless families moved in. Private security firms hired by landlords to repossess properties were confronted by IRA members
negotiating for squatters 'like the Godfather [with] an offer they
can't refuse'. The DHAC were denounced in the Dáil as 'reds and
fellow-travellers'. Its chairman, De Rossa, was equally confrontational in an *Irish Times* interview in June: 'We don't set out to
be respectable public figures. We want to force attention on the
problem and force action on it. Ours is only a short-term solution.
But I'd like to emphasize one thing. Our gripe is not with officials
or the councillors or Dublin Corporation. Our battle is against
conditions, against the system.' De Rossa recalled that DHAC
secretary Ó Cionnaith was 'a first-class organizer, in particular with
the media. I would have the idea to get the thing going, I would get
him on board and the thing would take off.' The demonstration at
the home of Kevin Boland in January 1968 was part of a strategy of
targeting Fianna Fáil, and noting the links between property developers and Taca, the party's corporate fund-raising body (or 'payola
racket', as the *United Irishman* described it). Boland hit back,
denouncing the DHAC as the creation of an 'illegal organization'.
Seán Ó Cionnaith's response was that he considered the 'British
Army, RUC and B-Specials' to be the only illegal organizations in
Ireland. Emulating Dublin and Derry, republicans established
housing action committees elsewhere. Costello threw his energies
into organizing the Bray Tenants' Association. There was increasing
activity in rural Ulster, with Liam Ó Comain involved in housing
protests in Limavady and liaising with Francie Donnelly about the
setting up of Republican Clubs in Co. Derry. In Belfast republicans
fought for rehousing for 160 families living in prefabricated bunga-
lows in Beechmount, and campaigned on the need for pedestrian
crossings and better street lighting in Turf Lodge. Agitation continued against the new Divis Flats complex, drawing condemnation
from local curate Fr. Padraig Murphy, who supported the development because it kept parishioners in the Falls area.

Reorganization of the IRA in the south-east had seen an older
militarist leadership replaced by supporters of Goulding. Now Sean

Walsh in south Kilkenny and Mick Dunphy and Sean Kelly in Waterford were among those who brought new activity to the area. Waterford was a 'factory town' with a large industrial working-class population and a strong trade union base. Kelly had been drawn into politics when trying to unionize his first workplace. During 1967 the city's activists established an advice bureau in a rented office on the quays. The setting up of a flat-dwellers association, housing action committee and local civil rights branch quickly followed. An activist recalled: 'We were the ministers for hopeless cases as well as people that got things done. After a short period of time people became aware if you wanted something done, be it officially or unofficially or dodgy or otherwise, you went to 115 the Quay.'

Costello had been upsetting the local status quo as a councillor in Bray. On several occasions he brought housing protesters into the council chamber and demanded that their problems be heard. When Wicklow's Labour TD died in January 1968, Costello was eager to contest the by-election. The leadership's suspicion of their younger colleague saw Mick Ryan appointed director of elections even though he and Costello 'did not get on'. On election day a donkey adorned with a placard stating 'Don't be like me: I voted Fianna Fáil last time' was paraded by Sinn Féin outside polling stations. Costello won 2,009 votes, coming fourth. Publicly republicans argued this was significant, especially in an area with little republican tradition, but there were tensions behind the scenes. Costello complained that Sinn Féin had 'let Wicklow down very badly' in terms of support and finance. But he also claimed that 'during the course of the by-election we found that the greatest single objection to voting Sinn Féin was the existence of the abstentionist policy'.

One consequence of the increasing activity of republicans and the left was anxiety about extremism. An *Evening Herald* front page after Sarah Place warned that 'Red Cells' existed in Dublin and were active in the DHAC. It was claimed housing agitation was the product of a 'well-known organised movement under the direction of a man who is alleged to have been trained by extreme elements in Britain and sent over here to exploit housing and other problems'. The person in question was a 'Dublin man with exceptional ability as an organiser' and was 'under constant surveillance'. The article ended with a doorstep interview with Roy Johnston, in which Johnston dismissed Garda activity, saying 'let them investigate away, it is their business not mine'. In May 1968 the Deputy Lord Mayor of Dublin Lauri Corcoran asserted to a union conference that there were 3,000 communists 'infiltrating . . . all walks of Dublin life'. The same month a demonstration by the Internationalists in Trinity against the visit of the Belgian King led to more media denunciation of student radicals. While the college republicans were highly critical of the Maoists, they helped lead a large protest march to the headquarters of the *Evening Herald* and *Irish Independent*. North of the border, Unionists were also playing the 'red' card. William Craig told the Northern parliament that civil rights agitation was the result of communist and republican conspiracy. Unionist hard-liner Major Ronald Bunting claimed that 'if anyone wanted a communistic, godless, Bolshevik, atheistic city then the opening of playgrounds on Sundays was the right way to start'.

Although most of the mainstream newspapers in Ireland were conservative, and several were closely linked to mainstream political parties, not all media coverage of republicans was hostile. Under the editorship of Douglas Gageby the *Irish Times* was generally a benevolent environment for left-wing employees. Dick Walsh from Co. Clare had reported on working conditions and strikes while living in London and after returning to Ireland became a staff journalist with the *Irish Times* in 1968. Walsh became friendly with Goulding and other republican leaders. The *Irish Times* political correspondent Michael McInerney was a former communist who was sympathetic to the republican left. Also working at the paper was Mary Maher, a young Irish American who edited the 'Women First' column during 1968. Maher had covered the Bodenstown commemoration of 1966 and became closely associated with republicans, marrying Des Geraghty, who had recently left the Labour Party to join Sinn Féin, in early 1969. Roy Johnston wrote a series of articles on science for the paper during 1967. Current affairs magazines such as *Hibernia* and *Nusight* also gave space to the political and social ferment.

The impact of left-wing republicanism was becoming evident at RTÉ. Producer and activist Eoghan Harris produced and directed a documentary called *The Testimony of James Connolly* during 1968. Some of RTÉ's current affairs output also caused government unease. In May 1968 the religious affairs programme *Outlook*, presented by Fr. Austin Flannery, had discussed the housing crisis with a panel including Mick O'Riordan and two members of Sinn Féin. Fianna Fáil was enraged, with Kevin Boland calling the programme 'grossly distorted' and Charles Haughey dismissing Flannery as a 'gullible priest'. Concerns within RTÉ about the left-wing tone of some of its programmes led the station's Director General to introduce strict restrictions on political involvement by station employees.

The civil rights movement in Northern Ireland started to heat up during 1968. The Northern Ireland Civil Rights Association's new executive included republicans Rebecca McGlade, Kevin Agnew and Frank Campbell, and RUC intelligence recorded that 30 of the 70 people present at the AGM in February were 'known republicans or IRA'. During April, 400 republicans attended a banned commemoration in Armagh, which ended with several arrests. NICRA condemned the arrests and the ban. In a climate of growing militancy, and conscious of the example of civil rights marches in America, the NICRA leadership sought to expand its campaign. By this stage the sole Unionist on the NICRA executive had resigned in protest at the description of Northern Ireland as a 'fascist state'. During 1968 the Brantry Republican Club helped organize an eight-month occupation of a vacant council house in Caledon near Dungannon. The squat drew headlines when local MP Austin Currie became involved and the squatting family was forcibly evicted in front of the TV cameras. The publicity garnered by the Dungannon events was a huge boost to a more militant civil rights strategy, which republicans were urging. In Derry housing action protesters disrupted the opening of the new Craig-avon Bridge. In early August, Currie, Labour councillor Jack Hassard and Republican Club leaders Brian Quinn and Tom O'Connor presented a major survey into discrimination in Dungannon to the *Irish News*. Momentum began to build from there with increasing calls for the adoption of civil disobedience as a tactic. Currie approached Fred Heatley about involving NICRA in a protest march from Coalisland to Dungannon. Republicans were enthusiastic about the idea. Communist Betty Sinclair was much less so, and only after extended discussions was it agreed to fix 24 August as the date for the march. Sinclair was convinced the march would be seen simply as a nationalist demonstration, no matter how NICRA presented it. Loyalists announced they would hold a counter-demonstration in the centre of Dungannon and the RUC attempted to reroute the NICRA march, but the organizers refused on the basis that their march was not sectarian.

An internal republican document explained that civil rights was of 'overriding importance' in the struggle to 'educate and organise the people for the achievement of a Republic'. Tactics adopted could include 'marches, meetings, sit-ins, sit-downs [and] boy-cotts'. If marches were stopped then protesters were to 'sit down, occupy roads, be carried off physically – no resistance – [and] in this way expose the violence of the police'. Another tactic could be the 'occupations of central squares . . . at peak hours, with press tipped off'. It was important to ensure the 'maximum participation of women and children'. The document argued that the 'success of such techniques in USA, India, Czechoslovakia' showed 'the power of an organised and disciplined people'. It was also important not to display 'party banners or tricolours' and judge carefully the effect on 'Protestant public opinion and opinion abroad'. A disciplined movement with a wide basis of support would be able to 'undermine the popular basis of Unionist rule'. In fact the IRA had been informed of how 'fragile' support for civil rights was within the unions and of emerging hostility to the agitation from Protestant workers by the Belfast communists in early 1968. But on 24 August members of the IRA acted as stewards for the

2,000 marchers in Dungannon with 'the bulk' of the Northern membership, including McMillen and McKnight, present (though Southern volunteers were ordered not to attend). Old habits died hard. As the march approached Dungannon McGurran ordered IRA volunteers to 'break ranks, you are on a protest, not a route march'. While the RUC later credited the IRA's stewards with a 'high degree of discipline', the republican strategy was a risky one. Stewards had orders to prevent trouble but also to encourage non-violent confrontation; 'prevent the crowd getting near the police [but] make them think they want to fight the police . . . let them get angry'. However, the 'more you stopped them the more they wanted to attack'. The marchers halted in front of the RUC cordon separating them from the centre of Dungannon and 1,500 loyalist demonstrators. Hassard addressed the crowd, telling them many Protestants like himself supported civil rights. Other speakers included Sinclair, Currie and Fitt. Despite NICRA's intentions the support given to the march by organizations such as the Hibernians and the presence of nationalist marching bands gave the event a distinctly communal flavour, as did Fitt's description of the RUC as 'black bastards'. Despite some minor stone-throwing the day ended peacefully. McMillen felt that the march had been a 'disappointing anti-climax'. Others agreed, with Goulding finding that some republicans 'objected to the attitude of the civil rights marchers in Dungannon when confronted by the police. They said the police cordon should have been broken.' This was also the view of groups like the Young Socialists. Despite these tensions, the importance of the civil rights tactic was brought home to young republicans like Sean Curry after listening to discussions between McCann, Anthony Dornan and others on the bus back to Belfast.

In the aftermath of the Coalisland march a number of Derry activists, including Melaugh, McCann and Bridget Bond, discussed the possibility of a march in their city. The fluid nature of Derry radicalism meant that the proposed march was organized by a coalition of republicans, Young Socialists and housing activists, not NICRA, which did not have a branch in the city. NICRA agreed to the proposal and a date for the march was fixed for 5 October. Goulding told Ulster Television viewers on 27 September that the IRA was 'actively' supporting the civil rights movement and civil disobedience, though he denied they controlled NICRA. Their ultimate aim remained a 'united socialist republic'. Unionist MP John Brooke countered that this proved that the IRA had become 'completely perverted by communism'. The route chosen by the Derry marchers, from the Waterside to the city, and their determination to break any police ban made trouble inevitable. When loyalists promised to counter-march both demonstrations were banned and nationalists like John Hume withdrew support from the protest. Republicans then decided to up the ante. At an IRA meeting in south Derry it was agreed that in the event of the RUC blocking the marchers' path they were to push any politicians or dignitaries present into the police lines. This would ensure that the first people to receive a 'busted head from a peeler's baton' would be newsworthy. Again a contingent of the Belfast IRA travelled to Derry, where about 400 people took part in the march, which was confronted by the RUC in Duke Street. An evocative image from TV footage of the march is of Eddie McAteer, the Derry Nationalist Party MP, Gerry Fitt and other notables marching under a civil rights banner being carried by Johnnie White and another republican. TV viewers saw Fitt and others batoned as the RUC ran amok. Water cannon drenched marchers including Anthony Coughlan and those who had come from Dublin. Two of the first arrests were of Fred Heatley and Belfast IRA man Martin Meehan. News of the events spread to the Bogside where major rioting broke out that lasted well into the night. Across Ireland people in living rooms and pubs were 'transfixed' by the television pictures from Derry. Over the next week demonstrations took place in London and Birmingham, and in Dublin a republican march to the British Embassy ended in clashes, with petrol bombs thrown at the building.

McMillen would later argue that the Derry march had 'done more for the minority in the six counties [than] IRA physical force campaigns had been able to do in fifty years'. Republicans had helped unleash a new movement and now pushed for the setting up of local civil rights groups and marches in other areas. But the civil rights strategy was undoubtedly also producing polarization. In Ó Tuathail's view, 'no one could control it' after 5 October. Protests continued in Derry, with a demonstration of 2,000 in late October, a sit-down of 3,000 in early November and a march of 15,000 later that month. On that demonstration Johnnie White and three other activists symbolically breached RUC lines on Craigavon Bridge, while marchers virtually took control of the city centre. But every civil rights event faced loyalist counter-protests and working-class Protestant opinion seemed to be hardening. In Derry loyalists had attacked Catholic shirt factory workers after the third demonstration and there were increasing clashes between Catholic teenagers and youths from the Fountain. Despite republican efforts the image of the movement was quickly monopolized in public by a range of non-republican personalities from Currie, Hume and the Labour Party's Ivan Cooper to Gerry Fitt and Eddie McAteer.

The Derry Citizens Action Committee was founded at a meeting on 9 October. White and Finbar O'Doherty were members of the DCAC but were outnumbered by supporters of Hume and local moderates. Liam Ó Comain was critical of McCann for refusing to sit on the new body, thus making it easier for Hume and his supporters to gain control. Mass Catholic support for civil rights inevitably gave it the appearance of a nationalist revolt. On 30 November 5,000 joined a NICRA march in Armagh, with Denis Cassin as chief steward and republicans again in the front ranks. Despite the march being legal the RUC allowed hundreds of Ian Paisley's supporters, many openly armed with clubs and sticks, to occupy the town centre. The police then halted the march. Clashes were avoided but locals confronted police and loyalists in the aftermath of the demonstration. Armagh youngster John Nixon was enthused by the fact that the local 'great and the good', including priests and his schoolteachers, were taking part in the marches.

As well as marking the emergence of a newer generation of

nationalist politicians the October events gave a boost to the far left. In Belfast 2,000 students had marched in protest at the Derry events. At Queen's a meeting led to the setting up of People's Democracy, influenced by the French student radicalism of that year, civil rights and a variety of socialist and anarchist ideas. At its core were Michael Farrell and his Young Socialist comrades, who felt that NICRA was not militant enough. A 21-year-old student from Tyrone, Bernadette Devlin, emerged as one of the most forceful of PD's public speakers.

While most eyes were turned north during October, Fianna Fáil suffered a political humiliation in the South. The government had called a referendum in order to abolish the proportional representation voting system and replace it with a first-past-the-post ballot. This was seen as a purely political manoeuvre that might lead to indefinite Fianna Fáil government. Fine Gael, Labour and the trade unions all called for a no vote. Sinn Féin also joined the campaign, though it expressed 'some embarrassment' that it was on the same side as Fine Gael. Fianna Fáil's arguments became hysterical, with one TD claiming that only communists wanted to retain PR. This was disproven when the electorate voted by 3:1 to maintain PR. Many felt that the arrogance of the younger ministers and their association with the Fianna Fáil fund-raising body Taca had backfired on the party.

Meanwhile the government was preparing its own response to the growing street protests. A new Criminal Justice Bill sought to give Gardaí much greater powers in prohibiting demonstrations and arresting those deemed to be or have been engaging in 'conduct likely to lead to a breach of the peace'. Republicans saw the bill as being aimed at their initiative, and the leadership decided that the fight against it could be the basis for extending the civil rights issue to the South.

Sinn Féin held its Ard Fheis in December. Noting events in the North and the defeat of the PR referendum, Mac Giolla referred to October as a 'truly historic month . . . that will have a significant effect on the future course of both parts of the country'. Aware that support within the party was still less than the two-thirds required to change the abstentionist policy, the IRA leadership had decided on a new approach to the old problem. Before debate on motions calling for the end of abstention could begin, Garland proposed an amendment that would 'set up a commission of persons representing both branches of the movement' to examine how the new political situation 'may be turned to the advantage of the movement'. This so-called 'Garland Commission' would advise on changes at the following year's Ard Fheis. Costello, in a speech seconding the amendment, rubbished abstentionism to the chagrin of not only those seeking to maintain the policy but also his leadership allies who hoped to avoid overt conflict. The amendment passed. A less contentious suggestion came from Tipperary 'that in future the Easter Lily be supplied with adhesive backing'.

In early December the Northern premier Terence O'Neill, under huge pressure from both Unionist hard-liners and the civil rights movement, had outlined a reform package and asked for a chance to put it into practice. Within NICRA there were conflicting views on how to respond. It was agreed to suspend marches for a period but PD disagreed and argued for stepping up the pressure with a march from Belfast to Derry modelled on Martin Luther King's 1965 march from Selma to Montgomery. Some NICRA members, such as Kevin McCorry, argued very strongly with student republicans in Belfast that the march would end in disaster. But many were unconvinced and there was considerable rank and file republican enthusiasm for the idea. NICRA called on its supporters to provide support for the marchers. Mac Giolla had confidently predicted that after October republicans were witnessing the beginning of the disintegration of Unionist rule in the North and Fianna Fáil power in the South.

All were sure that after 1968 Ireland would never be the same again.

4. 1969: Backlash

'In different parts of the country units of the IRA (and Sinn Féin) are
uneasy about the new left-wing policy of their leadership and about
the violent methods that are being adopted in the destruction of
private property. Their uneasiness needs to be brought to the surface in
some way with a consequent fragmentation of the organization. It is
suggested by the Department of Justice that the Government should
promote an active political campaign in that regard.'

Department of Justice memorandum, 18 March 1969

The year 1969 began dramatically. The People's Democracy march
from Belfast to Derry was under way, encountering opposition in
several towns before being ambushed at Burntollet Bridge on
4 January. Loyalists led by Major Bunting, including off-duty
B-Specials, attacked the marchers, injuring dozens. This news
sparked off major rioting in the Bogside and barricades went up
along with a newly painted slogan: 'You are now entering Free
Derry.' Meanwhile, housing activists were squatting with a family
of five in Derry's Guildhall. A few days later in Dublin 1,000
people attended a meeting in the Mansion House to protest against
the Criminal Justice Bill. Speakers warned against giving Fianna
Fáil the same powers as those of the Unionist government in the
North. The following weekend 10,000 joined a civil rights march
in Newry and rioting followed that saw seven RUC vehicles
destroyed. In Dublin protesters blocked traffic outside the GPO
to highlight the case of Dennis Dennehy, jailed and on hunger
strike for squatting with his family. A message from the Guildhall
occupiers was read out proclaiming that 'the struggle is the same:
North and South'. Running battles on O'Connell Bridge between

Gardaí and protesters followed another 2,000-strong Dublin Housing Action Committee march on Saturday 18 January. In Cork housing demonstrators disrupted a Fianna Fáil dinner at which Taoiseach Jack Lynch was the guest, and there were nine arrests when the Cork HAC took over City Hall the following week. In Dublin veteran Joe Clarke was escorted from a government ceremony to commemorate the fiftieth anniversary of the First Dáil after he interrupted a speech by President de Valera, raising the Dennehy case. Outside, 3,000 took part in another day of housing protests; meanwhile the Labour Party conference pledged itself for socialism, and against coalition. While the DHAC protested outside Fianna Fáil's Ard Fheis, inside there was considerable dissatisfaction expressed about Taca and the Criminal Justice Bill, which several speakers compared unfavourably to repressive legislation in the North. The month ended with more than 70 protesters still squatting in Derry's Guildhall.

Republicans were centrally involved in this agitation. The housing committees in Dublin, Derry and Cork were largely republican led. Sinn Féin was pushing for the campaign against the Criminal Justice Bill to be the focus for civil rights agitation in the South. Following the rioting in Derry republicans were to the fore in the organization of vigilante patrols in the Bogside. Republicans provided food and shelter to the Belfast–Derry marchers as they made their way across Co. Derry. In Maghera the marchers were billeted overnight in the Brackaghreilly Hall, while IRA members, armed with shotguns, stood guard. The *United Irishman* suggested that 'whatever else the march has done it has shown up the corruption and violence at the heart of society in the six counties'. Anger over the brutality at Burntollet certainly influenced the militancy of the crowd in Newry. That march was called by People's Democracy but supported by NICRA, with local republican Dan Moore as the chief steward. Most of the Belfast IRA were present, again to act as stewards, but on this occasion once the RUC tried to reroute the march, republicans reacted, leading the rioting. Joe McCann, seen steering one of the RUC vehicles into Newry's canal, was among 24 arrested. The Derry and Newry events signalled that Catholic protest had developed a momentum of its own.

IRA activity continued in tandem with street politics. When Dublin security men hired by a Mountjoy Square landlord arrived to evict squatters, they found a group of men armed with hurleys waiting for them and thought better of the eviction. Landlords considered 'particularly vicious' were also being 'made to pay a price'. One, a garage owner, had several of his cars burnt out. During March 1969 another landlord had his car firebombed outside his home on the Howth Road. In that case things almost went badly wrong. While one man poured petrol over the car, one of his comrades threw a firebomb without warning, which narrowly missed him, hit another car and bounced back on to its original target, eventually setting it on fire. In early March the IRA burnt a German-owned farmhouse at Ferran's Lock, Co. Meath, as part of their opposition to what they called the 'chequebook conquest'. Shortly afterwards the IRA in Cork firebombed a minibus that was being used to take republican prisoners to trial in Limerick. An IRA man was badly injured during the operation and received extensive burns. The Special Branch believed that 'landless men' in Meath and Galway were supplied with Molotov cocktails by the IRA for use against 'large landowners'.

In June the IRA destroyed property on the Mannin Estate in Ardrahan, Co. Galway. They demanded that the estate be 'acquired by the Land Commission and divided up among the thirteen neighbouring smallholders'. They also threatened that if a landlord in Oughterard evicted an elderly tenant he would be held 'personally responsible'. Property belonging to the Toome Eel Fisheries Company on Lough Neagh was burnt during a dispute. On 11 June, when questions were to be asked in the Bundestag about the Ferran's Lock burning, four farms in Meath and Louth were attacked and considerable damage caused. Three of the farms were German-owned while an ex-British officer owned the fourth, a 600-acre estate. In early July shots were exchanged between a German farmer and a group of raiders attempting to burn his mansion at Midleton, Co. Cork.

Later that month the IRA blew up farm buildings on a 900-acre estate belonging to an English farmer near Trim.

Meanwhile, one IRA member was pressing for an operation to raise funds. In 1967 Joseph Brady, an ex-British soldier, had been recruited into the movement and had become a training officer for the Dublin Brigade. During early 1969 Brady raised the idea of stealing the Book of Kells from Trinity College and holding it for ransom, but he found no support. On 24 March he broke into the college himself and, unable to gain access to the Book of Kells, stole the Brian Boru harp instead. A few weeks later he contacted the college and demanded £20,000. In April he was arrested while trying to collect the ransom and the harp was recovered from a sandpit in Blessington, Co. Wicklow. Within the IRA there was suspicion that Brady was a provocateur. Later in the year he was picked up at gunpoint but managed to escape, though not before being shot twice; as a result one of the IRA men was arrested and jailed. It transpired that Brady had been giving information to the Garda Special Branch since 1967.

Seamus Costello led a campaign to keep Brittas Bay beach in Wicklow free and open to the public. Regular pickets and protests led to clashes with private security men and arrests. Eventually an agreement was secured to allow public access and was celebrated by a Sinn Féin 'victory barbecue' on the beach. There were over a dozen 'fish-ins' organized by the National Waters Restoration League during the first half of the year. Crowds gathered to watch and support illegal fishing, with salmon cooked and distributed on the spot. One such event was attended by 1,500 people on the Boyne in late June on a river owned by Major D. H. Coddington, whose farm had been attacked by the IRA shortly before.

Eyes were turned towards the North again during the spring. The February Stormont elections saw both unionist and nationalist politics fracture. Prime Minister Terence O'Neill lost support to hard-line loyalists, while John Hume took Eddie McAteer's seat in Derry and People's Democracy candidates gained 25,000 votes. Republicans did not contest the elections, and some rued this as a missed opportunity. Easter saw large crowds attend commemorations across Ireland, particularly in the North. The 5,000 who turned out in Derry's 'biggest ever' parade saw the IRA defy a ban on carrying the tricolour. In Belfast Sean Garland was the main speaker, with McMillen reading the IRA's statement and Gerry Adams the 1916 Proclamation. Garland emphasized continuing support for civil rights, which had exposed the 'undemocratic and bigoted' nature of unionism and shattered its monopoly on power.

But the civil rights movement was fragmenting as it struggled to deal with the mass following that had developed since October 1968. There were dozens of local civil rights groups, many of them virtually autonomous. During the spring several marches were jointly organized by NICRA and PD, and stewarded by republicans. Privately the republican movement wanted to establish a civil rights committee 'under our control' that would 'set the tone or give the lead'. Publicly republicans argued that NICRA should avoid being used by aspiring nationalist politicians like John Hume and should instead fuse People's Democracy's 'anti-sectarian policies' with the unity of the established campaign. Republican delegates refused to vote for the relatively moderate Betty Sinclair as chair of NICRA and supported instead a PD call for a march through Belfast. But there was also an awareness that sectarian tension was growing and it was reiterated that Britain was the 'main enemy', not the unionists. This argument was complicated by the fact that the movement was resisting efforts to raise specifically socialist demands and insisting 'Catholic' unity be maintained. During February the RUC Inspector-General had claimed in the *Belfast Telegraph* that the IRA was fomenting 'civil disorder' in the North through the civil rights campaign, in line with their 1966 strategy document. Goulding denied this, claiming that republicans 'have not organized the Civil Rights movement and we have not infiltrated it'. Mac Giolla, however, admitted that 'most' of the stewarding at civil rights demonstrations had been done by IRA volunteers. Loyalists were convinced that civil rights agitation was a 'front for the regeneration of IRA activity'. Goulding's statement to the *Irish Times* in early February that 'if the civil rights movement fails there will be no answer other than the answer we have always preached . . . all constitutional methods will go overboard' would hardly have been reassuring.

A major debate was taking place within the republican movement about how to respond to a Westminster by-election in Mid-Ulster, caused by the death of the local Unionist MP. There was enormous pressure on republicans to field a candidate and, if successful, allow that person to take the seat. Tom Mitchell had won the seat in the 1950s and had taken 27,000 votes as recently as 1966. But he declined to go forward and Kevin Agnew, a Sinn Féin Ard Chomhairle member and well-known solicitor, was suggested as an alternative. During December 1968 Agnew had argued to the party Ard Chomhairle that if the abstentionist route was taken then there would be 'no republican movement in Mid-Ulster in a month's time'. Mac Giolla suggested that a non-republican candidate representative of 'all non-unionist opinion' might be a better option, and Labour's up and coming Conor Cruise O'Brien was suggested as such a unity candidate. Garland considered that a NICRA personality such as Fred Heatley or Frank Gogarty, who would be 'amenable' to republicans and under no obligation to abstain, should be considered. Meanwhile Austin Currie had contacted republicans to see if they would back him. Garland felt that any nationalist candidate and 'Currie in particular' should not be allowed an open run, but there was some support for Currie among republicans in Tyrone. Bernadette Devlin was mooted as a possible alternative and Malachy McGurran and Costello met her to sound her out. By the time Devlin entered the race the local republicans were hostile, claiming that she accepted partition and was a 'West British advocate of dubious socialism'. But pressure was applied from Dublin to allow Devlin a clear run and Agnew was persuaded to withdraw. Johnston and Mac Stíofáin successfully convinced the Ard Chomhairle not to back Devlin publicly, though Costello dissented. In the event Devlin won 33,648 votes and the 22-year-old became the youngest MP ever elected to Westminster and an international personality overnight. Privately republicans rued that abstentionism had again prevented what might have been a landmark victory, feeling that had Agnew stood, he would have won.

Devlin's election coincided with what the *Irish News* called the 'most devastating wave of violence and civil strife since the 1930s'. There was intense rioting in Derry on 20 April during which over 200 people were hurt. Police badly beat a number of local people, one of whom, Samuel Devenney, was critically injured. In response NICRA called for solidarity demonstrations across Northern Ireland. In what he called 'an effort to draw off the large force of police who were laying siege to the Bogside', Billy McMillen authorized IRA units to firebomb ten post offices and a bus station across Belfast. The (unclaimed) attacks were carried out over a two-hour period and caused considerable chaos. The following day 2,000 people took part in a republican-led march on the Falls Road. Hastings Street RUC station was stoned and senior RUC officer Frank Lagan was attacked and beaten by protesters. The IRA's actions coincided with loyalist bomb attacks on the Silent Valley reservoir the same night, which many wrongly attributed to the IRA. On BBC radio Cathal Goulding warned that 'if our people in the six counties are oppressed and beaten up . . . then the IRA will have no alternative but to take military action against the police force . . . [we] have no alternative but to protect our people or allow them to be slaughtered and we are not going to allow them to be slaughtered'. Goulding's rhetoric implied that the IRA were ready to intervene militarily, but arms were in short supply. McMillen later claimed that the IRA in Belfast had just 24 weapons in early 1969, most of which were pistols. For their part British intelligence estimated that the IRA had 500 members in Northern Ireland in the spring of 1969. They considered that while the morale of the republican movement was 'good', arms and ammunition were 'in short supply' and financially the IRA was 'weak'.

The events provided Clann na hÉireann with a new focus. In Birmingham the Counties Association with the support of the Connolly Association had set up a Campaign for Justice in Northern Ireland, but republicans felt that neither the Counties Association nor the Campaign for Justice were 'doing the business', and so a more radical Birmingham ad hoc civil rights group was set up by Clann and local Trotskyist groups. A major focus was the disruption of the Northern Ireland Tourist Board's Ulster Week. Mass pickets were placed on Rackhams, Birmingham's most exclusive department store, where an Ulster exhibition was taking place. Stink bombs were let off inside the store, causing its evacuation, and IRA members placed an elaborate fake bomb inside an exhibit of a 'traditional Ulster cottage', labelling the device 'Ulster slum clearance'. There were major strides forward for Clann after the appointment of 27-year-old Gerry Doherty as national organizer. Civil rights also created interest in Irish America. A key figure was Brian Heron, a grandson of James Connolly. Heron had been an organizer for the United Farm Workers in California during the long and bitter struggle led by Cesar Chavez to gain rights for migrant grape pickers. In 1968 he helped found Citizens for Irish Justice in San Francisco, which inspired similar groups elsewhere. Musicians Tommy Makem and the Clancy Brothers agreed to fund an organizing trip by Heron to see if these groups could be coordinated. The result was the formation of the National Association for Irish Justice, which gained recognition as NICRA's US support group during 1969.

Back in Ireland, and despite increasingly frantic activity, the Garland Commission had overseen discussion at over 20 regional activist meetings. The result was a document entitled *Ireland Today*. Drafted by Johnston it stressed that British imperialism dominated Ireland, North and South. Ireland was changing, however, with the North 'shaken to the core' by the civil rights movement, resulting in the old Unionist power structure fragmenting. The achievement of civil rights demands would open the way 'for linking of economic demands to the national question'. The traditional institutions of the Catholic community, particularly the Nationalist Party, were also in crisis; 'gombeen nationalism' was on its way out. In the long run civil rights could pave the way to a 32-county republic.

In the South, despite the 'moribund . . . bureaucracy' of the trade union leadership, there was a new radical mood, expressed through support for the Labour Party and by social agitation. The republican movement had an opportunity to significantly influence events as it not only represented the 'great mainstream of the national and social revolutionary tradition' but also had the 'physical defence experience' that would be necessary to resist 'counter-revolutionary attack'. Agitation on housing and trade union activity had to be kept up, and organized to involve all existing radical political groups as well as 'trade unionists and homeless people'. The republicans were to become the driving force for a 'National Liberation Front' (the same title used by the Vietnamese revolutionaries). This new body would include republicans, Labour supporters, cultural activists and communists and embody the radical alliance envisaged in the movement's education programme of 1967.

Emphasis was also placed on the movement's need to intervene seriously in electoral politics. It was stressed that failure to take Dáil seats would allow Labour to reap the benefits of social agitation. *Ireland Today* examined the historical objections to electoral participation and concluded that safeguards could be built into the process to ensure that corruption did not set in, commenting that 'the elements which were missing in the twenties and forties have now been developed sufficiently to enable the movement, if it had TDs, to instruct them specifically on all key issues'. Refusal to face up to electoral participation could mean that the 'negative tradition of glorious failures' would continue to be the lot of Irish republicans. The reports of the various regional meetings added several points to the original document, such as the need to tackle the 'special position' of the Catholic Church in the South because of the negative effect this had on Northern Protestant attitudes. Rural members also wanted to know how the concept of a National Liberation Front (NLF) would apply outside of Dublin, Cork and Belfast where other left-wing groups simply did not exist. The danger that too great an emphasis on Dublin might alienate rural republicans was noted. However, a positive sign was that 'no significant support for a reversion to the strategy of the fifties' had been reported. This reflected the fact that many of those opposed to the left had effectively dropped out of the movement. But the 'general feeling' from most who attended the discussions was that the authority of 'the Republic should remain with the Army Council for the foreseeable future'.

During the summer of 1969 Goulding and Mac Giolla held several discussions with Bernadette Devlin, and it was agreed to stage a special conference to discuss the North at which she and Eamonn McCann would be invited speakers. Republicans believed that if the NLF emerged as a 'convincing' force then radical youth 'will be attracted to it and the apparent need for left-wing splinter groups to assert young radicalism against the alleged conservatism of more experienced revolutionaries will cease to exist so sharply'. The communists were to be a key part of the NLF and republicans were particularly interested in communist trade union work. Private discussions between IRA leaders and Mick O'Riordan continued regularly.

Some groups were beyond the pale of the proposed NLF. The Irish Communist Organisation, which had adherents in Dublin and Belfast, was dismissive of Sinn Féin's leftism. DHAC activist Dennis Dennehy was one of its members. In Cork Jim Lane and his comrades launched a paper called *Saor Éire – People's Voice –* during 1968, taking a broadly Maoist perspective. They wrote to Sinn Féin inquiring about membership of the NLF, but received no reply. The Dublin-based armed splinter group that had formed in 1966 was still active; it consisted of several elements, some of whom had become attracted to Trotskyist politics; another element was attracted by armed crime and the possibility of personal enrichment that this offered. Dublin criminal Christy Dunne was involved in procuring arms for the group. In Newry during early March the group took £12,000 in a bank raid during which shots were fired at the RUC. In the South neither the banks nor the Gardaí were equipped to deal with determined armed groups. The ability to obtain several thousand pounds at a time bred a certain 'outlaw' lifestyle and, as one of the group's leaders recalled, 'a lot of people [were] there for the adrenalin'. The pressures of living on the run and needing ready cash stimulated demands for more action. Many of the group still socialized on Dublin's 'strip' and plans for dramatic guerrilla actions were discussed as the drinks flowed.

The IRA, strapped for cash, had noted the splinter group's successes. Any serious future electoral intervention would require major funding. The Wicklow by-election of March 1968 had cost £933, and the borrowed £150 election deposit was still unpaid in 1969. It was also unlikely that serious arms supplies could be procured without finance. Goulding's fund-raising trip to the US in late 1968 had yielded just £865. Goulding, Garland and Ryan had been looking at Dublin Airport, where large sums in wages were delivered by Securicor. Rather than spend time discussing the morality of armed robbery with the rest of the Army Council they went ahead and organized a raid.

On 14 May Goulding picked up one of the Dublin Active Service Unit outside Quinn's Pub in Drumcondra. They drove to Ballymun, where the unit was briefed on the operation. The men were armed but ordered to avoid shooting if possible. At 9.15 a.m., as the Securicor van arrived, five IRA men, dressed in business suits, were in place. When the security man entered the administration building one raider held the door open for him while two others coshed him and threw ammonia in his face. The IRA men took two boxes containing £24,600 from the guard and made off in stolen cars; when one of the cars crashed its occupants hijacked a van and made their getaway. At first the Gardaí were reported to be baffled by the 'complexity and ingenuity' of the robbery, which they believed involved up to five resprayed and renumbered stolen cars.

The raiders buried the money and weapons in a field at Garristown on the Dublin–Meath border. However, the man who had rented the land for them did not know that it was conacre, which could not be ploughed. A local farmer noticed that it had been dug up and complained. As the Gardaí began searching the field the raiders were 'sitting . . . in Dublin biting our nails as they got closer and closer'. The Gardaí found £18,000, two revolvers and a shotgun. When asked to comment by the press, Goulding denied any knowledge of who was responsible but mentioned the splinter group in passing. Two young men, Roland Giles and Jimmy McCabe, were arrested and charged with the robbery. Although not a participant, Garland was convinced he had been identified and went on the run, removing himself from public activity.

Attempts to procure new weapons also led to a raid by IRA volunteers on the Sterling Engineering Works in Dagenham, England. The raiders were unsuccessful, and Cork volunteers Conor Lynch and Pat O'Sullivan, both of whom had previously been active in housing campaigns, were captured. The raid had not been sanctioned by the IRA leadership and two other volunteers involved were dismissed from the organization on their return to Ireland.

The Sinn Féin leadership was also discussing the internal politics of RTÉ. The movement took a dubious view of the station, arguing that its 'function is to brainwash and manipulate the people in the interests of the small group of politicians, businessmen and bishops who are the local managers for foreign capital'. According to the *United Irishman* a progressive exception was producer Eoghan Harris, a 'fly in the rather watery soup which is RTÉ'. During May there had been mass meetings of staff at the station to discuss the resignations of three producers, who complained that they were being restricted in their investigative journalism. The *United Irishman* argued that management could only be fought by 'conscious and open activity among large sections of staff . . . undercover conspiracies get nowhere and alienate potential and essential support'.

In June a general election took place in the Republic. Costello was strongly in favour of contesting the Wicklow seat. He argued that should it be won, then an extraordinary Sinn Féin Ard Fheis could be held to discuss the question of abstentionism. Costello warned that failure to contest the seat had grievously affected local 'morale'. The Clare organization also suggested fielding a candidate. But, to Costello's great frustration, Sinn Féin did not contest the general election, in which Fianna Fáil won a comfortable majority.

In July the *United Irishman* headline was 'Backlash' – a reference to the tactics adopted by the government during the election. Earlier that year the paper had noted the international revival of the right with the electoral victory of Richard Nixon in the US, the emergence of Enoch Powell in Britain and the resurgence of Gaullism in France. Internationally this backlash was often accompanied by populist denunciations of the left as elitist, deviant or foreign. This language of right-wing populism was already firmly entrenched in Irish politics by 1969. When the Dáil debated the Criminal Justice Bill some TDs angrily dismissed claims of Garda brutality and blamed the demonstrators themselves; 'if people did not want a cut head they should not be there'. Galway Corporation suggested withdrawing grants from students who took part in street protests. There were recurring scare stories about Maoist recruitment in schools. This rhetoric reached a crescendo during the general election campaign. Fianna Fáil speakers accused the Labour Party, which was expected to make gains, of wanting to force communism on the Irish people. Charles Haughey claimed that Labour favoured 'extreme socialism' and a 'materialistic concept of life'. Neil Blaney denounced the 'pseudo-intellectual Marxists, Maoists, Trotskyites and the like who have emerged . . . like carrion birds to pick the flesh of the Irish people'. Minister for Justice Michael Moran attacked the 'new left-wing political queers' from Trinity College and RTÉ. Prior to the election Moran had asked Peter Berry of the Department of Justice to supply him with information on the left and on the republican movement to be used during the campaign. Interestingly, given the developing crisis there, Northern Ireland was barely mentioned during the campaign.

Much of the republican movement's agitation had been explicitly targeting not just Fianna Fáil but 'the Taca boys, the real power in the party, [who] are making fortunes out of the big business that the sale of land has become in recent years'. The ultimate 'Taca boy' was its founding patron, Haughey. In May 1968 the *United Irishman* told its readers that Haughey was 'always a great man with the money making. Ask anyone around Raheny and they'll tell you who made a packet out of the fore-knowledge that the Green Belt was eventually to be built on, and who that knowledge was passed on to.' Matt Gallagher was singled out as among the property developers who were closely linked to Taca, and in January 1969 the *United Irishman* raised the issue of property dealings between Haughey and Gallagher. A Housing Action publication argued that 'the foundations of Irish society – the 1916 Proclamation and the First Dáil Programme – are sound. The Fianna Fáil top-storeys are crumbling – the woodworm of graft and the termites of speculation have eaten into their fabric.'

The relationship between republicans and Fianna Fáil became bitter. In February Sinn Féin and the Connolly Youth had picketed a Fianna Fáil meeting in Sligo. Members of the party emerged and attacked the pickets, beating several. Declan Bree was dragged along the ground towards the Garavogue River while several men shouted 'drown the bastard'. Protesters alleged that the Gardaí had stood by and watched. In response the IRA stated that it would defend the right to protest and would 'not hesitate to take direct action against any individual or group of individuals, who would attack these Irish men and women'. During a general election rally at Dublin's GPO, government minister Kevin Boland 'exchanged blows' with Sinn Féin protesters. From the platform he then blasted them as communists and 'psychedelic Maoists'. There were a number of clashes with uniformed security guards hired to protect Fianna Fáil's GPO rally as well as evict squatters and prevent pickets at Brittas Bay.

The republican relationship with the Gardaí, especially the 'Castle rats' of the Special Branch, always hostile, became more confrontational as they embraced street politics. The *United Irishman* nominated individual Gardaí for 'brute of the year' awards after clashes, with their photographs and numbers published regularly in the paper. During 1969 a Special Branch notebook was 'acquired' by the IRA. It contained the names of over 200 activists, including Des Geraghty, De Rossa, Mac Giolla, Sherlock and de Burca. The descriptions caused some amusement and annoyance. One IRA man, 'a real Dub', was described as 'red faced and country looking', while a female volunteer was called 'plump', prompting the riposte: 'I nearly starved myself for two weeks!'

Republican activity was also discussed at cabinet level. During

March the Minister for Justice had circulated his colleagues with a report on the IRA. Written by Peter Berry, it outlined the situation since 1962, when the IRA had been at a low ebb, militarily and financially:

In these circumstances the leaders became very receptive to suggestions from left-wing sources for a change in policy. By 1965 a strong liaison had been established with a number of intellectuals with marked communist histories and these men were given positions of authority in the organisation which facilitated them in indoctrinating the rank and file with the conviction that any occasions of social unrest could be exploited to establish the IRA as a dynamic political force on whom workers and small farmers could alone depend for improved social conditions. Coincidental with this indoctrination, the IRA leadership saw that it would be necessary, in order to establish and stimulate the interest of young or new members, to hold meetings and parades of a military character and instructions in the use of arms. By 1967 the leadership were gauging public reaction by statements issued to the public press and on public platforms in which they were openly advocating the establishment of a 'Workers Republic' and an eventual resort to arms for that purpose.

The report noted that since May 1968 the IRA had carried out a number of 'serious crimes' involving 'arson or the use of explosives', and that the Gardaí estimated that the organization had perhaps 1,200 members. Of particular concern was the fact that IRA statements justifying their actions were carried without comment in the press. Most newspapers no longer used the official designation 'illegal organisation' to describe the IRA, and 'a new and disturbing feature in recent times is the way in which the press in Ireland and the Television service in particular, lend themselves to publicising IRA and Communist spokesmen to whom they have given a new and false public image'. The report contended that public opinion was being influenced to a 'disproportionate degree' by a 'small number' of left-wingers in 'key positions' in the media.

In July a further memorandum noted the 'commando-style'

robbery at Dublin Airport and IRA influence in housing action, fish-ins and land campaigns. The Gardaí had prevented several attempted bank raids but the IRA was 'very short of money' and was likely to try again. The Gardaí were aware that there was unease within the IRA at its leftward direction and Berry urged that this be exploited so that the 'result would be (as in the Republican Congress Movement) a split in the IRA organisation and the communist element would become discredited'.

Also in July the bodies of Peter Barnes and James McCormack, executed in England during 1940 for their part in an IRA bombing campaign, were released for return to Ireland. The coffins were met at Dublin Airport by Mac Giolla and several veterans of the 1940s, along with an IRA colour party. A thousand people marched behind the coffins along Dublin's quays while another colour party in battledress led the cortège. On a sunny Sunday up to 10,000 people attended the reinterment outside Mullingar. A minute's silence was held for two Free Wales Army members killed in a premature explosion intended to target the investiture of Prince Charles, followed by a recitation of five decades of the rosary. Then four men in black polo necks and berets fired volleys from revolvers over the coffins. There were large numbers present from across Ireland who had dropped out or left the IRA and Sinn Féin. Jimmy Steele, of Belfast, gave a speech in which he launched what Goulding called a 'vicious' attack on the movement's turn to the left. He denounced the adoption of 'foreign' ideologies – 'one is now expected to be more conversant with the thoughts of Chairman Mao than those of our dead Patriots' – and poured scorn on 'politicians' and 'constitutionalists'. The venom shocked many of those present. The atmosphere was thick with tension and Mick Ryan could feel 'the ground moving' from underneath the leadership.

There had been inklings that something was afoot. Ryan had received reports from Ned Dempsey in Carlow that veterans Liam Burke and Myles Shevlin had been circulating in the area asking people what they thought of the leadership's policies. As Bobby McKnight circulated among local intelligence officers he heard again and again that 'communists' had taken over at HQ and that while Goulding himself was not a communist, he had been taken in by them. Goulding, however, was reluctant to accept these reports and especially reluctant to accept that Mac Stíofáin was spreading these rumours. Ryan had met Mac Stíofáin at his house in Meath during July and they had sat outside in the sun discussing abstentionism and other issues. Mac Stíofáin professed to have admiration for Ryan and Garland but stated that he would never accept people taking seats in Leinster House or the NLF concept. When Ryan disagreed Mac Stíofáin said, 'I'm disappointed in you, Mick, and a lot of other people will be as well.'

While the vitriol in Steele's speech was a shock and a sign that many people were unhappy with the movement's direction, he had said nothing about the situation in his home city of Belfast, where sectarian tension was rising during July. A particular flash-point was in Ardoyne, a local priest Fr. Marcellus Gillespie attesting that during July 'Catholics were as much to blame as Protestants' for the clashes. The Belfast Housing Action Committee began trying to find accommodation for families displaced by intimidation. Rioting in Dungiven, Co. Derry, where an Orange hall was burnt down, saw a man die after an RUC baton charge, and Derryman Samuel Devenney also succumbed to the injuries he sustained in April. IRA members were placed on defensive duty in Ardoyne and at Unity Flats during July. The RUC noted the presence of Belfast IRA officers Frank McGlade and Jim Sullivan in these areas. Billy McMillen later claimed that he resisted pressure to release weapons because 'we realised that the meagre armaments at our disposal were hopelessly inadequate to meet the requirements of the situation and that the use of firearms by us would only serve to justify the use of greater force against the people by the forces of the Establishment and increase the danger of sectarian pogroms'.

Confidence in the progress of the civil rights struggle in the North also underwent severe tests during July. Tempers were raised by William Craig's statement that civil rights protesters were 'the scum of Irish politics'. After rioting in Derry during mid-July,

Johnnie White helped set up the Derry Citizens Defence Association (DCDA), with veteran Sean Keenan as chairman and White as secretary, to organize preparations for the 12 August Apprentice Boys parade. In early August there was serious rioting on the Shankill Road between loyalists and the RUC. There were then more clashes at Unity Flats that developed into the worst rioting in Belfast since 1935. NICRA claimed that the police were allowing mobs to gather in loyalist areas while dispersing Catholic crowds with force. Nightly clashes, rumours of evictions and threats of more violence pervaded the city. McMillen and Malachy McGurran raised the likelihood of more trouble at IRA staff meetings from early summer. Ruairí Ó Brádaigh has claimed that Goulding told the Army Council that 'it is not our job to be Catholic defenders' and that the IRA would 'put it up to the official forces, the British Army and the RUC, to defend the people'. This contrasts strongly with Goulding's public rhetoric during 1969 as well as the accounts of other leadership figures. His later explanation for not sending 'extra' weapons to Belfast was that the IRA leadership was unsure whether, and where, violence was going to break out: 'we felt that if we, previous to the Twelfth [of July], had sent them into Belfast, into Derry, into Newry . . . there might not be any real fighting' and the weapons might be lost to the police or unavailable if trouble broke out elsewhere. The leadership believed that the 'best way for people to engage the police and B-Specials was the way that things developed in the Bogside' – in other words through mass protests and street fighting. Goulding admitted that, as it transpired, 'the only defence was armed defence'.

Barricades had already gone up in the Bogside before the Apprentice Boys parade and the DCDA had overseen the stockpiling of materials in case of attack. An estimated 43,000 milk bottles were unreturned from the area during early August. The IRA had decided not to use arms unless the RUC fired live ammunition first. The defence committee made little effort to stop Bogside youths from stoning the Apprentice Boys on 12 August. They in turn responded and Derry went up; the Battle of the

Bogside had begun. Petrol bombs rained down from the Rossville Flats and kept the police confined to the outskirts of the Bogside, from where they fired 1,147 canisters of CS gas. Radio Free Derry was broadcast from a transmitter in Eamon Melaugh's home in the Creggan. Republicans and members of the Young Socialists were involved in the organization of defence but the majority of the rioters were the local young. As the violence escalated Jack Lynch broadcast a message to the nation on RTÉ warning that the government could 'no longer stand by' if violence continued. This had the effect of heightening anticipation on both sides. The B-Specials were eventually ordered into Derry to back up the police, provoking a flood of refugees and the injured into Donegal as fear of an all-out attack increased. But before the Specials could be moved in, the British Army had arrived on the streets.

On 13 August McMillen ordered republicans in Belfast to organize demonstrations to 'get people on the streets' and take the 'pressure off Derry'. Joe McCann and Anthony Dornan led a march of 1,000 people to Hastings Street RUC Station. Republicans believed that police were due to leave there to go to Derry, and 'the idea was to keep them occupied for as long as possible'. The crowd stoned the station and at one stage tried to smash in its door with a makeshift battering ram. Nails were put into pieces of cardboard to disable police vehicles and whitewash and paint stockpiled to throw on their windscreens. IRA members were also present with arms. When the RUC attempted to disperse the crowds by driving armoured cars into Leeson Street, the IRA opened fire, wounding a policeman. McMillen authorized members of the Fianna to attack Springfield Road RUC station with petrol bombs. The RUC opened fire on the young republicans, wounding two. Large crowds on the Shankill looked on but did not join the fighting, which on 13 August in west Belfast was between nationalists and the RUC, not nationalists and loyalists. However, in Ardoyne, where again nationalists had attacked police to divert resources from Derry, the combustible sectarian atmosphere had seen Protestant crowds burn down a Catholic-owned pub and betting shop.

On 14 August McMillen and his adjutant Jim Sullivan ordered all IRA members on to defensive duties, sending small groups to various areas. One participant recalls about 30 IRA men and 12 women along with 40 Fianna boys and 15 to 20 girls being active on the Falls, and that their arsenal consisted of 1 Thompson sub-machine gun, 1 Sten sub-machine gun, 1 rifle and 6 handguns. A 'wee factory' for making petrol bombs was set up in a house in Leeson Street. The IRA began to hijack buses for use as street barricades. Clashes developed along the streets that led to the Shankill and by evening serious rioting was taking place. As loyalist mobs encroached into Catholic areas, the IRA exchanged fire with the police in Conway and Divis Streets. The RUC forced Catholics back towards Divis Street and mobs of Protestants, among them Shankill MP Johnny McQuade, followed, setting fire to houses as they progressed. As the loyalists approached from Dover Street, four young IRA men in the grounds of St Comgall's School opened fire, killing Herbert Roy, a 26-year-old from the Shankill, and wounding several RUC men. The RUC then sent Shorland armoured cars, equipped with Browning heavy machine guns, into Divis Street. They were pelted with petrol bombs and opened fire with tracer ammunition, raking Divis Flats and killing 9-year-old Patrick Rooney in his home. RUC gunfire from Hastings Street killed another Catholic, Hugh McCabe, an off-duty British soldier. Loyalists sniped from on top of mills and rooftops into the Falls, wounding several people. B-Specials were deployed across Belfast backing up the RUC. Police gunfire killed three more Catholics during the night in north and west Belfast.

The RUC and B-Specials seem to have believed that the IRA were heavily armed and proceeded very slowly. IRA members in turn tried to preserve ammunition by limiting their firing to single shots or short bursts. One man recalls that the idea was to 'just fire a few rounds up each street to drive them back, but then they came back and that's when I was shot ... that was B-men, they came out of the van and opened up on us from the side'. Unarmed IRA men ran along with others to take up their guns if they were wounded.

Those involved stank with sweat and their throats were parched with smoke; 'this must be what wars are like', thought one. The noise of the rival crowds was deafening, 'like a football match'. Rumours spread that the Irish Army had crossed the border and taken Newry. In Falls Park, through the haze of smoke, men with insignia on their caps were seen approaching. 'Free State Army Officers!' shouted someone and people began to cheer. It turned out to be the Order of Malta. At 5 a.m. on the morning of Friday 15 August, a group of IRA men, their faces black, lay exhausted on the ground in Osman Street, where they each got a bottle of water to slake their thirst. Palls of smoke rose over west Belfast. Their adrenalin and exhaustion produced fits of laughter. An old woman approached them, disgusted, and warned, 'Ye are laughing now but wait until they come in and shoot ye in yer beds!' She remembered the 1920s; they did not. Despite the folk memory of the pogroms then, the terror, panic and fear of 14–15 August was completely new to most people.

Early that morning the IRA weapons were dumped in Slate Street. There were just two socks of ammunition left and 'they weren't full'. McMillen, McGurran and Frank Card had been arrested in Kane Street and charged with possession of handguns and illegal documents. In total, 21 republicans across Northern Ireland were held under the Special Powers Act. British troops were now on the streets. Protestants attacked Bombay Street in large numbers and drove Catholics back, burning houses. A small number of IRA men were present at Clonard Monastery but were unable to prevent the attack. Gerald McAuley, a 15-year-old Fianna member, was fatally wounded by gunfire, the first republican killed in action since the 1950s. The Bombay Street burning highlighted the vulnerability of Catholics at a time when the fighting was thought to have ended and British troops had arrived. In Belfast 7 people were dead – 5 Catholic and 2 Protestant – while over 400 were treated for injuries, 108 of them for gunshot wounds. Over 1,800 families had been forced from their homes – 1,500 Catholic and 300 Protestant. About 150 houses had been destroyed. The IRA had suffered one dead and several wounded but on the Falls, at least, the feeling was that they had 'stopped them'. Gerry Adams felt that the IRA's actions had been 'crucially important' in halting the loyalists at 'decisive times'. With McMillen in jail, Jim Sullivan, who had played a prominent part in the fighting, took over as O/C while McKnight was sent south to get more weapons.

Elsewhere there had been fighting after civil rights rallies in Coalisland, Newry and Dungannon. In Armagh B-Specials killed a local man. In Newry republicans used stolen lorries to close off the town's main streets. Crowds attacked the police during two nights of rioting, while the post office was firebombed. When B-Special reinforcements arrived the local IRA withdrew across the border, burning down a customs post as they fled, but a premature explosion saw several injured with 19-year-old Colman Rowntree suffering bad burns. In Dungannon armed IRA members had been on the streets following shooting by the B-Specials but locals convinced them that opening fire would make the situation worse.

Among the IRA leadership in Dublin there was confusion. Goulding and Ryan had been taking part in a TV programme about the IRA being filmed in the Dublin Mountains. Coming back into Dublin, Goulding and Ryan stopped off to meet some supporters. Only then were they made aware of what was unfolding in Belfast, and they rushed to republican HQ at Gardiner Place. With the acting Quartermaster General unavailable, Goulding, shocked by the turn of events, immediately appointed Ryan to the position and ordered him to begin organizing weapons and men. Word was sent to available Dublin Brigade members to assemble in Billy Wright's boxing gym underneath his barber shop on Parkgate Street. In the gym Ryan read out a statement to the 27 men who had turned up and then called out a list of names for active service. Those present were anxious that their names be called out; 'you weren't worried about getting shot or being put in jail, the only thing you were worried about was would you do the right thing and not let the side down'. But the weapons produced did not inspire confidence. They included a Winchester rifle that reminded someone of the type used by John Wayne in *Rio Bravo*. Eventually four units were moved up to the border, with volunteers from Cork and Kerry placed in Donegal while the Dubliners were sent to Monaghan and Leitrim. Some of them were billeted overnight in councillor Seamus McElwaine's house in Monaghan; McElwaine's young son was roused to give two Dubliners his bed. They were told that Sean South and Feargal O'Hanlon had shared the same bed before the Brookeborough raid, information that produced decidedly mixed feelings in the men. Command HQ was established in Ballinamore, where another Dublin man was taken to a drainage tunnel by John Joe McGirl, who had been active in the IRA since the 1930s. Two rifles and a Thompson were taken out of the hide and given to the volunteer with the suggestion that 'you lads have more use for this than me'. The Dublin man admits feeling 'so inadequate . . . we hadn't a fucking clue'.

The units' orders were to carry out attacks to stretch the RUC and B-Specials and 'take the heat' off Belfast. On Sunday 17 August a unit attacked Crossmaglen RUC station using a stolen van packed with explosives that failed to ignite. Shots were exchanged with the RUC before the men escaped back across the border. With British troops on the streets of Belfast and the situation calming down, it was soon decided that more offensive action would make things worse. At the Castle Hotel in Dublin the IRA leadership agreed not to undertake offensive activities along the border; the presence and perceived influence at this meeting of republicans who were not IRA volunteers caused some resentment at the time. The units stayed in place for another few weeks. People were well aware that they were there, with one unit regularly sending into a local village for chips. In Ballinamore some of the men drank in McGirl's Pub while in battledress. By September they were finally ordered back; Tony Heffernan remembers being 'relieved' to go back home.

On 18 August Goulding issued a statement on behalf of the IRA 'acting in its capacity as Provisional Government of the Republic'. He claimed that the organization had 'been in action' in Derry and Belfast and that it had sent 'fully equipped units' to the North. Noting the IRA's support for the civil rights movement, Goulding stated that they had been 'reluctantly compelled into military action' by the onslaught of the 'Orange murder gangs'. In Derry the IRA had put themselves at the disposal of the defence committee and in Belfast had used 'their all too limited resources' to hold off the assault on the Falls. Goulding warned British troops that if they allowed themselves 'to be used to suppress the legitimate demands of the people' then they would 'have to take the consequences'. He then called on the 'Dublin government' to 'immediately use the Irish Army to defend the persecuted people of the six counties'. Irish military intelligence noted that 'as in Bogside, IRA now seem to be in control of barricade defence in Belfast. Reports indicate that such defence is on an organised, disciplined basis with elements of southern IRA taking an active part.'

Sinn Féin had decided that, if there was trouble in Derry, they would organize an open-air public meeting in Dublin and demand that the 'full resources of the state be used in defence of the Irish people in the six counties'. On 13 August 4,000 people marched on the British Embassy, and over the following days there were several thousand people in O'Connell Street each night demanding that *they* be armed. At the GPO Sinn Féin speakers called for a general strike and a boycott of British goods. MP Paddy Devlin, on his way to meet government officials in Dublin, told protesters that the 'only way we can defend ourselves is with guns . . . we need them'. Mac Giolla challenged the 'Free State Army' to use their weapons to defend the people in the North and that if they would not, then they should 'give them to us'. He called on the crowd to come to Collins Barracks and demand the arms; 3,000 people marched down the quays to the barracks chanting 'Give us guns' and several were injured in scuffles outside its gates. Fergus Whelan recalls 'the whole of Dublin was abuzz, people marching here and there demanding guns. Mac Giolla was outside Collins Barracks demanding guns, Bernadette Devlin was on the news urging all the young people of Ireland to come north to defend the Catholics. I was at a demo I think, in Collins Barracks . . . they said there would be buses at Parnell Square to bring people up to the North to fight. There was hundreds of people got on to the buses. I realized after the buses pulled out half of them were pissed.' By the time they reached Dundalk, 'most people had sobered up and started walking home'. Whelan and his colleagues slept in sheds and got the Belfast train the next morning. They made their way to the Falls after some mishaps and Whelan was dispatched to Turf Lodge for barricade duty. Eighteen-year-old Paddy Woodworth had also set off with a friend to go north. 'We didn't know where we were going, Derry or Belfast, we just thought when we arrived the struggle would be there. We didn't get lifts further than Dunleer, slept under a bridge there, we got cold and very wet and said fuck this and hitched back to Dublin. That was my Northern campaign.' In fact the IRA had hoped to use the buses to divert attention from their own units moving north at the same time.

Sinn Féin organized solidarity demonstrations across the South. In Westport Seán Ó Cionnaith called for people to hand over arms 'no matter how obsolete'. In Sligo a Sinn Féin speaker called for 'young men to come and fight . . . we will direct them where to go'. Kerry County Council called on the government to remove the ban on the IRA as a gesture of goodwill. Refugees were coming south and being housed in Gormanstown, Co. Meath.

The IRA had explicitly asked the 'Free State' government to intervene in the North and its propaganda was heavily centred on saving 'our people'. The *United Irishman* argued that 'Ulster must be coerced . . . if that is the only way to get Civil Rights and basic democracy for the Catholic and non-unionist population'. On BBC television an IRA spokesman insisted that if it had not been for his organization 'the people in the Divis Street area would have been massacred'. Goulding told RTÉ's *Seven Days* that his organization had the 'right to kill' B-Specials and 'Paisleyites' if they attacked nationalist areas.

Politically, republicans argued that the call for the abolition of Stormont made by the Labour Party and some civil rights leaders was a mistake. Direct rule from London would only increase British control over Ireland; 'less Westminster rule is required, not more'. Instead a 'democratic Irish structure' at Stormont could be utilized to bring about an all-Ireland settlement. The *United Irishman* warned that the movement should 'not lose its identity' and that activity on ground rents, public ownership of resources and the anti-EEC campaign should be kept up. In practice this was very difficult. The upsurge in nationalist feeling created opportunities for Sinn Féin but also caused problems. Membership was growing as application forms were given out at many of the demonstrations, but activity was disorganized and the *United Irishman* was not being properly utilized. Sinn Féin bemoaned the lack of a competent spokesman for TV or radio while Costello pushed for Sinn Féin to open its offices full-time, appoint new organizers and publish a weekly bulletin to keep the membership up to date on campaigns. But in Connacht 'local agitations [were] more or less abandoned' after the August crisis, and in Dublin rumours were current among the Labour left that Sinn Féin had brokered a secret deal with Fianna Fáil to abandon the housing campaign. Sean Dunne agrees that in practice that is what happened: 'We abandoned the homeless and ran up to the border.'

Some of those who had dropped out of the movement were reporting back. Liam Ó Comain had asked Cork border campaign veteran David O'Connell, working as a teacher in Donegal, to become active again during 1968, but was rebuffed. But Goulding appointed O'Connell O/C in the north-west during late 1969 despite Eddie Williams already having been given that position. Williams was loyal to the leadership while O'Connell would soon prove to be an ally of Goulding's critics. Bobby McKnight had been gathering weapons, and setting up a route for moving them from Dundalk through Newry, while Ryan was searching the country high and low for more. At one stage ITGWU General Secretary Michael Mullen was going to transport arms to Belfast by boat. Mullen, who had been an IRA internee during the 1940s and later a Labour TD, was close to both Goulding and elements in Fianna Fáil. Eventually nearly everything the IRA could get their hands on was sent north — about 96 assorted weapons and 12,000 rounds of ammunition in the immediate aftermath of

August. IRA members in the North believed that Southern politicians had supplied some of the weapons. Neil Blaney would later
claim that up to 25 TDs and Senators had made privately held
arms available during 1969. Republicans in Tyrone also received
guns from Fine Gael or 'Blueshirt' sources. All manner of weaponry
was assembled: there were .303s, .22s, shotguns, Webleys, 'Peter
the Painters' (Mauser automatics) and a pair of gold-plated automatics, like 'something out of *Patton*'. In Dublin a Chinese-made
AK-47 turned up, battered and looking like it had 'come down
the Ho Chi Minh trail'.

Republicans argued for maintaining the barricades in Belfast and
Derry, Costello stressing that the potential existed for the formation
of a new radical 'civil organization' in these areas. Mac Giolla
visited the Bogside and found enthusiasm for this idea. In late
August the Liberation Fleadh was held in the Bogside featuring
the Dubliners, Tommy Makem, Shay Healy and Eugene Lambert
of RTÉ's *Wanderly Wagon*. Young radicals like student Liz
McManus were drawn to the atmosphere of 'Free Derry'. By early
September republicans had lost control of the leadership of the
Derry Citizens Defence Association, due to the co-option of large
numbers of non-aligned nationalists, but arms training for young
republicans and members of the left-wing groups was provided
behind the barricades by IRA members from Cork.

In Belfast Jim Sullivan became chairman of the Central Citizens'
Defence Committee (CCDC) on the Falls; the British Army
described him as 'head of Nogoland committee' and a 'known
IRA leader'. The CCDC was an amalgamation of dozens of local
defence and relief committees that had sprung up behind the
barricades. It included IRA members as well as a cross section of
Belfast nationalism. Paddy Devlin was its secretary; Fr. Padraig
Murphy and fruit importer Tom Conaty were also committee
members. The committees organized vigilante patrols and set up
rotas for food distribution and transport in and out of barricaded
areas. Space above a shoe repair shop behind the Long Bar was
utilized as the HQ; groups would meet there before patrols to
receive their arms and ammunition, and 'Radio Free Belfast', a

pirate radio station, was broadcast from there. The sight of armed IRA members at barricades no longer raised eyebrows. Indeed, Sullivan admitted to the *Belfast Telegraph* that 'automatic weapons, revolvers and rifles' were being held for defence. Despite the British being aware that the IRA was moving in weapons, Sullivan met British GOC General Freeland on several occasions in late August. He was also part of a delegation that travelled to Westminster in September. However, Home Secretary Jim Callaghan refused to meet Sullivan because he knew he was an IRA officer, so Sullivan stayed in an anteroom while Callaghan met Devlin, Fitt, Conaty and Fr. Murphy.

In Belfast recruits flooded into the IRA; 'you could have filled Falls Park with the amount of people who wanted to volunteer'. There were recruiting classes every night in Billy Sullivan's house. Auxiliaries were set up to cater for older men and those who only wanted to take part in vigilante activity. While the nationalist community now had 'high expectations' of the IRA, they had 'not supported the organization in real terms for 40 years', and some republicans resented the fact that people who 'would have spit on you and refused to put [money] in your collection box' before August 1969 now expected to be provided with guns. There was also some contempt for the re-emergence of those – such as Jimmy Drumm, Seamus Twomey, Billy McKee and Joe Cahill – who had dropped out of the movement during the 1960s or even earlier; 'they thought the republic was going to be got without them . . . and they were afraid to be left out of it'. Soon these veterans were suggesting that the IRA leadership had failed to defend nationalists. Gerry Adams later recounted that he was 'perturbed and perplexed to find that extreme criticism of the Belfast leadership was being expressed most of all by republicans whom I didn't know or had only recently met'. Jim Sullivan reflected:

I don't think these people should have been accepted. I think they should have been chased, but it is very easy to say that now. I was part and parcel of the decision to allow them back . . . they blamed everyone from Dublin right down to Belfast Republicans, said they had been lax in providing means to defend people. I pointed out to them on many occasions that if things had been left to them there wouldn't have been a shortage of things to defend the people, there would have been nothing.

Remembering the IRA's popularity, veterans find the idea that 'I ran away' became a common slogan on Belfast walls ludicrous. The earliest reference to the slogan dates from April 1970, when Fr. Gillespie from Ardoyne told the British government's Scarman Tribunal that some men in his parish had told him the IRA were being called the 'I ran away' after August. 'I never saw it written on a wall,' recalls Sean O'Hare. 'That wasn't the attitude. People fell in behind the IRA, people stood behind them one hundred per cent. [That] was not painted on a wall in West Belfast, [it] would have been the talk of the place.' Sean Curry believes that the slogan comes from a taunt used by B-Specials during the Border Campaign: 'if anyone wrote it, it was Protestants . . . people on the ground at the time, some were a bit angry, but most praised people who did defend the area. They knew that if the men weren't there the area wouldn't have been defended.'

But dissensions that pre-dated August had been given a powerful emotional focus and were growing with the return of the older men to the IRA. In late August this group met and decided to take over the IRA leadership in Belfast. On 22 September they burst into a meeting in Cyprus Street and demanded that McMillen and the Belfast IRA sever their ties with Dublin until four Army Council members were replaced, and that several of their number be added to brigade staff. McMillen, just out of jail, was in a difficult position, as several of the group had arrived armed. He agreed to break links with Dublin, to abstain from attending the forthcoming IRA Convention and to bring several of the dissidents on to his staff. However, he had no intention of breaking with the leadership. Goulding sent Mac Stíofáin to Belfast to find out what was going on; but Mac Stíofáin was already in touch with Leo Martin, the Belfast intelligence officer who had allied himself with the leadership's critics. The dissidents discovered McMillen was still in touch with Dublin and began setting up their own command structure.

Meanwhile contacts had been established between republicans and representatives of the Irish government. During August the Irish government had established a cabinet subcommittee to deal with the Northern crisis, made up of Neil Blaney, Padraig Faulkner, Charles Haughey and Joe Brennan. They had £100,000 at their disposal to supply humanitarian aid to nationalists, which Blaney and Haughey effectively controlled. Goulding had been told that an individual in London was interested in supplying weapons. He travelled there and met Padraig (Jock) Haughey, brother of the Minister for Finance Charles Haughey, at the Irish Centre. Jock Haughey told him that money was available and Goulding suggested that at least £50,000 would be necessary. Haughey gave the IRA leader £1,500 in cash and told him more was to come. In Dundalk Bobby McKnight was approached by a local businessman and Fianna Fáil supporter, who informed him that £150,000 would be available for arms purchases provided the IRA stopped their activities in the South and abandoned left-wing policies. McKnight had instructions to play along and 'get as much out of them as you can'. He satisfied the businessman by telling him that 'all we're interested in is defence'. The IRA leadership was aware that feelers had been put out before the trouble erupted in Belfast. A Co. Derry businessman and friend of Neil Blaney had approached Francie Donnelly, the south Derry IRA commander, and inquired whether he was interested in equipment. Donnelly reported this to Dublin and was told to continue discussions with the contact, but there was no renewal of the approach until September. Then the man arrived with Captain James Kelly of Irish Army Intelligence, who had been working inside Northern Ireland since August and had made contact with Sean Keenan, Johnnie White and Eamonn McCann in Derry. To White he offered army instruction for volunteers in Donegal with the proviso that independent training would cease. The IRA leadership accepted the offer for reasons of morale and in the hope of acquiring new weaponry, and during September IRA volunteers from Derry were trained at Dunree Fort in Donegal by Irish Army officers. Captain Kelly was active in Belfast and spoke to numerous republicans including many of those who had returned after the August events. He was able to tell them that the Irish government was willing to provide arms and finance to members of the IRA and the defence committees. He was articulate and convincing, and even his IRA critics acknowledged his 'sincerity'. However, in reports to his superiors Kelly made clear that in his view thus far 'arms and support seem to have got into the wrong hands in Belfast', meaning elements hostile to the Southern government. Kelly favoured working with Hugh Kennedy of Bord Bainne, the Irish semi-state company, who was public relations officer for the Central Citizens' Defence Committee, and Tom Conaty.

The Special Branch believed that Charles Haughey had met senior IRA men during September and promised that arms shipments to the North would not be interfered with, if the IRA ceased their attacks in the republic. The Gardaí believed Haughey had facilitated shipments through Dublin Airport and Dublin Port. On one occasion Jock Haughey assisted with smuggling, as McKnight remembers: 'Two of us went down [and] Charlie's brother brought us into the airport, we'd a wee pickup truck we got a loan of, [and] he brought us in, and they put these big boxes on the truck, we had to take it away, the truck was fucking swaying from side to side [but] we had the right of way.' The men were not stopped or questioned before leaving the airport and they drove to a rendezvous nearby where Goulding had assembled a team who divided up the cargo – handguns and automatic weapons – and moved them to separate dumps.

During late September a meeting was organized in Lurgan to coordinate the defence committees. Considerable dissatisfaction with the IRA leadership was expressed. Ruairí O Brádaigh was present without Goulding's knowledge, as were several of the Belfast dissidents. Jim Sullivan, Paddy Devlin and Hugh Kennedy arrived at the meeting and made it clear that they were travelling to Dublin to see a government minister who was prepared to supply support. The three men met Charles Haughey at his home in Kinsealy, which Sullivan remembered as 'a massive house . . . two big steps up to it . . . a statue of a lion on either side of the door'. Haughey agreed that a bank account would be opened in Clones for funds for the defence committees. Money from the account was supposed to be paid weekly to the IRA and defence committees in Belfast. Realizing they were unlikely to receive their fair share, Goulding's supporters demanded access to the account at gunpoint. During October 1969 a Belfast IRA officer (who supported the Dublin leadership) was able to withdraw £4,000 from the account for the defence committees, while the dissidents also drew money from the fund.

It was becoming clear, however, that the money and arms were not going to be supplied willingly to those who supported the Dublin leadership. Donnelly was visited again by Captain Kelly and Seamus Brady, a former speechwriter for Blaney, and it was spelled out to him that four members of the IRA leadership – Goulding, Costello, Ryan and Johnston – would have to go before more money became available, and a separate Northern command would need to be established. The IRA leadership ordered units to 'accept guns if offered, keep them in dumps, follow the non-sectarian strife policy . . . and refuse political promise.' As Captain Kelly later explained: 'How do you expect a government in the South to give you arms and support if you are going to overthrow it? It's just not on.' After attending a meeting in Dublin's Shelbourne Hotel in October, Donnelly was not contacted again. The IRA leadership decided to go public on the affair. On 30 October a press conference was held in Dublin at which Séamus Ó Tuathail outlined the 'plot to take over the civil rights movement'. Blaney, Haughey and Boland were named as the promoters of the plan to buy off republicans and divert them from the real struggle, North and South. The *United Irishman* warned readers to 'beware these men and their Fianna Fáil gold', reminding its readers that 'twice in the past, prior to 1932 and again in 1957, Fianna Fáil climbed to power on the back of republicans on the pretext that they were sincerely trying to reunite Ireland'. Relations quickly soured. In early December Sinn Féin picketed an appearance by Blaney at the Golden Grill in Letterkenny; Fianna Fáil Senator Bernard McGlinchey emerged with a group of men and physically fought with them.

The promise of arms and money had the biggest effect in Belfast. Most of the new IRA recruits there had not been active in any form of politics before and large numbers of them were motivated only by a desire to defend their areas, or indeed to gain revenge for the attacks on their localities. They knew little and cared less about the history of Fianna Fáil repression of republicans in the South. Belfast buzzed with rumours of a 'shipment of weapons coming in on an airplane, enough to fill a hay barn'. The promise of arms and finance gave confidence to those opposing the Dublin leadership that they would be able to set up a viable alternative organization. But there were many new recruits to their ranks anyway. Many of those loyal to Goulding were also eager to take up offers of money or weapons, believing that Fianna Fáil could be outmanoeuvred. Left-wing volunteers were also swept up in the 'raw emotion . . . your streets were getting burnt, there was no time for doctrinaire talk'. However, most of those who had been active before August 1969 – including McMillen, Sullivan, McKnight, Mal McBurney and Denis Toner as well as the younger activists such as Dornan, Joe McCann, Seamus Lynch, Sean Mateer, Sean O'Hare, Sean Curry and Jim Hargey – remained loyal to Dublin. Gerry Adams was a notable exception, though his sister Margaret remained loyal to Goulding, as did her husband Michael McCorry. Initially the divide was not set in stone. One of those who stood guard while the dissidents confronted McMillen in Cyprus Street later went back to McMillen's side.

The August events had greatly accelerated the potential for a split and added new elements to it. As it became clear that a split was on the cards a major meeting of IRA officers was held in Billy Wright's gym where Goulding outlined the offer of finance from Fianna Fáil. Part of the purpose of the meeting was to determine who had been privately dealing with Captain Kelly or anyone else. Both Mac Stíofáin and Ó Brádaigh were restrained in their criticism. Only David O'Connell lost his temper, shouting, 'We want guns!' It was clear to a fellow delegate that 'he didn't care how he was getting them'. Whoever got them first was going to have a big advantage.

The race for weapons was on and any and every source was utilized. Anything that the IRA in Britain had was sent to Ireland. An arms dealer in Huddersfield was approached about providing substantial amounts of SLR rifles and Sterlings, and a meeting was organized with Costello and Gerry Doherty during November. In the event, Costello was unable to make it and Eamon Smullen, a London-based veteran who had rejoined the republican movement in 1969, went instead. The meeting was a police trap and Doherty and Smullen were arrested. During their trial, conducted under heavy security, Smullen's 1940s IRA record was recounted, as was a recent visit to Cuba. Smullen was sentenced to eight years and Doherty five. In a separate case a Belfast-born Protestant and member of the Communist Party, Barry Bruton, was sentenced to four years for persuading a friend to give him a rifle. In Belfast weapons were bought from Ted Pavis, a Protestant arms dealer who used his connections with a showband to smuggle guns from Europe.

Goulding and Costello approached Mick O'Riordan and asked if the Soviet Union would provide weapons. Costello was to organize a trawler crewed by 'select and reliable' IRA members who would pick up the shipment in neutral waters. During November O'Riordan informed the Soviets that the IRA's 'combat potential' had been weakened by its concentration on 'social protests and educational activity'. It needed weapons urgently. O'Riordan optimistically requested 2,000 AK-47 assault rifles and 150 machine guns along with over a million rounds of ammunition. But the Soviets were not inclined to supply arms at short notice to an unknown quantity like the IRA. KGB chief Yuri Andropov insisted that if arms were to be supplied then the 'secret of their source of supply' had to be preserved. Meanwhile the *United Irishman* launched a 'Dynamite Fund', aimed at Irish America, arguing 'bandages are not enough, defence is needed'.

The violence had created huge interest in the US but as yet it was unclear in which direction the new support would flow. Local Clan na Gael activists found Irish-American army veterans turning up on their doorsteps with handguns to send to Ireland. Bernadette Devlin's August speaking tour had attracted intense coverage, though her socialism alienated many. Goulding went to the US in November to try to secure the loyalty of Clan. He also sought allies elsewhere. Dominic Behan was working for the IRA on the east coast and was not reticent about their objective. In one address to a Philadelphia gathering he declared, 'We are over here looking for money to buy guns to spread the revolution.' Goulding was introduced to the actor Gene Kelly, who made it clear he would make a financial contribution as long as it was for arms. Goulding also raised money from the National Association for Irish Justice.

A number of important figures on the republican scene in New York, all of them Irish and several of them 1919–23 veterans, had already raised their own funds. National Association for Irish Justice activist Joan McKiernan recalled a meeting in the autumn of 1969 when many of the old guard made it clear that 'we don't want any money going over there until we know who is going to get it'. They were highly suspicious of the left. Goulding had met some of the older group including Liam Kelly, the former Saor Uladh leader, who eventually gave him his backing. However, in December Sean Keenan and John Kelly, a representative of the Belfast dissidents, arrived in America on a trip paid for by Irish government money. Initially the New York republicans were wary of Keenan and Kelly but the two men made useful contacts.

Small donations aside, weapons were going to cost money, and the only way to get the kind of money required to buy them was to steal it. Armed robberies were now back on the agenda. Costello appointed several officers whose job 'was to suss out info, intelligence, to get money to get guns. The word was out, we *have* to get guns.' The IRA robbed banks in Belfast and Omagh during October, and there were further robberies in Dublin and Belfast during December. Later that month an IRA man was arrested and a shot fired in an attempted armed raid on Wynn's Hotel in Dublin. IRA training was intensified as recruitment increased. Recruits came down from the North almost every weekend, as a Dublin activist recalls: 'Every Friday you met at 4 o'clock . . . you were in the deep of the fucking country at 10 p.m., you set up camp by 12, up at 6 next morning and then bang, bang, bang all day long.'

The Dublin republican splinter group had decided to develop their own political programme. On 15 August they had taken £800 in a raid in Baltinglass. Afterwards some of the raiders sat listening to radio reports of the Battle of the Bogside and decided time was ripe for a new organization. During September they robbed £8,000 from banks in Dublin and in Kells, claiming the raids in the name of the Saor Éire Action Group. Jim Lane and his Cork comrades had also gone to Northern Ireland during August and, despite past differences, spent some time with Eddie Williams and several IRA activists along the border. Lane and the Cork group were less than impressed when the Dublin gang adopted the Saor Éire title, causing a great deal of confusion not to mention drawing Garda attention to their organization.

In November the IRA complained to Sinn Féin that 'gossip' about political divisions was circulating freely in its ranks. Arguments about the IRA's performance were also becoming more public. The *United Irishman* reacted angrily to a critical article in the current affairs magazine *Nusight* entitled 'Where were the IRA?', claiming a more sympathetic piece by Anne Harris had been rewritten by editors Vincent Browne and John Feeney. But Goulding's position during August was defended by Padraig Ó Snodaigh in the Irish-language monthly *Comhar*. News of the divisions in Belfast appeared in the press in early December. Dick Walsh reported in the *Irish Times* that a majority of the IRA in the city had severed contact with Dublin and details of the September meetings were publicized later that month.

Sporadic sectarian clashes continued and people in Belfast were still regularly forced from their homes. Thousands of loyalists had rallied on the Shankill in early September and threatened to march on Unity Flats, only to be stopped by British troops. Five Catholic homes were burnt out in late September and the IRA had fired on loyalists at Unity Flats. A Protestant vigilante was shot dead after an argument with Catholics at a barricade in the same month, and another Protestant man died after a clash with Catholics in Derry. In mid-September the British Army had removed most of the barricades in west Belfast despite some opposition. In early October loyalists outraged by the abolition of the B-Specials rioted on the Shankill and again tried to reach the Falls but British troops dispersed them violently. The Ulster Volunteer Force opened fire, killing an RUC man, while British soldiers killed 2 loyalists and injured 60. Loyalists complained bitterly about army brutality. A UVF member was killed planting a bomb at a power station in Ballyshannon, County Donegal. Even though the IRA in the city was effectively split, both sides still cooperated in defensive work. Malachy McGurran was released from jail in early December and set about work, a 'clear thinker' who had been badly missed by the leadership over the previous three months. Also missing for much of the time was Sean Garland, who was now living in Glasgow, though travelling extensively on IRA business.

Preparation was taking place for both the extraordinary IRA Convention to be held in December and the Sinn Féin Ard Fheis to follow in January. There were now strong indications that a formal split was inevitable. Many of the younger IRA and Sinn Féin members were happy at the prospect. Eoin Ó Murchú remembers that he 'naively and wrongly thought a split would be a good thing'. Mac Giolla, on the other hand, was much more cautious, while Goulding and his allies would later blame Costello, who was more determined than ever to get rid of abstentionism, for pushing people into the other camp. Goulding claimed that Costello left a battalion convention in Leitrim to watch Bernadette Devlin being interviewed on television and also suggested that another officer had alienated local units in Clare and Kerry by his dismissive attitude. Ó Brádaigh also noted what he called Costello's 'arrogant' manner at this time. However, Costello was expressing views widely held among the younger membership that those who disagreed with the movement's direction should just leave. Mick Ryan was fearful about the prospect of a violent split and armed a number of volunteers for security at the convention. They were told to watch Mac Stíofáin and to take action if he looked like producing a weapon.

The convention took place in late December at Knockvicar House, in Boyle, Co. Roscommon. The leadership motion on the National Liberation Front was passed. This was followed by a debate on abstentionism. This too was passed by 28 votes to 12. There were accusations about opposition delegates not being transported to the meeting, but the leadership would have won the vote anyway. Because of the situation in Belfast neither group from the city was represented at the convention. The units in rural Ulster, Armagh, Tyrone, Co. Derry, south Down and Derry city supported the leadership. So did the majority in Dublin, Wicklow, Waterford, south Kilkenny, Mayo, Cork and south Kerry. Mac Stíofáin and Ó Brádaigh had the support of Louth/Meath and Longford/Roscommon as well as the dissident north Kerry organization. While most of Dublin remained with the leadership, the Active Service Unit split down the middle and some of the most experienced military activists left to support Mac Stíofáin. Despite Ryan's fears, the convention was not acrimonious. Mac Thomáis, who voted against the leadership, gave Sean Dunne and a number of other Goulding supporters a lift back to Dublin.

Later that night Ó Brádaigh and Mac Stíofáin held their own meeting and set up a new Army Council and established a new organization, the Provisional IRA. Their existence became public knowledge on 28 December, with a statement claiming the support of the majority of IRA volunteers. This was not the case, except in Belfast. Joe Cahill proposed they drop the claim to the IRA's name and use a new title instead, but his proposal was rejected. There were now two IRAs but still one Sinn Féin, which was to have its Ard Fheis in January. There was now a frantic scramble to secure dumps and the control of arms locally, and to bulk up support.

Goulding's IRA moved to undercut support for the Provisionals by setting up a separate Northern Command in early January. McGurran was made its commander and it publicly promised to place a special emphasis on 'the defence of those areas vulnerable to attack by government-inspired pogromists'. Describing the Provisionals as 'totally unrepresentative' of the IRA in general, a Northern Command statement asked that 'disgruntled' volunteers return to the movement and pursue their grievances through its structure. The IRA outlined its policy in a major statement in the January *United Irishman*, explaining that it was no longer an 'elitist force, divorced from the struggles of the people' but a revolutionary army, whose role was to 'assist the people in what is THEIR liberation struggle'.

The Sinn Féin Ard Fheis took place in the Intercontinental Hotel in Dublin's Ballsbridge on the weekend of 11–12 January 1970. It coincided with a rugby match at nearby Lansdowne Road between Ireland and South Africa. Costello had led pickets on the South African team's hotel in Bray, and on the first day of the Ard Fheis some of the 295 delegates joined the 10,000-strong demonstration at Lansdowne Road. The debate concerning the National Liberation Front went on for four hours and finally ended at 11 p.m. in a majority accepting the concept. The issue of entering parliament was discussed all day Sunday, and when a vote was finally taken at 5.30 p.m. there were 257 present. The motion needed 172 votes to gain the necessary two-thirds majority but received 153; abstentionism was safe for another year. Denis Cassin proposed a resolution pledging Sinn Féin's continued support to the IRA. Mac Stíofáin retorted that he owed allegiance to the Provisional Army Council, at which point he, Ó Brádaigh and a number of supporters began to walk out. Joe Clarke got on to his crutches and followed them as a supporter grabbed the microphone, shouting: 'Joe Clarke, the hero of 1916, is leaving!' There were scuffles during which Mac Stíofáin was punched. The Provisionals went to a prearranged meeting in Parnell Square where they announced the setting up of a 'caretaker' executive of Sinn Féin. The formal split was complete. The Provisionals' reasons for splitting away were listed as Goulding's organization's recognition of foreign parliaments, their cooperation with radical groups, the NLF policy, their adoption of 'extreme socialism', undemocratic internal methods, the 'let down of the North' and the opposition to abolishing Stormont.

The split produced mixed emotions. In Dublin Margaret O'Leary had 'no close friends' among those who left and felt the division was inevitable; 'we were leaving the conservative rear-guard behind and moving on'. Tony Gregory recalled that young activists 'didn't even think of the Provos as an option'. De Burca was delighted: 'I went home the day of the split walking on air.' On the other hand Mac Giolla conceded that some of those who had walked out had been involved in social agitation and felt 'very sincerely that abstentionism is the heart of republicanism'. His close friend Mac Thomáis was one of those who left. Most of those who had joined since the mid-1960s were enthusiastic about the NLF concept and had no problem with TDs taking seats if elected, though the split was not simply generational. The Goulding leadership retained the support of IRA veterans like Liam Leddy and Paddy Fleming, both 1940s chiefs of staff, Charles McGleenan, the former abstentionist MP for South Armagh, Gerry Dunlop, a Belfast man who had been sentenced to 20 years for involvement in the 1940s bombing campaign, and Newry's Joe Campbell. Goulding also retained substantial rural support including the majority of the movement in Northern Ireland. One man who later became a leading Provisional in Tyrone estimated that the 'overwhelming majority' of the local organization there remained loyal to Dublin. There was, however, considerable unwillingness to split at all in many areas, both North and South, with Wexford Sinn Féin asking for a meeting so both sides could go about 'patching up their differences'. Some individuals would take a long time to make up their minds which side they should take. But in Belfast, where the split was already several months old, and in Dublin to a lesser extent, the division was becoming bitter. An ominous sign for Mick Ryan was that his car had been stolen on the weekend of the Ard Fheis and was found on the Dublin Mountains riddled with bullets. He felt the atmosphere at the Intercontinental had been terrible, reminding him of 'a civil war', and his former comrades were like 'a family member who knew everything about you'. Goulding seemed to be more blasé, commenting that splits had never really worked in the past.

In fact, the split was to dominate republican politics for the next decade.

5. Defence and Retaliation

The Official IRA and the Northern Troubles, 1970–1974

'The war on the people will be turned into a people's war.'

Official IRA, Belfast, August 1971

Cathal Goulding and his supporters continued to refer to themselves as the IRA, despite Seán Mac Stíofáin's group also claiming the title. By the end of 1970 the terms 'Official IRA' and 'Regular IRA' were introduced by the press to differentiate Goulding's organization from the Provisionals. Goulding remained Chief of Staff, Costello was Director of Operations and Malachy McGurran became Northern commander. Sean Garland was abroad for most of 1970, still concerned about the possibility of Gardaí arresting him in connection with the Dublin Airport heist. Tomás Mac Giolla chaired the leadership body with Mick Ryan initially Quartermaster General. Billy McMillen represented Belfast while Sean Ó Cionnaith, Eoin Ó Murchú and several other local commanders were members of the extended Army Council. There were now also two rival Sinn Féin organizations, also labelled either 'Official' or 'Provisional' according to their military wings, or 'Gardiner Place' or 'Kevin Street' after the addresses of their headquarters. To confuse matters further the Officials continued to call their political organization in Northern Ireland the Republican Clubs.

The Official leadership did not believe that a revolutionary situation yet existed or that an armed offensive against the British was realistic. The role of the Official IRA within Northern Ireland was primarily defensive, a back-up to social agitation on both sides of the border, but it was recognized that rearming was vital, and the Official leadership publicly appealed at Easter 1970 for help so that the IRA could 'equip itself with modern weapons, to ensure that it will never again ask men to face armoured cars with short arms'. The British were aware that the OIRA had been seeking aid from both Cuba and the Soviet Union. The Soviets were extremely concerned about security and were alarmed by stories in the British press about Eastern Bloc arms finding their way to the North. They wanted assurances that there would be no leaks before they acted. Other sources were sought. Goulding had a contact in the Military Police at the Curragh Camp who informed him about the possibility of stealing a quantity of FN rifles. The raid was planned for 17 May 1970, and a unit led by Goulding set off to the Curragh. However, at the last minute the raid was aborted and Gardaí stopped the stolen lorry in which Goulding was travelling. He was arrested and charged, but the IRA put pressure on the lorry owner to withdraw his statement and the case collapsed. The incident led to questions as to why the Chief of Staff was personally leading an armed raid. Some saw it as an attempt to 'upstage' Costello, who was himself taking part in robberies.

Some of Goulding's earlier efforts in the United States were beginning to bear fruit. McGurran visited America during March and several lines of supply were opened up. Weapons bought as far south as North Carolina were being moved through Baltimore, Toronto and Montreal en route to Dublin. The IRA's supporters in Dublin Port were able to have the weapons, sometimes marked 'agricultural machinery', picked up safely. By the spring of 1970 small quantities of Garand and Springfield rifles, M1 carbines and .38 revolvers had begun to arrive from contacts in the US. British sources continued to supply ammunition, as did loyalist gun dealers. Goulding claimed during 1970 that the accusation that his supporters had 'gone soft' had been a 'big help' to rearmament as state attention had been focused elsewhere.

At Easter the division within the IRA was displayed publicly, with rival commemorations held in Dublin, Belfast, Derry and Cork. The Official IRA now admitted that there had been a shortage of weapons in Belfast the previous August. They claimed, however, that the fault for this lay mainly with those who had 'deserted the republican army' during the 1960s and only returned after August, when they became 'free with their criticism'. The Provisionals blamed the IRA's lack of preparation on infiltration by supporters of 'Marx, Mao and Castro' who had introduced 'foreign socialism' under the cover of republicanism. It was after Easter that the Provisionals began to taunt their rivals for adopting an adhesive lily, nicknaming them 'Stickeybacks', a term soon shortened to 'Sticks' or 'Stickies'. The Provisionals were christened the 'Pinheads' after reverting to using a pin to attach their lilies, but the name never caught on, most people referring to them as 'Provos'. In much of rural Ulster there was still only one Easter commemoration. Bernadette Devlin confirmed that in many such areas there was no split as the movement had remained almost completely behind Goulding. Intelligence sources at the US Embassy in Dublin concluded that 'most of those associated with the Republican Movement since 1962 remained with the "Officials" . . . who [have] retained most of the Movement's brains, trained men, money and arms as well as much of the movement's Dublin and Cork bases'.

In Derry city several thousand attended the Official parade in the city centre while the Provisional event held after Easter in the Bogside attracted only a few hundred. In Belfast, however, the Provisionals had turned out the larger numbers, reflecting their predominance, and it was in this city that the rivalry soon became bitter and violent. This was partly because those involved came from the same streets, had gone to the same schools, had worked together or were from the same families. During April Jim Sullivan was punched during a pub row with a Provo. The Officials responded immediately, McMillen kneecapping the Provisional involved outside the Celtic Bar on the Falls Road. A few days later the Provos ambushed McMillen, firing on him while he was driving his Volkswagen Beetle through Finaghy. The 'wee man' was unhurt but clashes escalated and a familiar pattern emerged: supporters of either group who were a minority in their own areas were victimized by their rivals. A truce was announced in early May after clergy had facilitated talks between McMillen and Provisional Billy McKee, but tension remained. Some members of the OIRA discussed the possibility of a pre-emptive strike against the Provos, but McMillen later explained that 'it would have been virtually impossible for us to explain in political terms [why] we had felt it necessary to kill twelve or thirteen republicans, after all these people had been our comrades in arms, it just wasn't on'.

The clandestine contacts between the Southern government and those who became the Provisionals were brought to public attention during 1970. By May Charles Haughey, Neil Blaney and Kevin Boland had either resigned or been sacked from government for their part in the scheme. Haughey along with Military Intelligence officer Captain James Kelly, Belfast Provisional John Kelly and Flemish businessman Albert Luykx eventually faced trial for their part in the operation. A jury, unconvinced that the men had not been working with official sanction, and caught up in the wave of sympathy for Northern Catholics, acquitted the four in Dublin's High Court. The Provisional IRA, stung by the allegations of connivance with Fianna Fáil and the 'Free State' military, issued a statement that dismissed 'press allegations' of assistance 'in the form of finance, arms and training facilities' as 'completely untrue'.

Outside the Lower Falls the main area of Official strength in Belfast was the Markets, though in reality 'no area belonged to anybody' and there were members of both organizations in every nationalist district. With the influx of new members the division of the city's brigade into three battalion areas, which were further subdivided into companies, was re-established. The 3rd Battalion area stretched the length of the Falls Road from the Divis Flats to Ballymurphy, with support concentrated in the Lower Falls (D Company), Beechmount (B Company) and Divis. The 2nd Battalion covered the rest of west Belfast, with Turf Lodge the centre of its strength. The 1st Battalion's area was centred in the Markets but spread over the rest of mainly Protestant east Belfast, with companies located in the Catholic enclaves of Short Strand and the Ormeau Road. Although the smaller group in the city,

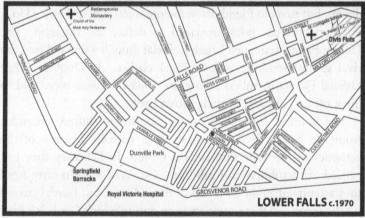

the Officials regarded themselves as the authentic IRA, better disciplined and organized than the 'breakaway group'. Many had a contemptuous attitude towards the Provos, seeing them as 'armed Celtic [Football Club] supporters', most of whom would never have been recruited into the IRA before August 1969. Sullivan was particularly dismissive, predicting in Dublin that the Provo organization would disintegrate within a few weeks. Another result of the August 1969 upheaval had been the setting up of shebeens in residential areas, as many pubs had been burnt down and people were avoiding drinking in the city centre. Among the first Official shebeens were the Cracked Cup in Leeson Street and the Liam Mellows Club in Verner Street in the Markets. Members also continued to frequent pubs such as the Long Bar and the Old House on the Falls, as well as the National Club in Queen Street.

Away from the tinderbox atmosphere of Belfast, conflict was mainly verbal, though there was sporadic violence in Dublin. Shortly after the split a group of Provisionals carried out an armed raid on an Official meeting in Ringsend. The raid became somewhat farcical after a female Official who knew the raiders personally lectured them on how ashamed of themselves they should be. The Officials claimed to have 'no fear' of such violence escalating, as they were the stronger organization in Dublin. During another confrontation outside Maher's Pub in Moore Street, guns were drawn, but two old friends from the pre-1969 Active Service Unit, now on different sides, managed to defuse the situation. The Dublin Fianna remained largely Official though a few did join the rival group, resulting in occasional clashes. At Dublin's GPO Official Fianna members selling the *United Irishman* were told to 'fuck off to Vietnam' by their Provo rivals.

The political atmosphere in the South had shifted somewhat from the heady days of August 1969, partially because of the activities of the Saor Éire Action Group. In February they had carried out a robbery in Rathdrum, Co. Wicklow. In early April they attempted a raid on Dublin's Arran Quay, but Gardaí arrived on the scene and there was a struggle during which Garda Richard Fallon was shot dead. This was the first killing of a Garda since 1942 and it caused outrage. (The Officials' *Nuacht Náisiúnta* deplored the 'orgy of sentimental twaddle and calls for repressive retaliatory legislation' that followed this incident, contrasting it with the lack of outcry over violence in police custody, during evictions and towards travellers. The *United Irishman* went further, claiming that a Special Branch officer, rather than the bank robbers, had accidentally shot Fallon. Cathal Goulding later gave evidence to court in support of Frank Keane, who was charged with the murder, claiming that Keane was a man of 'very high character' inspired by a desire to do the best for his country.) A major hunt was launched for the raiders and the names of seven Saor Éire suspects were published in the national press. The group's ambitions of becoming an urban guerrilla organization were severely damaged, but the group remained in existence, receiving some support from the Trotskyist Fourth International, which was also backing urban guerrilla groups in South America. Peter Graham, the Young Socialist leader, became Saor Éire's quarter-master. The group continued to carry out robberies, although with most of its members on the run it was already splintering and it lost an important member when Liam Walsh was killed while attempting to defuse an explosive device left near Dublin's McKee Barracks in October 1970.

The consequences of the IRA split were quickly overshadowed by the deterioration of the relationship between Northern Catholics and the British Army. There had been rioting in Derry following the Officials' Easter commemoration, followed by complaints about army brutality. The Official IRA in the city warned that 'action' would be taken against collaborators with the British. In Belfast there were serious clashes between young nationalists and the British Army during April. General Freeland announced that henceforth petrol bombers would be shot by his men. The Officials responded by threatening to kill British soldiers if civilians were shot. During rioting in Ballymurphy a group of OIRA men were driven into the area by the Northern Ireland Labour MP Paddy Devlin. They chose an ambush position and had orders to open fire if British troops used live ammunition. Devlin was cooperating closely behind the scenes with the OIRA, even offering to become a volunteer himself. Goulding advised him that he could be of better use in his political role, though some Belfast Officials suspected that Devlin was actually working on behalf of the Dublin government.

Street clashes became worse as the build-up to the 1970 Orange marching season began. The Officials advised their volunteers and supporters to 'exercise utmost discipline and self-control' and 'avoid sectarian strife'. Units were put on alert to defend areas against loyalist attack but also to prevent Catholics engaging in attacks on Protestants. Sullivan and others, armed with hurleys, had stood between rival crowds on the Grosvenor Road during April. The Officials suspected the Provos were using the sectarian rioting to build up their own base. At Bodenstown during June Malachy McBurney told the crowd of several thousand, nearly half of whom had travelled from the North, that the OIRA welcomed 'arms in the hands of Irishmen, not for use against the Protestant workers in the North, but for use against the British Army of occupation'. But later that month Belfast saw the worst sectarian violence since August 1969. Major rioting broke out during Orange parades on 27 June and the Provisionals opened fire on loyalist crowds, killing three men. Later that evening mobs attacked the Short Strand and the Provos killed three more Protestants during gun battles in the vicinity of St Matthew's Catholic Church. (One Catholic vigilante was killed by fire from his own side.) The defence of the Short Strand became a powerful recruiting tool for the Provisional IRA, and sectarian feeling intensified. Five hundred Catholic workers were forced out of the shipyards in the aftermath of the shootings. The Officials argued that 'the hatred and bitterness engendered by the killing of six Protestant civilians can only increase the likelihood of further pogroms'. On the ground, however, many felt that the Short Strand had been 'defended well' and the local OIRA unit had also been on defensive duty that night. More violence was expected and all Official units were put on alert. A large number of weapons, many of which had just arrived in Belfast, were brought into the Lower Falls for cataloguing and distribution.

On 3 July British troops raided 24 Balkan Street in the Lower Falls, having received a tip-off that weapons were being stored there. They found 1 sub-machine gun, 1 rifle, 15 pistols and some ammunition. As they withdrew locals tried to obstruct them. Stones

were thrown and the troops replied with CS gas. As the confrontation escalated, rumours spread that a man had been killed by an
armoured car. The Officials were desperate to avoid their arms being
captured. 'A decision was made very hastily to move out the bulk of
the weapons that was in the area in case they decided to raid larger
scale; in doing so some of the weapons became visible and the guys
that had the weapons decided to fire a few shots.'

As more troops were sent into the area the Officials realized
they would have to fight. Barricades were thrown up in Raglan
Street, Cullingtree Road and Leeson Street and armed OIRA
members were sent to take up positions. Buses were hijacked and
used to block off Albert Street junction. Jim Sullivan gave orders
to confront the army:

About 6 o'clock that night the order was given that the weapons and
the area must be defended. About 60–70 men were armed, local IRA
Volunteers, D Company. Each man was given a rifle, some people had
two revolvers, and some people had three revolvers! Some people had
two rifles and two revolvers, there was that much about then, at the
same time we were trying to get the weapons out of the area.

Many of the guns were just out of their packaging and there was
a rush to assemble them, one carbine falling apart when it was
fired. British troops initially withdrew under heavy gunfire. At
10 p.m. General Freeland issued orders to curfew the Lower Falls,
threatening to shoot anyone who remained on the streets. Minutes
after the curfew was imposed three soldiers were shot in Omar
Street:

It was purely coincidental, they were in the right streets at the right time,
they knew the streets, the backyard walls came in very handy. It's said
there was 2,000 Brits, I don't know if there was, there was a lot anyway.
You tried to pick a target. At one point weapons had to be cooled down.

As CS gas poured into the area British soldiers reported coming
under 'heavy and extremely accurate sniper fire' in Plevna Street.

By midnight 3,000 troops were surrounding the area and they entered in armoured cars, which eventually made firing futile. As the battle raged 'young lads in the area were still throwing stones, petrol bombs and bottles, they were actually pushing the volunteers out of the way at one stage'.

Over 36 hours the British admitted firing 1,454 live rounds, 1,385 CS canisters and 218 CS cartridges, killing three local civilians and a freelance photographer; 18 soldiers were wounded, 15 by gunfire. As the army entered the area they began extensive house searches. Men and teenagers were beaten and women abused. Dozens of homes were wrecked. To add insult to injury, two Unionist MPs were brought on a tour of the subdued area in the back of an army Land Rover. Trapped in a house near Sultan Street as troops approached, one Official consoled some younger volunteers that they were in 'a bad house'. 'We're in a bad fucking area!' was their reply.

The curfew was eventually lifted on Sunday morning, after women marched down the Falls Road, pushing prams and chanting, and broke through the British lines. The British knew that most of the 'more attractive' armaments had been spirited away 'before the cordon was fully effective'; some of these weapons ended up in the hands of the Provisionals. Five or six local Provisionals had been in the area at the beginning of the trouble and fired on the army but had then withdrawn. In the curfew's aftermath, after the streets had quietened down and arms had been dumped, a group of volunteers met up in Lincoln Street and, allowed alcohol for the first time in days, proceeded to 'get full'. They composed a song: 'The Provos never showed that night / They would rather sleep and leave us to fight . . . / But with hand grenades and carbine guns / We put the wind up Britannia's sons.'

The British Army had no doubt that what they described as 'determined and organized armed resistance' had been spearheaded by the 'Goulding faction'. McMillen was one of 337 people arrested in the curfew's aftermath and his home in Ton Street was ransacked by troops.

The Falls curfew was a key moment in the general alienation of

Catholics from the British Army. For the Officials it led to increased recruitment and a new sense of confidence. Their publicity declared that it had been the single biggest engagement between the IRA and 'British Crown forces' since 1916. *This Week* magazine noted approvingly that it was the 'Regular IRA, which for the first time since 1921 engaged in open combat; not with Orangemen . . . not with fellow Irishmen, but with the naked and overwhelming power of the Imperial forces'. There was a strong desire for revenge among local OIRA members; 'some of their mothers and fathers had been hurt . . . their homes had been wrecked'. They 'had got the buzz . . . [they] were out to cause harm to the army'. But the Official leadership did not believe that a military campaign was in the offing; instead volunteers were given permission for a limited number of retaliatory attacks on the British Army.

The problem for Goulding's organization was that in Northern Ireland reasons for retaliation were multiplying. In late July another Catholic civilian in Belfast was shot dead by troops. Approval was given for a retaliatory mine attack in Derry but then withdrawn, causing some local dissension. At an Army Council meeting held in Dublin's Dominican Friary, courtesy of radical priest Fr. Austin Flannery, McMillen asked for permission to kill three soldiers in response. The IRA men sat around a long table in a room dominated by a crucifix and a religious painting. One participant found the scene surreal:

There we were under a large cross, someone dying on a rock over there, and then any other business, and Billy McMillen . . . says we want permission for an operation, we want to execute three soldiers . . . we had a vote . . . we were like the Last Supper, and the big cross, and we all voting for the death of three fucking men, it couldn't happen anywhere else except Ireland.

Two gun and bomb attacks on the army followed, though no soldiers were killed.

By winter 1970 both IRA groups were carrying out gun and

bomb attacks without claiming them. The Provisionals' bombings came to light only when one of their members was killed in a premature explosion in September. To ensure Official volunteers did not carry out unauthorized operations 'weapons were not readily available to anyone . . . you had only two or three weapons floating about on the surface, the rest were in dumps that only two or three people could access. Very few people were able to take weapons without sanction.'

In Belfast Fianna members, boys and girls, learned a variety of bomb-making techniques. A basic nail bomb was developed, as McMillen explained to a reporter: 'You just wrap a couple of ounces of "jelly" around 30 or 40 nails and stick a fuse in it.' Grenades were tested inside a brick kiln in Beechmount, while there was a small shooting range in an Osman Street entry. Intelligence was built up on the British Army, the routes they travelled, their favourite resting places and the usual spots for their checkpoints. A support organization, the Auxiliaries, existed in every area where the Officials were organized. Sometimes these were men who would not have been recruited into the OIRA, though the 'Lower Falls Auxies were a serious team' led by 1940s IRA veterans. In Belfast both the Officials and the Provisionals also had to contend with a large group of non-aligned vigilantes, the Catholic Ex-Servicemen's Association, which had access to its own arms supplies. With 'one or two exceptions' OIRA members were forbidden to join British ex-servicemen's groups, but the two organizations occasionally created 'joint vigilante groups'.

Following the Falls curfew a number of defence committee vigilantes had been recruited into the Officials. One evening Joe McCann, OIRA leader in the Markets, asked Harry McKeown to wait near the Black Bull Pub for a young man. The man turned out to be Unionist hard-liner Major Ronald Bunting's son Ronnie, a former student and People's Democracy member. Recruits from Queen's University were attached to the Markets unit and McCann, as local O/C, was happy to recruit them. Some of his comrades were less sure, McKeown warning that 'those students are not like us, once they get their degree it will be up you and your politics'. McCann also encountered some disapproval for his recruitment of men with criminal backgrounds. Despite not hailing himself from the notoriously clannish Markets, McCann was accepted locally. Harry McKeown himself did not formally join the OIRA, as he now ran his own building firm, employing McCann 'when he turned up' and other OIRA members. He also allowed members to use his bungalow for billets and ferried people on active service in his Jaguar.

Most Official recruits in Belfast were working-class Catholic teenagers. Harry Donaghy, who joined the Fianna in 1970 at the age of 13, while aware of the difference between the Officials and Provisionals, felt that had he come from somewhere other than the Lower Falls he might have ended up in the other group. Volunteers were expected to be active in their local Republican Clubs, and Joe McCann himself was education officer of the Liam Mellows Club in the Markets. The OIRA also backed up Clubs' campaigns such as that for lower bus fares in Belfast. During November 1970 buses on the Falls were taken over by men who ordered conductors not to collect any fares and announced that 'people's buses' were in operation. The OIRA also continued fund-raising operations, stealing £4,600 from a bank in Strabane in September and £15,000 in what British Intelligence described as a 'well-planned' wages robbery in the Markets in November, shooting two security men in the process.

During November, fifteen OIRA members were arrested in Louth in possession of weapons and explosives, and a Dublin ASU member was sentenced to seven years in jail for the Wynn's Hotel robbery. In December Taoiseach Jack Lynch mooted the introduction of internment to deal with the threat of subversion. This was ostensibly in reaction to Garda intelligence that Saor Éire were planning to kidnap politicians, but the Officials claimed they were the real targets. Gardaí carried out raids on Officials in Kilkenny, Cork and Kerry. Meanwhile relations with the Provos continued to deteriorate. As Goulding drank with supporters in Dundalk after the Edentubber commemoration, shots were fired into Mark's Bar, narrowly missing him; the Provisionals were blamed, though it was felt that the shooting was not authorized by their leadership. In Belfast the Provos kept up a steady stream of abuse over the Officials' 'communist' politics. Describing them as the 'National Liberation Front', they complained about the 'evil' threat posed by 'trained agents' sent out by 'Marxist masterminds' to 'brainwash' young republicans. The rhetoric was accompanied by a renewal of physical clashes, particularly around rival paper sales. During December several Officials were taken from their homes at gunpoint in Ardoyne, held overnight and warned 'not to operate in the area'. After this 150 Officials, many of them armed, carried out a mass paper sale on the Whiterock Road, in the face of local Provisionals. The Provisionals, meanwhile, complained that their supporters in the Lower Falls were being beaten up.

Ironically it was action against the British Army that led to a fatal escalation of these clashes. Confrontations between young nationalists and the army in Belfast were now daily occurrences and the brutality of the troops alienated more and more Catholics. The OIRA carried out a number of attacks in response in Ardoyne and Ballymurphy. The Provos were upset about the Officials' action on what they considered their turf in Ballymurphy and tried to force an Official auxiliary, John McGuinness, to give them information about the whereabouts of arms. He was held down and shot in the neck, leaving him paralysed. The shooting was seen as a 'dirty, obscene' act and many wanted to retaliate for it. In Ballymurphy the OIRA continued to attack the Henry Taggart army base. Shortly afterwards a Ballymurphy Official was pistol-whipped by Provisionals and in retaliation the OIRA shot a local Provo in the arms and legs. Trouble spread to the Falls and two young Officials were kidnapped and beaten by a group of Provisionals in a disused chemist's shop in Albert Street. Two young Provos were then kidnapped by the OIRA and beaten. The Provisionals raided the Officials' Burning Embers Bar, where Sullivan was drinking with Paddy Devlin, and tried to burn it down. An emergency meeting of the OIRA command staff was being held in the Cracked Cup when 'the meeting place was hit with machine gun bullets, Thompson sub-machine guns both ends of the street, the place we were in, it was like raindrops falling on a tin roof'. Afterwards young OIRA members confronted Provisionals in Leeson Street and shot dead 26-year-old Charlie Hughes.

Talks between the two sides produced a truce. Seven hours later, however, a group of OIRA men who had spent the night on the mountains overlooking Belfast were coming down into Ballymurphy when they spotted Tom Cahill, a milkman and brother of leading Provo Joe Cahill, on his rounds. They shot and badly wounded him. The OIRA claimed that their men hadn't heard about the truce and it held, uneasily. An observer described the atmosphere as 'literally eerie. Knots of young and old men were gathered at all street corners, and even in broad daylight silent eye-to-eye confrontations seemed to be taking place.' The Officials claimed to greatly regret the death of Hughes and offered condolences to his family. But privately they felt the Provos had 'got their lesson'. One Official felt the Provos had been 'so naive, to think you can just walk in and fire bullets at somebody and then they'll run away crying, it just doesn't happen . . . it's sad, he was a good kid, Charlie Hughes, [he] should never have been put in that position'.

There were echoes of the Belfast violence elsewhere. In Bray, Costello led a group armed with iron bars in an attack on Provisional supporters. In some areas of rural Ulster, by contrast, relations remained relatively friendly even after the shootings in Belfast. In Tyrone both sides were 'neighbourly and polite' though not 'cordial' and in Lurgan and Portadown there was an uneasy 'mutual understanding'. During the spring there was a confrontation with the UVF after they raided an OIRA arms dump being stored in a house off the Antrim Road. The Officials kidnapped three loyalists from Sandy Row and threatened to shoot them if the weapons were not returned. The men were terrified, 'literally wetting themselves', but Joe McCann decided to release them. For one of the Officials present, talking to the prisoners was a 'road to Damascus' experience, as he discovered that the loyalists were 'working-class men like yourself'.

Street clashes continued between troops and nationalists, and the Provisionals killed a soldier in February 1971. From that point deadly violence escalated to a degree previously unseen. In Belfast the Officials carried out several attacks on troops, without claiming them; McMillen intimated to journalists that the Officials had killed one soldier in Ardoyne during February and another in Derry in early March. In April the OIRA sank a British naval motor launch, *The Stork*, off Baltimore, Co. Cork. They also blew up the British Ministry of Pensions Office on Cork's South Mall, claiming it was used for British Army recruitment. During May Fianna members stoned a Land Rover and drew troops into a chase; this culminated in an ambush in the Markets in which Corporal Robert Bankier was fatally wounded. The OIRA found that they had 'kind of stumbled into' an armed campaign with 'no great strategy, the Brits were coming in and causing havoc [and] you couldn't have sat and done nothing'.

In early July an open-air céilí was held by the Officials to commemorate the Falls curfew. Thousands of 'Óglaigh na hÉireann – Battle of the Falls 1970' badges were distributed. The event was also marked with violence: two soldiers were shot on the Falls, there was an attack on the army post at Tyrone House on the Malone Road, and the Fianna carried out dozens of nail bomb attacks on troops. Significantly, the Official IRA claimed these attacks and promised more, though the consensus among the organization's leadership was still that a 'revolutionary situation' had not yet developed. In a magazine interview Goulding outlined his thoughts on urban guerrilla warfare, drawing upon examples ranging from Black Hugh O'Neill's defence of Clonmel in the seventeenth century to the tactics of the Israeli Irgun and the Tupamaros in Uruguay. From his studies he had drawn a number of lessons. Firstly, there was a need to have at least passive support from the urban population, though through trade union activity this could be developed into a more active factor; 'it is not the same to attack a State with its full force intact as a State half paralysed with strikes'. Secondly, pointing to a failure of Connolly's Irish Citizen Army and the success of the IRA in Dublin during the War of Independence, he felt it was 'absurd' for the guerrilla to don a uniform out of a misplaced 'sense of chivalry'. Instead units should be disguised, mobile and attack without warning. Finally, he claimed that the helicopter and Ireland's 'bare' hills ruled out a successful rural guerrilla campaign.

In late July there were police raids directed at the Officials across the North, with 48 arrested including McGurran, Sullivan and McMillen. In early August the OIRA's Tyrone O/C Peter John Monaghan was also jailed. Among documents captured by the RUC during the raids was material relating to Britain, where the Officials were attempting to revamp their military structure. There were several new recruits through Clann na hÉireann, including some who had been active on the British left. Intelligence was also being gathered on the very lax security at army bases in England. One new recruit was Jim Flynn, a 26-year-old building worker from Crossmaglen. Flynn had contacted republicans in the Bristol area and met the Officials' main British organizer in Exeter railway station, where he offered his services to the movement.

The Officials were recruiting from smaller left-wing organizations at home as well. In Derry the Young Socialists were generally on good terms with the local OIRA, and during 1971 several of their activists joined the Officials. Young Socialist Terry Robson had become convinced that 'tiny groups of people scattered around the place [was] madness, if we are going to do anything . . . we will do it within an organization that has the capability of doing something'. Within months much of the Official organization in Derry was led by these new recruits. During July two men were shot dead by troops in Derry and the local OIRA were pressing for permission to retaliate. In order to maintain control over a growing unit, McGurran was moved up to Derry as a full-time organizer.

In early August, with the tempo of violence increasing, the OIRA claimed to have inflicted three fatalities on troops since May. As far as they were concerned the British could only 'blame themselves' for the deaths of their soldiers. Unlike the Provos, who were involved in much more widespread violence, the Officials reaffirmed that they were not engaging in an offensive campaign and were fully supporting the civil rights call to 'get back to the streets' in mass mobilizations. Such slogans became increasingly abstract after the night of Monday 9 August, when internment without trial was introduced in Northern Ireland. Hundreds of Catholic homes were raided and over 300 men arrested. The ghettos exploded and within four days 23 people were dead and hundreds injured as the North was engulfed in the worst violence since 1920. There were hijackings, burnings, bomb attacks and shootings, and thousands once again fled south. Five people were killed by the army in Ballymurphy alone on 9 August. Reports soon emerged of beatings and worse for those who had been interned. On the ground 'everyone just said fuck them, get into them . . . them bastards won't do that to our areas'. One of the biggest battles took place on Tuesday 10 August in the Markets, where Joe McCann and other volunteers occupied the Inglis Bakery and engaged in gunfire with a large force of troops. At one point the British announced that the gunmen had been trapped and killed, only to be embarrassed when it was discovered all had escaped. Loyalists had joined in the fighting, attacking nationalist areas. On the night of 12 August there were gun battles between the Officials and the UVF on the Grosvenor Road. On Friday morning the British Army reoccupied the Lower Falls in strength after severe gun battles with the OIRA. The Officials broadcast warnings of army and loyalist movements on Radio Free Belfast, which was being run from a variety of locations across the city. The ferocity of the fighting saw the Officials and Provisionals thrown into ad hoc cooperation in Belfast. On internment night both Officials and Provos were engaged in almost continuous exchanges of fire with the UVF in the Springhill/Springmartin area. Members warned each other of troop movements and 'pitched in' when the other organization was engaging the enemy. The first British soldier killed in Tyrone died in a joint Official/ Provisional ambush. On occasion both organizations there swapped ammunition and explosives.

Internment also marked the point when both republican groups 'turned into substantial organizations'. Recruitment to the Officials soared, especially in areas where they were already the main organization, and even in weaker areas like Ballymurphy there was a substantial influx. Thousands of Catholics and Protestants left or were forced from their homes and it became almost impossible to work any longer in the 'wrong' area; contacts between the two communities broke down almost totally.

In the aftermath of internment Costello oversaw the setting up of a small active service unit composed of McCann, Anthony Dornan and another Belfast Official. McCann's legend was growing, with a photograph of him during the Inglis Bakery battle published in *Life* magazine and also featured as an iconic *United Irishman* front page. McCann and several other OIRA members who were on the run were living in the Omeath area of Co. Louth, a traditional holiday destination for Belfast Catholics. After internment the Officials were given access to caravans there and McCann's wife and children moved to the area, but McCann regularly returned to Belfast. He dyed his hair blond and wore glasses, but still took risks, on one occasion walking his pet wolfhound around an army base near Albert Street to boost local morale. His attitude was evident when he and a comrade were going to see the movie *Soldier Blue*. While his friend studied opening times, McCann drew a handgun and opened fire on a nearby army checkpoint. Plans of movie watching were abandoned as McCann ran off laughing, his comrade roaring: 'You mad bastard, what are you doing!' Many who met McCann concurred with Padraig Yeates that he was 'an incredible character, the only genuine hero I ever met out of the Northern troubles'. But some felt he 'lacked discipline' and wasn't a team player.

In the months after internment gun and bomb attacks were general across the North. In late August the OIRA claimed to have killed four soldiers in attacks in Ardoyne, Albert Street and on the Springfield Road. Volunteers remembered 'things got a bit haywire, [there was] open warfare . . . weapons [were] left on street corners, in cars overnight, easily accessed . . . 24 hours a day, people driving and walking about looking for targets'. Teams of teenage boys and girls operating in couples left dozens of small incendiary devices in shops, bars and restaurants in Belfast city centre. The Fianna also carried weapons and scouted ahead of attacks. Targets for OIRA bombs included council offices, customs posts, pubs and shops that served soldiers, police stations and army bases. The OIRA killed a soldier in a landmine attack near Newry on 6 September. On 21 September they killed another in a sniping attack on Bligh's Lane army base in Derry. Off-duty soldiers were ambushed in pubs in Belfast city centre. For those involved there was little time for reflection on politics: 'Strategy didn't come into it, it was a day-by-day thing, [you] didn't have time to stop and think.' Activists on the run 'used to meet in the morning, decide what was going to happen . . . just what you were going to do that day and where you were going to sleep that night . . . all up and go every morning'.

On 22 September two Official Fianna members, 18-year-old Rose Curry and 17-year-old Gerard O'Hare, were blown up while preparing a mine in a house on Merrion Street. Curry's brother Sean remembered:

I had just left my mother's home, my girlfriend Eileen had come in and I was on the run so I wasn't at home much. We were going for a drink in the Old House, maybe a five-minute walk. We were just in the bar when we heard the explosion going up the stairs and we thought Jesus, I wonder who that was? There was so many explosions going on then. We had sat down and a friend of mine came in . . . Harry Hyland, and he was ashen, and he called me up and said you'd better get down to your house I think that's your Rose and Gerard O'Hare. Then it came to me, I had passed them fifteen minutes before, she was pushing a pram, and she waved and said see you later.

Curry, whose father John had been interned in August, was the first female republican to be killed in Northern Ireland. Gerard O'Hare also came from a republican family, his father Jimmy 'Skewbald' O'Hare having been interned during the 1940s. Eight thousand people followed their cortège after a Fianna colour party had fired volleys over the coffins.

On 5 October OIRA volunteers disguised as workmen delivered building materials to an army post on Cupar Street, which was being rebuilt following a bomb attack. The men were searched but after nothing was found they were given access to the post. Once inside they placed a bomb under the building material and left. It exploded, bringing the building down on the soldiers, killing one, and injuring several.

OIRA training was intensified with a 'semi-permanent' camp in Kerry and others in Dunleer, the Galtee Mountains, Wicklow and Galway. The development and storage of weapons was a dangerous business with the new Munster-based quartermaster losing a hand in an accidental explosion. There was increasing pressure on finance, with men on the run and in prison. At least £600 a week was needed for prisoners' dependents alone, and there was a huge increase in armed crime. During August the OIRA had taken £4,900 in a bank raid on the Ormeau Road and £15,000 in a raid on a dairy in Dublin. Banks and post offices had only rudimentary security, and were targeted for substantial sums, while 'bookmakers were usually handier when you wanted money in a hurry'. As a Southern volunteer recalls, this activity had attractions beyond the purely practical: 'It's impossible to describe the buzz that people actually get from it, OK, you're doing it for a cause, but still . . . to be in a car, come out of the bank, pick up the people, have a police car coming after you, you're speeding, relying on one driver to get you through . . .'

Leading Officials publicly offered the view that bank robbery was justified if the money was going to further the aims of socialism. The resurgence of nationalist feeling in the South meant that on occasion people carrying out robberies 'for the North' were actually applauded by customers. This attitude was also present in the Irish security forces. When a GHQ member was moving some rifles from Derry to Donegal he was stopped at a Garda checkpoint; the Garda looked in the boot and 'couldn't have missed' the rifles, but still waved the OIRA man on.

Life on the run brought various kinds of pressure for those involved; a Belfast activist recalls having to lie to his own family about the date of his wedding. It also brought problems for their organizations. As more men came south the pressure to find them work and billets increased. Transport union leader Michael Mullen assisted the Officials with this, though he often found that the men failed to show up for the work he'd arranged. Some volunteers drank heavily and caused trouble, and there was always the danger that they would dip into robbery proceeds for personal use. Dundalk's proximity to the border and the fact that many Northern republicans settled there meant that it developed a wild reputation, being nicknamed 'El Paso'. Mark's Bar in the town was an important rendezvous for the OIRA, used extensively by those on the run from the North. Dundalk-born British soldier Private Robert Benner was picked up by the Officials when he was visiting his fiancée during November 1971; he was shot dead and his body dumped near the border.

There was shock in left-wing circles in Dublin when Young Socialist Peter Graham was murdered in late October by Saor Éire members who were demanding he reveal the whereabouts of money and weapons. In fact most of the arms under his control had already been given to the Provisionals. It was not known at the time who killed Graham and his funeral saw a provocative speech from the British-Pakistani Trotskyist Tariq Ali, who warned that there would be revenge for Graham's death. In reality Graham's comrades had no way of retaliating against his killers. The Officials, who were being blamed by some, met one of Graham's friends to assure him they were not involved in the killing. During October the Officials were embarrassed when they held a press conference in Dublin featuring David Seaman, a former British Paratrooper who claimed to be a spy with information on British undercover activities in the South. It transpired that Seaman was a psychiatric patient and a fantasist.

Internment was taking its toll on the OIRA. In early October Jim Sullivan was captured in Belfast. Seamus Lynch was caught later that month and arrived in Long Kesh having been beaten 'black and blue'. Over 100 OIRA members had been interned and the British considered that they had been 'particularly hard hit'. With McMillen in Dublin, Bobby McKnight took over as O/C in Belfast, living a precarious life on the run. Paddy Devlin, now an MP for the new Social Democratic and Labour Party (SDLP), drove McKnight around Belfast, using his status as a politician to get him through roadblocks.

During the winter life in most Northern towns was over-shadowed by the intensifying Provisional 'economic' bombing campaign. The Officials condemned 'irresponsible bombing of public buildings during working hours', which they predicted would lead to civilian deaths. Sectarian tension meanwhile grew more intense. After Provisional bombs killed two people on the Shankill, workers fought each other in Gallagher's tobacco factory. Fifteen Catholics were killed in a loyalist bomb attack on McGurk's Bar in North Queen Street in early December. A week later four Protestants, including two children, were killed by a Provisional bomb at a furniture shop on the Shankill. OIRA attitudes to their rivals hardened again, with Seamus Costello stating publicly that 'we have no common ground, good, bad or indifferent, with the Provisionals'.

In contrast to the Provos, the Officials tried to target the property of establishment figures. The homes of businessmen on Belfast's exclusive Malone Road were burnt down by the OIRA while their families were held at gunpoint. During December the Officials blew up or burnt down property owned by unionists in Belfast, Derry and Newry. They also shot dead 65-year-old Senator Jack Barnhill at his home in Strabane, before destroying his home with a bomb. It was the first killing of a politician in Northern Ireland since 1922. The Official leadership declared that 'while workers . . . are subject to British military atrocities . . . the leading proponents of that policy must expect reprisals against them'. The impossibility of waging a 'clean' campaign was apparent, however, when an attack on Royal Marines in Newry saw one soldier badly wounded but several local women also hit by OIRA gunfire.

So as the new year began the Official leadership faced a dilemma.

Unlike the Provisionals, who declared that 1972 would be the 'year of victory', the OIRA made clear that a military victory was impossible. But the military situation made it difficult to achieve progress on other fronts. As a GHQ member recalls, 'there was so much to retaliate for, there was so much defence, we couldn't keep up, we were effectively in an unplanned chaotic armed struggle without having decided to be in one'. The idea of using military attacks strictly as back-up to a political campaign of civil disobedience, what one Official supporter described as 'mass civilian agitation, tempered with selective and non-sectarian military action', was unrealistic. A document captured by the British also pointed towards increased concerns within the OIRA over the impact of security measures: 'The entire security of our organisation is in danger. This emphasises that we cannot survive for much longer with present losses of men and stuff; only the ending of internment and repression will work here.'

Another cause for concern was the loyalist backlash. The UVF and local paramilitary groups were growing rapidly. Thousands of Protestant youths were becoming part of 'Tartan gangs' that clashed with nationalists and carried out sectarian attacks on Catholics. There was increasing violence in towns like Lurgan, where the family home of OIRA internee Martin O'Hagan was burnt out in early 1972. A local Tartan gang member was kneecapped by the OIRA in retaliation for attacks on Catholics. There was undeniable support for wider anti-Protestant attacks: in Strabane the killing of Barnhill had been seen as sectarian and was 'very popular' as a result. But McMillen and his staff are recalled as having been 'intensely concerned that anything they did could not be construed as an attack on the Protestant people'.

There was a strong perception in some areas that Dublin was not supplying adequate arms and equipment. Many units were still operating with Lee-Enfields, Thompsons and Sten guns. One estimate of the OIRA's armament in Derry city was two M1 carbines, two Thompsons, one Sten, two Lee Enfields, a Garand, a .303 hunting rifle, an SLR and a few handguns. Joe McCann complained that not enough 'gear' was being moved north, on one occasion getting into a shouting match with the Officials' Quartermaster General in Gardiner Street; his militancy led to him being the subject of numerous disciplinary hearings, which he often ignored. In north Armagh and Tyrone, units began raiding the homes of soldiers in the Ulster Defence Regiment (UDR) to capture SLRs and Sterlings. However, some older volunteers in these areas were happier with a more restrained policy. A Tyrone Provisional recalled that 'the typical Provo in 1971 or '72 was 18, 19, 20 years of age while at the same time the typical Official [in Tyrone] was maybe . . . 35 or 36'. Age and having families made a marked difference to most people's willingness to take risks.

In Derry the violence had developed a distinctive momentum of its own, with crowds of young men and teenagers known as the Derry Young Hooligans ritually fighting battles with soldiers on the edge of the Bogside. One member of the Derry command staff recalled:

[It] used to remind me of the Zulu warriors, standing up at the Roundabout in the Creggan . . . we could see the troops fighting down in William Street . . . Saturday at 3 o'clock like clockwork. You'd have Martin McGuinness and the boys over there, and the Stickies, which were in the majority at the time up on the hill. They'd be setting up operations, so we're standing there, do this and do that, move them in etc.

The existence of the no-go area of Free Derry gave the OIRA considerable leeway. The local OIRA usually patrolled Creggan in cars and kept weapons in these or in a dump behind a local chemist's shop. In January 1972 a 21-year-old British soldier visiting his fiancée was captured by the Officials in the Bogside. After questioning him they let him go unharmed and issued a statement explaining that killing the soldier would have served no purpose. The Provisionals responded by denouncing the Officials for their 'diabolical' action and accusing them of letting down the people of Free Derry.

On 22 January a civil rights protest at nearby Magilligan Strand had seen serious army violence and NICRA had called another march for Sunday 30 January in Derry. Malachy McGurran assured civil rights activist Bridget Bond that there would be no OIRA activity before or during the march. On the day of the march almost all the OIRA's weapons were left in Creggan because there were fears that the British might attempt an incursion there. Most members went on the demonstration unarmed. However, at an early stage two people were shot and wounded by troops and OIRA members took a .303 rifle from a car in Columkille Court and fired one shot in response. Later Paratroopers burst into Rossville Street and opened fire, killing 13 people and fatally wounding another. In Rossville Flats courtyard an OIRA man 'lost his temper' after seeing people shot and fired at troops using a handgun. Later that evening OIRA volunteer Mickey Doherty was slightly wounded in an exchange of fire with soldiers.

Across nationalist Ireland the response to 'Bloody Sunday' was ferocious, with three days of strikes, marches and rallies. At a demonstration outside the British Embassy in Dublin's Merrion Square, Seamus Costello announced that 'notice to quit' was being served on the occupants of the building. There were baton charges and attempts to rush the building with McGurran warning the marchers that the Gardaí would perform the same role as the Paras if the power of the establishment in Dublin was threatened. OIRA members tried to blow down the embassy door. One remembered:

We were in Omeath and Costello phoned us to go down to Dublin and organize a bit of turmoil . . . students told us that they were going to carry coffins, it was decided to try and put something inside one of the coffins, get as close to the embassy door as we could, it took a bit of doing, the coffin came back and forward to us a few times! . . . a few [coffins] were placed against the door, [Joe] McCann myself and two other guys put it up. It ignited, but the crowd had already attacked the Guards and everybody started to scatter. We hadn't planned our getaway too well and I ran back to the Shelbourne [and] into the arms of the Guards, who battered the crap out of me.

After two more days of marches and rioting the building was finally burnt down. Shortly after Bloody Sunday the OIRA killed former Para David Seaman and dumped his body in Armagh. They also killed Thomas McCann, a 19-year-old British soldier from Drimnagh in Dublin who had been home on leave. His body was found near the Monaghan–Fermanagh border.

Not surprisingly, Bloody Sunday led to further recruitment to the Officials. As one recruit explained, 'Bloody Sunday did it for me . . . I was the right age at the wrong time!' Weighing up the option of joining the Officials or the Provos he reasoned that he wanted to defend his local area but not destroy Belfast city centre. For his first operation he was given an M1 carbine and told to 'have a blatter' at an army post.

Defence of their localities was a strong motivation for many OIRA recruits. When one Official prisoner was told to go to an education class, he responded: 'Education for fucking what? I joined to defend my area and you told me I could.' After the Officials in Belfast's Unity Flats fired on loyalist rioters they explained that while they wished to 'avoid sectarian conflict' they had to 'protect the people of the area'. Other young recruits in this period were also swayed by day-to-day experience. One Newry teenager remembered 'getting the odd dig from the Brits, you can't go into town if you're with a girlfriend [or] you're humiliated, you're getting stopped going to school and your lunch box is being checked and they drop it, there [was] this build-up all the time of an anger'. Joining the OIRA offered him a 'sense of defiance and strength and power'.

The Official leadership had decided prior to Bloody Sunday that 'retaliatory action must be extended to include the assassination of top political personnel, the kidnapping of same and the destruction of property'. In Lurgan the Officials raided the home of a former Unionist mayor of the town and shot him while he was in his bath. He was dragged outside while his house was burnt down. The Army Council gave the go-ahead for an attack on the headquarters of the Paras at Aldershot in Hampshire. On the morning of Tuesday 22 February a blue Ford Cortina car, its boot packed with 200lb of explosives stolen from a quarry in Somerset, was driven into the base and parked outside the officers' mess. At 12.45 p.m. it exploded, flattening the front of the building and killing five women cleaners, a gardener and an army padre. The Officials initially claimed that they had killed at least twelve officers. They expressed regret for the civilian dead but argued that responsibility lay 'totally with the British authorities' while the attack showed the 'capacity of the IRA to strike back at the very hearts of those who impose a reign of terror on the Irish people'. Back in Dublin the Gardaí moved quickly, arresting Goulding, Ryan, Garland and Tony Heffernan, among others. But just three days after Aldershot, John Taylor, the Unionist Minister for Home Affairs, was shot six times in the head and body as he sat in his car in Armagh; miraculously he survived. The Officials were unapologetic about the shooting of the 'arch-bigot' Taylor. Goulding later reflected that Prime Minister Brian Faulkner might have been an even more enticing target, but that 'availability of target matters too'. The OIRA planned both 'prestige type' operations to illustrate the effectiveness of their targeted reprisals. On the day Taylor was shot the Officials bombed an army post in Dungiven, Co. Derry and claimed to have killed a soldier. At the end of the month the OIRA shot dead Police Sergeant Thomas Morrow in Newry after he responded to a hoax call. Mistakes, such as Aldershot, could not be dwelt on, a volunteer recalls: 'You couldn't step back . . . it was a dangerous thing to introduce doubt; if you introduce doubt then where the fuck do you end up?'

In early March British police arrested Noel Jenkinson, Finbar Kissane and Michael Duignan in London in connection with the Aldershot bombing; Jenkinson, 42 years of age from a Protestant background in Co. Meath, was identified as the key suspect. He had emigrated in the 1950s and been involved in communist and Maoist politics. During 1969 he joined the IRA in London. The police had traced the three men's involvement through the engine number of the Ford Cortina used in the attack. The men had been instructed to steal a car but had instead used a false driving licence to hire one. The same licence had been used in a case involving a car accident during 1971, and once the engine number was known the police were able to trace those who hired the car. Jenkinson was sentenced to 30 years in jail for the Aldershot bombing, with his co-defendants receiving lesser terms. By late 1972 there were ten OIRA men in jail in Britain.

One response to the upsurge of violence after Bloody Sunday was the abolition of Stormont by the British government and its replacement by direct rule – a move which, the Officials argued, simply consolidated British control. After the abolition of Stormont the Provisional IRA declared a 72-hour ceasefire, but the Officials continued attacks, shooting soldiers in Newry, Derry and Belfast. During an attack on troops in Leeson Street, a 24-year-old mother of one, Bernadette Hyndman, was shot dead. She had stepped out of her doorway as a gunman opened fire and was hit twice. During late February in Derry 16-year-old Official Fianna member Gerry Doherty was killed accidentally while using a defective weapon. In early March the OIRA in the city killed UDR officer Marcus McCausland. In areas where they were strong the OIRA had also been carrying out punishment attacks on 'anti-social' elements. There was controversy when a 15-year-old girl had her head shaved and was tarred and feathered on the Lower Falls after being accused by the Officials of informing. In response to the criticism they declared that 'she was lucky' that they had not shot her. Better publicity was derived from actions such as the hijacking of coal trucks near Newry. Most of the coal was emptied out on to the road for locals to collect, an OIRA statement saying the action was in 'support of the striking coal miners of England' and warning 'strikebreakers . . . that similar treatment will be meted out to them unless they cease these activities immediately'. This and similar OIRA actions led British Prime Minister Ted Heath to inquire if that organization had 'schemes to promote industrial action' in Northern Ireland along the 'lines of the recent miners' strike'. He was reassured that the sectarian divisions among workers made republican-inspired strike action of that scale unlikely.

In early April the Officials carried out an attack on a UDR patrol near Cookstown in an action designed to 'teach these bully boys a lesson'. On 10 April they killed two soldiers with a booby-trap bomb in Derry. In Belfast, however, there was a gradual reduction in offensive activities, the aim being to scale down activities in areas where there was 'relative calm' in the hope that 'peaceful, mass civil disobedience' could be revived. Any hope of this was soon shattered. Joe McCann's status as one of the most wanted men in the North had not stopped him regularly returning to Belfast; as one of his comrades recalls, 'He was an accident waiting to happen.' He attended the wedding of a close friend, who was also on the run, on the Falls in early April. Shortly afterwards McCann and a comrade had a narrow escape from the Special Branch in Belfast city centre. At 3.15 p.m. on 15 April British Army radios buzzed with reports that in 'Joy St/Hamilton St man shot maybe JOE McCANN details later'; confirmation soon followed that McCann was indeed dead. He had been due to meet a comrade in Kelly's Cellars pub but was spotted by detectives walking through the Markets. They called in Paratroopers who shot McCann several times as he tried to escape. As news of his death emerged, Belfast exploded with the worst violence since internment night. The British Army claimed that they were attacked on 84 separate occasions in the Divis Flats area alone in the two days after McCann's death. The Officials patrolled openly in Turf Lodge, driving around the area in a Land Rover bearing the legend 'Official IRA – mobile patrol'. A soldier was killed by the OIRA at Durham Street, and in Derry two soldiers were killed by the OIRA in separate sniping attacks. In Newry a detective was shot five times in the head and body after being lured by the OIRA into an ambush.

McCann's funeral was one of the biggest republican events in Belfast to that date. Over 5,000 people walked behind the cortège led by 21 OIRA companies marching in formation. In his oration Goulding warned that 'those who are responsible for the terrorism that is Britain's age-old reaction to Irish demands will be the victims of that terrorism, paying richly in their own red blood for their crimes and the crimes of their imperial masters'. Four MPs – Paddy Devlin, Paddy Kennedy, Paddy O'Hanlon and Bernadette

Senior Sinn Féin members outside Gardiner Place party headquarters, Dublin, early 1960s (Workers' Party of Ireland)

Roy Johnston, whose communist background and intellectual force were influential in the development of left republicanism in the 1960s; in 1966, when this photo was taken, he was IRA Director of Education

IRA volunteers training, Republic of Ireland, 1966; the photo appeared in a one-off republican publication called *The Separatist*

Dublin Housing Action protest, late 1960s. Leading Dublin IRA activist Jim Monaghan is third from front, facing camera (Padraig Yeates)

In Mark's Bar, Dundalk, late 1960s: Mark McLoughlin, Billy McBurney, unidentified, Billy McMillen and Paddy Devlin (Mary McMillen)

Civil rights march, Derry, 5 October 1968. Johnnie White, local
IRA officer, is second from left, carrying banner; to his right are
Nationalist Party MP Eddie McAteer and Republican Labour
MP Gerry Fitt (RTÉ Archives)

The reinterment of Peter Barnes and James McCormack, near Mullingar, July 1969 – a
stressful occasion for the Sinn Féin / IRA leadership. Cathal Goulding stands to the
left of the firing party (*Irish Press* Archives)

Joe McCann, photographed by police after his arrest in August 1969
(*The Plough*)

The Sinn Féin Ard Fheis at which the movement split, Dublin, January 1970.
Seamus and Maelíosa Costello are seated at back; Malachy McGurran is at front centre,
in profile (Workers' Party of Ireland)

Official Easter Commemoration, Dublin 1971. Marchers include Tony Gregory (centre, in dark polo neck), Margaret O'Leary (in white polo neck) and Liz Doyle (in cardigan and skirt) (Private collection)

The September 1971 cover of the *United Irishman*, featuring the iconic photo of Joe McCann during the Battle of the Markets the previous month (*United Irishman*)

The funeral of Official Fianna members Rose Curry and Gerard O'Hare, Falls Road, Belfast, September 1971 (Sean Curry)

OIRA members in Turf Lodge, Belfast, following the death of Joe McCann, April 1972; the jeep is marked 'Mobile Patrol – Official IRA' (*Irish Press* Archive)

Des O'Hagan, Tomás Mac Giolla and
Sean Garland in Moscow, October 1973
(*United Irishman*)

Bernadette Devlin MP and Galway
Official Sinn Féin activist Liz McManus,
early 1970s (John Carlos)

Female OIRA members, Bogside, Derry, May 1972 (Eamon Melaugh)

Mick Ryan and Cathal Goulding, mid-1970s (Private collection)

Billy McMillen giving the speech at Bodenstown, July 1973, in which he declared: 'We stand not on the brink of victory, but on the brink of sectarian disaster' (Mary McMillen)

Eoin Ó Murchú addressing an Irish Republican Clubs rally, Philadelphia, 1973 (Eoin Ó Murchú)

Devlin – attended the funeral. Imprisoned UVF leader Gusty Spence offered 'deepest and profoundest sympathy' to McCann's widow: 'He was a soldier of the Republic and I a Volunteer of Ulster and we made no apology for what we are . . . Joe once did a good turn indirectly and I never forgot him for his humanity.' Spence was referring to the release of the three men captured in Sandy Row during 1971.

Despite Goulding's threats the OIRA leadership was seriously considering calling a halt to offensive activities. They had already stated that RUC and UDR officers were not to be targeted except in clear cases of retaliation. Events in Derry in May 1972 brought this question to a head. Ranger William Best, a 19-year-old soldier, had returned home to Derry on leave from Germany. He ignored a warning from the Officials that he should leave Creggan. The OIRA had released a captured soldier in January but after Bloody Sunday this was unlikely to happen again. On 19 May Manus Deery, a 15-year-old, was killed by a British soldier. Deery's death sealed Ranger Best's fate: he was picked up the next day and shot dead. The killing sparked a major controversy in Derry, with angry protest marches to the Officials' headquarters and a mass meeting of 2,000 people at which Johnnie White was shouted down when he attempted to explain the Official position. Some of the reaction to Best's death was genuine shock at the killing of a local youth who had taken no part in British operations in Northern Ireland, but it was also politically driven, especially by the Catholic Church. Local priests stated that the OIRA were being 'used by international communism' and were not welcome in Derry. The Officials responded that they were 'not a Catholic organization'. The Provisionals jumped on the bandwagon, demanding the 'Marxist' Officials get out of Derry; 'Better Dead than Red' graffiti appeared in the Bogside. Johnnie White was summoned south to answer charges over the killing and was surprised to find real aggression directed towards him. While those in Derry felt that they had been fighting a clean war – 'it was us against the state rather than against the guys on the other side of the fence' – others had a more dubious view, seeing them as 'the Wild Bunch . . .

who were even at the best of times likely to do anything'. Some at GHQ felt that McGurran had become 'the spokesperson for Derry' and his judgement had been marred as a result.

A meeting of local O/Cs and members of GHQ was called to discuss a possible ceasefire at Mornington on the weekend of 27–28 May. The fallout from the Best killing was one factor: it was seen as reflecting a decline in nationalist tolerance for violence, while Aldershot highlighted the political pitfalls of military actions. But the growth of sectarianism was the major issue. The loyalist Vanguard movement led by William Craig was leading a general strike in protest at Stormont's suspension. The strike had won mass support among Protestants but was also accompanied by widespread intimidation. The Ulster Defence Association (UDA), which had emerged from various loyalist vigilante groups, and was not illegal, had held its first mass rallies during May, at which thousands of masked men paraded in military fashion. The number of Catholic victims of sectarian assassination was rising: 40 people would die during May alone. Despite their condemnations the Officials felt they were being tarred by association with the Provos' bombs, which killed fourteen civilians during the spring. Within the Dublin OIRA the view that any continuance of the campaign necessitated getting 'rid of the Provos . . . otherwise you were going to get involved in a war that you had no control over', amounted to an argument in favour of cessation. Ó Murchú recalls supporting the proposed ceasefire because 'the thing had gone completely overboard, defence and retaliation had meant that there was no stop to military action, there was no strategy, it was continually reactive'. At a very sullen gathering only Johnnie White argued completely against a ceasefire; while Costello was felt to be less enthusiastic he was not vocal in his opposition. Frustration was expressed by J. P. Mullan from Tyrone, who asked: 'Who can we shoot?' The answer was Special Branch officers, who would not be covered by the ceasefire terms. On 29 May the OIRA publicly announced an 'indefinite ceasefire' and stated that this step had been taken to avoid descent into full-scale sectarian civil war. They claimed that the move had come following representations by the

Republican Clubs. The statement demanded that all internees be released, that there be an amnesty for all political prisoners and that troops be withdrawn from the streets. The ceasefire was conditional and the OIRA maintained the 'right to defend any area under aggressive attack by the British military or by sectarian forces from either side'.

In Belfast the ceasefire 'went down like a lead balloon'. Many felt that 'we were going to look like wimps in the face of the Brits and cowards in the face of the Provos'. One Official prisoner remembers arguing against the ceasefire because he thought 'it was coming at the wrong time, and in some respects for the wrong reasons: [we] had allowed the Provos to set the agenda, we had become a bit inward looking and at the same time their sectarianism was a reason for our ceasefire'. A further problem was that 'there was practically no consultation with us as prisoners'. A myriad of arguments were used to sell the ceasefire, many of which presented it as a purely tactical move to gain a breathing space and win prisoner releases. As an OIRA officer recalls:

I was in Long Kesh at the time. It was more or less accepted. It was put across mostly as a tactic, that we would carry on with whatever activities we wanted to carry on with but this was a tactic to give us time to reorganize. It was reckoned that the Official movement had never been at war and to call a ceasefire was just an exercise; as long as the Brits kept doing stuff we could keep doing stuff back against them. Most people accepted it and a lot of stuff did go on afterwards.

One of the desired effects of the ceasefire took place: 75 Official internees were released in early June and the rest by the autumn. There was a view that the Provos were going to run themselves into the ground and that the OIRA, better organized and disciplined, would then renew the struggle.

A number of volunteers who opposed the ceasefire left the OIRA. Most who were unhappy simply dropped out, while a few, such as Francis Hughes in south Derry, eventually joined the Provisionals. There was particular dissatisfaction among the Belfast

Fianna. The Official Fianna had their own dumps, were carrying out their own operations and gained a reputation as a 'third army'. A meeting was organized in Dundalk between the Officials' GHQ and Belfast Fianna to discuss widespread rumours of unauthorized robberies and of feuding with Provos. The GHQ officers didn't want operations that led to 'young fellas getting shot', because while for a brief period the victim might 'be a hero . . . in ten years' time there's nobody that'll want to know about them'. GHQ staff also counselled restraint in dealing with their rivals, because though it might be tempting 'to hit some stupid trouble-some bastard . . . a row with a Provo is doing nothing to free Ireland'. The Fianna representatives expressed frustration that they were being criticized for doing things that the OIRA were also doing. One officer felt that the OIRA were happy enough to use the youngsters, but 'if they were caught, it's them Fianna again'.

In fact very little changed in terms of OIRA operations for some time. In Belfast particularly the OIRA was *more* active militarily than it had been in the month before the ceasefire. But after the ceasefire many Officials reported an increase in petty harassment by Provos who were calling them 'rusty guns' and accusing them of surrender. On 19 June Provisionals raided the Cracked Cup and in a scuffle 37-year-old Desmond Mackin was shot in the legs with a machine gun. Witnesses alleged that the Provos prevented aid from reaching Mackin, who bled to death. Mackin was not a member of the OIRA but was from a well-known republican family. His brother Brendan, an Official, had just taken part in a hunger strike in Crumlin Road and his son Dessie was a member of the Provos. His death led to considerable bitterness, and low-level confrontations between the rival groups continued on a day-to-day basis: 'You couldn't let anything go.' The Officials felt that some Provos, such as the Lower Falls O/C Brendan Hughes, did their best to avoid conflict, but they regarded many of the other Provos in that area as 'low-life' types.

The Provisionals called their own ceasefire on 26 June and several of their leaders were flown to talks with the British government. The OIRA criticized the Provos for dealing with the British and argued the talks were 'useless and irrelevant'. For a fortnight there was relative peace on the streets until the Provos resumed their campaign after confrontations in Lenadoon. The breakdown of the ceasefire led to intense violence, with over 70 people killed in the next month. In Belfast OIRA units were involved in dozens of shootings. On the night of 10 July they were involved in a three-hour gun battle with the UDA in the Lower Falls. The OIRA also killed two loyalists on the Grosvenor Road after they had stopped them at one of their roadblocks: the loyalists mistook the Officials for fellow Protestant paramilitaries and boasted that they had just killed a Catholic, whose body was dumped in the boot of their car. On 25 July the OIRA shot dead a Protestant, Arthur Kenna, who was part of a mob trying to invade Roden Street. The Officials also suffered several losses: 14-year-old Fianna member David McCafferty was killed by the British Army in Springhill while trying to drag a local priest to safety after he'd been shot, and two days later 17-year-old Official Gerald Gibson was shot dead by troops in Andersonstown. On 14 July Ted Brady, an officer in the Beechmount unit, was shot dead by soldiers during a battle in Oldpark. In Strabane 18-year-old Tobias Molloy, an Official Fianna member, died after being struck by a rubber bullet during a confrontation with troops. During his funeral, which featured an OIRA firing party, soldiers fired rubber bullets at the cortège and rioting broke out. Later that night the OIRA shot a soldier in Strabane. Billy McBurney was shot by loyalists in an assassination attempt, targeted because the British Army had alleged publicly that he was the OIRA's Finance Officer. Joseph Rosato, father of Official activist Tony Rosato, was shot dead in north Belfast. Initially the Officials blamed loyalists but suspicion soon fell on the Provisionals, who had perhaps been intending an attack on his son. Responding to the deaths of five of its supporters, the OIRA warned that 'retribution' would be exacted, but without civilian casualties.

But the month would be remembered for the deaths of 9 people, 7 of them civilians, and the injuries to 130 others caused by the Provisional IRA on 21 July, which became known as 'Bloody

Friday'. Standing on the Falls that morning a group of Officials speculated on the number of familiar faces driving by and commented that something big was up. Twenty bombs detonated within an hour, bringing havoc to Belfast city centre. The Officials argued that while the 'flame of sectarianism' had originally been 'lit by the British government and maintained by Orangeism' it was now 'being fanned by every bomb'. The Officials still claimed to respect the 'courage and sincerity' of ordinary Provisionals, but they warned that the inevitable outcome of the bombing campaign would be civil war. Bloody Friday gave the excuse that the British needed to penetrate Belfast and Derry's no-go areas. On 31 July, Operation Motorman took place, with 1,500 troops backed up by 300 armoured vehicles reoccupying Free Derry. Neither the Officials nor the Provisionals attempted to resist militarily. The Derry Officials instead tried to launch a campaign of civil disobedience. On the day of Motorman nine people were killed by a Provisional IRA bomb in the village of Claudy in Co. Derry. The Officials lamented that the people of Claudy were 'lost, for many, many years to the Republican cause'. There were still contradictions in local attitudes. Nine more people died in a premature bomb explosion at Newry customs station. Three of the dead were Provisional IRA members, one of whom, Oliver Rowntree, had left the Officials earlier in the year. His brother Colman had remained with the OIRA, and as a result Rowntree's funeral had *both* Official and Provisional firing parties and an OIRA statement praised the 'brave volunteers' who had died in the explosion. But in Belfast confrontation continued after the killing of a Protestant man, James Neill. Neill and another man had been involved in a car crash on the Springfield Road. They were picked up by rival IRA patrols, with each organization taking a prisoner. The Provos decided Neill was a loyalist spy and killed him. The OIRA questioned their prisoner, judged him innocent and let him go, arguing there was 'absolutely no reason to kill this man'. The Provos then accused the Officials of cowardice and the OIRA responded that they would not take life in such an 'inane cowboy fashion'.

Around this period the manner in which some units of the

OIRA were operating began to worry Belfast members. From early 1972 an English criminal, Kenneth Littlejohn, had been active with a group of Officials in the south Down area. Littlejohn had been introduced through an OIRA member's relative as 'a guy who arranges bank robberies'. He took part in a number of raids in the area during the spring and his brother Keith also became involved. The group carried out a robbery at the Hillgrove Hotel in Monaghan, after which Gardaí discovered an arms dump and made arrests. One volunteer became very suspicious of Littlejohn, who incessantly argued for robberies in Dublin, 'as if [he] wanted to make a few waves'. He noticed that Littlejohn and his colleagues were wearing new clothes and socializing a lot. He refused to go on robberies with them, but other local Officials continued to vouch for the Englishman. Littlejohn constantly sought information about OIRA operations and often brought people on drinking sessions while not imbibing himself. On 18 September, 32-year-old Edmund Woolsey, the owner of the Ulster Hotel in Warrenpoint, was killed by a car bomb. Woolsey was a supporter of the OIRA and his death set alarm bells ringing. Woolsey's car had been stolen and the RUC informed him that it had been found and he could pick it up at Glassdrummond. When Woolsey went to collect his car he was killed and several of his companions injured by a booby-trap bomb. The suspicion grew that Littlejohn had set up Woolsey in the hope of killing members of the Officials.

During October the Littlejohn gang robbed £67,000 from the AIB in Dublin's Grafton Street, the biggest robbery in the state's history, but their triumph was short-lived as they were caught within a few weeks. At their trial the Littlejohns claimed that they had been sent to Ireland to infiltrate the OIRA, which, after Aldershot, British Intelligence services had decided was the most dangerous paramilitary organization. They also claimed that they were asked to kill Garland, Costello and Seán Mac Stíofáin. The Official who first suspected Littlejohn still doubts this account: 'I think [Littlejohn] was a bank robber . . . an opportunist [who] got involved with the IRA and realized he got kudos back home by reporting this [to] get himself out of trouble.' But British Intelligence knew that the Littlejohns were coming to Ireland and did not inform the Irish authorities, which suggests some pre-planning.

In late September 20-year-old Patricia McKay, an OIRA member from Divis Flats, was involved in a major gun battle on the Falls, during which a soldier and a Provisional were killed. Provo leader Brendan Hughes remembered:

During the fighting I ended up in the same small house as her. The Brits had us pinned down with heavy gunfire from the direction of Conway Mill. She insisted on moving out and making a break for it . . . my only regret at her being in the Official IRA was that I could not order her to sit tight.

As McKay broke cover she was gunned down. The Officials warned that there would be 'merciless reprisals'. However, the scope for such action was becoming much narrower. Very tight control was being exercised over the ability of local units to carry out attacks, one volunteer recalling 'you couldn't lift a screwdriver without the permission of the staff'. One of McKay's friends joined the Provisionals as a result. The leadership policy was not applied uniformly on the ground. On one occasion a local O/C was approached in a pub by volunteers who wanted permission to open fire on an army patrol. He argued that a pre-emptive attack was not justified and refused to sanction it. The men were leaving disappointed when a member of the IRA executive arrived and they asked his view; 'Ah, go on and give 'em a blatter,' was the response. On 16 October the British Army shot dead the Officials' Tyrone O/C John Pat Mullan and another volunteer, Hugh Herron, near Coagh. At Mullan's funeral Goulding warned that the men's deaths would 'not go un-avenged'. When there was no major retaliation, frustration increased. There was also irritation over the policy of not claiming attacks, which simply allowed the Provisionals to take the credit for them. As an OIRA member recalled, 'When somebody in one area did a job and it wasn't claimed, nobody in other areas knew who did it. There was a general feeling that nothing much was being done.'

Opposition to the ceasefire began to coalesce around Costello and was expressed at the IRA Convention held in a seafront mansion in Dalkey, Co. Dublin, in October 1972. While much of the criticism was based around military policy, some members – like Ronnie Bunting, now O/C of Turf Lodge, whose unit included a particularly active group known as the 'dirty dozen' – were also hostile to the political direction of the movement. In Derry, despite the appointment of an O/C who was loyal to the leadership, 'there was no support for the ceasefire at all ... the Provos were continuing the war and we weren't and I suppose our egos took a fair knock at the time because we still felt we had the capability of continuing'. Costello and Garland argued that the 'national question' should now become the primary focus; they were opposed by Goulding and Mac Giolla, who urged continued concentration on civil rights and attempts to win Protestant support. The competing positions were presented and after protracted discussions it was decided that 'both documents be submitted to general meetings of each Command Area to assess their opinion'; each Command would then 'instruct its delegates on the attitude to adopt at a reconvened convention'. Delegates also heard Costello report that over the two years since the last convention the movement's income had been £92,000 – '£70,000 came as the direct result of operations and £22,000 from USA etc.' – of this £22,378 had been spent on weapons.

The question of the OIRA's political direction came to a head at a second convention held in the lead-up to the 1972 Sinn Féin Ard Fheis. From 10.30 p.m. on 9 December until the meeting's conclusion at 6 the next morning, 41 delegates debated the movement's direction. With 25 proxy votes allowed for those units whose representatives had failed to attend but whose mandated position was known, Garland and Costello's document seeking a return 'to the high road to the Republic' was approved by 48 votes to 18. Costello then proposed a new strategy document, 'The Way Forward', which outlined how the new policy might be implemented, including a return to more aggressive military activity. These proposals were supported by the majority of Northern delegates, but it was decided the document should be discussed by OIRA units before any changes in strategy were endorsed. Eoin Ó Murchú, who had strongly opposed the policy change, was dismayed at Garland's approach:

Basically Garland was saying one day it's civil rights and another it's republican[ism], and because we are not talking about the Republic we are leaving that ground to the Provos . . . then the whole confidence went out of the civil rights movement . . . if you accepted Garland's [position] it was logical to support Costello: if you wanted to compete for the republican high ground and civil rights was only a tactic, then you had to have an armed struggle, in cooperation with the Provos or not.

Despite the ceasefire the OIRA was continuing to seek arms supplies. During the summer of 1972 Ó Murchú was in Beirut, meeting representatives of the PLO to discuss shipments. With his pockets 'stuffed full of cash' he met Abu Jihad, the Fatah military commander, with promising results. There were two more meetings in Lebanon, which Goulding also attended; when Goulding began to emphasize the potential for conflict with the Provisionals, a subject the PLO were not interested in, the deal fell through.

There were still no arms forthcoming from the Soviets. KGB agent Oleg Lyalin, who had defected to Britain during 1971, informed the intelligence services about talks between the Irish communists and Moscow regarding aid for the Officials. In 1972 Mick O'Riordan made another request, pointing out that there had been no leak of information over the previous two years. He suggested that if the Soviets were still worried then the connection could be made through Cuba instead. During the autumn the OIRA did receive a shipment of Swedish Ljungman automatic rifles from their Canadian contacts. A small number of Armalite AR-18 rifles also arrived from US sources. In New York, an OIRA supporter, Patrick Purcell, was arrested on gun-running charges, having personally bought 56 weapons between June and December 1971; but the main organizer of the American shipments was an experienced and cautious man who avoided attention. During September, loyalist Ted Pavis, who had supplied arms and explosives to the OIRA, was killed by the UVF, who suspected him of stealing weapons from their dumps.

The British Prime Minister had been apprised in late August of what his intelligence services thought OIRA intentions were. Information derived from a 'delicate source' outlined the Officials' interest in 'penetrating the trade union movement and in industrial action' and their aim of cooperating with working-class Protestants. The British believed that the 'military potential' of the OIRA was 'unimpaired' despite their ceasefire but that while the organization had the 'capacity' to resume they feared touching off 'widespread sectarian fighting'. The Officials were also trying to professionalize their own intelligence gathering. In October all Command Intelligence Officers were circulated with a document instructing them to collate information on members of rival political groups, the security forces and journalists and to tighten their own structures against infiltration. Units were asked, 'Do you have members in the state services – the post office, state companies, local government – and do your members have friends or acquaintances in the government forces?'

In December the Official leadership responded to internal pressure by sanctioning several attacks on army bases with mortars that had been developed and tested at camps in the South. The results were mixed, with a number of mortars missing their targets and others failing to explode. A soldier was killed in Lurgan when a shell detonated while he was examining one of the abandoned mortars in Kitchen Hill. The attacks were unclaimed. On 15 December the Officials in Lurgan were waiting to carry out a robbery when an RUC patrol arrived on the scene. The police were delivering Christmas presents to a local child who had been injured by one of their vehicles earlier in the year. The OIRA attacked the patrol, shot dead Constable George Chambers and stole his machine gun. On the same day a part-time UDR man,

Frederick Greeves, was killed by the OIRA leaving his workplace in Armagh. In response to these attacks the Provisional IRA issued a statement querying the status of the 'NLF ceasefire', citing the Kitchen Hill attack and the 'Santa Claus killing' of Constable Chambers.

By 1973 the issue of sectarian violence was to the fore in Northern Ireland. During 1973 over 40 Catholics were killed by loyalists in Belfast alone. The community in which the Officials were based was under almost constant attack. In at least two cases loyalists killed the fiancées of OIRA members. Officials conducted patrols in areas like Bawnmore and the Ormeau Road to counter loyalist assassins. For some members of the OIRA 'under siege' in south Belfast, loyalists were the 'main enemy'. During April, Robert 'Scruff' Millen, a Protestant member of the Officials, was shot dead by the UVF while on vigilante duty in McClure Street. The Officials shot a loyalist in south Belfast in retaliation, but there was disagreement as to whether this was the best way to respond to sectarianism. Some thought that 'if retaliation took place it would stop it; it was just emotion, emotion ruled everything in the areas at that time, logical thought didn't come into it'. The other response was to try to convince at least some of the loyalist paramilitaries that these killings were counterproductive. Both the UDA and UVF at various stages claimed to be against sectarian assassinations, and there was talk among the Officials of joint patrols with the UDA in west Belfast. In Belfast a line of communication was established whereby Protestants or Catholics who found themselves in the 'wrong Long Bar' – there being two pubs of that name, one on the Shankill and one on the Falls – were escorted to Northumberland Street and handed over. Some Officials involved in retaliatory attacks on loyalists were also involved in talks with them.

Pressure also remained for attacks on the British Army. As Ballymurphy Official Mary McMahon recalls: '[Units] tried to assert themselves by having a shot at a soldier and it was always covered by the terms of the ceasefire, because there was never a day in the week when the soldiers didn't do something that didn't warrant [retaliation], you know, if that was your thinking.' For example in early March 1973, 12-year-old Kevin Heatley was shot and killed by the army in Newry. The OIRA responded with over a dozen attacks and a soldier was killed by a booby-trap bomb after being lured to a cottage at Mullaghbawn. In Armagh the Officials attacked a patrol in Ogle Street but as they made their withdrawal British soldiers in concealed positions opened fire, killing 18-year-old Peter James 'Jake' McGerrigan and wounding a comrade. Local people ensured that 'all the forensics and the guns and that were got away, as were [the] combat fatigues'. The Officials would strenuously deny the young men had been armed and on active service when they were shot. A day later the local OIRA quartermaster, 19-year-old Tony Hughes, was shot dead while moving weapons for a retaliatory attack. The Army Council gave permission for general attacks in response. During April operations were carried out in Armagh, Newry, Lurgan, Derry and Belfast. A bomb was placed in the car of a UDR mechanic who worked at Gough Barracks and he unwittingly drove it inside; it exploded at lunchtime, injuring nine people. Several activists were captured during the operations, among them Martin O'Hagan after a gun battle in Lurgan. The Officials claimed that they had killed 7 soldiers and wounded 20 more and warned that they would continue to 'retaliate for murderous attacks'. In reality, this was the last general use of the retaliation policy.

'The one thing that never stopped,' a Belfast volunteer recalls, 'was the robberies.' During August the OIRA stole several thousand pounds from the central postal sorting office in Belfast. An OIRA volunteer dressed in a postman's uniform took a taxi to the office where he jumped into the back of a delivery van and asked for a lift. Once the van had passed an army post the man pulled a gun and demanded to be taken to the Falls. The OIRA were waiting for the van and its contents were robbed. The amount stolen was a pleasant surprise, one participant recalling 'we didn't know what to do with it'. The volunteers involved got £5 each for their efforts.

In early June loyalists carried out a number of killings in west

Belfast. In response the OIRA picked up David Walker, a 16-year-old mentally retarded Protestant boy, on suspicion of being a loyalist spy. He was taken to the Lower Falls, questioned about recent murders, then shot dead and his body dumped in O'Neill Street. The Officials said nothing about Walker's death, but two OIRA men were arrested and one was jailed for life. In the days after Walker's death the UDA stabbed Catholic Senator Paddy Wilson and his girlfriend Irene Andrews to death. They claimed it was in response to the killing of Walker and later asserted that Wilson and Andrews had supplied information to the Officials.

One of the OIRA's supply lines was disrupted during July 1973 when Canadian police raided a flat in Toronto and found sub-machine guns. This led to Gardaí searching a ship at Dublin Port and discovering a ton of arms and ammunition, including Armalites. They then arrested a Monaghan man at Dublin Airport arriving on a flight from Canada. During the same month OIRA officer Pat Bracken, a 28-year-old joiner, was shot dead by the UVF in the Lower Falls. Trouble also flared again with the Provisionals in Belfast. Tension had been growing in Ballymurphy, where leading Provo Jim Bryson was harassing Officials. Bryson had acquired a legendary status within the Provisionals, though many Officials saw him as little more than a bully. Ronnie Bunting and others wanted action and a decision was taken to kill Bryson. Armed Officials were searching for him but he had been alerted and was also driving around in a car looking for them when he was ambushed by British troops. Bryson was fatally wounded and a comrade, Patrick Mulvenna, killed outright. The Provisionals immediately assumed that the Officials were responsible and widespread violence was predicted. In Crumlin Road Jail, Official prisoners were attacked by Provisionals. An emergency meeting was organized in Dublin between the leaderships of both organizations. Goulding, Garland, Ryan and McMillen met with David O'Connell and Brian Keenan in the Dominican Friary. During the meeting Costello arrived uninvited and with different priorities, as Garland recalls:

We just wanted to get the incidents stopped and [to] get on with our own thing. Dave O'Connell's attitude was we don't want anything to do with these incidents; we want to get on with the war. Our attitude was you get on with your war but you have to stop intimidating or wounding our members but for Costello it didn't matter that that was happening, he wanted a joint campaign.

Costello's attitude at the meeting was in marked contrast to his earlier position as one of the most outspoken critics of the Provos within the Official leadership. The result of the talks was a joint statement in which the Provisionals accepted that Bryson and Mulvenna had been killed by soldiers. It was also stated that 'differences between the two organizations had been exploited by the British' and that machinery was being established so that in future 'friction and hostility' would be eased. McMillen returned to Belfast seeking information on Keenan, who had risen rapidly in the Provos' ranks but was unknown to the Official leader.

During August 1973 Kenneth Littlejohn and a Newry man were convicted for the Grafton Street bank robbery. The affair continued to have repercussions in Co. Down, where the OIRA sought out an ex-member, Paul Tinnelly, who had remained active despite being expelled from the organization. Tinnelly came from one of the 'most prominent business families' in south Down, had been involved in the Border Campaign and claimed to be 'proud to have served the cause of Ireland rather than international communism'. The OIRA accused Tinnelly of having 'teamed up with British agents' who had played on his 'greed' and desire for 'easy money'. As they tracked Tinnelly they also killed Seamus Larkin, a former member whom they had previously kneecapped and banished from Newry. His body was found dumped near Omeath. The family of another murder victim in Belfast, 24-year-old Owen Devine, also claimed that he had been killed by the OIRA. Devine died after being shot in a derelict house off the Ormeau Road in August. It was alleged that the Officials had abducted him after he stole keys belonging to one of their clubs. Later that year the OIRA 'executed' Sean McAstocker in the Markets after they discovered he was part of a gang that had carried out several brutal killings. The OIRA also routinely kneecapped or similarly punished petty criminals in Belfast, Newry and Armagh. Sometimes beatings were administered with hurleys or the victim's limbs smashed by breeze blocks.

The OIRA leadership made it clear they did not rule out military action either for 'short-term objectives' or in the struggle for the socialist republic. However, they still argued that such a campaign was not realistic. There were serious disagreements about this on the Army Council. Costello felt that the defence and retaliation policy had been effectively abandoned. Some of those who agreed with Costello on the need for armed activity had little time for the Provisionals. Indeed, many of those who wanted action against the British were also eager to respond to Provisional provocation. But they felt that they would be left in the shadows unless OIRA activity was stepped up. Disillusioned members continued to drift out of the organization. Nevertheless efforts were made to solidify internal structures. During 1973 Mick Ryan, inspired by nineteenth-century Fenian infiltration strategies, had produced a manual, entitled *A Reporter's Guide to Ireland*, dealing with counter-interrogation techniques and intelligence gathering. It advised arrested volunteers to:

Simply deny everything. You are not a member of the IRA, never have been and don't intend to be. You know nothing about the IRA except what you read in the papers . . . the Special Branch will know you are lying for all you are worth but that does not matter. They cannot prove that in a courtroom so you just deny everything.

The guide asserted that IRA business 'should not be discussed in pubs or anywhere else where it could be overheard'. Intelligence officers should build up knowledge on individuals by collecting birth certificates, passports and ID cards. Emphasis was put on developing contacts with sympathetic members of the Gardaí and the Irish Army. The guide stressed that the state saw the OIRA 'as a much greater danger than, say, the Provisionals – in the long term – because we are committed to the overthrow of all that the army is paid to protect'. The Gardaí seem to have shared the Officials' view of their potential. In early 1974 an Irish government inquiry into internal security concluded that the 'greatest long-term danger to the security of the institutions of the State comes from the activities of the Official IRA and of political groups or associations connected with it'. Young volunteers had already begun to join mainstream political parties. One infiltrator was appointed to a position in the SDLP's Belfast head office and the Officials were able to gain access to that party's entire membership lists and much of its internal correspondence.

In Derry approval was granted for a retaliatory attack in January 1974 and Ebrington Barracks was chosen as a target. An OIRA volunteer from Armagh supervised the operation. A bomb was taped underneath the car of John Dunn, a 46-year-old Creggan man who worked as a cleaner in the base. It was timed to explode at lunchtime, but Dunn had been giving driving lessons on his lunch break to a fellow cleaner, 51-year-old Cecilia Byrne, and as they drove along Limavady Road the bomb exploded, killing them both. The OIRA denied any involvement in the bombing. That year saw the tempo of sectarian killings increase. During November 1973 the OIRA in Belfast had announced that it was setting up auxiliary defence groups to 'check all strange cars and persons' in areas where sectarian attacks had taken place. In Portadown the Officials opened fire on a loyalist mob trying to storm Obin's Street. During February the OIRA sealed off Bawnmore Estate in response to three loyalist killings. Many died in bomb attacks on pubs, with five killed in the Rose and Crown on the Ormeau Road in May. There were authorized and unauthorized responses by the OIRA. A squad was formed which had permission to carry out retaliation attacks on pubs frequented by the UVF or UDA. These operations were kept secret, even from fellow members, and were never claimed. After one attack on a loyalist pub in south Belfast a suspicious quartermaster inspected weapons belonging to the local OIRA unit to see if they had been fired. The OIRA were also blamed in early 1974 for the killing of Christopher Daly, an ex-internee who was involved in gun dealing.

In 1974, the Soviets finally authorized a limited shipment to the OIRA of captured western weapons. The guns, in waterproof wrapping, were submerged off the coast of Ireland and were then picked up by a trawler. From New York sources the OIRA also received silenced American M3 sub-machine guns, usually called 'grease guns'; in Belfast they were nicknamed 'spitting dummies'.

In May, while preparing a landmine for an attack on the army in Newry, Colman Rowntree and a comrade, Martin McAlinden, were surprised by soldiers and shot dead. Immediately after the funerals of the two men the OIRA shot a British soldier in William Street and carried out five more attacks on troops over the coming week. They claimed to have inflicted fatalities, though the British Army denied this. In early June the OIRA finally caught up with Paul Tinnelly when he returned to Rostrevor for a relative's funeral and killed him in a machine-gun attack. His family angrily denied the OIRA's allegations that he had been an informer. Tinnelly's brother met with a member of the Army Council to demand (unsuccessfully) that the claim be withdrawn.

Finance continued to be needed both for maintaining the army and for intervention in politics. The Republican Clubs and Sinn Féin were involved in three major election campaigns during 1974, for local councils in the South and two Westminster polls. During March the OIRA had taken £17,000 from the AIB in Newry. In July £4,400 was taken from the Hotel Blarney in Cork after four OIRA members booked in as two couples; at 5 o'clock in the morning they held up staff and emptied the safe. During August the OIRA stole £6,400 from a post office on the Falls Road. Late in the year several Officials were caught after a series of robberies in Belfast. In an effort to prevent robberies the army had begun escorting post office vans. The Officials contacted a post office driver and threatened to shoot his family unless he made sure an extra £40,000 was left in Grosvenor Road post office. After the van had made its delivery and driven off with its escort, the OIRA raided the post office and took the £40,000. The perception that the OIRA was being downgraded to a political fund-raising operation caused disquiet among some volunteers. The leadership stressed the importance of involvement in political activity, and indeed most leading Republican Club figures were also OIRA members; as one activist put it: 'If the O/C of the IRA was talking to the chairman of the Republican Clubs, he would be talking into a mirror.'

But many were still unhappy. In July 1974, Seamus Trainor, an Armagh IRA veteran of 42 years, resigned from the movement, complaining of OIRA military 'inaction'. There were several reasons for discontent: 'some people wanted operations to let the Brits know you still existed' while others 'wanted operations against the Brits to let the Provos know you still existed' and many volunteers questioned the effort being put into electoral campaigns. Sectarian attacks also continued to take their toll. During September a car driven by Tartan gang members ran down and killed Official Fianna member Noel Beckett off the Ormeau Road. The gang had made repeated sorties into the area trying to kidnap people off the street. Another Official Fianna boy, 16-year-old Pat McGreevey, was shot dead by the UVF in Clifton Street. In November 20-year-old Official supporter Geraldine Macklin was shot dead by the UDA at a shop on the Springfield Road. Many of those disillusioned with the lack of military activity were eager to retaliate against loyalists. Efforts to reorient the Fianna into other political activities had mixed results. In November a group of masked Fianna members took over a secondary school on the Glen Road to demand integrated education. They locked the teachers in a staff room and addressed an assembly of largely bewildered students. Some within the movement in Dublin thought that Fianna had become 'a joke'. There were suggestions from Fianna members in Dublin and Cork to reorganize with a more political focus.

Unlike most other areas of the North, where republican allegiance had drifted to the Provisionals, the Officials in south Down had maintained support. During August 1974 soldiers were shot in response to army harassment of local people. In October the OIRA in Newry carried out more gun attacks on British soldiers following the killing of a 16-year-old by the army. Relations between the Officials and the Provisionals in the town were increasingly tense. The local Official O/C recalled: 'The Provos' attitude was don't do what we ask, do as we tell you, and we would have had people coming to us because of that.' After widespread violence over the weekend marking the third anniversary of internment in early August, the OIRA accused the Provisionals of using 'young boys' to hijack and burn cars belonging to civilians. Two teenagers were kneecapped by the Officials as a result. In response the Provisionals warned that they would not allow their men to be 'assaulted or molested' by the OIRA. There was more bad feeling in Belfast when Provisional Martin Skillen was killed. Skillen, a former OIRA volunteer himself, had been in a fight with some Officials and had retrieved a gun from a dump and gone looking for them when he was spotted by troops and shot.

During August the OIRA took £50,000 in a wages raid at Clondalkin Paper Mills in Dublin; but in Galway an attempted robbery saw a clerk, 60-year-old Jeremiah O'Connor, shot dead. The killing was a major embarrassment to the Official leadership, who told supporters those involved were dissidents, though the same people had been involved in 'official' activities shortly before the killing. In Belfast the OIRA were involved in a gun battle with British troops in Ardoyne during which 66-year-old Maura Lavery was killed. In response to the killing of another civilian by the army the Officials shot dead a soldier, Private Philip Drake, near Craigavon on 26 August. In early September the OIRA robbed a bank in north Belfast; as the raiders made their getaway RUC inspector William Elliot was killed in an exchange of fire. On 5 November the OIRA shot a loyalist in Bawnmore. A few days later a gun battle erupted on the estate between the OIRA and the Provisionals, sparked off by a punch-up in the Boundary Bar. Despite this, the two republican groups still occasionally cooperated in actions against loyalists in the area. The British Army noted increased OIRA activity across Belfast during the winter. In part this was a result of the growing internal tension and a desire to keep volunteers loyal and active.

Between 1970 and 1974 1,270 lives were lost as a result of political violence in Ireland. Of these approximately 600 deaths were caused by the Provisional IRA, 350 by loyalists and 190 by state forces. The Official IRA had killed over 50 people, and the Official republican movement had lost 20 members in the same period. What was also lost was any illusion on the part of the Official leadership that they held the initiative in provoking a revolutionary situation in the short term. They had not wanted the war that had developed, which, as they had predicted, had blown off course any hopes of united working-class action.

6. Civil Rights not Civil War

'We stand not on the brink of victory, but on the brink of
sectarian disaster.'

Billy McMillen, Bodenstown, 1973

During the first five, intensely violent, years of the Troubles, the
Official IRA in Northern Ireland struggled to maintain social
agitation amid the growing violence. Their members fought elections, intervened in housing disputes, ran local cooperatives and
were the backbone of the Northern Ireland Civil Rights Association (NICRA). Numerous members of the movement were
jailed or interned and intervention in prison politics was another
focus of activity. They competed with their Provisional rivals in
the media as well as on the streets. But disagreements about the
nature of their struggle soon divided the Official movement, and
would eventually lead to another split.

Prior to the Falls Road curfew the Belfast Republican Clubs
were at the forefront of a widely supported rent strike, while in
Derry they were prominent in unemployment protests. Kevin
Smyth, who had helped set up a Club in Andersonstown, viewed
the barricades as 'an extension of the whole Civil Rights struggle
and the street demonstrations' and he and his colleagues took the
view that 'it could not be allowed to develop into a purely military
struggle between the IRA and the British army'. Despite growing
military commitments OIRA members continued with their Republican Clubs roles. Malachy McGurran combined his role as
Northern OIRA commander with that of chairman of the Republican Clubs, while Billy McMillen was vice-chair for most of 1970.
This was not lost on the authorities, who maintained their ban

on both the Clubs and the *United Irishman*, sales of which were periodically disrupted by the security forces.

The continued commitment to the civil rights campaign resulted in growing Official influence within NICRA, but only as the latter organization's importance declined. In 1971 NICRA's fourteen-person executive contained six Republican Clubs representatives, including McGurran and McMillen. The Officials within NICRA could also count on the support of Communist Party members and some independents such as Tyrone's Paddy Joe McClean. This bloc argued for NICRA to place greater emphasis on economic issues and demand the adoption of a Northern Ireland 'Bill of Rights' which would outlaw all forms of discrimination. They pushed for the civil rights demand of 'one man, one vote' to be developed into 'one family, one house, one man, one job'.

In Belfast and elsewhere the Officials were now the mainstay of local NICRA groups. In some areas it became 'difficult to tell the difference' between the local Republican Clubs and the civil rights branch. NICRA policy, such as opposition to the setting up of the Ulster Defence Regiment, began to mirror that of the Republican Clubs. Relationships with the other main NICRA factions had become increasingly fraught. Complaining of a left-wing takeover, several 'moderates' had resigned from the executive in early 1970. On the other hand, the mainly student-based People's Democracy was angry that NICRA refused to take a more stridently left-wing approach, such as condemning the influence of the Catholic Church in the South. Provisional supporters withdrew from NICRA, many bitterly dismissive of its attempts to seek 'British rights'. By early 1971 the last remaining Provisional supporter on the NICRA executive, Kevin Agnew, had been replaced as chair by Communist Andy Barr.

The emergence of civil conflict had a distinct social impact within Belfast's working-class communities. In areas of new housing, built to cater for the city's growing population, paramilitary activity became knitted into the social fabric. Official activist Martin Lynch would recall that prior to the violence of 1969, Turf

Lodge 'people did not know one another very well, neighbours didn't know neighbours in many cases. It wasn't until 1969 [that] people came together in large numbers and vigilante groups were formed and people talked to each other.' In May 1970 the Belfast Republican Clubs organized a Falls Fleadh with music and sports events. Among the bands that performed were the Dubliners, whose new bestselling album *Revolution* included several left-wing ballads. However, the success of the Falls Fleadh would not be repeated. The 1971 event faced local objections because of street trouble the previous year, and the Provisionals condemned its organizers for having allowed 'known and professed communists' to address young people. That year's event ended in tragedy, with the murder of an elderly woman and recriminations about drunkenness and rowdy behaviour. As Des O'Hagan recalled, there were only two opinions on the Fleadh – 'a unique urban people's festival or else a drunken orgy'. The politically charged atmosphere could also have a detrimental impact on social agitation. Mary McMahon recalled feeling that her local area, Ballymurphy, which was largely bereft of facilities, was a time bomb waiting to explode; the deteriorating relationship with the British Army meant that local energy was deflected away from social campaigns and towards violence.

The political conflict between the rival Sinn Féins was played out in the press. In public statements the Officials referred to their rivals as the 'Provisional Alliance' – attempting to portray a loose coalition of traditionalists, Belfast Catholic defenders and Fianna Fáil manipulators. Conversely the Provos used the term 'NLF' to refer to the OIRA and what was now called Official Sinn Féin. The Provisionals adopted the plan drawn up by Roy Johnston and Seán Ó Brádaigh in 1966, but shelved at the time by the leadership, as their core social and economic policy document. This 'Éire Nua' (New Ireland) document sought to remake Irish society along cooperative and federalist lines.

Away from the factionalism of Belfast the Officials, for a period, publicly adopted a conciliatory approach to their former comrades. As late as December 1970 Mac Giolla walked out of an

RTÉ interview when Ruairí Ó Brádaigh was not allowed to take part in the discussion. There were still attempts to bring the rival factions together. In early 1970 the Irish Workers' Party and the CPNI had unified to form the Communist Party of Ireland (CPI), the first orthodox 32-county communist movement since the 1940s, and the new party's General Secretary, Mick O'Riordan, was adamant that unity was also key for republicans. Throughout 1970 he was in contact with the leaderships of both groups seeking to organize a compromise; but both sides refused to send speakers to a unity meeting in Dublin. This was unsurprising on the part of the anti-communist Provisionals, who publicly proclaimed they would 'never come to terms with the Goulding IRA which is now Marxist and Socialist'. In contrast their aim was a 'free Ireland' based on 'Christian principles'. With delegates at the Official Sinn Féin Ard Fheis overwhelmingly voting to end abstentionism in January 1971, any faint hopes of a reunion came to an end. The Liberty Hall conference also saw the National Liberation Front strategy reaffirmed, and while the escalating Northern conflict loomed large, debates focused on Southern campaigns. McGurran was the only leadership figure to express reservations about abandoning abstentionism at that point, though a few Official activists had remained supporters of the policy. In some areas there was still unease that the split had occurred at all: Easter 1971 saw several commemorations in the North take place under a unified banner. And some who had taken the Provisional side still sought an understanding, with Kevin Agnew, speaking in Swatragh, calling for the movement to reunite. In the United States former IRA Chief of Staff Sean Cronin echoed these sentiments.

Despite the large number of potential recruits now being drawn to the Provos, the Republican Clubs continued to grow in number. A number of young activists, most of whom had joined after the split, were becoming prominent, among them Margot Collins, a teacher based in Newry who was briefly dubbed 'the new Bernadette'. The Willy Orr/Betsy Gray Republican Club in Ballymurphy is recalled as 'quite an intriguing mix' of local people and ex-students: 'We were going to have the revolution the next day [while] people who had been around a bit longer thought it mightn't happen tomorrow, you know.' With Provisional Sinn Féin only marginally active beyond acting as a military support group, to outsiders the Clubs continued to be the public face of republican politics.

On his return to Ireland in early 1971, Sean Garland demanded a harder public line be taken with the Provisionals. At GHQ he had a strong supporter in Eoin Ó Murchú, who recalled: 'After the split a decision was made that [we] wouldn't exacerbate [it] by engaging in argument, which was a big mistake. It meant all the arguments against us, all the crap about 1969, was left unanswered . . . every dishonest comment was given maximum coverage and we were fighting the split, particularly in rural areas, with one hand tied behind our backs.' The Army Council replaced the moderate Seamus Ó Tuathail as *United Irishman* editor with Ó Murchú in May 1971. There followed a notable hardening of the paper's stance. Garland replied to appeals for 'republican unity' by ruling out agreements with the 'elements who had derided' left-wing policies. At that summer's Bodenstown observances, McGurran contrasted the words of leading Provo David O'Connell, who the previous year had warned that British forces would never again run riot in Irish streets, with the Belfast Provisionals' behaviour during the Falls curfew, when they had stood aside while the OIRA had defended the area.

The first two major studies of the IRA were published in 1970. The Officials gave a warm reception to J. Bowyer Bell's *The Secret Army*. Goulding was effusive when describing Bell's work as 'not just a book about the IRA, but a book for the IRA'. In contrast, Tim Pat Coogan's *The IRA* was damned by Goulding for its 'patronising pseudo-objectivity'. The *United Irishman* claimed that 'Coogan's Cook-In' was riddled with 'factual error, misleading comment and ill judgment'. The Officials also felt Coogan had given 'excess publicity' to the Provisionals and was 'fanning the flames of division' in his role as editor of the *Irish Press*. Certainly the paper was dismissive of the Officials, an editorial claiming that it was 'silly, eyes-elsewhere, socialist policies' that had left Belfast

Catholics undefended in 1969. After an unsatisfactory meeting between Coogan, de Burca and Mac Giolla to discuss the newspaper's coverage, Official Sinn Féin called for a boycott of the publication. (The US Embassy, for their part, felt that on political matters the *Irish Press* 'speaks for the Irish government'.) In contrast the *Irish Times* was seen as broadly sympathetic to the Officials. The paper's political reporter, Dick Walsh, socialized with members of the Official leadership, giving them background assistance and advice. Then Sinn Féin General Secretary Tony Heffernan recalled: '[Walsh's] views were sought out and respected, not just [for] the political ideas but the presentation of ideas.' The journalist helped write several important speeches, including Goulding's funeral oration for Joe McCann. *Hibernia* magazine regularly featured articles by leading Officials, with supporter Anne Harris writing a regular back-page column. The *United Irishman* criticized student magazine *Nusight,* and its young editor Vincent Browne, as aiming to 'titillate rather than activate' a 'cosy . . . middle-class liberal readership'. The Northern newspapers were in the main pro-unionist or, in the case of the nationalist *Irish News*, decidedly wary of the Officials. However the Belfast *Sunday News* on occasion featured sympathetic articles. The paper's news editor, Jim Campbell, had been on good terms with leading OIRA figures since his involvement in republican politics as a teenager.

While the Officials' political sophistication won them friends in the media, on the ground selling such nuanced positions as opposing the abolition of the Stormont parliament, while demanding its wholesale reform, was a harder sell. The Officials stated that it was preferable for Northern Ireland to be administered by an 'Irish' institution than succumb to unelected rule from London; this was felt to be consistent with the need to 'weaken imperial control' as a prerequisite to unifying the country. In contrast, the Provisionals and a large swathe of nationalist opinion had a simple message: the Northern parliament should be abolished immediately. In the face of this, Republican Clubs activist Brian Brennan recalls that attempting to explain Official policy was like 'trench warfare in every Catholic street in west Belfast'.

Unionism, meanwhile, was divided between Unionist Party leader Brian Faulkner, who became Northern prime minister in early 1971, and hard-liners such as William Craig and Ian Paisley. (Paisley had won seats at Stormont and Westminster in 1970.) The Officials generally saw the fracturing of unionism as a sign of the civil rights strategy's success. Realignment had also taken place within nationalism, the major development being the launch of the Social Democratic and Labour Party in August 1970. The SDLP included people from labour backgrounds, such as Gerry Fitt and Paddy Devlin, alongside younger nationalists who had become prominent through the civil rights campaign, including John Hume and Austin Currie. On the left, People's Democracy, with Michael Farrell its dominant figure, had adopted a more structured Marxist ethos and was initially critical of the Officials for concentrating too much on the national question to the detriment of uniting Catholic and Protestant workers. However, in many areas there was a friendly relationship between the two organizations. In Armagh several Fianna members had their first introduction to the pamphlets of Mao and Lenin in the PD shop, which adjoined the town's Republican Club premises. After internment, the PD line shifted dramatically to support for the Provisional armed campaign and criticism of NICRA's 're-formism'. People's Democracy began to argue that the Protestants represented a reactionary colonizing bloc, like the French in Algeria. By late 1971 the fracture was complete, with the PD pulling out of NICRA and helping establish the Provo-supporting Northern Resistance Movement.

The much smaller Irish Communist Organisation was also challenging Official policies, taking the view that responsibility for the Northern conflict lay 'at the door of the Southern ruling class' and that the choice was between a 'secular social democratic British state' and the 'reactionary 26-county Catholic state'. Claiming to be applying Stalin's writings to the national question, the group now argued that there were two historic nations in Ireland – Protestant and Catholic – each entitled to self-determination. The organization accordingly changed its name to the British and Irish

Communist Organisation (BICO). They argued that the Officials were 'chiefly responsible' for the Troubles, having led NICRA into 'a policy of sectarian confrontation'.

Some Official strategists also delved into Marxist ideas on cultural identity and revolutionary theory, but came to different conclusions from BICO's. In 1971 Sinn Féin published Eoin Ó Murchú's pamphlet *Culture and Revolution in Ireland* in which he accused the British of historically conducting a 'campaign practically amounting to genocide' in Ireland, leading to the near destruction of Irish culture. The material values of 'Anglo-American' imperialism were being fostered through the education system and the mass media. This process could be countered by looking to a Gaelic past that, Ó Murchú stated, underlay not only native Irish but also the Anglo-Irish and Orange cultures. From a fostering of these roots republicans could conduct a 'cultural revolution', which would see imperialism overthrown by the 'culture of the Irish working class'. This meant support for the Irish-speaking regions of the Gaeltacht and the promotion of Irish language and culture. Some were worried by the Maoist influences in Ó Murchú's work, and its dissemination at Official education seminars met resistance, but Goulding was a strong supporter. In January 1971 at the Ard Fheis, his defence of working with young people who offered 'extreme solutions to an extreme situation' was at least partly in reference to Ó Murchú. Billy McMillen was among those who argued that 'without the [Irish] language there could be no revolution'. In 1970, when the noted Irish-language writer and former IRA internee Máirtín Ó Cadhain died, the OIRA provided the colour party at his funeral; and the Officials would name a new drinking club in Gardiner Place after him.

There were differences within the movement on cultural issues. At the 1971 Ard Fheis Belfast activist Tony Rosato questioned the widespread use of Irish in speeches, as many Northern delegates could not understand it. By 1971 OIRA colour parties featured men with long hair and flared trousers, while Fianna activists in the North often dressed in the 'boot boy' style of half-mast jeans, 'suedehead' or longish hair and bomber jackets. In Armagh's

Drumarg Estate members of the rival Fiannas were distinguished by different-colour bomber jackets: green for the Officials and black for the Provos.

The Catholic Church, an institution that had underpinned nationalist culture for over a century, was seen by many Officials as having taken sides in the republican split. Belfast priest Fr. Des Wilson would publicly admit that some clergy and bishops felt that the Provisionals were much 'less dangerous' than the Officials. Bernadette Devlin concurred, stating that during 1970 many rural Northern clergymen were 'falling over themselves' to endorse the Provisionals in preference to the Officials. Nonetheless at least one cleric, Fr. Vincent Forde from south Down, joined the Official movement and British intelligence feared the possibility of an Official alliance with 'radical socialist priests' in the South. The November 1971 Sinn Féin Ard Fheis outlined a series of demands aimed at ending religious control of education. It also called for equal pay for women and backed the legalization of contraception and an end to the ban on divorce. Sean Mulready, who had been victimized by the Church while working as a teacher during the 1950s, congratulated Sinn Féin on moving far ahead of all other Irish political parties 'including the Communist Party' on matters of social reform. To more cautious members Official Sinn Féin stressed that 'no one' would be 'forced' to divorce. The 1971 Dublin Easter commemoration was notable for the absence of the rosary, though the prayer was still said at most local Official commemorations elsewhere.

Labour's Conor Cruise O'Brien was seen by many as the serious intellectual force on the left of Irish politics. As trouble in the North intensified, his views became more stridently anti-nationalist. In October 1971 Mac Giolla accepted O'Brien's challenge to a public debate in University College Dublin. O'Brien charged that Sinn Féin was only the public expression of a 'secret and illegal army'. However the Officials might protest the difference between themselves and the Provisionals, the outcome of all their activities would be fascism. O'Brien contended that the Protestants of the North had the right to a separate state and were not settlers, like the

French-Algerian *colons*. Mac Giolla argued that 'no republican ever regarded the Protestant workers as *colons*' and that 'the only *colons* were the Ascendancy class . . . the "Horse-Protestants"'. He stated that 'there are not two nations but two classes in Ireland . . . the exploited and the exploiters.' The Sinn Féin president maintained that republicans wanted unity between Protestant and Catholic but no section of the nation had a right to secede from it. The following year Cruise O'Brien's influential deconstruction of nationalism, *States of Ireland*, was described by Mac Giolla as 'pro-Unionist and pro-Imperialist'.

For most Official activists, let alone the ordinary population, these debates were inaudible due to the sound of gunfire that engulfed the North after August 1971. Substantial numbers of local activists, many of them not IRA members, were rounded up when the British launched internment. On 9 August Séamus Ó Tuathail had been staying in Billy McMillen's house, having cycled to Belfast that day. Despite being warned that a round-up of republicans was on the cards, Ó Tuathail decided he needed a rest and was arrested by a party of British soldiers in the early hours of that morning. By late August he was giving Irish classes in Crumlin Road Jail and smuggling out articles on conditions there for the *Irish Times*. Following the round-up, Mickey Montgomery and Paddy Joe McClean were among a number of prisoners singled out for special interrogation techniques. McClean remembered being forced to stand spreadeagled until he collapsed and was beaten, being choked, handcuffed and hung up off the ground. He heard mock firing squads 'executing' people and death marches being played. He was 'convinced he was to be killed' because the authorities would surely not allow anyone to survive and expose what was happening.

Early in September 10,000 people rallied against internment at Belfast's Casement Park. Republican Clubs called for the ostracizing of British troops, and for a national rent and rates strike, to hit the Unionist government 'where it hurts'. In Derry the development of the 'no-go' areas gave the Officials an opportunity to put their policies into action behind the barricades. Street committees were set up and local people were encouraged to elect representatives to oversee the running of their areas, ensuring rubbish was collected, barricades maintained and crime kept under control. The Provisionals denounced the idea as 'Moscow-style communism'. In contrast Goulding, on a visit to Free Derry, stated that behind the barricades the 'saplings of freedom' were being planted in an area where there were 'no Gestapo, no RUC [and] no Free State Special Branch'.

Scores of people attached to the Official movement were being detained between Crumlin Road Jail, Long Kesh and the *Maidstone* prison ship in Belfast Harbour. By Christmas 1971 there were enough OIRA internees to form five Republican Clubs in Long Kesh internment camp. They were still outnumbered by several hundred Provisional internees. As a non-aligned prisoner P. J. McClean was made secretary of the Long Kesh camp council, and in an illustration of the widespread support for the internees he was elected as a delegate to the GAA's annual congress. The makeshift huts that housed prisoners in Long Kesh were in poor condition – 'leaking, permanently wet' and overrun with mice. In October there had been an escape attempt and in response the authorities had cut food supplies. Some of the internees burnt the canteen in protest and, in the ensuing riot, troops severely beat several prisoners.

Most prisoners, internees and sentenced, were initially held in Crumlin Road Jail. There the rival republican O/Cs Seamus Lynch and Martin Meehan knew each other from work as dockers and agreed to coordinate escape plans. Unlike their Official colleagues, all the Provisional prisoners on the *Maidstone* went to mass, with the exception of Ted Howell, who was nicknamed 'Ted the red . . . the Sticky Provo'. The Official prisoners started several riots on the ship to demand transfer to Long Kesh, eventually succeeding; but when they arrived at the run-down huts, one recalls, 'We were sorry we fucking left the *Maidstone*!'

In Long Kesh the prisoners established command structures that replicated those of their organizations outside. Lynch was elected camp O/C of the Official internees. He encouraged the setting up of education classes and reading, making a public appeal for donations of books, while the Provisional prisoners mainly engaged in drilling and weapons classes. The Officials' greater emphasis on political education was apparent when Provisional internees approached OIRA education officer Art McMillen to ask him to lecture them on their Éire Nua policy. Lynch ran a strict regime, arguing that it was 'very important to maintain discipline in [the] cages to keep people from getting depressed'. One threat to morale was the worry that girlfriends or wives were having affairs, and a number of men on the outside were given punishment beatings by the OIRA on suspicion of this.

Among the sentenced Official prisoners in Crumlin Road, Peter John Monaghan of Tyrone was elected O/C with Brendan Mackin of Belfast his second in command, the view being that a rural O/C and an urban adjutant would be a good mixture. Monaghan had been interned with Provisional leader Billy McKee during the Border Campaign and Mackin knew McKee from childhood. The rival sides fielded teams in soccer and Gaelic football matches, and there was also cooperation over the issue of political status. During May 1972 a hunger strike for recognition as political prisoners began, Monaghan and Mackin taking part for the Officials alongside McKee and Frank Card for the Provisionals. The OIRA officers in the prison had decided on taking part in the strike, which lasted until mid-June, despite the wariness of the outside leadership. It was in Crumlin Road that initial contact was made between the Officials and UVF leader Gusty Spence. During 1970 Billy McMillen had introduced himself to Spence when he was briefly jailed after the Falls curfew, but it was with Monaghan that Spence had his first 'in depth' conversations about politics. During 1972 paramilitary structures in the prison were modified to accommodate the new UDA prisoners. This group were led by Jimmy Craig, recalled by Official prisoners as a criminal not overly concerned with politics, and a 'totally different kettle of fish' to Spence.

During 1972 the Officials established *Saoirse* as a new campaign for prisoners' rights. It demanded education, regular visits, civilian clothes and productive work for political prisoners. *Saoirse* also campaigned for general penal reform, with many in the Official movement endorsing the view that 'ordinary prisoners are unconscious political prisoners'. In Dublin the Officials set up a National Anti-Extradition Committee to protest at attempts to extradite Michael Willis back to Northern Ireland, where he faced ten years in jail. Willis, an OIRA prisoner, had escaped from Crumlin Road in May by hanging on to the underside of a bin lorry.

Prison life was substantially different for republicans in the South and for a period they benefited from the upsurge in nationalist feeling. IRA prisoners had access to alcohol in Mountjoy Prison, with one Official recalling that his cell 'was like a brewery'. There was little tension between Officials and Provisionals in the prison initially. The factions shared drink and reading material including a well-thumbed copy of *The Secret Army* signed by inmates from both factions. Both sets of IRA prisoners took part in a major riot in Mountjoy in May 1972. An Official prisoner remembers that the focus on a list of prisoners' demands came as an afterthought, the riot having been provoked by the sacking of a sympathetic warder who had allowed some Provo prisoners to visit a pub while being transferred to court:

There was no plan, even though the papers claimed there was. Al Ryan [a Waterford Provisional] leapt up on the back of one of the screws and roared, 'Give me the fucking keys, you bollocks!' . . . the prison was gone up in 25 seconds . . . Martin Cahill [a young Dublin criminal later to become known as the General] was running around wearing these white Arab robes, like Lawrence of Arabia . . . he had this big iron bar and he was going around smashing all the pipes and there was steam coming out of them and water and he was smashing the radiators as well . . . The ordinary prisoners let out some real madsers from the hospital wing . . . The politicos had to try to get . . . these other real loo-las . . . back in their cells.

Following the riot republican prisoners began to be transferred in greater numbers to Portlaoise Prison. There during the summer of 1972 three OIRA men went on hunger strike in protest at restricted visits. By late 1972 the Officials in Mountjoy were a small minority and relations with the Provisionals worsened. While on remand 19-year-old Official Tony Moriarty found one group of Provisionals 'extremely hostile' and was physically threatened, though an older group took him 'under their wing'. In the military prison at the Curragh, Official and Provisional prisoners collaborated on an escape during October 1972, though they were soon recaptured.

Over the following years, however, the growing tension between the rival republican factions was mirrored in the prisons. By 1973 the numbers were now decisively in favour of the Provisionals, who had several hundred prisoners compared with 52 OIRA men in Long Kesh, 5 in the Curragh, 6 in Mountjoy and 14 in England. There were several clashes between the outnumbered Officials and the Provisionals in both Mountjoy and Portlaoise. The worst trouble arose when the Official prisoners in Mountjoy dissociated themselves from a campaign by the Provisionals for segregation of political prisoners. The Officials' O/C Ronnie Deehan argued that it was their duty to spread 'Republican political ideas' among ordinary prisoners and not take a 'holier than thou' attitude to them. Several Official prisoners were attacked as a result, and Provo Éamonn Mac Thomáis had to intervene to try to guarantee their safety. Despite increasing trouble between the Officials and Provisionals on the streets, Mackin and others managed to maintain a mainly peaceful relationship in Long Kesh: 'There was an unwritten rule that inside Long Kesh we shouldn't be bringing in the whole thing of what was going on outside.'

Emphasis was also placed on nurturing contacts with loyalists. In Long Kesh this occurred through the education process in classes conducted by the Open University. Several OIRA prisoners were taking degrees along with loyalists during 1974. During 1973 the Officials in Long Kesh had began producing a journal, *An Eochair* ('The Key'), featuring articles, poems and songs smuggled out of jail. The prisoners used *An Eochair* to link the Northern conflict to struggles in places like South Africa and Palestine and to the 'Indian people of the USA'. Another issue dealt with was feminism, with the men advised that use of language like 'chick' and 'bird' contributed to the oppression of women.

The Irish conflict was a source of curiosity to the international left, with growing numbers of foreign groups making contact with the Officials. An American radical recalled that 'Sinn Féin had a huge profile internationally and it was part of the revolutionary world tour that every left-wing backpacker that managed to find their way [to Ireland] would go to'. In late 1970 New Leftists Jerry Rubin and Stew Albert, who had been defendants in the famous Chicago Seven trial that followed the 1968 riots in that city, were invited to Ireland by the People's Democracy and shown around Belfast by the Officials, before being deported. Bob Purdie, a Scottish member of the International Marxist Group, ended up staying with McMillen in the Lower Falls shortly after the curfew. He recalls the area having 'sandbagged army posts, armoured cars and foot patrols everywhere'. The differences in approach between the international radicals and the republicans could lead to confusion, as Purdie recalls:

Billy had been in jail and released only two or three days before I met him. We were walking past the sandbagged post in Cullingtree Road, which was manned by a black soldier. I asked if they had tried to 'get at' the soldiers, meaning trying to propagandize them as the US anti-war movement was doing with GIs. He immediately became very evasive and said, 'I'm only out of jail and I haven't got meself turned round yet. Anyway they always go around in patrols.' I realized he had misunderstood 'get at' and explained my meaning. He stopped dead and said, 'That's a good idea.'

In Belfast during 1971 the OIRA did distribute a letter to British soldiers calling on them to desert, warning that they would soon be used to police the working class of Britain on behalf of the rich. In the immediate aftermath of Bloody Sunday, two members of the Queen's Lancashire Regiment, Colin Demet and Michael Hawkins, deserted and handed over their SLRs and uniforms to the OIRA. Demet and Hawkins were then produced by the

Officials at a press conference in Dublin, where they outlined their disgust at the army's tactics in Belfast. Both men had an uncomfortable time in Dublin and they eventually returned to Britain and gave themselves up, enduring harsh imprisonment as a result.

The Officials also sought out their own international political links. In late 1970 and early 1971 Máirín de Burca attended conferences in Jordan and Kuwait organized to discuss the Palestinian issue. The Amman event was described as a 'guerilla Disneyland', with leftists from all over the world attending.

Official visits abroad were monitored closely by the authorities. Malachy McGurran was particularly well travelled, undertaking extensive speaking tours of the US and Europe. British Prime Minister Edward Heath personally intervened in an attempt to halt a 1972 McGurran tour of Sweden. Among the complaints British officials raised with their Scandinavian counterparts was that this 'senior Official IRA officer active in the North' had 'affiliations with the Trotskyist Fourth International' and 'his main contribution to IRA policies is his international outlook. Guevara is one of his heroes.' Nonetheless McGurran was allowed to undertake the tour. Contacts were not exclusively with the Marxist left. In late 1971 the British Young Liberals contacted Sinn Féin to say that their chairman Peter Hain was visiting Dublin and wished to meet representatives of the 'political and or/military wings' of the movement.

With many republican supporters in America having defected to the Provisionals, the Officials had to develop a new US network that incorporated traditional and left-wing support. In mid-1971 the Irish Republican Clubs of the US and Canada were launched. The IRC comprised Irish-born republicans, older Irish left-wing emigrants, younger Irish Americans, some of whom had been active in the New Left, and American leftists with no Irish connections. Some of the Officials' efforts were geared towards winning support away from the Provos. They published a statement in the New York *Irish Echo* outlining Official military actions during August 1971, claiming that the OIRA had inflicted at least 'six fatalities' on the UVF and also killed several soldiers. During the winter of 1971 Mac Giolla undertook a major US speaking tour, appearing alongside veteran 'labor' priest Fr. Charles Owen Rice in Pittsburgh. In Boston he gatecrashed a press conference by former British Prime Minister Harold Wilson. After Bloody Sunday the IRC helped form a broad Anti-Internment Coalition in New York, leading large protests outside British airline offices; John Lennon and Yoko Ono were among those who took part. McMillen visited America the same month, drawing a large crowd for a speech in Philadelphia during which the organizers made a point of referring to him as 'commander'. He also led the IRC contingent in New York's St Patrick's Day parade. Though de Burca was refused a visa to visit the US that autumn, Ó Tuathail was able to carry out a coast-to-coast speaking tour that raised over $12,000. The IRC also took part in several demonstrations against the Vietnam War, demanding 'US out of Vietnam, Britain out of Ireland'. However, the Official leadership were anxious the IRC should not confine itself to the far left, instructing their American supporters that they 'must avoid hard-line doctrinaire positions'. The IRC's function was 'to strengthen the base in America in support of the Irish Anti-Imperialist struggle'. This would be done 'not in terms of Vietnam or the Blacks', because an 'overemphasis on your role in American radical politics can weaken your base among the Irish working class in America'. By late 1972 there were Irish Republican Clubs in fifteen North American cities.

In Britain Clann na hÉireann was also reorganized after the split. The Clann had preempted Sinn Féin's abandonment of abstentionism, members voting in early 1970 for seats to be taken in all three parliaments. Birmingham and the English Midlands remained the group's most active area. Emigrant advice centres, modelled on Sinn Féin citizens' advice bureaux, were set up, activists often dealing with the problems of Asian immigrants as well as those of the Irish. In late 1969 Padraig Yeates had helped set up *Site Action Press*, a paper for building workers that exposed dangerous conditions and low wages in the industry. A protest campaign calling for the freeing of republican prisoners in British jails included the occupation of Aer Lingus offices in Birmingham. Following the Falls curfew in July 1970, Yeates met Bowes Egan, who had stood unsuccessfully as a PD candidate for Stormont. Egan asked Yeates to accompany Frank 'Butch' Roche, a Saor Éire supporter, in an attack on the House of Commons during a debate on UK accession to the EEC. Roche and Yeates made it into the Strangers' Gallery, Yeates recalls, as Anthony Barber, the Chancellor of the Exchequer, rose to speak:

[Roche] waited for a few minutes and I thought he might have lost his bottle and I was wondering would I be up to it, when he stood up, pulled the release on the first canister and threw it, shouting: 'Here's a present from the Falls, you bastards.' It landed right in front of Barber. Roche then threw the second canister, which was another superb shot and landed beside Barbara Castle on the Labour front bench. At first nothing much happened, except Roche was dragged away, and then the canisters started to spurt gas and pandemonium broke out. Some of the MPs thought it was a bomb and rushed for the doors. Castle was first out. I never saw a woman in high heels move so fast . . . People in the Strangers' Gallery thought it was great fun . . . Although I had told nobody in Dublin about the incident beforehand, in case they tried to stop it as a piece of left-wing adventurism, there were no repercussions.

Roche received a one-year prison sentence for his part in the incident. Clann's political profile was aided by the MP Bernadette Devlin, who contributed half the costs towards Yeates going full-time as Clann organizer in 1971. As Clann grew, relations with the Connolly Association worsened, both groups aware they were 'fishing in the same very small pond' for members and influence. The older organization secretly blocked the republicans from hiring halls for meetings. Relations with Irish associations and county associations were also problematic, with Clann members barred from selling papers in some Irish community centres.

In the aftermath of the Aldershot bombing the police clamped down on Clann, with dozens arrested and their homes raided. Seamus Collins lost his job after being featured in hostile press reports while a few members left, disgusted at the carnage. However, the impact was not all negative, Collins recalls:

For a long time afterwards I was paid compliments over Aldershot because I got up at [an Easter] commemoration and refused to condemn it. I remember Provo elements being hostile to me in a club and a man saying no, no, that man had the guts to stand by Aldershot. It made me uncomfortable that Aldershot got me out of a tight situation.

One consequence of internment and the violent atmosphere in Northern Ireland was that previously less prominent activists came to the fore. Margaret McNulty, whose husband Trevor, a leading New Lodge Official, was interned, recalls that, with the men 'either on the run or inside', women took a more prominent role, 'organizing groups, protesting, picketing, then looking at facilities in the areas, seeing what was needed, and different things were set up'. The Official leadership hoped that 'returning to the streets' by breaking the ban on illegal marches might provide a new focus for agitation. Their ambitions were buoyed by what seemed to be a rising appetite for mass political campaigning. Several thousand people marched outside Belfast in early January 1972 and six more demonstrations were held that month, culminating in Derry on the 30th. After the Bloody Sunday massacre in Derry the focus was on a huge turnout in Newry a week later; with an estimated 25,000 taking part in this protest, many were satisfied that the British Army had failed to drive the movement off the streets.

Following the OIRA's ceasefire and the release of internees there were major efforts to revive open Republican Club activity in Belfast. By August there were 25 Clubs organized in the city, with approximately 600 members, selling 6,000 copies of the *United Irishman* a month. Five cooperative 'People's Shops' sold basic foodstuffs at reduced prices. The shops also became a target of loyalists, and a woman was killed in a bomb attack outside the Leeson Street co-op in October 1972. Activists also ran children's play centres and film shows, and organized a 'Paras Out' campaign in Ballymurphy and a 'Festival of the Oppressed' folk concert. Another major effort was to get education classes up and running. It was felt that former internees had already attained a level of political education and that efforts should be concentrated on other members. As part of the post-ceasefire re-evaluation, education documents examined the difference between 'elitist' military action and mass revolutionary violence. Among the questions discussed at education meetings was, 'Did Aldershot enable the British to say "Now we are quits for Derry"?' One IRA O/C was shocked when he first heard a member of the leadership denouncing 'terrorism'.

The link between political and military activity sometimes created problems. In August 1972, fifteen members of the Warrenpoint Republican Club resigned, informing the Dublin leadership that local OIRA 'militarists . . . looked down' on them. They also claimed that the Crossmaglen O/C was a 'gangster' and that another local unit were a 'gang of criminals'.

Many Northern activists were beginning to feel that some in the movement's Southern leadership were divorced from the reality of the conflict. In Armagh John Nixon recalls being upset when de Burca lectured a group of young volunteers on how ordinary British soldiers were victims of the system as well. 'I said hang on a minute, these people are shooting us right, left, and centre and raiding our homes and beating our people . . . and you're coming up here to preach to us and then heading back down to fucking Dublin. What the fuck do you know about?' Differences were also evident to Sean Kelly from Waterford when he addressed the 1972 Easter commemoration at Carrickmore, Co. Tyrone. He found that people 'didn't give a shit, they didn't want to hear it, the helicopters came down and drowned it out. Now if you were up there and had the Brits up your back morning noon and night [you] wouldn't want to hear it either. I was a tourist.' Within the movement in the South, attitudes to the violence varied. Some felt that the OIRA was engaged in a 'race to the bottom' with the Provisionals, which could only lead to more disasters. Others 'quietly cheered' when a soldier was killed, even by the Provisionals. Many Southern members had little idea of the extent of the OIRA's activities in the North. The Aldershot bombing and the killing of Ranger Best caused soul-searching for some but were defended vigorously by others.

Anne Harris, writing in *Hibernia* two weeks after Aldershot, described the negative reaction to the bomb in the South as the 'most nauseating show of hypocrisy from the Irish middle class to date':

It was quite clear that it took courage and determination to enter the headquarters of the technological savages who are maintained for colonial repression by the Crown . . . In Ireland the three political parties help keep the natives quiet. But if that should fail there is always the refined gentleman standing at the bar of the officers' mess in Aldershot. In the last analysis the Irish poor face the Paras. That is why, although I'm depressed about the deaths of the five waitresses, I am also sickened by the hypocrisy of the establishment reaction.

The Aldershot bombing was just one of many incidents that inspired growing ideological division among the Officials. Many of these debates were coloured by the use of concepts drawn from the international left. Two major competing views emerged. One, based on Marxist 'stageist' theory, held that a 'revolutionary situation' could be brought about only by achieving a series of goals: equality, then national freedom, then social freedom, and eventually socialism. Those who held this view prioritized the rebuilding of the civil rights campaign and the push for reform within Northern Ireland. They tended to place a great emphasis on the need to split unionism and win Protestant working-class support. Premature military action only increased sectarianism and gave the British the excuse to introduce more repression. Once sectarianism had been overcome new political alliances built around a united working class, North and South, would push for a united Ireland. Only then would the movement concentrate its entire energies on achieving socialist revolution. This, broadly, was the view of Goulding and Mac Giolla, among the leadership of the Official movement, and of some of its leading intellectuals, such as Eoin Ó Murchú and Eoghan Harris.

Others believed the outbreak of violence in the North had resulted in the civil rights struggle being replaced by a direct confrontation with British imperialism. This analysis held that it was possible to push towards a revolutionary situation in the immediate term by political action combined with armed struggle. Adherents of this analysis, most prominently Seamus Costello, stressed that republican-socialism's greatest icon – James Connolly – had concluded that British state interference in Ireland must be removed as a prerequisite to wider social change. Winning Protestant support was not considered likely as long as loyalism held sway over that section of the working class. While critics denounced this as sectarian 'ultra-leftism' its supporters held that the 'national question' could not be ignored.

On both sides there were those who saw the question in terms of international left-wing conflicts. Ó Murchú recalls he 'rather romantically' looked upon the divide between the stagism of Goulding and Mac Giolla and the more urgent militarism of Costello as 'Stalinism versus Trotskyism'. Some in the movement happily adopted such labels while others were repelled by them. Many activists remained 'eclectic' in their ideological approach, Padraig Yeates recalls: 'You took what you thought was useful and left the rest.'

While division over the merits of a stageist approach would come to dominate internal Official politics, other related arguments also raged. These included whether Ireland's economic, political and cultural situation was that of a colonized country or a developed capitalist society. In 1970 a *United Irishman* article linking the political situations in Ireland and Palestine concluded that 'it is difficult to see how strategies of the Third World, which have invariably consisted of national liberation campaigns, can fail to apply in Ireland'. Some Officials, such as Sean Garland, were reading the works of Third World liberation theorists, particularly Frantz Fanon, whose *The Wretched of the Earth* drew upon his experiences as an FLN operative during the Algerian War of Independence. Fanon's thesis held that the poorest among the rural and urban masses – dismissed in traditional Marxist theory as the reactionary lumpenproletariat – could become a revolutionary vanguard if properly mobilized.

Although these debates were arguably at their most intense among the movement's Dublin-based leaders and ideologues, they also impacted on the North. The Derry OIRA, some of whose members had a background in organizations such as the Young Socialists, came in for particular scrutiny for 'ultra-left tendencies'. During a short sojourn from Derry, Terry Robson had become education officer for the Co. Antrim Clubs, but was suspended for urging his unit to refuse to sell the September 1972 *United Irishman*. That issue carried an article by Eoin Ó Murchú which described Bernadette Devlin, Eamonn McCann and Michael Farrell as 'Provo-Trots' who had helped turn 'civil rights into civil war'. Ó Murchú charged that the Provos' 'insane' bombing campaign had been urged on by the 'parasitic sub-life' of the Trotskyist movement. The article drew much criticism and the Official leadership discussed whether Harris might have partly written it. The OIRA Army Council minutes for 8 October noted: 'It was further agreed that we advise B. Devlin that the article attacking her in the Sept *U.I.* did not in any way reflect the opinions of the editorial comm[ittee] or the leadership: the writer alone was responsible.'

In Belfast there were also those concerned with instilling a distinct brand of pro-Soviet Marxism within the movement. After his release from internment, Des O'Hagan had become an increasingly influential figure. A member of the IRA and then Saor Uladh during the 1950s, the Belfast man had emigrated to England after serving time during the Border Campaign. There he studied at the London School of Economics and joined the Communist Party. Active as an Official auxiliary in the Lower Falls, he was nicknamed 'the Devil' after a run-in with local clergymen. O'Hagan attained public recognition during his imprisonment, authoring a series of 'Letters from Long Kesh' published in the *Irish Times*. On his release the Dublin leadership recommended that he be given greater authority in Belfast, and he was elected on to the army executive in late 1972. O'Hagan was unashamedly supportive of the USSR and hostile to

Trotskyism. This Soviet orthodoxy was opposed by Belfast Clubs members such as Ronnie Bunting, who had a background in People's Democracy.

After the May 1972 ceasefire the leadership was intent on renewing efforts at reaching out to the Northern Protestant working class, emphasizing the role of the Provo campaign in intensifying sectarian division. Within the leadership McGurran voiced a note of concern, warning 'there is always the danger that you would concentrate all your efforts . . . in getting through to the Protestant working class, and find the Catholic working class has been led astray behind your back'. At Carrickmore in July 1972 Mac Giolla made a major speech, partly written by Dick Walsh, in which he stated that the Provisionals' military activity had destroyed the momentum of the civil rights campaign. In doing this they had played into the hands of the 'forces of Imperialism'. According to the Sinn Féin president, the key task was to prevent a sectarian civil war and to enlist Protestant workers' support for the republican cause:

People have talked about the Provisionals trying to bomb one million Protestants into a republic; but they would not – could not – and no one can – and no one as far as we are concerned would try – to bomb them into a socialist republic. That would be the ultimate contradiction and the ultimate stupidity. We need those million Protestant working people on the workers' side in the Irish revolution.

The speech had a significant impact within the movement. In Derry it was decided to resume efforts to contact loyalists despite the fact that a previous attempt 'ended in near disaster'. In March 1973 the Clubs began a major campaign against sectarianism, taking out an ad in the *Irish News* declaring 'Sectarianism kills workers' and distributing leaflets on the theme that 'republicanism is secular, socialist, separatist'.

During the same period British civil servants were discussing how they 'might draw the sting from groups such as the Officials wavering between political activity and violence'. They considered 'the extent to which the Officials could be weaned from violence' by 'concessions' such as the legalizing of the Republican Clubs, while noting that the group's 'new supporters are more politically orientated than the old supporters'. Secretary of State for Northern Ireland William Whitelaw was wary of such an approach, asserting that 'some gunmen are pathological killers'. Those seeking rapprochement won out, however, and the Republican Clubs were made legal in April 1973. In response the Officials announced plans to contest the forthcoming District Council elections. All 83 candidates took a 'people's pledge' that they would not take their seats while internment existed. Despite their legal status the Clubs faced security-force harassment, with several candidates arrested and their homes raided during the campaign. Neither South Derry's Francie Donnelly nor Armagh's Tommy McGleenan could campaign openly because of threats from the army. In Belfast there were clashes with the Provisionals, who were running a boycott campaign. In the end the Clubs gained just 3 per cent of the vote, winning 10 seats. There were some encouraging signs: in Newry they took 11 per cent of the vote, and in Belfast Jim Sullivan and Ray O'Hagan were elected and a substantial vote of 9,500 first preferences taken in the Falls area. In Derry the Clubs received 6 per cent overall but took 16 per cent in Creggan where Mickey Montgomery became the first republican to win a seat in the city since 1921. Claims that the Ranger Best killing had ended support for the Officials in Derry were obviously mistaken.

A few weeks later a separate election was held to choose representatives to negotiate new power-sharing governmental structures for Northern Ireland that would include an 'Irish dimension'. The Clubs fielded fewer candidates and saw their vote fall to 1.8 per cent. Rural constituencies provided the most support, with James McDaid taking 2,923 votes in Fermanagh-South Tyrone while four Belfast candidates mustered only 3,728 between them. The Officials did receive a morale boost when Francie Donnelly, having been disqualified from the South Derry Council for refusing to take his seat, was returned in the subsequent by-election, beating an SDLP challenger. His campaign was supported by local MP Bernadette Devlin, who had recently married a Tyrone Official, Michael McAliskey.

At a meeting in late July the lessons of the elections were considered. Widespread intimidation of voters by the Provisionals was reported from parts of Belfast and especially in Crossmaglen. Their accusation that the Officials were collaborators was also thought to have hurt the Republican Clubs' vote. It was felt the Officials' anti-sectarian statements were seen as 'too accommodating' to unionists by some voters. Others felt the Clubs were 'too closely associated with violence' and that the OIRA's claim to have killed seven soldiers during the spring had actually 'lost us votes'. Internal problems had also created difficulties. In Armagh city the Official director of elections did not even agree with contesting them and made no effort to organize the area. After the Council elections the Clubs had found it difficult to motivate activists to canvass for the Assembly poll. More problematically it was noted that some voters did not take the Clubs 'seriously as a political party: they regarded us more as a mixture of social workers and militarists'. It was admitted that the Officials' use of voter impersonation had helped up the total poll, 'particularly in the Belfast area'. The Belfast director of elections recalled 'umpteen dud votes . . . people weren't interested in voting so we voted for them. Vote early and vote often.'

The Official leadership believed that getting involved in a campaign against the building of an orbital road in Belfast had potential to bridge the sectarian divide. Up to 14,000 people were to be uprooted for the huge project, which would pass through parts of the Lower Falls, Short Strand, Sandy Row and the Markets, and the Officials believed that both Catholics and Protestants could be mobilized on the issue. A great deal of time and energy was spent on pickets and road blockades over the next two years. The OIRA announced that they had built up 'dossiers of information' on the various companies involved in the project and offered their services to the campaign. Attempts at cross-community cooperation were also made by NICRA, which began to campaign for the release of all political prisoners, loyalist and republican. But Kevin McCorry reported a 'lack of interest' among Club members towards NICRA, with even executive members not turning up for meetings. In Derry the majority of the local membership had decided that involvement with NICRA had 'shackled' the movement. The Officials were already noting that even 'many of our own members . . . doubt the credibility of our anti-sectarian stand'.

Even more contentious were efforts to engage with loyalist paramilitaries. In late 1972 the UVF dismissed appeals from the Sinn Féin president by sneering, 'Mac Giolla, get your priorities right. You are no more interested in the working-class Protestant than the man in the moon.' The Officials recognized that the leadership of loyalism was 'overwhelmingly reactionary' but maintained that the UDA and the UVF represented a 'new factor . . . an effort by the Loyalist working class to set up their own organisations' and 'a very faint flicker of hope'. Goulding was very anxious for contacts to be established. Harry McKeown already had some connections to men who had joined loyalist groups through his construction business. Encouraged by Goulding, McKeown set about organizing a meeting for the Official leadership and the UVF. In this he sought the assistance of his friend Kevin Myers, a young journalist. Myers socialized with members of the OIRA, who found him very left-wing and anti-British in his attitudes. On the UVF side there was also interest in talks; leading Belfast UVF man Billy Mitchell recalls that his organization's leadership were interested in seeing face to face what made their 'enemy tick'. Mitchell had also read Rosita Sweetman's strongly pro-Official *On Our Knees*, published in 1972. Sweetman's twin sister Sue was an activist in Official Sinn Féin in Dublin.

In early 1974 the OIRA leadership wrote to the UVF leadership:

It is our belief that ultimately the solution [can] only be found in the 32-county context of a Socialist Republic . . . if our organisations were to cooperate in any way, we would retain the right to try to persuade you of our point of view but we renounce the use of force to push anyone into a United Ireland. We only accept the use of force in defence of working-class homes or communities. Make no mistake, we may well need that force in defence of working-class demands. Recent experience has shown that we are all 'natives' to the British Army when we oppose the policies of a British Tory Government.

Shortly after this letter was sent, a delegation from the UVF including Mitchell, Jim Hanna and another of the organization's senior figures were met in Monaghan and brought to Dublin. At a hotel in Chapelizod they spent several hours in discussion with Goulding and Garland; Mac Giolla also entered the talks briefly. As Mitchell recalls: 'We got the impression they were people we could do business with. Most of the talk was social and economic stuff, not the constitutional stuff.' On the Saturday night the loyalists and their wives accompanied the Officials, including Billy McMillen and Des O'Hagan, to Slattery's Pub in Capel Street. The UVF men were unsure what to do when 'Amhrán na bhFiann' was played at closing time. They began to stand up, but O'Hagan made a point of not standing and McMillen told the UVF men they didn't have to either. A level of contact was maintained, but when news of the meetings began to seep into the press the loyalists furiously denied that there had been any contacts, while the Officials confirmed talks had occurred. During this period the UVF men had also met members of the Provisional leadership, a fact that caused outrage when news of it also leaked out. The talks led to internal ructions in the UVF and were a factor in the killing of Jim Hanna by members of his own organization in April 1974. During this loyalist feud, Billy Mitchell hid out in McKeown's home.

Some of the Official leadership saw the internal disputes within loyalism as indicating a left–right divide. The Official press enthused whenever the UVF's *Combat* quoted an article from the *United Irishman* or used left-wing rhetoric. Des O'Hagan contributed an article to the UVF journal on internment under a pseudonym 'Long Beard'. The Officials also saw evidence of new thinking within the UDA. After two of its leading members, Tommy

Heron and Ernie 'Duke' Elliot, were killed during internal feuds, the Officials speculated that they had been 'working against Fascism in Loyalist ranks'. However, Mitchell felt that the Officials were 'probably looking at the UVF through rose-tinted glasses' and that the loyalists who had met the Official leadership were 'not representative of the UVF or the Loyalist community'. Despite its occasional leftist rhetoric, *Combat* also stressed opposition to 'communism, the enemy of the working class' as well as featuring an article supportive of the British National Front and white rule in Rhodesia. It reiterated that the UVF was equally opposed to both the 'Papist Provisional Alliance' and the 'Marxist Republican Movement'.

A powerful reminder of the strength of a mobilized Protestant working class came in May 1974. Since the beginning of that year, after agreement at a conference at Sunningdale, some Unionists, the SDLP and the cross-community (but mainly middle-class) Alliance Party had been operating a power-sharing government. In opposition to this arrangement, many grassroots unionists, the DUP, Vanguard and the Orange Order had come together under the umbrella of the United Ulster Unionist Council. This group both reflected and fuelled widespread Protestant unease with the 'Irish Dimension' of the Sunningdale Agreement. Behind-the-scenes contacts between the UUUC, loyalist trade unionists and paramilitaries culminated in a general strike organized by the newly created Ulster Workers' Council. Two days into the stoppage, on 17 May, UVF car bombs in Dublin and Monaghan killed 33 people. After thirteen days, with all essential services threatened with closure and loyalist paramilitaries openly on the streets, the power-sharing Assembly collapsed.

During the strike the OIRA helped coordinate relief efforts within nationalist areas, bringing in supplies of food and fuel. On the ground in Belfast many Officials feared pogroms or even a loyalist coup. Extra weapons were moved into areas in preparation for attacks, and plans were drawn up for barricading and holding nationalist districts. The OIRA made it clear that it was 'prepared to cooperate with other groups in defence of areas' but would not participate in 'offensive activities of a sectarian nature'. Preparations were made in south Belfast for cooperation between Officials and Provisionals to hold the Lagan Bridge and evacuate local Catholics down the railway line into the Markets. At a meeting of the Official leadership to assess the impact of the strike, McMillen reported that the organization had 'responded very well' in Belfast. While many Catholics were frustrated that the 'Brits were not moving against the Loyalists' they seemed to have confidence that the 'movement would protect them in the event of sectarian clashes'. In Armagh, however, fear of sectarian attack had led many Catholics to accept the British Army in areas where they would have normally met a hostile reception. In Derry, Catholic workers were attacked when they tried to go to work and some families were also forced out.

In the US the momentum of the Irish Republican Clubs had faltered and in 1973 just $8,448 was sent back to Ireland. The organization was riven by disputes between the more traditionalist Irish-American activists and young left-wingers who wanted support for issues such as abortion and gay rights. The Official leadership were concerned about the flow of money and counselled compromise. The most successful fundraisers were a Club composed of New York transport workers led by Liam Kelly. As part of a longer-term plan, the movement opened a pub in Berkeley, California, during 1974. Several American supporters of the Officials emigrated to Ireland during the early 1970s including Helena Sheehan and Ellen Hazelkorn. There was some suspicion of their motives and the OIRA carried out investigations into the backgrounds of these emigrants.

Clann na hÉireann also had to take stock of the new situation after 1972 as the worsening violence saw enthusiasm and interest fall away. The organization faced constant police attention and attempts at infiltration. At various stages Mac Giolla, McGurran and Seán Ó Cionnaith were also served with exclusion orders from Britain. Clann tried to build a wider base, setting up an Emigrants' Campaign, demanding the vote for emigrants and protection for Irish workers from unscrupulous landlords and employers. But the turnout for Clann protests began to dwindle as the British left shifted its focus away from the Northern Irish conflict and towards other causes such as anti-racism. There was an emotional response to former Clann activist Michael Gaughan's death on hunger strike in May 1974. The Clann newspaper *Rosc Catha* admonished the Irish community by asking: 'Where were you? . . . rightly or wrongly . . . this 24-year-old boy died for you.' Clann members hoisted a tricolour over Lambeth town hall and flew it at half mast to mark Gaughan's death.

On many occasions Clann members were raided after Provisional bombings. Clann condemned these bombings not for 'moral or pacifist' reasons but because they were 'politically and strategically wrong'. After 21 people were killed in the Provo bombings of Birmingham pubs in November 1974 Clann denounced the 'disgusting outrage' and, in an atmosphere of rising hysteria, distributed leaflets in Irish bars and clubs arguing, 'You didn't do it, you didn't plant bombs, don't put your heads down, hold them up.' However, the bombs had a major impact in alienating British people from the Irish cause and led to a police crackdown on all Irish republican groups. Jim Flynn was among the Officials arrested and held for eighteen days in solitary confinement before being deported to Ireland. Eventually three more Officials – Gerry Doherty, Danny Ryan and Brendan Phelan – were also sent back to Ireland.

During this period the Officials identified a new source of funding. The Inland Revenue allowed building contractors to settle their tax affairs at the end of the year. Rather than pay tax on a weekly basis the subcontractors were granted tax exemption certificates, which enabled the main contractor to pay in gross without income tax being deducted. Harry McKeown was one of the first to realize the potential of the scheme. If false certificates were produced then contractors could present a figure to the authories and pay a percentage to the OIRA. An anarchist group and BICO members were recruited to help print the first false certificates. As the official certificates became more sophistated the OIRA devised new ways of obtaining plates from which to forge them. With major building work starting to take place in areas like the Lower Falls and the Markets, the tax exemption rapidly became a major source of funding for the Officials. They expanded the operation to the British Midlands and to Bristol, also providing security on sites there. Another source of income came from the local drinking clubs, which were becoming much more professionalized. Clubs now operated in the Lower Falls, the Markets, Turf Lodge, Beechmount, New Lodge, Whiterock and Ballymurphy. In Twinbrook the OIRA were asked to intervene in a row between two factions of the ex-servicemen's organization over the running of their drinking club. The Officials took the opportunity to gain a say in the running of this club themselves.

There were two British general elections during 1974 and the Republican Clubs contested both, again complaining of widespread harassment. The Irish government's assessment of political developments in the North suggested that the SDLP would lose support to republicans and that the Officials would benefit, because they 'were not as closely identified with the atrocities and violence of recent years and were in general more active politically than militarily'. However, the Clubs polled just 2.1 per cent of the vote in February. In the October Westminster poll the Clubs' vote rose slightly to 3.1 per cent. The SDLP's Gerry Fitt accused the Clubs of costing his party seats by only standing in nationalist areas.

Tension had been growing in Long Kesh over the conditions for the more than 1,000 republican and loyalist prisoners held there. There were complaints about the quality of food, visiting rights and cutbacks on parcels from outside. The Clubs helped establish the Belfast United Workers Group to organize industrial action on the issue. In September it was decided to stage marches and block roads across Belfast, involving supporters of all paramilitary groups. The Officials optimistically stated that for the 'first time since the [1932] Outdoor Relief riots' there would be cross-community protests on the streets of Belfast. At the last moment the loyalists called off their participation and only nationalist areas saw protests.

In Long Kesh the 'cages were pretty boiling' after several incidents and the Provisional prisoners had decided to burn their huts in protest. The Officials agreed to participate, while the UVF and UDA declined. The Provo O/C Davie Morley assured Officials that his men were not interested in having a battle with the loyalists, and that their prisoners would be left alone. On 20 October P. J. Monaghan called the Officials to 'emergency drill' and told them that the huts were to be destroyed. The men set fire to Cage 21, grabbing their coats and jackets and tearing off pieces of wood for weapons. Within 'five minutes [the] place was ablaze' as large parts of the camp were set alight and fences knocked down; 'the place all burned down around us'. As the prisoners retreated on to the football pitches hundreds of soldiers entered the camp backed up by dog units, firing CS gas and rubber bullets. A helicopter came in low over the prisoners, spraying CR gas. There was vicious hand-to-hand fighting, as John Nixon recalls: 'It was the first time ever that I had seen mass fighting on an open scale, 18 years of age, it scared the heart clean out of me.' Sean Curry was hit in the face by a rubber bullet and awoke in the UVF compound having been dragged in by loyalist prisoners for his own safety. Many prisoners were seriously injured and denied medical treatment. Nixon got a 'heavy beating . . . they told me it was for my own good'. Once the camp was secured the men were forced to stand for hours spreadeagled and then had to sleep outside for four weeks. Soldiers destroyed the Officials' prison library and many of their possessions. During this period loyalist prisoners threw tobacco and food into the republican prisoners' cages. A 5,000-strong march in support of the prisoners by the Belfast United Workers ended in rioting on the Falls.

By the end of 1974 the Official leadership was aware that their position was making little advance in the North. While 3,000 people attended a May unveiling of a monument dedicated to OIRA volunteers Tony Hughes and Jake McGerrigan in Armagh, the performance of Republican Clubs candidates in the area illustrated how little support had been gained beyond this active base. The Unionist Party had split but, rather than move to supporting republicanism or the left, the Protestant working class had been drawn towards the Democratic Unionist Party (DUP) and loyalist paramilitaries.

The crisis in the North had dominated Official political considerations since late 1969. However, the movement had also set its sights on radically changing Southern society.

7. Towards the Revolutionary Party

'In world revolutionary history only one form of organisation has
proved itself capable of organising the people to achieve victory. This
was the Bolshevik Party of Lenin . . . If we accept that we need and
must have the support of the mass of the Irish people, the working
class, and if we accept that we will not be able to develop the political
consciousness of all the people then the way forward is through the
development of a cadre of leaders in a conscious disciplined political
revolutionary vanguard organisation.'

Sean Garland, 1973

Events in Northern Ireland overshadowed Southern political life
in the early 1970s, and much OIRA activity in the South was
focused on providing military, political and financial support for
comrades in the North. Sinn Féin in Dublin experienced dramatic
growth, from just 9 cumainn in 1969 to 23 by early 1973, and the
picture was similar elsewhere in the South. The party was also
successfully reorganizing in areas severely affected by the split. By
mid-1971 the North Kerry cumann had enough members to set
about establishing a new branch in the west of the county. Many
new recruits dropped out of activity after a short period, however,
Goulding commenting 'that from every ten that come, maybe we
retain anything from three to five'.

Overt conflict with the Provos was relatively rare in the South.
Most among the Official leadership were keen to maintain this
situation, even ordering members to refrain from heckling at their
rivals' events. But contact between the former comrades was inevitable. The Felons' Club, a shebeen run in the basement of the
Kevin Barry Hall in Dublin's Parnell Square, remained a late-night

drinking venue for both wings. One Official recalled that in the club current politics 'were not meant to be discussed . . . but you sang your songs and you drank your drinks'. Some Officials were prone to dismissing the smaller faction in the city as politically naive 'cowboys' and of little long-term consequence. As in the North, however, the split intruded on families and friendships. Dublin activist Nuala Monaghan remained with the Officials while her husband Jim joined the Provos; Pat and Peigín Doyle, son and daughter of 1930s Dublin IRA man Archie, took the Provisional and Official sides respectively.

An interested observer of the ructions within republicanism was the US ambassador to Ireland John D. J. Moore. In his communiqués to Washington on the 'high priority' subject of an 'increasingly active' left wing in Ireland, the ambassador argued that the communists were attempting to 'capitalize on the lingering sentimental affection felt for the IRA' among the Irish public. In early 1970 Ambassador Moore sent a 'rundown of Communist and Communist-Front Organizations in Ireland' to Washington. This communiqué noted the observation of a 'highly placed official in the Irish Police' that 'communism has made more progress in Ireland in the last two or three years than it made in the previous thirty or forty years'. But the actual numbers involved were still small, Moore quoting estimates that the Communist Party had around '200 members plus about 100 fellow-travellers', that there were 100 Maoist Internationalists and around 40 in the Irish Communist Organisation. The Trotskyist League for a Workers' Republic (LWR), which was active within the Irish Labour Party, was estimated to have a membership of only 30. The Irish Voice on Vietnam, the Irish Campaign for Peace and the Ireland-USSR Society – groups, Moore noted, that had been central to 'several anti-war demonstrations at the Embassy' – were classified as mere 'front organizations' for communist subversion. In order to counter such agitation, funds were requested for a publicity campaign promoting President Richard Nixon's administration.

The British were less troubled by the potential of the Irish republican left wing. A Foreign Office intelligence report stated that the Officials' attempts to create a National Liberation Front were 'extremely unlikely' to succeed:

Although overdue for social reform, Ireland is markedly stony ground for Communism. In the first place, extremists and malcontents have an anti-Communist safety value in traditional Republicanism . . . The Republic is the antithesis of the classical Communist society: it is rural, bourgeois and clerical. The Church especially has great influence on opinion and most Irish, educated by the Church, regard even pink Socialism as atheistic dynamite. The Russians and their fellows are the legions of hell.

Nevertheless Official Sinn Féin activists were increasingly to the fore in demonstrations against America's war in Vietnam. The party's vice-president Máirín de Burca was prominent in many such protests, eventually spending several weeks in prison during 1971 following an incident in which cow's blood was thrown on to the US Embassy's facade.

The Officials also reinvigorated the campaign demanding public ownership of Ireland's fisheries. A new wave of fish-ins were planned, aimed not only at the remnants of the Anglo-Irish aristocracy but also the 'new rich of Fianna Fáil' whose interests the National Waters Restoration League felt minister Neil Blaney was most concerned to safeguard. Fish-ins occurred around the country, Lough Ree, Waterford and the Boyne valley seeing particularly intense activity. The protests also reached Donegal, with activists conducting salmon drift-net fishing in privately owned sections of Inver Bay. In May 1970 the Starry Plough flew over the battlements of Lismore Castle, Waterford, after a group of Officials barged their way into the Irish demesne of the Duke of Devonshire. A July occupation of Slane Castle led by Donnchadh Mac Raghnaill, chairman of the Boyne National Waters Restoration League, resulted in Gardaí storming the building and making arrests. The class rather than nationalist aspect of the campaign was emphasized in County Cork when Joe Sherlock led a fish-in on a section of the Blackwater owned by Fianna Fáil Senator Kevin O'Callaghan. Protesting about this infringement of his property rights, the senator stated that his father had bought back these 'dispossessed' O'Callaghan lands in the 1930s, adding that his family had taken the Jacobite side in the 1641 rebellion. The National Waters Restoration League was not impressed, replying that prior to the Cromwellian conquest fisheries were not the property of clan chiefs but 'were held in common by the people under native law', adding that its campaign would continue 'whether the owner be a Senator or an absentee landlord, a Duke of Devonshire or a native aristocrat'. Séamus Ó Tuathail's *Stolen Waters*, a pamphlet collection of the 'Poacher's Guide' articles, was one of the Official movement's fastest-selling publications. Addressing a Donegal fish-in, Máirín de Burca stated that there was a unity in the struggles of 'such outwardly disparate groups as the fishermen of Inver, the cement strikers of Drogheda and Limerick and the oppressed of the Falls and Bogside'. The Official IRA remained committed to backing up these protests, blowing up a salmon weir at Ballincollig during one dispute.

With an eye on stemming the growth of the Provisionals the Officials stepped up activity throughout rural Ireland. In Galway the Connemara Civil Rights Movement was active on issues of emigration and rural development. Although not a creation of the republicans, the Connemara Civil Rights Movement had applied to join the NLF. Eoin Ó Murchú was appointed full-time organizer for the Gaeltacht, the movement supplying him with radio transmission equipment that enabled Saor Raidió Chonamara to begin broadcasting in May 1970. A Small Farmers' Defence Association was set up to help generate rural agitation, with Ard Chomhairle member Tom Kilroy appointed organizing secretary. Elsewhere republicans had become involved in a dispute between the small community of Montpelier/O'Brien's Bridge, straddling the Clare–Limerick border, and the government. Ignoring local protests, the Department of Education had announced it was closing the community's primary school. Sinn Féin arranged for it to remain open without departmental funding, with Brian Patterson, former chairman of the Queen's Republican Club, taking over teaching responsibilities in early 1970. Several other republican teachers followed over the next year until the school was finally closed. In County Galway agitation against the construction of a golf course at Oughterard reached its height in the first months of 1971. Local activists picketed the developers' businesses, demanding that the land be divided up among local small farmers. Meanwhile the OIRA sabotaged building machinery and warned that the developers would be held 'personally responsible for depriving people . . . of their natural right to live in Ireland without fear of unemployment and emigration'. Later that year the OIRA again destroyed machinery on the site, firing shots over the heads of Gardaí who disturbed them.

The housing action campaign, by contrast, was now in decline, due to a combination of activists' concentration on Northern issues and the Gardaí's adoption of a more belligerent approach. As the Officials rearmed, squats were increasingly used to store weapons, a situation that precipitated a large-scale confrontation in 1970. During 1969 housing activists had occupied two empty four-storey houses on Pembroke Road in the leafy south Dublin suburbs. The properties, owned by a leading Dublin jeweller and by property developer Matt Gallagher, had been used by the Dublin Housing Action Committee (DHAC) to house several homeless families. In late May 1970 workmen forcibly evicted squatters from the Gallagher property. A 'frantic call' was received in Gardiner Place; Sean Dunne immediately gathered together a dozen activists, who rushed over to Pembroke Road only to find the house deserted. Unbeknown to them, a homeless man from the adjacent squat had produced a gun and frightened the evictors off. Within minutes of the activists taking repossession of the property a voice, amplified by megaphone, was heard demanding, 'Throw out the gun.' Gardaí had surrounded the area and began to move in, Dunne recalls:

We threw everything we had at them, plates, dirty nappies. We lost each floor as the police came in; we went up, and up and up, and we got stuck up in the kitchen . . . fronting out on to where the American

Embassy was and we were all singing 'We shall overcome' and I was holding the door and next minute an axe came through the door and the door swung open and I was caught behind the door, lucky for me because the police came in with crowbars and they bate ten kinds of shite out of everybody.

Injuries included broken ribs and a fractured skull. Those protesters not hospitalized were produced at the High Court, where it was demanded they give an undertaking to stay out of the property. But, as Dunne remembers, 'The minute we got out we ran back into it.' He oversaw defensive preparations:

We . . . [barricaded] it, we put railway sleepers against the door, we dug trenches, we put nails in cement, we made petrol bombs, of course . . . in the IRA we learned how to do this. We put acid in it. Of course the CP didn't want that violence, so we had an argument and we stashed them up on the roof. We were prepared for war on this one.

Well over 100 Gardaí surrounded the barricaded building and after a week of preparations launched a pre-dawn raid. Riot shields were deployed for the first time in the force's history and, under specially constructed corrugated-iron shelters, the Gardaí advanced into a hail of bottles, bricks and smoke bombs. They attempted to gain entry using power saws but met with a sustained shower of missiles. After hours of violent confrontation the protesters surrendered. That night, as the squatting families were being removed from the second Pembroke Street house, the OIRA's Dublin Active Service Unit was in action, burning down offices owned by the Gallaghers on Baggot Street, causing an estimated £250,000 worth of damage.

Although housing protests would continue, for many activists the Pembroke Road siege marked 'the last hurrah of the squatter'. An internal Sinn Féin report stated that after the siege the DHAC 'disintegrated' as attention was focused on events in the North. The housing action committees also had to accept there was growing disquiet that squatters, particularly in council properties, were merely 'queue jumpers'. Concerned by the campaign's decline, de Burca had called a special meeting of leading housing activists, including Sean Dunne and Proinsias De Rossa, in December 1970. Little was agreed upon and during 1971 the campaign reverted to opposing evictions and finding housing for those fleeing the Northern violence. There was also decisive action by government, with the Forcible Entry Bill becoming law in September 1971. It increased both Garda powers and the penalties on those who transgressed property rights. The new law clearly targeted housing action committees and the activities of the National Waters Restoration League, with Minister for Justice Micheál Ó Móráin referring to fish-ins as a 'form of intimidation' when proposing the new legislation. The summer of 1971 would see the last major fish-ins.

As the arrest of activists became more frequent, Sinn Féin sought to develop less confrontational forms of agitation. In September 1970 the party called upon people to stop paying ground rents, publishing a pamphlet called *Ground Rent is Robbery*. Ó Tuathail was central to the formulation of this new agitation, making clear at the campaign's public launch that 'means that might be considered by some illegal' would be used when deemed necessary. During early 1971 cumainn in Dublin and Waterford began forming 'Flat-dweller Associations' to represent people living in privately rented accommodation. The initial aim was to 'pressurise the Government into establishing a rents tribunal, similar to the one operating in England, to enforce a statutory scale of rents and minimum conditions of maintenance'. This campaign drew some students and young white-collar workers into the party.

While most activists turned their energies towards the North, de Burca was increasing her involvement with the fledgling Irish Women's Liberation Movement. De Burca argued for Sinn Féin to adopt a feminist agenda, though she found her male comrades, with the exception of Mac Giolla, largely uninterested. Nonetheless the party did distribute the Women's Liberation Movement booklet *Irishwomen: Chains or Change*, and the internal Sinn Féin newsletter *Nuacht Náisiúnta* recommended it to 'every woman in the movement and all men who really know what Socialism is all about'.

Internal unease at the perceived primacy of nationalist politics over social agitation resulted in several Dublin activists resigning from Sinn Féin in the aftermath of the 1971 Ard Fheis. Among those who left to set up the Socialist Party of Ireland (SPI) were former leading figures in the Dublin Housing Action Committee. Most were also OIRA members who had already left following disputes over the movement's political direction that surrounded the 1970 IRA General Army Convention. In order to help fund the new party, SPI supporters robbed £1,000 from a post office in Ballymun. Despite some allegations of intimidation, relations between SPI members and their former comrades remained relatively good, with several rejoining Sinn Féin within a few months. The new group would eventually adopt a view on the 'national question' strongly influenced by the British and Irish Communist Organisation's 'two-nations' theory. It was openly pro-Soviet and unashamedly adopted Communist iconography. But outside of Ballymun, where it campaigned consistently on local issues, the SPI failed to make a discernable impact and never numbered much more than a few dozen activists.

The Wolfe Tone Society had been severely affected by the split, with many members attempting to steer a neutral course between the rival wings. Anthony Coughlan remained prominent within the group although his perceived influence with the republican leadership was now causing problems. A disgruntled Sinn Féin activist had to be assured 'Tony Coughlan was not a member of the Republican Movement' in order to prevent him resigning. The perceived threat of EEC membership now dominated the society's concerns. Most of the left and the trade unions opposed entry, while Fianna Fáil, Fine Gael, business and farmers' groups supported it. Republican anti-EEC rhetoric made appeals to cultural nationalism while predicting that membership would have dire consequences for the Irish economy. It proved difficult to motivate members on this issue, *Nuacht Náisiúnta* accepting that the EEC was 'probably the subject best calculated to raise a yawn'.

But with factory closures and unemployment rising, claims that membership would lead to 'fierce competition for jobs between locals, dispossessed small farmers and Continentals with work permits' had some resonance. Cumainn were instructed to form broad-based anti-EEC 'action groups'. Goulding hoped the campaign could be used to reinvigorate the National Liberation Front strategy.

At all levels members were encouraged to work closely with the Communist Party. Some young activists held dual membership of Sinn Féin and the Connolly Youth Movement. Attempts were also made to enlist left-wing Labour dissidents. Sinn Féin supported a 'Socialist Unity' conference during March 1971, from which a new grouping, the Socialist Labour Alliance, emerged. The Officials did not wish, however, to build a movement that was confined to the left. Goulding proposed that the party 'write to organisations catering for small shopkeepers', pointing out to them the dangers of the EEC and the threat of supermarket takeovers in the hope 'that they may become part of the opposition' to the European Community. After Mac Giolla had criticized left-wing organizations a request from de Burca to have this 'thrashed out' was dismissed by her colleagues, who felt 'that Sinn Féin should not get involved in the internal doctrinaire wranglings of various left groups'. Even so, the importance of developing an understanding of left-wing politics was still the primary purpose of the movement's internal education. Among the guest speakers at a major seminar held at Lough Sheelin in Cavan in late 1970 was Ruth First of the African National Congress, who spoke on the Cuban revolution. A lively level of critical debate was encouraged at educational meetings. Dublin activist Tony Gregory recalled asking Roy Johnston why a middle-class person was lecturing about the working class. Johnston responded that 'it's not what class you're from that matters but the one you're allied with'.

Despite the desire to gain influence with organized labour, evident as far back as the IRA's 1966 strategy document, little progress had been made. Sinn Féin helped organize protests against the 1970 Trade Union Bill that sought to regulate unions and curtail strike activity, and in the same year 'active support' was also provided to striking workers during a long-running cement strike. The OIRA destroyed premises, machinery and vehicles belonging to two Dublin building companies that were supporting strike-breaking. There was also a firebomb attack on a strike-bound haulage company in Dublin. During 1971 the Official leadership decided to put their trade union activities on a more solid footing, setting up a Republican Trade Union Group with ITGWU official Des Geraghty as its key figure. This new arm of the move-ment would soon make an impact within RTÉ. At the station Eoghan Harris was chairman of the Workers' Union of Ireland branch as well as producer of Irish-language programme *Feach*. He had already raised hackles among the RTÉ authorities for appear-ing on the *Late Late Show* passionately denouncing the EEC, as well as for helping produce the station's internal left-wing journal *Feedback*. The 1969 controversy that led to the resignation of three producers had politicized many at the station, with RTÉ employees feeling they 'had to take sides' in the wider political debate. Harris and his allies John Caden, Oliver Donohue and Fergal Costello were among a group of station employees sus-pended for taking part in an April 1971 anti-redundancy picket of the Eurovision Song Contest in Dublin. Donohue, an active trade unionist who had joined the Labour Party while a student in UCD, was invited by Geraghty to a meeting in the North Star Hotel, which he recalls 'turned out to be a meeting of those sympathetic [to] or members of Official Sinn Féin'. Among those in attendance was Paddy Whelan, leader of the bricklayers' union BATU and a long-term republican activist. Donohue recalls being impressed by Whelan, who made a 'passionate speech welcoming this move of republicans into the trade union movement . . . he also talked about getting away from the gun'.

Violence in support of union militancy remained an OIRA tactic, however. In July 1971, during a strike at the Silvermines in Co. Tipperary, armed men held up security guards and placed bombs on the electricity transformers. These exploded, causing extensive damage. While planting the devices, 20-year-old Cork

OIRA member Martin O'Leary was electrocuted and suffered extensive burns. His comrades drove him to hospital in Limerick, where he died a few days later. Goulding gave the oration at O'Leary's funeral; describing him as a 'prototype' of the 'modern revolutionary', Goulding warned that '[if] the forces of imperialism . . . repress, coerce and deny ordinary people their God-given rights . . . then it is our duty to reply . . . in the language that brings these vultures to their senses most effectively – the language of the bomb and the bullet'.

With the OIRA increasingly active in the North there were fears that Goulding's speech heralded a 'new phase' of armed action in the South. As a result of his speech Goulding was arrested and charged with incitement to cause explosions. The case was adjourned several times as the OIRA made a concerted effort to intimidate the jury, getting the addresses of several members through tenants' association contacts and visiting them at their homes. An RTÉ tape of Goulding's speech was found to be blank and ten jurors failed to show up for Goulding's trial, at which the historian John A. Murphy gave evidence on the Official leader's behalf. Goulding was eventually acquitted.

In December 1971 the Sinn Féin leadership decided to intensify their involvement within the unions. The leadership adopted a Seamus Costello proposal that an 'Industrial Sub-Committee' be appointed to coordinate the activities of a 'Republican Industrial Development Division'. Lar Malone, a prominent member of the Dublin OIRA, would become RIDD's leading organizer. Malone envisaged the new organization having the 'dual purpose' of conducting policy research and providing a support network for Northern OIRA members in the South. At an initial RIDD meeting Malone was happy to see a number of people he had not known to be involved in republican activity. Malone, Oliver Donohue, Des Geraghty, John Caden and Fergal Costello, a CPI member, were elected from the floor on to a committee to draw up a document outlining the department's goals. Eoghan Harris also attended some of the early meetings. Malone had met Harris once previously, when appearing on *Feach* to discuss credit unions.

Malone recalled Harris as 'a capable fellow, very clever . . . if a little egotistic'. Other Official activists were also instructed by the movement to involve themselves in RIDD, among them Sean Dunne. He recalls how involvement 'was sold' to OIRA members: 'This is an army operation, it's going to be run like a fucking army cell. Now we're not going to be shooting anyone, but we will if we have to, we are going to be involved in our trade unions, and get people into committees, we're going to do industrial espionage, to lean on people, we're going to do whatever it takes, to be in there with the working class and the trade unions.'

Fergus Whelan, son of BATU leader Paddy, recalls sometimes being called by his 'army section' to attend meetings that turned out to be RIDD events: 'It was in no way military but there was a crossover of personnel . . . some of the ways we would meet in secret was also based on the paramilitary system . . . it certainly was covert but not illegal.'

Despite the escalating violence in the North, debate at the October 1971 Ard Fheis had been preoccupied with the forthcoming referendum on Ireland's membership of the EEC. In his presidential speech Mac Giolla stated: 'The government in Dublin cannot be regarded as pro-Irish; it is an anti-Irish government . . . preoccupied with an attempt to sell out to another empire, the New Empire of Monopoly Capitalism, the Common Market.'

Galway delegate Liz McManus proposed an amendment that any anti-EEC alliance with business interests should be ruled out, with a clear alternative of a 'Socialist Workers Republic' being offered instead. Speaking as a guest, Bernadette Devlin supported this position, but Seamus Costello came out strongly against it. A rousing speaker, he argued: 'If we lose this [referendum] we can pack up as revolutionaries and that applies whether we are Socialists, Trotskyites, Communist Party or anything else.' McManus's amendment was defeated by an overwhelming majority.

Although the party's mood was confident, the leadership was unhappy with the continued sapping of movement energies by the Northern conflict. Mac Giolla bemoaned to his fellow party leaders 'the complete inactivity on social issues in most of the country'. On 30 January 1972, while Ireland was transfixed by Bloody Sunday in Derry, de Burca was aiding a woman who'd been arrested after being evicted, along with her child, from their home. She recalls:

Everybody was of course upset but I just thought the Brits aren't down here and this woman is in jail because she put a roof over her own head and the head of her child and the Brits have nothing to do with this . . . The days were gone that I could get very exercised about the North except in terms of social attitudes and social problems . . .

Nonetheless de Burca took part in the protest outside the British Embassy a day later and was among several demonstrators injured in baton charges.

One of those disillusioned by the rising mood was Roy Johnston, who resigned from Sinn Féin and the OIRA during January 1972, the killing of Senator Barnhill having confirmed to him that the movement had gone too far in its 'reversion' to militarism. He informed Goulding first, and they parted 'on relatively good standing . . . on talking terms'. Johnston would eventually join the CPI, hoping 'that there might be some sense to be found there'. The departure from the republican movement of a man once dubbed a dangerous communist infiltrator was regretted by British officials, senior diplomat David Blatherwick noting: 'A pity. Communist influence was a force for good – i.e. less v[iolence] . . . more scribbling in Ireland.'

The Official IRA's May 1972 tarring and feathering of a 15-year-old girl in Belfast for fraternizing with British soldiers also had repercussions. The feminist activist Dr Moira Woods shaved her head in protest and picketed Gardiner Place. What gave her protest added significance was that Woods was living with Cathal Goulding. Trinity educated, Woods had been married twice by the time she met the OIRA leader. Her previous husband, Bobby Woods, had died in 1970 leaving substantial property interests in Dublin, including the building that housed the British Embassy on

Merrion Square. During 1971 Goulding had moved into Woods' home in the exclusive Ailesbury Road area. The relationship caused considerable unease among some in the OIRA leadership.

In spite of internal tensions, Sinn Féin was presenting a more dynamic image than its main rival on the left, the Labour Party, which had been convulsed by infighting. Left-winger Jim Kemmy resigned from the party and set up the Limerick Socialist Organisation, which adopted a 'two-nations' perspective in relation to Northern Ireland. Within Labour the Young Socialists faction angrily complained of the party's inactivity, with Una Claffey stating that the republican movement had been the only organization to consistently oppose the EEC while the Labour Party 'had passed pious resolution after pious resolution and done nothing'. Many Young Socialists drifted towards membership of Sinn Féin, as did several former Maoists when the campus craze for Mao's 'little red book' began to wane. The Officials' innovative use of media was an added attraction for left-wingers looking for a new political home. Utilizing RIDD's connections within RTÉ, the movement had established an anti-EEC radio station in Dublin; the first words broadcast were those of United Irishman Henry Joy McCracken: 'The rich always betray the poor.' The party also funded propaganda films about the anti-golf-course protests in Oughterard and the threat of the EEC made by playwright John Arden and his wife Margaretta D'Arcy, both Sinn Féin members. However, neither an influx of members nor cutting-edge propaganda could persuade the Irish public to back the republican approach to the EEC: on 10 May the Irish electorate voted to join by nearly 5:1.

Despite the movement's radical politics and often bohemian social life, its leadership could not ignore the conservative mores of wider Irish society. When on the country's most popular light entertainment show, the *Late Late Show*, celebrity priest Fr. Michael Cleary explicitly claimed that the Provisionals represented the authentic IRA while the OIRA were 'communist inspired and controlled', the Officials felt they had to react. Sinn Féin General Secretary Tony Heffernan wrote to Archbishop McQuaid of Dublin to complain: 'Fr. Cleary's remarks have been a source of great distress to our members, the majority of whom are practising Catholics.' Indeed, Goulding had been at pains to stress on occasion that the Officials were 'not reds'. In late December 1971 he and Mac Giolla visited McQuaid, and according to the archbishop a 'very relaxed and cordial' discussion took place. Afterwards McQuaid declared that the 'Marxist' label should not be applied loosely to the Officials, as they were chiefly interested in 'social justice'. Nonetheless the Officials' growth in the Republic resulted in British Intelligence reassessing the threat posed by a group which, in their view, had 'attracted a large number of habitual "protesters" to themselves'. A 1972 security assessment of the Republic of Ireland stated:

They are worse armed and numerically fewer than the Provisionals, but more vocal and politically sophisticated . . . The Officials have a considerable following in the Universities and a number of sympathisers in the press and radio: in general they attract the left-wingers present in most Western societies . . . They represent the greatest internal subversive threat at present (the energy of the Provisionals is turned to the North) and in the longer term: but this threat is not yet a real danger to the State.

However, British ambassador John Peck in Dublin feared the worst if the 'long road' to a peaceful settlement was not taken:

At the end of the other long road . . . for the Republic there will be a gradual erosion of the democratic and economic structure of the nation and the dominance of two rival factions of violent men, the one aiming at the creation of a Marxist Republic of Ireland, the other at a State founded upon Irish nationalism but in structure probably not so different: even if they have to fight it out, the end of the road is another Cuba.

Jimmy Jordan, a building worker and former Maoist who joined the party during 1972, found 'orthodox Shinners', republican socialists, people who were close to the Communist Party's thinking, Trotskyists and those interested in the 'two-nations' idea, all included among the membership. Increasingly, however, there was division between those broadly supporting Seamus Costello and a hard-line Marxist grouping led by Eoin Ó Murchú. Many of the arguments between these groups were fought out at monthly Dublin members' meetings where up to 200 activists would observe and participate in debate. For Ó Murchú 'the reality was a choice between a serious, tightly disciplined party operating along the lines of Ard Fheis decisions, or a constant state of flux'. The often bitter internal debates enthused some but disheartened others. One of the Dublin members who dropped out during the early 1970s remembers: 'I couldn't take any more of this infighting . . . there was an awful lot of personality clashes, nothing was clear any more.'

Disputes with other left groups could go beyond polemic. In early 1972 the Connolly Youth Movement wrote to Gardiner Place to complain of the 'fascist tactics' employed by Sligo Sinn Féin activists and the party's Connacht organizer Breasal Ó Caollaí. These related to alleged physical threats against Declan Bree, who was attempting to reorganize the Connolly Youth Movement in Connacht. This was not the only problem in the west. In May 1972 the Dublin leadership called for the expulsion of John Arden and Margaretta D'Arcy. According to a letter to the Dublin Comhairle Ceantair they had made remarks after a performance of one of their plays at UCD in which they attacked 'everything for which the movement stands', including its maintenance of an 'illegal nationalistic army'. Specifically they accused the OIRA O/C in Galway of giving gelignite to 'a local contractor so that he . . . could carry out an action'. D'Arcy was expelled later in the year and Arden resigned. His resignation letter included a stinging condemnation of the University College Galway Republican Club over their 'cowardly' failure to support an elderly Oughterard woman who faced eviction. It concluded:

I would not wish any further to impede you in your political careers . . . You have good work yet to do, talking big and keeping quiet: and there are many masters of your craft already seated in the Dáil ready and willing to instruct your apprentice legislators when, in due course, they creep into Leinster House.

Adding to head office's headaches about the state of the movement in Galway were contacts between local members and Socialist Workers Movement (SWM) activists, and the participation of other members in 'freelance' robberies, the latter activity leading to two expulsions. By 1973 both the city's cumainn and the area's Comhairle Ceantair had been disbanded, leaving only the UCG Republican Club in operation.

The influx into Sinn Féin of members with a diverse range of views necessitated a re-examination of the movement's ideological direction during 1972. Derry Kelleher, who temporarily replaced Johnston as director of party education, is recalled as 'a bit like a bumbling professor', promoting an esoteric mix of 'Republicanism, Christianity and Marxism'. After the OIRA ceasefire, however, it was Sean Garland, combining his roles of party national organizer and OIRA Adjutant General, who became the driving force behind internal education. Garland was an avid reader, and attempted to encourage his Army Council colleagues to read Marxist texts, with varying degrees of success. Garland was drawn to Lenin's concept of a revolutionary party, views forcibly presented in a May 1971 *United Irishman* article, 'Building Revolution'. In this he clearly defined that 'revolution' for him meant 'the change of state power from one class to another', and that the Official movement was still a work in progress; '[at] this point in history our movement must have a national liberation and socialist character', but its 'central goal was political power for the working class'. He returned to this theme at Bodenstown in June 1972, telling the crowd of several thousand that the republican movement sought to 'build a revolutionary party based on the reality of the principle of Tone', which would lead a revolution against 'the imperialist, the capitalist, the foreign gangster and his native lackey'. Those who stood in their way included 'the man who helps a tottering regime by his appeals to sectarian violence . . . the sniper of the ultra-left . . . the Social Democrat intellectual or opportunist, who pretends to socialism, but once scratched by reality reveals his desire only for power'. In Garland's view a revolutionary party would be built 'not by emotional appeal but hard argument and long debate'. However, the IRA was still central: 'Let no one take . . . any suggestion or even hint [that] the army of the people will not be used and when necessary fully employed to defend the interests of the working people.'

Key to the building of such a party was the education of party cadres. During 1971 the Officials had acquired farm cottages in Mornington near Drogheda, Co. Louth. The buildings were renovated into a complex of small lecture rooms and sleeping huts that could accommodate 28 people. This 'Mornington School' was to serve as a training centre in 'revolutionary theory'. It was put into immediate use, holding lectures for OIRA and party education officers. Work began on drawing up a movement-wide education programme. By August 1972 John McManus was the education committee chairman and Padraig Yeates its secretary. McManus was a Wicklow GP and former Labour Party member who had joined Sinn Féin in Galway, where his wife Liz was a party activist. Other committee members included Dubliners Tony Gregory and Andy Smith, Newry's Sam Dowling, and Garland. Some of the lecturers had particular expertise, such as Des Geraghty, who spoke on 'Industrial Organisation'; by contrast, Helena Sheehan recalls that she 'learned everything [in her lectures] . . . just before I gave them.' The education committee recognized that for 'new and young members (many from the North) with little formal education and probably even lacking in basic academic discipline like reading a book or making notes from reading' the need was to 'gain familiarity with the habit of study and confidence (but not overconfidence) in expressing their ideas to others'. Mornington had its own library, which included the works of Marx, Lenin and Connolly along with numerous Irish and international works, including Bowyer Bell's *The Secret Army*. International reading material ranged from Ho Chi Minh and Mao to Machiavelli. Education officers were instructed to use copies of education committee lectures in order to conduct courses at branch level. To oversee the education committee and the Mornington School, Des O'Hagan was employed as a full-time party director of education.

Maintaining a regime that lent itself to an appreciation of Marxist theory proved difficult. O'Hagan reported 'negative attitudes', with some members having to be reminded the school was 'not a rest home for tired revolutionaries'. The director of education drew up a set of house rules that allowed for time to 'relax on the beach or play football' between lectures, but 'rowdyism' was banned and it was stressed that Mornington was not 'a holiday camp'. In theory there was to be 'no drink brought to the school, no Gambling, no dancing after the pub closes' and all were to be in 'bed by a reasonable hour'. Those transgressing were 'liable to be sent home'. These stern rules were not always enforced, as Mary McMahon recalls: 'It was great to get out of Belfast and get away from all the hassle and shite, it was our Butlins, you know, it was fabulous, but for most people you went through it in an alcoholic haze . . . I mean some people went to the pub on Friday night and didn't emerge again until Saturday night.' Some lectures are recalled as 'just fucking nonsense', with O'Hagan bewildering and boring many a student with his lecture on the theory of dialectical materialism. But many activists who attended Mornington, or the 'school for terrorism' as some jokingly called the venue after it appeared in a British tabloid scare story, found it a rewarding experience. Largely due to Mornington, a greater degree of ideological cohesiveness developed in the movement. The message was driven home to activists that theory without action was pointless while lack of theory led to 'malpractice', the cost of which was dramatically outlined in the education committee's publication *Foghlaim*; 'erroneous theory for us is different than for example . . . a left faction – their mistakes don't finish in a cemetery'.

Garland and Costello had emerged from the OIRA's internal debates as the leading proponents of a major re-examination of movement strategy. Costello was hugely popular among the membership of Sinn Féin's five North Wicklow cumainn, and had been active in the North, mixing with OIRA volunteers eager to return to full-scale operations against the British. Having personally combined successful political and military activity himself – he remained a prominent figure in Wicklow local politics, sometimes packing the county council chamber's public gallery with supporters – he saw no contradiction in openly pursuing both. Garland had spent much of the preceding two years abroad and now sought to reverse the trend that was seeing the Officials losing ground to Provisional militancy. Goulding would recall Garland as 'depressed' during this period: 'Sean had an idea that we went too fast with the ceasefire. He was deeply affected by the Provo split.' Garland and Costello produced an IRA policy document entitled 'A Brief Examination of the Republican Position: An Attempt to Formulate the Correct Demands and Methods of Struggle.' It sought to re-emphasize the Officials' commitment to the 'National Struggle':

In this country more and more events of the past few years demonstrate that the struggle for democracy is also the national struggle since it is . . . British power and influence that maintains the undemocratic structures and it is the Nationalist population that suffers under this system.

The document suggested the movement's current policy was possibly leading to a departure from core republican values and was 'dangerously close to accepting arguments made by Conor Cruise O'Brien and those who propagated "the 2 Nation theory"'. To accept such a position, it argued, 'even in part, leads one inevitably to the position where . . . we expect and look to the British army to play a progressive role in Ireland. What a position for republicans!' In fact, it argued, the 'National Question' remained central and this was one of the reasons 'why the Provos are still a force today and why they will not fade away for a long time yet'. During this period Garland was involved in numerous discussions with the American Trotskyist Gerry Foley. Recalled as an intense, 'small, solemn-looking owl of a man, with large glasses', Foley spoke several languages, including Irish. He developed friendships with McGurran and Garland, and later with Costello. Foley re-called Garland as the most 'interested in socialist theory' of the Official leadership and as a 'complex personality, a sort of Hamlet ... very much tied to Goulding and Mac Giolla personally' but unsure about their strategy. In Foley's opinion the debate within the Officials in late 1972 was between support for a 'Castroist' national liberation struggle and a 'Stalinist' stages approach. At the time debate was raging among Trotskyists globally on the use of armed struggle. Much of the British far left took a position of unconditional support for violence carried out by 'national libera-tion' movements. Foley adhered to another strand of thought, which placed emphasis on the building of mass revolutionary parties. Garland found the concept of building a mass revolutionary party particularly appealing, seeing the concept as a way to move beyond the increasingly bitter debate between those espousing the 'stages theory' and others seeking to dispense with it.

Meanwhile Eoghan Harris had asserted himself as the main intellectual force within RIDD. His winning charm and sharp polemic gained him many admirers, and a nickname: 'the thin blue flame'. However, even among fellow adherents there was some amusement at the leather-jacket-wearing Harris's regular declarations that he was a 'Stalinist'. RIDD had grown to include dozens of active trade unionists, leading members continuing to meet as an ad hoc executive. This group had begun to develop a role in researching movement policy. Developing this role brought Harris and other RIDD figures into increased contact with the Republican Club at Trinity College Dublin. Paul Sweeney joined the Club during 1972, having been 'recruited by Eoghan Harris [and] convinced that the revolution might actually happen'. He was impressed by Harris's 'tremendous ability to get young people up and going and doing intellectual work ... getting it discussed and disseminated around'.

Even though RIDD contained a substantial number of OIRA members, Harris and others with a Labour Party background were shaping the movement's 'big debate' – what was the 'national question'? As leading member Oliver Donohue puts it, 'To still talk of the British Imperialism as the enemy of Ireland was outdated and simply not accurate because at that stage . . . it was American monopoly capitalism that was ruling the world. If you look at what was happening in Ireland, the surplus value of the Irish working class was not being used to line the pockets of the British aristocracy.' The acceptance of this analysis within RIDD provoked a cultural shift within the movement in Dublin, as Sean Dunne recalls: 'All of a sudden everyone is talking about Eoghan Harris and we're singing . . . American Wobbly songs, "Joe Hill" and all. The culture had changed from "The Boys of Kilmichael" to "Casey Jones".' Goulding was generally supportive of the RIDD view of how the republican struggle should be redefined. The OIRA Chief of Staff also developed a close friendship with Harris, and told others that the Cork man was a 'genius'.

The thinking emanating from RIDD was evident in a May 1972 memorandum outlining the group's views on the 'two great current problems' facing the movement: the loss of the EEC referendum and 'the sectarian pogrom which the Provisional Alliance seem determined to provoke'. The document argued that all cooperation with the Provisionals should be ruled out as they were entering 'their mad-dog last convulsions'. Instead it called on contact to be made with loyalist Vanguard leaders. The Derry OIRA, whose perceived Trotskyist connections were a source of concern to RIDD, were also a target. An outlandish proposal for a 'mass temporary evacuation of the Bogside and Creggan [to Donegal] . . . in the tradition of the great ghetto evacuations' concluded that 'the logistical problems are great, but not as great as the problem of leadership'. Two sentences at the end of the four-page document dealt perfunctorily with the possibility of setting up a 'national Anti-Redundancy Campaign' – the main issue that the Official leadership hoped the trade union group was pursuing. A 1972 draft internal party report on the Small Farmers' Defence Association also illustrated RIDD thinking:

Farmers' . . . disregard of Sinn Féin turned to hate due to the EEC campaign and the apparent increase in prices obtained by farmers [following the referendum] . . . the farming community is getting smaller. *This move from the land may be a good development from the revolutionary movement's point of view* . . . in approx. 10 years there will be no such thing as a small farmer . . . When that stage comes . . . it might be found necessary by the revolutionary movement of the time, to organise worker against farmer . . . As there is a long-standing ill feeling between workers and farmers, this friction could be very easily developed. However in the meantime . . . it is the job of a revolutionary movement to try and organise these discontented people now into an organisation which will oppose the plans of the capitalist system.

By late 1972 a perceived lack of activity by RIDD was a cause of concern for the Official leadership. RIDD members were also accused of overstepping their authority. While honeymooning in England, Oliver Donohue had approached Clann activists, inquiring about *United Irishman* sales and the 'political affiliations' of their membership. This prompted the leadership to remind RIDD members that until the group's position was formalized, they 'did not represent the movement' and merely had an 'advisory capacity'. Following a meeting between party leaders and RIDD it was agreed 'after some difficulties' that the group's 'activities would be organized through the movement'. These strictures prompted a short-lived resignation by Harris and Donohue. Eventually a compromise was reached whereby the relationship between the two organizations was held to be one of 'full mutual cooperation'.

Alongside RIDD, Eoin Ó Murchú and those aligned with him also strongly espoused a stageist approach. Several of the activists identified with this tendency, including Tony Moriarty, Sean Dunne and Helena Sheehan, shared a house on Dublin's north side. Sheehan recalls that among this group the *History of the Albanian Party of Labour* and Mervyn Jones's biography of Stalin, *Joseph*, had a 'cult status'. Ó Murchú's use of the *United Irishman* to propagate his views was widely criticized. Obscure political jargon, personal attacks and the inclusion of a poem in Irish dedicated to Sheehan prompted a number of cumainn to complain to head office. Sales had also fallen greatly from the average 50,000 a month in 1970. Other activists recall being perturbed by what they saw as the English-born Ó Murchú's attempts to be 'more Irish than the Irish themselves'. In late 1972 the leadership eventually replaced Ó Murchú as *United Irishman* editor with the Derry *Starry Plough*'s Jackie Ward.

The RIDD and Ó Murchú groupings shared a fear that 'Trots' were attempting to infiltrate the movement. Harris, 'in a black leather coat [and] looking terribly fierce', is recalled lecturing one Galway meeting on 'our Trotskyite deviations and Social Democratic instincts [which] had to be purged out of us if we were to become true revolutionaries'. O'Hagan, no fan of Trotskyism himself, recalls meeting Harris and Donohue in Des Geraghty's house, where Harris started 'to rant about the Trots. I looked at him in stark raving fucking amazement . . . I said to Geraghty, "Is he mad?" Geraghty replied, "He just goes on like that."' On one occasion Goulding requested that a number of Dublin Comhairle Ceantair members meet Harris. On arriving at the meeting Harris let it be known that he wished to talk to IRA members only, necessitating Liz Doyle's exit. She recalls Garland laconically asking, 'Are you feeling Harrised?' Garland also took to describing meetings between Goulding, Harris and other RIDD members as the 'Army Council in exile'. One RIDD member suggests that 'if Harris had been allowed to sit in Sean Garland's company for two fucking seconds the game would have been up'. In order to avoid such confrontations Harris sometimes waited in an adjacent room to give advice to his allies when OIRA meetings were taking place.

On the Army Council, Goulding, Mac Giolla and Ryan were now identified with the stageist approach, with Garland and Costello on the other side of the debate. McGurran was torn between the two, while McMillen was loyal to Goulding's position but aware of the demands for greater militancy from those under his command. By the time of the December 1972 Ard Fheis the OIRA convention had endorsed the Garland/Costello position. This directive was delivered to the Ard Chomhairle, with non-OIRA members not even seeing the political motion they were proposing till the morning of the Ard Fheis. At the conference the impact of the ceasefire and debates within the OIRA was clear. Goulding did not make a speech and no statement from the OIRA was read out. Garland's oration dwelt on the organizing of a revolutionary party rather than on Northern Ireland. It had been decided not to distribute the competing Garland/Costello and Goulding/Mac Giolla documents, but Costello took it upon himself to hand out a document outlining the position 'that the ending of partition was essential to the fight against imperialism'. Delegates supported the key political motion, which stated: 'The main obstacle confronting us in this struggle is the stranglehold of British Imperialism . . . any final settlement must be on the basis of a total withdrawal of all British military, political and economic control from Ireland.'

Other motions called on the British to commit to 'total' withdrawal at 'an early specified date' with a full implementation of a Bill of Rights during the 'interim period'. The removal of all sectarian elements in the Southern constitution was also demanded. The Derry delegates were particularly vocal in their support for the reassertion of the 'National Struggle' in traditional republican terms. In the polarized atmosphere even the appearance of Derry's Terry Robson, making a speech with his 'long hair, combat jacket and Che moustache', was enough to provoke revulsion in some Dublin delegates.

The Garland–Costello alliance broke down very quickly. A leaflet on Northern policy based on the Ard Fheis resolution was drawn up, but then shelved. Gerry Foley recalls feeling the divide as due to Costello wanting 'to go for armed struggle full stop', a position the Wicklowman felt the resolution endorsed, but which Garland opposed. Garland was still close to Goulding and Ryan, and Costello's behaviour since winning the internal OIRA debate had rekindled concerns about his arrogance. Goulding, now 51, was coming under increased pressure from his colleagues to either abandon his painting business or step aside as Chief of Staff. There was no clear agreement on who might replace him, with Costello, Garland and Ryan all potential candidates. Ryan, known as the 'bald eagle' in Belfast, was seen as someone who took the struggle in Northern Ireland 'very seriously'. Costello had a definite following but his support among Southern OIRA officers was limited. Garland was seen as having 'tremendous integrity and great authority' but as being a 'hard man to get on with'. For many OIRA members he was the movement's 'leading political figure' and Goulding's obvious replacement. However, Garland's insistence that the movement abandon titles such as Chief of Staff, his loyalty to Goulding and his belief that policy could be directed from his present position meant there would be no immediate change at the top.

A priority for Garland was establishing a weekly paper for 'the Republican voice to be heard on the day-to-day issues'. He had planned to launch such an enterprise in early 1972. But it was mid-1973 before the first issue of the tabloid *Irish People* appeared. Séamus Ó Tuathail was hired to edit the publication, named after its Fenian predecessor of the 1860s. Among its early scoops were exposés of corruption in the Irish Hospitals Sweepstake and naming the developers responsible for poorly built council houses. The December 1973 'Christmas Special' bore the headline 'Exploited for Christ' and detailed the conditions endured by those working for the Catholic Church in its colleges and laundries. Ó Tuathail's independent editorial line provoked complaints, and circulation was poor with only around 5,000 copies sold per week. In contrast, *United Irishman* sales had stabilized at 45,000 per month.

With most of the Official leadership not envisaging a return to large-scale military action in the near future, Costello was becoming more isolated. His supporters blamed a 'Goulding–Garland–Ryan' alliance for keeping him out of the movement in the capital and they recall him becoming 'fed up' with his 'one-man battle'. On top of the political problems, rifts were also emerging between Costello and senior comrades over fund-raising and the definition of legitimate targets. Party General Secretary Tony Heffernan recalled being uneasy when Costello expressed the view that 'shooting Unionists, if you shoot them because they are Unionists, is not sectarianism'. The Dublin OIRA leadership were also angry at the Director of Operations' unwillingness to authorize robberies. Speculation was rife that he was 'putting [jobs] in his back pocket to do later' and then informing Northern OIRA units that 'those fellas [in Dublin] was doing nothing'. There were also rumours Costello 'was going bogey' and retaining funds for himself. By March 1973 the differences were such that Costello threatened to resign as Sinn Féin vice-president.

Until mid-1972 the Dublin OIRA, with Gerry Parker as O/C, had continued to regularly back up social and political agitation with military activity. In the summer of 1971 Gardaí arrested a number of Dublin Officials in connection with arson attacks on British property. Later that year in Dun Laoghaire a bomb exploded at Cumbria Flats, property targeted by housing action protesters. In early 1972 three activists were arrested trying to set fire to a landlord's property after he had evicted a pregnant woman. Cooperation between industrial and IRA activists saw a haulage company owner, who was involved in a strike in Co. Kilkenny, shot in Armagh and his supermarket blown up.

Recruitment into the OIRA had continued after the ceasefire. After a few months in Sinn Féin one young woman was asked to join the IRA, and despite 'having no interest in guns' but a 'romantic New Left thing about armed struggle' she accepted. A 'very ritualistic reading' of the army constitution, which included offences punishable by death, was conducted at a class for new recruits held in a council house in Finglas. It was made clear to all recruits that 'if they wanted to join the IRA they had to be involved politically'. One member recalled that they were to be the 'iron fist' within the movement. At OIRA meetings the politics of new Sinn Féin members were discussed and decisions made on whose progress in the party should be halted. Another post-ceasefire Sinn Féin member recalls being approached in 1973 by a leading party figure, not notably associated with militarism, and asked if he was prepared to join the OIRA. When the recruit argued that an armed campaign in the North was of no interest to him, he was assured that his role would be in providing funding for political activity through robberies. Dublin OIRA political education now carried a new emphasis. One activist who attended an education meeting in Billy Wright's Boxing Club remembers the message of the evening as:

Lads, there is no more military training on assault weapons or any of that stuff; if there is going to be military training it will be with short arms. We are not going to fight a conventional war with the British army. If we are going to fight a war it is going to be a class war on the streets of Dublin.

For Southern activists the priorities of the Northern membership could surprise. In the North young people usually joined the OIRA first and were then instructed to join their local Republican Club. Tony Gregory recalls a trip to Belfast to give an education lecture as an 'eye-opener . . . they wanted guns . . . there was a difference between what they were at and what we were told they were at'.

In February 1973 Sinn Féin contested its first Southern general election in twelve years, fielding ten candidates. The party manifesto put 'people before profit' and advanced a programme described as 'unambiguously socialist, undeniably republican'. A feature of the campaign was the prominent role played by RIDD and newer party members, among them former Young Socialist Charlie Bird, who managed the Sinn Féin campaign in Dublin South Central. If elected, candidates pledged to sign their salaries over to the movement; but none were successful. Seamus Rodgers in Donegal received the party's highest first-preference vote of 2,436, or 8.65 per cent. No candidate in Dublin broke the 5 per cent barrier. Costello came second last in Wicklow with 1,966 votes. Overall, Fianna Fáil gained votes but lost seats and a Fine Gael–Labour coalition emerged victorious, with Liam Cosgrave of Fine Gael becoming Taoiseach. It was the first time in sixteen years that Fianna Fáil was out of office. The *United Irishman* attempted to put the best gloss on the poor Sinn Féin performance, declaring the party's 15,000 votes had come despite the 'bans of RTÉ and bias of bourgeois commentators'. For many, the lesson was that the party needed to define itself more clearly as socialist and to professionalize campaigning techniques. Discussion also centred on the adverse impact of OIRA activity, with internal election analysis pointing to canvassing by Northern members as 'counterproductive'.

Discussion on how electoral performance could be improved fed into an ongoing debate on the need to reorganize the movement. Following the December 1972 Ard Fheis a 'structural commission' including Costello, McMillen, Heffernan, Tony Moriarty and John McManus (there to give a non-OIRA perspective) had been established with a remit to 'examine the organisational structure of the Movement'. Although not directly involved in the commission's deliberations, Garland was the main motor behind the push for wholesale changes. The possibility of establishing a formal alliance with the Communist Party of Ireland – consistent with the National Liberation Front concept – had foundered because Northern CPI members feared that a direct link with republicanism would be disastrous for party support among Protestant workers. Ó Murchú recalls that this 'pushed Garland to decide that this avenue is closed so the movement would go alone to become the revolutionary party of the working class'. Garland argued during this period that the movement should be 'primarily political and any military activity should be strictly subordinate'. Debate now centred on whether Sinn Féin or the OIRA should be the 'superior organisation'. The commission's discussions drew upon international models. One proposal was that Sinn Féin be developed as a mass movement with the OIRA an inner 'revolutionary party', similar to the position of the South African Communist Party within the ANC. After seven months the commission, without reaching an agreement, presented 'Discussion Documents on Organisation and Structure' for circulation among the membership. In the documents Sinn Féin was referred to as 'Group A' and the OIRA as 'Group B', to circumvent the legal implications of using the term IRA.

Document No.1 set out the case for the 'building of a single structure/revolutionary party type organisation'. It argued that in 'world revolutionary history' only the concept of the revolutionary party, a 'tightly organised vanguard of conscious revolutionaries', had proved successful. This party had to 'subscribe to the doctrine of Democratic Centralism', which meant once policy was decided it had to be 'enforced without compromise throughout the organisation'. In the pursuit of 'ideological clarity and unity', members would be expelled rather than be allowed to compromise policy. Highlighting the differing views within the commission, a 'Critique of Document No.1' followed. It pointed to the Communist states 'where revolutionary parties of this type are in control' in warning that adopting a 'tightly knit Revolutionary Party' model would lead to 'the emergence of a guiding Elitist type intellectual vanguard who feel that only they know the true road to Socialism and who therefore must direct the movement'. The critique argued that the 'revolutionary genius of the Irish people' could produce its own methods of organization.

In the light of this critique of the 'revolutionary party' model, Document No. 2 looked to make improvements 'without changing the fundamental structure of either organisation'. However, a number of disadvantages in the present structure were outlined. These included that some members of Group A complained of an elitist and a scornful attitude being displayed to them by members of Group B, and that 'decisions were taken outside of Group A'. It was felt that the advantages of the present system included the attraction Group B had to 'militant young people', and ending it as a 'separate entity could create a vacuum which possibly would be filled by the Provos or some other such group'. Maintaining two separate organizations was also seen as conferring advantages in terms of security and deniability. Finally, 'Document No. 3' outlined a 'suggested model for a Revolutionary Party'. There would be a division of labour within the party whereby some members were 'required for technical operations (whatever they may be)' while others would concentrate on civil rights work, trade unions and research. 'Ideological unity and clarity' was to be promoted through the 'insistence in the educational programme on one policy'. Determination was to be shown by the leadership in insisting on 'unity' and the need to 'overcome and expose elements, no matter how high they may be in the party organisation, who refuse to carry out the policies'. The Ard Chomhairle would have 'overall direction and control of the policy and work of all branches of the Movement, including Group B'. The discussion documents were distributed on a 'strictly confidential' basis, a covering page carrying the warning that 'on no account' were they to be 'shown to or discussed with those outside of the Movement'. However, the documents were accidentally distributed to people on a mailing list of prospective Clann na hÉireann members in the UK. Even more embarrassingly the British Army came into possession of a copy and leaked it to the *Belfast Telegraph*.

Meetings to discuss the documents were held throughout the country in October 1973. Costello came out against many of the aspects of the revolutionary party concept, including democratic centralism. He used a meeting in Derry to renew his rapport with activists there, highlighting to them his problems with the proposals and with some members of the leadership. Many activists feared that the proposals would lead to a running down of the OIRA's structure and authority within the movement. The debate reached no definitive agreement but by late 1973 a process of reorganization had begun. Prior to this Garland had presented a paper on 'The Organisation of the Proletariat's Armed Forces' for discussion at an Army Council meeting in Co. Kilkenny. This was a communist document dating from the 1930s about how political and military organisations could be merged. Largely at Garland's instigation the Army Council passed a resolution committing it to transforming the movement into a Marxist party run on Leninist principles.

In Dublin the reorganization debate coincided with a crisis of leadership within RIDD. Through RIDD Lar Malone had also been attempting to forge a formal alliance between the CPI and Sinn Féin at a Dublin level. Malone recalls that as well as the political benefits of an alliance he also hoped to 'eventually get money and weapons from Russia'. To promote these aims he lobbied for the co-option of CPI member Fergal Costello on to the Dublin Comhairle Ceantair as an observer. Having felt he had secured endorsement for such a move, Malone recalls being shocked when it was voted down at a Comhairle Ceantair meeting: 'I said that's it, I'm finished with that, I was raging.' Malone and several other like-minded members of the Dublin OIRA resigned. Some of this group were among a thirteen-man unit that undertook a £14,000 robbery of Heuston Station in Dublin in September 1973. Barber Billy Wright was arrested by Gardaí, having provided a car and disguises for the robbers. During questioning Wright broke down and told Gardaí that assisting them meant he was a 'dead man'. There were conflicting accounts of who planned the Heuston heist, and when Mick Ryan attempted to investigate the background to it, some of his comrades stymied the inquiry. Whatever its origins, the robbery's proceeds were handed over to Goulding. Gardaí sought Malone for the robbery but with the help of the movement he fled to Holland.

With Malone gone RIDD members' dogmatic approach was causing increased problems at Dublin members' monthly meetings, leading some activists to demand 'get rid of RIDD'. Goulding's answer to this problem came in the form of Eamon Smullen, who had been released from prison in England in February 1973. Aged 48, he had extensive trade union experience after years of agitation on the building sites of London. He was also a firm believer in Soviet Communism, taking pride in having joined the British Communist Party *after* the invasion of Hungary in 1956. Goulding initially appointed Smullen as the new director of RIDD. After Gerry Parker, who was wanted for a robbery in July, went on the run to the Continent, Goulding appointed a new Dublin O/C who was widely seen as ineffectual and resigned the position after only a few months. Goulding turned to Smullen again, appointing him Dublin O/C around the same time as he received the formal title of Sinn Féin Director of Economic and Industrial Research. Smullen oversaw a restructuring of RIDD's relationship with Sinn Féin. All RIDD activists were now to become party members, but many wished to maintain political anonymity. There was a long history of republicans losing jobs because of their political affiliation, while in RTÉ and other sectors of the civil service

employees were contractually barred from party-political membership. It was decided that such persons could be issued with party
cards without being publicly active, and 'would be responsible
directly to Eamon Smullen on behalf of the Ard Chomhairle'.

Attempts by the Officials to link up with international communism were a source of concern for the British and Irish governments. In a secret internal communiqué the British Foreign Office
noted: 'The Irish government are increasingly worried by the
long-term threat of the Official IRA which is penetrated and
supported by international communism and its helpers.' It was
decided that Edward Heath should play upon this fear in an attempt
to persuade Jack Lynch to think again about allowing the Soviets
to establish a diplomatic mission in Dublin. The British Prime
Minister sent a telegram to his Irish counterpart, which stated:

We now have proof that Soviet officials posted to this country were
engaged on preparing contingency plans of sabotage and subversion to
be implemented in times of crisis. I am sure that this latter aspect of
Russian activity will be in the forefront of your mind, not least because
the Soviet journal 'New Times' recently remarked approvingly upon
the aims of the Official IRA, which they defined as 'the overthrow of
reactionary governments in the North and South of the country' . . . In
this connection you should know that a recent defector has told us that
the KGB are taking a close interest in the Irish situation . . . The setting
up of official Soviet representation in Ireland would be a significant
indicator that the Russians intended to exploit the situation. If they did
establish an office at least half the Soviet staff would be KGB officers.

Nonetheless, with the Irish government eager to promote international trade, within two years the Soviets would have an embassy
in Dublin.

In October 1973 Official Sinn Féin secured an invitation to send
delegates to the Congress of International Peace Forces to be held
in Moscow. The trip was seen as critical to building relations
directly with the Soviet Union. In Moscow nearly 3,000 delegates,
representing communist and national liberation organizations from

144 countries, met under the shadow of events in Chile, where the military, with CIA backing, had overthrown the left-wing government of Salvador Allende on 11 September. Allende took his own life rather than fall prisoner as planes bombed the presidential palace. Over the following month an estimated 2,000 trade unionists and left-wingers were killed as the military regime set about enforcing its authority. As South America's first democratically elected Marxist president, Allende's radical policies had been the international left's leading example of how much reform could be achieved without a resort to revolutionary violence. This ideal was now shattered. October's *United Irishman* carried Goulding's view: 'At what point in history was it ever possible to say to the power hungry and the rich: stop, you have had enough. One cannot ask the tiger for mercy. Chile has established beyond contradiction that the path to revolution through mass action and politics must be backed by the determination of those involved to use physical force to achieve political power.'

The Irish delegation in Moscow included not only Mac Giolla, Garland and O'Hagan representing Sinn Féin but also CPI members, journalists and students. Particular importance was placed on meetings with officials of the Communist Party of the Soviet Union, Garland recalling: 'Once you got them to talk to you, then others would follow.' At one of the conference's fringe meetings Mac Giolla addressed an audience that included representatives of the ANC and other guerrilla organizations. He stated that Ireland had for centuries been oppressed by the world's 'greatest imperialist power', but had 'never surrendered'. However, the country now had 'less economic independence than the neo-colonial countries of Africa and South America', with most industry and natural resources 'in the hands of Anglo-American and other foreign monopolies and multinational companies'. O'Hagan recalls discussing with Soviet 'South American experts' the damage they believed the Chilean Trotskyists had done in undermining the Allende government. Mick O'Riordan was also with the Irish delegation, the CPI General Secretary insisting on attending a meeting where Sinn Féin papers were presented to Moscow

University, causing resentment from Mac Giolla and O'Hagan. The Soviet 'peace movement' acted as a cover for the work of the state intelligence services, the KGB undoubtedly using the event to consider how effective the Official republican movement, with its trained military cadre, might be as a Cold War ally. Many of Garland's comrades felt he was politically influenced by his visit to Moscow. Padraig Yeates recalls feeling that Garland 'had seen the system working. Until then he would have seen a lot of merit in the Trotskyist thing.'

In sections of the OIRA, unease at the ceasefire was festering. Northern volunteers 'on the run' conveyed to Southern comrades their displeasure at the lack of action. The malcontents were increasingly drawn to areas such as Bray and north Munster, where support for Costello was strong. At leadership level Ó Murchú's militant opposition to Costello was a growing problem. At one GHQ meeting Costello lashed out at Ó Murchú, denouncing him as nothing more than a 'bluenose, wine-drinking Trinity shit'. Goulding and Garland felt it necessary to ask their younger comrade to 'tone down' his criticism of Costello. While Costello longed to reopen full hostilities with the British, most of his fellow leaders wanted to focus on Southern agitations, Goulding writing in the international newsletter *Eolas* that:

The most vital thing, we believe, is to develop a popular struggle in the South to complement the struggle in the North . . . to safeguard the struggle in the North it is therefore essential to mount a massive campaign in the South to oust the collaborationists.

By the time of the 1973 Ard Fheis Costello was reduced to a minority of one on the Army Council on many issues, but he could still depend on a sizeable reservoir of support among both the Sinn Féin and OIRA membership. The fault lines within the movement were starkly visible among the 360 delegates who gathered in the basement of Liberty Hall for the November 1973 Ard Fheis. In his presidential address Mac Giolla called for a union of the 'forces of the left', which would 'strictly exclude those who are more interested in mouthing slogans or scoring debating points than doing solid work'. In the South this union could 'fill the vacuum' created by Labour's coalition with the 'class enemies' Fine Gael. He still hoped the Provisionals 'might yet be persuaded to halt their campaign and thus allow the people once more to impose their authority on the situation'. But he also made clear where he stood on the debate over the 'National Question': 'We must . . . continuously re-emphasise what is the "National Question" and what is the "National Struggle". It is all about the ownership of the wealth of the country.' While British Intelligence's impression of the Ard Fheis was of 'a gathering of hairy academics in woolly sweaters' with an average age of 'no more than 30' who partook in 'level-headed, orderly and articulate' debate, behind closed doors the discussions turned bitter. In a prearranged move, Costello supporters from Donegal put forward an amendment to the political motion seeking to replace the primacy of the stageist approach with calls for 'national unity' and 'revolutionary demands'. Delegates from Derry and north Munster supported the amendment, Johnnie White disparaging the leadership's attempts to replace 'working-class demands' with 'bourgeois reform'. Ó Murchú hit back, decrying his opponents' inability to see that seeking reform was central to the revolutionary struggle, and Mac Giolla condemned the amendment's supporters' 'failed tactics', turning on the north-western delegates who, he claimed, had been unable to organize the people of Free Derry and now wished to 'leave the homeless homeless and the unemployed unemployed while they waited for the instant revolution of the International Socialists'. (Ironically, the movement's organizer in Derry during the period in question had been Malachy McGurran, who supported the leadership position.) The Donegal amendment was defeated. John McManus had voted against the amendment but now tabled his own, seeking the removal of a line in the political motion linking Sinn Féin's aims to the socialism 'presently being built in the Socialist countries'. Others also attacked this endorsement of 'bureaucratically imposed state capitalism', Johnnie White denouncing the leadership as 'simply another facet of the

CPI'. O'Hagan and Garland both came out strongly for retention of the line and the amendment was voted down.

RIDD influence was evident in a walkout by some delegates as the agriculture debate began. From the platform Dermot Nolan condemned the RIDD approach, dismissing 'the idea that small farmers would be driven off the land in a few years' and arguing that 'it was impossible to have a revolution in this country without a united workers' and small farmers' movement'. On the contentious issue of whether republicans could accept a reformed Northern Irish police force, Costello overwhelmingly carried the day: his amendment ruling this out was carried by 181 votes to 41. His popularity also saw him head the poll for the Ard Chomhairle and be elected vice-president. Crucially, however, he could not stop delegates voting to approve the implementation of the principle of democratic centralism as the party's new core organizational principle. A radical policy platform emerged from the Ard Fheis in which total opposition to the EEC was reiterated and proposals on economy-wide agreements between government, unions and employers were dismissed 'as an attempt . . . to induce the working classes to substitute their fight for political and social emancipation with a vaguely defined concept known as social partnership'.

Outside the Ard Fheis hall Ó Murchú received 'serious threats' from Costello supporters, and in the immediate aftermath of the event the North Munster Comhairle Ceantair passed a resolution condemning 'certain members of the Ard Chomhairle' for an Ard Fheis speech criticizing the Provos 'which in some people's mind can be looked upon as "informing"'. Other cumainn now called for decisive action against perceived internal enemies. Dublin's McKee cumann passed a motion demanding the party refuse membership to 'Trotskyites and militarists'. The Robert Millen cumann complained that the party bookshop sold Trotsky's writings but didn't stock Stalin's *Selected Works*. On the other side of the debate it was Dun Laoghaire's Markievicz cumann which led the way in confronting the leadership position. Contrary to instructions, it provided names of possible local election candidates to newspapers. Worse still, the three prospective candidates – Mick

Plunkett, Dan O'Riordan and Osgur Breatnach – were Costello supporters.

A belief among some activists that the leadership had rigged the Ard Fheis votes fed into the growing unease that had emerged during the debate over the Group A and B documents. This led to activists dropping out of the movement, among them Dublin OIRA members Tony Gregory, Noel and Marie Murray and early RIDD member Bill O'Brien. The hardening attitudes also saw Séamus Ó Tuathail, who had attempted to remain neutral in the leadership arguments, replaced by O'Hagan as *Irish People* editor. Others were thrown out as the leadership began to move against Costello. Derry's Terry Robson, who had seconded the controversial Donegal Ard Fheis amendment, was one of those summarily dismissed. Costello, however, would be afforded the full rigour of IRA law.

The first days of 1974 saw the instigation of both an OIRA committee of investigation and a party inquiry into Ard Fheis vote rigging. Leading figures travelled around the country to compile evidence of Costello's contraventions. OIRA units received lectures on all 'Vol. Clancy's' (Costello's codename) offences throughout his service, while members were told privately that Costello had stolen money and connived in allowing volunteers who opposed him to be captured by Gardaí. One volunteer recalled feeling that 'if they had all that on him going back to the fifties how come he was in a position of power now?' On 21 February 1974 an IRA Court of Inquiry dismissed Costello, also taking his car and wages. He requested a full court martial hearing.

On 5 April witnesses were escorted at short notice to Mornington for Costello's court martial. Bridget Makowski, a Costello defence witness, would later recall being frisked as she entered Mornington while armed volunteers with walkie-talkies patrolled the area. The IRA court and prosecution witnesses, among them Goulding, Garland, Mac Giolla, Ryan, O'Hagan, Ó Cionnaith and McGurran, gathered in one schoolhouse; in another house were Costello and those aiding his defence. When the hearing commenced, McGurran, who had replaced Costello as Sinn Féin vice-president, formally read the charges. Costello was accused of engaging in conduct that undermined the IRA, misappropriating army funds and faction building. Part of Costello's defence was that his accusers had undermined him by their own vote rigging. Without even calling most of the defence witnesses, the three IRA judges found Costello guilty of all charges and he was summarily dismissed 'with ignominy'. In the opinion of his supporters, Costello hadn't stood a chance, Makowski later stating: 'Jesus could have testified on Costello's behalf and it wouldn't have changed the verdict.' The former Chief of Staff and his supporters left immediately. It was a dramatic end to over 20 years of IRA membership, during which Costello had been at the forefront in pushing for the organization to adopt left-wing policies and immerse itself in politics. But he was now breaking with his former comrades, believing they were shirking their duty to conduct an armed struggle against the British.

Costello was still a member of Sinn Féin and faced a separate party inquiry, relating to his 'general unsuitability', in late April. Costello had appealed, by letter, against the composition of the panel – Seamus Lynch, Jimmy McKeown and Bert Twomey – who had been selected to hear the case. He argued that 'at least two of them are members of Group B' and 'could be instructed' or 'feel obliged to uphold whatever case is made by Group B at the inquiry'. Costello had been provided with a 'written summary' of the IRA investigation but was not aware of the specifics of the Sinn Féin case. Northerners Larry Carragher and Ivan Barr were ordered to give testimony that they had received voting lists of who 'would constitute a good militant Ard Chomhairle' directly from Costello. The Ard Chomhairle found Costello guilty and decided by 17 votes to 3 that he should be suspended for six months, during which time he could not seek re-election or attend meetings of Wicklow Council or Bray Urban District Council. Letters supporting Costello began arriving in head office, while the Rockfield Park Tenants Association in Bray called for him to be allowed to stand in the upcoming election. Costello himself publicly called for an extraordinary Ard Fheis to debate his situation. The prospect of losing the political base he had created was unthinkable. On 21 May he announced that 'in accordance with the wishes of the people' he would contest the council elections as an 'Independent Sinn Féin candidate'. The press release publicizing his decision appealed to 'the people of Wicklow' to support other Sinn Féin candidates and stated that he intended to resume his party activities at the end of his suspension.

In the June local elections Costello topped the poll in Bray and was re-elected to both the Urban District Council and County Council. Supporters from around the country had worked for him and his election literature had prominently supported Sinn Féin. Sinn Féin ran 75 candidates nationally and won 14 seats, most of them in rural towns. Joe Sherlock topped the poll in Mallow, as did Liam Ahern in Clonakilty and Paddy Gallagher in Waterford's Ward 3. In Waterford the three Sinn Féin candidates gained 1,376 votes between them, 10.3 per cent of the poll, and narrowly missed out on two extra seats. None of the four candidates in Dublin got more than 1,000 votes, however, and outside of Waterford the Sinn Féin vote remained overwhelmingly rural. At a discussion on the results in Mornington, Waterford's Sean Kelly was dismayed to find more concern over internal movement politics than election analysis. He would recall that for many activists 'parliamentary politics was . . . not what the party was about'.

The Ard Chomhairle dismissed Costello on 13 July, citing his continued attendance at Wicklow County Council, his re-election campaign and lobbying for an extraordinary Ard Fheis. At the same time the Army Council ordered volunteers 'not to associate' with Costello and stated that they were 'duty bound' to report any communications from him or face 'instant dismissal'. Moves were made to dismiss any remaining Costello supporters, with Ronnie Bunting among those expelled, while many others left of their own accord. However, a small band of Costello supporters fought a rearguard action within the party up until the 1974 Ard Fheis. Costello's problems allowed the Ó Murchú faction to seize control of party organization and education within Dublin.

For Ó Murchú and his comrades, control of recruitment allowed them to fully indulge their obsession with the threat of Trotskyist infiltration of the movement. Prospective members' previous involvement in left-wing politics was a cause of serious concern. Introductory lectures on Irish history, the republican movement and socialism could be unfriendly affairs with many members rejected before the end of a six-month probationary period. New recruit Paddy Woodworth, who had been inspired to join Sinn Féin in part by the bloody events in Chile, recalls classes in Gardiner Place delivered by Dublin education officer Tony Moriarty:

He used to sit and singe a cigarette packet with a lit cigarette . . . talked constantly about the danger of Trotskyism . . . They [fellow prospective members] were the unfriendliest, coldest – I don't remember ever going for pints with them afterwards. We all went our separate ways . . . There was a very cloak-and-dagger feeling about the Gardiner Place building at the time because stuff was going on in other rooms, other groups were meeting in other rooms, and even if people weren't, they liked to give that impression.

Since not all those seeking membership were successful, activists remember feeling 'privileged if you were accepted'. Once in, a very high level of commitment was expected. In late 1973 Moriarty had instituted a compulsory lecture series for Dublin cumainn education officers. The almost year-long course was to be an 'experiment in Revolutionary political education' that sought to create 'solid hard-core conscious revolutionaries in Dublin'. Lectures were to be conducted on the Russian, Chinese, Vietnamese, Cuban and Albanian revolutions as well as Irish and European history. It was the 'compulsory essay' aspect of the course that raised most concern. That many of the essays were on subjects of controversy within the movement led to fears that members were really being tested on 'where you were on the Stalinist spectrum', and after heated debate these concerns eventually caused the course to be terminated.

Argument over the direction of the movement was fierce among the up to 300 members in Dublin, and was conducted in the language of the Communist purges of the 1930s. Ó Murchú's group decried their opponents as 'Trotskyite ultra-leftists', 'dilettantes' or 'right-wing militarist Costelloites', while they in turn were described as 'Stalinists', 'reformists' and 'agents of Moscow'. Some members recall 'an intense atmosphere of mutual suspicion', which was exacerbated by the claustrophobic nature of the movement. Members often lived in shared 'movement houses', and their little spare time not taken up with political activity was often spent socializing together. Summary arrests and house raids were common, as were Special Branch visits to members' employers. But many also recall feeling a sense of belonging and the many occasions when 'the craic was marvellous'. However, despite attempts by the leadership to rein in Ó Murchú's group, by the end of 1974 the infighting and departure of Costello supporters had made its mark; the number of cumainn operating in Dublin declined from 25 to 19, with nearly 50 members leaving during this period. Out of 103 people who had applied for membership that year only around 30 had become active. The Ó Murchú faction was unrepentant, their 1974 Dublin AGM report stating:

Our Direction was meant to shock . . . some of us could benefit from a course on How to Win Friends and Influence People – but anyone who cannot distinguish between political ideas and the personalities through which they are expressed cannot be described as a revolutionary.

Their strategy document did contain some important ideas. It admitted that the movement had 'little or no contact' with the mass of the Dublin working class and that this had to be remedied. Cumainn in working-class areas were urged to intensify their involvement in tenants' organizations. In south Finglas a 'golden opportunity' to intervene on the issue of the 'disgraceful' condition of newly built houses was pointed out. The 'south-side flat-dweller belt' was also to be the subject of a major campaign by the Flat-dwellers Associations. There was a need to reorient the movement to systematic local work.

Ó'Murchú's faction was not the only grouping rising to

increased prominence. In the months after the 1973 Ard Fheis the several dozen RIDD activists had been restructured into an 'Industrial Department' that comprised 'specialist cumainn' whose memberships were based on particular groups of trade unions. The September 1974 OIRA General Army Convention received a report that seven such cumainn had been established in Dublin, one in Limerick and one in Cork, with an organizing committee in Belfast to oversee the activity of 'specialist clubs'. Among the new secret cumainn were Dublin's William Thompson cumann, named after the nineteenth-century Irish socialist pioneer, and the Ned Stapleton cumann, named after the communist activist and friend of Smullen who had died in January 1973. A third was named after Joe O'Connor, another wartime comrade of Smullen's who had also died that year. The Thompson mainly comprised members of the ITGWU, with Des Geraghty its leading figure, while the Stapleton was mainly based on the Workers' Union of Ireland and included Harris and Donohue. Many university Republican Club graduates, several of whom had taken up posts in the civil service and semi-state companies, were absorbed into the special 'research groups'. According to the General Army Convention report, research groups were operating in Dublin, Belfast and Limerick and had aided workers in a number of disputes.

The covert nature of RIDD was maintained. All Dublin OIRA members were now ordered to join these new secret cumainn. Most of these men were manual labourers whose unions the Thompson catered for, while clerical staff joined the Stapleton. This led to some seeing the demarcation between the two cumainn as being one for OIRA members and the other for 'new movement intellectuals'. There was some confusion over whether they fitted into the movement's structure as part of Group A or Group B, with one leading member of the Industrial Department recalling seeing them as the 'real Group B'. However, the leadership had decided that the Industrial Department was attached to the party. As both the operations of the OIRA Dublin Brigade and Industrial Department were the direct responsibility of Smullen, who took the position vacated by Costello on the Army Council, their exact relationship to the leadership was largely academic. During 1974 the Department published *The Great Oil and Gas Robbery*, which outlined how the 'Irish Gombeen class' was selling off Ireland's 'human and natural resources'. In the longer run the Department's research section ambitiously aimed to 'know more about the economy of this country than any political or economic organisation . . . [and] . . . use this information as a weapon in the battle to give the ownership of Ireland to the people of Ireland'.

The tactics of the Industrial Department were outlined by Smullen. As most unions had rules forbidding 'factional activity', the Department's covert operation was tightened up. Smullen authored a document on how groups within unions were to work. Members should endeavour to 'take a leading part' in workplace politics, becoming shop stewards. Knowledge that such 'a machine' existed but that they could not 'prove that it exists' could be used to coerce union officials. In the workplace there were to be constant endeavours to raise the political consciousness of workmates. However, 'policies which are perhaps correct in principle but which do not attract the active support of a substantial number of workers must be examined very carefully'. Connection to a 'research department' was seen as a great asset in terms of the workplace: a 'member who wishes to know what profit a boss made last year; if the boss is the director of other companies . . . is usually supplied with this information very quickly'. As a result, 'workers soon understand that the party member can be depended on to supply all sorts of information not readily available . . . all sorts of information can be supplied on all questions touching working-class lives'.

The Industrial Department constantly sought new recruits by 'targeting people that were coming up through the trade union movement'. However, their ability to forgo normal party work provoked some resentment of 'secret' members, Dublin activist Margaret O'Leary recalling: 'I wasn't interested in a second layer of so-called intellectuals. [It was seen as] sort of alright for the people in the cumanns to go out and do the slogging work while the other people made the decisions.' Fears were also expressed about the possibility of some members having votes in both geographical and 'specialist' cumainn.

The Industrial Department's views were expressed through the *Irish People*'s 'Anne Devlin' column. It sparked a major debate when it attacked feminism for downgrading class struggle. In a published reply, de Burca provocatively responded that the article was the 'usual Trotskyite bullshit', knowing its author would be irritated by the term. She decried the idea that 'everything must wait for victory in the class struggle' which was of little use to a 'woman with broken bones or worse, broken spirit from a brutal husband'. Industrial Department members were unconcerned by the criticism, one activist recalling that they saw themselves as 'modernist, untraditional or unemotional, pragmatic people who were clearly trying to break with the past'.

For some party activists farmers were part of that past. There remained a dedicated group who attempted to keep the Small Farmers' Defence Association's rural agitation going, but by late 1974 an internal report stated that 'as an organisation the FDA is defunct' with the few branches that still existed operating independently. Nonetheless in the rural constituency of Cork North-East, Joe Sherlock received 5,363 votes in a November 1974 by-election. Many of these votes were gained in the small town of Mallow with Sherlock's key role in a successful campaign to maintain the local hospital proving to be crucial. It was a positive return for the ITGWU shop steward at the Mallow beet factory, who had been assiduously building a base of support in the area since 1967. The performance came despite Labour minister Michael O'Leary stating during the campaign that Sherlock was a 'subversive'.

August 1974 saw Sinn Féin welcome over 200 of its international allies to Ireland for an 'Anti-Imperialist Festival' held over two weeks in Dublin and Belfast. Government concerns about the event fed into tabloid outrage, with headlines branding the event a 'Festival of Terror' and an 'IRA Terror Summit'. Interpol was reported to be on high alert and several delegates were refused entry to the country. Among those who did make it were representatives of ZANU guerrillas from Southern Rhodesia, Basque, Welsh, Breton, Quebecois, Puerto Rican and Scots nationalists, and left-wingers from across Europe. Speaking from a Liberty Hall platform draped with a banner declaring 'Our Fight is Your Fight', Tony Heffernan told them they would see 'not just the Ireland of the tourist brochure, but the Ireland where 5 per cent of the people own 75 per cent of the wealth'. In the North they would encounter all the 'repressive apparatus' of imperialism while in the South they would see a 'classic neo-colonial state'. For the next two weeks delegates were treated to lectures in both cities, historical tours and late-night drinking sessions. Des O'Hagan told delegates that the preservation of the Irish language was part of the struggle against an 'Atlantic culture' fostered by 'barbarous Hollywood'. Guest speakers included figures from the wider left, such as John de Courcy Ireland, Matt Merrigan and Padraig Ó Snodaigh. However, not all leftists were happy with the event. The British and Irish Communist Organisation picketed Liberty Hall, declaring that Official Sinn Féin was a 'sectarian nationalist body', while the Provisionals organized their own lecture for festival delegates. Despite their animosity to the Officials, BICO's theories were having an impact. The group's theoretical literature was eagerly read by many activists, particularly those attached to the Industrial Department. John McManus recalled BICO as 'tremendous intellectually, lobbing bombs into all our assumptions about things; we opposed them very often but at the same time a lot of their ideas became our currency as well'.

Republicanism of all shades was also being subjected to savage criticism by Conor Cruise O'Brien, the minister with responsibility for broadcasting. His 1974 Labour Party conference speech had placed responsibility for the continuation of internment in the North squarely with the Provisionals. Soon after taking office, Cruise O'Brien had set about tightening Section 31 of the Broadcasting Act, which outlawed interviews with members of paramilitary organizations and their supporters. This caused resentment within RTÉ. Rodney Rice, a journalist at the station who was close to the Officials, contacted de Burca about the possibility of taking legal action against Section 31. However, it was Harris as a producer of the station's current affairs flagship *7 Days* who publicly confronted the minister. A special programme dealing with intern- ment was broadcast in October 1974, and featured interviews with three ex-internees and footage of British troops violently dispersing rioters. Cruise O'Brien felt that Section 31 had been breached and personally took the matter up with the head of RTÉ current affairs. After an internal RTÉ inquiry Harris was transferred out of current affairs and the programme editor was reprimanded. Newspapers gave the controversy much attention, as they did concerns over the degree of control Cruise O'Brien was attempting to exert on all programming. Despite the tougher government line, RTÉ continued to attract radicals as employees, several of them with backgrounds in the Official movement. Among those joining the station during 1974 were Patrick Kinsella, a former Dublin Comhairle Ceantair member, and Charlie Bird, who was told about a research job with *7 Days* by Harris.

As 1974 drew to a close Costello's supporters saw their last faint hopes of salvaging their leader's position within the Officials disappear. The 1974 Ard Fheis saw 700 people pack the Town and Country Club in Dublin's Parnell Square on 29–30 November. The Starry Plough hung behind a speaker's platform, from which for the first time in over a decade Costello would be absent. Only two minutes' walk away in the Gresham Hotel he awaited the outcome of his final attempt to be reinstated. Some of his sup- porters were turned away at the door. In the hall, Nicky Kelly put forward a Wicklow motion that Costello be reinstated. Maelíosa Costello made an impassioned speech on behalf of her husband. Ó Murchú followed with a strong denunciation that he recalls may have gone 'over the top'. The motion to reinstate Costello was defeated by 197 votes to 15. It was left to Garland to reiterate a warning against Costello's attempts to 'subvert' the movement. He cautioned that Costello's line would vary:

If, for instance, he thinks that you want only political activity, he will tailor his approach to this, and if on the other hand he thinks that you are primarily interested in bombs and bullets he will tell you of what should be done in this field promising all the time he will be able to supply all needs . . . [He] has gathered to himself a collection of individuals who are either past members of our organization or the Provisionals or Saor Éire. We are confident that such a combination will not go anywhere but will, because of the motley crew that makes it up, finish up eating each other as all such unprincipled combinations do . . . We are a revolutionary organisation, and we will not shrink from taking whatever action, popular or unpopular, to assist on the road towards revolution.

8. 'Brothers Fighting Brothers'

'Ar laoch, ar gCurai, ar sciath cogadh, ta se ar lar. Seasaimis an fod mar
sin, ar naghaidh leis an sean namhad, ce go bhfuil gadhair na
mbreathadoiri ag tagaint faoin ar gcosaibh.'

('Our hero, our Champion, our shield in battle has fallen. Let us stand
our ground nonetheless, facing our ancient enemy although the traitor
dogs snap at our heels.')

Cathal Goulding, 30 April 1975

For over a year Costello had been preparing for a leadership coup
within the Official republican movement, or, failing that, for the
establishment of a new organization. As the leadership of the
Dublin OIRA alleged, Costello had been allowing volunteers to
research possible heists for the purpose of funding his own schemes,
and several of these men were caught carrying out robberies in
Dublin and Limerick during the autumn of 1974. He also
attempted to utilize the Officials' US arms network for his own
project. By August Costello was having detailed discussions with
supporters at the Fairways Hotel in Louth on the breakdown of
OIRA loyalties area by area in the event of a split. He proposed a
greater emphasis on the national question, a more proactive military policy and the maintenance of the traditional dual military/
political structure rather than the creation of a unified 'vanguard
party' as proposed by Garland.

It was only in December 1974, during the week after the Ard
Fheis, that his plans emerged into public view. The entire Wicklow
Comhairle Ceantair, three cumainn in north Munster, and
members in Dun Laoghaire and Dublin announced their resig-

nation from Official Sinn Féin, all airing similar complaints: a lack of democracy within the movement, the abandonment of the pledge not to take seats in the Northern Assembly and the alleged rigging of the Ard Fheis. Over 100 Southern members left during this period, although many had not been active for months. In Wicklow Sinn Féin was reduced to just one cumann, in Bray, chaired by John McManus, and the local OIRA was left with the county O/C and one volunteer. The Official leadership dismissed talk of mass resignations as a 'paper war to confuse [the] general public', and there was an element of truth in this: outside of Wicklow, north Munster, Dun Laoghaire and Ballymun, Costello's supporters were a small minority. Northern volunteers 'on the run' comprised a substantial chunk of his active support in the capital, along with a few others including Border Campaign veteran Tony Hayde.

About 25 Costello supporters defected or were expelled in Dublin, and these people formed the core of the new Irish Republican Socialist Party (IRSP), launched on 8 December in the Spa Hotel in Lucan. Around 80 activists from across Ireland were present. Earlier at the same location Costello had secretly set up a new military organization at a meeting of around 45 people. Among those attending the military meeting, according to the OIRA's intelligence, were Ronnie Bunting, Seamus O'Kane, Johnnie White and Teresa Gallagher. Costello was elected Chief of Staff, with White his adjutant general, of an organization that would eventually be known as the Irish National Liberation Army (INLA), though that title was not announced until 1976. Meetings to organize the IRSP followed in Dublin, Belfast and Derry.

The driving force behind the IRSP was a desire for a more active military policy. There was also frustration at the Official leadership's stressing of the need to build cross-community support – 'Ring Road socialism', as Costello dismissively termed it. This was allied to a desire to respond to loyalist attacks. Many Officials were not satisfied with the limited, unclaimed operations undertaken by the OIRA and at least some wanted to respond indiscriminately. 'Come with us, lads,' one IRSP member is recalled telling his former comrades in south Belfast, 'and you can shoot as many Prods as you want.' One Official argued that the IRSP were going to differentiate themselves 'from the Provos on the basis that they were left wing but [they] were going to shoot Prods, whereas the Provos were right wing and were going to shoot Prods'. Opinions differed on Costello's hopes for the new army. Some felt that he would have been happy with a more proactive version of the OIRA's 'defence and retaliation' policy, but many in the IRSP clearly desired a campaign to rival that of the Provisionals.

Northern support for the IRSP was concentrated in Belfast and the north-west. Costello's supporters were clearly the majority in Derry city and most of the local OIRA followed him into the new organization. A small number of local activists, including Mickey Montgomery, remained loyal to the Official leadership and a much depleted OIRA structure was maintained in the city. Co. Derry saw a number of important defections and the IRSP split had a bigger impact locally than the Provisional split had done. In Strabane, local leader Ivan Barr refused Costello's overtures, despite some sympathy for his position. In Belfast Costello had been popular with most of the organization. He had visited the city on a regular basis and, unlike many of the national leadership, personally took part in Republican Clubs activity. Costello made a point of eliciting information about conditions on the ground; 'he didn't tell you what he was thinking but he really listened to what we were thinking . . . in retrospect maybe he was canvassing for support'. However, when it came to the crunch he attracted only a minority of the Official organization in the city. Divis Flats was the only unit to defect en masse, after a combative meeting with Seamus Lynch representing the Belfast command staff. The important Beechmount unit, numbering about 30 volunteers, saw only 4 leave. Among those in Belfast who did leave for the IRSP were some of the OIRA's most experienced 'operators', including Anthony Dornan and Sean and Harry Flynn. Former volunteers from Ballymurphy, Whiterock, the Upper Springfield and Turf Lodge, including some of the 'dirty dozen', helped form the 'backbone of the IRSP' in Belfast. In many cases they had not only taken on the security forces but had been to the fore in confronting loyalists and the Provisionals. The Official leadership's 'barrack room' discipline, including threats and punishment beatings to keep people in line, in fact 'drove some people away' when Costello's alternative presented itself. Many pro-Costello dissidents accused McMillen of having not relayed to the Army Council the level of disaffection in Belfast with the ceasefire restrictions, but loyalty to the 'wee man' was extremely strong and the core areas of the Lower Falls and the Markets remained with the Officials. In total the OIRA estimated defections in the city at about 40 volunteers.

In Long Kesh over 20 men, including Thomas 'Ta' Power, Hugh Torney, John Nixon and Robbie McConville, announced their loyalty to the IRSP on 12 December. (McConville was an OIRA member from Divis Flats whose mother Jean had been abducted and killed by the Provos two years previously.) Nixon felt there was 'a sense of tragedy' about the split, as the Officials were a small minority in the camp and had built up a unique camaraderie. The IRSP supporters initially occupied a section of the OIRA compound, but tension soon built up over access to food and water and eventually the IRSP supporters had to be moved to a separate cage, away from the 70 or so Officials.

There was suspicion that some OIRA members who had shifted their loyalty to Costello were continuing to operate within the Officials and, as the IRSP tried to expand, persons loyal to the Official leadership infiltrated meetings. This bred further paranoia: in Belfast Mary McMahon was among those thought to be a possible Costello supporter; and the Officials had to issue a statement pointing out that Belfast's Kitty O'Kane was not the same person as the Derry woman affiliated to the IRSP. By late February Costello was claiming that his new party had 700 members; Bernadette McAliskey, who had aligned herself with the group, privately and more realistically estimated the IRSP's strength as between 200 and 300.

The Officials launched a propaganda offensive against the new group, describing it as comprising three elements: 'a criminal sectarian gang, a few willing to be guided by latter-day messiahs, and those imbued or manipulated by the principal distraction of our time, violent ultra-leftism'. Many Officials were dismissive of the political understanding of those who followed Costello and tended to stress the role of 'articulate, educated ultra-leftists' like Terry Robson in influencing impressionable younger volunteers.

The far left were enthused by the emergence of the IRSP, seeing it as having the potential to become a mass revolutionary party. In February 1975 the Socialist Workers Movement's Brian Trench helped prepare a speech for Costello at a Dublin public meeting, and the SWM later narrowly rejected a suggestion to merge with the new party. People's Democracy also welcomed the formation of the IRSP, and some of its members joined it. Those alienated by the Officials' increasing embrace of Eastern Europe saw the IRSP as potentially 'anti-Stalinist'. Others hoped it would provide an open forum for various tendencies to cooperate. But few within the IRSP, beyond those with a background in the leftist groups, had any knowledge of Marxist ideology. Costello was wary of over-reliance on such theory, with his political reading largely restricted to the *United Irishman* and Connolly's pamphlets. Within a month of its foundation the IRSP declared: 'We're not Trotskyite . . . Connolly, Lalor, Davitt and Pearse are good enough for us.' Some suggested that the far left saw the IRSP as a shortcut to a working-class base and to an armed wing, which their own organizations wanted but lacked.

From early 1975 the Provisional IRA had been observing a ceasefire after talks with Protestant clerics and contacts with the British government. This had caused unease among some of its members, a few of whom joined the IRSP. The Official Army Council welcomed their rivals' curtailing of hostilities and called for the British to respond by releasing all internees. The British and the Provisionals cooperated in the setting up of local 'incident centres' to monitor the ceasefire in nationalist areas. The prospect of Provisional talks with the British alarmed unionists and, fearing a sell-out, loyalists upped the pace of sectarian killing. The Provisional IRA claimed the right to respond and the ceasefire became more honoured in the breach than in the observance. The year 1975 saw 206 people killed, 174 of them civilians.

The Officials and their new rivals contributed to the violence, starting a few days after the IRSP was set up, when a meeting of its supporters in New Lodge was broken up by OIRA members who pistol-whipped a number of those present. Across Belfast IRSP supporters were being threatened and beaten up by early January. Ronnie Bunting, by now a west Belfast schoolteacher, and five others had been 'taken into custody' by the OIRA and questioned about stealing weapons. Claim and counterclaim followed, with the OIRA alleging that IRSP members had committed robberies using the Officials' name and were attempting to embezzle movement funds. In Newry the OIRA carried out a punishment shooting on a Costello supporter who was planning to raid an arms dump. An internal OIRA report circulated in March 1975 stated that the situation in Belfast had 'steadily deteriorated from polemics to shootings as the IRSP commenced a systematic campaign of seizing weapons from the IRA'. It also claimed that IRSP members carried out a number of sectarian attacks in the first months of 1975, leaving two Protestant civilians dead. For the OIRA this provided an ideologically sound reason to take offensive action: 'These attacks have led in turn to Protestant extremist attacks which have claimed the lives of four Catholics. It is here that the Costello aim of provoking virtual civil war, in order to break the overall ceasefire position, is seen in its clearest light.'

Some in the Official leadership thought the smaller group 'could be wiped out': those who had witnessed the birth of the Provisionals at first hand were particularly adamant that the same mistakes should not be made again. Worries over further defections and the membership's resolve were provoked by Donegal Sinn Féin's condemnation of the movement's attitude towards the IRSP. The Officials therefore had to convince sections of their own membership of the IRSP's malevolence, a task aided by an IRSP statement lauding the Provisionals as a 'genuinely anti-Imperialist force ... [whose Army Council made] principled

efforts to secure peace with justice'. For many this confirmed the
treacherous nature of the new group. For others there was a sense
that once again 'brothers [were] fighting brothers' as personal
friendships and family relationships were sundered. Men who had
been interned and on active service together were now threatening
to shoot one another.

On 20 February a three-man OIRA squad attacked Hugh
Ferguson as he worked on a building site in the Whiterock area,
where he was the local IRSP leader. They had been ordered to
wound the 19-year-old, but in the altercation that unfolded Ferguson was shot four times and died. The 3-year-old son of Republican Clubs councillor Bernie McDonagh, who was playing nearby,
was also hit by gunfire. McMillen was upset about the death but
realistic: 'Unfortunately he was a game kid and wouldn't take it
lying down. He put up a fight and was killed by accident.' Publicly,
however, the OIRA denied they were responsible. Costello gave
Ferguson's funeral oration to a crowd of only 200, mainly 'young
boys with a sprinkling of older men and women', who dispersed
'rapidly' after the burial.

In his oration Costello denied that the IRSP had a military wing,
but his organization responded to Ferguson's death by launching a
series of revenge attacks. The Officials' Turf Lodge Social Club
was firebombed, a number of OIRA members were wounded
and on 25 February Belfast OIRA Quartermaster Sean Fox was
killed by a sniper near Divis Flats. The funeral of the 32-year-old
former internee, attended by 2,000 people, was turned into a show
of strength, with over 800 men and youths marching in formation
behind the coffin. In his oration Goulding warned that 'the threats
of a few misguided and confused malcontents will not stop us
now'. Anger was intensified later that day by a bomb attack on the
Bush Bar in Leeson Street, which had been packed with OIRA
members including Goulding and Mick Ryan. Although the UVF
claimed the attack two weeks later, in the immediate aftermath it
was blamed on Costello's supporters.

As trouble escalated McMillen gave orders for 'full-time men'
to guard the Officials' HQ at Cyprus Street, bringing 'soft shoes

and bedding' with them. Entrances to local areas were to 'be watched 24 hours a day'. It was stressed that there was to be 'no drinking' by the guards. Intelligence was desperately needed, according to McMillen's notes, on where members of the new organization lived and which pubs they frequented. A squad was organized to 'raid certain houses', but McMillen was unsure whether to create a 'special unit' to deal specifically with the IRSP or just mobilize 'every area full-time'. What was clear was that there was now going to be an 'all-out effort to destroy this group'.

Tension was also growing in Dublin. Those prominent in the debates leading to the split feared for their own security. Helena Sheehan, Eoin Ó Murchú's wife, recalls 'going to bed every night fearing that they would be coming for him and worrying about the kids, locking them in [and] having kitchen knives in the bedroom'. On the other side of the divide, Tony Gregory slept with a hatchet under his mattress. Then the feud reached the capital. At 10 p.m. on Saturday 1 March Costello and Malachy McGurran were in the RTÉ studios debating the ongoing violence. Less than an hour after the debate's conclusion, on the other side of the city, Garland and his wife Mary were returning home to Ballymun from a night at the theatre. They had married only four months previously, Dominic Behan officiating as best man. As the couple walked to their front door two hooded gunmen emerged. As Garland remembers: 'When I realized what was happening I turned and ran but then . . . I was shot in the leg and I fell.'

The OIRA leader had been shot six times and was thought unlikely to survive. Tony Heffernan, who was working at a by-election in Galway, remembers the 'sense of shock such a thing could happen down here [in the South]'. Another activist recalled: 'Garland had a lot of loyalty. When he got shot even people in the trade unions were saying could they do anything to help, people you wouldn't think knew him.' Costello's condemnation of the attack as the work of 'enemy agents' was dismissed by the Officials. They accused him of rallying 'these elements under his blood-stained flag'. Garland's survival and his alleged response when asked if he wished to see a priest as he lay wounded – 'I need a doctor, not a fucking witch doctor' – added to the 'iron man' image that had first become attached to him after Brookeborough. The attitude of his assailants, he thought, was: 'Just kill the cunt and that will fucking do it, he's finished therefore the whole lot's finished . . . But [they] had no conception of what was involved, it wasn't just an individual.' During his convalescence he was visited for the last time by Gerry Foley, whose Trotskyism was now anathema to the Officials. Whatever his would-be assassins thought about the possibility of Garland's death hastening the end of the feud, Foley felt otherwise, arguing that the death of this 'sincere revolutionist' would not only 'evoke a strong reaction' but also remove the leader 'most likely to have the stature and objectivity to rise above the factional frenzy that has gripped the "Officials"'.

Only hours after the gunmen struck in Ballymun, Paddy McAllister was shot and critically wounded in the Officials' Twin-brook Social Club in Belfast. Two days later, on 3 March, an IRSP member was seriously injured in Turf Lodge. On the 5th, in the same area, Ronnie Bunting was driving a car with an armed IRSP member when he was shot at by a sniper; Bunting received a slight neck wound. This was followed on the 6th by an attack in Beechmount that left two Officials wounded and a 5-year-old boy injured. Sinn Féin claimed that the IRSP had formed an assassination group to kill members of its leadership. Many IRSP members sought refuge in the Divis Flats, which became known as 'the Planet of the IRPs'. The violence, and also internal pressure from McAliskey and others, seemed to be having an impact when on 7 March the IRSP announced the 'stand down' of its organiz-ation in Belfast. On BBC television McAliskey described how the party had attracted every 'tupenny, hapenny gangster' in Belfast, a remark that provoked much resentment.

There were elements among the Officials who felt that the IRSP were on the run and should be finished off. In one incident Harry McKeown was informed by IRSP members that they wished to return stolen weapons to the Officials. He offered to stay with the IRSP members in order to ensure the safety of one of their comrades, who would be in the custody of Officials while the weapons were handed over. But McKeown withdrew his offer when he was warned by an Official that they had no intention of returning their 'hostage' alive.

The two organizations agreed that union leader Michael Mullen would act as a mediator. On 10 March the Officials announced an 'amnesty' for IRSP members who dissociated themselves from that party. Although the IRSP dismissed the amnesty as 'sick', there was a feeling among the Officials that the strategy of violence twinned with conciliatory gestures in public was working. An internal Official report claimed that over 20 members of the IRSP had renounced their involvement, including national executive members Teresa Gallagher and Joe Sweeney. Both organizations were also feeling pressure from the hard-pressed Catholic ghetto communities. In the previous month nineteen people had been killed, the majority of them Catholic victims of sectarian attacks. A group called the Turf Lodge Peace Women had been founded to lobby for a halt to the violence. Initially their peace calls were welcomed by the Officials and Goulding met with the women. On 15 March Mullen announced he had successfully negotiated a 'truce' in order for talks to begin. The days leading up to Easter were somewhat calmer, with the Officials only recording failed attacks against Seamus Lynch and Tony 'Tonto' Maxwell. The IRSP claimed there were at least six attacks on its members in the same period. That year's Easter commemorations at Dublin's Glasnevin Cemetery hosted three separate Republican observances – by the Provisionals, the Officials and the IRSP. In contrast 250 people attended a rare joint Official–Provisional commemoration in Ballymacnab, Co. Armagh.

The Official commemorations heard militant speeches decrying the IRSP and its 'assassins'. Costello had earlier announced that due to Official intransigence no talks had begun and the IRSP was to reform in Belfast on 1 April, with members returning to their homes and workplaces after accepting assurances of protection from 'several groups'. The stage had been set for another violent cycle. On 2 April an IRSP member was seriously wounded in what the Officials claimed was an act of self-defence by two of their volunteers, and the tit-for-tat attacks began again. A group calling itself the People's Liberation Army claimed responsibility for firebombing Andersonstown Republican Club on 3 April; the PLA was the armed wing of the IRSP, though the party denied it had such a wing. On the night of 5 April Danny Loughran, a 20-year-old IRSP member, was shot dead near Divis Flats. Loughran had been with his wife, who heard the four attackers shout 'Official IRA' before opening fire with a machine gun. Within hours an attempt had been made on the life of Des O'Hagan in which he was slightly injured. On 12 April 23-year-old Paul 'Cheesy' Crawford was shot dead by men in a passing car as he sold the *United Irishman* on the corner of the Falls and Springfield Roads. As Crawford's coffin left his home a volley of shots was fired by OIRA volunteers. At his graveside O'Hagan warned: 'The people who direct and organise these killer squads cannot expect to continue with their crimes.'

Two days after Crawford's death Seamus Lynch was fired on as he drove to hand in his application papers for forthcoming convention elections. A few days later Lynch's friend, IRSP member Sean Flynn, was shot and wounded by the OIRA.

Even at the height of the conflict some people on both sides managed to maintain amicable relations. In early April the Provos launched an attack on OIRA members in the Markets. Official Robbie Elliman was wounded in the attack on Mooney's Bar, as was his drinking partner Anthony Dornan, by then a leading member of the IRSP. When three members of the Ormeau Road OIRA decided to defect to the IRSP, the local OIRA unit ignored urgings from the leadership to punish their former comrades, even going as far as warning them of planned attacks.

In the midst of the fighting the Officials were trying to run an election campaign. A 'Constitutional Convention' had been established to ascertain what system of government would be most acceptable to Northern Ireland's population, and an election to the convention was held on 1 May. The *Irish Times* commented that the feud 'could not have come at a worse time' for the Republican Clubs, whose key demand was an end to violence. It would be difficult for the Clubs to take the two or three convention seats they might have hoped for. (The IRSP and Provisionals, meanwhile, called for a boycott of the election.) A proposal for the replacement of the RUC by a 'new Civic Police Service' was central to the Clubs' platform. Entitled 'The Police and You', and unveiled on the day Hugh Ferguson was shot, the plans envisaged a force that would be unarmed, full-time, unionized and answerable to 'civilian control bodies' comprising trade unionists, community representatives and police union representatives. Contrary to the demand of some nationalist politicians, recruits would be selected on the basis of suitability rather than to achieve religious balance within the force. It was stressed that the RUC's sectarian record made it unacceptable.

The Officials were increasingly exercised by the Provisionals' use of the new incident centres to coordinate their local activities. It was felt that the British Army was allowing the Provisional IRA to take over the policing of the ghettos in place of the RUC. The Officials denounced the 'Royal Ulster Provisionals' and stated that an 'unreformed RUC [was] totally unacceptable, whether accompanied by former anti-civilian bombers or not'. During the ceasefire some Provisionals were being allowed to carry personal weapons, and two Lurgan Officials were 'arrested' by armed Provos in February. One Belfast OIRA O/C recalls 'a visit from the local major from the barracks' who asked him, 'Have you a list of men for me?' The Official asked what for, and the officer replied, 'But you're the O/C of the area.' The OIRA man demurred, while the soldier reiterated, 'We need a list of people who will be policing the area.' The OIRA man recalled, 'I thought he was crazy. Only afterwards I realized he had gone to the wrong group.'

The election campaign was marked by more sectarian violence, with pubs a favoured target. Several of those attacked were Official haunts. A man was fatally injured in another attack on the Bush Bar and four injured in an attack on The Oak in March. Jim Sullivan was in the Bush Bar during the second attack when the

OIRA fired shots at the fleeing gunmen after they wounded two people standing outside. On 11 April the Jubilee Bar was sprayed with machine-gun fire, but a bomb left inside by a UVF gang was disposed of by an OIRA volunteer, who carried it outside and threw it on to a railway line. A British Army patrol then came upon the scene, shooting a loyalist gunman dead. Although diplomatic contact had been maintained between OIRA and UVF leaders, the loyalists had come to the conclusion that the Officials were a major threat. This view was made explicit in a UVF document released to journalists, which stated that although the 'number one short-term enemy of Ulster' was the Provisional IRA, 'the most dangerous and deadly enemy long term will be the Official IRA and its Marxist-Leninist associates'.

The Officials and UVF could agree that the IRSP's militancy and 'ultra-leftism' were an immediate threat to both. The March edition of the UVF magazine *Combat* carried an article denouncing the IRSP's 'sectarian activities' and directed particular vitriol at the 'renegade Protestant Ronnie Bunting'. The Officials were described as 'non-sectarian', and it was concluded that the Provos would probably end up backing the IRSP. The analysis mirrored that of the Officials, and indeed had origins in the *United Irishman* and UVF/Official contacts. The *Combat* article provoked praise and a front-page headline in the *Irish People*: 'UVF names the killers'. The IRSP claimed collusion had gone further, announcing the Officials had given sixteen of their members' names and addresses to the UVF. On 8 March UVF members entered a house in north Belfast and shot 23-year-old student Michael Adamson dead. Justifying the murder, *Combat* claimed Adamson was a former Markets OIRA member who had defected to the IRSP. Adamson was not claimed by the IRSP, but he had been an OIRA member until 1974. Both the Officials and the IRSP claimed that their enemies had security-force backing. In reality there were numerous arrests on both sides; seven OIRA members were caught with weapons and charged with offences including attempted murder in late April alone. Meanwhile the UVF undertook attacks that raised tension at crucial periods.

The violence contributed to a disappointing last-place showing for Sinn Féin's 22-year-old candidate Renee Prendergast in the Galway West by-election of early March. Tony Heffernan recalls being worried by the long-term consequences of the Officials being 'seen by the public as some sort of fucking cowboys going around shooting one another. People that otherwise might have joined said they were not getting involved in that sort of thing.' The leadership decided that the feud had to end. Garland recalled coming to this conclusion while recovering from his injuries: 'We had to stop it in order to preserve ourselves, because we were going down the road where it was just a gang fight. Nobody was winning.'

Pressure was also being felt from the participants' own communities. After the Officials refused to send a representative to a meeting on the feud, the Turf Lodge Peace Women criticized their 'callous indifference to the sufferings of the working-class people'. The IRSP attempted to capitalize on the changing atmosphere, announcing their 'support groups' had been asked to halt attacks, resulting in the People's Liberation Army declaring a four-day truce. The Officials continued to refuse direct talks with Costello, but the number of attacks from both sides decreased.

There was meanwhile a spate of Official–Provisional violence in the border area. In February leading Newry Official Eugene Tremers was shot outside his home. A week later Provisional Michael McKevitt and a colleague were kneecapped by the Officials in Dundalk. In April a bomb injured seventeen people near the Officials' newly opened club at Trevor Hill, and senior Official Larry Carragher was wounded in a gun attack in Newry. In response the OIRA abducted five Provisionals, beating and kneecapping them. The dispute could easily have escalated, as the local OIRA O/C recalls:

There was fourteen people shot in that particular period but nobody was killed . . . some boys called to me and said, 'Look, do we shoot them in the head or what?' I said, 'There is nobody dead yet, so shoot them in the legs'; but if we had wanted them dead they would have done it as simple as that.

After more incidents on both sides of the border the Provisionals approached a local priest to mediate an end to the violence. He helped establish a liaison process that lasted for a number of years, ensuring disputes between the local factions were 'sorted out before the guns came out'. This violence was a further embarrassment for the Republican Clubs' election campaign, as were accusations by Ivan Cooper of 'mafia-style' Official intimidation of SDLP members in Strabane. Cooper blamed the OIRA for beating up James Hume, brother of SDLP leader John Hume.

On Monday 28 April 1975 Billy McMillen visited the Cyprus Street HQ. There he instructed Seamus Lynch to contact the IRSP and inform them the Officials were halting all attacks in order to allow peace talks to progress. The news was quickly relayed to local OIRA O/Cs. McMillen then drove with his young wife Mary to a hardware shop on Spinner Street; they had been married just eight weeks before and were decorating their new home. The couple were spotted by two armed IRSP men: Brendan McNamee, a former Provisional, and Gerard Steenson, a teenage former Fianna member. As the McMillens returned to their van, Steenson approached and shot McMillen a number of times at close range. A woman who worked in the hardware shop described to a newspaper how McMillen

was lying on the pavement with his feet in the van. There was a hole the size of a 2p piece in his neck. I saw him trying to breathe and as he breathed his neck caved in ... A few minutes later a woman came into the shop and said: 'I'll have six rolls of purple wallpaper, please.' I felt sick. I felt like smashing her face in and throwing her out of the shop. He was still lying out there on the pavement outside.

Although McMillen's killers fled in a black taxi, a rumour that their getaway vehicle was a yellow Cortina spread quickly among the numerous armed OIRA men in the Lower Falls area. This led to the shooting of an innocent Armagh man driving such a vehicle. On hearing of the killing, Costello hurried out a statement in the name of the IRSP National Executive condemning the shooting 'without reservation' and placing the blame with 'the British Intelligence Services and possibly ... other sources with a vested interest in a continuation of the conflict'. The idea of British involvement found a ready audience among some sections of the left, but not in Belfast. The following day's *Irish Times* led with the killing, while the *Irish News* carried five columns and several large notices of condolences for the fallen 'O/C Belfast Brigade Official IRA'.

Two days later several thousand people walked behind McMillen's coffin as it processed up the Falls, flanked by a ten-man OIRA colour party wearing black leather jackets and berets. Most of the Official leadership were present, along with Mick O'Riordan of the CPI and representatives from a variety of organizations, including UCG Students' Union. In Milltown Cemetery Goulding's oration alternated between heroic rhetoric and rage. Speaking in Irish, which many of the audience would have barely understood, he proclaimed:

Our hero, our Champion, our shield in battle has fallen. Let us stand our ground nonetheless, facing our ancient enemy although the traitor dogs snap at our heels ... Soldiers and people of Belfast, the task now is yours. Our hope is in you. Not soft or easy the task before you without Liam Mac Maoláin as chief over you. You are now like children without a father, like the Fianna without Fionn.

Continuing in English, his comments were more direct:

An Orange junta sent Liam [Billy] McMillen to prison because he fought for separation. The Provisional Alliance attempted to assassinate him because he held socialist principles and fought for civil rights. The RUC and the British Army of occupation harassed and hounded him because he was a socialist republican. A small, mad band of fanatical malcontents, the sewer rats of Costello ... finally laid him low.

In Belfast the immediate impulse was to 'get [the] people responsible'. The night of McMillen's killing three OIRA members were arrested after forcing their way into the home of leading IRSP member Jim McCorry. In Dublin a massive escalation was planned, as a senior Dublin Brigade member recalled:

Billy McMillen was shot and after that it was [Costello's] whole team has to go . . . we're going to take out about twelve men in Dublin in two houses, arrangements are made, dates are picked, the weapons are secured, then it's called off at the last minute . . . Goulding says that's called off but Seamus has to go.

The Army Council had decided that rather than widespread killing 'there was two people that were going to go instead, Costello and Larry White'. White was a Saor Éire member from Cork who had been implicated in the Garland attack and violent confrontations with local OIRA members. But even in the emotionally charged aftermath of McMillen's death the Official leadership was adamant that paramilitary activity would remain subsidiary to politics. Rather than select the 'militant' Jim Sullivan, or another OIRA member of his generation, as the new Belfast O/C, Goulding turned to a younger man, Seamus Lynch, the Constitutional Convention candidate for the North Belfast seat, who was felt to be 'a safe pair of hands'. Goulding approached Lynch on the day of McMillen's funeral about assuming command responsibilities. After a week of discussions, during which Goulding and Garland assured Lynch that the movement intended to prioritize political development in Belfast, he accepted.

The political damage that the feud inflicted was starkly illustrated in the disappointing performance of the Republican Clubs at the Constitutional Convention election. Their 17 candidates received only 14,515 votes in total, winning no seats; unrealistic hopes of an electoral breakthrough, held by many in the movement, were dashed. The Ard Chomhairle concluded that 'a combination of apathy among the people, Provo intimidation and the conflict with the IRSP had adversely affected our vote'. The Unionist Party and the SDLP emerged from the election as the biggest blocs.

They would now attempt to hammer out a new constitutional settlement in Northern Ireland.

The issue of abstentionism from Northern council chambers now re-emerged as an issue for the Clubs. The leadership wanted elected councillors to take their seats, but met strong opposition from Northern councillors and members. However, McGurran attended a meeting with the Ministry of Home Affairs on prisoner issues in June, and the Clubs' two Belfast councillors were given permission to attend corporation transport planning meetings, although it was decided not to publicize this. By late October the party leadership privately succeeded in persuading all the Northern councillors, bar Barney McKeown in South Armagh, to take their seats.

Although sporadic clashes between the Officials and the IRSP dragged on into the summer, the violence would not again reach the ferocity of the spring. Instead the Officials targeted Costello himself. Just after midnight on 7 May Costello and Seamus O'Kane were driving two Waterford SWM members home after a public meeting in the city. A motorbike pulled up alongside and the pillion passenger raked the car with machine-gun fire. The IRSP leader managed to outmanoeuvre his attackers, escaping with only a slight injury to his hand. The Officials denied any role in the attack, claiming that Costello's accusations were an attempt to 'discredit' them. The Officials were now talking peace: Mac Giolla issued a statement the following week stating that the feud was only serving British interests and allowing for the harassment of political activists. An uneasy truce was now in place between the two organizations and talks would drag on for several weeks. The IRSP had succeeded, despite the OIRA's efforts, in establishing a position for itself within the paramilitary subculture. When the IRSP's Brendan McNamee was shot dead in early June it did not spark off another bout of violence, despite accusations of OIRA involvement. (In fact the IRSP man had been killed by his former comrades in the Provisionals.)

The killing was not over. At 12.15 a.m. on 10 June, Larry White was walking down Mount Eden Road in Cork city eating chips and drinking a bottle of lemonade. As he ambled along an OIRA man, disguised in a wig and false moustache, opened fire with a silenced M3 sub-machine gun. White was hit several times, and was dead within an hour, aged 26. The event provoked outrage in Cork, which had not witnessed a politically motivated killing in decades. White was given a paramilitary funeral at which his brother condemned media speculation over republican involvement, instead blaming Gardaí. However, within days five Officials had been arrested. Believing that the case against them was insubstantial and likely to collapse, some of the suspects turned down the movement's offer of evacuation to Cuba. But four of the five were convicted of murder and sentenced to life imprisonment. There were allegations of Garda brutality and of confessions being forced under duress during questioning lasting until the early hours of the morning. One of those sentenced to life – Bernard Lynch, a leading Cork Sinn Féin member – was later freed on appeal. At least one local Sinn Féin member who had felt assured that the OIRA had been 'retired' resigned over the killing.

On 22 June a device planted near the railway line in Sallins, Co. Kildare, exploded 25 minutes after a special train carrying 300 Official supporters had passed en route to Bodenstown. While planting the device a UVF gang had been disturbed by a local man, Christopher Phelan, whom they stabbed to death. Gardaí initially suspected the IRSP, arresting six members including Costello. The IRSP were also initially blamed by the Officials, creating even more hostility towards the 'gangster from Bray' and his 'trendy lefty' support.

The numbers at the competing Bodenstown ceremonies showed that the Officials had not disintegrated as Costello had rashly predicted. Three hundred had attended the IRSP event in early June, while an estimated 5,000 took part in the Official commemoration. The Official leadership were in no mood to compromise with Costello. Despite the OIRA's denials, the Waterford assassination attempt had been carried out by its recently restructured Operations Department. Volunteers were selected who could be brought together at short notice from various brigade areas to operate directly under the command of the Director of Operations. In the Waterford attack the logistics were organized locally and the SWM public meeting chosen as a likely opportunity to kill Costello, but the would-be assassins were Northern operatives. A week later in Dublin a group of OIRA members were arrested in possession of weapons and charged with conspiracy to commit armed robbery. The group of young men from Dublin, Armagh and Down were typical of the units that would become the hallmark of OIRA operations in the South. Most were jailed, though one of the men left the country while out on bail while another served his sentence under an assumed name. Embarrassingly for Sinn Féin, Sue Sweetman, education officer of the Jemmy Hope cumann, found herself charged with perjury when attempting to post bail for the men. Shortly after the men's arrival in Portlaoise they and other OIRA prisoners were involved in a violent confrontation with warders and Gardaí.

In bringing together the new non-geographically based active service units the OIRA leadership was acting on the recommendations of an Operations Department report, which stated:

It is a fact that there has been no effort made to plan a Dept. We can talk about the other aspects of ops, but if we don't see the need to set up a proper dept we will always fail. Finance must be made available to not only hire transport etc, but to buy it (it can be garaged and only used when needed). When it becomes known it can be sold and new transport bought ... Most of the ops in the South are of a specialist nature yet nothing has been done to train Vols in this field, or very little. There has been a reluctance to involve new blood on ops, which leaves at this moment a vacuum (due to arrests etc) ... Research into police methods has been almost nil. More use of police radios might have helped here. Note: The most important deciding factor in selecting vol. for training for this dept should be their political status and loyalty to the movement. Too often men are selected because they are supposed to be 'hard' men.

Operations in the South were to be authorized by GHQ, with close attention paid to possible political impact. (Many activists in Waterford had expressed concern at how the killing of Costello would have affected Sinn Féin's progress locally.) Trusted Fianna activists, some as young as 15 years of age, were recruited to replenish the ranks. In early 1975 Goulding had appointed a new OIRA organizer in Dublin and discussed with him the need for a tight loyal unit in the city. Another key figure in the reorganization of the Operations Department was Jim Flynn, who had joined Sinn Féin's Lalor cumann in Dublin after being deported from England. Operatives were paid nominal amounts of between £5 and £10 per mission. The Director of Operations, a Belfast man referred to as 'McLaren' in OIRA documents, was on a weekly wage of £30 and had his rent paid. Meticulous planning went into each operation, with robberies only authorized if the funds to be raised were considerable. It was believed that 'inside intelligence was always the best' and funds were available to pay for it. A contact in Dublin's Sheriff Street postal sorting office allowed the OIRA to simply walk out with a bag of money orders before anyone realized that they had been robbed.

The new GHQ strategy created some dissension among Dublin OIRA members. Ó Murchú felt that by 1975 the Dublin Brigade had 'no role to play'. He recalls that 'in a sense there was two Dublin units' – one about 50–60 strong and a 'tighter one of about 20'. Under democratic centralism, all discussions on policy were supposed to take place within specified party and IRA structures; and once decisions had been made by a democratic vote of the leadership, or at Ard Fheiseanna, they were to be adhered to at all levels with clandestine promotion of policy changes banned. Despite the acceptance of these rules throughout the movement, early 1975 had seen rifts intensify again within Dublin Sinn Féin. The new Comhairle Ceantair chairman Jim Sherry and his supporters were vying with the Ó Murchú grouping for control of the executive. Both groups were also contending with the growing influence of the Industrial Department. Despite the ban on factions, a Dublin activist recalls a meeting of 'all the supposed communists or Marxists in the movement', with 'Harris on one hand and Ó Murchú and Moriarty on the other', to debate the movement's direction: 'There was 30 or 40 people there, or more, and I can still see this argument there in the hall with Moriarty and Ó Murchú arguing in support of republican socialism on one hand, and on the other hand Harris and Donohue, a kind of two-nationism.'

The internal arguments were complicated by activists' overlapping membership of various sections of the movement: some were members of OIRA units and secret industrial branches as well as party cumainn. Fierce debate was accompanied by whispering campaigns accusing rivals of everything from 'sexual deviance' to being Garda informers. Accusations that Padraig Yeates was an 'ultra-leftist' and Trotskyist led to the leadership taking the extra-ordinary action of issuing a statement to all Dublin cumainn stating: 'Padraig is and has been a loyal member of the Republican Move-ment . . . anyone using these kinds of smear tactics in future . . . will be severely reprimanded.' Eoghan Harris displayed particular panache in manipulating debate among the competing groupings. The Corkman's personal persuasiveness as well as his closeness to Goulding and Smullen aided his growing influence, which caused resentment among some: 'All these things that were getting voted on in the party, and the army even, were just getting overlooked. Democratic centralist decisions were being taken on things and they were getting overrode the next morning by Harris.'

It was Jim Sherry's group that ultimately brought about Ó Murchú's departure. During March, Sherry and Dermot Nolan reported to the leadership comments made by Ó Murchú in a Mornington lecture to Dublin education officers. Ó Murchú alleged that there had been 'inept handling of the IRSP issue by the leadership' due to their 'petit bourgeois backgrounds' which resulted in a 'natural reaction against working-class politics'. When questioned on his assertions, Ó Murchú had stated that the leader-ship contained 'only about four Marxists'; he highlighted the fact that Cork's Joe Sherlock was a practising Catholic and argued that 'such people . . . would baulk at full Marxist politics'. He also complained that, 'If £3,000 could be allocated by the Ard Chom-hairle for arms, then a similar sum should be allocated for the training of education officers at the Leningrad Institute.' The leadership launched an investigation and, despite a tape record-ing of the controversial Mornington lecture 'malfunctioning', Ó Murchú resigned from Sinn Féin in early April and joined the Communist Party. A number of other Dublin members left with him.

Sherry had less success curtailing the influence of the Industrial Department. Within the industrial cumainn those members who were critical of the political line defined by Harris and Donohue were being sidelined. Some members were simply no longer informed when meetings were taking place. Alan MacSimoin, a Thompson cumann member, stated in a resignation letter to the leadership that he found the movement's new policies incompat-ible with his 'libertarian communist views'. During this period Industrial Department operation was also becoming even more clandestine. Meeting venues were kept secret and some went to great lengths to hide their membership, to the point of absurdity. As Dublin member Eric Byrne recalled, 'There would have been dramatics about hiding membership cards under the carpet and that . . . an awful lot of that bollixology didn't ring true to me.'

As head of economic research, Eamon Smullen had become a central figure in policy formation. He was seen as having been 'tested in the fire' during his imprisonment in Portlaoise and led an ascetic, frugal lifestyle that won him respect from those with IRA backgrounds and admiration from younger industrial cumann activists. His critique of Costello's organization, 'What is the IRSP?', was distributed to members. In it Smullen dismissed the defectors as 'stooges' of the establishment who had under-mined the movement through their support for 'Trotskyite infil-trators'. He argued that Costello's supporters in Derry had 'strutted about behind the barricades and devised one daft scheme after another, always ideas which did not involve long, consistent, seri-ous work'. In contrast Smullen counterposed those involved in 'industrial trade unionism' among the working class, which was 'the breeding ground for revolutionary ideas, for serious political organisation'.

Harris, by now a close confidant of Smullen, was looking for new internal targets in his drive for ideological purity. One party activist recalls Harris stating, 'We have got rid of the militarists, we have got rid of the Trotskyites, [and] next thing . . . we get rid of the social democrats.' Along with another ally from the Industrial Department, Eugene Murray, Harris addressed an education seminar in Trinity College at which Nolan and Sherry were present. They had made no secret of their dislike of the Industrial Department ideologue's approach:

We turned up and sat at the back and Harris said, 'The topic of today is . . .' and then suddenly started shouting, 'No, No, No, No, get those chairs out of there, get those chairs out of there, you are too comfortable!' We were sitting there breaking our fucking hearts laughing, all his little minions were running around with the chairs. 'Go outside and bring in the hard chairs!'

While some found such dramatics ridiculous, for others Harris was the 'driving force in the party', pushing the Industrial Department to question Sinn Féin's approach to issues like the EEC and multinational investment. Smullen introduced discussion on some of these concepts to a meeting of Northern delegates at Mornington in late June. The Economic Affairs Department published *The Public Sector and the Profit Makers* during 1975, outlining the case for the extension of the state sector in the areas of energy, oil, gas and mines, the establishment of a state construction company and 'expansion of the state into food technology, processing and marketing'. The basis for making all these demands possible was the nationalization of the banks.

The Resources Protection Campaign, launched in late 1973, had become a key area of Sinn Féin agitation. The RPC had emerged from a Sinn Féin initiative to bring together groups on the left in a broad campaign demanding the nationalization of mining and energy rights, which were mainly being sold to US multinationals. The campaign initially drew heavily upon the work of the Trinity College Resources Study Group which had called for 'nationalisation without compensation' of the Irish mines under the slogan 'Chile took it back – so will Ireland!' In Galway the local RPC was particularly active under the chairmanship of UCG Republican Club member Eamon Gilmore, and several trade union leaders now endorsed the RPC's aims. Sinn Féin sought to gain influence in the wider left milieu via the RPC, supporting sympathizers like Labour's Una Claffey for election as the campaign's organizing secretary. Meetings had also begun between Sinn Féin, the Communist Party and the Labour Party's Liaison of the Left group. Initially these meetings had been organized through the Wolfe Tone Society, but the Official leadership decided to remove this group from involvement in these contacts, instead putting them under control of the Industrial Department.

One area of concern was the involvement of Seamus Costello in the local resources campaign in Bray. Given the balance of forces in the town, Sinn Féin could not have barred the IRSP from involvement even if they had wanted to. This led to the surreal situation whereby, while the organizations were feuding in Belfast, Sinn Féin and IRSP members were attending fund-raising socials together in Bray. The leadership ordered the Bray Officials to exclude Costello's supporters, and Paddy Woodworth was summoned to Gardiner Place to explain why they would not. There he found himself in a 'roomful of glowering strangers', and after he explained the Bray position he was told forcefully by Smullen that, 'It is people like you who don't realize the necessity of taking tough decisions and when necessary taking up arms – it's people like you who are going to end up in the stadium in Chile.'

The feud with the IRSP was also fought out in the press. In his oration at the grave of Paul Crawford, Des O'Hagan had drawn attention to journalists 'motivated solely by hate' of the Officials. The *Sunday World*, to which Eamonn McCann and Gery Lawless were contributors, had reported early in the feud that Officials were leaving in 'droves' with Costello. In contrast the Belfast *Sunday News* told its readers that only a 'few' activists had left the Officials, that many of these had already been expelled for 'gangsterism' and the Officials were 'better off without them'. The Officials were particularly angered by the coverage of the feud in *Hibernia*, whose assistant editor, Brian Trench, was a member of the SWM. He had already been informed during 1974 that he was 'persona non grata' at Official events. De Burca protested to *Hibernia* that its 'assistant editor belongs to an organisation which is in open association with the IRSP'. During this period Trench was told that the Officials 'were going to take physical action against me' and believed that he was being followed. McCann had also been warned by McGurran that the Official leadership had discussed taking action against him.

Most of *Hibernia*'s reports from Belfast were penned by Jack Holland, who had family and social contacts with the Officials, and a concrete reason to dislike them: his cousin Paul Tinnelly had been shot dead by the OIRA the previous year. Holland was informed by a leading Official that his 'career as a journalist in Dublin would be quickly brought to an end' if he continued to write critical reports. During the feud Conor O'Clery of the *Irish Times* described how two of the paper's reporters had received phone calls from OIRA members. They informed them that journalists might expect a visit from 'the boys' and that a 'close eye' was being kept on their coverage. Leading Officials met *Irish Times* editor Fergus Pyle to complain about Northern reporter Fionnuala O'Connor's coverage of the feud, but Pyle defended his journalist's independence.

The belief that the media was biased against them led the Officials to emphasize the importance of their own press. An internal document on 'Propaganda' was produced, its stated purpose to 'underline the importance of propaganda in the struggle against imperialism. A highly effective propaganda machine operates in Ireland on *behalf of* imperialism; an equally effective machine must be constructed to operate *against it*.' The document asserted that 'no matter how "liberal" or "objective" any newspaper is, it will in the final analysis be true to its class'. The *Sunday World* and the *Irish Press* and *Sunday Press* gave a 'distorted version of

Republicanism'. Socialism was also 'obstructed by the Provisional/ Trotskyite press which is objectively in alliance with the Protestant-supremacist press'. To counter this it was the 'task of the Republican Movement to expose the lies, name the liars and tell the truth'. This was to be achieved by acquiring the equipment necessary for the movement to print its own publications, and by establishing a Republican Propaganda Department. The movement's press was to take a 'thorough investigative approach', presenting stories in a manner understandable to the working class while offering space to opponents 'who wish to debate'. It concluded that 'the techniques of the "soft sell" have no place in the selling of hard politics'.

The party's press had become explicitly pro-Soviet. In late 1974 the *United Irishman* began a series of articles praising Communist states, such as Romania, where 'poverty [was] only a memory'. This provoked some members, like Frank Gallagher from the fishing town of Killybegs in Donegal, to refuse to sell the paper. Gallagher had earlier raised questions as to how Soviet super-trawlers putting Irish fishermen out of work could be progressive. Other members were uneasy about the *United Irishman*'s defence of the crushing of the 1956 revolution in Hungary. In response to such criticism the 'Propaganda' document stressed that in future the 'positive achievements of the Socialist countries' should be related 'in a matter of fact way, free of hysteria or exaggeration'. Great interest was also shown in developments in Portugal, where a revolution, led by left-wing army officers, had overthrown the dictatorship. Sinn Féin members visited Portugal as guests of the Armed Forces Movement and met communist and trade union activists.

In the autumn of 1975, after continued squabbling, the faction led by Jim Sherry was expelled from Sinn Féin for 'breach of party discipline'.There was a period of trepidation after their exit, as Dermot Nolan, who was part of the Sherry faction, recalls: 'We were looking under cars in the morning.' Sherry and Nolan soon joined their former adversary Ó Murchú in the CPI.

The dissidents' fears were not without foundation. In early

October former OIRA member Billy Wright was shot in a machine-gun attack at his barber shop in Cabra. The gunman escaped by hijacking a passing coal truck, and Wright died seventeen days later. The attack was carried out by OIRA members who accused Wright of being a Garda 'informer'. In September an off-duty Garda was shot dead while giving chase to armed robbers in Dublin. A number of Officials were arrested in the aftermath of the shooting but it was two ex-members, Noel and Marie Murray, who were charged with the killing.

In June Sinn Féin issued its first major pamphlet on women's issues, *The Rights of Women in Ireland*. Members such as Máirín de Burca and Pat McCartan were also increasing their involvement in the Prisoners' Rights Organisation, picketing the homes of Department of Justice officials to draw attention to conditions in Ireland's jails. The OIRA Easter statement had highlighted what it saw as an attack on Irish culture through 'TV and Radio to saturate the minds of our people with an alien capitalist ideology and an equally alien Anglo-American culture'. To counter this Officials were active in organizing cultural events, notably the Easter Week *Non-Stop Connolly Show* performed in Liberty Hall. This was a 24-hour play written by ex-member John Arden that dramatized the life of James Connolly. The cast included Jim Sheridan, who had been involved with RIDD, and Jer O'Leary, while those who helped organize the event included Geraghty, Harris and Goulding. Some members of the movement found such endeavours invigorating, though one recalls feeling that 'dying for Ireland in the GPO would have been less painful than sitting through some of that stuff'. The most ambitious cultural project was Sinn Féin's commissioning of director Bob Quinn to produce the feature-length film *Caoineadh Airt Uí Laoghaire* [Lament for Arthur O'Leary]. Filmed in Connemara, the film's plot followed a group of actors rehearsing a play based on an eighteenth-century poem recounting the tale of an Irish aristocrat, Art O'Leary, who returns from service with the Wild Geese. Filmed in Irish and English and avant-garde in style, it was seen as an educational tool as well as entertainment. Mac Giolla praised the film as '[not being] another exercise in futile probing of myths, but essentially a comment upon reality in the present Ireland of 1975 ... Courageous campaigns of resistance, however noble their inspiration, will fail like the gesture of Art O'Leary if they ignore realities ... romantic acts of heroism or defiance may inspire people but will never organise them.' The censor gave the film a general certificate for viewing in its Irish version but not in the English. It was shown by Sinn Féin cumainn throughout the country.

In the North the year had seen an intensification of the sectarian slaughter, with 70 Catholics and 41 Protestants killed in sectarian attacks between February and September. In June an off-duty UDR man and two Protestant civilians were shot dead by the Provisional IRA at Killeen on the border. Loyalists killed a youth in Rathfriland, claiming he was an OIRA member. On 31 July three members of the popular Miami Showband were murdered as they crossed the border by a UVF unit that included serving UDR men. The Provisional IRA in Belfast openly attacked Protestant civilians in retaliation for attacks on Catholics. On the weekend of 14 August, eight Protestants were killed in Belfast, including four in a gun and bomb attack on the Bayardo Bar. Two days later a loyalist car bomb injured 35 people on the Falls. In its aftermath the Citizens' Defence Committee asked Belfast Corporation for help in housing repairs and workmen began deliveries almost immediately. One, Sammy Llewellyn, was bringing in hardboard when he was stopped by Provisionals and asked for identification. When they discovered he was a Protestant he was beaten and shot dead. The so-called 'Good Samaritan' killing caused widespread revulsion on the Falls. It also angered the local OIRA, who clashed with the Provos shortly afterwards.

By mid-1975 the Official leadership had concluded at a meeting in Mornington that while civil war was not 'inevitable' and the British government still had no intention of 'pulling out' of Northern Ireland, London was willing to 'tolerate and, in some cases, even encourage' a 'terror situation' that would force Nationalist and Unionist politicians into power-sharing. This would aid the 'overall fundamental British (and USA) intention – the safe incorporation of Ireland within the Western bloc'. However, as elements within the Provos and the loyalists were 'hell bent' on provoking civil war, there were four 'pragmatic considerations' that were paramount for the Officials if this occurred: '[a)] Not to appear in the '69 light no matter how erroneous the PA [Provisional Alliance] line on this is; b) To save as many lives as possible; c) To save our personnel and the movement; d) To ensure the continuity of our political line.' It was stressed that while the movement recognized the 'current attitudes' of Northern Protestants, 'we, as republicans, cannot at any time regard them as enemies . . . unity of the working class is a prerequisite for the socialist republic'. By August the Republican Clubs had organized anti-sectarian meetings in Derry and Armagh and were distributing thousands of 'sectarianism kills workers' leaflets. Ironically these activities were often curtailed by the threat of sectarian attacks.

'Defence and retaliation' was still OIRA policy but permission to launch attacks was rarely forthcoming. One exception was the shooting of a soldier in Newry in May, retaliation for the injuring of two people by the British Army during a street protest. In July the OIRA launched a series of attacks on the Green Howards regiment, wounding three soldiers. Following these incidents the Newry O/C received an unusual house call:

My door knocks and there was the commanding officer of the Green Howards at the door and he handed me this envelope. He said, 'That's for you . . . I don't want any more of my soldiers shot.' I said, 'I'm political,' [but] he said, 'Now read that.' It said . . . we would like to have a chat.' I had to laugh but I showed it to Mick [Ryan] and he said, 'Well, go along and see what they have to say.' I took Joe Campbell and we met them in Ballyedmond Castle [Hotel] . . . we actually came to an agreement that they would leave us alone if we would leave them alone. They never bothered us at all – no searches, roadblocks or that at all.

However, the OIRA still felt it appropriate to back a Republican Clubs campaign against the blocking of border roads with a

20-minute gun attack on an army observation post at Carrickas-
ticken Road.

In Belfast there was also the occasional retaliatory attack. After
a Fianna member was badly beaten up by soldiers, the OIRA
attacked troops in the south of the city with a grenade and one
soldier lost a leg. In June the OIRA had confronted an undercover
unit after a car crash on the Falls and shots were exchanged; the
OIRA made off with documents and weapons from the crashed
car. The documents contained detailed descriptions of local
Officials, Provisionals and IRSP members. The Officials put the
material on display at a press conference, and a photograph of two
OIRA volunteers brandishing a captured Ingram machine pistol
appeared in the *United Irishman*.

Robberies continued even during the feud, with £1,400 taken
from the Royal Victoria Hospital in January and £7,050 in two
raids in Coalisland in March. Numerous robberies were carried
out by the OIRA in south Armagh, south Down and Louth, with
targets including local banks, post offices, building sites, labour
exchanges, and Dundalk train station. Criticism of the OIRA's
robberies by the local Provos was met by a rebuttal stating that
while 'bombings of pubs are anti-working class and anti-social . . .
the robbing of banks and wealthy establishments is a well established time-honoured revolutionary tradition practised by the
Fenians and revolutionary groups throughout the world . . . it
hurts none but the wealthy and establishment'.

In Dublin Jim Flynn was proving to be an imaginative operator.
Tipped off by a porter about the sums held in the Gresham Hotel's
safe on weekends, he booked in under a false name. At midnight
he held up staff at gunpoint and stole £5,000 in jewellery and cash.
Hotel staff gave a false description of the raider to Gardaí, as the
OIRA operative had demanded.

The OIRA continued to carry out punishment attacks, with
shootings and beatings in Derry, Strabane and Newry. One victim
in Newry was warned that he was 'lucky he was not executed'.
Local reaction was often based on political rivalry. In Strabane the
Provisional IRA condemned the Officials' kneecapping of five

local criminals. As tension mounted the OIRA shot two Provo supporters, and the Provisionals tried to shoot an Official in response in late September. There was also simmering hostility in Derry over an incident in which the OIRA had lost handguns to the Provos while preparing for a department store robbery. During May both sides had abducted each other's members at gunpoint until a truce was worked out. In Belfast a 17-year-old Provisional, Martin McMenamy, was killed accidentally by his own side during an altercation with Officials in New Lodge on 8 August. The frequency of such confrontations was increasing in the city. A 15-year-old Official Fianna boy, Patrick Crawford, was fatally wounded in one of these incidents, in mysterious circumstances. Crawford's mother Martha had been accidentally shot and killed by the Provisional IRA in 1972.

Late summer saw two Catholics, who were returning from the All Ireland semi-final, shot dead in Armagh, while the Provisionals killed five Orangemen in a rural hall in Tullyvallen. The OIRA in Newry argued that there was security-force collusion in local loyalist attacks, including one on a volunteer in Warrenpoint. But they also stressed that those who carried out attacks on Protestants could not absolve themselves of responsibility for recurring attacks on Catholics. The OIRA proposed talks between all paramilitary groups in an effort to end what they saw as the slide to civil war, a call rejected immediately by the UDA. While the sectarian killings continued, the OIRA publicly ruled out revenge attacks, arguing that 'invariably the totally innocent [were] the random victims'. Armed OIRA members did mount roadblocks in Belfast and Newry in an effort to halt the attacks, warning they would 'get the sectarian killers . . . no matter what side of the community they come from'. Photographs of an 'OIRA gun girl' covering colleagues with an Armalite appeared in the press. Unionist politicians complained that the OIRA had set up roadblocks openly in Newry. But there was less welcome publicity on 10 October when, during a wages robbery at a building firm in west Belfast, OIRA members shot and killed 24-year-old Sean McNamee.

Tension between the Officials and the Provisionals remained

high. The larger organization was suffering demoralization in the ranks due to the lack of concrete gains brought about by its ceasefire, and was stung by Official taunts about being the 'Queen's own Provos'. A measure of the hostility was expressed in the contemporary statement of one Provo that 'if I had a gun with one bullet and I had to choose between a Stick and a Brit, I'd blitz the Stick'. Internally, the Official leadership informed members:

[There] can be no doubt that in the present period of defeat the Provisional membership must re-examine their politics and the more thoughtful and principled elements within them realise the need for socialist politics. For their current and past leaderships however there is no positive way forward.

9. The 'Pogrom'

'The Catholic nationalist xenophobics were going to do to us what
they plan to do with one million of our Protestant fellow countrymen.
But we survived.'

Máirín de Burca, Bodenstown, June 1976

As darkness fell in Belfast on Wednesday 29 October 1975 many
Officials were returning home from work, while others settled
down to their tea and a night in front of the television. In the
Cyprus Street Club Des O'Hagan was setting up a projector
for the showing of *Caoineadh Airt Uí Laoghaire*, to be introduced
by Eamon Smullen. In McKenna's Bar in the Markets, Robbie
Elliman and two comrades were among the regulars enjoying a
pint. Suddenly one of the group, Jim Millen, saw three masked
men burst in through the front door:

One of the gunmen shouted 'Freeze.' He had an Armalite. He . . . was
aiming at Robbie Elliman's chest. He fired six or seven shots and then
the three men ran out. I was lying on the floor and I told the barmaid
to call an ambulance. I knew Robbie was dead.

Elliman's killing was the beginning of an hour-long onslaught.
Approximately 100 gunmen attacked members of the Officials
across Belfast. In Beechmount Sean O'Hare was pursued by gunmen who fired at him as he made a dash for safety into a house.
The British Army soon arrived, and when O'Hare told them that
his life was in danger he was advised to 'fuck off'. The householders
called for help and O'Hare made his escape to a waiting car,
through a crowd that included the gunmen. Around the same time

in New Lodge, a wounded Dan O'Hara was desperately trying to push his children to safety after answering his door to a gunman. Some recognized their attackers as Provisionals but in general confusion reigned. In New Lodge Margaret McNulty thought the gunmen were IRSP members as there had been trouble with the 'Irps' earlier that month. Kevin Smyth, wounded in his living room, thought that loyalists had attacked him. Many of those who had escaped injury hurried to Cyprus Street and other Official social clubs. There the scale of the assault began to emerge: Ellis McKnight using her body to shield her husband Bobby after he was shot in the hallway of their house; Carol and Davy McGranaghan shot at their home; Alec McManus wounded when he answered his door; Dan Mulvenna shot six times. In total 31 people had been attacked in just an hour, in locations from Andersonstown to Turf Lodge and Ballymurphy to the Ormeau Road. Robbie Elliman was dead, nineteen were wounded, and Catholic Belfast was convulsed with shock.

Many Officials felt there had been an unusually sparse troop presence that evening. Tommy Flanagan had been taken from his home in Ardoyne by armed Provos and transported in a car that was stopped at an army checkpoint; while searching the passengers, soldiers noticed he was barefoot but showed no interest. Flanagan managed to run away as the car was waved on. Seamus Lynch, a prime target for the Provos, was missed because he had been in Dublin and was on his way back to Belfast when the attacks occurred.

When it was ascertained that the attackers were Provos, the implications of retribution were discussed at an emergency meeting in Cyprus Street. O'Hagan called for widespread retaliation to show the OIRA were 'willing to be equally [as] ruthless' as their attackers. McGurran, the most senior OIRA member present, counselled caution. He argued for confining retaliation to Belfast and for launching a propaganda offensive. A Republican Clubs press statement issued that night condemned the Provisionals for 'allowing their madmen to let off steam by shooting Republicans' but asked that there be no 'senseless retaliation'. The Provisional IRA issued their own statement shortly afterwards, justifying their action against a 'criminal group' who they accused of 'murder, arson [and] gangsterism' and of bringing 'terror to the Nationalist community'. So began a pattern of allegation and counter-allegation that would continue throughout the following days of bloodshed.

The Official leadership advised their Belfast members to stay away from their homes and workplaces. Provo volunteers similarly withdrew from areas such as the Lower Ormeau Road, Markets and Lower Falls. These precautions proved justified when attacks resumed the following evening. Gunmen burst into the home of John Kelly in Beechmount and opened fire, killing his 6-year-old daughter Eileen. The Provisionals apologized for the killing, saying that their intended target was the girl's father. Six other men were shot and wounded that night, five of them associated with the Officials. The OIRA were also looking for targets. They knee-capped an 18-year-old female Provisional at her workplace on the Ormeau Road; she was one of a number of young women targeted. On Friday afternoon they killed one of the men they held respon-sible for the attacks. Seamus McCusker, the Provisional IRA's Northern Director of Intelligence, was gunned down as he left the Artillery Flats complex on the New Lodge Road, but the OIRA did not claim the killing and the Republican Clubs actually con-demned it. That evening an attempt was made on McGurran's life by gunmen travelling in a black cab, while the Gem Bar was machine-gunned. Tom Berry was shot dead during a clash outside Sean Martin's GAA Club in the Short Strand. The 26-year-old OIRA member, who came from a Protestant background, was preparing to ambush Provisionals when his gun jammed. Despite the fear that tightened its grip on the Catholic ghettos, journalists noted that children still continued to walk the streets in Halloween costumes.

Attacks continued over the weekend, with Official-supporting families forced out of their homes in several areas. Some houses were daubed with white paint, marking them out for attack. Many of the displaced sought refuge in the relative safety of the Lower Falls, while others travelled south. There were similar forced

evictions of Provisional supporters in Twinbrook, Bawnmore and
the Lower Falls. The war of words continued. At press conferences
McGurran alleged a 'dirty deal' between the Provos, the British
Army and elements of Fianna Fáil. Northern Secretary Merlyn
Rees's explanation of the violence as 'a battle for military control
of areas' caused by the Officials moving into Provo territory was
described as 'ludicrous'. The strong stance on national reunification
taken at that week's Fianna Fáil Ard Fheis was considered significant, an interpretation supported by the unionist *Belfast Newsletter*,
which commented that 'it is a grim coincidence, and perhaps more
than a coincidence, that the Provo Frankenstein was, the same
night [as the Fianna Fáil Ard Fheis], launched against Leftwing
Republicans, who are feared as the greatest long-term threat to
the whole political and financial set-up in the "gombeen" southern
State'. Some journalists reported that Provo attacks had been
launched from incident centres while troops were stationed nearby,
seemingly unconcerned.

The main thrust of the Provisionals' justification for the assault
was that the Officials had been targeting small businesses in nationalist areas. They claimed the OIRA had carried out over 20
robberies of the Andersonstown post office, robbed that area's
Ulster Bank into closure, and raided the Falls Road post office
fourteen times in six months. At a Belfast press conference, Provisional Sinn Féin president Ruairí Ó Brádaigh accused the
Officials of acting like 'Communists all over the world' in
attempting to 'gain control of the streets' towards the aim of
establishing a 'totalitarian Marxist social republic'. Kevin Smyth
had recovered enough to watch TV from his hospital bed and saw
Ó Brádaigh's interview: 'I think that annoyed me more . . . than
being shot.' Other Provisional leaders openly announced that their
aim was to 'get rid of the NLF'. Seamus Ó Tuathail felt that
the Belfast Provisional leader Billy McKee was seeking to take
advantage of the IRSP split and McMillen's death to enforce
control of the Catholic ghettos but suggests that 'McKee made the
mistake of thinking the Officials had nothing left'.

The Officials tried to step up the media war. A delegation of women travelled to Dublin to picket the Provisional Sinn Féin offices, and in Short Strand women marched protesting that republicans were killing one another while their area was under loyalist threat. By the end of the week nerves in Catholic Belfast were shredded. Pubs and clubs frequented by either group's supporters were targeted daily for arson attacks and bombings. On 3 November former Official internee Jim Fogarty was shot dead, aged 22, in front of his wife in their Whiterock home. According to Fogarty's brother, when troops arrived 'they just laughed at his dead body'. In a move reminiscent of the OIRA's offer to IRSP members earlier that year, the Provos announced a three-day amnesty for those willing to formally dissociate themselves from the Republican Clubs. But there was no let-up in attacks, with OIRA member John 'Mario' Kelly shot dead in Newington on 9 November. OIRA members were determined to hit back, burning down the Provisionals' Green Cross office on the Springfield Road and attempting to kill Provo spokesman Seamus Loughran. Nineteen-year-old Provisional Paul Best was shot and critically wounded in Andersonstown. The Provos accused the 'NLF' of a 'wave of terror' which included shootings, bombings, beatings and the eviction of opponents' families from their homes.

On 11 November the violence dramatically escalated. John Brown, a well-liked 25-year-old OIRA member and former boxing champion, was shot dead on his mother's doorstep on the Ormeau Road. He had returned there, against orders, to see his pregnant wife, and was spotted by local Provos. They alerted others from Short Strand, who shot Brown fifteen times with a machine gun at close range. A few hours earlier Provisionals had entered a workshop on the Falls Road, where they singled out 19-year-old apprentice joiner Comgall Casey. He was forced to kneel down and, although he pleaded that he was not a member of the Officials, he was shot in the head. That afternoon another 19-year-old, Jackie McAllister, was gunned down while waiting for a bus on the Springfield Road. McAllister's mother Ethel had been among the women who picketed the Provisional office in Dublin. The OIRA also claimed a victim, armed men bursting into a house on the Falls Road and shooting Owen McVeigh dead. The 28-year-old had no connection with either republican group and his killer is reported to have exclaimed, 'Christ I'm in the wrong house,' as he made his escape.

With their members under severe pressure the OIRA sought to up the ante. They believed that the Falls Taxi Association, whose black cabs offered a cheap alternative to public transport in west Belfast, was closely connected to the Provos and had carried gunmen involved in Provisional attacks. On 12 November OIRA gunmen entered the Hawthorne Street Social Club and shot dead Michael Duggan, the director of the FTA, as he played billiards. The killing shocked taxi drivers, who announced a strike until after Duggan's funeral and called for an immediate end to the killings.

The Clonard-based Redemptorist Fr. Alec Reid had been working hard to bring about a truce. At an early stage Reid had approached Officials in Cyprus Street and, despite being told to 'fuck off', followed one of them to Beechmount and made some headway in impressing upon him that he was genuinely trying to bring the conflict to an end. Other Catholic churchmen had voiced their fears that the British Army was allowing 'civil war' in the Catholic community to continue. The Officials, so often the target of the clergy's ire, had been scathing of the clerical response. Jim Sullivan attacked the 'deafening silence' of the clergy who had 'condemned lesser things from the pulpit'. When in the wake of Duggan's killing Reid and fellow cleric Fr. Des Wilson visited Cyprus Street with news that the Provisionals sought a truce, O'Hagan recalled thinking, 'You would not be here unless the Falls Taxi Association head had been shot.'

Eventually a meeting was set up in Wilson's home in Springhill. Three representatives of each organization sat at either side of a table, the Provo delegation a generation older than their OIRA counterparts. For an hour both sides spoke only through the priests, never directly to each other. Eventually, during a break for tea, Provisional Jimmy Drumm asked Sean O'Hare how his father Paddy, a 'forties man', was keeping. O'Hare responded, and slowly dialogue developed. A ceasefire to end what the *Irish Times* called the 'bloodiest fighting between republicans since the Civil War' came into effect at 4 p.m. on 13 November. Behind the scenes a formal mediation scheme was established. This would develop into a system whereby complaints concerning members of both organizations were dealt with in writing. The clergymen oversaw regular meetings between the rival groups' representatives. They aimed to deal with serious incidents on the day they occurred, and to respond to lesser infringements within three days. Each side had to agree to discipline the members concerned and, if admitting blame, to express regret. Both groups also had to ensure that 'complaints and replies contain no words which the side to whom they are addressed would deem disrespectful'. The mediators would then file copies of the complaints.

The sixteen days of what the Officials labelled a 'pogrom' had seen over 100 armed attacks, 11 deaths and some 50 injuries. The Officials had been on the receiving end in the majority of incidents, losing seven members or supporters, along with little Eileen Kelly. Twenty-four people faced charges directly resulting from the feud. During arms raids and arrests the OIRA had lost a number of weapons, including the Ingram they had captured from a soldier in June. At John Brown's funeral Frank McGlade accused the 'Royal Ulster Provisionals' of carving out a 'niche in history alongside the Free State Army of the twenties'. It soon became an article of faith for the Officials that 'the Provos were in cahoots with the Brits', who had given them permission to carry out 'housekeeping' during their ceasefire. Some linked the Provo attacks to the counter-insurgency tactics promoted by Brigadier Frank Kitson, previously used in Kenya and Aden, which involved backing one enemy faction against another. The Officials would increasingly see the 'Pogrom' as evidence of the counter-revolutionary nature of the Provos, and other observers noted that the violence had helped the authorities in some ways. The *Irish Times* suggested that there were 'spin-offs in the feud for the British Administration' because the 'organisation they fear most in the long-term, because of its Marxism, [was] under attack . . . [while] the energies of the Provisionals are absorbed'.

The Provos' incident centres had operated throughout most of the violence, but the Officials also benefited from the army's laissez-faire attitude. An OIRA operative recalled 'going around pieced up' while being waved through checkpoints. The feud also played into British assertions that the violence was motivated not by politics but by rival criminal gangs. Seven days into the attacks Rees announced that he was withdrawing special category status for paramilitary prisoners. With republicans sidetracked by what most outsiders saw as gang warfare, little heed was given to voices raised in opposition. On the day Michael Duggan was shot, Rees announced the closing of the Provisionals' incident centres.

The events defined the Officials in Belfast for years to come. 'Everybody thinks the 29th of October lasted for three weeks,' says one activist. 'It lasted five years; it lasted five years, every weekend.' Remaining friendships between individual Provos and Officials broke down, replaced in some cases by 'pure hatred'. Family relations were also damaged, some irrevocably, with relatives unable to sit together in the same room. OIRA strategy was redefined. '"Defence and retaliation" took on a whole new concept,' says Mary McMahon. 'Up till then it was against the Brits. Post-1975 it was against the Provos.' Now OIRA intelligence was directed to find out where local Provisionals signed on for social welfare, so they could be targeted there, and where their aunts and grandmothers lived, as that was where they were likely to hide during feuds. Internally the OIRA lauded the 'very effective military response' of their units and claimed their willingness to target 'non-military "operatives"' had helped force the Provos into talks.

Tension between the rival organizations remained high in the feud's aftermath and a single punch-up would have a 'ripple effect' that threatened to reignite the fighting. In February 1976 Paul Best died of wounds received in an OIRA gun attack the previous November. The Officials' Tony Maxwell was shot and badly wounded on the Falls. The clerical mediators declared themselves 'disturbed by the trend of recent events', noting several 'serious breaches of the truce'. They recommended that weekly meetings of the leaders of both organizations take place and that local representatives also meet with them. A particular feud-resolution etiquette had developed: the side that had been the victim of an attack did not take part in mediation until after they had first responded in kind. Nonetheless the process did help ensure that that year's Easter commemorations passed largely peacefully. But vandalism and breaking of windows continued to be routine:

When you looked back on it you wonder how your family lived with it, what my wife had to put up with – she was attacked physically in the street and she wasn't interested in politics; my kids were attacked, my sitting-room window broken maybe six times with bricks when my children were young.

For Kevin Smyth it was a 'very peculiar existence, constantly on alert, always expecting something'. In Andersonstown party activity invariably meant 'there was constant ongoing fights: every time you tried to sell the United Irishman, every time you gave out leaflets, there was pushing and shoving, almost soccer hooligan-style bang-ups, not always caused by the Provos I must say'. People stuck even more rigidly to their own drinking clubs, and a claustrophobic situation developed.

Within days of the truce, Pogrom, a Republican Clubs pamphlet outlining the course of the violence, was being distributed. Written from an unashamedly partisan perspective, it carried no mention at all of OIRA activities. In New York the Officials' American supporters had taken out an ad in the Irish Echo demanding that the Provos 'stop murdering Irish Republicans', and the Officials believed that the 'intense pressure on the Provisional leadership from the United States contributed substantially to ending the attacks'. In Belfast, however, Smullen's assertion that the Officials were 'winning the propaganda war' had cut little ice with those on the receiving end of the violence.

For the most part the violence did not spread south, though an argument between a Dublin Official and a relative who supported the Provos resulted in OIRA members bursting into the Provisional's south-side home and shooting him in the leg. A Dublin

OIRA man was arrested moving weapons for Belfast outside Drogheda, though a colleague managed to escape. While the association with violence may have been offputting to some, it reassured others of the importance of their political affiliation, a Dublin member recalling, 'It was scary but it was exciting . . . you felt this was something you could be really committed to. People were willing to give up not only parts of their lives but their whole lives, they were that committed to it.'

The scars left by the feuds were reflected in speeches at the January Sinn Féin Ard Fheis. Seamus Costello was described as a 'traitor' who had tried for years to 'subvert or destroy' the movement; but the Officials had rid themselves of 'the opportunists, the instant revolutionaries, the sectarian bigots' as well as the 'cowards who fled, not to greener but to safer pastures'. The leadership expressed frustration that there were still some members who saw the events of 1975 as a 'quarrel between Irishmen'. Instead it was reiterated that the Provos were a counter-revolutionary force, the creation of Fianna Fáil, set up to derail progressive politics in Ireland. Mac Giolla warned that any member with 'latent sympathy for acts of terrorism' would be 'ruthlessly dealt with'.

Fifty-five people, mostly civilians, were killed in Northern Ireland in the first six weeks of 1976 as a result of the continuing Provisional and loyalist campaigns. The most shocking sequence of events occurred in Armagh, where five Catholic brothers from two families were killed by the UVF on 4 January. A day later Provisional IRA members stopped a bus carrying workers at Kingsmills. The men were lined up and asked if there were any Catholics present. They instinctively tried to shield their one Catholic workmate, assuming that the gunmen were loyalists; but the Catholic was told to leave and the eleven Protestants were gunned down at close range, only one surviving. The attack was claimed by the 'South Armagh Action Force'. In Newry the Officials stated: 'There is no SAAF . . . just the sectarian killers of the Provisional Alliance.' Two thousand people attended a protest against sectarianism organized by Newry Trades Council, whose president was Republican Club leader Tom Moore.

During the summer a mass movement briefly emerged after three young children were killed when a Provisional IRA man, fatally wounded by troops, crashed his getaway car into them. Thousands of protesters, mainly women, both Catholic and Protestant, demonstrated for an end to violence. Official Sinn Féin joined the protest marches in Dublin though the organization was equivocal about the movement. Mac Giolla warned that 'middle-class do-gooders' would kill the movement 'stone dead' by aligning it with the authorities. Though it illustrated that many people were weary of the violence, their religious tone and failure to criticize the state forces made the 'peace people' a short-lived phenomenon.

Sinn Féin still lacked a strong electoral base in the South, and in order to change this the fifteen cumainn in Dublin had to be motivated into systematic local activity. Denis Foley was appointed as full-time coordinator of elections in an effort to professionalize local organization. An opportunity arose with a by-election in Dublin South-West during June. The constituency contained Ballyfermot, described as 'Dublin's most concentrated working-class area'. Tomás Mac Giolla received 1,679 votes, or 7 per cent, which was double the Sinn Féin total in 1973. It was decided that he would remain active in the constituency and prepare for future elections. Among new recruits in the area was Noel McFarlane, who had written the well-received *Down the Corner*, a look at Ballyfermot from the perspective of a local teenager. In Finglas the problem of substandard housing was leading to increased activity at the party's new permanent office in the area. The area maintained a strong Official IRA tradition and the party's advice centre was subject to constant Special Branch surveillance. In late 1976 Smullen was chosen by Finglas members as area candidate for the next general election, but declined, as did Garland, both men preferring behind-the-scenes organization to public office; Proinsias De Rossa was selected instead.

The Sinn Féin leadership were eager to reorient the party to Southern political work, feeling there was growing disillusionment at the Labour Party's role in government amidst high levels of unemployment and inflation. The chairman of the Resources Protection Campaign's trade union group, Pat Rabbitte, accused Labour of 'betrayal' of its 'principles and objectives' and argued that the 'capitalist system cannot fulfil the needs of the working class'. Discussions between Sinn Féin, the Communist Party and the Labour Party's Liaison of the Left resulted in a joint policy document, *The Economic Crisis: The Left Alternative*. It argued that 'private enterprise' had 'totally failed' to provide for the needs of the majority of Irish people. In early February 1,000 people attended the public launch of the 'Left Alternative', an ad hoc alliance of the three groups, at Dublin's Mansion House. There were speakers from all of the groups and an air of enthusiasm at the prospect of unity on the left. The three organizations also cooperated in the organization of Dublin's May Day march. Members of the Left Alternative met to discuss the formation of a civil liberties organization, to highlight the Fine Gael–Labour coalition's increasingly repressive security policy, and in July the Irish Council for Civil Liberties (ICCL) was launched; among the executive committee of the council were several members and supporters of the Officials.

By 1976 Sinn Féin dominated the leadership of the 55,000-member Union of Students in Ireland, Eamon Gilmore and Johnny Curran having been elected president and education officer, respectively, in January. The Officials' dominance was contested by a variety of opponents, who often seized on their pro-Soviet politics. The USI was affiliated to the International Union of Students (IUS), which was composed mainly of student unions in Communist countries. Through the IUS, delegates from Romania, Iraq and the USSR attended USI conferences and the USI had a full-time representative at IUS headquarters in Prague. As a result many of the debates at the USI Congress took on an international flavour. Sinn Féin's opponents tried unsuccessfully to have a motion condemning repression in the Eastern Bloc passed at the 1976 congress. The Officials complained that their college opponents represented a 'right-wing Trotskyite alliance'. Sinn Féin advised its student members to 'devote as much time to student affairs as to international affairs' in order to offset 'scare headlines' in the press. But the link with the IUS was seen as valuable by Sinn Féin. It provided contact between the movement and future Eastern Bloc cadres, outside the influence of the Irish Communist Party.

There was also tension within the Left Alternative, despite the early optimism about left-wing unity. Sinn Féin accused the Communist Party of caucusing before Resources Protection Campaign meetings and distributing lists of their candidates for election. Competition between the organizations was inevitable, as the communists saw themselves as providing the disciplined Marxist core to any alliance while Sinn Féin were still seen as 'petty bourgeois'. But the Officials had greater ambitions, as demonstrated by the use of the slogan 'Sinn Féin – The Workers' Party' on display in banners at Easter and increasingly on leaflets and posters. The RPC trade union group was dominated by Industrial Department cadres, with Oliver Donohue, Paddy Gillan and John Caden in leading positions during 1976. The Industrial Department's promotion of Sinn Féin policy at the expense of cooperation with the other affiliated groups was a source of concern to some within the party. Bray's Liz McManus argued that 'the tactics recently adopted [in the campaign] . . . have had the effect of alienating support' and that 'tried Marxist principles for operations within broad fronts' had been abandoned. But Smullen and his allies felt they were the main intellectual force within the campaign and were adamant that the other groups should not reap the benefits of Official expertise and effort.

During 1976 the Industrial Department's Research Section unveiled a number of policy documents, including *Rapid Rail for Dublin*, aimed at providing cheap and accessible public transport for the growing suburbs of Tallaght and Blanchardstown, and *Full Employment by 1986*, which set out a vigorous expansion of the state sector into job creation and development of natural resources. Sinn Féin also argued for a new state construction company, because of the failure of private firms to ensure adequate standards for houses. The party stated that 'we want the state sector to expand until it has obliterated all private enterprise'.

The Industrial Department strongly supported a proposal from the Dublin Port and Docks Board that an oil refinery be set up in Dublin Bay. The environmental activists of An Taisce and a range of community groups, led by councillor Sean 'Dublin Bay' Loftus, opposed the project. Sinn Féin was dismissive of environmental objections and argued that the refinery would both create desperately needed jobs and could eventually be taken into public ownership so that Ireland would have its own independent oil and gas industry. Sinn Féin members on Dublin Trades Council were instrumental in getting that organization to row in behind the refinery project.

Anti-refinery campaigners had complained bitterly about a *7 Days* programme broadcast in November 1975 and produced by Harris, which they claimed was heavily biased in favour of the refinery. The programme had featured Smullen prominently. Harris was also central to the writing of two new pamphlets: *The Banks* and *Tony O'Reilly's Last Game: A Case History of Irish Capitalism*. O'Reilly's career was said to have 'enshrined all the ambitions of gombeen Ireland' and he personally all the 'avarice, greed and stupidity of that class'. Some thought the tone of the pamphlet too personalized, but Harris explained that the 'working class needs someone to hate'. Significantly, in the pamphlet's introduction Smullen took aim at those who blamed foreign capital for Ireland's difficulties. While he stressed that Sinn Féin wanted 'state companies in place of the Tony O'Reillys', in the interim 'productive multinationals' were preferable to 'protected Irish sweatshops', because in the long term the working class would 'rid themselves of both'. In this view, industrialization 'foreign and Irish . . . strengthened the working class' as it helped create 'its own gravediggers'. The Industrial Department were also pushing for change in the movement's Northern policies, Harris circulating a document called 'From Civil Rights to Class Politics' which argued that civil rights had now been attained in Northern Ireland.

Within Sinn Féin there were mixed attitudes towards the Industrial Department. Its members cultivated a certain image, 'wearing working-class clothes like they'd just come in off the building site

. . . it was very irritating . . . for a lot of people who realized it was a bit of an act'. Cynics dubbed the Department's Ned Stapleton cumann the 'Led Zeppelin cumann'. There was a strong macho tendency among department members, and several activists were involved in the martial arts. The penchant for secrecy and conspiracy alarmed Paddy Woodworth: 'It was very creepy, very creepy. I frankly found . . . the Harris faction a far more frightening phenomenon than the IRA itself.'

During the 1976 Ard Fheis debate on women's rights, department members proposed a motion concentrating on equal pay but ignoring other legal restrictions on women. Máirín de Burca, who had gained national attention with a successful case against the exclusion of council tenants and women from jury service, countered that just because contraception and crèche facilities were demanded by middle-class women did not mean that they would not also benefit workers. The Industrial Department, contemptuous towards what it saw as liberal, middle-class concerns regarding gender and the 'lumpenproletariat', pushed for one of their supporters to replace her as Sinn Féin's election candidate in Dublin Central. Former Sinn Féin vice-president Derry Kelleher resigned in July 1976, citing the Industrial Department's activities as his reason. Kelleher would accuse the Industrial Department of having instructed members to curtail strikes on factory construction sites as part of its 'master plan', never discussed with the party leadership, to speed up the 'proletarianisation of the countryside'.

The sixtieth anniversary of the 1916 Rising was a very different affair from that of ten years previously. In the run-up to Easter, Minister for Justice Paddy Cooney argued that the Provos' violence and the Officials' 'Sino-Hibernian' Marxism represented equal threats to the state, and a commemorative parade in Dublin by the Provisionals was banned. The Officials condemned the fact that a government of 'opportunist Labour and blue-shirt Fine Gael' had decided to 'completely ignore the 1916 Rebellion' as part of its 'policy of apologizing . . . to the British Government and the intransigent elements of Northern Unionism'. The Officials organized 40 commemorations of their own, North and South, none of which were prohibited. An Official IRA statement lamented that the anniversary was 'not marked by the secularism, socialism or egalitarianism' of the Rising's leaders but by an 'almost unprecedented wave of sectarianism, authoritarianism and materialism'. While condemning the Provos' campaign, the Officials opposed the ban on the Provo parade, arguing that the government's 'attack on the right of peaceful assembly, allied to the stringent censorship operated in RTÉ, helps glamorise rather than expose the perverted ideas of the Provisionals'.

Official Sinn Féin made a concerted effort to distance itself from any connection with political violence, condemning the Provos' assassination of British ambassador to Ireland Christopher Ewart-Biggs in July as a 'gross act of terrorism' and refusing to ally itself with the campaign set up to call for a reprieve for Noel and Marie Murray, ex-members sentenced to death for killing a Garda in 1975. While the *Irish People* argued that the couple should not be executed, the party avoided association with the issue. After a Garda raid on the home of activist Nuala Monaghan, she was advised to keep a 'low profile' during the Dublin by-election. The distancing of the party from violent militancy brought about the resignations of Jack Lynch, from Cork, during March and Mickey Montgomery, from Derry, in December. In the longer term both Lynch and Montgomery would join the IRSP, as did some other former Officials, such as Goulding's daughter-in-law Mary Reid.

Some contacts survived the ideological rift between the Official movement and the IRSP. Following the March robbery of £200,000 from a mail train in County Kildare four IRSP members – Nicky Kelly, Osgur Breatnach, Brian McNally and Michael Plunkett – were arrested. All were former Officials, and despite evidence of Garda brutality in forcing their confessions the four were convicted and sentenced to lengthy prison terms. During their trial and subsequent high-profile appeals the group were aided by a radical lawyers' group based in Dublin's Church Street, with Sinn Féin activist Pat McCartan initially prominent in their defence. The idea for such a heist had a long pedigree, having been discussed by Ryan and Garland during the mid-1960s.

The phasing out of special category status by the British government affected the Officials' approach to prisoners. In January greetings had been sent to the Ard Fheis from OIRA prisoners in Long Kesh and Portlaoise. The message from Long Kesh asserted the 'right of political prisoners to political status'. Jim Smyth, a member of the OIRA prison leadership, argued that as they had 'fought long and hard to secure their rights' they were not prepared to 'take a retrograde step' and give them up. The Ard Fheis had endorsed a motion to fight against the removal of political status. However, the fact that Provo and IRSP prisoners benefited from a status that put them above common criminals was hard to accept for many activists. During the debate de Burca had stated that 'to ask for special status for the murderers of men, women and children is anti-republican, anti-socialist and anti-people'.

An article on prisoners' rights in the March *United Irishman* seemed to reflect de Burca's view. It argued that 'all prisoners of a corrupt system are political prisoners' and that to call for special status was elitist. There were complaints over the tone of the article and the prisoners asked for guidance on the matter from the Official leadership. The general opinion among the leadership was that free association was the most important right while clothes and prison work were 'matters for negotiation'. But OIRA prison spokesmen argued that to abandon any of the special category privileges would be to accept criminal status. The prisons issue remained a live one because OIRA volunteers continued to be sentenced. Several had arrived in jail because of the feuds with the IRSP and the Provisionals, and the continuing robberies. During May a Craigavon Official was jailed for nine years for armed robberies and involvement in shootings, and four more were arrested after holding a family hostage during an attempted raid on the Ulster Bank in Banbridge later that month. In July three Lurgan OIRA men were jailed for a post office robbery in the town. The Officials continued to raise money by other means as well, running a construction company in Belfast, providing security at building sites in areas of Official influence, and continuing exploitation of the tax-exemption scam, which produced thousands of pounds in revenue for the movement as well as for Harry McKeown and his accomplices.

A Stormont security think tank during March had noted that the OIRA possessed the ability to involve itself in 'non-sectarian revolutionary violence', and in October British Intelligence suggested that the Officials were 'capable of selective sabotage' but that their military capacity was now 'slight and localised'. In fact the year had seen important changes in the OIRA's structures. Discomfort with Goulding's refusal to abandon his painting business and assume a full-time role came to a head. There was frustration about his heavy drinking and failure to contribute seriously to leadership discussions. He was replaced by Garland after an Army Council vote in summer 1976. Long dismissive of the IRA's titles and formal military structure, Garland was reluctant to adopt the title of Chief of Staff; but he was now undoubtedly in charge. Goulding kept his place on the Army Council and the two remained friends.

Garland set about finalizing the changes that were intended to turn the movement into a Leninist revolutionary party. It was envisaged that the Official IRA would become a 'special department', strictly subordinate to political needs and out of public view. It would have a defensive role, primarily but not exclusively in the North, and be concerned with fund-raising and intelligence gathering. Existing unit structures were maintained in Belfast, Lurgan and Newry. All activity was to be strictly controlled by the leadership, with punishment attacks having to be authorized by the command staff. Loosely defined units comprising several dozen members were maintained in Dublin, Cork and Waterford. In Dublin the GHQ staff remained, with most of its members also holding important positions within the Sinn Féin organization. However, Operations Department members were ordered to distance themselves from open party activity. Garland strongly encouraged the use of the term 'Group B' rather than IRA. There was to be no further public manifestation of the Official IRA, no

Easter statements or claims of attacks. If arrested, Group B members were to deny any links to Sinn Féin. If jailed they would serve their sentences as ordinary prisoners, though their dependents would be looked after as in the past. In the North, prisoners sentenced before the end of special category status would retain that privilege but those jailed afterwards were to accept being regarded as ordinary prisoners.

OIRA units were briefed on the changes and, while some expressed unease, one Dublin member recalls his unit were enthusiastic, feeling 'it was the way to go'. When five prisoners faced charges over clashes at Portlaoise their solicitor asked that the 'biased and dangerous' term 'Official IRA prisoners' not be used about the men. After January 1976 lists of prisoners no longer appeared in the *United Irishman*. Public manifestations of the OIRA did not disappear immediately. At the Easter commemoration in Newry, where there had been complaints about the behaviour of the Parachute Regiment, Seán Ó Cionnaith warned that the 'army of the people' would 'retaliate' if aggression by British troops continued; and later in the year the OIRA carried out a number of gun attacks on security forces. They also continued vigilante activity and punishment attacks. At the funeral of 19-year-old OIRA volunteer Gerard Gilmore, who was shot dead by the UDA at the Boundary Bar in Belfast's Bawnmore in July, the RUC arrested members of the colour party; early August saw the OIRA retaliate with a gun attack against troops on the estate. OIRA members had also fired on the British Army elsewhere in Belfast on 9 August; 'having a blatter at the Brits' on internment night had remained a tradition in the post-ceasefire years. In other areas there were also OIRA warnings to criminals and the security forces. But gradually all public statements ceased.

In October, as part of the general move away from the trappings of a traditional republican military organization, the Irish Democratic Youth Movement (IDYM) was launched, replacing the Fianna as the Officials' youth wing. After April no more youths had been recruited into the Fianna in Belfast. There was a great deal of resentment among Fianna members in Belfast at this. They felt that the majority of their members had stood by the Officials during the recent feuds, and that they were unfairly accused of being militarists. When a compromise (that the Fianna in Belfast form the basis of the IDYM) was rejected, they stood themselves down. Initially over 100 Belfast ex-Fianna members joined the new group, although some of them drifted out quickly.

By 1976 Soviet Bloc Communism was the dominant ideological influence within the Officials. Party delegations frequently travelled beyond the Iron Curtain, and party representatives were in regular contact with Eastern Bloc diplomats, attending receptions at the Bulgarian and Soviet Embassies in London. Soviet ambassador to Ireland Anatoly Kaplan was a guest at the Davitt commemoration in Dublin, and during September Sinn Féin met representatives of the North Korean government in Brussels. A Sinn Féin office was also opened in Rome after discussions with the Italian communists. Links with liberation movements continued with representatives of the Namibian SWAPO brought on a tour of Ireland while Sinn Féin members visited Cuba, Ghana and Vietnam. During July 1976 a second Anti-Imperialist Festival was held in Dublin with Palestinian, Angolan and Rhodesian guerrilla groups represented.

Activity had also been maintained among the immigrant support groups. The Irish Republican Club organized for Ó Cionnaith to address a Congressional Committee on the subject of civil rights in Northern Ireland in late 1975, and de Burca toured the US during the winter of 1976, visiting 20 cities and raising £1,286. Contacts with Democratic Congressman Lloyd A. Barbee, who attended the Dublin Anti-Imperialist Festival, led to the Wisconsin State Assembly passing a citation praising Official Sinn Féin's policies for peace. British Labour MPs Audrey Wise and Joan Maynard agreed to invite Tomás Mac Giolla to speak at Westminster. Despite condemnation from Tory MPs who had called for a ban on the visit, with one describing Mac Giolla as the 'scum of the earth', he met several Labour MPs and spoke at the 'Communist University' organized by the British CP in London in July. Mac Giolla also attended an International Liberation conference in

Algiers, where he condemned the 'viciously fascist' activities of the Provos. This theme was echoed by Goulding at the Anti-Imperialist Festival when he warned delegates that although the Provos were seeking support in Africa and the Middle East as a national liberation organization, they were not. Sinn Féin also worked to frustrate plans by a British Troops Out Movement delegation to meet Irish trade unionists. English TOM organizer Paddy Prendiville complained that neither the Dublin nor the Belfast Trades Council would meet the delegation as a result.

British Intelligence noted that the Officials were carrying their 'bitter competition' with the Provos to an international level. They felt that the Officials had achieved 'qualified success' in gaining international recognition, and they were worried about links with the Soviets, who could utilize the common travel area between Britain and Ireland for espionage purposes. The British considered that there were at least three KGB agents operating from the Soviet Embassy in Dublin. Surveying the international scene, the *United Irishman* was optimistic that the examples of 'Cuba, Vietnam, Mozambique and Angola' proved that 'the flood tide of Socialism is surging forward to sweep away the remnants of a system history has marked for obsolescence'. While Chile and South Africa proved that capitalism would not concede without a fight, the 'Socialist flood will engulf [it] all the same'. But the movement's leadership were not simply going to wait for socialism to reach Ireland. The Officials were about to commit themselves to a radical policy re-direction that would aim at building the Irish working class into a force capable of establishing socialism.

10. A Historic Mission

'Sinn Féin – The Workers' Party is the historical product of the French
Revolution. In turn, the product of our party in history must be the
creation of an Irish Industrial Revolution ... [This] in turn means the
emancipation of the Irish working class so that it can carry out its
historic mission – the construction of socialism in Ireland.'

Eamon Smullen, January 1977

There was no dissension among the Official Sinn Féin delegates
gathered in Dublin's Mansion House in January 1977 as they
ratified the party's rather unwieldy new name: Sinn Féin The
Workers' Party. The debate had been well choreographed, with
twelve cumainn, drawn from every region, placing motions calling
for the change. One delegate, speaking in front of the Ard Fheis
slogan 'Working for Peace, Planning for Progress', attempted to
capture the significance of the new name, declaring it 'the end of
the Griffith era and the beginning of the Connolly age'. For
Industrial Department cadres the new title signified their ideological ascendancy; Northerners hoped it would appeal to the
Protestant working class; and Garland and others saw it as a statement of the party's place within the international struggle between
labour and capital. Facing into a Southern general election, there
was also a more practical reason to welcome the development: 'The
Provos were killing people and they were getting the publicity, and
the [Sinn Féin] name was becoming synonymous with death and
killing.' An *Irish Times* editorial welcomed the 'promising' if 'cum-
bersome' new party title. It also noted that 'that shadowy organisation' the Official IRA had not delivered a public message to the
Ard Fheis, but neither had it announced its disbandment.

Although media attention focused on the addition of 'The Workers' Party' to the party's name, the January 1977 Ard Fheis saw a no less important development with the publication of *The Irish Industrial Revolution*. At just over 150 pages, this was the fruit of Eoghan Harris's endeavours to provide the movement with a comprehensive economic plan, backed by a historical narrative from a scientific socialist perspective. Although advertised as the sixth title in the Research Section's series 'Studies in Political Economy', *The Irish Industrial Revolution* was more wide-reaching and had a far greater impact than any of the previous booklets. The document was distributed by Industrial Department members, but had not been submitted to the Ard Chomhairle previous to publication, a cause of disquiet among some at the Ard Fheis. Industrial Department attempts to influence the movement's direction without reference to its decision-making structures had already contributed to Máirín de Burca's decision not to seek re-election to the Ard Chomhairle and her resignation as general secretary. She had been increasingly disturbed by the intensity of Industrial Department cadres: 'They examined people's every word, every gesture almost, were they Stalinist or weren't they; if they weren't they did their damnedest to get them out of the party.' Some leadership figures had seen the new booklet prior to publication. Smullen had worked closely with Harris, and Garland had also read a pre-publication copy and requested changes.

The Irish Industrial Revolution contained two distinct sections: an economic history of Ireland from the seventeenth century onwards, written mainly by Harris, and 'a systematic plan for the making of an industrial Ireland', which had been worked on by a number of Research Section members under Harris's direction. The history section exposed as a 'fable' the idea that Ireland's past was one of 'inevitable poverty'. Instead, in vitriolic language, Irish history was presented as the story of the rise of a 'gombeen' class of Catholic strong farmers, professionals and merchants. The 'National Bourgeoisie' had finally gained state power with the 1922 Treaty and their 'bloody triumph' in the Civil War. The losers in this rise to power were not the British, whose capitalist system the National

Bourgeoisie would administer in Ireland at less expense, but 'the populist Fenian movement, the labourers and cottiers and finally the Irish working class'. In the course of this narrative the radical credentials of Daniel O'Connell and Arthur Griffith were debunked while the revolutionary aims of figures such as Michael Davitt and James Connolly were re-emphasized. Southern Irish capitalists were depicted throughout as lazy, cowardly and backward, their symbiotic relationship with the Catholic Church holding back the economic potential of the country and its working class. This was contrasted with the capitalists of the north-east and their industrialization of Belfast.

Independence had simply allowed the National Bourgeoisie to demonstrate their inadequacies. Behind de Valera's protective barriers and without direct British interference they still failed to industrialize Ireland. By the late 1950s 'Irish capitalism was like a raddled and blowsy prostitute, long past her best'. The opening of Ireland to international investment by Sean Lemass was merely the National Bourgeoisie selling out to US monopoly capitalism 'while retaining a minor share in any profits that could be beaten out of the servants'. However, this process of multinational development was not condemned out of hand. Those with knowledge of 'elementary dialectics' could grasp the 'progressive tendencies' that multinational investment was encouraging. As an unintended consequence it was producing what native capitalism had failed to do, 'a highly organised and militant working class'. As Marx had predicted, 'advanced capitalism in Ireland was creating its own gravediggers'. This meant that the movement's view of the Industrial Development Authority and the EEC would have to change from opposition to qualified support, based on a belief that both institutions were aiding Ireland's entry into the 'world capitalist network'. The growing state enterprise sector, consisting of companies such as the ESB, Bord na Móna, CIÉ and Aer Lingus, was identified as the other key conduit of progressive change. The 'struggle to defend, consolidate and expand the state sector' should be seen as 'the single most vital task confronting the organised working class at the present time'.

A variety of groups were identified as standing in the way of the working class's ascent to power. Firstly there was the 'tiny financial oligarchy' of individuals who occupied directorships in both banking and industry and used the major political parties to 'hold state power'. This group was encouraging US economic penetration and attempting to drag Ireland into the 'Western Alliance'. On the supposed left were social democrats seeking to divert the working class from revolutionary change. The 'ultra-leftists' were damned for their 'neurotic phobia' of bureaucracy and unrealistic demands for instant solutions. The small farmers, referred to as 'transitional farmers', would have to accept that their economic role was defunct and take their place among the urban working class or in collective farming endeavours.

The Irish Industrial Revolution's economic plan was a broad-stroke attempt at formulating policies that would consolidate working-class economic power over the next decade. It was based on the premise that the population would become younger during the 1980s, due to the ending of emigration brought about by Irish economic growth and capitalism's global crisis. This would, for the first time since the Famine, see Ireland's population structure begin to resemble the European norm. (Labour and Fine Gael calls for the legalization of contraception were criticized as a long-term attempt to halt such a development.) In order to cater for this young population, and economically enfranchise it, the plan sought to achieve full employment through the creation, by 1986, of 330,000 new jobs in the state sector and 81,000 in the private sector. In a renunciation of the central plank of Sinn Féin economic policy since Arthur Griffith, economic growth would not be fostered by protectionism but by Irish products competing in international markets. A 'rapid increase in productivity' would be brought about by massive state investment and 'large scale rationalisation of production'. In most industries state companies would be given a dominant role. This industrial utopianism was neatly summed up by the pamphlet's cover, which depicted two boys happily playing with a dog on the beach in front of the impressive outline of Dublin's Pigeon House power station. There could be no mistaking the message that industrial development equalled a bright future for the urban Irish population.

Although its measures were never formally adopted as policy, *The Irish Industrial Revolution* redefined SFWP ideology. Many members, particularly those attached to the Industrial Department and the paramilitary structure, eagerly adopted its thesis. As one activist recalls, 'The *Industrial Revolution* was our Bible, it won people over.' The brutal simplicity of its core demand, for rapid industrialization through central planning, showed a debt to Stalin. It also drew liberally on the output of the British and Irish Communist Organisation, and on the work of mainstream historians such as Joe Lee and John A. Murphy.

An attraction for some activists was how much the pamphlet 'annoyed the party's enemies'. Left-wing journals carried competing reviews and letters on the subject well into the summer. Having recently become the editor of the CPI paper the *Irish Socialist*, Eoin Ó Murchú used his contributions to rejoin ideological battle over the importance of the 'national question'. He argued that the pamphlet was a 'massive revision of republicanism, in that the role and significance of British imperialism in Ireland is minimised', and concluded that it was 'Left in form but Right in content'. The booklet received a more favourable reception from economic historian Cormac Ó Gráda, who hoped it would act 'like a dose of salts on the kind of woolly and utopian thinking about history that too often has influenced the Left in Ireland'.

The pamphlet and its reception were symptomatic of a deterioration in relations between SFWP and the Irish communists. In March 1977 the Communist Party privately distributed a memorandum, written by Ó Murchú, that criticized the changes in the SFWP's ideological position. The memo accused SFWP of describing small farmers and small businessmen as enemies of the working class, posing as a Marxist-Leninist party internationally, and dismissing the national question as 'mythical'. It also claimed that SFWP had 'rich financial resources (not raised by members' subscriptions, emigrant support groups or any kind of fund-raising campaigns)'. SFWP dismissed the Communist Party's allegations in a point-by-point rebuttal, which was also distributed internationally. On the issue of the movement's ideology, the reply stated: 'While the teachings of Marx and Lenin figure largely in our educational curriculum and play a large part in the formulation of our ideology and organisational principles, we never claimed to be a communist party.'

In early 1977 resentment towards the Industrial Department had seen another group of Dublin members resign, among them Jim Sheridan, Sean Dunne and Jer O'Leary; many went on to join the CPI. One cause of this was the Industrial Department's decision to vote Labour Party and communist representatives off the Resources Protection Campaign executive. Arrangements were made to pack meetings electing delegates to the RPC's annual general meeting in Dublin's Ormond Hotel; at the latter event, previous allies of SFWP were shocked to find themselves being voted off executive positions in favour of inexperienced SFWP members.

Smullen, Harris and Oliver Donohue toured cumainn throughout the country to promote *The Irish Industrial Revolution*. The Industrial Department cadres' self-proclaimed role as the 'progressive wing' of the party resonated within a movement that had spent more than a decade challenging tradition. Nonetheless, in many regions debate was fierce. One member recalls bringing his concerns to Garland: '[I] said this is bad Marxism and inaccurate history and Garland said, "Yeah, you could be right about the details, but we need a working-class history of Ireland, a history of our class. None of us agree with this document 100 per cent."' It was not until October 1977, following a prolonged period of strife within the leadership over the Industrial Department's role, that Tony Heffernan provided the most forceful internal critique of the document. Heffernan called for the history section to be deleted and for consideration of whether the entire booklet should be withdrawn. He dismissed the document's style as 'bigoted, hysterical and sectarian' and claimed that it totally ignored 'the role of British Imperialism in Irish history'. He feared the logical conclusion would be for the party to adopt the 'two-nations theory'. He disputed that industrial development automatically equalled social progress and attacked the 'writing off of the farming community' as impractical. Finally, Heffernan denounced the document's tone: 'People in [other] organisations are not merely criticised, but denounced for holding attitudes which were until a short time ago held by our party.' Despite this criticism, in December 1977 the Ard Chomhairle, at the proposal of Garland and seconded by Goulding, voted to produce an edited but unexpurgated second edition.

Apart from Smullen, few within the party leadership had much idea how the Industrial Department functioned. Its leading members' obsession with secrecy had resulted in Smullen receiving an early 1977 commitment that 'trade union plans' would no longer be referred to in internal party reports. The Department's clandestine nature was such that the Coiste Seasta (steering committee) found it necessary to formally demand a complete list of industrial cumann members. By this period these several dozen activists were organized into the three Dublin-based industrial branches, with smaller groups active in Cork and Belfast and with aligned influential figures in most areas. There was also concern over the Industrial Department cadres' attempts to foster independent links with the Soviet Embassy. Eagerness to develop fraternal relations with the Eastern Bloc also saw Industrial Department member Patricia Redlich play a leading role within the Ireland-GDR Friendship Society. Disappointingly, elements within the Soviet Communist Party who had been given a copy of *The Irish Industrial Revolution* to review by an Industrial Department member visiting the Black Sea resort of Yalta were unimpressed by the publication. Debate was also provoked by the attitude adopted by Industrial Department members within the Irish Council of Civil Liberties. De Burca claimed that Smullen was organizing block voting by his supporters on the ICCL executive without the authorization of the party. The central issue here was Industrial Department attempts to get the ICCL to remove its support from a symbolic hunger strike calling for the transfer of republican prisoners from Portlaoise Prison to the Curragh. This debate had seen Heffernan and Ó Cionnaith strongly oppose the Industrial Department's position, but the majority of the leadership rowed in behind Smullen's view that the 'standing and credibility' of the ICCL was being endangered by its association with 'Provo activities'.

During preparations for the June 1977 general election the Industrial Department flexed its internal muscle. For some time there had been attempts to sideline the party's candidate in the Rathmines area of Dublin, Peigín Doyle, with a whispering campaign that she was suspect due to her brother's involvement with the Provisionals. Her position as SFWP candidate was taken by Eric Byrne, who had the support of the Industrial Department. De Burca, although no longer on the Ard Chomhairle, was still the choice of most of the leadership as candidate for the Dublin North Central constituency. She had the highest profile of any party member in the area and had received a respectable vote in 1973. However, the Industrial Department succeeded in replacing her at the selection convention with Ray McGran. Mac Giolla reported 'that there may have been some irregularities in the convention', resulting in an internal party investigation. But McGran was confirmed as the candidate, a decision which led to de Burca ending her 22 years of membership of the party, decrying the fact that a 'clique' controlled party policy. *Hibernia* magazine felt that the only 'odd thing' about de Burca's resignation was that it was 'so long in coming . . . just how a committed pacifist could work alongside prominent members of the Official IRA Army Council for so long is something of a mystery'. In all, sixteen SFWP candidates, five of them in Dublin and all of them male, contested the June election.

Nationally SFWP fought the election on a policy platform of a 'massive' increase of employment in the state sector, investment in public housing, introduction of universal free public medical provision, the removal of religious control of education and state ownership of natural resources and the banks. The numbers out of work in the Republic had reached 106,000 by mid-1977, and party propaganda focused on the need for radical solutions if an economic downturn was not to result in a return of mass unemployment and emigration. The party's radio election broadcast summed up the message:

We have the most serious crisis in a generation on our hands. With a projected population growth of half a million by 1986 and a job need of up to 40,000 per year in the same period we are facing a daunting challenge indeed . . . Many people say that there is no difference between the Coalition and Fianna Fáil. They are quite right . . . We seek the support of conscious people who are not afraid to meet the challenge of our times by voting for the alternative policy and the alternative party in this election.

The election resulted in Jack Lynch's Fianna Fáil, whose manifesto had promised to slash taxes and increase private-sector employment, achieving its most impressive result since 1938, winning just over 50 per cent of the first-preference vote. Significantly Fianna Fáil received the support of over 54 per cent of skilled workers, compared to just 11 per cent for Labour. The SFWP performance was disappointing. The party's 16 candidates had garnered 27,203 first-preference votes in total, an average of only 4.4 per cent support in the constituencies contested. In Dublin only Mac Giolla in Ballyfermot and Andy Smith in Dublin South Central gained over 5 per cent support, and the highest left-wing non-Labour vote in the capital was gained by the Socialist Party in Ballymun. Outside Dublin there were some promising performances, with Joe Sherlock receiving 9.5 per cent in Cork North-East and Paddy Gallagher 10.6 per cent in Waterford. Both these candidates, as well as Donnchadh Mac Raghnaill in Louth, outperformed Labour rivals. In Cork the campaign was dogged by continuing bitterness over the 1975 OIRA killing of Larry White.

In the aftermath of the election the *United Irishman* felt able to claim that SFWP was 'without a shadow of a doubt, the main working class party in Ireland'. A more sober internal review of the election pinpointed the need to surmount a remaining public 'credibility gap', which was best done by focusing on local activity rather than the expensive strategy of upping the party's profile by fielding a large number of candidates. It was felt that a strategy of attempting to keep rivalry with Labour as amicable as possible was preferable, in order to maximize the likelihood of receiving transfers from Labour voters.

The poor results also provoked a major reorganization of the party leadership. Heffernan had decided to resign his general secretary position and a new General Secretary role was created for Garland, ratifying his primacy within the movement's political and military wings. Mac Giolla had given up his ESB job and would now combine his role as president with editing the *United Irishman*. Des O'Hagan was appointed Director of Elections in addition to his existing role as Director of Education.

During the election post-mortem some in the leadership, notably Ó Cionnaith and Ryan, saw an opportunity to curtail Industrial Department influence. An election report drawn up by the Research Section was suppressed and *The Irish Industrial Revolution* was defined as not SFWP policy but rather an 'economic plan . . . worked out in the light of economic resolutions passed at various Ard Fheiseanna'. However, it was an indiscretion by Harris that presented his critics with their clearest opportunity.

Earlier in the summer of 1977 SFWP member Paddy Woodworth had been waiting for a bus in Ballsbridge when Harris and his wife Anne pulled up in a car and offered him a lift. During the drive to Bray Harris disclosed to Woodworth his concerns about some members of the party leadership. Woodworth recalled Harris explaining that the party's primary problem was that there were 'green people [i.e. nationalists] still in charge', namely Mac Giolla, Ó Cionnaith and Heffernan, and until 'we get rid of these people we will never make it as a communist party'. Not an Industrial Department member, and already sceptical of Harris's influence, Woodworth was amazed at what he had heard. Such an attempt to influence a member against figures in the leadership clearly contradicted the tenets of democratic centralism. Woodworth recalls feeling

really outraged, because we took the thing about being in a Leninist party very strongly, meaning if you were in a branch in Galway and

I was in a branch in Clare I would not tell you about my views about Mac Giolla, the only place I could say my views was in my cumann, then up to Comhairle Ceantair then to Ard Chomhairle . . . that was the only way, otherwise you were factionalizing.

Woodworth discussed Harris's comments with John McManus in Bray. A few days later Mick Ryan called to see Woodworth at the Project Theatre, where he worked. He was questioned about the allegations and, aware of Ryan's seniority within both the OIRA and the party, stressed that Harris had not meant 'eliminated' when he spoke of getting 'rid of' the three men. In July Ryan took the matter up with the Coiste Seasta. A letter requesting that Harris explain his accusation about members of the leadership being opposed to the 'further development of our policies' resulted in two replies. In the first Harris claimed he was not a member of SFWP; Smullen explained to the Ard Chomhairle 'that the denial of membership was to protect his job' at RTÉ. In a second communication Harris denied making the remarks, attributing them to a 'third party'. A leadership delegation of Ryan, Goulding and Smullen was authorized to meet Harris and inform him that any 'reoccurrence would lead to him being disciplined'. Smullen continued to defend his ally, requesting that due to his status as a secret member Harris's name be deleted from party records referring to the allegations. Eventually Goulding and Harris met one-to-one. According to Goulding's report, Harris continued to deny the allegations. It was 'impressed upon him the serious view [with] which the Ard Chomhairle took the matter'. The fact that Harris was only reprimanded for a contravention that would normally have been cause for expulsion was a sign of the influence of the Industrial Department, but the incident also aided those opposed to its influence. Woodworth would later be scolded by an RTÉ producer and SFWP member for having 'single-handedly put a stop to political progress in the party for two years'.

The Labour Party's removal from government had heralded another bout of introspection and internal strife. Out of the now defunct Liaison of the Left emerged a new Socialist Labour Party, formed around trade union leader Matt Merrigan and TD Noel Browne. The SLP made a number of unsuccessful approaches to the SFWP leadership about joint initiatives, but there was interaction between SLP and SFWP members in campaigns and policy discussion in Dublin. Meanwhile the Communist Party, freed from an obligation to maintain a semblance of good relations with the Officials, intensified its contacts with other republicans. During 1977 meetings were held between the CPI and representatives of the Provisionals and IRSP on the possibility of establishing an anti-imperialist 'broad front'. Neither of these republican groups wielded any significant influence in the South, although Provisional Sinn Féin had several rural councillors. The talks were roundly condemned by SFWP and furtive attempts by the communists to involve them were stridently rebuffed.

Seamus Costello's participation in these meetings was brought to an abrupt end when on 5 October the IRSP chairman was shot dead as he sat in his car in Dublin's north inner city. Although many suspected OIRA involvement, SFWP publicly condemned the killing as an act that 'in no way served the interest of the Irish working class'. The IRSP had failed to make any electoral impact: Costello had won just 955 votes in the June general election, outpolled in Wicklow by SFWP's John McManus. At the time of his death Costello was the party's only councillor and with his passing went any chance that his followers would ever exert an organized influence beyond the paramilitary underworld. None of the Official leadership were present among the 2,000 mourners at Costello's funeral, who included Bernadette McAliskey, local Labour, Fine Gael and Fianna Fáil TDs, the CPI's Mick O'Riordan and Provisional Sinn Féin's Ruairí Ó Brádaigh. In her oration Nora Connolly O'Brien declared Costello 'the only one who truly understood what [her father] James Connolly meant when he spoke of his vision of the freedom of the Irish people'. Two men were arrested after INLA volunteers fired a volley of handgun shots over the coffin.

*

The late 1970s marked the height of SFWP influence in the student unions, with a number of mostly undisclosed SFWP members holding full-time elected positions in the Union of Students of Ireland. Among the SFWP members to achieve high USI offices during this period were presidents Eamon Gilmore and Gerry Grainger, education officer and later vice-president Padraig Mannion, and vice-president John Ryan. While SFWP were rarely in the majority on USI executives, they could usually rely on the support of other student leaders and the party exerted a defining influence.

The party's other avenue of youth recruitment was through the Irish Democratic Youth Movement which, as the decade advanced, developed branches beyond Dublin and the North. The group also began to seek recruits within third-level colleges. The IDYM's orientation towards street politics met with SFWP disapproval, with Smullen criticizing a confrontational protest outside a Fianna Fáil Ard Fheis. While Mornington's use by other sections of the movement waned, IDYM members from around the country regularly met at the venue to hear lectures by O'Hagan and Garland. The group's annual congress attracted notable guest speakers such as Seán MacBride and the ITGWU leader Michael Mullen.

The IDYM's encroachment into colleges was opposed by the SFWP students, who had voted against amalgamating with the IDYM, and became a point of contention among the party leadership. As IDYM recruitment was largely restricted to a handful of technical and teacher training colleges, where 'the majority of students are working-class [and] are studying practical subjects relevant to society', the SFWP leadership concluded that the IDYM could have a useful role to play. Over time the IDYM, like the Fianna before it, generally provided recruits for the 'army', whereas university graduates tended to gravitate towards the Industrial Department. However, the organization's lack of development became the focus of regular criticism from the Ard Chomhairle.

The lack of cohesion in the movement's youth recruitment strategy undermined the SFWP position within USI. A 1979 internal report noted the deficiencies:

The position of the party within USI is undoubtedly strong in terms of power. The Officer board and principal staff positions are filled by people who are, at least, sympathetic to the Party's position . . . This position is deceptive, however, for although the leadership of the Union is controlled by the Party, the college position has become weak. A number of colleges are now controlled by Fine Gael – who have replaced Fianna Fáil – and the majority of colleges are now controlled by non-politicals, who cannot be relied on. Even worse, the next two years will see the departure of three-quarters of the present Party membership from USI. *At present there is virtually none to replace them.* As it takes 2–3 yrs to train a person for competency in USI, it is quite likely that unless a number of people are recruited in the coming year the party will lose control by 1981. Apart from the value of controlling a large organisation with a good public image, the Party should also prioritise retaining control of USI as a means of influencing and attracting left-wing students, and training party members for work in trade unions etc afterwards.

The USI report was correct in emphasizing the importance of student recruitment. Many former student members had maintained their party affiliation as they moved into jobs within state companies, the civil service and trade unions. The post-1973 recession had accelerated a growth in white-collar union membership as the middle classes saw their standard of living recede; in the 10 years prior to 1976 membership of Ireland's 46 white-collar unions had increased by 71 per cent. By the late 1970s over 60 per cent of the total workforce were union members and the growth in union bureaucracy to cater for an increasingly professionalized membership provided more employment opportunities for young SFWP-aligned graduates.

The recruitment of left-wing graduates was encouraged by ITGWU General Secretary Michael Mullen. ITGWU official and SFWP member Noel Dowling recalls Mullen's enthusiasm being largely born of pragmatism:

He had the view [that] lefties, or people that thought they were, would make great trade union officials because they would work their arses off night, noon and morning because the harder they worked, they believed, the closer the revolution would come. Now Mickey [Mullen] never believed that, but it was [a] good tactic none the less.

Mullen continued to be personally close to Garland as well as the new Minister for Health and Social Welfare, Charles Haughey. Mullen's move towards recruitment from student unions rather than from among shop stewards resulted in some resentment and a joke among ITGWU members that their union 'was being killed by degrees'. Within the Industrial Department there was also some criticism of the graduates as 'people that never had to get their hands dirty on a building site, [that] never saw the inside of a jail, [who] didn't really have to take the rough with the smooth'.

Some of the new trade union officials had been SFWP members for several years. This category included Eamon Gilmore, who after two years as USI president took up a job with the ITGWU. Others only took up party membership after securing a union position. This was the route taken by another former USI president, Pat Rabbitte, who left the Labour Party and joined SFWP after becoming the ITGWU official responsible for organizing senior management-grade members. At the ITGWU Gilmore and Rabbitte joined Des Geraghty, who by the end of 1980 was editing that union's publication *Liberty*, assisted by another SFWP graduate, Dee McGarry. In Cork, party member Doc Doherty oversaw ITGWU activity in the city's port.

The influx of SFWP-aligned officials brought a fresh intellectual rigour to trade unionism that won others over. Union of Professional and Technical Civil Servants member Seamus Cody had been active in the Socialist Labour Party before becoming disillusioned by the infighting. He recalls:

There was a cutting edge to debate in the trade union movement. There was a Sticky ideology that was much more [than] party membership; people were participating in the debate on the side of the Workers' Party who could not have joined. The most controversial debate would have been around the national question. The only people who were prepared to stand up and articulate a non-national position with any critical mass was the Workers' Party . . . It just opened up a sphere of influence for the party among skilled semi-professional workers – in the media etc, there was a category of people that were very attracted to the party's message.

The Workers' Union of Ireland (WUI), second only to the ITGWU in membership, was initially the union most influenced by the SFWP Industrial Department. At the union's 1978 annual conference Harris delivered a speech in which he declared himself a 'turncoat' on the EEC issue and demanded delegates dismiss a motion calling for a boycott of the upcoming European Parliament election. The Industrial Department was solidifying its influence within the WUI, pushing its support of national wage agreements while strongly criticizing moves to affiliate the union with the Irish Council for Civil Liberties because of the latter's perceived nationalist posture on Northern Ireland. Aer Lingus worker Liam Maguire and RTÉ's John Caden were Industrial Department members who rose up the WUI ranks, followed by other SFWP members. Although the political affiliation of such figures was often obvious, a pretence of secrecy was maintained. When a *Hibernia* article alluded to the existence of a 'well organised SFWP caucus' within the WUI, the magazine was threatened with legal action and forced to print letters from both Maguire and Caden's solicitors stating neither was a member of any political party.

The Industrial Department was a driving force behind the movement's shifting view on the EEC. In November 1977 the Ard Chomhairle had decided to call for the party to contest all five Irish European constituencies. At the March 1978 Ard Fheis the debate on whether to contest these upcoming elections was the main point of friction, with questions of finance rather than direct opposition to the EEC being the main argument of those against contesting.

SFWP's slow move towards political respectability was illustrated by the handful of IRSP picketers outside the meeting and by RTÉ's decision to broadcast delegates' speeches directly, rather than via the voice-overs used to relay the utterances of paramilitary organizations under Section 31 of the Broadcasting Act. Garland addressed the conference for the first time as party general secretary. His speeches had become the centrepiece of Ard Fheiseanna, as a delegate recalls: 'He was a mystical leader to some degree . . . everybody thought they were fucking great speeches and they sort of gave you a bit of time to sit back and listen to what the future struggle might be for you.' While Mac Giolla's presidential address had focused on the state of current party policy, Garland sought to restate the ethos underpinning the movement, linking Tone's attachment to the ideas of the French Revolution with the Fenians and Connolly's search for inspiration in Marxism. In Garland's opinion the historical tradition he outlined meant this was 'not a small isolated movement but a world brotherhood that stretches through developed and developing countries to the underdeveloped and underprivileged of the so-called Third World'.

Within SFWP such a 'world brotherhood' was increasingly associated with an alliance with the 'socialist countries' and Soviet-backed Third World liberation movements. Seán Ó Cionnaith headed the party's International Affairs Bureau, which spent a great deal of energy and effort on establishing links with such movements. A growing list of communiqués from various international groups were being read out at Ard Fheiseanna and observers from organizations such as the PLO were annual fixtures. During 1977 and 1978 Ó Cionnaith visited Poland and toured American cities as a guest of black activist Stokely Carmichael's organization. Links were also established with the Puerto Rican Socialist Party. During visits to London he would make courtesy calls and hold meetings with a hotchpotch of international contacts. These included the exiled leaders of the Iraqi Communist Party, though within a couple of years this link had been replaced by contacts with the governing Ba'thist party of Saddam Hussein. Closer to home the party continued to work closely with the Union Démocratique Bretonne within the Declaration of Brest grouping of European independence movements. Party members also visited the Basque region in Spain. Here SFWP found itself for a time in the contradictory situation of being linked to the faction of ETA that was continuing its armed struggle against the Spanish state while the Provisionals had contacts with the ETA faction that had renounced violence. Funds were raised to help the 'reconstruction' of Vietnam and to send medical equipment to the MPLA government in Angola. Garland visited Romania in October 1978, and relations were also fostered with the governing East German Socialist Unity Party. With the end of the Vietnam War, the focus of solidarity work had shifted from South-East Asia towards opposing the Apartheid regime in South Africa. Republicans had been prominent in the Irish Anti-Apartheid Movement since its foundation, and SFWP maintained a delegate on the group's executive.

The centrepiece of international work during the late 1970s was a trip by 23 IDYM and party members to the World Festival of Youth in Cuba in the summer of 1978. The festival was a massive event, with the Cubans playing host to more than 20,000 left-wingers from over 100 countries under a slogan of 'Anti-Imperialist Solidarity, Peace and Friendship'. The SFWP contingent staged a number of performances of a play directed by Martin Lynch and distributed party booklets and T-shirts, while taking full advantage of the tropical sun and cheap Cuban rum. SFWP members were among the founders of the Ireland-Cuba Friendship Society in 1979. There was more good news from Latin America in July that year when the Sandinista rebels overthrew a pro-American dictatorship in Nicaragua. SFWP sent 'warmest best wishes' to the new government. As an activist recalls, 'We basically saw the whole Cold War very much from the Soviet point of view . . . anti-Americanism was basically our world view.' Not everyone was comfortable with this, and motions from rural cumainn appeared at successive Ard Fheiseanna calling for the party to distance itself from Soviet Communism.

Domestically, SFWP was seeking to formulate a coherent position on a thorny issue that had emerged due to Ireland's economic development. In the face of growing energy demands the government had been considering diversifying electricity production, which, apart from turf-fired stations, overwhelmingly depended on imported coal and oil. The 1973 oil crisis concentrated minds on this issue, but it was not until the appointment of Desmond O'Malley as Minister for Industry, Commerce and Energy in 1977 that momentum gathered behind ESB plans for a nuclear power station at Carnsore Point, Co. Wexford. Announcement of the scheme provoked protest from a nascent environmentalist lobby and many on the left. A SFWP delegation met with Friends of the Earth in early 1978 but there was no meeting of minds and by August that year the leadership was reprimanding the *Irish People* for 'giving support' to environmentalists. Within SFWP suspicion of environmentalism had roots in the campaigns against a Dublin Bay oil refinery and the expansion of the capital's docks, projects supported by the party. In 1977 the party had welcomed the controversial Raybestos-Manhattan plant to Co. Cork, despite its dumping of asbestos materials, and criticized 'selfish opposition' to industrial development. The self-appointed leader of Dublin's conservation movement, Sean 'Dublin Bay' Loftus, continued to be a party hate figure and, according to the *United Irishman*, the 'greatest menace' to the city since 'the Black Death'.

SFWP's eventual decision to oppose the Carnsore project arose, in Smullen's words, from the view that, 'The party is committed to exploring the possibilities of all native sources of energy before foreign technology is brought in.' Prioritizing the native over the foreign was inconsistent with the general tendency of the party in these years; the fact that the technology in question was American made the difference. SFWP supported the 10,000-strong rally at the proposed power station's site in August 1978 and distributed a leaflet outlining the party's position.

The nuclear issue was discussed widely at party meetings. Smullen struggled with the obvious contradiction in opposing a scheme which promised to deliver, in the medium term, a massive increase in cheap electricity. It would not be until late 1979, and following an August rally by nearly 20,000 people at Carnsore, that SFWP's Research Section issued a pamphlet, *Nuclear Power and*

Ireland, which outlined a definitive position on the issue. This document expanded on views already aired in party media that the problem was not nuclear energy itself but the type of reactor proposed by the ESB, and hostility was expressed towards the 'element within the anti-nuclear lobby' who wished to 'turn back the clock' on technology. It was declared that safety in nuclear power generation was a higher priority in the 'socialist countries' and that Ireland should wait until techniques had been improved and then seek to purchase know-how from them, rather than purchase a reactor from the US. This position was strongly disputed by many in the party and by some of their international allies, but by this stage the worsening economic situation had made state investment in the Carnsore project a distant prospect.

Smullen, who was interested in liberation theology, developed contacts with a community of Jesuit priests based in Gardiner Street, just around the corner from the SFWP head office. The Jesuits were keen to develop this relationship, sending ten members of the order to the 1978 Ard Fheis. While common ground was found on issues of social justice, the priests expressed concerns over SFWP leaflets calling for contraceptives to be made available to persons of all ages and a poster supporting the legalization of divorce displayed on the front door of head office. Smullen got the divorce poster amended.

When Jack Lynch's extravagant plans for job creation began to fall asunder, the traditional affinity of many Irish Congress of Trade Unions (ICTU) leaders with Fianna Fáil meant they had little appetite for militancy. This created a vacuum of leadership which a newly revitalized Dublin Trades Council, heavily reliant on radical Labour, communist and SFWP shop stewards, was more than willing to fill. The trades council was a body to which affiliated Dublin unions sent representatives to discuss areas of shared interest, and Smullen and the Industrial Department had hoped for some time to turn it into a grouping capable of organizing workers. SFWP members, who 'had ideas and were younger' than most of the other delegates, brought a new dynamism to the body. Unions re-affiliated and the group's monthly meetings in Liberty Hall began to attract dozens rather than a handful of delegates.

In 1977 Smullen had supported the Dublin Trades Council taking over the organizing of the city's May Day parade from the previous year's ad hoc committee, and the council also staged protest marches. SFWP members were instructed to march with their union contingents rather than behind party banners. By 1978 left-wing Labour activist Mai Clifford had been installed as council president with leading Industrial Department member Fergus Whelan as vice-president. The party was also active in other trade councils, including those in Galway and Cork. In Waterford members were involved in organizing a September 1978 strike over the growing number of job losses; under the banner of 'Waterford Wants Work', 20,000 people demonstrated.

The *Irish People* became more influential following the installation of Padraig Yeates as editor in 1977. With exclusives on topics including child labour in a jam-making factory, multinationals paying for politicians' foreign trips and overpriced imported goods, the *Irish People* began to achieve a reputation for uncovering hard news stories, some of which were followed up by national newspapers and RTÉ. With their network of informants in the unions, state sector and paramilitary underworld, it was perhaps not surprising that Yeates and his journalists could access information others could not. The paper named building companies, often linked to Fianna Fáil, who were accused of shoddy workmanship on corporation houses. Facts and statistics on workplace safety, price increases and housing standards were collated from government documents or more secretive sources and presented to the readership in an accessible way. In March 1978 the paper revealed an internal Department of Labour report that showed up to 50 per cent of school leavers faced unemployment.

Editorially Yeates was not slavish in adherence to the party line, a fact which often had him at loggerheads with Smullen. But Garland was impressed by his editorship: 'He was an activist. He wasn't just sitting at his desk waiting for stories to come in but was on the ground talking to people and finding out about stories. I think members were enthused about the paper, it was a paper that was articulating what they felt about the party.' Sales had reached 15,000 by the end of 1977 and would grow to 25,000 by the turn of the decade. This increase was due in part to a new system of sales pioneered by Gerry Doherty during 1977. This involved the paper being distributed free in pubs followed by a collection and complemented by door-to-door sales. This 'Dublin Method' greatly increased circulation and the collections usually raised far more revenue than the 2p cover price. Other parts of the country were encouraged to adopt the system, but even when they did Dublin continued to account for roughly two-thirds of sales. While the *Irish People* grew in importance, the monthly *United Irishman* declined. Edited by Mac Giolla, the paper carried longer theoretical articles than the weekly and had a more distinctly republican tone.

The *Irish People* drew attention to an issue that would mobilize SFWP trade unionists. Partly as a result of the oil crisis, pre-tax industrial earnings had gone from being slightly above the average farmer's income in 1972 to being 93 per cent of the average farm income in 1977. Meanwhile the gap between the tax burden on farmers, who as self-employed workers reported their own income and tax liability, and Pay As You Earn (PAYE) workers, whose tax was deducted at source by their employers, was widening. While wages kept up with inflation, PAYE tax allowances did not – a dynamic that did not affect the self-employed sector. Perhaps most importantly, due to a lack of enforcement, farmers and others who reported their own income in practice paid little of the tax they owed – a fact that jumped out at *Irish People* journalist Seamus Phelan from a small *Irish Times* report of September 1977. The figures were stunning: £274 million, or three-quarters of the annual tax revenue, was provided by PAYE workers; the farming sector meanwhile contributed just £1.6 million, while receiving over £30 million in subsidies. Phelan was adamant that in the tax issue they had 'the story of the year if not the decade'. The next week the story appeared on the front page under the banner headline 'The Great Tax Robbery'. Over the next year Yeates continued to emphasize the issue, and discussion of how it could be brought to the fore became a constant theme in Gardiner Place. SFWP members were encouraged to start discussions on tax in their unions and workplaces. That the tax issue involved a conflict in which state employees were opposed to farmers was a source of enthusiasm for the cadres of the Industrial Department. Members who worked in the civil service wrote a pamphlet that was published in late 1978 as *Come On the Taxpayers!*, a title inspired by a banner unfurled by Dublin GAA fans during a match against Kerry in Croke Park. The pamphlet proposed that the tax system be overhauled to ensure that it forced 'farmers, self-employed, professionals and business firms to pay a fair share of their income and profits'. It called for the Revenue Commission to be reformed and empowered, and for the establishment of a state auditing company that would remove accountancy firms' ability to 'defraud legally'. It also demanded a cultural shift whereby 'tax dodging' would no longer be seen as merely 'pulling a fast one' but as a 'social crime' that 'takes medicine from the sick, money from the widow, teachers from the schools'.

Come On the Taxpayers! was circulated widely and members were fired up by its message; one recalls feeling that 'this was class war, the enemies were the owners of capital that were not paying their taxes and the farmers that were not paying their taxes'. The identification of PAYE workers as the core constituency for a new political campaign was pushed vigorously by the Industrial Department; Fergus Whelan recalls that 'at one stage we even made the decision to stop saying the worker class, instead referring to the PAYE sector'. SFWP members felt they had not only tapped into an area of existing public concern but 'refocused the pub talk' in urban centres towards the tax issue.

The influence farmers' organizations exerted over the government turned this concern into a revolt in early 1979. In February, after intense lobbying from farmers' groups, the government decided not to enforce a 2 per cent levy on farm produce. The decision caused outrage in the trade union movement and beyond. Dick Walsh in his *Irish Times* column described PAYE workers being 'mugged' by the levy deal. It galvanized militancy within white-collar unions, with one union leader declaring: 'The PAYE sector is paying for the running of a country in which farmers dictate to the government on budgetary taxation matters.' In response to the levy U-turn, SFWP-aligned shop stewards were to the fore in demanding a strike at Dublin Airport, while craft unions in the Dublin Trades Council called for a city-wide general stoppage.

As momentum was gathering around the levy and PAYE issues, SFWP held its 1979 Ard Fheis in Dublin's Mansion House. There delegates gave vent to their anger, one declaring that farmers had a tax system of 'pay as you like', while another demanded that land be confiscated if farmers attempted to carry out threatened production strikes. Mac Giolla, in his presidential address, attacked the EEC not as a threat to national sovereignty but due to the Common Agricultural Policy's funding of farmers. He also voiced unease over the effect that US multinational investment was having on Irish foreign policy; but any concerns that were voiced over motions supporting multinational development were swept aside, Seamus Phelan declaring that such development had to be accepted unless people were to be shipped 'like cattle out of [the] country'. The conference's 700 delegates voted to reinforce the ideological positions of *The Irish Industrial Revolution* and against motions seeking to re-emphasize more traditional republican goals. Several of these motions originated with Dublin's Anne Devlin cumann. During the debates Tony Heffernan clashed with Industrial Department members, and in the wake of the Ard Fheis he decided to resign from the party completely. *Hibernia* magazine, commenting on his departure, argued that 'the most vocal, and perhaps the only, remaining opponent of the Harris/Donohue intellectual takeover of the party has been silenced'. Heffernan had not clashed directly with this pair, however, as both had maintained their pretence of not being SFWP members and attended the Ard Fheis as 'observers'.

In response to workers' disquiet over the levy decision, and in an attempt to reassert their authority, the ITGWU and ICTU leaderships organized demonstrations around the country on Sunday 11 March. However, the Dublin Trades Council would not be placated and called its own general strike and march for Tuesday 20 March. Upwards of 50,000 took to the streets of Dublin on the 11th, and there were demonstrations in every major city and town. These protests only increased the appetite for strike action. During the days leading up to the 20th, more and more organizations, including trades councils, unions and the USI, called upon their members to join the work stoppage, and the ITGWU leadership were forced to throw their support behind it. An estimated 150,000 marched through the streets of Dublin on the day of the strike, with a further 40,000 in Cork and sizeable demonstrations elsewhere. At the head of the biggest labour protest in generations, Mai Clifford delivered a letter to Government Buildings demanding an easing of the 'intolerable burden on the working class'. The crowds that swept through the city carried banners declaring 'Farmers take all – Workers pay all' and 'Tax dodgers are social spongers'. In an enthusiastic address Whelan told the marchers, 'Today the most powerful lobby in Irish politics is born – the lobby of the Irish working class.'

The show of force by workers forced reassessments by the government and the ICTU leadership. Jack Lynch committed himself to tax reform and ICTU announced they would coordinate further action on the issue. 'Tax equity' was confirmed as a core SFWP policy, and this attracted growing support for the party from white-collar workers. The protests had the effect of drawing the government into playing a formal role in negotiations between unions and employers, which would eventually culminate before the end of 1979 in a 'National Understanding for Economic and Social Development' that enshrined wage restraint in return for government action on taxation, health, education and employment. SFWP broke with the hard-left consensus in its support for such cooperation between unions and the state, believing, as Seamus Cody put it, that 'centralised bargaining [was] a way of maximising workers as a class vis-à-vis the government'. This view pitted them against a shop steward-led 'New Liberty' grouping in the ITGWU and the CPI, which called for greater trade union democracy and an end to wage restraint. A decision was made to attack New Liberty publicly and link it to attempts to weaken the ITGWU. SFWP dock workers had taken a leading role in industrial action during 1977 and 1978, which had included the occupation of the port offices, during which the Starry Plough was hoisted and arrests made. This activity displeased the Industrial Department and Danny Ryan, the strike leader, eventually defected to the IRSP. The SFWP position, as articulated by Smullen, was that 'activities which fragment and weaken the trade union movement when the working class is under concentrated attack are basically anti-working class'. Hence unofficial strike action, widespread in the late 1970s, was often opposed by SFWP union members.

Within the Industrial Department two competing concepts of how the party should operate within the unions had emerged. Des Geraghty argued that cadres should run for senior trade union offices, while Smullen continued to emphasize gaining influence through behind-the-scenes persuasion. These divergent views led to tension between Geraghty's supporters, generally ITGWU members, and those, such as Whelan and Harris, who were loyal to Smullen's more clandestine approach. In 1981 Geraghty topped the first count in a six-way contest for vice-president of his union but was defeated on transfers, by 199 votes to 148.

The gap between SFWP and the Communist Party continued to grow, with the CPI adamant that they were international communism's representatives in Ireland. The Connolly Youth Movement continually frustrated attempts by the IDYM to formally join the pro-Soviet World Federation of Democratic Youth, even after the Soviet Embassy in Dublin was asked to 'pressurise' the intransigent Connolly Youth into giving their permission for IDYM affiliation. However, SFWP successfully developed links through the Soviet-aligned World Peace Council and the non-governmental Organisation of European Security and Cooperation, to which O'Hagan and Ó Cionnaith were delegates; and Soviet Embassy officials were regular visitors to Gardiner Place. SFWP was establishing itself as a respected voice within international communism just as that movement was beginning to rupture. While Garland, closely advised by O'Hagan, put emphasis on cementing relations with the East Germans and Soviets others were becoming interested in the 'Eurocommunist' ideas emerging from the Italian and Spanish communist parties. The concept of communism developing democratically within Western Europe and independent of a strict adherence to the USSR found its ideological inspiration in the work of the Italian Marxist Antonio Gramsci. It placed an emphasis on building broad alliances with groups such as environmentalists and women's rights campaigners, and democratic change rather than working-class revolution. The fissure between the Italian and Soviet positions had emerged publicly in Moscow in 1976, when the leader of the Italian party had spoken of his party's acceptance of a 'pluralistic system'. Echoes of these international collisions were being heard within SFWP. Des Geraghty used Eurocommunist concepts to question Smullen's hostility to farmers and support for a centralized economy. Other activists also began to read Gramsci and looked to Milan and Bologna rather than Moscow for ideological guidance. Although sceptical of the general direction of Eurocommunism, Garland, Smullen and O'Hagan favoured one aspect of this new thinking – its complete rejection of terrorism within democratic societies. This saw SFWP condemning the activities of groups such as Italy's Red Brigades, Germany's Red Army Faction and ETA, going as far as speculating that they were being financed by the CIA in order to discredit the European left. In response to the 1978 Red Brigade killing of Italian Christian Democrat leader Aldo Moro, the party's theoretical journal *Teoiric* analysed the 'deadly cul-de-sac of terrorism'. It contrasted the Irish and Italian responses, condemning sections of the 'Irish "Left" who are – to say the least – ambiguous on the terrorist question'. While such a response was expected from 'politically sick' Trotskyists, dismay was expressed at the CPI's focus on 'petty and hysterical criticism' of SFWP rather than 'facing the terrorist challenge' of the Provos.

As the Soviets began to view Eurocommunism as a heretical schism, the SFWP leadership sought to confirm their international credentials with strict adherence to the Moscow line. Any concerns over the 1979 Soviet invasion of Afghanistan were balanced by criticism of CIA and Chinese interference in that country. The attachment to international communism was such that party functions raffled memorabilia such as Vietnamese flags, allegedly flown from tanks during the fall of Saigon, and spent rounds of MPLA ammunition as prizes. SFWP also published a pamphlet about the Vietnamese 'Boat People' which attempted to refute allegations that refugees were fleeing that state due to 'massive political persecution'. Mick Ryan, the party press officer, told the *Irish Times* that 'one-party government would have to be a decision of the people' but that he could envisage 'a position where you might have only one party as an expression of the democratic will of the people'. The party's pro-Soviet orientation also led to the watering down of an *Irish People* exclusive in December 1979. The paper revealed that illegal arms sales to the Chilean dictatorship were being facilitated by British companies; the arms themselves were being sold by Poland but the desire to present the Eastern Bloc in the best light meant that the Polish connection was played down.

Despite the frostiness between SFWP and the CPI, Garland still yearned for some form of united left approach. To this end a SFWP talks team, separate from the Industrial Department, of Goulding, Mac Giolla and Garland began negotiations with the CPI leadership in August 1978. Mick O'Riordan had accepted assurances that threats of violence against CPI members in Dublin and Belfast should be forgotten, with the communists admitting that circulation of the 1977 international memo attacking *The Irish Industrial Revolution* had been 'bad'. The communists also accepted that SFWP was not in the business of forcing their officials out of certain trade unions. But the meetings came to an abrupt halt when Jer O'Leary and Sean Dunne, now CPI members, found themselves caught up in what the communists alleged was an 'IRA squad operation' by SFWP members against dissidents in the Dockers Pub in Dublin in December 1978. After the incident O'Riordan wrote a scathing letter to Garland 'suspending the present series of political discussions with your Party'. O'Riordan claimed that 'the political consequences' of the pub violence were 'disastrous for the Left. The method of criminal terror, reminiscent of the animal gang, in a public place must be condemned and its participants exposed. It also raises again the connection between your political apparatus and a secret army wing.' Despite further correspondence it was not until August 1979 that SFWP delivered a definitive response to the CPI's concerns, ironically condemning the communists for their links with 'terrorism'. Garland stated that what had occurred in the Dockers was a 'purely private affair' and not politically motivated. Only if the CPI issued an 'unambiguous statement on the question of terrorism' and there was an agreement reached on both parties' international links could they resume a 'principled' alliance.

The CPI's response made clear the possibility of such an 'alliance' was gone for now:

The essence of our difference and much of the tension arising from these differences is because in recent years your organisation has departed from commonly agreed policies on which our relationship was grounded. On the National Question, the EEC, the role of the state, the role of foreign multi-national companies, National Wage Agreements and Social Contracts, the issue of political status and other important questions you have changed your public positions. Your association with the Official IRA remains ambiguous and unexplained. It stands to reason that there can be no mutual co-operation until there is re-established common accord on major questions.

Despite these disagreements, there was still social and cultural interaction between left-wing activists. In Dublin much of this activity centred on the Project Arts Centre. The Project had developed from artistic cooperative ventures, with much input from left-wing activists, some of them aligned with SFWP. The party had on occasion also made small financial contributions. By 1977 the Project was staging productions by up and coming Irish writers and directors such as Jim and Peter Sheridan, and exhibitions by artists like Robert Ballagh. Smullen wrote Brecht-influenced plays expounding SFWP ideology, including a musical about youth unemployment called *Waiting for the Future*; one Industrial Department member compares these works to 'cracking a hazelnut with a 14-pound hammer', but recalls one particularly poor performance in Trinity being 'defended to the bitter end by Harris' and others.

The movement's publishing house, Repsol (short for 'Republican Socialist Publications'), produced the party's newspapers and pamphlets as well as a number of books not directly linked to party policy, such as Sean Cronin's biographies of Connolly and Frank Ryan and Dominic Behan's memoirs. Repsol had been incorporated as a company at the close of 1975 and its print shop was located at the rear of party HQ in Gardiner Place. In 1977 the company purchased modern printing equipment, but the machinery was left unserviced in a warehouse and became so rusted as to be inoperable.

The party managed to exert a strong influence over a major Irish cultural exhibition in London in March 1980. The 'Sense of Ireland' festival of exhibitions, plays and seminars, supported by over £600,000 of Irish government funds, was intended to act as an antidote to the bad publicity surrounding the country due to the Northern conflict. Current and former members of the Official republican movement were prominent in the festival's events. Donal Foley commented in his *Irish Times* column that the festival programme was so 'heavy loaded' with SFWP members that one academic had boasted that 'the Stickies control the seminars'. Harris delivered a paper entitled 'The Production of the Popular Image' in which he described the Irish media as 'a small elite, visibly well paid and equally visibly deficient in many of the intellectual and moral requirements that would facilitate political and social change', and castigated its failure to challenge the euphoria that had greeted the Pope's 1979 visit to Ireland and the rise to power of Haughey.

During 1978 the party decided to redevelop its Gardiner Place head office, which involved ending the leases of the other occupants and seeking to have a noisy piggery located at the back shut down. The basement tenant was reluctant to leave even after visits from party leaders, and only legal manoeuvring prevented SFWP from being forced to carry out a highly embarrassing eviction. The bottom-floor bookshop was extended and Ó Cionnaith took over its running. Among the leadership Garland, Ó Cionnaith, O'Hagan and Smullen were near-constant presences in Gardiner Place.

The party made a major effort to increase its representation and profile in the 1979 local and European elections, which took place against a backdrop of a deepening economic crisis and the tax marches. Industrial unrest had returned with a protracted strike by postal workers which saw violent clashes between Gardaí and pickets. The country was also suffering from the sharp global rise in oil prices. SFWP pointed out that the Fianna Fáil government had abolished wealth tax and slashed tax on corporation profits while maintaining the unjust PAYE system.

In total SFWP ran just over 80 local candidates, with 13 in Dublin, 9 in Cork city and 7 in Waterford. The party won 19 seats altogether, mostly in rural towns. The most impressive urban showing was in Waterford, where it achieved 20.2 per cent of the poll and saw Davy Walsh join Paddy Gallagher on the council. A breakthrough was also made in Cork city, where Ted Tynan took a seat. Joe Sherlock topped the poll in Mallow as did John McManus in Bray; and Liz McManus joined her husband on Bray council. But it was Mac Giolla's win in Dublin, representing the Ballyfermot area, that most enthused activists: SFWP finally had an elected representative in the capital. The election saw a rise in Labour Party support that was cautiously welcomed in the *Irish People*, which argued that if Labour 'had the courage to cut their links to big business and Fine Gael' they might become a valuable part of a left alternative. Labour took 4 of the Republic's 15 seats in the European Parliament, equalling Fine Gael, while Fianna Fáil took 6; the SFWP candidates all polled poorly in the European vote.

In November, following the defeat of Fianna Fáil candidates in November by-elections in Cork, Jack Lynch resigned, throwing his party into a bitter leadership contest that was eventually won by Charles Haughey. In contrast SFWP had been enthused by its candidates' performances in the by-elections: Ted Tynan secured 8.26 of the vote in Cork city, while Sherlock took 22.8 per cent in Cork North-East, coming third. The results drove home to the SFWP leadership that Sherlock was now a real contender for a Dáil seat. The party derived extra impetus from Haughey's rise. Shortly after becoming Taoiseach, Haughey appeared in a special TV broadcast to assert that 'we as a nation have been living away beyond our means' and call for severe cutbacks. The *Irish People* responded with disgust, noting Haughey's 'private island, his string of racehorses, his palace out in Kinsealy'. Smullen would sum up Haughey's Fianna Fáil as 'a party run by property speculators in the interest of property speculators'.

The party meanwhile continued to be divided over the influence and the secrecy of the Industrial Department. Margaret O'Leary, a head office worker and Garland loyalist, chose to outline these concerns at Bodenstown in June 1979:

We must ensure that the Workers' Party is not used by self minded people as a bandwagon for their personal ambitions and selfish pursuits. We do not want people who will wait until the moment of victory before admitting their membership of our Party. We need women and men, girls and boys, who will work openly and be proud to be known as members of the Workers' Party in their workplaces, in their unions, in their local associations . . .

O'Leary's reference to the party simply as 'the Workers' Party' reflected another ongoing debate. Since 1977 some members, particularly but not exclusively those aligned with the Industrial Department, had been making calls for the deletion of 'Sinn Féin' from the party name, and many members now referred to the party simply as 'the Workers' Party'. At the 1979 Ard Fheis delegates had supported a motion proposing a party-wide survey of attitudes on a new name. A letter from Liam Maguire to the Ard Chomhairle probably summarized the general view among members of the

Industrial Department: 'As a non-public active member of the Workers' Party I wish to convey to you my disapproval of the continued retention of the prefix "Sinn Féin" . . . it ill behoves a progressive industrial organisation which is presenting its policies on a platform of dialectics and economics to allow itself to be confused with a nationalistic and fascist terrorist gang.' While there was much opposition to the proposed change, particularly in rural areas, canvassers' experience of having to explain to the public the difference between SFWP and the Provos was a strong factor in support of change, which was supported by the majority of delegates in Galway/Mayo, Cork, Waterford, Wicklow and Dublin.

Many of those who strongly supported getting rid of 'Sinn Féin' were equally dismissive of the title 'Workers' Party' as being 'too narrow' and not capturing the full scope of the party. There was also concern over how the title 'Workers' Party of Ireland' would play in the North. A plethora of other suggestions were put forward, including 'the United Workers' Party', 'Workers' Party (Sinn Féin)', and 'Democratic Labour Party'. Mick Ryan had played a key role in conducting the survey and its final report bore the hallmarks of his concern for consensus. The report stated that 'selection of a new title is a particularly important and sensitive choice since it may be interpreted, inside as well as outside the Party, as a reflection of the outcome of an internal struggle between traditional and urban-radical forces' and concluded that a change in party title was not necessary 'for the time being at least'.

The matter would be debated at the March 1980 Ard Fheis. In the lead-up to this event the tax issue was once more to the fore, with ICTU organizing a massive demonstration that dwarfed even the 1979 protests. On 22 January 1980, in what the *Irish Times* called the 'biggest demonstration of organised labour in the history of the state', an estimated 700,000 people participated in 37 marches, including 300,000 in Dublin. A special edition of the *Irish People* distributed on the day declared 'the party which backs the PAYE workers is Sinn Féin The Workers' Party'. There was a huge sense of satisfaction that SFWP had been at the cutting edge of the issue.

Almost simultaneously, however, the party's involvement in student politics generated unwanted media coverage. There were bitter overnight debates at the USI conference on disaffiliating from the International Union of Students. At one stage Trinity student union president Joe Duffy led a walkout in protest at alleged SFWP control and ties with the IUS, which he decried as 'a puppet of Moscow'. Nevertheless, SFWP's Gerry Grainger was elected president and there were those who remained positive about SFWP influence. Indeed, in the opinion of the *Irish Times'* education correpondent it was 'the Sticky establishment [that] has been holding USI together'. But the 1980 conference would mark a high-water mark of SFWP influence. Not enough had been done to rectify the problems in student recruitment identified by the 1979 internal report. By the January 1981 Annual Congress of USI, SFWP had lost influence in many of the major colleges. The conference saw heavy criticism from the floor of the USI leadership for lack of consultation with the membership and the use of the union for party political purposes. This opposition resulted in a series of serious reversals for SFWP supporters. Outgoing president Gerry Grainger was defeated by Brendan Doris, a Maoist, while self-described 'radical Catholic' Joe Duffy was elected education officer. This resulted in an incoming officer board with no SFWP representation. The conference also voted to disaffiliate from the International Union of Students and to undermine the policy of promoting mixed-religion teacher training colleges in Northern Ireland.

The 1980 Ard Fheis in Liberty Hall witnessed the most heated debates since the departure of Costello. On the issue of the party's name, a plea by a North American Republican Clubs delegate that losing the Sinn Féin designation would 'pull the rug from under them' in collecting funds for prisoners produced an angry response from Ted Tynan: 'That's one dollar-lined rug, soaked in the blood of workers, that I don't want to stand on, and they can pull it any time they want.' Party justice spokesman Pat McCartan was more diplomatic, linking a call for change with what he saw as the need to discard outdated tradition: 'We trample graves. We march to Bodenstown. We sell Easter lilies and pub-crawl to collect money. It is time for the double-think to stop.' Mick Ryan called for more effort on winning people to party policy and less emphasis on this divisive issue. For many, Belfast delegate Jim Sullivan's intervention was crucial. The veteran OIRA commander declared that, 'Many of my comrades have died so that this organisation could live and I feel I'd be betraying them if I supported any removal of the "Clubs" or "Sinn Féin".' In the end over two-thirds voted to put off any review of the party name until after elections scheduled for 1982. The result prompted Harris to leave his balcony seat in the observers' section and walk out of the auditorium followed by, among others, Smullen. Motions were passed returning civil liberties, health policy and women's equality to prominence in the SFWP agenda, in a move away from narrow economism; a motion calling for support of nuclear energy was also defeated. Garland's address drove home the message that clandestine activity was damaging the party's image. Commenting on media speculation that SFWP was 'engaged in some form of conspiracy in relation to student and working class organisations', he stated that members were 'instructed to play a full and active part openly . . . we are not in the business of usurping or conspiring to take over other organisations of working people'. In his presidential address Mac Giolla emphasized that 'all the marching in the world will not change the present system while the majority of workers still vote for the parties that are exploiting them'. He also took the opportunity to offer greater cooperation with the Labour Party.

The Ard Fheis was meant to mark a watershed, with the reversals suffered by the Industrial Department prompting speculation that some of its leading cadres would leave the party. Members' energies were now to be focused on building up the party in terms of membership and support and away from what had become a divisive search for ideological certainties. To this end a new professionalism was to be brought to election preparations. Cumainn around the country were instructed to follow the example of areas in Dublin and set up so-called 'Constituency Councils' in order to provide a forum for those who wished to aid the party but not to join it. Election funds were to be raised on an ongoing basis and ring-fenced, rather than scrambled for in the run-up to a campaign. The first test of the new approach came in the Donegal by-election of November 1980, for which the party installed two head-office workers in the county for the duration of the campaign; but the result of 2,401 votes for Seamus Rodgers was a slight decrease on his support in the general election. A notable feature of the by-election was that two local multinational companies who attempted to donate £450 towards SFWP election funds had their money publicly returned.

While Garland and Mac Giolla and their supporters had wrestled back control within the party, there was still one arena of SFWP activity in which they had little influence: the Ned Stapleton industrial cumann remained active within RTÉ, with Harris as its central figure. Former SFWP-aligned student activists, including former *USI News* editor Joe Little, were also gaining employment at the station. Harris had been on the interview board that had decided to hire Gerry Gregg, a 22-year-old UCD graduate who became enthusiastic about SFWP politics: '[I] wouldn't have jumped until I went into RTÉ and the battle was joined and you were either Stick or Anti-Stick.' Other graduates were less susceptible to the party's charms. Fintan Cronin, a former BICO activist, joined the station in 1980 and recalls being approached shortly afterwards in Madigan's Pub by Harris and asked if he would become involved with SFWP. Cronin was 'suspicious of the Official IRA' but not 'unsympathetic to their ideology'. When he informed Harris that he was somewhat 'cynical about what they were at' he recalls the blunt response: 'We need cynics like we need a hole in the head.'

The Ned Stapleton members had an influence on RTÉ's output that belied their relatively small numbers. Producers John Caden and Eugene Murray were also attached to the SFWP structures in a workplace that did not officially allow party political activity. Much activity was focused on the station's WUI branch, which catered for producers and clerical staff. Debate within the WUI was fierce and much of the Ned Stapleton cumann's attention was focused on undermining the position of those perceived as 'Trots' or Provo supporters and general opposition to what were deemed as unnecessary strikes carried out by the National Union of Journalists (NUJ), with which the WUI had a tense relationship. Cronin's attitude towards the 'Stickies' hardened when they refused to back a call for strike action after a so-called 'Trotskyite-Provo' producer faced losing his job following an investigative report. This reluctance to take militant positions, due to politics or to what was perceived by others as careerism, resulted in SFWP members losing control of the RTÉ's WUI branch committee by 1980. However, Harris's confrontation with what he saw as tribal nationalism could also generate support. Gregg claimed that 'there was a silent majority view among programme makers, whose common sense made them responsive to the arguments of Harris . . . some of the leadership of the middle ground was given by the Workers' Party element'. That was the case on the divisive issue of the restrictions embodied in Section 31 of the Broadcasting Act. In theory SFWP was still opposed to Section 31; in reality, continuing tensions with the Provos had meant the party line was now closer to O'Hagan's assertion in the *Irish Times* that he didn't think 'any state could permit people who want to issue calls to terrorist activity to use the airwaves'.

The NUJ was often vocal in its opposition to Section 31. A number of SFWP members and supporters were active in this union, including Gardiner Place staff Padraig Yeates, Gerry Flynn and Paddy Woodworth, and there was mutual suspicion between them and what were termed the 'Harrisites' concentrated in the WUI. For some Ned Stapleton stalwarts Yeates was still tainted by his youthful dalliance with Trotskyism in Birmingham, while Woodworth, with others, shared distaste for the frequent mental somersaults of their Industrial Department comrades, 'the way the line would change like *that* and the ripple would go through and then they would all be perfectly reflecting what Harris was saying'. Within RTÉ the NUJ branch also contained a number of people formerly close to the Stickies, such as journalists Charlie Bird,

Patrick Kinsella and Rodney Rice. Former members and current activists played a role in preventing Section 31 from becoming an all-consuming obsession for the union.

The input of SFWP members in RTÉ was most controversial, and perhaps most successful, in regard to programme output. In late 1980 station chiefs decided to revamp their current affairs coverage and launch a new show to be broadcast four nights a week. *Today Tonight* would become the station's current affairs flagship, marked by a campaigning style of investigative journalism. From its inception the show was associated with people seen as sympathetic to SFWP, among them producer Tish Barry, and programme editor Joe Mulholland. Mulholland, a Donegal man and Francophile, had a keen interest in Marxist politics and personally knew some of the SFWP leadership, including Garland. Although Mulholland never committed himself to movement discipline, he did recruit a number of young reporters and journalists to the programme who were closely aligned with the Ned Stapleton cumann. These included Gregg, who joined *Today Tonight* in October 1980, Barry O'Halloran, Joe Little, David Blake Knox and later Una Claffey. Although a wide variety of views and strong personalities were represented within the programme staff, which also included Brian Farrell, Mary McAleese and Olivia O'Leary, cynics christened the programme 'Stickyline' in reference to the show it was replacing, *Frontline*. Mulholland fostered a cooperative editorial style, and the team met every Friday. Gregg describes these meetings as 'invariably lengthy' and 'often passionate'. Staff would debate ideas before a final decision was taken by Mulholland in open view of the entire team. Such an atmosphere was tailor-made for SFWP members who believed that 'there was a number of social, economic and political Aunt Sallys that needed to be attacked'. Early programmes included an incisive report on the effects of growing unemployment and an investigation into the horrific Stardust fire of February 1981, in which 48 young people died in a north Dublin disco.

SFWP influence within RTÉ was not confined to *Today Tonight*, and indeed Harris and other party members never worked directly on the programme. But critics complained that SFWP members were regularly interviewed on *Today Tonight* without their party affiliation being revealed. With SFWP members also involved in the production of RTÉ's most popular programme *The Late Late Show*, it was not unusual for activists to make appearances as members of the studio audience there as well. On several occasions this provoked discussion by the Coiste Seasta, who had not been informed about some of the appearances. Smullen was forced to claim that members regularly turning up without sanction was due to them having 'friends' working at RTÉ. It was eventually decided that head office had to be informed of any members' TV or radio appearances and was also to supervise the distribution of audience tickets. In early January 1980, 17-year-old Ballymun IDYM member Delores Clinch appeared on a *Late Late Show* youth panel and successfully embarrassed Fine Gael leader Garret FitzGerald with some informed questions on his party's housing policy. A few days later she was taken in for Garda questioning about her participation in the show.

Sales of the *United Irishman* continued to decline. Its title was increasingly thought anachronistic and in O'Hagan's view too easily associated with 'Provisional Alliance type publications'. Despite being on differing sides in a number of the party's internal debates, Garland and O'Hagan worked along with Harris, Paddy Gillan and Donohoe in launching a new monthly magazine to replace the *United Irishman*. Launched on 1 May 1980, with O'Hagan as editor, *Workers' Life* was intended to be a 'stand-alone broad-based labour magazine' aimed beyond the SFWP milieu. The magazine was sold in newsagents and included articles on sport, film and the arts as well as economics and trade union news. Its first edition included articles by rising party star Pat Rabbitte as well as a report by Joe Mulholland on developments in the French Communist Party. Although the original plan was for the magazine to provide a platform for a variety of views, Gerry Flynn, its sole staff reporter, recalls that it was not long before it 'deteriorated into highly censored-type stuff'. Articles dripped with praise of union leaders, and a profile of Joe Sherlock emphasized his trade union record but failed to even hint at any military phase. Such an approach was now uniform: SFWP's position was that it had no knowledge of the Official IRA's existence, and the party showed an increasingly marked reluctance to acknowledge that it had ever existed.

Although registered party membership was less than 2,000 across Ireland, by the early 1980s hundreds of 'associate' and constituency council members could be called upon to canvass during elections and to help out in major campaigns – a vindication of the strategy adopted at the 1980 Ard Fheis. In the Republic's third city, Limerick, an older inactive republican membership had been replaced by a new group of largely student members. Over a dozen activists, including Church of Ireland vicar Peter Tarleton, organized flat-dwellers' groups and campaigned on transport issues as well as building up *Irish People* sales in estates like Moyross. In Galway, conversely, student support had declined but had been replaced by a membership of more than 30 who were selling 600 *Irish People* a week. By late 1980 Dublin had a registered public membership of 137 organized in 15 cumainn. This number did not include the several dozen who held only Industrial Department or IDYM membership, or a group of recent recruits from the Socialist Party of Ireland and from Labour. Of the 137 members, 63 were manual workers and there were 42 working in white-collar occupations, including 7 teachers and a number of clerks and secretaries. About 70 per cent of Dublin members were men. The majority (86) were members of trade unions, mostly the ITGWU. What struck one member attending socials in Club Uí Cadhain, the party's own licensed premises underneath the Gardiner Place headquarters, was 'how working class they were. They all would have left school at 13 or 14, a lot of the socialism may have been fairly crude but it was socialism that came from a need, a necessity, something that was innate within them . . . it was a very real socialism.' However this was not the entire picture. Paddy Woodworth remembers sitting at Ard Fheis dinners beside members from West Cork who had stayed with the party 'because they were loyal to Goulding . . . I think they always assumed Goulding was organizing some extraordinary revolutionary movement that they weren't fully aware of, that would out-Provo the Provos when the crunch came.'

The problem of funding the party as it orientated itself towards electoral politics remained. In January 1981 the Coiste Seasta faced the stark fact 'that we were paying out more than we were receiving in'. There were suggestions that trade union executives be approached requesting finance and that each candidate also seek funding from their own union. The leadership claimed that in the Donegal by-election Fianna Fáil had spent £100,000 and Fine Gael £50,000 while SFWP's total outlay was £2,000; 'this is a clear demonstration of how money wins elections'.

SFWP was still on the fringe of Irish politics but its potential was not lost on its rivals. Labour deputy leader Michael O'Leary noted: 'Sinn Féin The Workers' Party is now attracting the young articulate working-class support, the very group we ourselves attracted in the late sixties.' In the Republic SFWP had succeeded in creating an identity which seemed to point to the future rather than the past. In Northern Ireland, however, the party's progress was more problematic: sectarianism continued to define political life.

11. Peace, Work and Class Politics

'Even to maintain pace in Northern Ireland you are achieving quite a lot. Given our politics, which are socialist, non-sectarian – an attempt to bring the two communities together – you are pleasing neither faction, and therefore it makes life difficult.'

Kevin Smyth, 4 August 1980

After Sinn Féin's January 1977 name change, the Republican Clubs in Northern Ireland became known as Republican Clubs – The Workers' Party. RCWP called for fully integrated and co-educational comprehensive schools, and wanted to abolish the 11 Plus examination because of its 'inbuilt bias' against working-class students. The party estimated that 20,000 new houses a year were needed to ameliorate the North's housing crisis and campaigned for the rapid construction of new integrated estates such as Poleglass on the edge of west Belfast. As part of this strategy, councillors Jim Sullivan and Bernie McDonagh met with the Northern Ireland Under Secretary of State in early 1977 to discuss housing strategy. A RCWP delegation also met the Department of Commerce in April of that year and claimed credit for winning a commitment to a new Belfast industrial estate. Meeting government ministers and inviting them to tour local areas and see the problems for themselves was a radical departure for a republican organization. While RCWP chairman Malachy McGurran stressed that a 32-county socialist republic was the Clubs' long-term aim, it was accepted that as an interim measure a local parliament elected by proportional representation would be acceptable as long as there was a Bill of Rights to outlaw discrimination and guarantee minority rights. The hope that new politics might develop was also nurtured by the declining number of Troubles-related deaths: 112 people were killed during 1977, a figure that was less than half the previous year's total and the lowest since 1970.

The Clubs emphasized economic issues in the build-up to the May 1977 local elections, in which they fielded 34 candidates, but the election drive was interrupted by another confrontation with the Provisionals. During the spring there had been tension in Newry, with the Provos complaining that their members had been 'sneered at' and beaten up by the OIRA. But the worst violence flared in Belfast on Easter Sunday morning when, as the Officials gathered at Beechmount for their parade, a bomb exploded, killing 10-year-old Kevin McMenamin and seriously wounding three other people. In the panic and confusion the Officials were convinced the Provos were behind the attack. Hundreds of marchers surged towards Milltown Cemetery and met the front ranks of the Provisionals leaving the cemetery after their commemoration. Vicious hand-to-hand fighting broke out in full view of the British Army in Andersonstown Barracks. During the clashes OIRA members opened fire, wounding two Provisionals. A few hours later John Short, an uncle of the dead boy, and Daniel Mateer, a family friend, were ambushed and shot in Whiterock; Short died of his wounds. Only desperate efforts by the mediators prevented escalation. It later transpired that it was the UVF who had planted the bomb in Beechmount.

The election campaign continued despite the disruption of a loyalist general strike in early May. Led by Ian Paisley and backed by the UDA, the strikers demanded a return to majority rule and stricter security measures. Paisley was very confident of repeating the success of the Ulster Workers' Council strike and even claimed that he would retire from politics if the stoppage was a failure. The Clubs supported the ICTU's 'stay at work' call, McGurran denouncing Paisley as a 'false prophet' leading the 'loyalist community further into the political wilderness' and towards sectarian confrontation. The *United Irishman* reported an exchange between McGurran and Paisley backstage at the Belfast BBC studios in which the RCWP chairman asked the DUP leader: 'How's the stoppage going, Ian?' He was met with the ironic reply, 'Well, you ought to know how hard it is to lead the working class, Malachy.' In its early stages about one in five of the Protestant workforce backed the strike, but despite widespread intimidation, including the killing of three people by loyalists, the stoppage soon faltered. Sullivan publicly congratulated workers who had 'defied UDA bullyboys' and predicted that the 'writing is clearly on the wall for the politics of the gunman in Ireland'.

RCWP took just 2.6 per cent of the total poll in the voting on 18 May, and had six councillors elected. Sullivan, McDonagh and Seamus Lynch were elected in Belfast and McGurran in Craigavon; seats were also retained in Magherafelt and Omagh. But the Clubs lost their seats in south Armagh and in Newry. Overall the results were disappointing and showed a decline in Official support since 1973. The Ulster Unionists remained the largest party with 179 council seats, while the DUP took 74. The SDLP's 113 seats made it by far the biggest non-unionist force.

Early summer brought renewed clashes with the Provisionals. In Newry the trouble was eventually resolved through mediation. In Belfast the Provos accused the OIRA of a series of armed raids and kneecappings in the Lower Falls. But the most serious violence occurred in the north of the city. In Bawnmore the Provisionals claimed that one of their members was shot by the OIRA. Trevor McNulty, education officer for both the Republican Clubs and Official IRA in Belfast, was involved in talks with the local Provos in New Lodge to prevent further clashes and felt confident that the trouble was over; but on the afternoon of 27 July McNulty was shot along with another Official, Joe Flood, as they left the Alexander House high-rise flat complex. As he lay wounded, McNulty was finished off with a shot to the head while Flood, although hit, managed to escape his assailants.

The Officials decided to hit back hard, killing three men within a few hours of McNulty's shooting. James Foots, a brother of prominent Provisional spokesman Malachy Foots, was shot dead in Unity Flats and his father wounded in the legs. Armed men kicked in the door of a house in Andersonstown and killed

30-year-old Daniel Cowan, who was unconnected to either group. The OIRA had been looking for a man who had previously lived at the address. Later that night Tommy Tolan, a leading Ballymurphy Provisional, was ambushed and killed while he himself was searching for Official targets. Twenty people were injured in attacks across the city, the majority of them carried out by the OIRA. Frantic efforts by the mediating priests – and, on the Provo side, a recently released Gerry Adams – brought a surprisingly rapid halt to the killing. Despite the mistaken killing of Cowan, the Officials believed that they had made the shooting of McNulty very costly for the Provos. There was also a sense that they had hit back for 1975. But McNulty's death was badly felt by the organization; as Lynch put it, 'You can create a gunman in weeks, but the loss of Trevor McNulty was a major blow.'

Despite the truce, hatred between the rival organizations remained intense. At McNulty's funeral O'Hagan described 'Provisionalism' as arising 'from a nauseating blood-mythology cesspool spewed up by its mad kin – Hitler, Franco, Mosley and O'Duffy'. Small-scale clashes remained an everyday occurrence and over the winter of 1977 Lynch met Adams on several occasions at Clonard Monastery to resolve local disputes. Adams believed that the 1975 attack on the Officials had been a 'major mistake' that had resulted in a backlash against the Provisionals. According to Lynch, Adams was also interested in the Officials' attempts to build a political base. The dominance of Adams and his supporters within the Belfast Provisionals was reflected in their increasingly leftist rhetoric. *Republican News*, edited by Danny Morrison, now claimed that the Provos were 'more revolutionary than the Stickies'. The Provos also recognized that the British were not on the verge of leaving Northern Ireland. Official publications noted the new prominence of Adams, the 'thinking man's Provo'.

On Belfast City Council Lynch found there was intense suspicion of him as a Republican Clubs councillor, and set about building up the trust of unionists. He began to cooperate with the Independent Unionist Hugh Smyth from the Shankill, who was linked to the UVF. He also built up a relationship with

Unionist MP John Carson, who would come to hold Lynch in the 'highest regard' for sparing 'no effort in trying to bridge the sectarian divide'. Lynch invited Lord Melchett, the Secretary of State for Education, Health and Social Services on a walking tour of New Lodge and accompanied him to various problem areas, finding him 'most sympathetic'. Over the next year Lynch, Sullivan and Eamon Smullen would meet Industry Minister Don Concannon to discuss the Clubs' economic proposals. The Clubs produced documents and proposals for industrial development and job creation, including a steel mill for Belfast harbour and a new industrial estate on derelict land between the Falls and the Shankill.

The Clubs were building something of a political profile partly by being the only organization stressing the need for working-class unity. In late 1977 they succeeded in having a motion supporting striking firemen passed at Belfast City Council, winning support from individual councillors from the SDLP and the Unionist Party, as well as independents. During 1978 a delegation of party councillors from Waterford, Cork and Kilkenny were brought to Belfast and visited the Shankill. In response to unemployment and the movement's changing position in relation to multinational development, the Clubs welcomed the news that American businessman John DeLorean planned a car factory in west Belfast and met representatives of his company.

A large part of RCWP's new profile was based on distancing the Clubs from association with political violence. The practice of colour parties wearing berets and combat fatigues at Bodenstown was ended, much to the annoyance of the Strabane OIRA unit who had been given the honour of leading the march in 1977 but withdrew when they were told they were to discard their battledress in favour of black trousers and white shirts. At commemorations dead volunteers were now referred to as 'party members' rather than by military rank, while Trevor McNulty was not claimed as a volunteer by the OIRA. Five OIRA members arrested with weapons during the feud gave no indication of their allegiances in court. At Christmas 1977 the *Irish News* carried greetings to the Official IRA's prisoners from their 'friends and comrades on Markets and Roden Street building sites' rather than from the Clubs, as had been traditional.

Controversies related to the prisons and to state repression became more prominent during 1978. The Labour government's Northern Secretary Roy Mason, a gruff former coal miner, was pushing a policy of 'Ulsterisation': the use of the RUC and UDR in front-line roles, with the British Army less prominent. The aim was to produce the elusive 'acceptable level of violence', which in reality meant a level of violence acceptable to public opinion in Britain – hence the desire to minimize the number of casualties sustained by British soldiers. Violence *was* decreasing, with Troubles-related deaths falling again in 1978 to 88, of which 46 were civilians, and the rest soldiers, police and paramilitaries. Loyalist killings were reduced to just 10 – among them Dennis Kelly, a member of the Officials in Portadown, killed by the UVF. Mason was convinced that a tough policy of imprisonment was crippling the Provisional IRA, and on more than one occasion he announced that the tide had turned against 'the terrorists'.

At the end of 1977 there were 35 OIRA prisoners in Long Kesh, 13 in Crumlin Road and 4 in Portlaoise. Ann Boyle was the sole female Official prisoner, in Armagh. There was little public indication of their existence. Meanwhile, attention was increasingly focused on a protest movement by Provisional and INLA prisoners. Since March 1976, men jailed for paramilitary offences had been imprisoned in eight new 'H-Block' compounds at Long Kesh. They were no longer entitled to special category status, i.e. recognition as political prisoners. Instead they were expected to wear prison uniform and conform to regulations as ordinary inmates. Some of the growing number of Provisional IRA and INLA members being jailed in the H-Blocks had begun to refuse to wear prison clothing in protest at their status. As a result they were confined to their cells for long periods, lost remission and various privileges and wore only blankets. This 'blanket protest' had begun to attract increasing attention during 1977 and was the subject of campaigns by locally based Relatives Action Committees (RACs).

In Coalisland in January 1978 a conference was held to coordinate this fledgling protest movement. The driving force behind the conference was Bernadette McAliskey, who, though no longer a member of the IRSP, had support from that party and the smaller far-left groups. Over 500 people attended the conference, which marked a broadening of the H-Block campaign. When news of the attendance of a number of RCWP activists became public, the party leadership assured its members that they had not been present in an official capacity and that it was party policy to 'not take part in conferences with such unprincipled groupings'. Club member Eugene Lyttle was instructed to withdraw from involvement in the Coalisland RAC. The Clubs emphasized that 'the people of this country need peace in order to achieve any other objective' and that a complete Provisional IRA ceasefire was the 'only hope for release of prisoners'. The most emotive arguments against involvement in the campaign were related to the Provisional IRA's activities. In February 1978 twelve people, all of them Protestant, were burnt to death in an incendiary bomb attack on the La Mon House hotel outside Belfast. They were among 28 civilians killed by the Provisionals that year. At the 1978 Ard Fheis Mac Giolla asserted that 'the Provos are engaged in a war against the Irish people ... can anyone say that the atrocities of the infamous Black and Tans were any worse? Despite the brutal record of the British Army and the RUC the vast majority of the people of Northern Ireland see them as their only protectors against the mad Provos.' Similarly, the case of a Provisional jailed for life for the murder of OIRA man Robbie Elliman was used to illustrate how 'such killers are not entitled to any special POW status'. The party leadership were also aware from their own prisoners inside Long Kesh that most Provisional inmates were conforming to regulations and not taking part in the protest. This encouraged the belief that the protest would fizzle out. But the conflict inside Long Kesh became ever more bitter as the authorities tried to prevent the prisoners from smuggling communications in or out. Resistance to forced body searches led to fights and beatings and 24-hour confinement.

During 1978 some Provisional and INLA blanket protesters began a 'dirty protest', refusing to slop out and eventually daubing their cells with excrement. More forced searches and hose-downs followed. Women prisoners in Armagh also joined the protest.

It was clear that many who were not Provisional supporters were sympathetic to the prison protest and concerned about allegations of ill-treatment of protesters. This was reflected in the Clubs' own press. The _United Irishman_ accused the RUC of torturing suspects in Castlereagh and of killing detainee Brian Maguire. The Northern Ireland Civil Rights Association (NICRA) stated that no one 'in their right mind would pass on information to the RUC or the UDR' when it 'may well find its way into the hands of Loyalist paramilitaries'. The UDR were still described as the 'new B-Specials'. A large proportion of the material published in _Ballymurphy News_ and Turf Lodge's _Starry Plough_ dealt with RUC and army harassment and brutality. Indeed, the Republican Clubs claimed to have been victims of this harassment when councillor Bernie McDonagh was arrested and charged with possession of explosives. There was some internal unease about the emphasis on these issues, with Smullen objecting to the _United Irishman_ headline 'RUC Hangmen' after the death of Maguire, but at the 1978 Ard Fheis a number of motions echoed the demand of Whiterock RCWP that an 'unarmed, community controlled police service' replace the RUC and policemen guilty of 'torture and murder' be put on trial.

Debates about the relationship with the state were to dominate internal discussion over the next two years, but the man who had led the Clubs throughout most of their existence would not be part of them. After months battling bone cancer, Malachy McGurran died in July 1978 at the age of 39. He had been active in the movement since joining the Fianna in 1953. Two thousand people attended his funeral in Lurgan. McGurran was a major loss to the movement. Padraig Yeates remembers: 'Malachy had a political acumen no one else had up there, or down here for that matter. Billy [McMillen]'s death was a tragedy but I think

Malachy's was an even bigger setback. He was a figure leading people in other constituencies took seriously, even Paisley.'

Following McGurran's death Seamus Lynch took over as RCWP chairman and SFWP vice-president, with Seamus Harrison taking over some of his responsibilities in Belfast. There were now two major ideological influences on the movement in the North, sometimes contending, sometimes complementary. Des O'Hagan, though living in the South, was influential with many of the Belfast rank and file. O'Hagan stressed that the party must reach Protestant workers: 'The cost will be measured not in terms of rejection by the so-called Loyalist working class but by the bigots in our own midst.' His bitter hatred of the Provisionals appealed at a gut level, as did his enthusiastic manner and ability to raise morale. The other major influence was the Industrial Department, with Brian Brennan the group's leading local activist. Smullen was also a regular visitor to Belfast, and though his personality was viewed as strange he was popular and influential. *The Irish Industrial Revolution* had been generally well received in the North and the Belfast Republican Clubs were asking for a reprint of the pamphlet in October 1977. Brennan argued that the extension of the British state sector into the Northern economy, as well as providing much-needed jobs, would act as a counterweight to international monopoly capitalism. The Belfast Research Section added an appendix to the booklet's second edition that stressed how multinational investment was 'objectively progressive' in Northern Ireland. But the Industrial Department's critical stance on the movement's republican heritage and the role of the OIRA caused tension, Brennan recalls. He viewed as nonsensical 'the idea that Group A and Group B could run parallel and pretend that Group A was dominant, when on the streets every decision being made had to have the imperial blessing' – i.e. the approval of the OIRA leadership.

The Industrial Department was building its own power base within RCWP in Belfast. Bobby McKnight had been edged aside from a leading position in the Ted Brady Club, which itself was eventually renamed Belfast Central as part of a move away from republican references. The Central branch included activists from several trade unions and a number of delegates to Belfast Trades Council. There were also RCWP members on the Newry, Dungannon and Craigavon trades councils. Members accustomed to clandestine activity often found it difficult to adjust to routine trade union work. During 1977 a representative of the American United Farm Workers, who were calling for a boycott of Californian fruit picked by strikebreakers, was brought on an Irish tour by SFWP. While the California strike was being discussed in Belfast, Brennan recalls, a leading member

picked up the phone to a guy in the unions on the docks and says, 'I want you to stop some grapes.' 'Oh, you want some grapes Seamus, how much do you want?' 'No, I don't want any grapes, I want you to stop grapes coming in.' 'How much do you want us to stop?' 'All of it.' 'ALL of it!' – and the conversation went on like that. So we discovered there was rogue California grapes being dumped into Belfast, and the boys were able to stop it.

Industrial Department cadres were to the fore in demanding the Clubs clarify their attitude to the northern state. At a June 1978 meeting in Mornington Smullen presented a document arguing that sectarianism in the North was 'not particularly bitter' if considered in an international context. It could be overcome, but 'it was necessary to try to look at every question through Protestant eyes'. Smullen was also adamant that the fear of 'antagonizing present support' was not as important as winning Protestant confidence. Several delegates agreed that the party still had a Catholic image in rural areas and questioned the value of its commemorations. Seamus Harrison suggested that the party's 'ambivalent attitude' to the police had to be resolved. But Strabane's Michael Donnelly reiterated that area's view that the RUC should be disbanded. Garland felt that Smullen had been too blasé about the seriousness of communal division in the North, and that there had been times in the recent past when a 'sectarian holocaust' seemed imminent. But he also raised the example of Italy, where the

Communist Party had come out in support of the forces of law and order and the need to combat terrorism. Garland stated that, 'We should have learned that it was only the state forces which could defeat Provisionalism.' There were recurring discussions on the need to update the 1975 document 'The Police and You' and recognition that the RUC were making efforts to improve their relationship with the communities they policed. The organization in Newry reacted to the perceived shift by moving an Ard Chomhairle motion that the RUC remained unacceptable and that the party continue to demand its disbandment.

The Clubs also agonized over whether support for devolved government within Northern Ireland gave the party a 'unionist' image. In theory the party supported a devolved regional assembly elected by proportional representation, with a Bill of Rights to guarantee fair allocation of jobs and housing. In contrast the Provos eschewed any interest in 'partitionist' institutions while the SDLP was hostile to devolution in the absence of power-sharing structures that guaranteed a nationalist role in government. When questions were raised about guarantees of minority rights under devolved government, RCWP responded: 'We are a non-sectarian secular republican party and we are not representing any minority group. We represent the large working-class majority.' The SDLP were increasingly depicted as a 'sectarian, right-wing nationalist' party, many of whose supporters acquiesced privately in the Provisionals' campaign. But there was also a desire among many of the rank and file for a reassertion of the party's republican roots. At Easter 1979, in Milltown, Lynch emphasized that the 'ultimate aim of republicans [was] the creation of an independent socialist republic. We live in a part of Ireland that has been bitterly and deliberately divided against itself by the foreign interests of imperialism.' He also condemned the 'criminal violence perpetrated against the working people by the British military machine'. Similarly, in Newry, Larry Carragher placed the Clubs in the tradition of 'Tone and Davitt, the Fenians and Connolly' and reiterated the demand for a '32-county socialist republic'.

The Republican Clubs had remained active in NICRA despite

the latter organization's decline as an active force in street politics – a decline graphically illustrated when only 50 people attended its 1978 Bloody Sunday commemoration. Of NICRA's 120 members about 50 were RCWP members, as were 3 of its executive. The Clubs hoped that NICRA would become 'a well organized pressure group' through which they could raise their arguments about prison reform. The other main force within the association, the Communist Party, had begun to take a much more sympathetic stance towards the H-Block protesters. Brennan and other Clubs members walked out of the April 1979 NICRA AGM when it adopted a motion supporting political status for prisoners, accusing the CPI of providing 'moral aid and support' to the Provos. The NICRA chairman, Paddy Joe McClean, was close to the Clubs' position and a key ally in these debates. But disagreement over the prison issue caused a majority of Strabane activists, including Ivan Barr, to leave RCWP; Barr later joined the Provos.

The Clubs continued to distance themselves from the OIRA. In March 1978, when police found weapons at the party's Cyprus Street premises, the Clubs claimed that the building was no longer used by them. This incident followed several weeks of clashes with the INLA in the Lower Falls during which a number of shootings and beatings took place. In early 1979 Mac Giolla and John McManus received visits from the Garda Special Branch, who alleged OIRA involvement in a feud in Belfast; Seamus Harrison assured the Ard Chomhairle that the party had 'nothing to do with any attacks or incidents'. In June that year OIRA volunteer Joseph 'Josie' McKee was shot dead by the UDA but was not acknowledged as an OIRA member. The Clubs' public response to the death of a former Official, Hugh O'Halloran, in an OIRA punishment attack in September 1979 was that it was a 'gruesome reflection of the breakdown in law and order' which showed the need for a 'professional police force [which] enjoys the support and confidence' of the community.

The one place where the party continued to acknowledge its prisoners was the United States. In New York Liam Kelly's Connie Green Club was able to attract a broad spectrum of Transport

Workers' Union activists to its fundraisers. During June 1978 at a dance in Queens the Club presented TWU president John Lawe with a spinning wheel made in 'Long Kesh concentration camp' by OIRA inmates. Seamus Lynch also stressed the movement's republican credentials during a speaking tour of nine cities in late 1978, during which he was presented with the key to Madison, Wisconsin; at the ceremony Lynch charged the British with being the 'major source' of violence in Northern Ireland. Ryan was also a regular visitor to the US, and Mac Giolla undertook another speaking tour in early 1980. The movement now ran two pubs in California, the Starry Plough in Berkeley and the Plough and Stars in San Francisco. The Irish Republican Clubs were utilized as a source of information, providing details for *Workers' Life* on the right-wing politics of Republican Senator Alphonse D'Amato, who visited the H-Blocks on a fact-finding mission in 1980.

In Britain the Clann na hÉireann had declined to around 100 members in 19 branches by 1977. While the organization was smaller than in 1974, it claimed to have become more politically aware and consistent. Clann's international secretary Andy Pollock organized a conference in March 1977 on the links between Ireland and international liberation struggles, and an annual event in Birmingham featured Irish music, poetry and debate. Writers Seamus Heaney and Donall McAmlaigh were among the participants in 1979, while journalists Dick Walsh and Rodney Rice were judges in the event's essay competition. Relations with the British Communist Party and Labour were complex. Though one member of the CP's executive, Marion Banks, was also in Clann, that party's links to the CPI meant that some leading members were opposed to Clann on issues such as the H-Blocks. The Labour Party presented even greater difficulties. It was affiliated through the Socialist International to both the Irish Labour Party and the SDLP. The Labour left was divided into several different factions, some of whom took what Clann saw as a pro-Provisional position on Ireland. Clann sent details on the politics of several Labour MPs to the party leadership in Dublin. These included Tony Benn, who had been uninterested when he was contacted in the early

1970s but now saw 'Ireland as a populist issue and wants in on the act'. Among the other Labour politicians commented on were Denis Skinner (seen as 'basically an honest man'), Neil Kinnock ('regarded as an opportunist') and Joan Maynard ('well meaning' though often 'a maternal picture of confusion'). Although party representatives met a Labour delegation in Belfast during July 1980, with the growth of the prisons issue there was a growing lobby within the Labour Party who found the RCWP position anathema. These would coalesce in the Labour Committee on Ireland, which received the support of leading figures on the Labour left including Benn, Maynard and Ken Livingstone and would support the H-Block campaign. Similarly the Clubs met opposition from the Haldane Society of Socialist Lawyers, whom they met in 1980. The Society were 'not impressed' by the Clubs' position on prison reform and felt that the party was giving 'unqualified support' to the RUC.

Amid the growing international focus on Northern Ireland's prisons, RCWP continued to emphasize the primacy of social issues, including the highest jobless rate since the 1930s. There was some optimism that electoral gains would be made in both the Westminster and European elections of 1979. In the autumn of 1978 the DUP had objected to long-standing Clubs activist Tom French being co-opted on to Craigavon Council as a replacement for McGurran. They forced a by-election in which French defeated the SDLP's Bríd Rogers by 1,759 votes to 1,456. The victory evoked euphoria among the Clubs, who had canvassed Protestant and Catholic areas in Lurgan and Craigavon; the result was heralded as a 'new era' of an alternative to 'sterile orange and green politics'. Such optimism was a hallmark of the Clubs' campaigning: although their support was overwhelmingly Catholic, they trumpeted their attempts to canvass Protestant support and continually spoke of breaking through the sectarian divide.

In the May 1979 Westminster poll seven constituencies were contested at considerable cost, with newspaper advertising alone coming to almost £10,000. Prior to the election Lynch was predicting 'major electoral gains', mainly at the expense of the SDLP.

The Clubs believed that the SDLP was breaking up, with a discontented social democratic wing led by Gerry Fitt in dispute with the pro-business wing led by John Hume. Paddy Devlin had already left to form the United Labour Party (ULP) while other former SDLP members founded the Irish Independence Party. Lynch stressed that 'the break-up of all sectarian parties must be welcomed by those anxious to see real class politics after decades of sterile sectarian debate'. Hope of the SDLP's decline was such that the *Irish People* declared RCWP were 'well placed' to become the 'largest publicly represented anti-Unionist force in the north'. In the build-up to the election the Clubs were able, sometimes with assistance from their loyalist contacts, to canvass Protestant areas of Belfast such as Tigers Bay. Canvassers got a friendly reception in some Protestant homes, but they sometimes carried weapons for protection and met threats and abuse.

Despite the optimistic predictions the election results were very poor and only Lynch saved his deposit with 1,907 votes in North Belfast. The Clubs' candidates received 1.7 per cent of the overall poll. In the European Parliament election a month later the Clubs' two candidates, Brennan and Francie Donnelly, took less than 1 per cent of the vote. Ian Paisley topped the poll while Hume, coming second, was the dominant nationalist figure. Paddy Devlin won just 6,122 votes for the ULP, while McAliskey won 33,969 votes on an anti-H-Block ticket. Her votes came despite opposition to her campaign from the Provos, who had once more called for a boycott, and showed that a base of public support existed for the prison protest.

The poor results fed into an ongoing internal debate about the political future of the Clubs. Brennan and his supporters argued that towns like Craigavon, Downpatrick and Bangor, not traditional republican strongholds, were areas where the party could 'create a new base'. In this view there were young skilled workers in these towns who wanted to shed the politics of the old ghetto. As part of building this new base it was felt all remaining ties to old-style republicanism had to be jettisoned. Most members of the Industrial Department's Belfast Central branch favoured dropping the Republican Clubs name during 1979. Brennan went so far as to claim that the 'vast majority of trade union activists' in the North agreed with the party's policies and were only prevented by the party name from supporting them. Lily Kerr, an ATGWU shop steward, counselled caution, arguing that we should not 'delude ourselves [that] changing the name is going to produce more votes . . . we'll still be known as Sticks'. Recalling these discussions one participant remembers feeling frustrated by the unrealistic view that the party did not 'need the votes in the Lower Falls or Markets, our new base is in Carryduff or Bangor', as these were 'places where we didn't even have a member, never mind votes'.

At a general meeting in Belfast in July 1979, many argued that changing the party's title would give the Provos a 'clear field under the Republican mantle'. Accusations by nationalist politicians that the party were becoming 'unionists' had stung some members. In contrast the majority at a South Down/Armagh members meeting favoured change, although some felt that the adoption of Sinn Féin The Workers' Party throughout the country was best. Resistance to the name change reflected the reality of RCWP's reliance on a dwindling Catholic working-class support base. In Belfast the party was still strongest in areas like the Markets, the Lower Falls and Turf Lodge. These areas, especially the Falls, had changed substantially since the early 1970s, partly through huge redevelopment projects that splintered and divided communities. The core membership was still made up of people who had joined the republican movement during the 1960s and their families. Registered party membership in Belfast during 1980 was just over 120, though much larger numbers of people could be mobilized at election times and for commemorative events. There had been an effort to 'tighten up recruitment' which saw only nineteen new members admitted in the previous year, after all of them had attended five education classes. Most members were male, manual or skilled workers or unemployed. There were a smaller number of clerical workers and teachers. Almost all were from Catholic backgrounds, with a few exceptions such as Liam Clarke and his partner Kathryn Johnston, in north Belfast. The SDLP's Brian Feeney recalled differences in style marking Officials out in the Catholic ghetto: 'They wore different clothes. Stickies tended to wear tweed jackets with some sort of Lenin badge . . . they were always neat and cleaner than the Provos, [who] went in for bomber jackets. The Stickies tended to be one strata above in the working class than the Provos.'

The hostility of the Provos, and to a lesser extent the INLA, reinforced the camaraderie and defiance of this small band. Recurrent bouts of trouble brought former members and supporters back into the fold, and a major factor in holding people to the movement was the fear that if an individual left they would have no protection against attack by the Provos. Even the children of activists faced schoolyard taunts and fights for being 'Stickies'. There were constant reminders of previous conflicts. Maureen Fogarty – the widow of Jim Fogarty, who had been shot in November 1975 – took her own life in March 1979. In October John McGuinness, paralysed since being shot by the Provos in February 1971, died after spending eight years confined to a wheelchair. Nor were clashes within the nationalist ghettos the only danger. In September 1979 Peter Heathwood, a leading Official and the secretary of the Lower Ormeau Community Association, was left seriously injured when UDA gunmen attacked him at his south Belfast home. On hearing the news his father Herbert died of a heart attack.

Outside Belfast the movement's fortunes varied considerably. In Newry attendances at the RCWP Easter commemoration were still measured in the thousands. The movement's Plough Club at Trevor Hill was flourishing, holding regular dances, Irish music sessions and lectures. A successful junior boxing club was also run from the premises. The strong local association of the party with the OIRA was a concern for the leadership, who felt there was a 'need for a better image' in Newry. The 'bones' of an organization remained in the villages of rural south Armagh, and there was still a very small branch in Derry city. While members in Belfast, the greater Lurgan area and Newry had some insulation because of the OIRA, west of the Bann there was less protection. *United Irishman* sellers were beaten up in Omagh during 1978 and members in Carrickmore intimidated by Provisionals. Nevertheless, Clubs councillor Frank McElroy became chairman of Omagh Council during 1978.

The party's opposition to the Provisional IRA campaign was reasserted in the aftermath of the Lord Mountbatten assassination and the killing of eighteen British soldiers at Warrenpoint in August 1979. Condemning the killings outright, Garland stressed that 'terrorism [was] the enemy of all'. O'Hagan in particular was developing an analysis of violence in the North that linked it to the view continental communist parties took of terrorist groups. Terrorist activity, in this view, gave the state an excuse to introduce repressive measures which were then used to curb progressive political activity. Hence terrorist groups, no matter what their rhetoric, performed a counter-revolutionary role. RCWP argued that this was obvious in Ireland, where the Provisionals had originally been financed by Fianna Fáil. The party's rhetoric was increasingly uncompromising, with O'Hagan arguing that 'the terrorist is ultimately a fascist'.

At a RCWP conference attended by 120 members in Newry in September 1980, Seamus Lynch argued that RCWP was 'no longer in the backstreets but a serious political party' and had to be clear where it stood on violence, devolution, policing and prisons. O'Hagan felt that 'the one area where we *seem* less than honest is the police' and that the party must 'be to the fore in demanding a modern, professional police service'. Marian Donnelly reported that in south Derry the party's support for devolved government had led to a decline in membership and support. Kevin Smyth argued that the experience of Unionist-controlled councils in Craigavon and Ballymena showed that the 'desire to discriminate' was still there, and that devolved government would give Unionists renewed power to discriminate. O'Hagan dismissed these concerns, arguing that the party should not worry about allaying Catholic fears regarding discrimination and that majority rule would ultimately mean rule by the working-class majority. Liam Clarke suggested that people were right to fear the security forces given their past record, and unless the party emphasized safeguards for civil liberties then many would be alienated by its support for devolved government. Smullen argued that the party 'must campaign for reconstruction and reform' of Northern Ireland and that recognition of the state was a prerequisite to cooperating with Protestant workers. In response Larry Carragher argued that if the party's goal was a republic then its 'long term aims should never be concealed'. Tom French, while agreeing with Smullen's view, felt that it would be 'disastrous' to say so publicly. Into this debate O'Hagan intervened again, stressing that many of the fears expressed were the 'result of our Catholic background'. For many members there was a sense that the key decisions had already been made and that those who argued against the leadership line were not listened to; if they persisted then they would be written off as 'Trots' or 'Provos'.

The Clubs' continuing attempt to develop a new analysis of the Northern conflict was attracting interest, particularly among academics. Historians Henry Patterson and Paul Bew, who had been influenced by BICO's analysis during the early 1970s, argued that the British state could play a progressive role in Northern politics and that the Irish left had consistently misunderstood the nature of working-class unionism: there was 'nothing inherently reactionary about the Protestant working class or, for that matter, a national frontier which puts Protestants in a numerical majority'. Patterson had been sounded out by Smullen to write a Northern section for *The Irish Industrial Revolution*, and was drawn into closer contact with the party. Eventually both he and Bew joined, deciding that the Clubs were the 'only significant group on the left with decent politics'.

Sales of the *Irish People* had declined from 1,200 to just 600 a week in Belfast and it was decided in early 1980 to launch a new RCWP paper, the *Northern People*, edited by Liam Clarke. Robin Wilson, a new member from a Protestant middle-class background, became assistant editor, and the pair became known within the party as 'Batman and Robin'. The *Northern People* attempted to replicate the *Irish People*'s formula and eventually supplanted publications such as the *Ballymurphy News*. The Clubs also encouraged greater use of the mainstream media. A number of supporters worked at the tabloid *Sunday World*; an internal report noted its reporters were 'continually looking [for] stories from us, but personal prejudice about the content and selling theme of this paper has prevented us from using its potential'. It was also noted that a surge in 'human interest' features had also seen BBC Radio 'coming to us looking for stories'. In order to foster such valuable publicity, branches were encouraged to focus on advice centre work and issuing press statements.

As in the South some members feared a 'growing gulf' between the ordinary membership and the 'educated elite' of the Industrial Department. This was a factor behind Brian Brennan's failure to be co-opted on to Belfast City Council in the spring of 1980: Mary McMahon was the popular choice to replace Bernie McDonagh. That 'Mary Mac' had spent ten years 'battling away' in Provo-dominated Ballymurphy, running the advice centre there since 1976, was a factor in her favour. Brennan's defeat was another reversal for the Industrial Department, following on from the 1980 Ard Fheis. Brennan eventually moved to Dublin, where he re-engaged in party activity.

The Clubs members on Belfast City Council developed a good working relationship with John Cushnahan of the Alliance Party. The Clubs now saw Alliance as 'clearly to the left of centre' and felt an agreement with them could help 'break [the] Tory Unionist stranglehold on the city council'. The Clubs also held meetings with the NILP and ULP to suggest a united campaign against cutbacks, and cooperated with Hugh Smyth of the new UVF-linked Progressive Unionist Party in support of a march on the Shankill to protest the cuts. However, Lynch failed to get elected deputy lord mayor in late 1980 after the Alliance councillors split on whether to support him. After Gerry Fitt left the SDLP and denounced the H-Block campaign during 1980, the Clubs' attitude to their old adversary changed rapidly, with a gushing interview by O'Hagan in *Workers' Life*. Eager to present a respectable image, O'Hagan and Lynch attended Northern Ireland Office receptions at Stormont. Party delegates at the Belfast Trades Council, supported by the communists among others, successfully opposed a motion calling for a protest against a National Front march in Belfast in early 1980, claiming that it would only give publicity to the group and that talk of 'smashing' the Front smacked of violence. When Belfast City Council debated a Unionist motion giving freedom of the city to the RUC and UDR, the Clubs councillors absented themselves for the vote.

Political life was increasingly overshadowed by the prison crisis. During 1979 SFWP had continued to downplay the issue, dismissing it as the preserve of 'middle-class dilettantes, academics and [the] supposed left' who wanted the Provos to 'do their dirty work for them'. Garland argued that there could be no question of 'political status . . . for people involved in acts of sectarianism that disgrace the name of humanity'. But during 1980 the H-Block campaign gathered momentum both North and South and attracted broader support; trade union leaders Michael Mullen and Matt Merrigan were among those now calling for political status. Loyalists carried out a number of killings of those prominent in the campaign, including the IRSP's Ronnie Bunting. In late October the profile of the protest reached a new level when seven H-Block prisoners (including former OIRA man John Nixon) went on hunger strike. As the strike dragged on into December, attendances at protest marches grew. In the South SFWP found that some of their own members 'were victims of propaganda and were sympathetic on humanitarian grounds'. These included councillors in Cobh and Bandon and members in Tralee who took part in H-Block protests or signed petitions of support. The party also found that many 'principled' international organizations were supporting the H-Block demands. They decided to respond by distributing to left-wing organizations worldwide an analysis by Garland of the prison issue and its political impact in Ireland.

H-Block: the Socialist Perspective conceded that as those in Long Kesh were convicted by non-jury special courts it was 'very probable that some [were] falsely imprisoned, either through forced confessions, or having been deliberately framed'. But it was also the case that 'many of the prisoners are guilty of some of the vilest crimes ever committed in Ireland'. The majority, over 670, of the prisoners in H-Block were not taking part in the protests, and that number included 190 who had abandoned the blanket protest. Garland argued that the Provos had 'staked all' on the prisoner issue in order to provoke 'emotional support'. In order to stir these latent passions the Provisionals had embarked on 'a very well orchestrated campaign . . . using slogans such as "Don't Let Them Die", ignoring the fact that it is the Provisionals' own organization which can alone decide whether the Hunger Strikers die or not'. Garland claimed that much of the hysteria about the strike was driven by 'Provisional supporters/sympathizers/ultra-left Trotskyists' in the media giving it 'more coverage than is necessary'.

This analysis of the hunger strikes was widely supported within the movement. Accordingly, no sympathy was expressed when three Provisional women prisoners in Armagh Jail joined the hunger strike in early December. In the magazine *Women's View* Mary McMahon claimed that the female Provos treated 'ordinary' women prisoners as their 'slaves' and 'refused to associate in any way with other prisoners, so much for their concept of sisterhood . . . Armagh, like the Kesh, is all about status, elitism and privilege.' But no matter how much the Officials attempted to dismiss the issue, the Armagh protest began to dominate feminist debates, often pitting former sympathizers against the movement. Attending the 1980 Socialist Feminist Conference in London, Margaret McNulty complained that the agenda had been 'sidetracked' by those seeking a platform for the H-Block campaign, though McNulty herself was held under the Prevention of Terrorism Act on her way home to Belfast. There was also a heated confrontation at the Council for the Status of Women Conference in Dublin, where SFWP supporters dismissed a report by Nell McCafferty on the Armagh protest. Former Official Sinn Féin member Margaretta D'Arcy, in a letter published in *Women's View*, harshly criticized McMahon's views on the strike as akin 'to the bigoted ravings from the DUP'. *Today Tonight*'s coverage of the strike was criticized by, among others, *Magill* editor Vincent Browne, who declared at a

Dublin H-Block Action Group rally that RTÉ was now being used by SFWP to further their 'very perverse political objectives'.

Disquiet over the leadership approach to OIRA prisoners was growing. In June 1980 Seamus Lynch had claimed: 'Our party has no political prisoners.' But there were nineteen OIRA prisoners who had special category status in May 1980, as well as a number serving their sentences as 'ordinary' inmates. In Omagh the party bookshop had to be ordered to stop selling H-Block literature. There was also considerable concern expressed at a packed meeting in Belfast, with many of the participants former prisoners them-selves. When the argument against political status was made, 'people were saying to themselves, well, what are you saying? That all of us that were there from 1969 on were all criminals? It just doesn't compute.' But the counter-argument was bolstered by the fact that the Provisional IRA and the INLA had killed comrades, friends and relatives of those present. The polarization around the issue led to more tension and clashes with Provos. McMahon's home was daubed with H-Block slogans during November. The tension finally eased when, on 18 December, the H-Block hunger strike was called off with one hunger striker close to death.

The party continued to try to encourage cross-community contact. A RCWP delegation including Seamus Harrison and Smullen met with Northern Ireland Office minister Adam Butler to discuss the economic situation in March. Unionist mayor John Carson attended a pensioners event in Andersonstown at the invitation of Mary McMahon. On another front RCWP entered talks with the United Labour Party about the possibility of forming a 'democratic left alliance'. During January Margaret McNulty, standing for what was now officially named the Workers' Party Republican Clubs (WPRC), received 936 votes in a council by-election in north Belfast, coming third in a contest won by Sammy Millar of the UDA. The result produced an optimistic prediction of a 'massive swing' towards the WPRC that would mean an extra seat in north Belfast in the forthcoming local elections.

A visit of Dublin city councillors to Belfast ended in violence.

Mac Giolla, one of the visitors, accused the RUC of allowing Ian
Paisley's supporters to wreck the event. The WPRC saw the
spectre of civil war being raised again by Paisley, who in February
1981 began leading thousands of supporters, many waving their
firearms licences, in the night-time rallies on the so-called 'Carson
Trail'.

Despite the obvious difficulties facing the Clubs, the four years
following the 1977 party name change are remembered by Seamus
Lynch as the 'best period' for the movement in Northern Ireland.
The Clubs had redefined their political positions to such a degree
that by the beginning of the 1980s an Official Unionist politician
could comment that some Clubs documents were like a modified
one of his own. The Clubs' stated position was that they were 'not
calling for, at this point in time, British government withdrawal'
from Northern Ireland, though they sought removal of soldiers to
barracks. What fascinated many observers was how in a few short
years both SFWP and the Clubs had moved from open alignment
with the Official IRA to publicly condemning all paramilitarism,
to the point where a Clubs spokesman could claim to the *Irish
Times*: 'We don't deny our origins. But there is no present connection with violence and there hasn't been for some time past. It's a
question of time, of people being convinced that when we say we
are opposed to violence we do mean it.'

Some within the movement, and among the inhabitants of
Northern Ireland's Catholic ghettos, knew better.

12. Group B

'Nobody, I hope, will deny the need for us to have fundraising units.
If we accept this then we must recognise that at some point in
time something may go wrong with dire consequences for all.
This is one reason why we need capable but unknown people
engaged in this activity.'

Army Council discussion document, 1977

On 26 April 1977 the progress of a Securicor van travelling between
Limavady and Coleraine in Co. Derry was halted by a spiked steel
chain laid across the road. After the van's tyres burst it was forced
to stop, and four armed men took over 20 bags of cash from it.
They took an isolated forest road to a quarry, where they began
stuffing the cash – £229,977, the largest amount ever stolen in a
robbery in Northern Ireland – into eight half-skinned deer car-
casses. The manager of Securicor in Derry was a part of the plot;
only when he was told that the men had made their getaway were
the police to be alerted. But an RUC patrol spotted the four
'hunters' and arrested them. At their trial in December 1977 it was
revealed that the heist had been carried out by an Official IRA
unit drawn from Craigavon, Lurgan and Banbridge.

While it had never publicly announced its disbandment, the
leadership of the Official republican movement encouraged the
belief that the Official IRA – now known internally as 'Group B'
– no longer existed. It was seen as imperative to put distance
between paramilitarism and the increasingly respectable SFWP.
There were no public indications that the organization still operated, such as statements or claims of responsibility. But a core
within SFWP was fully aware of its existence and operations.

Group B was also engaged in fund-raising activities in the South. During July 1977 £30,000 was taken in a hold-up of the cash office at Irish Meat Producers in Dublin. Two raiders, dressed in work uniform of white coats and hats, walked into the office and held up staff as they were sorting the weekly wages. In November, £25,000 was stolen when security men were held up while delivering cash to the Bank of Ireland in Westland Row. Two raiders escaped on a motorbike while another managed to get away on foot, despite a Garda chase.

Group B's most notable action during 1977 was the killing of Seamus Costello on 5 October. The INLA leader was hit in the head and chest at close range by three shotgun blasts while sitting in his car on Northbrook Avenue off Dublin's North Strand; he died almost immediately, aged 38. Costello had been spotted in the North Strand some time before by Group B members and it was noticed that he tended to park regularly in the same area. He was believed to have been meeting Willy Stacey, the leader of the Seamen's Union, to discuss an arms shipment. Stacey had performed favours for a number of paramilitary groups, including the OIRA, in the past. It is unclear if the union leader had prior knowledge of what awaited Costello. There were conflicting descriptions of the man responsible for the shooting. A man about six feet tall with dark hair and a heavy moustache was seen leaving Northbrook Avenue shortly after the shooting, but another witness described the gunman as being five feet six inches tall, wearing a suit and dark raincoat. Costello's killing was the first assassination of the leader of an Irish political party.

The murder provoked widespread confusion. Internal instability within the INLA bred suspicion that Costello was killed by someone in his own organization. The IRSP refused to be drawn on whom they suspected and allegations of loyalist involvement or 'pseudo-SAS' squads were bandied about on the far left. A phone caller claiming to be from Saor Éire claimed responsibility for the killing, though naturally many suspected the OIRA. The OIRA denied responsibility in private communication with the INLA, but Gardaí believed the OIRA had killed Costello, having received information on his movements from someone close to the INLA. Such was the residual affection for Goulding that many of Costello's supporters refused to believe that he could have authorized the killing. But in the view of the OIRA leadership Costello had remained a threat. A 1976 intelligence document had argued that the IRSP leader's 'egotism and arrogance' meant that he would continue to try to 'hinder the development' of the movement and concluded that 'while Costello is alive and well, the IRSP will live . . . and he will do all he can to throw it in our path everywhere and on every occasion he can'. The death sentence imposed on him by the Army Council during 1975 had never been lifted. The OIRA in Belfast had been promised retaliation for the killing of Billy McMillen and the circumstances had arisen to make that possible without the Officials being blamed. While there was much later speculation that Jim Flynn was the gunman and had acted alone, in fact he was part of a team set up to kill Costello. Steps had been taken to avoid suspicion. Unlike the 1975 attempt on his life, when a machine gun was used, Costello was killed with a weapon not immediately identifiable with paramilitaries. Shotgun pellets, unlike bullets, offered few forensic clues.

Similarly, in most of the robberies carried out by Group B sawn-off shotguns were now used to avoid obvious paramilitary association. But more sophisticated weaponry was also available. During the July 1977 feud with the Provos in Belfast, an OIRA man had been arrested in possession of an AK-56, a Chinese version of the AK-47 assault rifle. Earlier that year a number of operatives had been called to a meeting in Turf Lodge where they underwent a training class on the use of the AK-56. A small number of AK-47s had also been smuggled to the OIRA from their American contacts, and these had been used in attacks on the British Army in Newry during 1976. The organization was also at work in Europe. The Popular Front for the Liberation of Palestine – with whom exiled OIRA members had trained in the early 1970s – supplied arms to Group B, which were smuggled into Ireland through Holland. OIRA men living on the Continent also made contacts in the Croatian émigré community living in West Germany. The

Croats, seasoned arms dealers who had links to the wartime fascist Ustashe movement, were sympathetic to Irish nationalism and had originally made contact with the Officials through supporters in Australia. By 1979 East German sources had also produced a shipment of new weapons, which were brought into Ireland by truck. Senior OIRA members from Belfast visited Iraq in the early 1980s, having been approached by an Iraqi doctor. They returned with Saddam Hussein watches and other memorabilia, as well as ongoing contacts with the Ba'athists. Links with Palestinian groups brought about an exchange of weapons and Group B involvement in an abortive plot to kill a Zionist target in London. In Dublin, links with the Soviet Embassy were strengthened for both open and covert political reasons.

Group B smugglers made use of influence with dock workers in Southern ports. Newry was an important base for moving weapons into the North, though some units felt that local activists liked to keep the best 'gear' for themselves. During 1977 much of the organization's heavier weaponry had been moved to long-term dumps, stored in grease and placed in pipes buried in the ground. It was usually not necessary for a unit to have more than one rifle or sub-machine gun easily accessible. 'Shorts' (handguns) were more readily available for both protection and use in robberies. All arms use and storage was tightly monitored by the OIRA's Quartermaster Department, but local commanders, particularly in Newry, often ensured they had access to weapons beyond this control. Long-standing party members who were not in the OIRA were on occasion asked to aid in the storing of weapons. On one occasion a SFWP member was asked to find a place to hide arms in Co. Wicklow. Calling to the home of a member of the Industrial Department whom he also knew to be in the OIRA, the party member was disappointed to be told, 'Unfortunately I can't get involved in anything like that . . . we [were] told we are a specially unarmed wing of the IRA.' The SFWP member thought, 'How convenient – you have the status, but not the risk.'

The continued existence of the OIRA was well known to both

the British and Irish governments. In early 1977 Irish Military Intelligence noted that the OIRA had rearmed and considered that SFWP's political image was just 'a tactical manoeuvre to tide them over for the next couple of years'. In their view 'the OIRA/ Sinn Féin must be seen as essentially a revolutionary organisation and a serious threat in the long term'.

In May 1979 the leaked British Army intelligence document *Future Terrorist Trends* received widespread coverage because of its analysis of the Provisional IRA. Group B had been given a copy of the report by sympathetic criminals who had obtained the document in a mail robbery. It was decided not to publish its findings in the *Irish People* as they reflected too well on the Provos. However, *Future Terrorist Trends* also confirmed the continuing existence of the Official IRA, noting that it had 'striven, with a modicum of success, to expand its influence through legitimate political activity' and was 'maintaining links with left-wing subversive groups in Europe'. Although there were no indications that the OIRA was going to end its ceasefire, the organization was considered 'nevertheless ready to re-enter the campaign'.

Training of new recruits was ongoing, usually in the South, often in Co. Wicklow. Northern volunteers were brought to a car park in Sandymount, Dublin, where they switched vehicles and were driven to Wicklow. A leading member of the OIRA would give the volunteers a political lecture before they learned how to use rifles and handguns. One of their training officers noted how many of the recruits still expected to take part in a guerrilla campaign against the British Army at some point in the future, and this belief was encouraged in order to hold their interest. Despite this, an occasional frustrated OIRA volunteer still defected to the Provos or the INLA. Most young recruits were from the North, many having served an apprenticeship in the Irish Democratic Youth Movement (IDYM) before graduating to Group B.

The Dublin Brigade now numbered a few dozen members concentrated in Finglas and Ballymun on the north side and Ringsend and Crumlin on the south side. This structure was largely utilized as a source of intelligence and a support group for robberies, with actual operations carried out by the smaller Active Service Unit directly answerable to members of the Army Council. In Cork, Waterford and the Dundalk area, similarly, only a handful of volunteers were expected to directly assist with armed activity; the wider support network could be called on to assist robberies and was involved in other fund-raising ventures, such as smuggling at local ports. The Director of Operations, a position now held by a long-serving Dublin-based member of the Army Council, believed in carefully planning each raid, using insiders where possible. As a result, many of Group B's robberies were 'hand-over jobs' in which a security guard or post office clerk provided key information. On occasion Group B operatives simply had to collect the funds while the informants told the Gardaí that they had been the victim of an armed robbery. Most insiders were paid for their help. A great deal of organization went into the provision of safe houses, dumps to store stolen money and 'clean' cars. The view of the Director of Operations was that 'no one is any use in jail', and the necessity of avoiding both arrest and the use of lethal force during robberies was drilled into operatives. The Operations Department would often meticulously plan more than one 'job' over a period of a few months and then carry them out in quick succession.

Although answerable in theory to the Director of Operations, Jim Flynn, as the leading figure in the GHQ Active Service Unit (known to some as the 'fund-raising department'), sought an autonomous role in planning and carrying out operations. He preferred to carry out 'jobs' with operatives hand-picked from units on both sides of the border. He continued to work closely with 'McLaren', who was a former Director of Operations. Belfast native Leo Steenson, an IRA member since the 1950s, was also an important but low-key figure in the Dublin OIRA structure. One operative recalled Flynn as 'a shrewd man, a very shrewd man, [he] wouldn't take a chance, wouldn't let anybody else take a chance he wouldn't take, very game but you had to do it his way'. A Newry activist described him as a 'very tough, hard individual . . . fearless and athletic'. Garda detectives nicknamed Flynn, who was over six feet tall and well built, 'the Spider' because of his web of connections throughout the Dublin paramilitary and criminal underworld. They recognized that in the capital a 'tight' unit had been formed around ex-Clann na hÉireann members. Despite the sizeable sums he was involved in securing for the movement, Flynn led a frugal existence with his wife Margaret and young daughter in a corporation flat near Pearse railway station in central Dublin. If possible he would try to be at home in bed shortly after an operation. In the company of people he didn't trust, Flynn would talk about Gaelic football rather than politics. Many of his comrades, some with a degree of disdain, noted what one called a 'certain flamboyance' about his activities. 'Clint', as his detractors nicknamed him, was seen by some as a 'nasty piece of work' and an 'Alsatian' for members of the leadership. But Flynn was also regarded as a 'father figure' by a number of young SFWP activists in Finglas, looking out for them and giving them advice about personal relationships. He was genuinely interested in Gaelic football and went to see both Armagh and his hometown club Crossmaglen Rangers as often as possible. At matches he on occasion discussed football with Tomás Ó Fiaich, the Catholic Bishop of Armagh who had become a cardinal in 1978. Although Flynn had let his party membership lapse, he regularly met Goulding and other members of the SFWP leadership at lunchtimes in Cusack's Pub in the North Strand. Along with his close friend Gerry Doherty, the SFWP Finance Officer, he went on cross-country paper selling trips for the *Irish People*. Flynn's push for more control over operations meant his relationship with the Director of Operations was increasingly fraught. Nonetheless, both were pleased when in November 1978 Flynn led a five-man unit that robbed the CIÉ wages office in Inchicore, taking £150,000. During the raid the depot's staff were locked up in a canteen by the armed and masked raiders, who drove off in a CIÉ van, which they later abandoned. The Director of Operations was particularly happy at this robbery, which had been written off as impossible some time before.

Internally the level of secrecy was such that GHQ Group B

operatives were not to discuss operations even with other OIRA members. The overriding aim was to keep the organization out of the public eye and to avoid tainting SFWP. On one occasion a training officer was transporting weapons when he was involved in a car accident. The arms were not discovered, but as he was also prominent in SFWP the leadership decided to retire him from armed activity. The majority of the Dublin unit directly involved in operations were not party members, though several had been in the past. Some of those who had carried out operations for the OIRA in the early 1970s were now active in trade unions or other forums, and therefore they too moved out of direct involvement in Group B operations. It was getting harder to convince some activists to take the risks inherent in robberies; one remembers joking cynically about risking jail for 'piss-poor candidates that three bank jobs wouldn't get elected'. Greater political respectability and the emphasis the party put on condemning terrorism also meant newer recruits were less likely to be amenable to Group B activity, though IDYM activists were often drawn from family or local backgrounds where OIRA membership held a coveted status. Many OIRA members now only referred to themselves as the 'Organization', or 'the revolutionary party'.

Those OIRA members who were perturbed by the party's denunciations of crime and paramilitary activity were reassured privately that it was a very clever political game to fool the authorities and their enemies. The political loyalty of Group B members meant that they still felt SFWP was 'our animal and we needed to feed it' even if it disowned them. Such loyalty saw one Group B member in Dublin, Willy Kelly, serve his sentence for arms possession as an 'ordinary' criminal in Mountjoy. Similarly two Group B members jailed after an armed robbery in Dundalk during 1980 served their time as 'ordinary' criminals and avoided media attention. The logic behind this non-recognition was accepted by most. This policy was also aided by the idea, expressed by OIRA officers in Belfast, that 'as a Socialist organisation *all* prisoners should be our concern irrespective of their status or "crime", they are all prisoners of the system'. Therefore volunteers should not try to differentiate themselves from their fellow prisoners.

Another view was that ultimately a successful democratic-socialist revolution would have to be defended against a violent establishment reaction. This idea was so pervasive that even the OIRA's most vocal critic within the SFWP leadership, John McManus, could envisage a situation in which armed activity might be necessary, telling the *Irish Times*: 'The only role for the armed struggle is where a clear majority have expressed a view for Socialism which is being thwarted by a small group who are using means to stop it. You defend your gains by armed struggle rather than achieve them.' Among the wider left there was also knowledge of Group B existence, as journalist Brian Trench recalls: 'We would have been aware of it as much as anybody in the Dublin pubs would have known of it; it would have been known that they were involved in bank robberies.'

But as SFWP became increasingly outspoken in their criticism of political violence, they also became very sensitive to any association with it. The party demanded an apology when Belfast's Downtown Radio linked them to 'illegal activity' during 1980. The same year Garland responded to a journalist's questions about OIRA activity by asking, 'Where did it happen? When? I don't know of them and if anybody has information, why don't they go to the police?'

What the party called 'the struggle to get the funds to provide the Party with the wherewithal to carry out the socialist revolution' lay behind the campaign of armed robberies. Many accepted that with mainstream politics heavily funded by business interests, revolutionaries would have to look to other sources. In Northern Ireland some of the proceeds of Group B operations were utilized to fund local party activity, but a growing proportion was transported south, often by sympathetic railway workers on the Belfast–Dublin train. In Dublin these funds, along with those raised by the Southern Operations Department, helped pay headquarters staff and went towards offsetting Repsol's printing expenses as well as the company's contributions to party election funds. Repsol's management was closely tied in with the movement leadership, with Garland as managing director and Ryan, Padraig Yeates and Mac Giolla filling the other directorships. Repsol charged the party for printing but often did not collect these debts. Its financial workings were shrouded in secrecy and it rarely made returns to the state companies office. Knowledge of Group B's relationship to Repsol was restricted to a small number of people within the party.

Even Southern members who had concerns over the OIRA's activities found that, as one activist recalls, 'people were no longer talking about it' and that the issue 'was always dismissed as if it was a sort of prurient interest in somebody else's sex life or something'. With the party leadership explaining away any allegations of links with the OIRA as politically motivated attacks on the party, by the early 1980s some Southern party members genuinely believed that SFWP was no longer associated with an active paramilitary organization.

In the North, however, the OIRA had a much more open presence (in one West Belfast member's view 'it was on every street corner') and was simply referred to as the 'IRA' within the party, while the ghetto communities still spoke of the 'Officials' or the 'Sticky RA'. A close reading of the *Irish News* would still throw up an occasional reminder of the OIRA's existence. Obituary notices for Billy McMillen and Joe McCann appeared from 'Belfast Command Staff, Óglaigh na hÉireann' during 1977 and 1978, and for Gerry Gilmore from the 'staff and Vols of "I" coy, Bawnmore' in 1980. During 1978 several OIRA members caught after a series of robberies in Newry admitted their membership in court. Most of those actively involved in the paramilitary structure in the North were also members of the party, and were concentrated in Belfast, the Lurgan/Portadown area and Newry. In Belfast there was an Active Service Unit of around a dozen operatives, answerable directly to the command staff, which carried out robberies. In Newry these lines were more blurred, with armed fund-raising and extortion operations regularly undertaken even by those prominent in the local party. In all these areas the organization could rely upon a wider milieu of former members who still considered themselves 'Stickies' and would rally to the organization in times of strife.

In areas of the Lower Falls, Turf Lodge and the Markets the OIRA still exercised a measure of paramilitary control, and those who transgressed in these areas or crossed the organization elsewhere were still subject to OIRA rough justice. In August 1977 several OIRA members were arrested after a kneecapping in Moyard, and the resulting court case received press coverage because one of the men was Ronald Spence, a nephew of UVF leader Gusty. Ronald Spence's mother was a Catholic and he lived in a nationalist area. All the men told the court that they were no longer members of the OIRA, the standard claim for Group B members facing charges. Two young men who received life sentences for the killing of James Foots and Daniel Cowan during the 1977 feud with the Provos also denied having any political affiliations. In early 1978 INLA man Joe Heaney was beaten unconscious and shot five times in the legs by the Officials, and Colette Dornan, a sister of Joe McCann but now an IRSP supporter, needed nine stitches after being struck by OIRA members during a related row. After former Official Hugh O'Halloran was accused of hitting a woman in Ballymurphy, in 1979, OIRA members were ordered to give him a punishment beating; he was attacked with hurleys, but his assailants were drunk and beat him so badly that O'Halloran died from severe injuries to the head. Two of the men involved fled to Cork, but there was considerable disquiet about the killing and the Army Council ordered the men to return to the North or be shot. They gave themselves up to the RUC in Newry and received sentences of fifteen years and thirteen years. There was more internal unease in early 1980 when Twinbrook Republican Clubs member Mickey Russell died accidentally after a fight involving members of Group B. The RUC initially treated the case as murder, though a member of Group B was later acquitted on a manslaughter charge.

The uneasy peace with the Provos in Belfast was maintained only through regular mediation. During the tense summer of 1980, youths rioting after H–Block protests had thrown stones at the Officials' drinking club in Cyprus Street. In early September, during more disturbances near Divis Flats, the OIRA opened fire on the rioters and seriously wounded a youth, Joe McCabe. Although hit in the head, he survived. With the threat of renewed hostilities, OIRA members prepared weapons dumps and brought a renewed intensity to ongoing intelligence gathering on the Provos.

Such clashes were not confined entirely to the North. In Dublin, one Group B activist recalls 'many a standing battle with gangsters, [the] INLA, the fucking Provos', often over paper sales in pubs. When a Dundalk member was threatened while selling the *United Irishman*, a team of Group B members accompanied him on his next pub run. Those intimidating him were pointed out, held at gunpoint and pistol-whipped. A similar incident led to a serious controversy with the Communist Party. In November 1978 SFWP administrative secretary and Group B member Peter Kane was involved in a fight with estranged OIRA members from Ringsend. There was the suggestion that a former girlfriend and party member had been involved in setting up Kane for attack. On 17 December, as some of Kane's assailants and former Officials who had joined the CPI drank in the Dockers Pub, Jim Flynn arrived with two carloads of Group B members. He made a dramatic entrance and addressed the company ominously: 'Hello Dingle, hello Davy boy, Mr O'Leary and your friend.' According to the CPI's report of the incident, this was the signal for the start of an onslaught, with guns produced, pub doors secured and the two dissident OIRA men beaten on the heads with the blunt side of a hatchet. CPI leader Mick O'Riordan led a delegation to Gardiner Place to complain about the attack, also raising the status of a threat to Eoin Ó Murchú's life made by Eamon Smullen in 1976.

But the continuing armed campaigns of the Provisionals and the INLA meant that little attention was paid to the Official IRA, which the press often assumed was 'dormant' if not disbanded. One exception was *Hibernia* magazine, which featured an article on what it called 'the most shadowy of Ireland's paramilitary groups' in September 1980. *Hibernia* and its owner John Mulcahy had been the subject of critical articles in the SFWP press and were accused of 'felon-setting' by Smullen because of negative coverage of the party. Olivia O'Leary also raised the issue of the Official IRA in a feature on the progress of SFWP in the *Irish Times*. O'Leary had met members of the OIRA in south Belfast while working on an RTÉ documentary in 1976 and was aware that the organization still existed.

Another function of Group B was intelligence gathering. Political and paramilitary rivals came under scrutiny, as did prospective and current party members. Through contacts in the IDA and the Revenue Commissioners, Group B had access to information that Charles Haughey had not filed tax returns for several years, but it was felt that to publicize this would lead to the discovery of its source. Information was collected on a range of Catholic groups such as the League of Decency, the Public Rosary Movement, the Society to Outlaw Pornography and the Irish Family League, and links were found between these organizations and 'anti-Soviet' bodies such as the Irish Council for European Freedom and Irish Czech Society. Included among those considered anti-Soviet was Amnesty International's Louise O'Brien, who had campaigned on the issue of Russian Jewish emigration; the supposed 'Anti-Soviet pro-Jewish lobby' was seen as an extra element on the right. The environmental lobby, meanwhile, posed a particular danger because it could be used by American big business to persuade underdeveloped countries not to industrialize. Roy Johnston's membership of the environmental group Conserve was noted, as was the involvement of 'elite historian' Kevin B. Nowlan in the Dublin Civic Group. Names, addresses, car registrations and movements of members of these bodies were collected and crossovers in membership noted. 'Ultra-left' organizations – which were believed to be potential tools of a right-wing backlash, no matter how revolutionary their rhetoric – were also the subject of surveillance. A group called Revolutionary Struggle, which had members in Trinity College and in community groups in the Ballyfermot area, was considered virulently anti-SFWP. It was noted that members of this group had heckled Smullen during a May Day rally in 1976. Students Frank Connolly and Ursula Barry, who were believed to have become involved under the influence of Trinity sociology lecturer James Wickham, were seen as the 'most active' members of the group.

Although many of the traditional trappings of the IRA structure had been dispensed with, the Army Council continued to control the organization. With an increasing number of political decisions being taken within the party structures, the frequency of meetings decreased. At its core the council still included the same band of activists who had led the movement since the 1960s. Although Garland was operationally the leading figure, he refused to accept the title of Chief of Staff, which was retained by Goulding. Other leading roles on the Army Council and GHQ staff were carried out by figures such as Mick Ryan, Des O'Hagan and Seán Ó Cionnaith. Mac Giolla increasingly focused on the political development of the movement but maintained a position in the Group B leadership. Smullen continued to hold his Army Council position and combined the roles of Director of Economic Affairs and Dublin O/C. Following the death of McGurran, Seamus Lynch combined the roles of Belfast O/C and OIRA Northern Commander. Even among the Group B leadership, knowledge of specific fund-raising activity was shared on a strictly need-to-know basis.

Decisions about policy and the suitability of members for election to positions within the party were still debated and decided upon within OIRA structures. Once a decision had been arrived at, it would be relayed down the command structure at meetings of OIRA members, which were often held prior to SFWP cumann meetings. The existence of the dual structure was apparent to activists when they would turn up for a meeting 'and you'd find a meeting was just breaking up when you came in, [and] some would stay on and you'd see that there was a two-tier thing'. Most cumainn around the country still contained OIRA members, often holding senior office or respected as long-serving members. In most areas of the North, the process was simpler, as a former member recalled in the early 1980s:

On a Wednesday night we'd meet in the club as the Republican Club. The Club chairman would put forward points for discussion. The Secretary was there. The proposals were discussed and decisions were taken – all democratic. The Monday before, the same people would have met in the front room of a house as the Army. The Chairman was the O/C, the Secretary was the Adjutant. We sat down and decided what decisions were to be passed on the Wednesday night. Today it is less blatant, [but] the principle is still there.

Another party activist describes a similar dynamic:

The IRA was pulled to a meeting beforehand and said now when you go into Cyprus Street you are to vote for this. When Jimmy puts his hand up, you have to put your hand up, because that's the RA and that was the only time the RA was used . . . for threatening people, for robberies most of all [and] whipping us into line to vote.

The need to maintain the fiction that the paramilitary wing no longer existed had consequences for Group B members who were accused of crimes. In September 1978 Group B members carried out a robbery on the cash office of CMP Dairies outside Cork city. A female clerk was shot and wounded during the raid, in which £10,350 was stolen. As they left the dairy the raiders were surprised by detectives and over 30 shots were exchanged with the Gardaí before the gang surrendered. Five men, from Lurgan, Newry, Belfast and Cork, were arrested. The prosecution opposed bail because of the men's paramilitary background. Their membership of the Official IRA was mentioned at the trial but the defendants' orders were clear: they told their lawyer that the robbery had been solely for themselves and disavowed any connection with the OIRA. While awaiting trial they were not allowed to associate with their OIRA comrades in Portlaoise and were given none of the privileges available to paramilitary inmates. The OIRA prison O/C went through the motions of refusing to have anything to do with the men. It was not until after sentences of twelve years were imposed, by which stage publicity had died down and political damage had been minimized, that the men were allowed to join their comrades on the Official wing. The episode led to a dispute within the ranks of the prisoners themselves. One felt that the refusal to recognize their comrades and being ordered not to provide them with food or even newspapers was demeaning; orders were given to the prisoners from the Group B leadership to isolate the prisoner who raised these questions, and he eventually moved to the non-aligned wing of the prison.

By the early 1980s Flynn and other core Group B members were mostly in their thirties, and it was becoming more and more difficult to replenish Group B's ranks with young recruits in the South. One way around this was to collaborate with non-political criminals on robberies. There had been informal connections between criminals and the Official IRA in Dublin since the early 1970s. In some cases these criminals were personally friendly with OIRA members, while others were related to them through marriage or came from the same areas. One former leading member of OIRA's Dublin Brigade recalled discussions in the mid-1970s about the possibility of hiring weapons to criminals to 'let them do the job and take a cut'. By the late 1970s cooperation became more common, especially in inner-city Dublin. But despite the mutual benefits of such contacts, many in Group B were wary of the security risks involved in engagement with 'crims'. There was also friction when criminals attempted to place themselves on an equal footing with Group B, which was seen by its members as Ireland's only 'legitimate' armed organization. On one occasion Flynn became aware that the Dunnes, a Dublin criminal family who had contacts with Group B, had plans that coincided with his own of robbing a major jeweller in the city centre. It was agreed both groups would carry out the job together. On the day of the robbery the Dunne gang met Flynn and his operatives at the rendezvous in the rural townland of St Margaret's in north Co. Dublin. Flynn and his comrades produced guns and left the criminals tied up while they carried out the robbery themselves. As a result threats were made against Flynn, but Group B fired into one of the criminals' homes as a warning not to consider taking the feud further.

One Dublin criminal figure increasingly involved with Group B was Eamon Kelly. Originally from the north inner city but living in Crumlin, Kelly came from a family that had republican connections. He ran a carpet business in Naas which took out full-page advertisements every month in *Workers' Life* during 1981 and 1982. Kelly had a wide range of underworld contacts and used the name of the Official IRA to threaten his business and criminal rivals. Another criminal contact of Group B was Eamon Saurin, an armed robber who was wanted for murder in Birmingham. He also worked with the Dunne gang and other outfits. Immersion in the criminal milieu brought disadvantages as well as benefits. One Army Council member expressed frustration at trying to find out 'who is doing what for us'. But armed robbery quite suddenly became more difficult in the Republic – the total number of political and non-political bank raids declined from 228 in 1979 to just 38 in 1980 – due in part to better bank security and quicker response times by armed detectives, and in this climate dealing with criminals was becoming a necessity. For the time being at least Flynn had the personality to impose some order on these communications.

In the context of SFWP's growing acceptance of the Northern state, a relationship was developing between some OIRA leaders and their former enemies in the security forces. Prior to his murder Billy McMillen had reported to members of the leadership in Dublin that the RUC had made contact with the Officials and asked for a meeting with members of the leadership. This provoked discussion but no direct response. During the 1975 INLA feud Official fundraiser Harry McKeown was taken aback, having been arrested alongside another leading member, to be offered tea rather than the normal dressing down in the barracks. Through involvement in the building-site scams and other fund-raising activities McKeown made informal contacts with 'bent coppers' who aided his illegal enterprises. The relationship with the RUC had become a subject of concern to some during the later 1970s. When Ivan Barr's brother was arrested disembarking from a ferry in England, Barr contacted the leadership in Belfast. He was surprised to be told that a call would be made to a RUC contact, and his brother was subsequently released. It was explained to him that the leadership had met RUC officers during meetings arranged by the Corrymeela peace group, a Christian organization based in Northern Ireland that had been promoting community reconciliation since the 1960s. By the end of the 1970s their changed attitude towards policing made contacts between certain Group B members and the RUC more acceptable, and bred an acceptance that only the state forces could effectively deal with the 'terrorist' threat of the Provos and INLA. Jim Flynn was one of those who worried about these contacts, refusing to carry out operations if certain members of the Northern leadership knew about them.

General army conventions continued to be held on a roughly biannual basis. At these gatherings, which were attended by smaller numbers of delegates than in earlier periods, elections to the Army Council were conducted and the key debate continued to be how much control the paramilitary structure should exert within SFWP. Garland is recalled as continuing to work towards his concept of Group B being stripped of paramilitary trappings and becoming solely the 'technical' arm of the revolutionary party. Others were more attached to the historic significance of the IRA tradition and were concerned about the mounting influence of the Industrial Department, taking the view that if there was to be an 'elite' within the movement then it should be the Official IRA. Personality clashes also coloured debate. Ryan was wary of Jim Flynn and about the fact that he had been given the go-ahead to do certain robberies by other members of the leadership without reference to Ryan. Some, particularly those in the Industrial Department, questioned the extent of Ryan's commitment to Marxism, and Des O'Hagan is recalled dismissing him as a 'crypto-Provo'. To other activists, however, Ryan was 'as honest as the day is long' and had a 'strong sense of obligation' to members, worrying about the lack of accounting for sums being raised and spent. This debate was largely settled when Ryan departed to oversee movement activity in the United States in early 1981, but he was still voted on to the Army Council at a convention held that year.

In Belfast and elsewhere the organization carried out so-called 'insurance jobs', in which a unit would organize a fire in a business in return for some of the insurance claim. In the border area Group B members continued to be involved in low-level smuggling of diesel and commercial products from the North to the South. The other major source of income was the tax-exemption rackets in both Northern Ireland and Britain, and there were strong suspicions by the late 1970s that the British government was prepared to turn a blind eye to such racketeering in order to 'buy off' paramilitaries. The OIRA was able to muscle in on profits from the building of the new Poleglass estate at an early stage. As publicity mounted about the sums being made out of the building trade, British police from the West Midlands Fraud Squad were sent to Belfast to investigate the roots of the scam. Harry McKeown was picked up for questioning, during which he was asked if the concept for the scheme had originated in the USSR. During 1980 a report into the abuse of Housing Executive contracts, overseen by Judge R. T. Rowland, found that a building firm run by Group B members had been awarded a number of contracts from the Housing Executive. It was alleged that the British government was steering money towards firms connected with the group in order to encourage the OIRA to maintain its ceasefire.

In loyalist areas OIRA-connected building firms sometimes worked on sites where security was provided by companies associated with the UDA or UVF. Such relations dismayed some OIRA members, while others looked upon the contacts as working-class cooperation that was useful in decreasing inter-communal tensions. OIRA relations with the UDA were considerably soured, however, with the shooting of Josie McKee in June 1979. The UDA had been informed that McKee was a Provisional and killed him while he worked as a doorman at a pub in Belfast's Castle Street. The Official IRA telephoned a UDA leader and threatened to retaliate against their personnel. A meeting was organized between the two organizations in the Royal Bar in Belfast city centre to 'clear the air'. Five members of the OIRA met six members of the UDA, including Jim Craig and Bucky McCullough, and it was agreed to avoid conflict over the killing. In the aftermath of the meeting relations between Craig and a number of OIRA members became quite close. According to Harry McKeown, 'Craig was a fucking hood, but he was a likeable fucking hood.' Craig was allowed to drink in the Officials' Lagan Social Club and a number of other bars frequented by them. In turn McKeown and his associate also visited UDA haunts in loyalist areas. They tried to interest the UDA in the tax-exemption scheme – to little avail, the loyalists preferring basic extortion – and there were some financial dealings between Craig and the two men.

The UDA leader's familiarity with OIRA meeting places disturbed some in Group B. They were also concerned that not all the finance from the exemption rackets was being paid into OIRA coffers. The Army Council wanted tighter control over the scam and began to put pressure on McKeown and his Markets-based associate who was running it. They demanded that the printing plates for the exemption certificates be handed over. When these were not supplied in a useable form, the dispute became bitter. The OIRA initially planned to assassinate the men – who were also involved in a protection racket related to brothels in south Belfast, including one managed by associates of the UVF – but instead informed the Provisionals that the two were no longer under its protection. The men sought help from the INLA leader Gerard Steenson, even though McKeown had been close to the INLA man's first victim, Billy McMillen. The OIRA and the INLA were forced to meet to avoid a feud breaking out, and it was accepted that the two men were now under the INLA's protection. Despite the loss of these two operators – and the jailing of another key figure in the building-site rackets, Eamonn 'Hatchet' Kerr, for arms possession in 1980 – the OIRA continued to control building sites and tax exemptions in several areas of Belfast. The cash flow from these operations was not too adversely affected by the defections, as the members controlling them were less prone to 'dipping' into the funds. In order to place the financial side of Group B in the North on a more professional footing, a new Finance Officer (who was also a leading political activist) had replaced the long-serving Belfast Brigade officer Kitty O'Kane.

Incidents such as the jailing of Kerr caused concern within the organization, particularly to those who were now seeking election on a platform of opposition to violence. Although he was the dominant figure in the Northern OIRA, Seamus Lynch supported the primacy of political structures in party decision-making. But such considerations would take a back seat in early 1981 as Ireland faced its biggest political upheaval in nearly a decade.

13. Hunger Strikes, Haughey and Heroin

'Following on a decade of sectarian slaughter, murder and terror in Northern Ireland the H-Block hunger strike has been designed to close the era with a renewed crescendo of gunfire, killing and indiscriminate bombings. No matter what efforts have been made to dress up the issue in a humanitarian guise . . . its entire bloody purpose has been to stir up the flames of sectarian and nationalistic hatred.'

Workers' Life, January 1981

On 1 March 1981, Provisional IRA prisoner Bobby Sands began refusing food in his H-Block cell in Long Kesh. This new hunger strike had been planned for two months by prisoners who felt that they had been pushed into calling off the previous protest by promises of concessions that had not materialized. There was a new resolve among the Provo and INLA prisoners that this time they would not flinch until they achieved political status. It was decided to stagger the start of each striker's fast in order to maximize the duration of the protest. As with the first strike, the attitude of RCWP was absolute hostility to the strikers' demands for 'preferential treatment'. At Easter the party pointedly commented that neither Padraig Pearse nor James Connolly had sought special status while imprisoned. Furthermore, it now argued that there was 'no such thing as a political crime' in Northern Ireland. There was a conscious effort to play down the hunger strike in the *Northern People*. The paper argued that 'you can't eat a flag' and that the emotion over the protest was obscuring the reality of economic disadvantage. As rioting broke out after protests in nationalist areas, the Clubs accused the Provos of organizing most of the street violence, charged them with showing scant concern for people's quality of life within the ghettos and predicted that the working class would pay a 'heavy cost' for the 'quite cynical use' of young people by the Provisionals. They contrasted the fact that the hunger strikers 'could make decisions to live or die' with the fate of those on whom 'death was foisted' outside the jails. They had a salient example shortly after Sands began his fast when a young Protestant woman, Joanne Mathers, was shot dead by the Provisional IRA in Derry while calling to houses collecting a census that the Provos were boycotting.

In April Bobby Sands was elected an MP in Fermanagh-South Tyrone after beating Unionist Harry West in an emotional contest. RCWP did not stand in the election, but criticized the SDLP for stepping aside and allowing Sands to be the sole nationalist candidate. When Sands died in early May, RCWP argued that his death had been unnecessary and called on both sides to reconsider their positions. Over 100,000 people attended Sands' funeral. Three more hunger strikers would die during May, while 35 people were killed outside the jails. Street violence erupted in nationalist areas, with 16,000 plastic bullets fired by the army and RUC in that month alone. Three children were among those killed by plastic bullets. RCWP condemned army violence, claiming that troops were intent on terrorizing local areas, but their position remained that the Provos could end the violence by calling off the hunger strike. Once the strike was over there could then be a broad campaign for a radical overhaul of the entire penal system.

Council elections took place in the midst of the violence. The RCWP leadership accepted that in the 'present emotive climate' it would be 'difficult to retain or win seats outside of Belfast'. In the event, the party lost its three Belfast seats as well as those in Tyrone and Derry, polling just 1.8 per cent of the vote. The party did make some gains: Tom French held his seat in Craigavon and Paddy Breen won a new seat there. They also won a new seat in Downpatrick for Raymond Blaney. But in Belfast it was People's Democracy and IRSP members campaigning on an H-Block ticket who took the seats from Sullivan, Lynch and McMahon. Gerry Fitt also lost his council seat while Paddy Devlin narrowly retained his, marking a distinct shift in the nationalist working-class vote. For the Clubs losing seats to PD and IRSP candidates was a bitter blow, compounded when another vocal critic, the SDLP's Brian Feeney, took a seat in north Belfast. The SDLP accused the Clubs of an 'organised and orchestrated campaign of impersonation and intimidation' in an 'all out effort' to save the seats of their Belfast councillors. One SDLP election agent had to receive RUC protection after being threatened in the Lower Falls and the party claimed to have identified 'hundreds' of attempts by RCWP members to impersonate voters. People's Democracy canvassers were beaten unconscious by RCWP members at one polling station.

During the hunger strikes the Clubs had maintained contact with the Northern Ireland Office, which sought their advice on the prison crisis. They found Secretary of State Humphrey Atkins 'useless' on the issue. Mary McMahon recalls the meetings as intensely frustrating: '[spending] two fucking hours on a Saturday telling them where you thought the Provos had changed their position . . . then they would come and say, well, we don't think they have changed their position at all'. In early July a statement from the prisoners, issued through the Irish Commission for Justice and Peace, seemed to offer a possibility of ending the stalemate. The prisoners stated that they wanted no special privileges. Mac Giolla publicly welcomed the statement, arguing that it offered a way out of the crisis and that 'it was a clear invitation to the British government to deal directly with the prisoners'; but he also stated that 'goodwill is something we have never got from the British government' and that Thatcher 'obviously takes pleasure out of seeing them die'. Others in SFWP felt that Mac Giolla was faltering under the pressure of the emotional campaign, and a group of party activists in the ITGWU sent a letter to the leadership complaining about the tone of Mac Giolla's statement. For other members of the leadership such as Des O'Hagan there was no compunction about denying political status to a 'bunch of sectarian terrorists'.

This point was reinforced for members in the North by clashes with Provos. On numerous occasions party members had their windows smashed and the home of a supporter was petrol-bombed in Newry. In Downpatrick a Provisional who had just been released from prison was shot and wounded by the OIRA. Nineteen-year-old Henry Robinson, an OIRA member since 1979, was jailed for the attack; on arrival in Crumlin Road Jail he was badly beaten by Provisional prisoners. There were clashes in Lower Falls as Provos demanded that shops and pubs close for hunger strikers' funerals, while the OIRA ordered them to remain open.

One Belfast activist recalls feeling that the party should take a more conciliatory line towards the hunger strikers, and arguing strongly with one of his comrades about this; but shortly afterwards his friend was kicked unconscious by Provos on the Ormeau Road, and he asked himself why he should support their prisoners. When Kitty O'Kane flew a black flag from her home she was disciplined by the OIRA. When she eventually left the organization, a rumour was circulated that she had secretly provided money to the Provos. Many felt that the hunger strike was the 'last kick' of the Provos and this led them to believe it would be a good thing if they were beaten. Smullen, having spent several years 'on the blanket' in Portlaoise during the 1940s, believed that just as de Valera had crushed the IRA then, Thatcher would now crush the Provos. Others recall comment within the movement on the 'necrophilia' of the H-Block propaganda, the glorification of martyrdom and the black flags as representing 'fascism and death'. Garland felt that 'the Provo leadership could have ended the strikes, but it suited them, because they were developing a base. Thatcher just played into their hands, she was so fucking blind.' McMahon was particularly angry that the deaths occurring outside the jails were being completely written off in the atmosphere of the hunger strikes. But she also thought that RCWP 'failed to separate the hunger strikers as individuals from the hunger strike'. As it happened, four of the hunger strikers had been in the Official IRA at some point: Provisional Francis Hughes and the INLA's Patsy O'Hara, Kevin Lynch and Michael Devine. Bobby Sands had also considered joining the OIRA in his native Twinbrook.

Sands' death meant another by-election in Fermanagh-South Tyrone. The H-Block campaign put forward Sands' election agent Owen Carron against the Unionist Ken Maginnis, while the SDLP again stood aside. Less than a fortnight before polling, RCWP announced that they would also contest the seat, with Newry trade unionist Tom Moore as their candidate. The decision came after a heated debate during which Mac Giolla opposed standing, arguing that there was 'low morale' in the party's small organization in Fermanagh and a real danger of physical attacks on their members. The only reason to stand would be 'if we could stop Carron', but it was more likely that they would get a 'hammering'. There was 'no hope' of gaining any Protestant votes. Smullen argued for standing but did not agree with making prison reform an issue. Instead he felt the party should campaign strongly on the slogan of peace. Garland argued that they had 'talked for years about not being a Catholic nationalist party' but that they would deserve that designation if they did not stand now. They had to 'demonstrate that there was [a] party prepared to stand for class politics and socialism against all the odds'. Gerry Fitt was one of those who applauded the RCWP decision to fight the election, admitting that he had previously thought of them as a front for a 'paramilitary group'.

Tom Moore later recalled the campaign as

the best-fought election I was ever involved in, in terms of the high spirits of all those participating, and also in terms of the political response that we were getting. During the election we made a serious decision and we followed it up – to take our politics to every estate and every village throughout Fermanagh/South Tyrone. There was not an area that we were not seen in; there was not an area where we did not knock on as many doors as was possible.

During the campaign Moore accused Carron and Maginnis of being the 'high priests of sectarianism' and of ignoring unemployment while leading their supporters towards civil war. Unemployment in Northern Ireland had reached 108,089 in July and more job losses were predicted. There were a number of confrontations with H-Block canvassers in which 'hatred' was expressed towards the 'Stickies', but serious violence was avoided. Moore won 1.8 per cent of the vote, which the party described as a 'shred of hope' that revealed a 'committed anti-sectarian base on which we can build'. But Carron won the seat, increasing the H-Block vote.

Both the British government and Provos claimed victory at the ending of the hunger strike in October, after 10 deaths inside Long Kesh and over 60 outside. Through the protests the Provos had widened their support base, particularly among the young, many of whom adopted the organization's hatred of the 'Sticks'. Within RCWP the strikes had heightened an already fervent hatred for the Provos. There was little dissent when the Clubs branded the Provos 'Nazis' after their killing of the Unionist MP Reverend Robert Bradford in November, and a rise in sectarian killings during the winter was seen as the 'bitter and bloody legacy' of the H-Block campaign.

The impact of the hunger strikes on the party in the South was less pronounced. The biggest H-Block marches in Dublin drew substantial crowds of 20–30,000 people, but this was a fraction of the numbers who took part in the tax protests of 1979–80. H-Block prisoners won two seats in the June 1981 general election but these came in border constituencies. The March 1981 SFWP Ard Fheis had convened just as the protests were gaining momentum. In his presidential speech Mac Giolla had dismissed the Provos as 'the military wing of Fianna Fáil'. There was some dissension over a motion which, with some caveats on reform, endorsed the RUC and accepted assurances that 'rogue elements in the force' were being rooted out. But the focus was kept on Southern politics and preparing the party as an electoral force. Central to this was a resolution to draw up a 'Party Development Programme', with the purpose of 'building a mass working-class party which will be capable of achieving state power in Ireland'. Although their vociferous opposition to the Provos was striking a chord, the Industrial Department's power within the movement continued to wane. In the run-up to the Ard Fheis, the ability of the Ned

Stapleton and William Thompson cumainn to propose motions
had been questioned due to their lack of fully 'registered members'.
After Eoghan Harris addressed an 'economic affairs section' meeting in TCD it was decided that the Coiste Seasta had to be
informed about all 'such arrangements'. Harris and his followers
may also have been embarrassed by an *Irish Times* interview with
Conor Cruise O'Brien in which the former TD claimed that his
own intellectual influence was 'perhaps greater among supporters
of SFWP than Labour'. Although the views of those connected
with the Industrial Department had in fact become very close to
those of O'Brien on a number of issues, the party leadership was
still formally opposed to any association with the 'Cruiser'.

Industrial Department activists had been to the fore in struggles
with H-Block campaigners in the trade unions, as SFWP vigorously opposed motions supporting the prisoners' demands. Des
Geraghty argued strongly with Michael Mullen not to allow the
ITGWU's *Liberty* magazine to become a platform for H-Block
propaganda. Party activists refused to join strikes in the building
industry; one SFWP shop steward remembers bluntly informing
those planning a stoppage, 'I'm not giving a minute of my working
day to a bunch of murdering fucking bastards. I don't care if they
die of fucking starvation, I'll have nothing to do with it.' There
were also physical clashes with H-Block campaigners in Finglas,
where there were a 'right few digging matches with Provos; they
knew we weren't going to be pushed around'. Some members did
quietly take part in the H-Block protests, including a former
OIRA GHQ officer who felt that 'if Bobby Sands was prepared
to starve himself to death then who am I to say he was not a
republican?' SFWP councillor Tommy Foley took part in protests
in Tralee. Another who left to join the H-Block protests felt that
Sands 'was in jail for having a gun and every single one of us could
have been in the same position'. Some OIRA veterans living in
Europe were unnerved by what seemed to be a pro-British stance.
One recalled being perturbed at a meeting with Garland and
O'Hagan in a bar in Amsterdam during this period. In his view
'they were saying things to me like I was reading [in] the statements

coming out of the British Embassy . . . it was almost word for word'. But others privately 'applauded Maggie Thatcher' because they felt that the Provos were a 'criminal gang', for whom 'the hatred was overwhelming'. Paddy Gillan argued in *Workers' Life* that when the Provisionals 'say Brits Out they really mean Prods Out. Provisionalism is largely based on a black, sullen hatred of Irish Protestants and Protestantism in Ireland. This hatred has finally crystallised into the most malignant ideology ever to take root in this country.'

RTÉ was another arena in which the H-Block issue led to bitter conflict. There were major arguments among the team that worked on *Today Tonight* about the prominence the issue should be given. SFWP members were quite clear that 'some force had to stand up against the tom-tom drums' of nationalism. Gerry Gregg argued that 'dangerous juju [was] being thrown into the body politic' and that the 'death fasters' had to be confronted. The SFWP members felt that those politicians who opposed the strike, such as Gerry Fitt, should be given prominence. During the first hunger strike a non-SFWP-aligned team – Forbes McFaul, Paul Laughlin and Fintan Cronin – had produced a programme that included hunger striker Leo Green along with victims of IRA violence. Belfast native Mary McAleese was a reporter on *Today Tonight* during this period and felt that her efforts to discuss the mood within Northern nationalism were ignored. McAleese already knew and was hostile to the Officials, having met many of them while working in the Long Bar on Leeson Street, which had been owned by her father. Her cousin John Pickering was a Provisional IRA prisoner in Long Kesh and eventually joined the hunger strike himself. Though McAleese was not sympathetic to her cousin's politics, she felt that any debate on the issue was dismissed as propaganda for the Provos. Reluctance to believe that Bobby Sands could actually win the Fermanagh-South Tyrone by-election resulted in RTÉ sending a crew to cover the count only at the last minute. The SFWP faction, who thought the coverage of the first hunger strike had been too sympathetic to the H-Block campaign, were unhappy with some of the coverage of Sands' death. Over the evenings of

4–5 May, Forbes McFaul had presented *Today Tonight* reports
from Belfast that featured vox-pops from the streets of the Falls
and the Shankill in which intensely emotional views were expressed. He also presented the coverage of Sands' funeral on the
RTÉ News. After these reports, McFaul and his producer Cronin
were taken off the story, and a team made up of Una Claffey, Joe
Little and Tish Barry sent to Belfast in their place. In June Joe Little
and Tish Barry produced *Victims of Violence*, which concentrated
on the results of Provo and INLA paramilitary activity and was
eventually nominated for an Emmy award. After June the attention
given to the hunger strikes by *Today Tonight* declined notably.
Cronin contended that 'the coverage was determined by a
Workers' Party line, it was as simple as that'. Other critics of the
party nicknamed the show '*Today Tonight: the Workers' Programme*'.

Opinions on what was happening at RTÉ varied greatly according to political allegiance. Paud Black, the Fianna Fáil Mayor of
Cork, accused RTÉ of being run by supporters of the Provisional
IRA and of being *too* sympathetic to the H-Block campaign.
SFWP members were united in believing that they had many
enemies in the station. As one of them put it, 'We . . . knew the
political background of many of those in RTÉ, that they had been
active Provos, were active Provos or were members [of] Trotskyite
organisations that even fucking Trotsky hadn't even heard of, [but]
we had half a dozen people that were meant to be running the
organization.' For Gerry Gregg and others it was a matter of
opposing a 'looming' civil war being whipped up by the Provisionals. There was more controversy in December when Gregg
was the producer of a *Today Tonight* feature on Finglas that provoked
outrage from Fianna Fáil, and Gregg lost his position at *Today Tonight*
in 1982 after a programme, inspired by an article in the *Irish People*,
examining how Fianna Fáil was using the state agency Údarás na
Gaeltachta to consolidate the party's machine along the west coast.
Following pressure and complaints Gregg recalls getting a 'letter
from [the] controller moving me on to kids' programmes, so
I brought a Marxist perspective to kids' programmes'.

*

Away from the rarefied atmosphere of Montrose, party morale was high. A Finglas activist recalls 'a huge commitment' in a district where 52 per cent of those under 25 were unemployed. In 1981 the party did a survey among women in the area, and the issues of health and childcare had arisen repeatedly; as a result a party women's group was set up and became what one activist calls 'a good structure for introducing women with no political experience to politics'. De Rossa campaigned for state funding for a family planning clinic in the area. The campaign was not confined to the women's group, as long-standing activist Brian Whelan remembers: 'Imagine a hairy-arsed fucker like me sitting down talking to a load of women about contraception, but that was the name of the game.' In other parts of the country, Finglas was increasingly held up as an example of 'how to build a revolutionary party'. All the party's fifteen candidates in the 1981 general election were male and eight were blue-collar workers, including two carpenters, a docker, a factory worker and a labourer. Two were teachers. Mick White and Pat McCartan, both solicitors, and John McManus, a doctor, were the only professionals. The party campaigned for the provision of 120,000 new jobs by state companies, for a freeze on food prices and an extension of maternity leave, for childcare to be provided by all employers, and for major reform of the tax system to take the burden off the PAYE sector.

SFWP achieved a breakthrough with the election of its first TD, Joe Sherlock in Cork East. Sherlock took a seat from Fianna Fáil in an area where he had been building up a base since his election as a councillor in 1967. His long campaign to keep Mallow Hospital open had been commented on when the hospital played a key role in the aftermath of the 1980 Buttevant rail disaster. Although Cork East was seen as a rural constituency, a large part of the population was dependent on factory work, and most of the local SFWP members were employed in the Mallow sugar factory or the Mitchelstown creamery and bacon factory. On the night of his election Sherlock told his supporters in Mallow that 'we have only begun the real fight on the road to a socialist republic'.

Overall, though, the SFWP candidates won the depressingly

familiar figure of 1.7 per cent of the poll. Sherlock's 14.6 per cent was the highest vote the party secured, followed by Paddy Gallagher's 8 per cent in Waterford. Internally the party admitted that 'we had expected to take a seat in Waterford' and that not doing so was a major disappointment. It was at least partially due to the H–Block factor: hunger striker Kevin Lynch had won 3,337 votes in the city. But the party was happy with increased votes in Wicklow, through McManus, and Carlow-Kilkenny, through Sean Walsh. Sherlock's election was seen as the 'all-important breakthrough'. There were now 'people talking about us that never heard of us six months ago and we are now in the mainstream of Irish politics as never before'. There were 'no short cuts' to success; only 'hard slog' would 'bring Sinn Féin The Workers' Party to every household in the land'.

Having an elected member of the Dáil brought new problems. Neither Fianna Fáil nor Fine Gael was able to form a majority government and both were soon in contact with Sherlock, seeking his support. Sherlock complained that Fianna Fáil were engaging in 'scurrilous' tactics, putting personal pressure on him, alluding to a shared republican past. SFWP called (unsuccessfully) for the Labour Party to stay out of government and form an alliance with Sherlock and the two other left-wing TDs, the Socialist Labour Party's Noel Browne and Limerick independent Jim Kemmy. Sherlock voted against the nomination of Haughey for Taoiseach and abstained on the vote for Garret FitzGerald, who emerged as head of a minority Fine Gael–Labour government. Sherlock stated that he had no 'commitment' to the new coalition but would judge every issue as it arose. The party viewed the government as the 'lesser of two evils'. Privately Goulding opposed the decision to abstain on the vote for FitzGerald as Taoiseach, pointing to Fine Gael's Blueshirt history. Though no longer part of the day-to-day leadership of the party he still made his voice heard at Ard Chomhairle meetings.

When the coalition outlined a supplementary budget in July, Sherlock denounced it as 'savage' but abstained on the vote. *Irish People* sellers in Finglas reported 'adverse feedback' to Sherlock's abstention, and there were official complaints from cumainn in Waterford and Cork city. Mac Giolla was forced to explain the position in the *Irish People*. He argued that a Fianna Fáil budget would not have been any more progressive than the coalition's and that it was not opportune to bring down the government at this time.

In September, according to a Coiste Seasta note, Sherlock complained that party leaders were working out strategy without consulting him. Ironically, he shared a Dáil office with Neil Blaney and Sean 'Dublin Bay' Loftus, both regarded by SFWP as enemies. Perhaps surprisingly, Blaney was helpful in explaining how to work the Dáil rules. Sherlock had no secretarial back-up of his own to begin with. He found the Fine Gael TDs ignored him and Fianna Fáil regarded him as having stolen one of their seats. In December he raised the question of the huge subsidies paid to cattle exporters who exported live animals to the Middle East while jobs were lost in Irish meat factories. He was suspended from the Dáil for demanding a debate on job losses in the meat industry.

The coalition was unstable and, with another general election a real possibility, all SFWP cumainn were instructed to appoint a director of elections, raise funds, set up citizen's advice bureaux and organize supporters into 'constituency councils' to prepare for campaigning. All areas were to undertake door-to-door *Irish People* sales, produce a local newsletter, and establish 'solely SFWP campaigns . . . initiated totally by the local Party' for a 'Health Centre, a community centre, a swimming pool, a new bus route . . . even if you don't succeed you will have put the Party stamp on the issue'. In November Garland had argued that their task was 'to become a Workers' Party in fact as well as name . . . there is a class content in every issue and we must always put this to the fore'. The party had to 'persuade the vast numbers of working-class people who cast their votes for Fianna Fáil that they are voting against their own interests'. There was a need to 'be in contact with the people in every aspect of their lives. Not simply on polling day but within their local communities, their sports places, their streets, their public houses, their schools, their colleges.' In January 1982 the party launched the 'Campaign for the Nationalisation of the Banks', calling for public ownership in place of the 'present system whereby a small but immeasurably powerful group of bank directors and shareholders control the nation's wealth'.

On 27 January, Sherlock and Kemmy voted against the government's budget, objecting to measures including a new tax on children's shoes, and the coalition fell after sitting for just 35 days. As the party planned strategy for the election, John McManus argued for a five-point programme of demands on the Labour Party, including tax increases for the wealthy, in return for participation in a left alliance. Party literature pointed out that while large working-class suburbs such as Finglas, Ballyfermot and Crumlin had populations similar to those of Galway or Limerick, they lacked many of the facilities of the provincial cities.

In the February 1982 election the party again fielded fifteen candidates, and increased its share of the vote to 2.3 per cent. Sherlock held his seat and increased his vote slightly, while in Waterford the disappointment of the previous year was overcome when Gallagher was elected. In Dublin North-West Proinsias De Rossa also won a seat, coming in well ahead of Labour. Both Mac Giolla and Eric Byrne also polled well, though neither could win enough transfers to take a seat. SFWP had become the first party since 1957, apart from Fianna Fáil, Fine Gael and Labour, to have three TDs in the Dáil. The election resulted in another hung Dáil, with neither Fianna Fáil (81 seats) nor the outgoing coalition of Fine Gael–Labour (78 seats between them) able to form a stable government without additional support.

Initally SFWP called on Labour to stay out of coalition and help form a 'workers' opposition' to the two main parties – they pointed out that three of Labour's TDs had been elected on SFWP transfers – but the party claimed that Labour's hostility made its efforts to find a common strategy a 'non-starter'. Labour's hostility was real: Ruairi Quinn had commented that unlike SFWP, his party did not 'have anyone's blood on our hands'. Quinn also suggested that SFWP had opportunistically dropped unpopular policies: 'You don't hear them shouting now about an oil refinery in Dublin Bay.'

The re-election of Kemmy, the election of new independent TD (and former Official) Tony Gregory in Dublin Central, the strong SFWP showing and the parliamentary maths also raised suggestions of a new 'left alliance' outside of the Labour Party. In early March Kemmy and Gregory announced that they would be interested in forming a 'left bloc' with the three SFWP members. Although the five would have held the balance of power in the Dáil, the alliance did not come together. Gregory found the SFWP TDs reluctant to deal with him, presumably because of his support for Costello in 1975 and his views on the North, which they saw as pro-Provisional. Kemmy had his own worries about SFWP's heritage, and SFWP in turn distrusted his 'two-nations' view of Northern Ireland.

With the party coffers exhausted by two campaigns within ten months, the SFWP leadership were not eager for another general election and were prepared to see if concessions could be won from either FitzGerald or Haughey in exchange for the party's support, and commenced discussions with both party leaders.

During the talks the Federated Union of Employers and the Irish Farmers' Association warned that 'unrepresentative' organizations should not be allowed to influence the new government. Garland and Mac Giolla countered that the FUE and IFA had 'ruled the roost for decades' but that the working class would now have a voice in the Dáil. Haughey and his colleagues Ray MacSharry, Ray Burke and Brian Lenihan met the SFWP TDs along with Mac Giolla and Garland; private meetings also took place between Garland and Brian Lenihan in the Gresham Hotel. SFWP demanded promises on tax, unemployment and poverty. They raised the question of Haughey's opposition to devolution in Northern Ireland and their demand for a divorce referendum. Fianna Fáil promised to find a new owner for the threatened Clondalkin Paper Mills and if necessary to nationalize them. They also agreed to ensure laid-off Clover Meats workers in Waterford would be allowed their social welfare benefits, and promised to publish a comprehensive social and economic plan which SFWP could judge on its merits. On the strength of these undertakings, the party decided to support Haughey's nomination as Taoiseach. SFWP argued that FitzGerald was a 'prisoner' of Fine Gael's right wing and was committed to 'monetarist and anti-working-class policies' if in government.

Given SFWP's previous antipathy to Haughey, the deal gave rise to critical comment and to rumours of secret deals over the OIRA's prisoners and mysterious Middle Eastern contacts. On the day of the vote for Taoiseach the three SFWP TDs found themselves locked out of the Dáil chamber, and had to be given access by Fianna Fáil to the press gallery, from which they clambered into the distinguished visitors area and then actually jumped into the chamber before casting their votes. Labour leader Michael O'Leary acidly commented that their 'method of entry was somewhat unorthodox. But their eagerness cannot be in doubt.' In the *Irish Times* Dick Walsh commented that the manner of their arrival was nothing compared to the ideological 'hoops that they must have jumped through' in order to vote for Haughey. Sherlock said that the party was voting for Fianna Fáil because 'it appears to us to be the choice of the voters that there should be a Fianna Fáil government' and because another general election would 'not be in the interests of the working class'. He claimed that the party had 'done no deals' with Fianna Fáil but would judge 'every issue as it affects the interest of the working class'. Sherlock restated the party's opposition to any attempts to end Irish neutrality and their desire for a 'democratic, secular, socialist unitary state'; but SFWP would resist any attempt to coerce the people of the North into a united Ireland. The *Irish People*'s readers were assured that: 'Charlie may be back in the saddle, but he's wearing an SFWP bridle.'

Haughey was elected Taoiseach with the support of SFWP, Tony Gregory and Neil Blaney. Haughey had secured Gregory's support – which would have been indispensable if he had failed to secure the SFWP votes – with a £80 million plan for inner-city development. There was some internal disquiet over the SFWP decision to back Haughey, as Padraig Mannion recalls:

We were particularly unhappy because we knew exactly the nature of Haughey . . . he was personally dishonest . . . he was politically dishonest . . . his whole 'wrap the green flag round me' persona was a load of nonsense . . . if he thought 'wrap the Orange flag round me' was a better short cut for power he would have wrapped the Orange flag round him, he would have wrapped any flag round him; as we know, he would have wrapped [the] Dunnes Stores better value flag round him.

In the North, 'most' of the membership 'understood' why the decision had been taken and it was thought that it would have 'nil' effect on unionist perceptions of the party. But Fr. Michael Sweetman, an ally of 1960s Sinn Féin and long-time critic of Haughey, wrote to the SFWP leadership to signal his disagreement with the decision. Relations with the other two left TDs were also soured. Despite SFWP's own alliance with Fianna Fáil, *Workers' Life* accused Gregory of having 'turned his back on true socialism' by his deal with Haughey, which had put 'parish pump politics in an urban setting . . . on a lavish scale'. Kemmy, who supported FitzGerald for Taoiseach, presented a different problem. During 1982 his Limerick organization merged with the Socialist Party of Ireland and elements of BICO to form the new Democratic Socialist Party. Kemmy remained highly suspicious of SFWP's republican heritage, and when interviewed for *Workers' Life* by Gerry Flynn he made it clear that he regarded the continued existence of the OIRA as a problem. (The interview was not published.)

A further question presented itself for the new SFWP TDs: should their salaries be at the disposal of the movement? It was agreed by the leadership that the TDs' salaries were a 'personal matter and not for discussion'. The Waterford organization was in favour of TDs contributing at least part of their pay to the movement, and Paddy Gallagher accepted this, but it was agreed instead that the TDs were 'full-time workers' for the party and were thus entitled to keep their salaries.

The SFWP Ard Fheis took place in April in a mood of high confidence. Delegates gave a tumultuous welcome to the three

TDs, who were introduced on to the stage by Mac Giolla as he announced that 'the battle has only begun in the war of the classes'. The main debate at the Ard Fheis was over a proposal, introduced by Garland, to drop the Sinn Féin title and become simply the Workers' Party. Many Northern delegates claimed that the party was increasingly attracting Protestant members and that the name change would be of great help in this process. Others argued that being called Sinn Féin linked the party to 'terrorism' in the public mind. Jim Sullivan, who had argued strongly in the past against dropping 'Sinn Féin', now endorsed change, reassuring delegates that he regarded the WP as the same organization he had joined in Belfast as a teenager. Unlike in previous years there were no speakers against the motion, and there were only 13 votes against it from a hall of several hundred delegates.

The only serious dissension emerged over motions seeking to change the party's official attitude to the confrontation between the Solidarity trade union and Poland's Communist government, which had racked that country since 1980. Ted Tynan's opposition to a pro-Solidarity motion at Cork Corporation in January had provoked a hostile reaction among the local party rank and file, and one rural cumann demanded a statement from the WP in support of Solidarity. To the surprise of many of his colleagues, Smullen argued that the party should make clear it was 'in support of democracy' and 'against outside [i.e. Soviet] interference' in Poland. The leadership's official position was outlined by Ó Cionnaith in the party bulletin *Notes and Comments*. Ó Cionnaith claimed that Reagan and Thatcher's support for Solidarity proved that it was a counter-revolutionary movement. The Solidarity leadership was made up of 'Social Democratic, Fascist, Anarchist and Trotskyist' elements and was being manipulated by the Catholic Church and the CIA in an effort to destroy socialism in Poland. Ó Cionnaith compared the Polish opposition group KOR to the Red Brigades, the Baader-Meinhof gang and, most damningly for his readership, the Provos. But the debate re-emerged at the Ard Fheis with motions calling for support for Solidarity and its 'democratic' aims. Garland made it clear that the WP supported the introduction of martial law in Poland as the 'armed forces had to take the action they did in order to stop the country from sliding into anarchy and total chaos and ultimately into the hands of the imperialists'. Many WP members agreed. Union official Mike Jennings recalls feeling that 'if I had a choice of living in a country ruled by General Jaruzelski or the Pope, I would choose the General any day . . . I never saw [Solidarity leader Lech Walesa] as a trade union official, I could never see beyond his Marian badge.' The pro-Solidarity motions were withdrawn under pressure and the Ard Fheis endorsed the leadership view.

In May, Mac Giolla took 6,357 votes in a by-election in Dublin West, a strong showing which suggested that the WP president could take a seat at the next general election. During 1981 the *Irish People* had hammered away at political corruption in west Dublin, naming businessmen Patrick Gallagher, Gerry Jones and Fianna Fáil TD Liam Lawlor as beneficiaries of corrupt land dealings. In the run-up to the election the paper ran a story about another rezoning scandal involving Lawlor. Prior to the election Eoghan Harris had contributed what he called a 'soft script' for the WP's televised party-political broadcast. He argued that they should present the 'democratic and liberal' aspects of party policy so as not to alienate those who thought the WP was 'excessively workerist'. The script was meant to appeal not 'only to workers in Ballyfermot but [to] technical and white-collar workers . . . and also gather the support of teachers and journalists who will respect a party that is not afraid to quote Joyce'.

Despite the overwhelming support for the name change at the Ard Fheis, the party's new course was still a source of tension, illustrated in dramatic fashion by a 'major row' during an Easter commemoration social in Cork in early April. One group, around Ted Tynan, was against holding the event while another faction, led by Doc Doherty, was for it. During an oration by Mac Giolla, which Tynan described as 'inflammatory', arguments broke out that resulted in bottles and glasses being thrown and punches and kicks exchanged. Rumours abounded in Gardiner Place that guns had been, or nearly been, drawn. An inquiry was set up and party activity in Cork city suspended for its duration. The report found there were serious 'ideological differences' among the city's membership and that a 'total lack of education' among the membership had led to the 'degeneration of the party' in the city. John McManus argued that the party's Cork HQ, the Thomas Ashe Hall, was a 'dump' and should be sold. Tynan resigned his corporation seat, claiming that his decision was motivated by personal factors. The seat was taken by Cork East organizer John Kelleher.

The party's enhanced political profile brought added scrutiny. Prior to the vote for Taoiseach, Garland and Mac Giolla had been interviewed by Marian Finucane on RTÉ Radio's *Day by Day*. She asked them about the alleged connections between SFWP and the Official IRA. Mac Giolla claimed that as far as he knew the OIRA 'no longer exists'. On further questioning he said that if such a group did exist it had no association with his party. Garland claimed that Official Sinn Féin 'never had guns [and] never had any control over the Official IRA'. In January the Ard Chomhairle were informed that Vincent Browne of *Magill* magazine had been in contact seeking interviews for a feature on SFWP. The front page of *Magill*'s April edition, published just before the Ard Fheis, was headlined 'The Secret World of SFWP' and contained an exposé of the continuing activities of the Official IRA. Browne listed a number of killings that had occurred since the 1972 ceasefire and a number of cases in which OIRA members had been jailed for armed robberies. He argued that the OIRA was intimately linked to the SFWP leadership and that its Chief of Staff, Adjutant General and Dublin O/C were members of the party. Most notably, the main article suggested that a key OIRA figure had been responsible for the killing of 'a prominent individual in Dublin in the course of the last five years'. This figure was described as a former Clann na hÉireann activist who had been deported from England in the mid-1970s. This individual was also placed at the centre of the incident at the Dockers Pub and held responsible for several armed robberies. To those in the know, Jim Flynn was immediately recognizable as the OIRA figure in question, and the 'prominent individual' could only be Seamus Costello. The following edition of *Magill* contained a number of articles on the political development of the WP, dealing with its influence in the unions, RTÉ and the role of the Industrial Department. Browne argued that the party had undergone a 'political lobotomy' over the previous decade, moving from republican to pro-unionist. Examining the role of the party in RTÉ, Browne claimed that six of the *Today Tonight* editorial staff held WP sympathies and had succeeded in influencing the programme's output. Browne also, improbably, described SFWP as 'probably the richest party in the country, bar none'.

The WP leadership, stung, told members that Browne had been supplied with lies by embittered ex-members, who were themselves alleged to be responsible for some of the killings listed in *Magill*. The party suggested to the *Irish Times* that if Browne had information on criminal activities it was his 'duty' to go to the Gardaí. Garland claimed that he had 'no knowledge' of the Official IRA and to suggest that such a body was connected to the WP was 'laughable'. He explained that 'our total opposition to terrorism . . . the fact that we stood almost alone when the Provisionals were trying to create a civil-war situation with their hunger strike . . . explains in some senses the motivation behind the recent slander campaign'. Mac Giolla stated that the WP had 'nothing whatsoever to do with violence or violent organisations. The people with a vested interest in promoting such stories [were] increasingly no longer credible.' This became the party's standard reply to such allegations. The party made public statements about the possibility of libel actions, but Pat McCartan advised them of the 'disadvantages' such a case might involve. Mac Giolla turned down an invitation to debate Browne's allegations publicly in Trinity College, contriving a 'prior engagement'.

In the aftermath of the *Magill* articles Jim Flynn was questioned by Gardaí about the killing of Costello. This did not prevent him from organizing another major heist: in late May £300,000 was taken from Newry Head Post Office in an operation involving Flynn and local Group B members. The three-man gang used a

Royal Mail van to gain access through the office's security gates, then held up staff before driving off with the cash and transferring to a different car and making their getaway. Back in Dublin on 4 June, Flynn left Cusack's Pub with Leo Steenson, having met members of the Group B leadership at lunchtime. A man stepped out of a phone box and shot him three times in the head, chest and abdomen. The gunman then turned to Steenson, but his weapon misfired. He escaped with an accomplice on a motorbike. Flynn died 90 minutes later in the Richmond Hospital. He had been shot 100 yards away from where Costello had been killed.

The INLA claimed responsibility and singled Flynn out as having been responsible for Costello's death. They claimed that they had received this information from disgruntled members of SFWP who had left the party during the hunger strikes. The INLA also indicated that the atmosphere created by the *Magill* articles had made the killing of Flynn more 'publicly acceptable'. They warned that the WP leadership would be held responsible for any retaliation by the OIRA. The *Irish Times* received a statement from the Official IRA stating that their leadership deeply regretted the death of Flynn and were 'conducting an investigation to discover those responsible'. Within hours Browne received threatening phone calls and was placed under Garda protection. Browne rejected any connection between his article and the killing, saying that the rumours about Flynn were well known among paramilitaries and others in Dublin and that there was no justification for his murder.

Garda detectives noted panic and confusion at headquarters level in the aftermath of Flynn's murder. De Rossa claimed that Flynn had never been a party member and that he had heard that he was killed as part of an internal INLA feud. But Gerry Doherty, a member of the WP Ard Chomhairle, described Flynn as a 'staunch party supporter'. The dead man's family demanded an Official IRA funeral, but a compromise was worked out whereby he was claimed as a member by Clann na hÉireann. Several leading WP figures, among them Smullen, Ó Cionnaith and Flynn's close friends Doherty and Padraig Yeates, attended his removal in Dublin and funeral in south Armagh. As the coffin, draped in the Irish tricolour and the WP's Starry Plough, was driven through Dublin it detoured and paused outside Gardiner Place. It was then brought to the border under Garda escort and across an unapproved road into Crossmaglen. A large number of WP members from across the North and Britain heard Clann na hÉireann president Seamus Collins denounce the 'cowardly assassins' who had murdered Flynn and claimed that they were 'the same people who would see the streets of our towns and cities flow red with the blood of our people, the Irish working class'. The mood among Flynn's comrades was angry, and *Magill* reporter Gene Kerrigan was warned to leave the church or 'heads and cameras would be broken'. Group B members in Belfast were told that Browne's movements were known to the OIRA and that he was to be killed while on a boating trip; this would happen when the public commotion had died down so that it could not be used to damage the WP. Group B also discovered that some of the information for the *Magill* articles had been supplied by Belfast-based journalist Ed Moloney, who had been a Republican Clubs member. After the February election Moloney had written an article on the continuing activities of the OIRA for the *Irish Times*, but it was not published. Moloney made his material available to *Magill*; meanwhile, an *Irish Times* sub-editor passed on the article, without Moloney's knowledge, to the WP, and they recognized Moloney's material when the *Magill* articles appeared. Group B then told their contacts in the UDA that Moloney was an INLA intelligence officer. Luckily for him, the UDA's own investigations did not bear this out.

Some of Flynn's comrades acknowledged the difficult position the WP was placed in by his death. Yet the claims that he was not known to the leadership rankled: 'They should have stood up at that time and said he was one of ours . . . but I think Jim may have understood the dilemma they were in.' Money was raised within the movement to put up a headstone at his grave in Crossmaglen. Shortly before his death, aged 37 and feeling increasingly wary of life on the edge, Flynn had discussed his growing resentment with the 'arm's length' treatment given to him by some members of the

WP. Yet although Group B in the South depended heavily on his organizational skills, he continued to be held at arm's length in death.

In June Yeates resigned as *Irish People* editor. He had become dissatisfied with the paper, feeling it needed to expand in size and ambition. By 1982 the paper generated about £300 a week in net profits, but this 'all went into the bottomless Repsol pit to help pay other bills'. Yeates had lobbied to get at least some of the money 'ring-fenced so that we could develop the paper', but Garland was opposed to any new departures, seeing no need to 'change a winning formula'. Around the same time, the three WP TDs complained within the party of the 'tremendous task' they faced and the need for more secretarial back-up in Leinster House. Yeates agreed to become the WP publicity and research officer in the Dáil on a short-term basis until the position could be filled permanently, and in July Tony Heffernan became party press officer, having rejoined the WP a few months before. Garland told Heffernan that 'he wanted somebody [that] could keep an eye on the TDs'.

Their support for the Haughey government was causing some discomfort for the WP. Fine Gael taunted them as 'Fianna Fáil's little party' whose TDs 'broke [the] furniture and fittings of Dáil Éireann in their haste to vote for Charles J. Haughey for Taoiseach'. Eoghan Harris reported in a letter to the leadership that 'around my own workplace and in media circles [there was a] perception of us being anxious to vote for Fianna Fáil at all costs'. This feeling, he claimed, had 'congealed around Joe Sherlock'. Sherlock's relatively traditional republicanism was not universally popular within the party. There was also disquiet over a payroll tax (PRSI) increase in the Budget, which gave rise to strikes and embarrassed the WP, who were opposed to such measures. The TDs were instructed to make their support for the walkouts clear. De Rossa met Aer Lingus strikers and brought their union representative, former Official Sinn Féin member Frank Keoghan, into Leinster House. The WP TDs suggested 24 amendments to the Finance Bill, which was necessary to put the Budget into effect, and put down a private member's motion calling for a reduction of employees' PRSI to the 1981 level. The party believed that both Fine Gael and Labour were trying to 'entrap' it into bringing down the government. In one case Fine Gael moved a resolution that the government nationalize an ailing factory in Kilkenny, clearly hoping to embarrass the WP TDs; but they were able to support the motion as it was not an issue on which a lost vote would bring down the government. The WP noted internally that 'our approach has been and should continue to be to maximise our position to highlight [the] similarities between the Coalition and Fianna Fáil but more importantly, we should use our position to educate the working class of this country to a degree of political awareness of their status of a class, and be proud of that fact'. Members were reassured that their TDs were in 'total confrontation' with Haughey's Northern policy.

By the autumn the government was lurching from crisis to crisis, most dramatically the arrest of a double murderer at the home of the Attorney General, and Haughey was subjected to an internal leadership challenge. The WP did not relish a third general election in the space of just over a year. Many local party organizations were still in debt from the two previous contests, and activists were exhausted. There were particular problems in Waterford. Local activists had noted that Paddy Gallagher's popularity was 'slipping' and that the WP was seen to have 'promised a lot [but] not really [been] able to deliver'. Gallagher complained that the local party organization was 'obsessed' with his TD's salary. There was also resentment because he had gone on a Waterford Corporation trip to Romania. He argued that he had wanted to actually see a socialist country at first hand. Party members complained that they opposed such council 'junkets'.

Other party activists had also been visiting the Eastern Bloc in this period under different auspices. During early 1981 members had attended events in Budapest, Prague and Moscow, and a delegation of 20 IDYM and party members had visited East Germany for the communist youth camp organized by the Freie

Deutsche Jugend [Free German Youth] during the summer of 1981. They spent three weeks working for GDR railways and met similar work groups from across Eastern Europe, as well as the American communist Angela Davis. The delegation leader was USI Northern convenor Eugene Hickland, and among the Belfast activists was Henry McDonald, an IDYM member from the Markets. His memory of the work camp was of a 'carefully controlled but not unpleasant bubble', which soon became a 'hive of hedonism and bed-hopping'. The Irish delegation won the 'Best Brigade' award for their voluntary work on the railways despite competition from the 'human bulldozers from Siberia and the GDR'. During 1981 Repsol had been granted the franchise to import and distribute Soviet publications including classic Russian literature, periodicals, records and postage stamps in Ireland. In July 1981 Des O'Hagan had attended a 'Solidarity Conference for the Support of Iraq' in Baghdad. This had been organized after the Israeli air force had bombed Iraqi nuclear reactors. O'Hagan reported how an 'impressive and packed hall' heard Saddam Hussein explain the circumstances behind the 'barbaric raid carried out by the Zionist entity'. In the early stages of the bloody Iran–Iraq war the WP took the side of 'radical and socialist' Iraq. *Workers' Life* described Iraq as the 'most progressive country in the Middle East' and a 'modern industrial socialist society', in contrast to Iran and its supreme leader the 'religious fanatic' Ayatollah Khomeini.

Another divisive issue came to the fore during 1982 when anti-abortion campaigners succeeded in gaining a promise from both Fianna Fáil and Fine Gael to hold a referendum to insert a prohibition of abortion into the Republic's constitution. All forms of abortion were already illegal in the South, and were extremely restricted in the North. The SFWP Ard Chomhairle discussed the proposed amendment in March 1982 and decided to oppose it. An Anti-Amendment Campaign was established during the summer with the WP listed as a sponsor. Goulding's partner Moira Woods was one of the founders of the AAC, and she had asked him if the WP would support the campaign. He had said that they would, without first consulting the leadership. The association with the

AAC caused dissension among many on the Ard Chomhairle, in part out of a reluctance to cooperate with some of the other left-wing groups involved, many of whom were seen as hostile to the WP. Garland asked Woods to remove the party's name from publicity material. Goulding still felt the WP should be involved, as 'the right people are opposed to the amendment and the wrong people are for it', and he continued to attend AAC meetings. But WP health spokesman John McManus warned that in WP literature it was best to 'steer clear of the rights and wrongs of abortion'. The majority view among the leadership was that the party should oppose the 'sectarian' amendment but without getting involved in the AAC or endorsing abortion itself.

Meanwhile, the party's working-class supporters were increasingly affected by the spread of heroin abuse in Dublin. In the February 1982 election Provisional Sinn Féin's Christy Burke had won just 214 fewer votes than the WP's Michael White in Dublin Central. The only Provisional candidate in the capital, Burke was becoming identified with opposition to drugs, as was independent TD Tony Gregory. Selling heroin was seen as a largely risk-free endeavour for some Dublin criminals, who had previously been involved in armed robbery. Drug use spread rapidly among the young unemployed. By July 1982, 9 per cent of young people aged 15 to 24 in north central Dublin had tried the drug, the vast majority injecting it. A contemporary study found that 73 per cent of those using heroin were 'involuntarily unemployed'. With addicts spending up to £100 a day to feed their habit, petty crime exploded in working-class communities.

In late 1981 a two-part feature in *Workers' Life* on the 'heroin menace' argued that 'Ireland is facing its greatest single potentially destructive social problem since the Great Famine'. The reporter, Adrian Gallagher, claimed that there was one major heroin supplier in Dublin, a large family based in the south inner city; this was a clear reference to the Dunnes. His article concluded that 'drastic measures need to be taken and taken quickly to combat the heroin menace'. The key to that would be 'smashing the gangs' who were supplying heroin. During this period Smullen was approached by

one of his Jesuit contacts, who had set up an anti-dealer group in
the north inner city. The priest asked about the possibility of OIRA
protection for his group. Smullen agonized over the issue for several
days before telling him, 'We don't do that sort of thing any more.'
As the heroin crisis continued to intensify, anti-drug groups emerged
in both the north and south inner city, eventually coalescing as the
Concerned Parents Against Drugs. There was division within the
WP leadership over what approach should be taken to these groups,
especially since the Provisionals were soon involved.

De Rossa proposed that the party develop 'a well-reasoned
document on crime'. The Association of Garda Sergeants and
Inspectors had produced a document on community policing that
drew the party's interest. The AGSI had noted that 'crime can
only be prevented by a determined attack on the type of social,
environmental and recreational conditions (or lack of them) that
encourage the development of these tendencies in the first place'.
Garland suggested meeting the AGSI to discuss these issues. He
also felt that the party had to assess its relationship with the Gardaí.
A WP delegation met the Prison Officers' Association to discuss
prison overcrowding and rehabilitation, while asserting that they
would oppose new bail restrictions. De Rossa was asked to raise
Garda surveillance of Gardiner Place in a meeting with Minister
for Justice Sean Doherty, whom McCartan had described as a
former member of the 'Special Branch political police' at the 1982
Ard Fheis. In *Workers' Life* Eric Byrne and Pat Brady argued that
socialists had failed to realize the importance of crime. The issue
was 'not [the] figment of the imagination of conservative politicians', though these politicians were adept at 'exploiting the fears
and anxieties of the working class'. Socialists needed a 'realistic
strategy for reducing crime and, in the meantime, ensuring that
the police service actually serves the people'. Furthermore 'the
notion that the Gardaí are the unreformable agents of repression'
was no longer adequate.

In September 1982 a private Special Delegate Conference, held
in Liberty Hall, endorsed changes in the party's leadership structure, on recommendations that emerged from the Party Develop-

ment Programme. There were over 600 delegates in attendance but no media present. The Ard Fheis remained the supreme decision-making forum, while the Ard Chomhairle became the Central Executive Committee and an Executive Management Committee fulfilled the old Coiste Seasta role. A new Executive Political Committee became the political decision-making body in between annual conferences; it was to 'concentrate on the political issues' and not on matters such as 'whether we have our permit for the national collection'. Numerous specialist committees were established. Part of the reasoning behind the changes was the perceived danger of too much concentration on electoral politics, and too much power being concentrated in TDs' hands.

The party's strategy for national economic revival, 'An End to the Crisis', was published in October. Written by the Research Section, its central contention was that 'private enterprise has failed to deliver the goods in the past' and that 'there is no reason to suppose that they will deliver the goods in the future'. The plan reiterated the WP position that state industry was the key to job creation.

By that time, the death of a Fianna Fáil TD and the serious illness of another left the WP holding the balance of power, and the party was considering the prospect of bringing down the government. Fine Gael pushed all-out to force an election. The WP backed Haughey in two key votes in the Dáil in October, but it was increasingly obvious that Fianna Fáil's plans to reinvigorate the economy would involve severe cutbacks that would go against WP policy. At the WP Ard Chomhairle it was argued that if an election looked likely the TDs should launch a strong attack on Fianna Fáil's 'Thatcherite policies'. Voting against the government on this basis would 'upstage' the forthcoming Labour Party Conference. On 3 November the crisis came to a head and the WP TDs announced that they would vote against the government. They argued that Fianna Fáil had broken its pledges on public spending and health cuts. Fianna Fáil lost a confidence vote by 80 votes to 82, a new general election was called, and what Dick Walsh in the *Irish Times* called a 'Hitler–Stalin pact of sorts' had come to an end.

14. Fight Back!

The Workers' Party 1982–1989

'There is no secret about our purpose. It is to win state power for the
Irish working class.'

Pat Rabbitte, Kilmainham, Easter 1986

In November 1982 the WP faced into its third Southern general
election campaign in eighteen months. The party's hopes of leading
the Republic into an age of post-civil-war politics were emphasized
in an innovative election broadcast. Featuring a long-distance
runner making his way through Dublin streets towards the Dáil in
a red Workers' Party T-shirt, the broadcast emphasized the party's
post-nationalist agenda and call to embrace industrial development.
In it De Rossa declared that 'freedom is only a flag unless it's flying
over new hospitals, new schools and new factories. Freedom for
us is full employment, full stop.' Paddy Gallagher reassured voters
that 'new technology shook up the old ways but it's cleaner, faster,
produces more ... the computer can be controlled, can carry a
message of hope'.

The party fielded 20 candidates, and with some £40,000 still
owed for printing costs from the two recent elections, a bank loan
of £100,000 was taken out to help fund the campaign. The results
were mixed: the WP vote increased to 3.3 per cent nationally, and
Mac Giolla was elected for the first time in Dublin West, but
Sherlock and Gallagher lost their seats, for a net loss of one seat.
De Rossa almost topped the poll in Dublin North-West with
nearly 20 per cent of the vote, and overall the party's vote in the
capital had increased from 15,748 to 29,155 in nine months.

Sherlock and Gallagher both lost out to Fianna Fáil; given that FF lost six seats overall, this was arguably a damning political verdict on the WP's decision to support Haughey's government. The party's election post-mortem found that in Waterford some had complained that Gallagher, whose vote dropped dramatically, had not done a 'Gregory deal' and got concessions for the town, a point emphasized by Fianna Fáil during the campaign. Losing his seat had personal implications for Gallagher, who was not re-employed in his old job: 'Here I was a high flier one day, [and] the next morning signing on in Ballybricken labour exchange.' Sherlock alleged that Fianna Fáil had bought rounds of drinks in rural pubs and even paid off some constituents' electricity bills in an effort to win back their second seat in Cork East.

Fine Gael meanwhile had received their best vote since 1927 and opened negotiations with Labour leader Dick Spring. While the *Irish People* pleaded 'Don't do it, Dick', Mac Giolla met Spring and put it to him that if Labour stayed out of government it might force the two conservative parties together. Spring expressed the fear that with voters seeking stability Labour would be 'swallowed up' if they forced another election. Mac Giolla concluded the meeting by telling Spring that the WP would 'oppose Labour constantly' if they went into coalition. Undeterred, Spring entered a coalition with Fine Gael, with Garret FitzGerald as Taoiseach. The WP was indeed hostile to the new government from the start, but the political realignment offered opportunities, as Tony Heffernan recalls: 'It was the ideal territory for us ... if Labour [had been] in opposition we would not have had anything like the same potential for growth at all.' The coalition was to preside over five years during which Ireland was hit hard by the international recession. When the government took office, unemployment stood at 187,000; by 1987 it would be 237,000. Emigration returned with a vengeance while the government implemented the first major health cuts since the foundation of the state. The relationship between the unions and the government was adversarial, with occupations and protests against closures leading to arrests and jailings. The public sector unions struck against cutbacks and teachers undertook their first national strike. In March 1983 the *Irish Times'* Olivia O'Leary provided a withering commentary on Labour in government, claiming that Garret FitzGerald found them 'most amenable . . . whenever he remembers they're there'. The WP blamed Labour for cuts in food subsidies, the abolition of free school transport and the introduction of local service charges. But the WP had greater ambitions than simply replacing its left-wing rival. According to an internal party analysis, 34 per cent of working-class voters chose Fine Gael while 45 per cent voted Fianna Fáil. The party's publicly stated aim was to win the majority of these voters to itself.

Despite the scale of the political task it had set itself, immediate post-election WP debate was overshadowed by a dispute over the party's international positions. The November election manifesto had included statements supporting the Solidarity trade union in Poland and arguing for recognition of the state of Israel. Both positions ran counter to party policy. The controversial material had been written in the main by Eoghan Harris and Oliver Donohue, who were concerned that the party's vocal opposition to Solidarity could lose them votes. At leadership meetings Smullen defended his Industrial Department colleagues, arguing the WP should be 'opposed to military rule [and] believe in free trade unions', while making clear that he 'had always' supported the USSR. He said the manifesto was inspired by the 'need to cover [the] party in the media'. Tom French agreed, feeling that the WP 'shouldn't be seen to say that we can't criticise Socialist countries'. But most members of the Ard Chomhairle were highly indignant that positions at odds with party policy had been included in election material. A clarification and restatement of the position on Poland was published in *Notes and Comments*. The statement concerning Israel was even more inflammatory, considering the involvement of WP members in the Irish Friends of Palestine and commitment to supporting the PLO. That year had seen Israel's invasion of Lebanon and the massacre of Palestinian refugees by Israeli-backed militia in Beirut. The party's support for the Palestinians had caused some unease, with the Chief Rabbi of Ireland informing Mac Giolla at a meeting in October 1982 that he felt the WP's position was 'anti-Semitic', according to a Coiste Seasta note. Claims by those behind the pro-Israel statement that it was intended to protect the party from such a charge were dismissed, and support for the PLO 'as the sole legitimate representative of the Palestinian people' was reiterated. The affair reignited questions about the Industrial Department's politics, with Ó Cionnaith expressing the view that some in the Department had adopted BICO's position of support for Israel. (At the same time, ironically, there was cooperation between WP students and members of the Iraqi Ba'ath party in UCD, both agreeing to exclude mutual enemies from solidarity campaigns.) Several members of the Ard Chomhairle asked Smullen why there were still secret members; not for the first time, he explained that this was due to the 'conditions of employment' of those concerned.

Concerns had also emerged over the functioning of the party in parliament. Heffernan, who had been directly appointed by Garland to work with the TDs, had already warned that the party had no clear idea on 'what we want to do in the Dáil'. De Rossa, similarly, complained at leadership meetings that 'we have TDs but we don't know what to do with them'. Most agreed it was important that the WP 'maintain our revolutionary image' and not 'confine our activity to the parliamentary area', but others felt there were 'dangers [in] street politics'. Des Geraghty believed the party's main problem was that 'a very small number of people [were] doing a massive amount of work'. There was concern over giving parliamentary representatives too high a profile, with fears expressed that 'we can't trust the TDs', but Garland was adamant that it was 'the party [that] decides what is going to be said' in the Dáil.

For nearly two years a party subcommittee had been considering the changes required for 'building a mass working-class party which will be capable of achieving state power in Ireland'. They sought to give effect to the 1981 Ard Fheis decision that the party would bring about revolutionary change by winning a Dáil majority rather than through the operation of a clandestine vanguard.

Electoral activity was no longer seen as merely an opportunity to propagandize but as the fundamental theatre in which the foundations of the revolution would be laid and final victory achieved. The subcommittee's March 1983 report stated a goal of increasing the party's membership vastly, to between thirty and forty thousand. Such growth 'will enable us, during the course of the struggle to win state power, to lay the foundations for a total revolution necessary to ensure that once state power has been won, that not only can it be defended, but that the revolution itself will be seen as the creative product of our class'.

In order to achieve this aim, the party would follow a more relaxed version of democratic centralism in order to allow 'for maximum participation by the membership in the democratic processes'. Emphasis was placed on curtailing the influence of the Industrial Department and Research Section, with the party's specialist committees empowered to develop policy. It recommended that 'health and social policy' be emphasized as much as 'economic or industrial policy'. The Economic Affairs Committee would still be 'important' but should only produce 'concise documents', which would be scrutinized pre-publication by the party centre. 'As far as possible' all branches were to be geographically based with only the Executive Political Committee allowed to make exceptions. Members were to join only one branch and partake in open party activity unless excused by the Ard Chomhairle. There were new guidelines for involvement in unions and other organizations:

Our participation in these organisations must be seen to be democratic and constructive and in no way conspiratorial or elitist . . . Every effort must be made by Party members to dispel any misgivings fellow workers may have about conspiratorial methods of work which opponents of the party are always quick to exploit.

Other organizational initiatives included the appointment of a full-time party fund-raiser, though the idea of a levy based on members' income was discounted. Internal power would be maintained within the Ard Chomhairle, which would meet quarterly, while the Executive Political Committee, which consisted of 14 members selected from the Ard Chomhairle, would meet on a monthly basis. All TDs not elected to the Ard Chomhairle were to be co-opted on to the body. It was reiterated that canvassing for Ard Chomhairle elections was 'prohibited'. Particular emphasis was to be placed on recruiting women as members, and the age of full membership would be reduced to 15.

Efforts to sideline the Industrial Department continued on other fronts. When Smullen requested that Fergus Whelan and Patricia Redlich be given special delegate status to the 1983 Ard Fheis, Garland asked why they couldn't simply come as delegates from their party branches. Smullen argued that Redlich's status as a member of the executive of her union meant she should be a delegate. Garland countered that there needed to be an 'assessment of these people' and their worth to the WP. Others openly questioned what contribution the 'non-geographical' branches were actually making. By the summer Des Geraghty and Rosheen Callender had transferred from the Industrial Department's Joe O'Connor cumann to a geographical branch in Dun Laoghaire.

The abortion issue remained to the fore in national politics in spring 1983. In the November general election, Democratic Socialist Jim Kemmy and Labour's Michael D. Higgins were subjected to campaigns that labelled them pro-abortion and contributed to them losing their Dáil seats. The coalition government had succumbed to the campaign to place a 'pro-life' clause in the constitution and a referendum had been set for September 1983. With Fianna Fáil also rowing in behind the anti-abortion lobby, only 13 of 166 TDs voted against holding the poll. At the May 1983 Ard Fheis, Mac Giolla condemned those 'craven politicians' who had caved in to 'ultra-Catholic' pressure. On the actual issue of abortion – as opposed to the question of a constitutional amendment – the party maintained a degree of ambiguity. An Ard Fheis motion supporting the extension of the 1967 British abortion act to Northern Ireland was defeated amid claims that it was contrary to WP's support for devolution.

As both pro- and anti-amendment campaigners stepped up their activity, the WP's refusal to become actively involved with the Anti-Amendment Campaign drew criticism from within the party; but the majority view was that the WP should run its own campaign on the basis of defending civil liberties and pluralism. A Mac Giolla radio interview in which the party president seemed to suggest the WP opposed abortion caused Des O'Hagan to point out that 'Tom French could not say one thing in Lurgan and Tomás Mac Giolla another in Dublin'. In the run-up to the referendum the party's line hardened. The *Irish People* argued that the proposed change gave an embryo the same rights as a pregnant woman and that if it were passed a rape victim could potentially be prosecuted for seeking an abortion. But the party continued to stress that it was not seeking legalization of abortion. The leadership argued internally that the key issue was stressing the nature of the groups behind the pro-life campaign. Many of these groups, funded by American right-wing organizations, were intent on using the abortion issue as a means to halt reform of family law and legalization of contraception. Goulding maintained a semi-independent line on the issue, accompanying Moira Woods to anti-amendment events and sharing car journeys with Eamonn McCann, one of the 'ultra-left' with whom the party was normally anxious not to associate. The campaign was tough and emotive and activists who took part in the campaign recall that there were 'no wishy-washy liberals' on the ground. Nonetheless thousands of leaflets and posters were distributed and WP activists canvassed door to door, arguing that the amendment was an attack on 'democracy and tolerance' as well as a hypocritical diversion from the reality of life for thousands of Irish women. The amendment was passed by a 2:1 majority, though in Dublin the margin was narrower; Fianna Fáil's Michael Woods attributed the high 'No' vote in some working-class districts to the WP's efforts.

By-elections during 1983 indicated that the party's electoral appeal was continuing to grow. Seamus Rodgers had polled respectably in Donegal South-West in May, and Michael White came third in the Dublin Central by-election in November, taking

13 per cent of the vote – more than double the vote of the Labour candidate. The latter constituency covered the poorest areas of the north inner city, though White's largest share of the votes came in the less deprived but solidly working-class areas of Cabra and East Wall. Sinn Féin's Christy Burke took 7 per cent of the vote – a strong showing, which the WP Ard Chomhairle described as 'saddening' – but about half of Burke's transfers went to the WP, which led them to conclude that the vote was not a hardcore Provo one. After the by-election Fianna Fáil established a committee, headed by Liam Lawlor, to work out strategy to counter the WP's growing popularity in areas of local authority housing.

Another area of strength for the party was Dun Laoghaire, where Eamon Gilmore was the local public representative. Despite the district's middle-class image, there were nearly 5,000 people out of work in Dun Laoghaire during 1983. Activists made a determined effort to build up *Irish People* sales in every working-class estate, as local member Colm Breathnach recalls: 'The intention of it was to keep regularly in contact with people and change them into voters, then supporters, then members.' Through the advice centre network the WP found that there were still over 900 local authority houses in the area that did not have a bathroom or indoor toilet.

Rivalry with the Labour Party was intense, particularly in Dublin, and the WP was quick to hold Labour responsible for controversial government proposals to introduce local service charges, which the WP saw as double taxation on workers. In Crumlin, a local activist recalls, relationships between the WP and Labour 'would have been officially cordial but actually poisonous'. In Ballinteer, similarly, it was 'daggers drawn' between the organizations. In 1983 De Rossa publicly outlined what he saw as the difference between the two parties: 'The Labour Party have no ambitions [to] transfer power from one class to the other. They are looking for a cooperation or a partnership between the classes . . . we are looking to transfer power from the capitalist class to the working class.' Labour's role in government caused disillusion among some of its own activists. In Tipperary town a number of

Labour members defected to the WP in late 1983. Among them
was Christy Kinahan, an activist for over eighteen years, who
explained that Labour had now become 'indistinguishable' from
the conservative parties and 'totally irrelevant' in terms of 'class
struggle'.

The rivalry with Labour was also being played out in the unions,
particularly the ITGWU. Michael Mullen had died in November
1982 and the new union leadership, dominated by John Carroll
and Christy Kirwan (a Labour senator), was hostile to the WP.
Des Geraghty, one of the union's six National Group Secretaries
and the best-known WP trade union figure, challenged the
ITGWU leadership in electoral contests on three occasions over
the next two years. An Irish speaker and traditional musician,
Geraghty was an affable figure who belied many of the 'Sticky'
stereotypes, *Irish Press* journalist Proinsias Mac Aonghusa describing
him as 'the acceptable face of the Workers' Party', but this did not
prevent the ITGWU leadership from making strong efforts to
ensure he did not win national office. During a 1982 poll for union
vice-president all 360 ITGWU delegates were sent a circular that
named 26 officials as WP members or sympathizers and claimed
that there was a plot to take over the union. Although relations
between the unions and the Labour Party deteriorated during the
coalition years, strong personal rivalries and fears that the WP's
officials' dynamism would see them take the top union jobs were
factors in the anti-WP feeling.

While the burden of taxation continued to be borne by the
PAYE sector, the campaign for reform was in decline. In April
1983 150,000 workers had taken to the streets in another day of
protest. Frustration at the lack of progress on the issue had seen
Waterford Glass workers withhold their PAYE and PRSI payments, a campaign that spread to other workplaces. The Irish
Congress of Trade Unions (ICTU) condemned that move, arguing that it could not support non-payment of tax. The WP also
argued against this tactic, and the campaign eventually fizzled out.
While there were confident assertions that the tax campaign could
be sustained, it effectively ended with 'low key' support for a

national day of action in January 1984. In Dublin just 8,000 turned out where 100,000 had marched the previous year. There were dozens of small-scale industrial disputes, often over redundancies, but the level of strike action, official and unofficial, declined steadily between 1982 and 1987. The need to respond to the decrease in militancy was at the centre of discussions among the WP leadership during 1983. Geraghty worried that it was becoming 'difficult to motivate' workers as many were saying 'to hell with their job' and accepting redundancy. The so-called black economy was growing, particularly in the construction industry: with 40,000 building workers unemployed, many were prepared to work for contractors who neither recognized unions nor paid tax. The WP leadership argued over how to translate party policy into local needs. Some suggested highlighting the call for a state construction company. Others felt that many 'people do not believe full employment is possible' and that workers in general were demoralized. Some were prepared to admit that the WP had an image problem. A survey had found that the WP were seen by many as 'recent converts from violence . . . gloomy, depressing' and 'staid'. Even Dick Walsh, a sympathetic observer, noted the somewhat 'turgid' nature of the party's rhetoric. Gerry Doherty worried that the WP could not motivate supporters as it was no longer a 'campaigning party', citing what he saw as a lack of effort in the campaign against water charges. In fact the WP leadership were divided on how to oppose local charges. They encouraged people to refuse to pay and to defy threats of prosecution, pointing out that fewer than 5,000 people had paid property tax out of the 75,000 who owed it and that there was at least £20 million owed by farmers in rates. Sherlock suggested that the WP should actively 'obstruct' collection of the charges, but most were not in favour of directly breaking the law. Some feared that the radical street politics of the 1970s had been replaced by an emphasis on getting TDs elected. John McManus meanwhile worried that the WP was too associated in the public mind with council tenants, stating that 'his constituents living in private accommodation did not see us as their party'.

One initiative – pioneered in Finglas and taken up with success elsewhere – that did help the party's image was to campaign for state-funded family clinics to provide facilities for smear tests, breast examinations and contraception. The WP had found widespread demand for such facilities through the work of its local women's group, and similar groups were set up in other constituencies. Women were still a minority within the WP, comprising about 30 per cent of the membership during the early 1980s. Leading figures such as Triona Dooney and Liz McManus maintained a very critical approach to the 'liberal/bourgeois element' in the feminist movement, which was seen as concentrating on 'superficial' aspects of women's oppression rather than on changing society. McManus told a Newry conference that 'without socialism even the possibility of achieving [gender] equality is not there'.

The WP continued to be hampered by publicity that linked the party to armed activity. In May 1983 Minister for Justice Michael Noonan stated that the Official IRA was still active, and Tony Heffernan was forced to deny any 'connection' with or 'knowledge' of the OIRA on behalf of the WP. In June an acrimonious court case saw a claim that Eamon Kelly was a member of the Official IRA reach the front pages of the *Irish Times*. Even more damagingly, in January 1984 a story broke linking the party with the printing of counterfeit five-pound notes, revealing that Gardaí had searched Repsol's printing works at Gardiner Place during November and were seeking the assistance of one of the company's print staff. The WP issued a statement denying any involvement in illegality. They explained that Gardaí had 'visited' their premises as part of a city-wide trawl through printing works and the party had given 'every possible assistance' to them. The statement reiterated that the WP was a 'bona fide political party . . . committed to democratic policies' and financed through 'raffles, collections and social functions' as well as members' subscriptions. They stressed that no 'senior member' of the party was missing 'nor to our knowledge is anyone being sought by the police'. Party members were assured that it was no coincidence that the Garda visit had come a week before the Dublin Central by-election.

That rival politicians sought to embarrass the party was unquestionable. Michael Noonan's confirmation of the existence of the OIRA had come on the day the WP Ard Fheis commenced in Dublin, but the written question to which he was responding had been submitted six months before. The WP contended that attacks on the party by *Magill* and the new *Phoenix* magazine were motivated by the same people who championed 'the Provisionals' drive for respectability'. What even the WP's enemies could not dispute was that, whether it existed or not, the Official IRA was not publicly killing anybody. Meanwhile, around the same time as the Garda raid on Gardiner Place, the Provisional IRA had killed a trainee Garda and an Irish soldier in Co. Leitrim; six people had been killed with a bomb at Harrods in London; and members of the INLA had shot dead three Protestants at a gospel hall in Armagh. The party's media supporters attempted to aid the WP in shedding any hint of a violent image. In December 1983 Goulding was interviewed by Mary Maher in the *Irish Times*. In her introduction Maher stated that the Official IRA had 'formally disbanded after a declaration of a ceasefire in 1972'. In fact there had never been an OIRA statement of disbandment, and the *Irish Times* had reported on OIRA statements until 1976. Dick Walsh continued to write sympathetically on the party for the *Irish Times*, where he became political editor during 1985, and in 1983 Padraig Yeates joined the paper as a freelance reporter.

Despite continuing suspicion about Eurocommunism, formal relations were established with the French, Spanish and Italian communist parties in the early 1980s. Meanwhile, the party continued to identify with the Soviet Union. The WP mourned Soviet premier Leonid Brezhnev on his death in November 1982 as an 'outstanding political leader and ardent fighter for peace', sending congratulations to his successor, Yuri Andropov. The party also publicly opposed the expulsion from Dublin of three Soviet diplomats accused of espionage in September 1983. As the issue of nuclear disarmament became central to superpower relations, De Rossa explained that 'we have to accept that the USSR has no vested interest in maintaining the deployment of nuclear weapons' whereas the United States had 'a vast military-industrial complex which depends on the continual development and production of these weapons'. O'Hagan was in regular contact with the Soviets due to his chairmanship of the Irish Committee for European Security and Cooperation, a WP-run body that was linked to an international organization established to publicize Moscow's view on the arms race. The Soviet Communist Party and the WP formally established fraternal relations during 1983, and at the year's close Garland, Ó Cionnaith, O'Hagan and Seamus Harrison visited Moscow and Estonia at the invitation of the party.

During the same year Garland and Ó Cionnaith had visited North Korea. The visit had been arranged through the North Korean ambassador in Denmark, with whom the WP had been in contact for several years. North Korea had developed an ideology based around Marxism and a personality cult of its leader, Kim Il-sung (whose writings were promoted in bizarre full-page ads in the *Irish Times* during this period). Garland recalls:

We had all these stories about North Korea but we met them anyway. [We] weren't under any illusions but at the same time what I seen, or we seen, was like there was a small country divided, it was very much isolated, blockaded economically, politically, militarily, and they were trying to do what they could themselves . . . We pointed out to them for instance putting full-page ads into the *Irish Times* of Kim Il-sung's thoughts was a waste of money because nobody fucking read them. They were paying £5,000 . . .

During their visit Garland and Ó Cionnaith met Kim Young Nam, Secretary of the Central Committee, and visited several parts of the country. *Workers' Life* reported that they were 'particularly impressed' with what they saw, visiting schools, health centres and factories. Of the port of Nampo they reported that 'the standard of living is quite high and the shops are well stocked . . . the people are well dressed and there were no indications of the sort of poverty that we witness daily in this country'. Paddy Woodworth recalls that Garland on his return was 'quite open about the strangeness of the Kim Il-sung regime'. When Woodworth wrote an article for *Workers' Life* noting the more bizarre features of North Korean life Garland admonished him: 'Ah come on now Paddy, I'm looking for support from these people.' (The article was not published.) In June 1984 the WP organized a visit to Ireland by the North Korean ambassador to Denmark during which he met representatives of a number of business and semi-state enterprises. Garland visited North Korea again during the autumn of 1984, this time with Mac Giolla and Seamus Lynch, meeting the 'Dear Leader' Kim Il-sung himself. The meeting was reported in the English-language *Pyongyang Times* of 29 September. A month later the *Sunday Tribune*, picking up on the piece, gleefully reported that Kim had praised the WP's struggle to remove 'the British occupation forces' from Ireland and that he was pleased that the WP had 'struck deep roots among the broad masses'. Mac Giolla was quoted as saying that 'just as there was one Korea and one Korean people so there was only one Ireland and one [Irish] People'. Embarrassed, the WP suggested that Mac Giolla's remarks were mis-translated.

In February 1984 the party held a Marx Centenary Conference that featured lectures from Paul Bew, Henry Patterson, Ellen Hazelkorn, Geraghty and De Rossa. Patterson argued that 'the radical political break which the WP has made with the traditional positions of "Irish Marxism"' put it in 'a pre-eminent position to make Marxism a real force in Ireland'. The extent to which party members actually embraced Marxism varied. Prospective members still attended introductory classes as part of a six-month probationary period; many dropped out before completing it, and others were so put off by the whole process that they never commenced it. Some were deemed unsuitable, and there was particular suspicion of prospective members who had been involved in other left-wing groups. Repsol continued to hold the franchise for the distribution of Soviet literature and publications in Ireland, placing over £12,000 of orders in the three years after 1982, while Garland informed a Soviet contact that they had 'made significant advances in bringing Soviet books, magazines and records to the Irish people'. Holidays to Yalta on the 'sun-scorched Black Sea' and others parts of the USSR were available through the WP's office and were advertised in *Workers' Life*.

The other side of solidarity with the international left was illustrated by the WP's opposition to Reagan's visit in June 1984. Widely seen as a cynical move in a US election year, the visit drew large protests. The WP supported the Campaign against Reagan's Foreign Policy, which included the CND as well as Church, refugee and Latin American solidarity groups. Party members were instructed to engage in 'peaceful and non-violent protest' and to 'avoid all contact' with the rival Reagan Reception Campaign, as this was supported by the Provisionals and various Trotskyist groups. When Reagan addressed the Dáil, Mac Giolla and De Rossa walked out in protest along with Tony Gregory.

The need to mould socialist theory into practical policy in recession-hit Ireland had been the focus of the April 1984 Ard Fheis. In his presidential address Mac Giolla raged against the 'small number of people' who controlled the country's finances. He mocked Fianna Fáil for copying WP economic policies, which called for greater investment in state enterprises, and called upon Labour Party members of 'great integrity' to 'recognise that their future and the country's lies with us'. Garland was pleased to announce that party membership had grown by 30 per cent in the preceding year, but this was not enough. Wexford member Dave O'Grady recalls of the Ard Fheiseanna of the 1980s:

You had the sophisticated developed political thinkers, you had these charismatic political figures who were being promoted in the media, you had the hard-line men, you had the solid working-class genuine Dubs, and then you had the people coming from the far-flung regions who were politically very committed and ideologically very sound but who had been working this out very much on their own, real mavericks within their own area . . . The effort to unite all these disparate groups into some kind of cohesive, coherent whole meant the flavour of every Ard Fheis was unpredictable and the line that was to be adopted was never clear until you were actually in the middle of the weekend . . .

There remained differing views at leadership level on how social-ism would develop in Ireland. Privately Goulding maintained that 'armed struggle is necessary for the revolution', telling a researcher during 1984:

There is only one country in the world that got there [to socialism] through elections – Czechoslovakia, and only because it was surrounded by powerful neighbours. Look at Chile. Allende got in, but then got murdered. The most important role of physical force is defending gains. There is a need for a revolutionary morality. No Marxist can be against the use of force.

Such views barely percolated down to the rank and file. Ordinary members often left the decisions on political direction to the leadership, as one recalls: 'I used to often laugh because the party went on so much about the membership owning the party . . . at times the membership were actually very passive.' In the newer branches there were often only a few members who kept in regular contact with the party centre. 'All splits and discussions took place at leadership level,' a member recalls. 'You could be in the WP all your life and not know about them. Democratic centralism was like a military structure.'

In Leinster House De Rossa and Mac Giolla asked hundreds of written and verbal questions and put down nine private member's bills during the five-year life of FitzGerald's government. Both men were widely praised for their work rate and diligence, even by the party's critics. De Rossa was named Dáil 'backbencher of the year' by *Magill*, and his public struggle with a pronounced stammer was admired. The men's profile is recalled by Heffernan as 'hugely important to the credibility of the party. You suddenly had TDs that could be on the news.' The leadership considered that the party's Dáil image was good, but feared that many voters failed to link their TDs to the WP itself. O'Hagan became closely identified with the view that the development of a separate par-liamentary party would be 'divisive'. He held that parliament was only a 'prop to capitalist society' and WP TDs were not constituency representatives but 'delegates from the party'. O'Hagan considered the walkout during Reagan's speech as a good example of the WP using the Dáil to highlight revolutionary politics. Geraghty, however, reminded his colleagues that in Waterford Gallagher had lost his seat at least partially because he was seen as having neglected his constituency work.

In the European elections of 1984, the WP won 4.3 per cent of the vote in the Republic. The party had hoped for a better result, particularly in Dublin where Des Geraghty took just under 7 per cent. Liz McManus won 3.45 per cent in Leinster and Jimmy Brick only 1.1 per cent in Connaught-Ulster (described internally as a 'disastrous' result). In Munster Sherlock won 5 per cent, polling poorly outside of Cork. Peter Kane thought the somewhat disappointing results came about because 'we were negative about the EEC', despite the party's formal enthusiasm. Canvassers reported that the party was seen as 'anti-farmer' and by implication anti-countryside. Also worrying was the strong showing in Dublin by Sinn Féin's John Noonan, characterized by an internal WP report as an 'almost illiterate, unknown candidate'. The report also noted that 'the Provies seem to have high votes where WP votes are also high' and were 'taking a substantial working-class vote from us'. According to Kane's figures the WP's budget for the election was one-fifth that of the Labour Party and less than half that of Sinn Féin.

It was apparent that the Irish left was still very much a minority. In the *Irish People* Dick Walsh pondered the paradox: unemployment stood at 215,000 and an estimated one million were living on the poverty line; almost 500,000 workers were organized in trade unions; the Republic had a very young population; yet the left still struggled to win votes. Mac Giolla complained that the media 'peddles *Dallas* and *Dynasty* as escapist opium' while promoting the 'greedy, dehumanising ethics of so-called free enterprise'. By 1984 the party realized a new youth wing was needed as 'nothing was being done' by the IDYM. This led to the setting up of Workers' Party Youth, with branches in Belfast, Downpatrick, Dublin, Cork and Ballina. It organized concerts and fund-raisers,

Official IRA gunmen, armed with an Armalite rifle and Ingram machine pistol, Belfast, July 1975 – three years after the OIRA's ceasefire announcement (*United Irishman*)

Official Sinn Féin Industrial Department members marching in Dublin on May Day, mid-1970s (Workers' Party of Ireland)

Officials and Provisionals clash at Milltown Cemetery, Belfast, April 1977
(*Irish Press* Archives)

Fergus Whelan addresses ICTU tax protest, late 1970s (Workers' Party of Ireland)

Delegates at the World Festival of Youth, Havana, 1978, including Eamon Gilmore at far left, Jer O'Leary beside Gilmore, Martin Lynch (bearded, right) and Margaret O'Leary (beside Lynch) (Private collection)

Sinn Féin The Workers' Party Ard Fheis, 1979: Jim Sullivan, Eamon Smullen and Sean Garland (Derek Speirs / Report)

At the 1982 SFWP Ard Fheis: Eoghan Harris (with pipe), his Industrial Department colleague Liam Cassidy, Oliver Donohue (with full beard, to the left of Cassidy) and Pat McCartan (standing behind lamp) (Derek Speirs / Report)

Tomás Mac Giolla introduces the SFWP TDs elected in February 1982 to that year's Ard Fheis (from left): Paddy Gallagher, Joe Sherlock and Proinsias De Rossa (Private collection)

Leaving the Soviet Embassy, Dublin, mid-1980s: Proinsias De Rossa, Tomás Mac Giolla and Sean Garland (front); Seán Ó Cionnaith, Seamus Harrison, Mary Garland, Des O'Hagan and Seamus Lynch (back) (Workers' Party of Ireland)

Tomás Mac Giolla and WP members protest against health cuts, Dublin, 1987 (Workers' Party of Ireland)

WP members at Jim Larkin statue, O'Connell Street, Dublin, 1987 (from left): Eric Byrne, Mick Whelan, Eamon Gilmore, Mike Jennings, Pat Rabbitte, Tomás Mac Giolla (Workers' Party of Ireland)

Des Geraghty speaking at Workers' Party Ard Fheis, 1988 (Eamonn Farrell / Photocall)

Proinsias De Rossa, held aloft by colleagues Pat McCartan, Eamon Gilmore and Gerry Doherty, celebrates his election as MEP in June 1989 (*Irish Independent* / National Library of Ireland)

Workers' Party members Marion White and Feargus Mac Aogáin canvass with presidential candidate Mary Robinson in Dun Laoghaire, November 1990 (Feargus Mac Aogáin)

At the 1992 special WP Ard Fheis to determine the future of the party (left to right):
John Halligan, Cathal Goulding, Sean Garland and John Lowry
(Eamonn Farrell / Photocall)

Familiar faces, new party: Liz McManus, Proinsias De Rossa, Kathleen Lynch and
Eamon Gilmore of Democratic Left, 1992 (Eamonn Farrell / Photocall)

campaigned on low pay, youth unemployment and solvent abuse, and produced an educational video entitled *From Sinn Féin to the Workers' Party*. Fearghal Ross, De Rossa's son, would become the youth organizer. The WP also secured funding from the National Youth Council to employ Ken McCue as Youth Development Officer. McCue suggested that there was an opportunity to reassert party influence in the USI, reporting that it had been 'destroyed and discredited by Trots and Provos . . . presently the national body is so weak that it is there for the taking'. Despite McCue's ambitions the WP was largely uninterested in student activity and the few student members it had were directed into local party work.

With finance a constant problem much of the party's social scene now revolved around events to raise money. Every meeting heard reports of unpaid printing bills, overdrafts and *Irish People* debts. All WP branches had to organize socials and raffles and take part in the annual national collection. Among those who performed at such fund-raising events were Niall Tóibín, Dermot Morgan and Ronnie Drew. Club Uí Cadhain was the focus for much of the Dublin fund-raising efforts, hosting events several nights a week. It was also a place where members would gather after paper sales, marches or meetings. The club also attracted a local clientele, some of whom 'would not have been highly regarded in their own community' and only drank there 'because they were barred from other places'.

The growing tension between party cadres and the union hierarchies was evident at the April 1985 Ard Fheis as Des Geraghty made the strongest attack on the ICTU leadership at a WP event in years, describing them as 'pseudo-socialists to the right of Fianna Fáil on social philosophy'. In part this rhetoric reflected the decline in Smullen's influence and his long-held strategy of not antagonizing union leaders. In his presidential speech Mac Giolla connected the rise in youth crime and drug abuse to the lack of 'honesty, integrity and justice' in Irish society. Nowhere was this more evident than in the 'hypocritical double dealing that goes on all the time in Leinster House'. The only long-term strategy to prevent 'new additions' to a teenage criminal 'subculture' was the creation of jobs and the provision of education and training via emergency state investment. He claimed that in some working-class areas the Gardaí were as mistrusted as the RUC were in the North, and called for 'joint action' between communities and the police in tackling crime as well as an independent civilian-run Garda complaints board. Garland stressed that the growing social problems also presented an opportunity: 'We must be able to turn to our advantage every sign of discontent with this system, to gather and turn to the best account every protest, no matter how small.'

Smullen increasingly found himself on the losing side in leadership debates. An attempt in early 1985 to organize a meeting of WP activists in the building industry was stymied by a demand from Garland that it be organized through ordinary party structures. When Smullen recommended Fergus Whelan as a delegate to the WP Dublin Regional Council his choice was roundly rejected by Garland, Kane and Ó Cionnaith as 'divisive'.

The WP performed strongly in the local elections of June 1985, winning 35 seats and 7.3 per cent of the vote. The most impressive results came in greater Dublin, where nine seats were won. Mac Giolla was joined on Dublin Corporation by McCartan, De Rossa, Eric Byrne, Eamonn O'Brien and Andy Smith; Labour by comparison held just two seats on the Corporation. On Dublin County Council the WP gained two seats, for Pat Rabbitte in Tallaght and Terry Delaney in Greenhills, and Eamon Gilmore was elected in Dun Laoghaire. Three WP seats were won in Bray, making it the second largest party locally; the party also had two seats on Cork Corporation, two on Galway Corporation and two in Waterford. Sherlock polled a huge 3,441 first preferences to hold his seat on Cork County Council. Seats were also won in more than a dozen other regional towns.

Fierce opposition to local service charges was one factor in WP success. In Fermoy, councillor Tadhg O'Donovan had faced jail for refusing to pay his water tax. On Waterford Corporation the WP councillors had successfully moved a motion to reject the local charges and instead raise taxes on the wealthy. In other areas members were to the fore in organizing the public burning of rates books. The WP considered that it had made 'water charges the tax issue [and] tax the class issue'. Some of the newly elected councillors, like Kathleen Lynch in Cork and Jimmy Brick in Galway, were seen as potential Dáil candidates. Lynch's election allowed the WP in the Cork South Central constituency, with 17 members, to set up 2 new branches and sell 700 *Irish People* a week, some 200 of them door to door. In Co. Kildare the WP had established small branches in the towns of Maynooth, Athy and in the growing suburbs around Leixlip. The Leixlip branch, which Catherine Murphy joined during 1984, was highly active: 'There was so many issues in a place like this – fair taxation, childcare, transport. We all took it seriously . . . it was a mix of people with a big bunch from west Dublin [because] that is where a lot of people around here are from.'

The Dun Laoghaire WP, which Feargus Mac Aogáin joined, was 'a real campaigning party, and that was the kind of party I was interested in, a party that had people at its heart, you were actually doing something for people rather than sitting in a room or office and discussing what you would like to do for people'. In Ballybrack 17-year-old Stephen Lewis would normally be told to get his parents when canvassers found he was too young to vote, but when Geraghty and Gilmore called to his house during the 1985 campaign they engaged him in discussion. Lewis, on the dole, listening to The Smiths and watching 'Britain being turned into a police state during the miners' strike' was open to left-wing politics: 'The fact that Gilmore had an interest in my opinions also made me think, "This is the party."' The results renewed confidence in the party, as an activist recalls: 'People were of the view if we keep this up we will outstrip the Labour Party . . . we felt that we were harder working and more pertinent to the working class.'

The election successes had come despite a number of local problems. In Waterford a split within the local organization, partly connected to members taking opposing sides in an inter-union docks dispute, had caused a number of activists, led by Mick

Dunphy, to form a rival Waterford People's Party, which contested
the local elections and had a councillor elected. In Mallow the
party leadership felt that there were two council seats to be won
but Sherlock had refused to accept a running mate, arguing that it
was vital for him to poll ahead of Fianna Fáil's Ned O'Keeffe in
order to put himself in the running for the next general election.
At a meeting to discuss the issue he threatened to resign if the party
fielded two candidates, and Garland concluded that Sherlock's 'sole
aim seems to be to win a Dáil seat for himself'. Despite what the
leadership considered his 'disgraceful' attitude, and his use of a
'clique' to attain 'total power and control' in the local party,
Sherlock eventually got his way.

While the WP had taken votes from Labour, the overall left
vote had not increased at all. Dick Spring reacted bitterly to the
election results, writing to the RTÉ authority alleging that the
Labour Party had been subject to attacks by a group 'whose values
on democracy and free speech would hardly commend themselves
to the Irish people'. Labour also made a complaint about *Today
Tonight*'s coverage of the elections to the Broadcasting Complaints
Commission, alleging WP influence. Spring did not even bother
to reply to letters from the WP urging discussions on a joint left
strategy.

In most urban areas the WP were still well ahead of Sinn Féin.
The one exception came in Dublin Central, where Christy Burke
beat White to a council seat. The Sinn Féin success was largely
due to Burke's association with the anti-drugs movement, with
the Provos now providing physical support for campaigns against
dealers. Gerry Doherty was worried, suggesting that the WP were
now 'perceived as an establishment party in the inner city'. There
was no doubt that the party was fully aware of the scale of the
heroin problem. The *Irish People* had carried a sympathetic interview with the Concerned Parents Against Drugs (CPAD) in
Fatima Mansions, and the paper's former editor Padraig Yeates
co-authored *Smack*, a vivid account of heroin's spread through the
capital, published in 1985. Action against drugs pushers was popular
and De Rossa conceded that 'the Provos' activity [was] winning

them votes' but he argued that the WP also had 'to go after the working-class vote which is going to Fianna Fáil and Fine Gael'.

There were also those who did not wish to compete with the Provos for support and who expressed distaste at the anti-drug campaign. Paddy Gillan argued in *Workers' Life* that Sinn Féin was recruiting from the 'traditional reserve army of reaction' and that the CPAD anthem 'Build a Bonfire' contained 'more than a hint of incipient fascism'. There was an 'obvious lumpen complexion' to Sinn Féin and if economic conditions worsened 'the consequent growth in the lumpenproletariat will encourage a more overt expression of fascism by the Provisionals'. Mike Jennings recognized that 'the CPAD did us an enormous amount of damage' but felt that the WP had to oppose 'glorified vigilantism': 'It was the correct position ethically but short-sighted politically. The stated position of the CPAD was that you did not involve the Guards. We were saying how the fuck do you oppose criminality and not involve the Guards?' Finglas activist John O'Neill recalls what he feels was a strategic mistake: 'We should have had pickets on Garda stations, highlighted the issue but directed it away from vigilantism, but we disengaged . . . there was a real problem for working-class people and we said because the Provos are involved we're not going to get involved.'

An internal party information leaflet for WP candidates outlined points to make when the issue of crime arose on the doorsteps: 'there were no instant solutions to crime; unemployment and poverty were factors; businessmen can rip off £2 million and go scot-free, if you rob a car you go to jail. BUT we must be very strong against crime which involves personal injury or attacks on old people etc.' The WP opposed greater powers of arrest and detention for the Gardaí contained in a proposed Criminal Justice Bill. Noting the suspicious death in custody of a man in Co. Cavan during 1982 and accusations that the Gardaí had forced confessions from people, the party argued that 'new Garda powers put the innocent at risk'.

In late 1985 the party in Dublin found an issue that gained it widespread publicity. WP councillors moved a resolution calling for a ban on slot machines in casinos. The idea had not actually been discussed before Eric Byrne, its originator, put it forward at the Corporation, but once it gained momentum the party took it up with gusto. The WP argued that the proliferation of these machines helped 'create misery' in areas blighted by unemployment, with families facing 'slot-machine extortion'. The party placed pickets on casinos and eventually Dublin Corporation voted to refuse to grant licences to the gaming-machine operators, despite strong opposition from Fine Gael. In Co. Dublin, however, both Fianna Fáil and Fine Gael councillors bowed to pressure from the casino owners to stop the 'attempt by the Workers' Party to undermine private enterprise'. The campaign was also tried, with varying degrees of success, in Bray, Waterford and Cork. While a small matter in comparison to the drugs crisis, the slot-machine campaign offered local branches a populist issue on which to increase their visibility.

So-called moral issues continued to cause problems for the government. In the Dáil, De Rossa and Mac Giolla supported the coalition's Family Planning Bill, which legalized the sale of contraceptives to those aged over 18, despite reservations about its limited nature. Another key social policy concern of the WP was the push for a referendum to end the constitutional ban on divorce – a cause that had been officially adopted at the 1982 Ard Fheis. A divorce bill put forward by the party in 1983 had only won the support of one other TD, Tony Gregory. De Rossa stated in early 1986 that divorce was the 'most important social and family law issue facing Irish society', with an estimated 70,000 broken marriages and no right to remarry. The coalition finally introduced its own divorce bill and the summer of 1986 saw another bitter referendum. The government was split, with several Labour and Fine Gael TDs opposed to divorce, while Fianna Fáil, in theory neutral, in effect campaigned against the bill. The Catholic hierarchy made clear their opposition. The anti-divorce campaign effectively utilized fear about the effects of legalization on poor families, propaganda that was not countered by the divorce lobby. The WP campaigned under the slogan 'Civil Divorce is a Civil

Right', and were later acknowledged by the Divorce Action Campaign as 'in some areas . . . effectively the only representatives' of the 'Yes' campaign. The party leafleted 20 major towns 'from Tullow to Donegal' and campaigned on the issue in all but 2 constituencies, but the amendment was comfortably defeated, with 538,279 voting for and 935,844 against. In Dublin, significantly, the vote was narrowly in favour of divorce. The WP argued, optimistically, that the result showed that 'there is an increasing number of people willing to make up their own minds and not be dictated to by the Church. This is progress.' But the party also acknowledged that 'some of our own supporters voted no'. In the referendum's aftermath local branches were instructed to ask those who had cooperated with them in the campaign to join the WP.

The bifurcation between the movement's Northern and Southern branches became more pronounced during the 1980s as the WP became increasingly hostile to irredentism and more deeply involved in mainstream Southern politics that was often far removed from the experience of the North. Many Southern members admired their comrades in the North: 'We were in awe of Belfast . . . [they] made us fucking stronger . . . you have to take your hat off to these people.' Members who went there found canvassing both nationalist and loyalist areas an 'invigorating' experience. Lucia O'Neill recalls that in Belfast 'the hospitality was unreal . . . probably because they didn't have many friends. They were real characters, really enjoyable.' But there were others who expressed the growing Southern alienation from all things Northern. Eric Byrne's attitude was 'Cut them off. We didn't want to know them . . . we didn't want Northern Irish people to come down and help us campaign because they were an embarrassment to us, their Northern accents; we didn't want people to identify them with the WP.' Another Dublin activist remembered, 'Quite honestly I would be afraid of some of them, they were big rough men. They were so bad that they could not let them knock on doors; they done postering but were never allowed to canvass.'

By the mid-1980s the party's image had undergone significant changes. Most branches were no longer named after republican icons. Although 'socialism' now clearly took precedence over 'republicanism' in the party's ideology, a strong commitment to the older concept was still expressed by some. Easter commemorations continued to be held at Kilmainham Gaol in Dublin, in Cork and Waterford. Members marched to Bodenstown every June, although now only in their hundreds. Selling Easter lilies remained party policy, though some felt that the practice should be abandoned. Any branch that did not sell lilies was told to make up the funds in other ways. Members were reminded of the party's heritage by the honouring of veterans at Ard Fheiseanna. There continued to be varying views on the Irish language and the GAA, with some resenting any expression of what they saw as nationalism. On the other hand, some Dublin members established a Cumann Gaelach, which organized trips to Ráth Cairn in the Meath Gaeltacht.

The most pressing issue concerning the WP 'republican heritage' continued to be allegations of Official IRA activity. In late 1985 Labour minister Ruairi Quinn told Hot Press that he believed that the OIRA existed and that its Army Council had an influence over the leadership of the WP. The WP countered that Quinn was whipping up a 'red scare' to cover up his party's 'appalling record' in government. Worse was to come in March 1986 when a Today Tonight special examined the funding of paramilitary organizations in the North. The first segment of the 90-minute programme dealt with the Provisional IRA, INLA and loyalist groups. The second concentrated on the Official IRA's connections to racketeering in the building industry, forgery and fraud. RUC Chief Superintendent Bertie McCaffrey was shown stating that it was the OIRA that had 'started off' paramilitary involvement in racketeering and that they were 'still very, very active in that sphere'. McCaffrey added that he believed some of this revenue was going 'towards the political end of things'. SDLP politician Brian Feeney charged that 'the Official IRA is engaged in the same activities as the Bolsheviks were before 1917, when Stalin was in charge of raising money for them . . . it was considered perfectly legitimate, before 1917, to stage robberies; [they] were called revolutionary expropriations.'

As no Southern WP figure was prepared to take part, Seamus Lynch appeared at short notice on a link from Belfast to respond to the allegations. A visibly nervous and annoyed Lynch alleged that the programme was the result of internal RTÉ politics. He stated that the programme's presenter, Pat Cox, was on the verge of joining the newly formed Progressive Democrats, producer Mick McCarthy was a 'republican sympathizer' and researcher Fintan Cronin had been seen in the company of 'known' Provos in Belfast. Lynch denied any knowledge of the Official IRA and said anyone with evidence of illegality should contact the police. Mac Giolla suggested to the *Irish Press* that the programme certainly 'gave the lie to suggestions about all the influence the Workers' Party is supposed to have in RTÉ' and contended that it was motivated by Spring's threats against the station after the local elections.

An internal WP report alleged that following Spring's 1985 criticisms, producer David Blake Knox had been removed from *Today Tonight* and replaced by Mick McCarthy. Programme makers with 'strong personal ties' to the Labour Party had demanded a programme linking the WP to racketeering. It was felt that it had been made clear to Joe Mulholland that if he wanted his own career to progress within the station 'he was going to have to deliver'. It was claimed that Belfast Provos had acted as 'researchers' and 'spotters' for the programme makers. Another internal report alleged that a youth featured in the programme as a victim of an OIRA punishment beating had in fact been assaulted by the Provos. When Pat Cox was appointed general secretary of the Progressive Democrats shortly afterwards, Eamon Gilmore asked: 'If RTÉ allows the general secretary of the Progressive Democrats to make a programme about the Workers' Party will they now accord the same opportunity to Sean Garland to make a programme on the Progressive Democrats?' Many were happy to believe that the programme 'was a hatchet job' but not all party members were mollified. Councillor Christy Kinahan and a number of those who had recently joined the party in Tipperary resigned, arguing that *Today Tonight*'s accusations had not been adequately dealt with. (Internally it was claimed that Kinahan had actually left because he was upset over failing to be picked as Dáil candidate for the general election.) The Broadcasting Complaints Commission rejected the WP's criticisms of the programme.

The *Today Tonight* programme appeared a week before the 1986 Ard Fheis. De Rossa told delegates that members were 'seething' at RTÉ's 'outrageous smear'. In his presidential address Mac Giolla took another approach, saying that despite the programme being an 'attempt to stand truth on its head' he was 'proud that our party had achieved a position in our society where it was seen by our enemies as a real threat'. He said the WP had 'deadly enemies in the leadership of the Labour Party' because 'they have abandoned . . . Larkin [and] Connolly and they hate us for exposing this'. More surprisingly, he also took the opportunity to welcome the formation of the Progressive Democrats as it set down 'clear lines of battle where friend and foe are more easily identified'.

Despite the party leadership's claims to be unaffected by allegations of links to criminal activity, those opposed to the WP were aware that the exposés were causing unease. In late 1986 the *Sunday Tribune*, edited by Vincent Browne, ran a feature on the Official IRA over two issues. It contained new material on links between Dublin criminals and the OIRA as well as on racketeering in the North. The WP informed their members that the articles were an attempt to discredit them with a general election in the offing. For many party members, such revelations were far removed from their experience; one Dun Laoghaire member recalls that 'my view on it was that the ruling class was trying to undermine us [because] we were developing in working-class areas'. The WP leadership did not have to try very hard to convince their members that media exposés of the Official IRA were politically motivated.

In January 1987 the government fell when Labour withdrew its votes from the coalition over proposed budget cuts. The following general election campaign was dominated by debate about how to solve the economic crisis. Fine Gael and the Progressive Democrats were adamant that public spending cuts and 'fiscal rectitude' were necessary. The PDs, with their monetarist agenda, were the media's election sensation. Fianna Fáil rejected what they described as the 'Thatcherite' policies of both Fine Gael and the PDs and campaigned under the slogan 'Health Cuts Hurt the Old, the Sick and the Handicapped'. The WP concentrated on presenting a 'real alternative' to the Labour Party. In Galway the WP made it clear that they did not want supporters to give transfers to Labour's Michael D. Higgins, despite his anti-coalition stance and left-wing reputation; he was not to be allowed to 'pose as pro-working class on the doorstep'. Prior to the election the ITGWU leadership had stated that officials of the union who stood as candidates would have to give up their jobs if elected – a move that the WP claimed was aimed at the four ITGWU officials who were standing as WP candidates, Rabbitte, Gilmore, Mike Jennings and Seamus Rodgers. (In the past several ITGWU officials had become Labour TDs and had been granted leave of absence; Dan Spring had been on leave from the ITGWU from 1943 until his death in 1981.) The WP fielded 28 candidates and produced 75,000 posters, 120,000 general leaflets and 2 million canvass leaflets. Mike Jennings recalls: '[Dick] Spring said who are these fellas? We seemed to be everywhere, harrying the Labour Party big time.' Their party-political broadcast was widely considered the strongest of the campaign. Scripted by Eoghan Harris and based on the *Mastermind* quiz show, it featured 'Jimmy Macken', a 'redundant worker' who was questioned about Fine Gael's economic policy. 'Macken' answered that it was 'to attack the poor *before* the election', while Fianna Fáil's economic policy was 'to attack the poor *after* the election'. Asked where the WP would make cuts, he answered 'in profits, in wealthy tax-dodgers' income, in subsidies to fly-by-night firms'. What was party policy on tax dodgers? 'New institutions . . . the kind of ones with high walls around them.' The party's aim was 'a country without poverty. People with pride in their work. A kind of country no young person would want to leave.' The WP also tried to address their negative image in rural areas, removing a reference to farm subsidies from the text of the election broadcast. The *Irish People* carried an interview with Irish Creamery

Milk Suppliers Association leader Donal Murphy, who argued in favour of a land tax and for a 'clear policy on farmer taxation, not least so that the problems relating to the urban-rural divide in taxation are sorted out'.

On election day, the biggest story was the great success of the Progressive Democrats, a party consisting largely of Fianna Fáil defectors who ran on a pro-market, anti-corruption platform and took fourteen seats in their first general election, mainly at the expense of Fine Gael. The WP won four seats, with Mac Giolla and De Rossa re-elected, Joe Sherlock regaining the seat he had lost in Cork East, and Pat McCartan taking the last seat in Dublin North-East after a nail-biting contest with Charles Haughey's son Sean. The party gained 3.8 per cent of the poll nationally, an improvement of half a percentage point over the previous general election. The WP vote in Dublin now exceeded that of Labour, which was badly punished for its part in the coalition government and received its worst vote nationally since 1933. Also satisfying for the WP was the fact that Sinn Féin had performed very badly, despite its decision to take seats if elected. According to one survey, 60 per cent of WP voters were under 35 years of age, and 77 per cent were manual workers or unemployed; both figures were the highest of any party represented in the Dáil. WP voters were also three times more likely to live in local authority housing than the average voter. The party's candidates, in contrast, were mostly professionals and concerns about the class backgrounds of candidates were particularly to the fore for Industrial Department cadres, a group that had done much to attract some of these professionals into the party in the first place. New TD Pat McCartan continued to be a key target of their 'workerist' ire. The fact that McCartan had joined a yacht club in Dun Laoghaire was a source of great embarrassment to many WP members. McCartan would repeatedly fail to gain election to the Ard Chomhairle and be the subject of continued internal sniping.

The left was still very weak, with the combined vote for the WP, Labour and Jim Kemmy's DSP just 10 per cent. Despite Labour's setbacks the party still held 12 seats; and the WP's vote in Dublin had increased by only 7,633 since 1982. There was a sense that a chance for a major electoral breakthrough had been missed. Peter Kane argued that 'there can be no doubt that the general public believe we did very well by doubling our seats. This can also be interpreted as an indication of how marginal we were thought to be prior to the poll.'

Fianna Fáil fell just shy of winning a majority of seats, but in the absence of any mathematically and politically viable alternative it eventually formed a minority government. Initially there had been speculation that Haughey would again seek the support of independents or even the WP TDs. On the question of whom the WP would vote for as Taoiseach, Garland suggested that Fianna Fáil had been 'progressive in some respects', such as their opposition to the privatization of semi-state companies. But after Haughey stated that he would implement '90 per cent' of the Fine Gael budget once in office, De Rossa made clear that this was '90 per cent too much'. Instead the party voted against both Haughey and FitzGerald for Taoiseach and suggested that as the conservative parties were a majority they should come together and allow a left–right divide to emerge. They also called for a united left approach in the Dáil with Labour and Kemmy of the DSP. Despite the often bitter rivalry at local level and the oft-stated desire to replace Labour as the leading party of the left, there was a recognition within the WP that this was not going to happen any time soon. With Labour out of government the WP's attacks on the party might well become counterproductive and alienate potential support. Furthermore, the hostility of large sections of the Labour Party to the WP meant that if Labour, as in the past, refused cooperation then they and not the WP would be seen as blocking left-wing unity. Garland told *In Dublin* magazine that any realignment had to 'include the Labour Party . . . a united left approach is going to secure some kind of benefit all around'. But some within the WP were less keen on an alliance with Labour; Pat Rabbitte argued that Dick Spring 'could easily join one of the conservative parties'. In any case it soon became clear that Labour were not interested. Kemmy was also wary, regarding the WP's answers to his questions on their relationship to the Official IRA as 'inadequate'. Although the other left independent, Tony Gregory, was keen on an alliance, the WP were hostile. A WP election leaflet in Dublin Central had accused him of having 'a pact with the Provos' and of being 'irrelevant' on national issues. Gregory eventually abstained on the vote for Taoiseach, seeing Haughey as the 'lesser evil'.

In a complete abandonment of their election manifesto, Fianna Fáil in April 1987 implemented what the *Irish Independent* called the 'toughest, strictest budget in a decade' introducing drastic cuts, particularly in health. Later that month at the WP Ard Fheis the 'cuts mania' was roundly condemned. Mac Giolla sensed the growth of a 'new and ugly' abuse of the poor, unmarried mothers and the unemployed and a deliberate campaign to divide the working class: 'What once wouldn't be whispered for charity's sake is now snarled openly by people who are bewildered and desperate for solutions to their own problems: blame the poor, blame those on welfare . . . cut them off, make them do useless work for the dole, let them take the boat.' The Irish business class were hell-bent on destroying state assets through privatization and dragging Ireland into NATO. He singled out Independent Newspapers owner Tony O'Reilly and the 'Privateers and Destroyers' of the PDs as key assistants in this project.

The health cutbacks provoked widespread protests by nurses; in June, 40,000 demonstrators in Dublin were addressed by Rabbitte and Des Geraghty. The issue provided opportunities for WP branches to renew street activity. There were pickets of Fianna Fáil TDs' clinics and a series of public meetings and petitions to build on the anger over the cuts. The WP hoped that disillusion over Fianna Fáil's conversion to 'Thatcherism' would cut into the ruling party's working-class base. During the autumn of 1987 Fine Gael leader Alan Dukes pledged that his party would not bring down the government while it continued its economic policies, in recognition of the dire state of the economy and the need to confront this. The *Irish People* in contrast argued that Fine Gael was supporting the government because 'Fianna Fáil are implementing basically what are Fine Gael policies' with the support of that party and the 'benign neutrality' of the PDs.

Meanwhile, the WP took a considerably more benign view of another exercise in economic consensus-building. In October 1987 a Programme for National Recovery was agreed after discussions between the ICTU, employers, farmers and the government – the beginning of 'social partnership' in Ireland. Included within the PNR was a commitment to pay rises for public service workers close to inflation level and a one-hour decrease in the working week. Labour was highly critical of the deal, Spring describing it as a 'con trick' in which pay rises would be offset by public sector job losses and further cutbacks; this in part reflected the acrimony that had developed between Labour and the unions during the coalition years. The WP, in contrast, cautiously welcomed the PNR as a 'significant if modest advance' and compared it with the Fine Gael–Labour government's refusal 'to talk to the trade union movement in this way'. If some of the promises about tax reform and job creation were vague, 'the trade union movement at least deserve credit for diverting Fianna Fáil from an undiluted Thatcherite approach in certain areas'. The deal won the support of ICTU despite the opposition of a majority of its constituent unions; the block votes of the ITGWU and the Federated Workers' Union of Ireland made the difference at an ICTU special delegate conference.

The WP's trade union officials had been crucial to pushing for a 'Yes' vote within ICTU, reflecting the party's long-standing support for centralized agreements that allowed 'class' demands to be made on a national basis. Geraghty recalls:

We had a totally failing capitalism, high unemployment, high emigration, high inflation . . . so how [were] we going to swing things around? Localized collective bargaining, which could only deal with wages in particular plants, was not in my view a real long-term option for us . . . so I was very much an advocate that we would get in with government and employers [and] start playing out an agenda that we would do x and y provided a, b [and] c was delivered.

Those in favour of the PNR explicitly warned that the Irish trade unions would be marginalized as the unions in Britain had been if they did not accept the deal. The WP's trade union influence was strongest among full-time officials who were very keen to avoid the unions being sidelined. Nevertheless there was considerable opposition within the unions, with some arguing the leadership had been 'snookered by Haughey'.

The WP, which claimed 3,000 members in 1987, launched a new recruitment campaign that year aimed at creating a 'mass' party. Every WP voter was to be treated as a potential member. Building greater membership would have taken some of the pressure off hard-pressed activists – Mike Jennings recalls being 'out six nights a week and Saturday and Sunday mornings' on party business – but would also inevitably have altered the character of a party in which a member who did only one night's work a week was considered 'inactive'. There was meanwhile a realization that a new generation of leaders would have to come to the fore. In September 1987 the 63-year-old Mac Giolla announced that he was stepping down as party president, after a quarter of a century. Even traditionally hostile papers paid tribute, the *Irish Press* noting his 'courage in helping to bring about the transition from gun to ballot' and the *Irish Independent* praising his 'dignity'. His position would be contested by vice-presidents De Rossa and Sherlock.

Among the international observers who had attended the April 1987 Ard Fheis was Igor Sokolov, representing the Communist Party of the Soviet Union. Sokolov's party had recently embarked on a programme of rapid change. Mikhail Gorbachev had been elected CPSU General Secretary in March 1985. Worried by the stagnation of the Soviet economy and society, he had embarked upon a dramatic reform agenda. By early 1987 it was already clear that Gorbachev was a very different figure from his predecessors, and a more positive view of the USSR had begun to develop in the West. The coming to power of Gorbachev coincided with a solidifying of WP–CPSU relations. In early 1986 Garland had again attended the CPSU Congress in Moscow, and in May 1987

De Rossa, Garland and O'Hagan visited Moscow to meet the Soviet Committee for European Security and Cooperation. Later that year Eugene Lagutin of the CPSU Central Committee visited Ireland on a tour organized by the WP, which included a public meeting in Dublin where he lectured on the progress of the Soviet reforms. Inside the WP there was near-universal enthusiasm for the changes taking place in the Soviet Union. Garland reported in December 1987 how 'since April 1985 there has been a continuous campaign to eradicate corruption, bureaucracy and stagnation' in all areas of Soviet life, with officials now speaking openly about the 'wasted years' under Brezhnev. The 'breadth and depth' of Perestroika could be gauged from Gorbachev's speeches, and while there were fears that the process might still be halted, wide support had been mobilized for it within the CPSU.

Relations were also maintained with North Korea. During 1986 De Rossa and Garland had gone to Pyongyang for a conference on nuclear disarmament, travelling via Moscow where they also spent a number of days. De Rossa claims to have been unimpressed by the Asian country – 'a completely unreal society and unreal situation, where people were basically treated as children not as adults at all' – but he understood the WP's relationship with North Korea as part of 'making friends . . . with the party in the Soviet Union'. The Soviets for their part also analysed the WP. In the view of the Second Secretary at the Dublin Embassy, D. S. Molodtsov, there were two major tendencies within the WP – 'Marxist-Leninist' and 'Social Democratic'. Since the WP had 'crystallized from the left wing of Sinn Féin', a 'petty bourgeois nationalist party, where Marxists played a certain, but not dominant role', it was not yet a fully communist party. An 'R. Geraghty' (probably a reference to Des Geraghty) was described as the 'chief ideologist' of the social democratic wing, Garland as a 'buffer' between the two wings, O'Hagan as a 'cementing unit' and Ó Cionnaith as a 'solid' Marxist.

As violence increased in Northern Ireland during 1987, there was also increasing tension with the Provos in the South. In September

De Rossa called for people in Finglas to shun Sinn Féin after the killing of a local man accused of being an informer. In November, the killing of eleven Protestants attending a Remembrance Day ceremony in Enniskillen, most of whom were old-age pensioners, had a major impact on Southern attitudes to republican violence. In Dublin 50,000 people signed a book of condolence for the dead and there was a minute's silence observed across the state. Within the WP it was noted that 'post Enniskillen we are in a new era'; the party's task was to 'make the most of it' and give revulsion at the carnage a 'political significance'. The WP proposed a motion in Dublin Corporation calling on all paramilitary groups to end their campaigns; it was passed unanimously.

Four days after the Enniskillen atrocity, Eoghan Harris distributed a document, titled 'Television and Terrorism', among WP members and colleagues in RTÉ. He argued that the ongoing campaign against Section 31 of the Broadcasting Act was led by three groups: a 'tiny tantrum' of liberals who believed in absolute freedom of speech, middle-class 'hush puppy' broadcasters who supported the Provos, and 'honest' journalists who believed abolishing Section 31 would undermine the paramilitaries by depriving them of a grievance and allowing journalists to question them directly on the national airwaves. Harris argued that, because of a 'leaky national consensus' on political violence, 'the Provos can draw and often win any such interview . . . even if the interview takes place within minutes of film of the most appalling atrocity'. His defence of Section 31 was shared by many of the party's members in RTÉ, but not by the WP itself. In March McCartan had put down a Dáil motion seeking to annul Section 31, arguing that it remained an undemocratic measure. Tony Heffernan responded to Harris by writing an internal WP analysis that argued that while the party's policy on scrapping Section 31 and replacing it with anti-incitement legislation was not perfect, it was better than supporting more censorship, which could be extended to 'those who advocate strikes [or] advocates of class conflict'. Section 31 also offered the Provos a chance to 'complain about their martyrdom'. But Heffernan suggested that the WP should not campaign on the issue because 'there is nothing politically to be gained for us in adopting a high profile on it ... any election canvasser will confirm that it is not an issue that is raised on the doorsteps to any extent at all'. He worried that the Harris document had unhelpfully resurrected the 'whole controversy about alleged WP influence' in RTÉ. In an *In Dublin* interview around this time Harris outlined his philosophy, arguing that 'Michael McDowell [of the Progressive Democrats] comes on television and in the language of fiscal rectitude can condemn a couple with six kids to semi-starvation for the rest of their lives. That phrase, fiscal rectitude, covers up crimes against humanity. There should be a Concerned Parents against Michael McDowell.' On recurring accusations of OIRA activity, he claimed that 'there is a big distinction between embezzlement and fraud, on the one hand, and mass murder on the other ... you have to put robbery in a social context and it's not number one on my list of heinous crimes'. He also suggested that 'any working-class party that doesn't have a theory of force is in trouble. I joined a revolutionary republican organization ... there was a good chance of the working class getting state power in Ireland ... but I don't believe that we will be allowed to do it peacefully.'

Within RTÉ the party's cadres were under pressure. Gerry Gregg had already been embroiled in a row over a *Today Tonight* special produced by him on the history of Fianna Fáil. John Caden, now producing and editing the Gay Byrne radio show, was in dispute with the Federated Workers' Union of Ireland over his role during a strike in October 1987. Harris himself had resigned from the FWUI after Enniskillen, claiming that the union in RTÉ was not sufficiently opposed to the Provisionals' campaign. Harris and Gregg were already preparing for a future beyond the station, establishing an independent production company called Iskra, after Lenin's newspaper in pre-revolutionary Russia. Among the company's first productions was a documentary on the life of Conor Cruise O'Brien. Iskra also began production of a series called *Workers' Lives* detailing the social and cultural history of Irish labour.

*

Relations with the anti-drugs movement, always tense because of the involvement of the Provisionals and WP skittishness about 'vigilantism', deteriorated further in 1987 and 1988. De Rossa described the Concerned Parents Against Drugs as being similar to the 'Ku Klux Klan' and named a CPAD activist as a Provisional IRA member in the Dáil. There were angry scenes at meetings in Finglas and Ballymun when the WP gave out leaflets denouncing CPAD as a 'Provo front' and demanded speaking rights for De Rossa as local TD. At one meeting he successfully addressed the crowd despite an attempt to physically push him off the platform.

Another difficult issue on the ground was relations between the travelling and settled communities. The WP called for funding for serviced halting sites, recognizing that the expansion of unofficial sites led to 'friction with the local community'. The Workers' Party Youth worked with the Dublin Young Travellers Development and Education Group in Dublin, and Club Uí Cadhain hosted travellers' rock 'n' roll nights. In Finglas members managed to prevent a meeting, called over complaints about local travellers, becoming a march on their halting site. A member present at the meeting recalls:

The people we were asking to vote for us, the same people, wanted to hang [Travellers]. We wouldn't leave, [we] kept explaining to people this isn't the fucking answer . . . I take my fucking hat off to De Rossa, people roared and shouted and [were] spitting at him and us, [but] we never got physical, we stood our ground and got up one after another and said our piece.

De Rossa managed to defuse the situation, making clear that the Council was ultimately responsible for the problem. In Navan the WP's Seamus McDonagh was 'split open' when hit by a stone while interceding in a row between local people and travellers.

De Rossa, who easily defeated Sherlock in the election for party president, told the 1988 Ard Fheis that he was calling on Dick Spring to 'sit down and talk about how we can defend the working class of this island'. If Labour's leader did not respond, the WP would 'not stand around waiting. We will drive forward whether he wants to come with us or not.' De Rossa warned that socialism was under 'vicious attack . . . even in those societies where our comrades have won victories'. The WP had to confront 'reaction . . . on the streets, in the factories, at the dole queues, in the colleges, in the universities, in the media . . . wherever we are presented with the opportunity to deal deadly blows at the vicious criminal immorality of capitalism'.

Mac Giolla used his final presidential address to compare Ireland with the USSR:

We are regularly told that we have freedoms here which they haven't got in the Soviet Union. [One is] freedom of movement . . . our young people are currently availing fully of this at the rate of at least 30,000 a year . . . We also, of course, have freedom of the press . . . if you own a press. Soviet citizens have a right to free and immediate medical care . . . but Irish citizens who have the money, have the right to jump to the head of the queue . . . it is the same with education: free in the Soviet Union; available here in full only to the rich . . . whatever restrictions there were in the Soviet Union on individual freedoms are fast disappearing as Mikhail Gorbachev leads an unstoppable surge towards freedom of expression, criticism and movement.

Numerous international communist observers were present and East German President Erich Honecker sent 'warm greetings', wishing the WP 'every success in your discussions'. The PLO provided the Ard Fheis's main guest speaker. Observers noted how little open discussion took place at the conference, though there were sharp exchanges on the issue of abortion referral. A motion that would have pledged the party to assist a woman with an unwanted pregnancy in 'whatever action she decides to take' was opposed by several delegates, including Joe Sherlock. One argued it would be 'disastrous' for the WP to be seen as pro-abortion.

After the Ard Fheis De Rossa began a tour of WP branches North and South to review the organization's strengths and weaknesses. Following the Ard Fheis, *Making Sense* was launched. It was a new 'political and cultural review' edited by Paddy Gillan, filling the gap left by the demise of *Workers' Life*. In the first issue, in response to a question on whether the Official IRA had finally disbanded, De Rossa dismissively replied, 'When did Fianna Fáil disband its army? When did Labour disband the Citizen Army?'

De Rossa also held talks with Dick Spring on left-wing unity. The WP's call for more cooperation with Labour was not universally approved of inside the party, but the leadership argued that while the 'primary' task was building the WP, the influence of socialism could be extended by cooperation with other 'principled organizations'. This cooperation had to be 'handled very carefully' on issues that united those opposed to 'Thatcherism, Haugheyism and terrorism'. Happily for the party in Waterford the breach with the People's Party was finally healed in May, with councillor Martin O'Regan rejoining along with his supporters, giving the WP three seats on the Corporation.

The WP had also begun to see growth in the greater Dublin area. Leixlip, Co. Kildare, had a population of 15,000 people living in what *Making Sense* described as 'modern housing estates tacked on to an old village centre'. In 1988 it attained town commission status, and in the subsequent election for town commissioners the WP won 21 per cent of the vote and had its two candidates, Catherine Murphy and Colm Purcell, elected. The WP had developed a strong profile in the town, campaigning for regular public transport and facilities in areas where 'they [had] built houses and nothing else'. De Rossa argued that the Leixlip results showed a new potential for the left. Most of the town's residents were homeowners, yet the WP and Labour combined had taken 40 per cent of the vote there. He stressed that Gorbachev in the Soviet Union was showing that socialism needed a 'shake-up from within' and it was also time for 'innovative and imaginative change'. There were suggestions that the WP should begin to seek votes outside its traditional base. Some felt a ceiling was being reached in working-class areas: 'The votes weren't there . . . because 50 per cent of the council estates would vote Fianna Fáil anyway regardless of what they did or did not do.' In Dun Laoghaire Gilmore became involved in resident associations in the upwardly mobile estates of Blackrock and the party began to see some return for effort in these areas. In *Making Sense* Gilmore argued that many people felt that the WP offered a 'gloomy stereotype of a People's Republic'. Socialists had to reassess some of their strategies given the high rate of home ownership in the Republic and the facts that many workers had private health insurance and most parents valued the contribution made by the churches to their children's education.

The discussions were influenced by the party's view of the rapid changes in Eastern Europe. Visits by WP members to the USSR were now regular and travel arrangements were usually made (and sometimes subvented) by the Soviet Embassy in Dublin. Some members took courses at the Lenin International School and the Higher Education Institutes in Moscow. In October 1987 Garland and Des O'Hagan met representatives of the Chinese Communist Party as guests of the CPSU at the seventieth anniversary celebrations of the Bolshevik Revolution in Moscow. The Chinese explained the opening up of the Chinese economy while stressing that they intended to remain a socialist society, and agreed to send a delegation to the 1988 WP Ard Fheis. There were also meetings with representatives of the Syrian and Japanese communists. In July 1988 De Rossa and O'Hagan attended a disarmament conference in East Germany addressed by Honecker. Talks between Garland, O'Hagan and Zadim Zagladim, the head of the CPSU International Department, led to an invitation to any WP member who required medical treatment not available in Ireland to apply to the USSR for it.

O'Hagan reported on developments at the CPSU conference in July 1988. Gorbachev had delivered a 'tough, frank message' on the problems that 'conservative managerial methods' posed to continuing reform. There were clashes at the conference when Boris Yeltsin, considered 'too diligent in attacking the city's bureaucracy' was heckled by 'anti-Perestroika elements'.

During the same year a delegation from the North Korean Workers' Party visited Dublin at the WP's invitation. Led by Kim Yong Sun, a director of the International Affairs Department, the Koreans hoped that their visit would 'contribute to further strengthening friendship and cooperation between our two parties'. A WP delegation that included Garland, O'Hagan and Seamus Harrison travelled to North Korea, via Moscow, in September 1988 to witness celebrations of the fortieth anniversary of its revolution. A huge series of commemorations and parades took place, partly to upstage the South Koreans, who were staging the Olympic Games. The WP delegation met with President Kim Il-sung and his son and heir apparent, Kim Jong-il.

In January 1989, with a European election looming, unemployment at over 240,000 and 40,000 people emigrating per year, De Rossa again raised the prospect of left unity, suggesting a 'Rainbow Coalition' of the WP, Labour, the Democratic Socialists, and church and campaigning groups. Labour was again wary, its conference ruling out alliances with the WP. The WP welcomed the proposed amalgamation of the ITGWU and FWUI into a new union, to be Ireland's largest. FWUI leader Billy Attley was considered much less hostile to the WP than some of his ITGWU counterparts.

As the WP prepared for its 1989 Ard Fheis, intended to showcase the party's European election campaign, the media noted a 'whiff of Perestroika'. The RDS delegates were surprised at the extent of the shift articulated in De Rossa's presidential address, to which Harris had contributed. De Rossa began by describing the 'vast upheavals in [the] Soviet Union' as 'a great movement of socialist renewal and regeneration', and went on to stress the need to 'challenge some sacred cows' at home:

In economic terms it is clear that the people of this country do not at this time want public ownership of the means of production . . . they want a market system . . . If that is what they want, we will not stand in their way . . . Socialism as we see it is not anti-market, anti-enterprise or anti-individual . . . work will be well rewarded and the lazy penalised – that means dole spongers as well as tax dodgers, short-day shirkers as well as bosses.

The WP would support 'public ownership only when the public wants to own something'. Some people, De Rossa acknowledged, will find such a statement surprising from a socialist party. That is only one of the surprises we have in store for capitalism in Ireland. Because the last thing a certain kind of capitalist wants is a socialist party which believes in enterprise and energy.

Yet De Rossa also stressed that capitalism 'with its emphasis on the price of everything, distorts our lives and our relationship with each other and with our world', and ended his speech by declaring: 'Capitalism, comrades, must be tamed, caged and starved until it withers away.' The WP's ambition was to become the 'principal socialist opposition party' in Ireland by 1992 and to 'prepare for government' by 2000.

De Rossa's embrace of 'market socialism' and use of terms like social democracy and 'dole spongers' shocked many activists, who had had no inkling that such change was in the offing, though Harris had first outlined some of its themes at a party education seminar in Belfast the previous summer. Reading it beforehand, Heffernan had warned De Rossa there was likely to be a hostile reaction. Some felt that the party president had been 'mesmerized' by Harris. De Rossa himself felt the speech was part of taking the WP on to 'the next stage of its evolution . . . I knew it would ruffle feathers . . . the party had elected me and I had an obligation to lead the party in the direction which I thought they wanted to go, and in which I had an obligation to lead them.'

The speech provoked a strident critique in *Making Sense*, where Ellen Hazelkorn and Paul Sweeney argued that socialism was about the 'control of state power, and the means of production, distribution and exchange by the working class'. In contrast social democracy had historically sought 'accommodations with capital . . . without challenging the distribution of resources within those societies'. They stressed that 'in our eagerness to be seen as "relevant" and "modern" the pitfalls of electoralism and populism must be studiously avoided'. This was the most forceful public criticism of a WP leader's speech that had ever appeared in a party publication.

The European elections meant the debate was not engaged immediately. For the first time in the WP's history the campaign featured posters in which the leader was pictured: a full-length photograph of De Rossa, in stylish suit and coat, walking on a beach and offering 'A Breath of Fresh Air'. In May Haughey called a snap general election, to coincide with the European poll, in the hope of winning an overall majority. This worked to the WP's advantage as the party's energetic European campaign had boosted its profile in Dublin. The WP's general election manifesto stressed traditional themes: 'the Socialist Alternative' promised a 'sustained assault on . . . power and privilege'. Supporters were urged to give their second preferences to Labour and the party called on Labour to urge its voters to transfer to the WP. In Galway, in contrast to 1987, Jimmy Brick and Michael D. Higgins agreed to a transfer deal. However, Spring rejected the calls for an overall electoral pact, claiming that the WP was 'clearly aiming to take seats at Labour's expense'. As the campaign heated up, Haughey accused the WP of promoting the 'failed economic dogma of socialism' and warned of the dangers of the left holding the balance of power. The day before the election, Fianna Fáil took out a four-page advertisement in the *Cork Examiner* which featured an article entitled 'Left turn: No Tanks' – a reference to the Tiananmen Square massacre that had taken place less than a fortnight earlier. Under a photograph of De Rossa it argued that people 'cannot risk the welfare of Ireland at the hands of the left', which was 'Marxist in its ends, Stalinist in its means'. An apology was successfully demanded on De Rossa's behalf.

This attempt at a red scare did not work. In the general election the WP won seven seats, an increase of three, and 5 per cent of the vote, an increase of 1.2 percentage points over 1987. In the capital the party won 11.4 per cent of the vote and six seats, beating Labour on both measures. The party's new TDs were Pat Rabbitte, in Dublin South-West, Eamon Gilmore, in Dun Laoghaire, and Eric Byrne, in Dublin South Central; the latter two took their seats from Labour. De Rossa and Mac Giolla both increased their votes while McCartan, who had been only narrowly elected in 1987, topped the poll in Dublin North-East. Having seven TDs entitled the WP to full secretarial and debating facilities in the Dáil and to £50,000 in state funding. The funding was particularly welcome as a loan of that amount had been taken out to help fund the election campaign, while De Rossa had taken out a personal loan of £50,000 for the European effort. Contrary to Haughey's hope of achieving an overall majority, the election left Fianna Fáil with four fewer seats, and he was eventually forced to form a coalition with the Progressive Democrats, who had lost eight of their own fourteen seats. This development was welcomed by De Rossa, who heralded it as 'a logical rationalization of the grossly overmanned right-wing sector in Irish politics'. He predicted that Fine Gael would join this right-wing bloc after the next election, resulting in the electorate having a clear choice 'between the humane policies of socialism and the unbridled greed of capitalism'.

The results of the European poll, which came in a day after the general election returns, were arguably even more dramatic for the WP. De Rossa – who, as part of the party's campaign opposing the Single European Act in 1987, had argued that the EEC was 'clearly based on preserving and developing capitalism in Western Europe and developing this area as a power bloc' – topped the poll in Dublin. As one member recalls, 'it was emotional . . . Dublin [was] having a mini revolution, that is exactly how it felt. I remember being in the RDS [with] fucking red flags and singing the "Internationale" . . .' Gilmore confidently predicted that the Republic would have a socialist government 'before the end of this century'. Fianna Fáil's working-class base was being eroded and 'people are starting to look at themselves as either Tories or Lefties'. For most WP members the results induced an unbridled sense of achievement bordering on euphoria at what many saw as the long-awaited electoral breakthrough.

15. Workers Unite!

'Workers are being told to vote not according to their class interests
but according to what the leaders of the two Tory camps want.
They want to maintain their power and privileges as rulers of two
supposedly hostile religious groupings.'

Seamus Lynch, 1982

Northern political life was dominated by ongoing violence, but
with the H-Block issue 'out of the way', in Mac Giolla's words,
the Workers' Party hoped there were fresh possibilities for class
politics. During 1982 the party had taken a position diametrically
opposed to the nationalist consensus over proposed educational
reforms that included the amalgamation of the two Catholic
teacher training colleges with Queen's University and Stranmillis
College, forming a single integrated teacher-education centre.
There was uproar in the nationalist community and the Catholic
hierarchy led a strong campaign against the proposals, which Sinn
Féin's Owen Carron described as an 'assault on the heritage, tradition and faith of the Catholic people'. The WP saw this reaction
as 'hysteria' and, while opposing any cuts in spending, supported
the concept of an integrated teacher-training college. Other issues
also set the WP against the North's religious blocs. The party
welcomed a European Court of Human Rights ruling that brought
Northern Ireland's laws on homosexuality into line with Britain's,
the *Northern People* describing it as a 'historic victory for the Gay
community'.

The first electoral test for the WP in the North was the poll for
a new 78-seat Northern Ireland Assembly – the first attempt to
establish a devolved governing institution in the North since the

short-lived assembly of 1974 – in October 1982. The WP were committed to taking their seats if elected, unlike both the SDLP and Sinn Féin. The SDLP, worried about the fact that some unionists were hailing the Assembly as a 'new Stormont' and under pressure on their flank from an increasingly confident Sinn Féin, announced that their candidates would not take seats in the Assembly if elected. Sinn Féin, meanwhile, opted to contest their first Northern Ireland election, but on an abstentionist basis. The WP made a determined effort to reach across the sectarian divide to as many voters as possible, canvassing in areas where they'd never canvassed before. The Belfast leadership resisted a suggestion that Joe Sherlock travel to Derry to help canvass, feeling the WP's Dáil support for Haughey might have an adverse effect on unionist voters, but Sherlock did campaign in the north-west.

Overall the WP gained 2.7 per cent of the first-preference vote, with Tom French receiving 2,826 votes in Armagh, McMahon 2,493 in West Belfast and Lynch 2,516 in North Belfast; in each case the party missed out on a seat by around 500 votes. The two most popular parties in the election were the Ulster Unionists and the Democratic Unionists, with the SDLP the largest nationalist party. More than half of WP voters gave their second preference to the SDLP, while 28 per cent gave second preference to the Alliance Party. In Belfast the transfer rate by WP voters to Alliance had been particularly high, helping that party win two seats. Alliance's relatively strong showing, with ten seats, was welcomed by the WP. The amicable relations between a revolutionary socialist organization and the largely middle-class Alliance confused some; but as Assembly member (and later Alliance party leader) John Cushnahan put it, 'What [was] more revolutionary in Northern Ireland than to be non-sectarian?' Indeed Cushnahan's perceived bias towards the WP saw him described as a 'closet Sticky' by some Provos.

But the story of the election was the 64,000 votes won by Sinn Féin, over 10 per cent of the poll. The swift turn to electoral politics by Sinn Féin amazed those who remembered having to literally fight their way past them into polling stations during the

1970s. Now the WP joined the SDLP in accusing Sinn Féin of engaging in the widespread practice of fraudulently casting votes in another person's name. The *Northern People* explained the Provos' success as based on 'sections of the young, unemployed, lumpen working class' who had been 'offered an intoxicating brew of rebellion . . . against being thrown on the scrap heap by job segregation, by de-industrialisation and by a born to fail education system'. Reaction to the results within the WP was mixed. There was general agreement that the Provos were 'replacing the SDLP in nationalist areas'. A despondent Tom Moore felt that 'extremism' was growing among nationalists and that things did not look good for class politics. Not everyone was so downhearted. Following the elections Fr. Alec Reid called into the WP offices in Belfast to commiserate on their lack of success. Des O'Hagan responded that the WP's 17,000 votes meant: 'There was more communists in Northern Ireland than there was in the whole of the UK!'

Seven per cent of WP voters had transferred to unionist candidates, and this was taken as evidence of the party winning some Protestant support. The WP continued to offer platforms for unionist views, with *Workers' Life* carrying interviews with Shankill councillor Hugh Smyth of the Progressive Unionists, the UVF's political wing, Harold McCusker of the UUP, and Alan Black, the sole survivor of the 1976 Kingsmill massacre. Seamus Lynch provided a testimonial for a bail application on behalf of a UDA member in late 1983, but that did not prevent the UDA from complaining the following year that the Northern Ireland Office promoted the Workers' Party, despite its having an armed wing, and that the WP had merely diluted 'their communism to a style more acceptable to society'. The party continued to stress the need to resist bigotry on both sides, opposing the DUP's refusal to countenance Sunday opening of leisure centres and raising the case of a young single mother expelled from a Catholic school in Maghera.

In 1985 Lynch met John McMichael, the UDA's military commander, at a social function in Belfast. The UDA was still a legal organization, despite its involvement in scores of killings, usually under its cover name 'Ulster Freedom Fighters'. Contacts between the two men continued during 1986, Lynch and his wife travelling nervously on one occasion to McMichael's house in Lisburn for dinner and discussion. The UDA killed six people that year, including a Protestant woman married to a Catholic and a 76-year-old Catholic grandmother. Lynch stressed to McMichael that sectarian killings had to stop but felt the UDA man was prepared to discuss ways to move forward politically. McMichael gave Lynch a draft of a discussion document, which the latter then commented on. In early 1987 the UDA published the document as *Common Sense*, outlining a scenario for peace with an assembly and executive elected by proportional representation, a written constitution and a Bill of Rights. The WP offered a cautious welcome to the proposals, as did the SDLP.

The party continued to develop its small base within the North's trade unions. Lily Kerr was prominent in health workers' union NUPE, Downpatrick councillor Raymond Blaney was a member of the executive of COHSE, and Eugene Hickland was union president at the New University of Ulster. Despite having lost their council seats in 1981, both Lynch and McMahon continued to work extremely hard at community level. Culturally the party also tried to make an impact. 'Poets and Pints' evenings were held in the Lagan Social Club in the Markets, featuring poet John Hewitt, writer Sam McAughtry and music by Tommy Sands. Meanwhile, Seamus Lynch's younger brother, Martin, was emerging as one of the North's leading playwrights, his productions moving from WP Clubs to mainstream theatres and television.

In early 1983 Garret FitzGerald and his Foreign Minister Peter Barry, worried about the rise of Sinn Féin as an electoral force, met Mac Giolla and De Rossa and invited them to take part in the New Ireland Forum, which had been established to discuss how 'lasting peace and stability' could be achieved through the democratic process. All who rejected violence were welcome to attend. The leading Northerners – Seamus Lynch, Mary McMahon,

Seamus Harrison and Des O'Hagan – voiced strong opposition to participating, and while there was some Southern support for taking part, on the grounds that the WP must be seen to be supportive of peace efforts, ultimately the leadership voted not to attend and attacked the process as an effort to save the SDLP. In *Workers' Life* O'Hagan described the Forum as part of a decade of 'physical and psychological assault on the Northern Protestant population, masterminded by Roman Catholic Dublin'. It was this 'vicious sectarian nationalism' that had 'spawned both the terrorist and the Forum'. The WP's alternative was to call for 'democratic devolved government' in the North, despite the fact that this virtually guaranteed unionist rule, with a Bill of Rights to guarantee there was no discrimination.

Violence took another party member's life in March 1983 with the mysterious murder of WP member Eamonn Kerr, who was shot at his home off the Lower Falls. Kerr was laid to rest in the Official Republican plot at Milltown, his coffin draped in the Starry Plough. The following month saw the WP contest an Assembly by-election in Armagh, caused by the disqualification of the SDLP's Seamus Mallon because he held a Senate seat in the South. The SDLP called for a boycott in protest at Mallon's disqualification, Sinn Féin sat out the poll and rival unionist parties felt that the UUP would easily take the seat. Hence there were just two candidates, with the WP's Tom French confronting 'Mrs Thatcher's local agents' in the UUP; French polled a creditable 4,920 votes but lost by a wide margin.

The next electoral test came in the June Westminster elections. The WP contested fourteen seats under the slogan 'Reject Terror – Reject Thatcher'. The party upped its rhetoric against Sinn Féin and the DUP, claiming that a vote for either party encouraged the 'pursuit of final solutions [with] the stench of Nazi pogroms and obscene racialism'. McMahon appealed to the 40 per cent of West Belfast voters who did not vote, arguing that many of these people felt that no party represented their interests. The WP complained bitterly that it was denied a TV broadcast because it had polled less than 5 per cent in the Assembly elections, and failed to get this ruling overturned in a court hearing. The WP polled poorly, taking just 1.9 per cent of the vote. Their top vote-winner was Tom French in Upper Bann.

Sinn Féin's rise continued as the party took 13.4 per cent of the Northern Ireland vote, only narrowly shy of the SDLP. Gerry Adams won a seat in West Belfast, benefiting from the fact that Gerry Fitt had left the SDLP and stood against his old party, splitting the nationalist vote. Sinn Féin's success produced pessimism within the WP, Lynch commenting to the BBC that 'as a result of the polls today Northern Ireland has taken a step back'. Although the party's canvassing in Protestant areas was again noted, Mary McMahon felt that the emphasis on winning over unionists came at the expense of more plausible vote-winning efforts in nationalist areas:

The most you could hope for in a solid Protestant area like the Shankill was 4–500 votes, which was great, but you were never going to win a seat. And while we rightly were working for this Protestant working-class vote there was no comparable effort to try to secure the Catholic working-class vote. It was almost taken [for granted] that whoever voted for us in Catholic areas would just do so ad infinitum, and there was no need to try to work at it. Now there was a huge non-voting electorate in West Belfast, so it wasn't that everybody was signed up to tribes.

Henry Patterson and Paul Bew addressed the dilemma the WP faced in trying to win Protestant support by suggesting that 'the WP cannot hope, in the medium term, for more than the interested attention of sections of the Protestant working class'. But for both men part of the WP's attraction was that though it had been 'reduced to a hard core of support within Catholic areas' it continued to 'expose the gap between the verbose professions of generosity and non-sectarianism of both constitutional and unconstitutional nationalism and the rather seamy reality'.

The electoral success of Sinn Féin only increased the hatred between the rival organizations. Annoyingly for WP members, the Provos were now employing socialist rhetoric, with Gerry

Adams arguing that his election victory meant the 'Irish working class [were] now off their knees'. The *Northern People* likened the Provos to the Orange Order with their marching bands, military-style uniforms, bonfires, arrogance and intimidation. At the same time O'Hagan compared the 'manic logic' of the Provos to the tactics of the Italian Red Brigades and other 'latter-day Trotskyist' terrorist groups, claiming that the methods of these groups showed a 'surprising degree of congruence', perhaps inspired by CIA involvement. Smullen reserved particular venom for journalists of the 'establishment and ultra-left [who] continually glorify the people responsible for the terrorism . . . the torturers, the knee-cappers and the droppers of concrete blocks on the limbs of men and women'. He claimed that 'when captured these people are "always innocent" – the foul deeds are always committed by someone else'. This attitude had practical implications for WP members interested in highlighting cases like those of the Maguire family, wrongly jailed for bombings in England. McMahon remembers:

> If you tried to raise those issues [it] was a no-no. It would be shot down in flames, [you] nearly would be accused of being a Provo. Anything that could have brought us into engagement with wider numbers of people, but that the Provos were supporting or complaining about, you just were not allowed to go there.

It also became WP policy not to share platforms with members of Sinn Féin, which led to a refusal to engage in a number of community groups. Despite the poor electoral results some in the South were just 'grateful' that the Northern party was 'still in existence'. Others felt the fact that they were 'an irritant to the Provos' was a good enough reason to stay active. The bitterness towards the Provos had been visible to all in December 1983, with the broadcast of Independent Television's *World in Action* programme about Gerry Adams, 'The Member for West Belfast'. The documentary was an exposé of Adams' role in the Provisional IRA. Among the hostile commentators featured were Seamus Lynch and Des

O'Hagan, who related a story that while in Long Kesh Adams had claimed to them that he would 'wade up to his knees in Protestant blood' to achieve a united Ireland. (Adams strongly denied this allegation.) Mary McMahon also appeared, described as a 'community worker', denouncing Provo punishment attacks. A symbolic shift came with Cathal Goulding's public endorsement, 'with reservations', of the use of 'supergrass' evidence to secure convictions for terrorist offences in an *Irish Times* interview the same month. Since 1982 large numbers of people had been jailed in the North on the word of former paramilitaries. Eventually most of these cases collapsed, but Goulding argued that the supergrasses had to be judged 'not in the tradition of informers against the people ... but of gangsters informing on gangsters' and asked 'which is the greatest evil, the bomb in the dance hall or pub, or the supergrasses?' Shortly after Goulding's statement the WP in Belfast issued a statement that it opposed supergrass evidence. But opposition was not a high priority and Goulding's views were shared by many in his party.

Physical clashes with Provos continued to be part of everyday life for WP members. After the 1983 elections shots were fired into supporters' homes on the Lower Falls. On internment night in August that year a Belfast WP member was beaten unconscious, his car burnt out and the windows of his house smashed. Violence also came from loyalists. In November Davy Nocher, a party member and former OIRA prisoner, was shot dead by the UVF in Newtownabbey in a random sectarian attack that also wounded a teenage girl. Nocher was buried without paramilitary trappings and at his graveside O'Hagan told mourners: 'Those who murdered Davy did so in the hope of provoking more brutal murders, but Davy Nocher was a member of the Workers' Party because he knew the futility, the insanity, the inhumanity and dreadful hate that sectarianism creates.' Following Nocher's death the WP denied allegations that they were downplaying the sectarian nature of the attack because they had contacts with loyalists.

The WP polled poorly again in the 1984 European elections in June, taking 1.6 per cent of the vote. All politics in Northern

Ireland continued to take place against the backdrop of political violence: 72 people were killed in 1984, 38 of them civilians. The Irish government had published its New Ireland Forum report in May, making it clear that a united Ireland remained the favoured outcome for Fianna Fáil, Fine Gael, the Labour Party and the SDLP but that a federal arrangement or joint authority might also be acceptable. The WP rejected these conclusions in their response to the report, *The Case for Devolved Government in Northern Ireland*, which again emphasized that class was the most significant division in Northern society. Kevin Smyth felt this downplayed the strength of communal division:

There was this naivety that there was only a working-class community. You have to recognize reality as well, that there are two different communities that have developed in their own ways with their own dynamics and maybe you are going to have to have interim arrangements. Or at least look at having interim arrangements – but we were not allowed to debate that.

In 1984 members of the Industrial Department's Research Section produced a draft document entitled *Northern Ireland: From Reformation to Revolution*. A Northern version of *The Irish Industrial Revolution*, it amounted to an even stronger renunciation of traditional republicanism than the original pamphlet. Garland, who was heavily influenced by O'Hagan's belief in a continuity between early Irish republicanism and later communist thought, was adamant that there was 'no way in which this can be published', and the pamphlet did not see the light of day. O'Hagan, who lived in the North full-time from the mid-1980s, became the party's leading Northern ideologue. He shared with Patterson, Bew and other intellectuals linked to the party the belief that attracting working-class Protestant support was now the WP's primary medium-term goal.

The May 1985 council elections, in which the WP ran 28 candidates, saw a measure of success for the party despite an overall share of just 1.6 per cent of the vote. Lynch won back the North

Belfast seat he had lost in 1981 and the WP retained its seats in Craigavon and Downpatrick. There were also increased votes in Enniskillen and Cookstown. During the campaign a hoax bomb was placed under the car of one candidate, there was an attempt to burn the WP advice centre in Lurgan, and Lynch's office in New Lodge was petrol-bombed. Clashes were sometimes spontaneous though on some occasions youngsters were egged on to harass or stone WP canvassers. An activist recalls:

We always blamed the Provos, and I think in the Provos there is a certain swagger that gave them a right to abuse those people that didn't have any great deal of popular support. That said, there was people on the Official side that every time they saw a Provo would want to push him off the footpath, so it wasn't all one-sided.

Seamus Lynch recalls being approached by Gerry Adams and his entourage while canvassing with Mary McMahon in the early 1980s. Adams smiled and held out his hand saying, 'Ah, how are you doing, Seamus?', to which McMahon responded, 'Fuck off, you murdering bastard!'

Unionists reacted to the arrival of Sinn Féin on local councils by disrupting meetings and attempting to exclude the party's representatives. On Craigavon Council the unionists put forward a motion that all representatives sign a pledge denouncing terrorist violence. The SDLP added an addendum that loyalist and state violence be included, but the unionists refused to accept this. WP councillors Tom French and Paddy Breen declined to sign, along with the Sinn Féin and SDLP councillors. After an attempt by unionists to block their entry to the council chamber, the RUC were called and physically removed Breen and the SF councillors. Behind the scenes the WP leadership in Belfast was furious: 'For our people to be seen to be in any way supporting the Provos is highly dangerous.' Lynch complained that the Craigavon WP 'have not left the sectarian camp and refuse to do so'. Mac Giolla concurred, declaring the best solution was to 'get rid of the lot of them', but felt this was impractical in the circumstances. The WP and SDLP councillors won a legal case against their exclusion and the matter was laid to rest.

In 1982 Clann na hÉireann had begun pursuing a strategy of establishing itself as a left faction within the British Labour Party. Any Clann members who were not already in the Labour Party now joined; the eventual aim was to have activists elected as councillors and even MPs. This was seen as necessary because the WP's opponents were already organized within British Labour. The increasingly active Labour Committee on Ireland was seen as a 'Provisional/Trotskyite' group; the best organized left faction within the Labour Party, the 'Militant tendency', was Trotskyist, and therefore also beyond the pale, despite being seen by the WP as having a 'reasonably correct analysis of the Provos'. There was general WP support for Neil Kinnock's efforts to combat the Militant tendency after he took over the leadership of the Labour Party in 1983. Another rival lobby group, the Campaign for Labour Representation in Northern Ireland, supported the extension of the British Labour Party to Northern Ireland. Clann felt that BICO were providing the 'direction and dynamic' for this group and extrapolated from this a view that Jim Kemmy was 'already organised' in British Labour while 'we are not'. Clann lobbied strongly to prevent Gerry Adams, who was addressing a fringe meeting at the 1983 Labour conference, from being allowed to enter the main body of the event. As for delegates who had attended the Sinn Féin MP's speech, they were described in *Workers' Life* as 'ghouls or voyeurs who would equally be at home with the Yorkshire Ripper as they were with Adams'.

A major part of the activity of the Campaign for Peace and Progress, as the Clann grouping inside British Labour was called, was to oppose motions calling for British withdrawal from Northern Ireland. As Seamus Collins recalls, 'We would oppose things like Troops Out very successfully around Birmingham. A lot of English people would be shy until a big booming culchie voice got up and then they would think, well, if an Irish person opposes it, we can too.' Harry Barnes, MP for North-East Derbyshire, was a sponsor of the campaign and Clann supporters were elected to Labour Party offices in Birmingham, Wolverhampton and Reading. One of the WP's strongest critics was Clare Short, the Birmingham MP who was a prominent supporter of Troops Out and had family connections in south Armagh. But Collins and Short worked together on local issues, and Collins considered Short 'a big-hearted decent woman. I campaigned, believe it or not, to have her selected as a candidate . . . she said Seamus is alright on everything except Ireland [and] I said Clare is alright on everything except Ireland.'

By the mid-1980s the WP was publicly supportive of moves to make the RUC a community police force. Party representatives argued that despite its faults the force was 'more humane . . . more disciplined and more democratically controlled' than the 'Provo gangsters'. In early 1984 a WP delegation had held talks with the RUC Chief Constable Jack Hermon; critics were quick to point out that at the same time the High Court in Belfast was hearing that the Official IRA had a 'huge' interest in building-site tax-exemption scams. One police officer, when speaking to a researcher during this period, explained the changed relationship between the Officials and the RUC by saying that 'gone are the days when we need an Army backup when we go into an Officials club'; the police were now 'cordially received' and offered drinks. Some party members successfully applied to the RUC for licences to carry handguns, and this bred situations that made others uncomfortable, as Kevin Smyth recalls:

I'm not criticizing the people that got them, because some felt a threat to their lives, but for some people it became a macho thing. It used to make me very angry and sick seeing them take out these guns and put them on the table at meetings. I think the only people they impressed were themselves.

Mary McMahon initially welcomed the development as 'one way of protection' but she became concerned about those receiving licences: 'The cops couldn't have been doing the checks they were supposed to; you didn't know who had them, legitimately and illegitimately.' The party's relationship with the RUC was just one facet of an increasingly respectable image. WP delegations, usually involving Lynch, O'Hagan and Seamus Harrison, met government ministers and civil servants regularly. Secretaries of State Douglas Hurd and Tom King also met delegations from the party. Party representatives, working from several advice centres in nationalist areas of Belfast, became adept at negotiating with the Housing Executive and funding bodies. For their political opponents, particularly in the SDLP, such activity also raised issues about how such a marginal party could fund such professional local operations.

The WP's desire for respectability was hampered by events within the ghettos. Sinn Féin made it their business to ensure any reports of activity by 'Mac Giolla's guerrillas' were given publicity. The WP's public position, reiterated time after time, was that the OIRA did not exist and that people who had information on illegal activities should contact the RUC. More often than not it was McMahon who presented WP rebuttals on television, her response the same blunt exasperation that she expressed towards sectarian killings. One former OIRA prisoner recalls the reaction to such denials:

People would be saying, 'Are they treating us like total idiots?' Because they knew. It didn't do the Workers' Party any favours. Okay, they might have got a couple more invitations to the Northern Ireland Office or Stormont, or [had] the police falling over themselves to congratulate them, but in areas like these it done them absolutely no good at all.

For McMahon, attempting to balance her community work with the need to present the party's line on this issue was unsettling:

We were never ever able to deal satisfactorily with the question 'What has happened to the Official IRA?' We waffled around it at every election, and between elections the IRA would come back to bite you and we would say it was an individual or an accident, [then] we would forget about it. It was never, ever dealt with.

The party continued to parade at Easter to Milltown Cemetery, marching behind the tricolour and the Starry Plough. Most of its members proudly wore Easter lilies. But the term 'republican' was no longer widely used in party publications. In his media appearances Seamus Lynch was always at pains to point out that the WP was not a republican or nationalist organization but a 'socialist party'. In Belfast, however, the party's links to its roots were still important. Many WP members talked about 'the movement' in the same way as they had when they joined the IRA in the 1960s. There was no public indication that there were prisoners linked to the party, but for the families of those still in jail a minibus was put on once a week from the WP offices to Long Kesh to visit the twelve long-term prisoners held at Compound 20 and in 1984 a WP delegation had met ministers to discuss the plight of long-term prisoners. Group B operatives jailed during the 1980s were not accorded recognition, and on release there were no party structures to accommodate former prisoners. One long-term prisoner recalls being given £100 on his release and thanked for his service; but he felt that he 'needed more than a pat on the back' as his options for work and education were limited. The remaining prisoners were still under OIRA discipline. Pat John Kelly, a life-sentence prisoner, objected to cooperating with prison authorities on a particular issue and was expelled from the OIRA compound. He returned from meeting visitors to find his possessions had been removed from his cell and he was persona non grata with the OIRA inmates. When Eddie Rooney, a postgraduate student at Queen's, began researching a thesis on the Officials in the early 1980s the prisoners were instructed not to talk to him. A rare public reminder of the OIRA prisoners' existence had come in 1983 when Liam McAnoy wrote from Long Kesh to *Fortnight* magazine in response to an article by Sinn Féin's Danny Morrison. McAnoy said he shared Morrison's sense of alienation from the 'Protestant state' of Northern Ireland and understood why many had responded with violence. But he argued that the Provisionals' campaign would merely prolong the agony of both communities. In early 1986 four OIRA life-sentence prisoners renounced their special category status after being given assurances on release dates and were moved from Long Kesh to Crumlin Road Jail.

Negotiations between the governments in London and Dublin produced the Anglo-Irish Agreement in November 1985. The Irish government hailed the agreement as giving it a say in the running of Northern Ireland and as helping to end nationalist alienation. But the deal recognized that Northern Ireland would remain part of the United Kingdom as long as a majority desired this and promised increased security cooperation between London and Dublin. The SDLP welcomed the accord, as did the American government, which promised investment to help encourage economic growth. Fianna Fáil and Sinn Féin attacked the deal as copperfastening partition. Both unionist parties immediately denounced the deal as a treacherous compromise and withdrew 'all support and cooperation' from the British government. A mass rally of over 100,000 in Belfast saw the beginning of the 'Ulster says No' campaign. New organizations such as the Ulster Clubs were formed to coordinate resistance to the deal as loyalists turned to street politics on a scale not seen since the 1974 Ulster Workers' Council strike.

The Agreement also provoked a heated debate among the WP leadership. The Northern leadership was overwhelmingly opposed to it, Seamus Harrison arguing that it had 'nothing in it to benefit the working class' and would only 'worsen the sectarian divide'. But Tony Heffernan felt it would be a 'mistake politically in the South to be seen to be totally negative about it'. Peter Kane feared opposition would align the WP with the Provos and with Haughey. Goulding's instinct was to oppose but Garland, though uneasy, thought the WP's image with unionists would be damaged by alignment with Haughey. After a narrow majority vote the leadership determined that the WP TDs would vote for the Agreement.

In the Dáil debate on the Agreement Mac Giolla's attitude to Fianna Fáil's opposition was caustic:

There is only one thing worse than Provos and that is armchair Provos. I stood behind Kevin Boland's barbed wire and looked out for a couple of years from it . . . it left me rather cold to Kevin Boland's commitment to the harassed people of the six counties . . . I also stood before Deputy Haughey's three colonels in the military courts in Collins Barracks. That left me rather cold in regard to Deputy Haughey's commitment to civil rights.

While complaining that the Irish government seemed to be 'conducting negotiations on behalf of the SDLP', Mac Giolla explained that the WP was voting for the Agreement in the hope that it might lead to an opportunity for peace. But the problem remained that 'it is an agreement between London and Dublin, and, unfortunately not between the Shankill and the Falls'.

Unsurprisingly there was some confusion reported among the WP membership as to their exact position on the Agreement. In Belfast the party explained that they were only 'reluctantly' in favour of the deal and warned working-class Protestants not to be misled by the former 'loudmouthed close allies of Thatcher'. Loyalist protests over the winter saw an upsurge in violence. There were strikes and riots, RUC officers' homes were firebombed in loyalist areas, and there were several killings of Catholics, mostly by the UVF. The WP acknowledged that in general the RUC had stood firm against the loyalists and felt this showed that reform of the force was succeeding.

As unionist opposition to the deal hardened, the WP's attitude also underwent revision. At the 1986 Ard Fheis, where a quarter of the 600 delegates were from the North, Mac Giolla launched a major attack on the SDLP's leader, stating that he had to 'seriously question John Hume's commitment to peace' and suggesting that the SDLP were 'happy to see the Protestant people in turmoil'. Concern was also increasing over American influence on the Agreement, with Mac Giolla claiming there was a 'sinister Catholic nationalist plot afoot and Washington is behind it'. The unionist protests caused huge disruption but failed to bring down the Agreement. There was more trouble over the summer of 1986 as several

Orange parades were re-routed and loyalists again clashed with the
RUC. The WP now argued that the Anglo-Irish Agreement had
failed and should be put in 'cold storage' while the democratic
parties came together to discuss the future.

In November 1986 Sinn Féin decided to abandon abstentionism
in the South, a victory for Gerry Adams. A small group led by
Ruairí Ó Brádaigh left the Provisional movement. They suggested
that an influx of former members of the Officials into the Provos
after the hunger strikes had been partly responsible for what they
saw as a betrayal, but Adams dismissed their claims that the movement was going 'Sticky'.

Adams had been urging his organization in the South to emulate
the WP's community politics; but one of the WP's successful
Southern campaigns drew adverse comment when it was pointed
out that despite their opposition to gaming machines in Dublin,
the same machines were in operation in their drinking clubs in
Belfast. Embarrassed, Seamus Lynch denied that the WP had any
drinking clubs. In fact the party ran the Lower Falls Social and
Recreational Club, the Lagan Club in the Markets, the Rosebud
in Short Strand, the Turf Lodge Social Club, the Victoria in North
Queen Street and the Plough in Newry. One Southern WP
member found drinking in the party's Belfast clubs a strange experience, 'like a bad 1970s workingman's club . . . lights flashing, cheap
tables and chairs . . . women saying don't go near the Dublin men
[and] fights breaking out'. In this hothouse atmosphere minor
disputes were often intensified into bitter arguments among
members.

The sympathy of foreign socialists and revolutionaries towards the
Provisionals was a persistent source of dismay to the WP. Soviet
coverage of Northern Ireland tended to echo a simple anti-British
line, and the WP put a great deal of effort into convincing the
Soviets that any public support for the Provisionals was mistaken.
On one trip to Moscow Garland had a heated exchange with the
editor of the Soviet paper *New Times* over articles he felt were
favourable to the Provos. During 1985 the WP contacted the

Nicaraguan Embassy in order to complain about the invitation of Gerry Adams to a diplomatic reception. In 1986 the WP strongly objected to an article in the Soviet journal *International Affairs*, and Garland submitted a long rebuttal, which was published in June 1987. The party's efforts may have had some effect: the strong condemnation of the Provisionals' Enniskillen bombing by the Soviet news agency TASS was seen by some as evidence of 'closer ties' between the Soviets and the WP, and one month earlier, on a WP-sponsored speaking tour, CPSU representative Eugene Lagutin made clear that the Soviets did 'not believe that terrorism will solve anything'. Lagutin stressed that while historically the conflict may have had colonial roots 'everyone in Northern Ireland now has a right to call it home'.

The party's network in the United States continued to decline. By 1987, when Ó Cionnaith visited 20 US cities, many Irish Republican Club members were involved in solidarity movements with Nicaragua, Palestine and South Africa. American WP supporters opposed the MacBride Principles, which sought to discourage American companies investing in Northern Ireland unless businesses gave a commitment to hire Catholics. The WP attacked the idea as 'crude, simplistic [and] sectarian', arguing that it would simply cause more unemployment in the North.

If getting their message across was difficult overseas, in Northern Ireland it was almost completely drowned out by an upsurge in violence. In 1987 106 people would die violently due to the conflict, the worst total since 1982. Twelve of these deaths came in a bloody INLA feud, and several of the dead had begun their paramilitary careers in the Official IRA. Thomas 'Ta' Power, once an activist in the Markets, was killed by a faction led by Gerard Steenson, who as a teenager had killed Billy McMillen in 1975. Steenson was then himself gunned down. Tony McCloskey, a participant in the Armagh OIRA ambush in which Jake McGerrigan died in 1973, was kidnapped and brutally tortured before being killed. There was private glee at Steenson's death and few tears within the WP when the SAS killed eight members of the Provisionals in Loughgall during May 1987, though one of those killed was a cousin of a long-time Official activist. The INLA feud spawned a new republican paramilitary group, the Irish People's Liberation Organisation (IPLO), with several former Official Fianna members prominent in its leadership.

Working-class unity remained elusive, despite high unemployment and Tory cutbacks. The WP entered the June 1987 Westminster election campaign again claiming that class politics could overcome these problems. One prospective election candidate in 1987 was Sue McMenamin, a Protestant from the Shankill Road who had married a Catholic from Ballymurphy during the 1960s. Her son, Kevin McMenamin, had been killed in the UVF bomb attack on the 1977 Easter Commemoration, aged nine. Gerry Fitt, now a peer in the House of Lords, called for a WP vote despite certain 'reservations' he had about the party. The party hoped that at least some of his former supporters in West Belfast would turn to it on polling day. The WP affected an aura of confidence, with O'Hagan predicting a 'massive turning' to the party by 'serious and intelligent voters'. The eventual WP share of the vote was 2.6 per cent. The party's consistently poor returns led some to conclude that a strategy review was needed, but raising questions about electoral stagnation often led to accusations of being a 'pessimist'. The results also meant it was hard to convince people to stand, as Mary McMahon recalls: 'The joke was you went to Maguire's bar [and] drank somebody stupid . . . tried to get them to say they'd be a candidate and then run back across the road and get them announced . . . before they had time to change their minds.' Kevin Smyth recalls that 'the fact that we were receiving so few votes was causing a drain on resources and a drain on morale. We would build up this euphoria for a month or two before an election, and like a bad hangover the reality would set in when the votes were counted.' Margaret McNulty, who stood in several elections, recalls that 'it was like beating your head against a brick wall but you still did it'.

Despite the WP's poor electoral showings, the party's politics had an impact on wider understandings of the conflict. *Fortnight* magazine regularly carried articles by writers and journalists associated with the WP, including Martin O'Hagan, John Hunter, Kathryn Johnston and Robin Wilson. Martin Lynch had his own weekly column in the *Irish News* from 1982, and former party member Henry McDonald's career was advancing at the *Irish News*. The *Sunday World* remained an outlet for WP publicity and its populist analysis of the political situation was often in line with the party's positions. The paper steered clear of any reference to the activities of Group B, but its exposés of criminal activity by other loyalist and republican paramilitaries was not without its costs: its Northern editor, Jim Campbell, was badly wounded in a UVF shooting in May 1984. In 1987 former *Northern People* editor Liam Clarke published *Broadening the Battlefield*, a study of the use of the hunger strikes by Sinn Féin to develop their political base. Henry Patterson's *The Politics of Illusion*, a history of the relationship between Irish republicanism and socialism, was published in 1989. Patterson had been co-opted on to the WP Ard Chomhairle in 1986, and his access to Goulding, Garland, Lynch and Harrison allowed him to produce the most in-depth account of the movement to date.

As rumours spread of secret talks to bring about a Provisional IRA ceasefire, the WP's position was that there could be 'no dialogue' with terrorists. This position was reinforced in the minds of party members by the murder of WP supporter Emmanuel Wilson, a father of four, in June 1987. Wilson was abducted, shot four times and his body dumped in an alleyway. In response the WP described the Provos as 'fascist animals' whose methods were 'similar to Nazi activity against their political opponents in the Germany of the 1930s'. De Rossa and Garland attended Wilson's funeral. At Bodenstown shortly afterwards Goulding declared that 'Emmanuel Wilson has now joined McMillen, Fox, McNulty and many more' in the ranks of those who died for socialism.

In the wake of the Enniskillen bombing in November the WP called for full support for the RUC to 'eliminate these Fascist killers from our society' and upped its propaganda against perceived sympathy towards the Provos within the British Labour Party. Mac Giolla, Dick Spring and Jim Kemmy jointly signed an appeal to

Neil Kinnock to recognize that the 'campaign of sectarian violence waged by the Provos is the greatest obstacle to creation of unity between working people'. A WP delegation including De Rossa and Lynch travelled to the House of Commons and met Labour, Plaid Cymru and Conservative MPs. WP speakers continued to address fringe meetings at British Labour conferences, John Lowry, a former IDYM member who was emerging as a leading figure in the Belfast party, making clear at one that 'the Provisionals' concern for civil liberties doesn't apply to their own gunmen, nor do we hear many calls for inquiries into this shoot-to-kill policy'.

The spring of 1988 had seen a marked increase in violence. In March the SAS shot dead three unarmed members of a Provisional active service unit in Gibraltar. At their funerals in Milltown Cemetery, loyalist Michael Stone fired into the crowd, killing three people. Two days later the Provisional IRA killed a 21-year-old Protestant woman, Gillian Johnston, in Fermanagh. The following day, at the funeral of one of Stone's victims, Provo Caoimhín MacBrádaigh, two British Army corporals who had driven into the cortège were disarmed, beaten and shot dead by the Provisional IRA.

In early 1988 it became known that John Hume was meeting with Gerry Adams. De Rossa described the meetings as a 'despicable attempt to create a sectarian Catholic nationalist front'. But a motion at the WP Ard Fheis calling for the repeal of Articles Two and Three of the Republic's constitution, which claimed Northern Ireland as part of the 'national territory', was withdrawn because of opposition from the floor. A 'secular, socialist unitary state' remained WP policy. There was a new focus by the WP on the rights of Northern unionists. At the Ard Fheis Mac Giolla described Northern Protestants as 'a living people whose courage and endurance have seen them take the genocidal butchery of 200 small farmers and workers in Fermanagh without retaliation' and praised the 'awesome display of tolerance and forgiveness' of Fermanagh Protestants as 'they knelt among their dead after Enniskillen'. Unionist leaders were urged to talk to democratic politicians to ensure they were not isolated.

One of those who welcomed Mac Giolla's speech was the UUP MP for Fermanagh-South Tyrone, Ken Maginnis. Describing Mac Giolla as having kept 'the best wine to the last', Maginnis said the WP 'had come a long way'. He expressed some reservations that the WP was funded through racketeering and the 'odd bank robbery', but felt there was 'absolutely no hindrance to coopera-tion' on certain issues. Many in the party regarded this praise as evidence of success, but McMahon would later describe it as 'almost a kiss of death . . . the Unionists loved the fact of this little party in the Catholic ghetto that had guns and stood up to the Provos, there was no doubt about that. [But] that was never understood as damaging to us.'

Similar concerns were voiced when a delegation from the WP attended a commemoration for British soldiers killed by a Provo bomb in Lisburn, and there were calls for representatives to attend commemorative events only for their own members or for all those killed as a result of the Troubles.

In August 1988 the WP marked the twentieth anniversary of the civil rights movement's early marches. As well as stressing the role that its members had played there was also an attempt to evaluate the impact of the movement. Brian Brennan argued in *Making Sense* that NICRA had not failed, but that a combination of ultra-leftism and Provisional violence had seen it forced off the streets. Former NICRA chairman Paddy Joe McClean made similar points, determined to 'nail a lie which is being put across to a younger generation . . . that the civil rights movement failed [and] that its logical successor had to be "the armed struggle"'. In Tyrone McClean was a particularly vociferous critic of the Provisionals. His sons sometimes felt the results of his out-spokenness playing Gaelic football when players on rival teams would single out 'the Sticks' for rough treatment.

The Enniskillen atrocity had reawakened Southern concern over Northern Ireland's ongoing violence. WP members were central to the development of the broad-based campaign group New Consensus, which was set up to 'challenge ambivalence' about IRA violence in the South; among those involved were former members of the Progressive Democrats, historian John A. Murphy and members of Fine Gael and the Labour Party. These campaigns intensified during 1989 with the twentieth anniversary of the beginning of the Troubles. The *Irish People* gave over its pages to a number of guest writers to discuss attitudes to the North. Jim Kemmy argued that because of the violence 'less and less people here really want or expect a united Ireland'. Journalist Eamon Dunphy felt Southerners should 'tell the nationalist community it has behaved disgracefully' and no longer deserved their sympathy. Fr. Denis Faul, in contrast, suggested that a phased release of paramilitary prisoners could undercut the ties of many people to the Provisional IRA and other groups.

In March 1989 De Rossa condemned the killings of two senior RUC men near the border, saying they had been 'murdered trying to bring peace'. During the same month the new WP president called for a re-examination of Articles Two and Three of the Irish constitution in his iconoclastic keynote address to the Ard Fheis. While reaffirming that the WP stood for the 'unity of the Irish working class', De Rossa argued that this class had 'more than one tradition'. He launched another strong attack on John Hume, describing him as a 'tribal leader' who 'says tribal things very slowly and very quietly', and claimed that the 'Protestants of the north have won the moral war ... despite all the Provo provocation there has been no Protestant murder campaign on the scale of the Provos' genocidal war'. Unionists would not be 'bullied into a state with huge unemployment, no divorce, a miserable health service and teeth pulled on three months' notice'. Unlike the other aspects of De Rossa's presidential address, his comments on the North caused little internal controversy; but the SDLP countered that surely the WP's own 'dubious' history proved that paramilitary violence 'could be abandoned' through discussion. De Rossa did not refer in his address to the fact that loyalists had killed 79 people since 1986. Random sectarian shootings were now common, as in late 1988 when WP supporter Gerard Cullen was badly wounded in Short Strand. In early 1989 the UVF and UDA killed ten people, among them a Sinn Féin councillor and high-profile solicitor Pat Finucane, in cases that strongly suggested collusion with members of the security forces. The impact of loyalist paramilitary attacks was not generally reflected in the WP's statements.

In May the WP contested 38 seats in the North's council elections and won 2.1 per cent of the vote. For the first time since 1981 the party had success west of the Bann, with Davy Kettyles elected in Enniskillen and Gerry Cullen in Dungannon. However, the WP also lost seats in Down and Craigavon. Sinn Féin's vote fell in several areas and they lost sixteen seats. On the basis of this and of the poor vote for Sinn Féin in the Southern general election, *Making Sense* optimistically concluded that the Provisionals were being reduced to a 'lumpen core around west Belfast'.

August 1989 saw the twentieth anniversary of the arrival of British troops. The WP held the Provisionals responsible for '20 years of murder' and argued that the British government should withdraw soldiers to barracks and allow the RUC the central role in combating paramilitary violence. A documentary on the life of Jim Sullivan was shown on UTV in September. *Sullivan's Story*, made by Gerry Gregg's Iskra, featured WP members Francie Donnelly, P. J. McClean and Rebecca McGlade. The documentary repeated many of the key tenets of the WP's view of the Troubles, stressing the cross-community nature of the civil rights movement and the involvement of Fianna Fáil in the birth of the Provos. It failed to mention that Sullivan had been a senior IRA officer in Belfast for most of his life and that he was adjutant of the Belfast IRA during the violence of August 1969. Sullivan, wheelchair-bound and in bad health, was filmed in front of Tone's grave at Bodenstown staring at the tricolour and lamenting:

Things for which Tone worked, and that which he strived to achieve, unity between Protestant, Catholic and Dissenter, is further away than ever has been in Irish history. Today you see Loyalists killing Catholics, Provo nationalists killing Protestants. I feel ashamed, this flag has been sullied, it's drenched in blood . . . I personally could never look up to this flag again.

Between 1982 and the end of 1989 a total of 680 lives had been lost in Northern Ireland due to the conflict. The WP had failed in its attempts to garner significant support among the Protestant working class. Within the nationalist ghettos the party's members and politics had been increasingly marginalized while Provisional Sinn Féin rose to prominence, by 1989 holding 43 Northern council seats compared to the WP's 4. For stalwarts of the Belfast party, such as John Lowry and Des O'Hagan, pessimism was not an option – the WP had survived another bloody decade and had succeeded in keeping alive an alternative to sectarian politics. But for a smaller group of Northern activists there was growing frustration at what they saw as their comrades' inability to adapt to the changed circumstances.

16. Special Activities

'The continued growth of the party in the public domain makes
"special activities" more hazardous for the party . . .'

Workers' Party to Communist Party of the Soviet Union,
September 1986

By the time of the killing of Jim Flynn in 1982, Sean Garland had
long shed any emotional attachment to the traditional trappings of
republican paramilitarism, as had Eamon Smullen, Des O'Hagan,
Seamus Lynch and a semi-retired Cathal Goulding. The party's
up-and-coming politicians, meanwhile, were wary of the taint of
a secret armed wing. This was the context in which approximately
30 delegates, booked as 'the Irish National Foresters', gathered in
the Sheelin Shamrock Hotel in Co. Cavan on 18 and 19 June
for an Army Convention; among them were senior WP figures
including Northern elected representatives and party president
Tomás Mac Giolla. Northerners raised concerns that a resurgent
Provisional movement, eager to assert its authority within the
nationalist ghettos, would embark on another 'pogrom' against
party members. Some called for a major rearmament in order to
counter this threat, and defensive plans were discussed. There was,
however, little appetite for retaliation against an increasingly erratic
INLA for the Flynn killing and the costly feud such an action
would provoke. Discussion was dominated by the question of how
to raise money to fund the WP, whose finances were at a critical
point following the two recent Southern elections. The push for
more funds would have to be balanced against the need to decrease
Group B's public profile, meaning a major increase in armed
robberies was ruled out. The meeting agreed the organization

would diversify its fund-raising activities as well as downgrading its paramilitary structure, thus continuing the move towards becoming a 'special technical group' under the direction of the party. It was a position the majority of activists accepted; as a former Group B operative recalls, 'We seen the party had to be financed [or] they could not have got the electoral success . . . It [the OIRA] had become a practical thing, really just a fund-raising group.'

Local Gardaí had succeeded in bugging the hotel, which had been used previously by Group B and had also hosted a number of Provisional IRA meetings. A senior Garda Special Branch officer later stated that during 1982 the Official IRA 'streamlined their organization to take them into the years that were to follow'. Formally the OIRA no longer had a separate recognized existence; instead, 'the way they looked at it internally was that they knew who they were, they were not overly concerned at what others thought, so they were just known as the central operational unit within the movement'. Their role would continue to be 'raising finance [and] vetting members who were joining the [political] organization'. This intelligence was shared with the Northern security forces, but it is believed that the Southern government was not informed of the specifics of the 1982 Convention due to Garda mistrust of Haughey and his ministers.

The US Central Intelligence Agency, which had maintained contact with Gardaí monitoring the Officials since the 1970s, took a closer interest after the WP TDs became crucial in supporting the 1982 Haughey government. WP members' trips abroad were closely monitored, with Garland's activities of particular interest; CIA agents cooperating with Gardaí informed their Irish colleagues that they regarded Garland as 'effectively an agent of the Russians'. The impact of CIA–Garda cooperation would be felt during 1983 when three diplomats at the Soviet Embassy in Dublin were expelled as suspected KGB spies based largely on information supplied by the Americans. At least one of the men had been in close contact with Group B. During this period a WP member who worked as a journalist recalls being asked by an employee of the TASS news agency to gather intelligence on US economic interests in Ireland.

Flynn's killing necessitated a restructuring of Group B's Operations Department. Control of activity was now divided between the Director of Operations based in Belfast, who oversaw all Northern robberies, and the Dublin-based operations unit. The Southern unit was directly answerable to a select group of Army Council members, while the Northern Director of Operations held a position on the Belfast command staff. Mindful of the threat to the WP's Southern political activities resulting from Group B operatives being arrested, the majority of armed robberies were carried out by the Northern unit.

Much of the Dublin Group B unit's activity increasingly focused on providing intelligence and logistical support for criminal networks, particularly the group headed by Eamon and Matt Kelly. By the early 1980s the Kellys had gathered around them a group of young criminals drawn from Dublin's north inner city. Some of the young men were sympathetic to the WP's anti-establishment politics, but the primary reason for their alliance with Group B was the percentage of proceeds they received from joint activity. Kelly's gang numbered over a dozen core operators; it specialized in armed robberies of cash and drink deliveries but was willing to turn its hand to most criminal enterprises, including the burning of properties for insurance claims and counterfeiting. Group B's expertise and firearms were useful to the gang, which also benefited from a stark decline in competition as most other Dublin criminal gangs became involved in the burgeoning heroin trade. Most Group B operatives looked upon the alliance with the Kelly gang as a tactical necessity, but there was disquiet about links to the drugs trade and Eamon Kelly's use of the threat of the Official IRA to back up his extortion rackets. The latter issue was of particular concern in the summer of 1983, when the Kelly brothers became embroiled in a highly publicized court case concerning the liquidation of their Dublin carpet businesses. Witnesses testified to the brothers' involvement in violent activity, large-scale fraud and intimidation. Eamon Kelly's connections to the Official IRA were also highlighted. One activist recalls his feelings during this period: 'They were people living off the working-class people, parasites. I couldn't bring myself to sit down with them. Eamon Kelly done a lot of things but he was not a volunteer ... [but] they were using the name of the Official IRA. We knew things were going on but we turned a blind eye to it.'

Group B continued to recruit from the Southern party membership, mostly from those who had been in the IDYM. One man recruited into the Dublin 'organization' – 'you didn't call it anything, Group B or whatever' – during the early 1980s recalls that Group B was divided between a small number of operatives who were focused on 'funds' and the remainder which 'became the revolutionary group within the party; basically you'd get called to a meeting which had a military-style structure and you'd get told who to vote for at Ard Chomhairle'. On another occasion, he remembers, 'We were asked to a meeting and addressed by a person and asked to keep an eye out for money, not huge amounts of money, reasonable amounts, money you can see being moved, blah blah, come back and tell us and we'll have a look.'

Some still recognized the Officials as a force within certain working-class districts of Dublin. In a 1983 court case a north-inner-city shopkeeper admitted he turned to the group for protection against local criminals. Conflict with the Provos sometimes involved violence, as a Finglas WP member recalls: 'If I had got a hiding off the Provos ... I would have gone to the branch and told them and there wouldn't be a discussion but it wouldn't happen again. People would leave the meeting and things would happen but it wouldn't be spoken about.' Another activist recalls: 'After Provos started getting out of jail in Finglas, they started picking on people, [and] those of us who did have a bit of muscle went down and kicked fuck out of the Provos. Ordinary party members would have been intimidated. But the fact there was a group there stopped them.' Despite the decision not to retaliate for Flynn's killing, Group B did not allow the IRSP a free hand in Dublin either. Following threats by IRSP members against a north-east Dublin activist while he was selling the *Irish People*, a group of armed men visited the pub where the harassment occurred and a pistol was put to the head of an IRSP activist as a warning that the intimidation should halt.

The Group B leadership was anxious to find a method of funding the WP that would not involve violence or undue publicity. By 1983 bogus punt and sterling notes, counterfeited by Irish and British criminal and paramilitary groups, were increasingly circulating in Dublin. With a number of skilled printers within its ranks, Group B was already involved in counterfeiting items including car taxation discs and company cheques. When a decision was made to embark on a major currency counterfeiting operation during 1982, the organization's leadership was intent on making it large-scale and professional. A Repsol printer set about perfecting a plate that could print high-quality copies of Irish £5 notes. A Scottish member who made inquiries with a sympathizer in the British print union SOGAT learned that the paper used for sterling notes was held in a British government facility in Cheltenham, and inquiries were made into the possibility of robbing this facility, though suitable paper was eventually secured elsewhere. Major expenditure was put into ensuring the best printing machines were available for the operation. One press was imported from London and another bought in Cork by a party member in early 1982. A third machine, owned by Repsol, was removed from Gardiner Place, necessitating the knocking down of one of the building's walls. By mid-1983 the three presses were installed in a warehouse in Hanover Quay near the Dublin docks. The intention was to print hundreds of thousands of notes that would be distributed during the Christmas period, mainly through Group B's underworld contacts. The Gardaí became aware that a major forgery operation was planned and conducted several raids in the Dublin area; on 16 November 1983 they discovered high-quality counterfeit £5 notes with a face value of £1.7 million, along with the printing presses in the warehouse. They also found a plate that had been used to print a WP publication. This led them to conduct a four-hour search of the Repsol offices at Gardiner Place on 26 November; there they found printing plates for Irish Life cheques, driving licences and car taxation discs. After recovering fingerprints from the Ringsend warehouse the Gardaí sought Repsol printer Bryan Lynch but found he had left Dublin. Lynch went on the run and spent several weeks in Belfast before eventually being spirited to East Germany, a country he had previously visited as a member of the Ireland–GDR Friendship Society. The breaking up of the counterfeiting operation was a major setback for Group B and generated as much adverse publicity as more violent fund-raising activity.

The movement's armed wing in Belfast remained sizeable. This was seen as necessary to ensure the protection of members, provide muscle for racketeering and prevent the Provos, seeking to promote their own political wing, from pushing the WP off the streets. With all paramilitary organizations now heavily involved in racketeering Belfast was divided into various areas of influence. The Markets, Lower Falls and Short Strand were considered 'Sticky strongholds', while in Twinbrook, Turf Lodge, the Ormeau Road, Poleglass, Bawnmore and the vicinity of WP social clubs local groups of volunteers had a visible presence. Other rival groups' turf was often demarcated by wall murals but, as befitted the organization's clandestine nature, the Officials opposed these glorifications of paramilitarism. For Belfast volunteers the effect of the 1982 Army Convention was limited; 'they just told us we have to be more secret'. One Belfast activist, when recruited into Group B, noted the almost complete overlap of membership with his WP branch. Clashes with rivals continued to be commonplace. In 1982 a Poleglass IRSP member claimed to have been interrogated at gunpoint after a gang of Officials forced their way into his home. A dispute in Turf Lodge saw armed OIRA members force a family from a house they had earlier been encouraged to squat in by the Provos. Spur-of-the-moment confrontations with rival paramilitaries also occurred with guns sometimes produced and fired.

Efforts were made to be less conspicuous. A specially trained operations unit of around a dozen hand-picked volunteers from across the city was utilized for most robberies. Younger volunteers continued to be recruited into the Belfast unit but there had been changes in modes of operating. In the 1970s, after a successful robbery operatives would often go drinking in one of the party's clubs where they would be met by knowing cheers and congratulations. By the 1980s the teams were ordered to avoid the clubs and keep a low profile after robberies. But OIRA activities occasionally came into public view. In February 1983 the OIRA was blamed for an abortive kidnapping and ransom attempt on a postmaster's son in Andersonstown, and the murder of long-time OIRA activist Eamon 'Hatchet' Kerr the following month ensured more intense media focus on the organization. Kerr, who had been released from prison in June 1982 after serving a short sentence on an arms charge, had been sleeping when a group of men burst into his home, pistol-whipped his wife and shot him five times in the chest. At his funeral Des O'Hagan denounced the media for blackening Kerr's name by linking him to building-site racketeering and claimed that Kerr had been a man dedicated to the 'fight of the working class for class power. His life was hard work, bringing no monetary rewards, no personal gains, but only personal sacrifice.' The circumstances of Kerr's death were mysterious. Both the Provos and the INLA were quick to disclaim any involvement and there was little hint of Official retaliation afterwards. The RUC told the inquest into Kerr's death that his killing was 'not sectarian and not political'. Rumours circulated that Kerr had had an altercation with a fellow OIRA member on the day of his death.

The OIRA continued to carry out punishment attacks, partly in response to intimidation of WP members or at the insistence of members of the local community. Several such beatings were carried out on youths in the Lower Falls during the summer of 1983. A recurring theme was the defence of party property against local teenagers, particularly during August when annual internment bonfires took place. Often egged on by the Provisionals, drunken teenagers would attempt to attack 'Stickie' clubs or individuals. The OIRA would occasionally put on a show of strength or fire shots in the air to make clear they would not be intimidated. On other occasions the suspected perpetrators were tracked down and either beaten or shot, leading to a litany of local complaints. Local businesses were asked on occasion to provide 'donations' to support the local WP social club or prisoners' families; refusal to pay sometimes meant violence was utilized in order to secure the requested funds.

The building-site tax-exemption scam – now overseen by Robert 'Black Bob' McKeown, who had returned to Belfast from Britain in 1979 – had become even more lucrative for Group B. Although he shared a surname with Harry McKeown, who had run the scam before defecting to the INLA, Black Bob was not related to his predecessor and his approach to the scam differed starkly. Whereas Harry McKeown's primary concern had been making money for himself, Black Bob was fastidious in ensuring the funds made it to the 'organization'. One member of the RUC anti-racketeering unit set up in 1982, RUC detective Kevin Sheehy, recalled:

[Black Bob] was intelligent, articulate and respected as a businesslike figure by major building firms, the workforce and financial institutions: e.g., banks . . . [The Officials] also used banks, financial advisers and financial markets to invest their profits. They were the first paramilitary group to appreciate the importance of converting fraudulent money into legitimate business: e.g., pubs, clubs, shops, private building projects. These businesses employed professional staff, kept financial records and made required audits to Inland Revenue.

Be-suited and professional in manner, Black Bob didn't look out of place visiting building company executives to assure them of the benefits of cooperating with the 'organization'. He could provide the companies with skilled men to work as subcontractors who would finish the job on time, to a high quality and without labour disputes. Most Official-connected building workers were 'doing the double', claiming unemployment benefit as well as working, and this allowed Group B to ask for 'contributions' of up to 25 per cent of the worker's wage. Group B could also ensure the sites would not be molested by other paramilitaries or criminal gangs. Employing firms connected to the Officials was not an impediment to building contractors securing work from the Housing Executive, the leading investor in local construction. The Northern Ireland Office's overriding concern was the completion of projects, and Official sympathizers working within the Housing Executive promoted the use of Group B-connected firms.

The success of Black Bob and his comrades was such that for a period in the early 1980s the Officials 'controlled' sites throughout Belfast, with a virtual monopoly in the inner city. With other paramilitaries developing their own tax and building-site protection scams, the operation could not have functioned without the use of force. The OIRA attacked other paramilitaries who tried to muscle in on sites or damage equipment. Business relationships with loyalist paramilitaries, particularly with the UDA, had been maintained, and on Official-connected sites in Protestant areas UDA-connected firms provided 'security'.

By 1983, with the RUC's anti-racketeering unit increasingly alert to the use of stolen and forged exemption certificates, Group B started to establish front companies that would fold before paying taxes due to the Inland Revenue. Where bogus certificates were used they were claimed to have been passed on to Official companies by those subcontracted by them. Utilizing contacts in the English underworld, Group B paid for the incorporation of Broadmine Ltd, registered to an office in Dagenham, Essex, and Black Bob used the Broadmine tax-exemption certificate on a number of Belfast sites.

In January 1984, after a year investigating the fraud, the RUC charged Black Bob, along with several other Group B members, with conspiring to defraud the Inland Revenue. The Belfast High Court heard that the Official IRA was involved in a 'huge' fraud in the building industry. One of those accused, Anthony McDonagh, was named as the leading 'enforcer' of the tax scam operation and, incorrectly, as the officer commanding the West Belfast OIRA. After an extended period out on bail, McKeown, McDonagh and three others were eventually convicted in late 1985, receiving relatively light sentences. Because all had returned 'guilty' pleas, the details of the case initially received little publicity. The men had also applied (unsuccessfully) in March 1984 to have references to the Official IRA removed from the evidence. Although Official IRA tax scam operations continued, the break-up of Black Bob's operation was a major blow to Group B's fund-raising.

The Newry district remained a key area for Official IRA activity. In the early 1980s, amidst accusations that too much funding was being retained locally, much of the area's leadership was replaced by a group of men recently released from prison. The new younger leadership followed direction from the organization's Dublin centre, but the couple of dozen active volunteers in the area retained a degree of operational autonomy.

With the local North Armagh OIRA unit dwindling, its operatives were now placed under the control of the Newry-based command staff and were also utilized by the Belfast-based Director of Operations. This handful of experienced volunteers based in the Portadown/Lurgan area, nicknamed 'the drum' within the organization because of its tight structure, played a key role in a number of robberies in the Newry area, including one which netted over £100,000 in cash and cheques from a security van in November 1983 and a similar operation which saw £25,000 grabbed by two armed men on a motorbike during a night-safe-deposit drop-off in June 1984.

In August 1984 Group B was linked to a failed kidnapping of the teenage sons of a postmaster in Belfast. In September two Belfast activists were arrested in a hijacked taxi following the robbery of £10,000 from the Larne–Stranraer ferry. Worse was to follow during November, as Group B's alliance with the Kellys' gang broke down irrevocably following an argument during a Saturday meeting in Club Uí Cadhain. The row erupted after Eamon Kelly demanded that Finglas WP activist Pat Quearney stop playing a slot machine. The following evening Eamon Kelly returned with a number of his associates and waited outside the club. When Quearney arrived he was stabbed three times in the heart. The critically injured WP member was rushed to hospital, where he was placed under Garda protection and subsequently gave a statement.

The incident caused consternation among Group B activists, several of whom had been long-term critics of the criminals who had violently attacked their comrade. With the 25-year-old Quearney a leading activist in his constituency, De Rossa became embroiled in the arguments about how the incident should be dealt with. Several activists demanded violent retribution; the Kelly brothers are said to have offered over £15,000 in compensation to the movement. A party member recalls De Rossa and Garland being in favour of leaving the matter to the Gardaí rather than seeking retribution. Eamon Kelly was charged with grievous bodily harm, malicious wounding and assault. In court Quearney named Eamon Kelly as the assailant, and Kelly was found guilty and sentenced to ten years in jail. The WP would later assure members: 'Kelly's only connection with the Workers' Party was that he occasionally frequented a social club in Gardiner Place, which is also used by some members of the Workers' Party.'

The case brought an end to the Kelly brothers' involvement with Group B, but the matter would resurface a year later when the Court of Criminal Appeal quashed Kelly's conviction and ordered a retrial. The new trial heard that one of the prosecution witnesses had himself been convicted of manslaughter following the 1974 Galway robbery in which Jeremiah O'Connor had been killed, and that he had changed his original statement. There were also accusations that WP members had been ordered by Cathal Goulding to testify that Kelly was Quearney's assailant. The judge noted that the testimonies had been marked by an 'undertone of fear'. Kelly claimed that he could not have been in 'the IRA club' on the night in question, having been barred from it in 1982, and that it was his brother Matt who had fought Quearney. Another gang member testified that he rather than Kelly had carried out the stabbing. Quearney again swore that it was Eamon Kelly, whom he had known 'for years', who had attacked him, but the charges of GBH and malicious wounding against Kelly were dropped and his sentence was downgraded to three years for assault.

During the May 1985 local elections there was a series of altercations involving WP canvassers and some locals in Twinbrook. The Officials retaliated against those they believed had threatened election workers, with locals claiming that a teenage girl was among those beaten up. Several weeks later the Officials shot a Twinbrook man three times in the legs. The victim claimed that he had been warned this would happen after the elections. Later in August, on internment commemoration night, Belfast Officials had to produce guns in order to ward off rioters from a number of WP social clubs. Some days later two youths, who had previously robbed bonfire material from an Official-protected building site in the Short Strand, were beaten. One had his hands broken with a lump hammer after being abducted by two men from his workplace. These incidents led to community disquiet and, in response to the Short Strand beatings, a protest march on the local WP social club. Responding to allegations of anti-social activity proved difficult for the Officials, with their political wing unable to defend the reputation of an organization they publicly claimed did not exist. The Official IRA continued to organize voter impersonation for the WP during elections, but with Provisional Sinn Féin doing the same, and increasing government clampdowns on the practice, it was no longer as successful as it had been in the 1970s.

Also during 1985, a disagreement developed between Group B activists and the owner of a Newry bureau de change. The bureau de change owner wrote to De Rossa and Mac Giolla claiming that he had loaned £6,000 to the Newry WP and that they were refusing to repay the loan. He also claimed a series of cheques cashed by party members in his business had bounced, that his office had been robbed of £5,000, and that an employee had been approached by WP members and told he would be shot dead by two men from Dublin if they were not given £10,000. The letter also stated that a signed affidavit detailing the case had been entrusted to the businessman's solicitor and would be made public in the event of the Officials carrying out their threat to kill him. The local Provisionals learned of the incident and, keen to cause maximum embarrassment to the WP, passed the details of the case on to an RTÉ *Today Tonight* team researching Official IRA activity for their programme on paramilitary racketeering.

The *Today Tonight* programme had been conceived in early 1985 by a group of RTÉ staff who argued that a WP 'freemasonry' had stilted programming and silenced opponents 'through an orchestrated campaign of gossip and innuendo'. The programme was initially to focus solely on Official IRA racketeering; but in the interest of balance, a concern of series producer Joe Mulholland, it was decided other paramilitary groups' activities would also be examined. The project provoked interest outside RTÉ, with representatives of the government assuring the journalists of their full backing and the Department of Justice offering them armed protection during their research. Former *Today Tonight* journalist Mary McAleese organized a meeting between programme researcher Fintan Cronin and Charles Haughey, who expressed pleasure and surprise that the programme was emerging from a 'nest of Sticky vipers'. In the North, assistance came from an eclectic range of sources, including the SDLP, sections of the RUC and the Provos.

While the WP's enemies were adamant that the Officials' activities should be exposed, particularly relishing the fact that this was to be done on a programme strongly associated with the party, leading WP members made polite inquiries with Mulholland as to why he was allowing such a programme. Less politely, Cronin's files in RTÉ were rifled through and his bank statements stolen; threatening calls were made to his home and to his mother, and RTÉ received bomb threats. As a precaution, very little of the programme's research material was kept at RTÉ. The researchers were also followed, Cronin recalls: 'At one stage Pat [Cox] and myself were in Buswells and they had a guy walking up and down outside and [he] was identified to me as a member of the Official IRA. Another time a guy with a big bushy beard came up to us and feigned to pull out a gun on us.' The team was also harassed while in Belfast: phone calls were made late at night to the reporters' hotel rooms and files were stolen from producer Mick McCarthy's room. On one occasion the research team hastily travelled back across the border after the RUC informed them they had intelligence that their lives were in immediate danger. The pressure had an effect, Cronin recalls: 'We did think they would shoot us.' The day before the programme went out, Cronin found himself face to face in the RTÉ canteen with a number of men whom he knew to be members of the Official IRA. The group had obviously been invited to lunch by sympathizers among the station's staff. The same day Cronin's wife's workplace received a bomb threat.

The RUC was helpful to the programme makers, although one high-ranking officer informed them that a superior had instructed him that his interview – in which he accepted that much criminal activity previously attributed to the INLA had in fact been carried out by the Officials – could not be broadcast. Cronin believed the interview to be 'one of the best things we had', but it was not transmitted. Although the claim of an 'unspoken RUC policy not to embarrass the Officials' by not naming people as members in court was broadcast, other claims, including one that armed OIRA men were sometimes allowed through RUC roadblocks, were not. Cronin developed the view that the OIRA was 'a protected species' in Belfast and that 'their criminality was often overlooked by the NIO [Northern Ireland Office] and RUC'.

The programme made much of the recent incidents in Newry, although there was no reference to the businessman's previous involvement with Group B. This man had disclosed further information on Group B funding including the existence of a joint Newry AIB account, in the names of a local WP member and 'Sean Gartland', that was used to launder funds that originated with the Officials' clubs in California.

That a public WP figure such as De Rossa had been dragged into controversy surrounding Group B strengthened calls within the movement for a reassessment of the organization's role. Seamus Lynch and his supporters wished to see Group B reduced to small groups of activists with access to weapons, and completely removed from political decision-making within the party. As legal funding methods were developed, Lynch envisaged Group B units coming together only when necessary to protect party members. Among

Group B's Belfast leadership one name suggested for these units was the 'April 15th Organisation', a reference to the date of Joe McCann's death. Although the general concept of reducing the numbers of active Group B members was adopted, the idea of completely dismantling the OIRA organization grated with some long-term activists. Many retained an ideological commitment to armed republicanism, and the combination of these remaining ideological bonds and the necessity of raising funds meant that Lynch's concept was not adopted. Some Group B activists were largely unconcerned about the impact the organization's existence might have on political development. As one puts it:

We just done our thing and let them do their thing; we didn't let it overlap, didn't want to be seen too much . . . As far as we were concerned we were at the heart of the movement, we were feeding it; you don't bite the hand that feeds you.

The party's 'dire' financial situation was prominent in leadership discussions during 1986. Ard Chomhairle members were asked to take personal responsibility for ensuring their areas' debts to the party centre and to Repsol were met. Garland now began exploring the possibility of getting funding from the Soviet Union. In July 1986 he wrote to the International Committee of the CPSU to seek support for Iskra Productions, a 'Marxist film-making enterprise which commands the Party's full support'. Among journalists listed as linked to Iskra were Gerry Gregg, Eoghan Harris and John Caden. Though Iskra functioned in an 'environment hostile to a Marxist analysis', Garland felt there was a commercial appetite for 'stories' that may 'embody a critique of Western society'. In early August 1986 Garland notified the CPSU that he, along with De Rossa, would be attending a nuclear disarmament conference in Pyongyang, North Korea. Garland requested a meeting with representatives of the CPSU Central Committee during their return trip via Moscow to 'discuss how our two Parties' relationship can be further developed and strengthened and to examine other possible areas of cooperation'. (Years later, Garland would explain the approach to the Soviets by saying that the CPSU was 'a fraternal party' and that he 'didn't see anything wrong with asking friends for help . . . the CIA had been financing parties all around the world for generations now'.)

A long letter on the WP's situation was presented to CPSU representatives in Moscow. It opened with 'fraternal greetings' and an analysis of the situation in Ireland, North and South. In the North the WP believed that the British and Irish governments, in close alignment with 'Washington', were attempting to impose a political solution. Potentially these moves could provoke 'extreme Unionist elements and the Provisional IRA' into 'a major escalation in terrorist violence which will result in many thousands dead'. Meanwhile, 'Monopoly capital' was pushing the EEC's Single European Act, ratification of which would diminish 'Irish neutrality and sovereignty'. Against these forces, the WP was attempting to educate and mobilize the working class 'to act in their own interests'. While accepting that 'at the end of the day it is our own activity . . . which will be the determining factor for victory', and that the 'bulk' of party resources would 'have to come from the people on whose behalf we are struggling', the WP was nevertheless seeking international assistance. This appeal was placed within the Irish revolutionary tradition that stretched from Wolfe Tone and the Fenians to the Irish Volunteers, all of whom had 'worked to build allies abroad for support and solidarity'. The letter went on to outline an ambitious five-year development plan for the WP which included the setting up of a full-time 'party school of political education' at Mornington. A relaunch of the weekly party paper was also envisaged, alongside an expansion in numbers of full-time party organizers and researchers, and increased resources to fight an estimated eight elections. In total the five-year plan's cost was estimated at IR£3.45 million. Total current annual party income was estimated at £120,000, made up of £76,000 collected in members' subscriptions, £30,000 through the national collection and £12,000 from special levies on local branches. The letter gave the WP's Soviet comrades a candid appraisal of the party's current funding arrangements:

Expenditure over a 12-month period is £325,000 which covers wages, offices and publications. The bulk of the shortfall has been met by 'special activities' of which it is not possible to detail here because of reasons we are sure you will understand. The 'special activities' are unable always to be effective and so on occasion the party has had to seek loans from individuals and financial institutions for specific activities. This has meant an accumulation of debt with financial institutions of approximately £100,000, the interest alone is crippling. Further the continued growth of the party in the public domain makes 'special activities' more hazardous for the party, which has more than enough enemies in the establishment ready to pounce on mistakes and difficulties.

With these considerations in mind the concluding section of the letter stated that 'we would respectfully request a grant of one million pounds (Irish) over the proposed five-year development period in order to assist us in this vital and urgent task, which we believe will be of benefit to the world struggle for Peace, Freedom and Socialism'.

Garland recalls that he and De Rossa composed the appeal and presented it at the Oktyabrskaya Hotel: 'De Rossa was there, he typed the letter, he insisted, he said he was a better typist than I was, I didn't give a fuck who typed the letter.' De Rossa's recollection, however, directly contradicts that of Garland. He would later contend that he never saw such a letter, let alone signed one, and that his time in Moscow had been just a stopover on the way back from North Korea. He had visited Gorky Park and gone to the ballet and had a meeting concerning Repsol but was not privy to any discussions involving funding.

In February 1987 CPSU International Department deputy chief V. Zagladin sent a memo to the Central Committee describing the WP as the 'most influential and promising left force' in Ireland. However, with the Soviets involved in a period of delicate détente with the West he felt there were drawbacks to granting the WP's request for funding. Zagladin pointed out that the roots of the WP in the 'nationalist movement Sinn Féin', whose 'other wing . . . still goes on with terrorist acts in Northern Ireland', meant that it was the 'focus of attention' of Irish, British and US intelligence agencies and therefore it would be 'impossible to conceal the fact of our considerable direct financial support'. The need to maintain fraternal relations with the Irish Communists was also noted. It was advised that the Soviets should 'discuss the possibility of rendering assistance in other forms without payment in hard currency', such as 'preparation of staff', provision of study books or 'printing works, equipment and paper'.

The WP's need for funds remained acute. In 1987 it was decided that the party rather than Repsol should take full responsibility for funding election campaigns. Leading WP members personally secured large bank loans and set up a 'development fund', while the now run-down cottages at Mornington were mortgaged. Repsol sought to become the sole agent for the distribution of Soviet oil and coal in Ireland, and other such schemes were discussed. However, few of the goods offered by the WP's international allies – including North Korean Christmas decorations and clothing – would provide the basis of fruitful commercial ventures. One Belfast operative reported that they were to distribute North Korean 'mouse skins', which left activists nonplussed until someone realized that it was actually *moose* skins that he was referring to. Commercial ventures were also central to discussions between WP leaders visiting China and that country's Communist Party officials. Chinese delegations visited Ireland as guests of the WP; one was brought around the Midlands to meet officials of the semi-state Bord na Móna. The WP also organized introductions to Irish government representatives for delegations from China and North Korea.

Group B was linked to a May 1986 robbery of £60,000 from a Dublin bus garage. The robbery was professionally executed, two operatives wearing bus driver's uniforms making their way to the garage's pay office and, once inside, pulling on balaclavas and producing pistols. As with most Group B operations, the Gardaí believed that the robbery could not have been successfully carried out without a level of inside knowledge.

In the Belfast ghettos clashes with Provo and INLA supporters were still routine. Punishment attacks also continued, with youths beaten up in Turf Lodge in October 1986 and the windows of their homes smashed after they were accused of anti-social activities. These attacks were preceded by the posting of warning notices in local shops that the 'Belfast Brigade Official IRA' would take action to halt the joyriding 'epidemic'. The pressure to keep Group B out of the media spotlight meant that in Belfast criminals were increasingly used for operations, as a member of the city's command staff recalls:

Slowly but surely a team started to come in that weren't Officials but really had balls to burn as long as they were getting a percentage ... they had nothing in common with us, so we took percentages ... The attitude was, 'Fuck it then, I might as well take bits from that.'

Despite the RUC's anti-racketeering measures and increased competition from other paramilitaries, the OIRA continued to run building-site scams. During 1986 there were particular problems with the INLA, who tried to muscle in on rackets in Short Strand; after Group B badly beat a local INLA member their rivals backed off. When the ITV investigative programme *The Cook Report* inquired into paramilitary racketeering during August 1987, they succeeded in getting an interview with Black Bob McKeown. McKeown had agreed to participate after discussing the matter with RUC man Kevin Sheehy and gaining agreement that he would be anonymous and be allowed to explain the difference between the Officials' fund-raising (to support political activity), and the Provos' (to support violence). He revealed relatively little on Official IRA activities, instead talking about other paramilitary groups' involvement. The programme ended up focusing mainly on the UDA's crude extortion rackets. One of the programme makers would admit, 'We intended to expose both loyalist and nationalist rackets but we soon discovered the "Sticks" are a lot more sophisticated about things. They seem to run legitimate businesses and we could not find a figure who was blatantly racketeering or anyone who would point a finger at [someone] who was. Their power base is too strong.' Critics noted the involvement of a former WP member in researching the programme. But McKeown's comrades were unimpressed: he was threatened with being shot, and moved to Wales for his own safety.

It was becoming ever more apparent to Group B volunteers that leadership figures were cementing a relationship with the RUC, and that Group B could increasingly rely on lenient treatment by the courts and police. After one robbery in south Belfast an operative had seen an RUC patrol in the area and expected to be chased but nothing happened. In the Newry area the détente between the RUC and the Officials was also evident, as one activist recalls: 'They weren't going to let anybody off right up front but they weren't going to come in heavy on them. But they knew that activity was going on.'

There were rumours of party members who had been caught drink-driving escaping charges, and of policemen being entertained in WP clubs. Some activists worried about how such things looked within the nationalist population. One recalls: 'It done no good seeing Special Branch staggering out of clubs at two or three in the morning or drink-driving charges getting dropped. If it had an effect on me like that, what effect did it have on ordinary people that did not have a Marxist orientation?' Another member recalls driving behind a leadership figure one night who 'was absolutely blocked out of his skull, I was petrified, he was stopped by the cops . . . he was drunk, he had a gun, and he was let drive on.' Group B members were unhappy that some activists were receiving training in the use of legal weapons from the RUC. Others recall some Northern leadership figures arguing that cooperation with the RUC was correct not only tactically but also ideologically, as some of their police contacts professed to be 'socialists' as well. The party's enemies consistently claimed that the WP had some form of agreement with the police. Indeed, Group B members had been given clearance to tell police directly about Provo activity. Although some activists were uncomfortable with this, hatred of the Provos and the belief that the state could be used as an ally to defeat terrorism meant many Officials approved of the relationship with the RUC. A document produced by the Group B leadership that caused some dismay stated that Official activity on Bloody Sunday in 1972, which included the firing of retaliatory shots at the Paratroopers, should be admitted. The idea provoked heated discussion but was not acted on.

The growing cooperation between the Officials and the RUC may well have played a role in the murder of Emmanuel Wilson in June 1987. The Beechmount resident was abducted in a black taxi and interrogated by members of the Provos' internal security department before being shot as a police informer. Wilson's Provo killers were aware of the 35-year-old's connections to the WP, as both a registered party supporter and a member of Group B's intelligence network, and would later claim he had also informed on OIRA activity. RUC sources stated their belief that Wilson could only have been killed with the agreement of the Officials as the Provos would not have risked an all-out feud, but the killing provoked heated demands for retaliation. Officials, many of them armed, gathered in Cyprus Street the day Wilson's body was found, demanding the organization hit back. But Seamus Lynch, concerned that a feud with the Provos would cause severe political damage to the WP, told a hurriedly convened meeting that he would play no part in authorizing a response, driving his point home by stating, 'If I'm shot I want no retaliation.' His position dismayed many volunteers who felt that one of their organization's fundamental roles, the protection of members, was being critically undermined. Members were pacified in the short term by a promise that retaliation would happen after a few months once those directly involved in the killing had been identified. The long-standing mediation process between the two organizations was activated and within a few days the Provos were able to make a public statement that 'we do not foresee any possibility of conflict between ourselves and the Workers' Party's military wing'. Meanwhile the WP highlighted to journalists the lack of retaliation as a clear indication that the Official IRA was now defunct.

Tension over the OIRA's liaison with the RUC would boil over during a meeting of senior Belfast Group B members shortly after the March 1988 killing of the two British army corporals who had driven into a Provisional funeral cortège. Activists were shown photographs of the mob attack on the corporals' car and its aftermath by a senior Official accompanied by a leading Group B intelligence operative. As one of those present recalls, they 'threw photos down and the corporals weren't cold. And they were photos from a helicopter, quite obvious they were from a helicopter.' Several of those present objected when asked if they could identify members of the mob that had attacked the corporals' car. The meeting broke up in disorder as several volunteers angrily criticized the leadership's contacts with the British security services.

Although the WP continued publicly to condemn loyalist terrorism, secret links had been maintained with the UDA, even as a new generation of largely apolitical and rampantly sectarian leaders came to the fore in that organization. These younger men replaced figures such as John McMichael, killed by the Provos in 1987, and Jim Craig, killed by his own organization in October 1988. Liaison was particularly important when leading Group B figures purchased a pub adjacent to the Seymour Estate, a UDA stronghold in south-west Belfast. The strong suspicion that information on mutual enemies was changing hands at meetings between Group B and loyalists troubled some within the WP, but connections were maintained.

In late 1986 two younger Group B operatives travelled to North Korea and trained alongside specialist units of the Korean People's Army. The following spring around a dozen Group B operatives travelled to Pyongyang for several weeks of intensive weapons, combat and intelligence instruction. The men's journey, via the USSR, was assisted by the KGB and elaborate measures were taken to conceal their real destination from western intelligence agencies. To aid these precautions each man wrote a series of postcards and letters while in Moscow which they dated over the coming weeks; a Moscow-based Group B activist sent these greetings on during the men's stay in North Korea. While training with the Korean People's Army the activists met with members of African military forces. It was unclear to what use the North Koreans believed the men would eventually put their training, which included use of heavy machine guns; some volunteers believed it was 'just an exercise in keeping them [Group B members] happy'. Others were informed the training was to establish an elite 'assassination squad' as part of a plan to 'stand down' the wider organization. Group B also utilized their connection with North Korea to import around two dozen .32 automatic pistols during the late 1980s, collecting the weapons from North Korean diplomats in Paris.

Group B's relationship with the intelligence agencies of communist states also resulted in the organization becoming involved in the distribution of forged United States $100 notes. Although it is unclear where the batches of counterfeit US currency which initially came into the possession of Group B during the mid-1980s originated from, most activists believed the notes were printed in the USSR. By the late 1980s Gardaí had become aware that Group B was in some way connected with the distribution of forged dollars. They were informed by CIA agents that the US authorities believed the KGB had instigated the plot but that the notes were possibly produced in North Korea. The Americans would later inform their Irish contacts that Group B had been awarded the 'European franchise' for distribution of the 'Superdollar', which was also being disseminated by separate networks in the Far East and Middle East. Group B activists based on the Continent initially aided the transportation of counterfeit dollars to Britain and Ireland; in the late 1980s the counterfeit currency was transported directly from the USSR to Ireland. On one occasion a group of veteran WP supporters treated to a holiday in a Black Sea resort transported notes back concealed in the lining of their coats and in money belts. As the USSR became increasingly unstable the transportation of the currency became more problematic; a confrontation between Group B's permanent representative in Moscow and the emerging Russian mafia resulted in the loss of a large quantity of notes.

Group B used a network of activists and criminal contacts to exchange the Superdollars in Ireland and Britain for genuine currency. Most of those who undertook this activity were allowed to keep a percentage of the proceeds. The operation was highly successful, with around one million dollars' worth of the notes estimated to have been distributed by the organization during this period. CIA agents liaising with Irish security operatives informed them they feared billions of dollars' worth of the fake currency had been produced and believed the scheme to be a 'serious threat' and 'a genuine attempt to undermine the US economy'. During 1990 the Belfast organization would establish five four-man teams who set about exchanging the Superdollars throughout Ireland. In order to prevent fingerprint detection volunteers sprayed their hands with a liquid solution called 'second skin'. Despite the precautions, the sheer volume of high-quality forged $100 bills being exchanged in Irish financial institutions raised suspicion. When a bank stopped exchanging the $100 notes and there was a police raid on a Belfast Group B operative's house, the operation was suspended.

While Group B's relationship with the North Korean intelligence services intensified, direct dealings with the KGB were becoming more problematic as the CPSU continued on its course of détente with the West. A December 1988 CPSU memo from KGB president Vladimir Kruychkov to the CPSU Central Committee reported that 'Comrade Garland' had requested of the resident KGB officer in Ireland that five 'reliable and trustworthy' WP members be given 'specialised training' in Moscow in order to 'strengthen' party security. Kruychkov recommended that the WP be given 'a positive answer', but despite the Soviets characterizing Garland as *doverytelni*, a 'trustworthy contact' who was familiar with the KGB Resident in Ireland Vladimir Vasilyevich Minderov, they decided against granting his request. A January 1989 KGB memo to the CPSU Central Committee outlined their reasoning:

Additional examination with the help of KGB specialists showed that despite the confidential relations between the CPSU and the WP, to satisfy the petition would mean a serious risk. Any leakage of information about our participation in staff preparation of this kind for the WP of Ireland, and it is difficult if not practically impossible to conceal these actions, would lead to serious complications in Soviet–British relations. We can inform S. Garland it is not possible to comply with his request at present but at the same time we should stress we would invariably like to go on strengthening our fraternal relations with the WP of Ireland.

Despite such reservations, the CPSU would eventually provide nearly £70,000 in direct payments to the WP, handed over directly by the KGB to Group B operatives in Moscow in 1989.

Although the Officials had not carried out a fatal attack beyond their own ranks since 1977, a 1988 British government briefing paper stated that the Official IRA 'still exists as a significant force'. The Belfast organization continued to be treated with caution by the Provos, as a Provisional intelligence document from this period indicated:

- No real political party structure. Political leadership of Lynch, McMahon and Lowry, and then a structure beneath them of approx 50 thugs.
- These thugs have no politics – not even WP politics.
- Isolated within and feared by communities – almost universally 'everyone knows the sticks'.
- Long record of anti-social and criminal activity.
- The structure is really a self-protection league. Anybody can join this league (in some areas) – including hoods that are afraid of the IRA.
- Collusion with Loyalists.
- Access to weapons – legal and illegal. Brits/RUC never interfere with them – role of fifth column.
- The drinking clubs in each area are the main focus of WP activities.
- In each area there is a hard core of activists, and an outer circle of hangers-on. Familie [sic] ties play a part here – very similar to criminal families.

- Media sympathetic – it's impossible to get an anti-stick story into papers.

The report went on to name the 'Sticks' in Turf Lodge, New Lodge, the Markets, Twinbrook and Lower Falls, the list coming to over 55 men – with a note that the organization's membership in several other areas of the city had yet to be compiled. Official IRA activities were outlined and points of friction with the Provos were noted: 'In Belfast the IRA and the Sticks have an agreement not to shoot each other. If there is any agro there's a mediation process to go through. The Sticks in the Markets are abusing this system to give protection to any hood in the area by claiming them as a "party member".' The report claimed that the OIRA was expected to take 'real heavy action against anyone who offends any member'.

While there were few obvious signs of Group B activity in the South by the late 1980s, Southern WP members who travelled North quickly realized that it was different there, as a Finglas member recalls: 'In Belfast it became clear to you very quickly that it was not as clear-cut as people were saying. There was a quasi-military structure about the whole thing and people would be roaring in your ear about it anyway, they'd be pissed and they'd be screaming this and that.' A Dun Laoghaire WP member recalled that 'we enjoyed going to the North, the camaraderie in the clubs and hanging around with hard men. You could not be there long without knowing the army existed.'

Another Dublin activist says that 'without Group B they [the Belfast WP] wouldn't have been able to exist ... Politics in the North is not civil society, it's fucked up, there was a war for the hegemony of the working-class areas, and the Sticks wouldn't lie down and go away.'

With the WP leadership claiming no knowledge of any paramilitary links to their party, it was a moot point how many Southern members were aware of Group B's existence. Dublin WP activist Colm Breathnach recalls, 'By the late '80s the level of knowledge of the army's existence correlated with how close to the centre you were and how long you were in the party.' Despite the growing pressure since the mid-1980s to wean the party off reliance on Group B funding, a Belfast Official recalls his caustic view of the party leadership's position: 'They all knew but didn't want to know. As long as the money was coming in.'

17. The Flight from Socialism

'The age of heroes is dead and gone.'

Proinsias De Rossa, February 1992

On the night of 9 November 1989, television viewers across the world were transfixed by the fall of the Berlin Wall. Four months previously Solidarity had swept to power in free elections in Poland, the country's communist regime finally succumbing to the popular revolt which had dogged it for nearly a decade. October had seen the ruling Hungarian communists vote to reconstitute themselves as a Social Democratic party. The Eastern Bloc's political upheaval accelerated in the weeks following the fall of the Berlin Wall, with mass demonstrations bringing about the largely peaceful demise of communist rule in Czechoslovakia and Bulgaria. By the end of December Romanian dictator Nicolae Ceausescu and his wife had been violently deposed and executed.

The WP had supported Gorbachev's reforms, but the collapse of regimes previously promoted by the party left many members questioning their own ideological commitments. In an *Irish People* article following the collapse of the Berlin Wall, De Rossa attempted to reassure them: 'Much of the media coverage of events in eastern Europe has been superficial and simplistic. What we are witnessing is not the collapse of socialism but birth pangs of a new, more democratic and stronger socialism.' He stressed that his party had not been 'attempting to reproduce particular forms of socialism existing in any other country' but rather trying to learn 'both from the successes and mistakes of socialists in other countries'. He also took a swipe at political opponents who were revelling in the fate of Europe's communist regimes:

Right-wing politicians in this country are in no position to be smug about the exodus of people from the GDR. Proportionately more people have emigrated from Ireland in the past year than from the GDR. The same politicians here claim the exodus from the GDR is an indication that socialism has failed. Curiously they do not conclude that the exodus from this country shows that capitalism has failed.

The WP's election success emboldened its public representatives. With seven TDs the party now had Dáil group status, which provided a sizeable state subvention and parliamentary privileges including greater speaking time. Gilmore used his maiden Dáil speech to attack service charges and the government's failure to properly finance public housing. On Dublin County Council WP councillors tabled a motion calling for the establishment of a judicial inquiry into allegations of widespread political corruption in the planning process, but the motion failed in the face of Fianna Fáil and Fine Gael opposition.

In a break with previous practice Labour leader Dick Spring agreed to the activation of a Left Cooperation Group with De Rossa to aid the coordination of their activities in the Dáil. Détente was not evident in the ITGWU, however, with newly elected WP TDs Pat Rabbitte and Eamon Gilmore finding themselves summarily dismissed from their jobs by the union hierarchy. The TDs launched a legal action and mounted a picket on the union's Liberty Hall offices, but the decision stood. Agreement had already been reached between the leadership of the ITGWU and WUI to amalgamate at the beginning of 1990 to form a new organization – the Services, Industrial, Professional and Technical Union (SIPTU). It was with one eye on the political balance of this new union that Rabbitte used his July address at Bodenstown to declare that 'ominous shadows' now hung over the ITGWU leadership due to their hostility towards the WP.

The party played a central role in organizing the 'Peace Train' protest against Provisional IRA attacks on the Dublin–Belfast railway line. Two special trains ran on the line to much media fanfare on 28 October; passengers included representatives of most of the political parties, and the large number of WP supporters included De Rossa and Seamus Lynch. The protest allowed the WP to focus on the Provos as the main source of violence in the North and to strengthen its own anti-violence credentials in the South.

The party struggled to cope with the reverberations from the collapse of international communism. During 1989 the communist group in the European Parliament had split into hard-line and moderate factions. After initial half-hearted inquiries about De Rossa joining the Party of European Socialists were rejected by that grouping's Irish affiliates, Labour and the SDLP, the WP leadership decided to join the Left Unity Group, which consisted of the French, Portuguese and Greek communist MEPs and was seen as hostile to Perestroika. The alignment would become a bone of contention among the party leadership, with Gilmore and Rabbitte vocal in their view that the party should have aligned with the Italian communists and should prepare to follow that party's stated objective of eventually joining the Socialist group.

There was a growing consensus within the party that changes had to occur in light of the collapse of the communist bloc, and once again it was Eoghan Harris who attempted to harness this. During the late 1980s Harris had begun to question his previous commitment to the interpretation of Marxism that had under-pinned *The Irish Industrial Revolution*. Having been an outspoken critic of social democracy, he was now beginning to suggest that it was the only viable platform for progressive politics. This view-point, which had formed the basis of a speech he gave to a 1988 WP summer school in Belfast and had underlain De Rossa's 1989 Ard Fheis address, was further developed in an address given by him at a fractious WP Dublin regional education seminar in November 1989. Despite a cool reception from party members, Harris's argu-ments found a degree of favour with Smullen, who felt that events in Eastern Europe had 'made many of us begin to examine carefully articles of faith that we had accepted for years'. Activists remember Smullen being 'absolutely shattered' by the revelations of corrup-tion in states like Romania.

Harris gathered his thoughts into a short pamphlet entitled *The Necessity of Social Democracy*. What emerged was a disjointed but savage attack on 'Left' politics and a demand that they be discarded in favour of what he called 'Social Democracy', which, according to Harris, had been the actual intention of Marx and other early communist writers. Harris stated that 'silence and suppression of self killed socialism' and 'that the individual person – not the crowd, collective or class – is the subject and the whole point of history'. While boldly stating that socialism was 'dead', having committed 'suicide', this was not the end for 'socialist values', which could now 'rise from the ashes as a democratic political idea'. But the term 'socialism' had to be discarded, just as the term 'republican' had been, 'like nuclear waste'.

Harris argued that the working class 'admire people like Smurfit, Goodman, Tony O'Reilly. Only Trots think otherwise.' His prescription was that the party must remove itself from 'Left circles', where he claimed a soft approach to nationalism was the norm. Declaring 'I am a Marxist. Marxism to me is, first and foremost a moral system', Harris held that his politics had always been defined by 'Dialectics' – 'change through conflict' – and using this approach the Research Section had from 1974 to 1979 'in a dozen pamphlets . . . carved out an original theory of Irish political economy which rejected state socialist economics, the politics of "national" labour and the whole mess of Republican socialism'. De Rossa's 1989 Ard Fheis speech had continued this process and 'saved our bacon' in the run-up to the general election.

The polemic closed with comments that would greatly anger his opponents within the party. Harris stated that 'as a person who deals with [the] media my impression is that the word "Left" is as attractive as the word "AIDS"'. He noted several elements of 'left luggage' that the WP would need to 'dump' and areas where the public perceived the WP to be wrong: 'Criminals are not victims of oppression. Alienation is a patronising myth of middle-class academics. Entrepreneurs are not evil.' Pursuing 'left unity' was useless; 'the public never talk about it'. Colleagues recall Harris taking a different tack privately, arguing that the adoption of social democracy would not be a dilution of the party's socialism but Marxism in a new guise; 'the iron fist in the velvet glove'.

Harris now faced the problem of how to get such an incendiary thesis out to the party membership. Fergus Whelan's initial suspicion, upon reading the pamphlet, was that the Industrial Department cadres would 'all be expelled before the week is out'. Harris delivered a copy for publication to *Making Sense* editor Paddy Gillan in mid-December 1989, and Gillan brought it to the attention of the party leadership. It was not well received. At a testimonial dinner held for Cathal Goulding in early January, Des O'Hagan mocked the 'new social democrats', leading to a confrontation with Smullen that resulted in the Director of Economic Affairs walking out of the event. Now aware that *The Necessity of Social Democracy* was circulating behind the scenes, Harris wrote a letter to Garland demanding its publication. He focused his ire on what he termed the 'SIPTU Tendency', a grouping around Des Geraghty and TDs Gilmore and Rabbitte. Harris harangued the group, who had been derided as social democrats by the Industrial Department in the past, as careerists who were using the WP for advancement in politics. For their part most of the 'SIPTU Tendency' looked towards figures such as Ellen Hazelkorn, Henry Patterson and Paul Sweeney as the source of a new 'Democratic Socialist' ideology, which emphasized the primary role of the state in economic development but questioned concepts such as democratic centralism. For veterans such as Garland and O'Hagan, and those loyal to them, both groups' call for an overhaul of WP ideology seemed to be an attack on the Leninist 'revolutionary party' they had striven to build. Despite these reservations, in late January the Executive Political Committee (EPC) agreed that an edited version of *The Necessity of Social Democracy* would be published in *Making Sense*.

The party was now in the throes of a major debate on the way forward. Special delegate conferences were held during February to discuss the WP's ideological future and the impact of events in Eastern Europe. Among the contributors was Paul Sweeney, who argued that the party had to be more democratic but maintain a

Marxist economic approach, while Oliver Donohue and Brian Brennan spoke on behalf of the Harris thesis. Donohue's claim that the WP had never actually been a 'socialist' party led to heckles. De Rossa's son Fearghal and Dun Laoghaire member Colm Breathnach spoke in support of a 'Third Way', 'a socialist theory and practice that can take us beyond the failed paths of "actually existing socialism" and social democracy'. It was also a response to concerns that the party was facing a split along Social Democrat/Marxist-Leninist lines. At the Munster conference Ó Cionnaith, now WP campaigns manager, expressed the view of many veteran leaders that the way beyond the current ideological strife was to strengthen protest politics and reiterate revolutionary goals:

The fight for the trust of the people and a willingness and confidence to offer leadership on every issue which touches their lives, is a day-in, day-out commitment for socialists such as us, who want to see the present dominant thinking turned around, or, in other words, who want to bring about a revolution in popular thinking which will make the Workers' Party the biggest party in the Dáil. That is revolution. We are revolutionaries. And revolutionaries have obligations.

In the run-up to the Ard Fheis, Harris's supporters blamed the 'SIPTU Tendency' for delaying the publication of *The Necessity of Social Democracy* so that Ard Fheis motions calling for its ideas to be debated could not be tabled prior to an early March deadline. Harris lobbied De Rossa, calling for WP meetings to be convened across the country to discuss his ideas. De Rossa was largely unsympathetic. In a letter to De Rossa Harris described Gilmore and Rabbitte as 'student princes' – a reference to their involvement in the USI – and 'bunnies' while the WP's Marxist-Leninists such as Garland, Ó Cionnaith and Peter Kane were dismissed as the 'Koreans'.

With Harris's new thesis meeting stiff resistance, Smullen took the decision, without consulting the party leadership, to publish *The Necessity of Social Democracy* in a special edition of the Research

Section journal *The Wealth of the Nation*. The document, the first
WP pamphlet to bear Harris's name, was distributed through the
post to party branches and the media. In his foreword Smullen
wrote:

The continuing crisis of socialism calls for more than cosmetic changes
such as prefixing 'democracy' to socialism. This pamphlet argues that
the word 'socialism' is now a brake on progress. It proposes a return
to the revolutionary roots of social democracy and a commitment to
'revolutionary reformism', defined as reformist struggle conducted with
revolutionary zeal for democratic ends . . . Social Democracy, in this
sense, offers a third way between conservative and careerist, between
discredited state socialism and so-called 'democratic socialism', which
. . . treats the party member not as a person at the hub of history, but as
a cog in a constituency machine.

The first glimpse that the public, and many WP members, had of
Harris's new ideas was Fintan O'Toole's warm response to *The
Necessity of Social Democracy* in his *Irish Times* column of 8 March.
Declaring Harris 'about the only person in the country who merits
the description of political ideologue', O'Toole juxtaposed this
'vigorous embracing of social democracy' with recent claims by
Fine Gael leader Alan Dukes to represent the same political ideology and concluded that 'the mantle of Social Democracy looks
like being something that will have to be fought over rather than
merely assumed'. But the WP leadership had no interest in wearing
any mantle bestowed on the party by Harris. With their authority
challenged, Marxist-Leninists, reformers and De Rossa all agreed
that action should be taken against Smullen, who recorded his
view of the March EPC meeting shortly afterwards:

I sat down at a big polished table in 30 Gardiner Place . . . The meeting
had been called to discuss the coming Ard Fheis – nothing about me on
the distributed agenda . . . When the meeting started De Rossa stabbed
first: 'Eamon Smullen has disobeyed a party order by publishing a document called *The Necessity of Social Democracy* . . . I therefore propose that

he surrenders his party card and leave.' Then Brutus stabbed and it was an unkind cut. Sean Garland said: 'I second that proposal.' Why did he have to stab? He has bullet scars on his body and his hair has turned grey in the long struggle. He cannot have any real fellow feeling with Trendies. Rabbitte and Gilmore were sitting there and were keen enough to use the knife. He could have left it to them. The Northerners sat tense, silent, worried.

After some debate the meeting adjourned. Smullen went to Garland's office to tell him he expected De Rossa's motion to pass and wished to arrange a time to hand over his keys to Gardiner Place, but Garland tried to persuade him to appeal the decision. By the time the meeting resumed Mac Giolla and Goulding had arrived. Mac Giolla, referring to the party constitution, declared that the EPC did not have the authority to rule in the matter and it should wait till the following day's Ard Chomhairle meeting.

That meeting opened with a letter from Harris denouncing the 'student princes' who, he claimed, were using the 'Third Way' grouping in a plot to push out the 'old guard'. This was Harris's last act as a WP member, as he had announced his resignation from the party shortly before the Ard Chomhairle meeting began. De Rossa put forward a motion, seconded by Rabbitte, calling for Smullen to resign from the EPC and as chairman of the Economic Affairs Committee. Smullen rejected this, saying as editor of *The Wealth of the Nation* he had the right to publish what he wished, and eventually a Goulding amendment that Smullen be suspended from his positions until the Ard Fheis was approved. The meeting then decided to appoint De Rossa the replacement chair of the Economic Affairs Committee, a move that confirmed to Smullen that the WP president was completely in alliance with the 'ex-student group'.

The internal squabble soon became public knowledge, the *Irish People* reporting that 'open debate' was taking place within the WP and that Harris had resigned from the party. The affair also spawned numerous newspaper articles revelling in the inner turmoil of an organization whose workings had for so long been hidden. The *Irish Times* referred to the departure of the WP's 'leading ideologue'. A WP statement referred to Smullen's suspension as being the result of a 'serious breach of party discipline'. Harris attempted to play down talks of a split within the party, stating: 'I am an intellectual and I feel it is my duty to present these ideas, and when I could try no more, I felt I should step back and allow the debate to continue. I have no desire to affect the party's historic mission to bring peace to Ireland.' Brennan's resignation statement later that week was more acerbic, with De Rossa and the 'Siptu group – Messrs Geraghty, Gilmore and Rabbitte' condemned for their 'suppression of the social democracy document'.

At the Ard Chomhairle it was decided that in conjunction with the review of party ideology a reappraisal of organization structures and policy programmes should also be undertaken. This process was intended to conclude with a special Ard Fheis that would endorse the most wide-ranging changes since the early 1980s. However, the Harris affair continued to dominate media coverage of the WP in the lead-up to the April 1990 Ard Fheis. Opening the event, Garland called for the weekend's discussions to be constructive and 'devoid of bitterness of a political and personal character'. Such a call was particularly important with the WP's enlarged Dáil presence meaning much of the Ard Fheis would be covered live on RTÉ television.

The following day's debates on party democracy and organization saw Garland's hopes dashed as the party had its first public fracture since 1974. Smullen's bizarre entrance – carrying a duty-free bag and a length of blue rope – contributed to the air of tension. From the podium Pat Rabbitte condemned Harris and his latest ideas, stating that social democracy had largely failed in Britain and elsewhere. While claiming to have 'great admiration for Eoghan Harris's talents', Rabbitte attacked him for using them to 'create division in the party'. He welcomed the organizational changes which ended 'secret' membership, stating that it had been misused 'by a small number of people to build a party within a party'. Several delegates spoke in support of democratic-centralist decision-making, saying its opponents merely wished to replace it with parliamentary control, 'middle-class' or 'yuppie' takeover. Others linked democratic centralism with Eastern Europe and called for it to be discarded. Anger exploded in the hall when Jimmy Brick, one of the four WP vice-presidents, mounted an impassioned defence of Smullen and Harris. Brick condemned the attempt to expel Smullen, declaring that 'at least show trials were heard in public'. He had considered resigning earlier but loyalty to the party had prevented him; now, after hearing the 'lies' of the 'triumphant tormentors as they mocked and humiliated Eamon Smullen', he ended his nineteen years of party membership. Slow handclaps greeted the end of his speech as another delegate marched to the front of the hall and ripped up his own membership card. John McManus dismissed Brick's outburst, adding: 'Those people who are hot under the collar about this are the very people who have persecuted the likes of me in this party over the years.' Donohue labelled Gilmore and Rabbitte the 'Ceausescu twins' and accused them of contact with Eastern European student leaders who had trained secret policemen. The session ended with a majority of delegates backing the retention of democratic centralism but reformers claiming that they had succeeded in having the concept's 'democratic' nature re-emphasized.

In comparison to the divisive events preceding it, De Rossa's presidential address held out a vision around which a new unity could be formed. Its opening lines, in which De Rossa declared, 'I am a socialist; socialism is not dead,' marked a clear break with Harris. The 1989 Ard Fheis speech was now recast not as a stark rupture with the past but rather an attempt to prompt debate. De Rossa accepted that 'Stalinist' Eastern Bloc communism had received a 'mortal blow' but that the WP espoused a different kind of socialism based on 'participative democracy'. He dismissed Fianna Fáil's recent attempts to appear concerned with environmentalism as just a 'new green flag to wrap around their jaded politics', contrasting their rhetoric with the reality of Fianna Fáil councillors 'abusing their powers to rezone and destroy green belts'. There was also criticism of the SDLP and a demand that all the island's 'nationalist parties . . . go much further down the road of harsh and self-critical reassessment of Ireland's nationalist and Catholic political culture'. In light of a recent Supreme Court ruling that the Irish constitution's Articles Two and Three constituted a 'claim of legal right' to the territory of Northern Ireland, De Rossa called upon all 'democrats in the Republic' to 'cooperate on securing the deletion of these articles'. He also demanded that Fianna Fáil's 'ambivalence' towards extradition of terrorist suspects be confronted: 'Those who kill, maim and destroy, by bomb or bullet, and claim to be doing it to achieve a united Ireland ... should be extradited to face trial.' This onslaught on nationalist shibboleths overshadowed De Rossa's calls for a universal minimum income, integrated education and highlighting of a new industrial policy that accepted the existence of a 'mixed economy'. What was not lost on those suspicious of the parliamentary group's growing influence was his support for a 'federal Europe' and praising of the 'new dimension' WP general election success had brought to Irish politics.

The following day, Smullen issued a public statement claiming that 'the newer additions to our Dáil strength began, as soon as they were in place in the House, to campaign to remove all decision-making to a parliamentary party, or rather to a part of it'. It was because of these people, who he accused of having little experience beyond 'the unreal world of student politics', that Smullen had now decided to resign. Attempts were made to the very last to keep Smullen in the party, but Garland summed up the weekend's events by telling delegates, 'If the time has come to part with old comrades then so be it.'

In the days following the Ard Fheis a couple of dozen members, including Donohue and Fergus Whelan, joined Brick and Smullen in resigning; but other Industrial Department cadres decided to remain with the WP. The WP's political direction was now largely in the hands of certain TDs, and their allies, rather than those loyal to the 'revolutionary party'. But the parliamentary group was still far from totally dominant, as emphasized by McCartan's failure to be elected on to the Ard Chomhairle. Also, to the resentment of some TDs, the man who took over Smullen's Dublin Group B responsibilities, a Garland loyalist, began to have a greater prominence within party committees. Those sceptical of the parliamentary group's direction also continued to hold a number of important party officerships, with Seamus Harrison remaining as treasurer, Peter Kane as national organizer and John Lowry as chair of the International Affairs Committee. With internal party education now less intensive, education director Des O'Hagan was seen by the reformers as a hard-liner whose influence was largely restricted to the Belfast area. Members were now encouraged to enrol in third-level courses, particularly those dealing with industrial relations, rather than depend on the party for political education.

The parliamentary group's growing influence was welcomed by an *Irish Times* editorial following the Ard Fheis. It called upon Labour and the WP to put aside 'partisan hostility' in favour of cooperation while taking a swipe at 'democratic centralism' as a 'fatally flawed' doctrine and an unwelcome hangover from the party's attachment to Eastern European communism. The editorial bore the hallmarks of Dick Walsh's thinking, and Walsh returned to the theme in his next weekly column. This narrative of dynamic public representatives opposed by a staid party 'old guard' was nurtured by the parliamentary group. The TDs' activity in the Dáil ensured they had a wider resonance among the public and Southern membership. With seven TDs the WP could now propose legislation, and their first bill, proposing measures to improve conditions for part-time workers, was defeated only after Fianna Fáil gave assurances that they would implement a similar law. WP TDs were also using Dáil time to highlight what they perceived as the twin political evils embodied by Haughey's Fianna Fáil – financial corruption and opportunist nationalism. Mac Giolla cited 'a suspicion which I hope has no basis' that the sprawling area of Blanchardstown in west Dublin was being denied shopping facilities due to the property developer seeking to build a shopping centre nearby being an 'old friend' of Minister for the Environment Padraig Flynn. Mac Giolla also unsuccessfully lobbied Haughey on behalf of Orangemen seeking to stage a tercentenary commemoration of the Battle of the Boyne at the event's site in County

Meath. A flow of state and EU funding allowed the parliamentary group to directly employ secretaries and advisers. Party press officer Tony Heffernan continued to lead the Dáil backroom team. Among the new WP employees based at Leinster House was Heffernan's assistant Eugene Hickland, a former IDYM activist, who had been appointed by head office and was a strong supporter of Garland. Older hands brought back included Padraig Yeates, who became De Rossa's assistant in Brussels, and Rabbitte's Dáil secretary Máirín de Burca. The reorientation of members and public contact to a party centre based in the Dáil rather than Gardiner Place was also evident in the new WP internal newsletter, *News and Views*, which listed Dáil and TD contact details as well as those for party offices.

Some WP activists had been developing relations with Labour Left, a grouping within the Labour Party seeking to promote a more left-wing agenda. These contacts included discussions on a joint approach to the upcoming presidential campaign. Initially some had attempted to promote the idea of approaching Noel Browne as a left-wing unity candidate, but Dick Spring was opposed to Browne and on 1 May Labour launched the campaign of its nominee Mary Robinson in Limerick. Robinson, a barrister, academic and former independent senator, was a veteran liberal campaigner on contentious issues including access to contraception and gay rights. She was presented to the media by Jim Kemmy, whose Democratic Socialist Party officially merged with Labour that day, and was flanked by members of left-wing groups including the WP. However, there was division within the WP over what role the party should play in the Robinson campaign. De Rossa took the lead in negotiations with Labour on a 'common policy platform and strategy' for the election, and in the summer of 1990 WP branches were asked to consider four approaches to the presidential election: '1) To ignore it, and not campaign, 2) Endorse Mary Robinson and not campaign, 3) Have joint campaign with Labour, 4) Endorse Mary Robinson and run an independent WP campaign.' Branches' views were to be relayed to the party centre by 21 July. In late July De Rossa announced to the *Irish Times* that the WP was to mount its own campaign in support of Robinson 'while working closely' with other groups supporting her candidacy. Some in the party felt that De Rossa had decided to support Robinson before the issue had been fully argued out. The young members behind the 'Third Way' strategy were the most vocal critics. Heated exchanges between De Rossa and his constituency chairman John O'Neill saw the TD threaten to walk out of a meeting when O'Neill remarked that 'members should not find out Workers' Party policy in the *Irish Times*'. There was also unease among some members at the prospect of campaigning for a candidate who was 'not talking class politics'. In Dun Laoghaire Colm Breathnach made it clear he would not canvass for Robinson as she was 'not a socialist'. A largely unspoken compromise was reached whereby members were not expected to canvass if they did not wish to. This was a new departure for a party with as disciplined a structure as the WP; Breathnach recalls, 'the main problem was the army people were not happy with us because we had breached democratic centralism'. In Finglas Brian Whelan recalls it as 'the first time I had a problem getting people out to canvass. [It was the] first time De Rossa came to us with a fait accompli, we wanted to discuss it first, but it was probably 60–40 to support her.' He remembers the period as: 'TDs stressing power, becoming strong, "my seat", [which was] alien to us, it's a Workers' Party seat.'

With Robinson competing against Fianna Fáil's Brian Lenihan, backed by £1.3 million of campaign funding, and SDLP veteran Austin Currie running for Fine Gael, most political commentators agreed that she stood little chance. WP branches were encouraged to use the election to promote their 1991 local election candidates and 'women's issues'. In Dun Laoghaire canvassers were encouraged by the support for Robinson, particularly in middle-class areas and among women, both constituencies in which the parliamentary group were keen to increase support. Robinson's appeal was seen as linking into wider cultural changes in the Republic, such as a weakening of clerical influence. The euphoria unleashed in the summer of 1990 by the appearance of the Republic of Ireland football team in their first World Cup also seemed to point to a new definition of patriotism. The party's Bodenstown commemoration was postponed from July until September to facilitate people watching the games. Three consecutive *Irish People* front pages charted the team's progress in Italy, though De Rossa declined a place on the government jet to watch the quarter-final in Rome.

As Robinson's campaign gained momentum it attracted support from the Green Party as well as the involvement of Eoghan Harris as a media adviser. There had been no rapprochement between the former WP ideologue and his erstwhile comrades. During the summer the *Irish Times* had printed a distilled version of *The Necessity of Social Democracy*, ensuring Harris's ideas continued to be a source of controversy. The July/August issue of *Making Sense* contained a series of articles attacking Harris's new thesis for historical inaccuracy, misreading of Marx and 'threadbare populism'. Ill feeling was again on public display following Smullen's death in early October. Aged 66, the former Director of Economic Affairs died suddenly while on holiday in Italy with his long-term partner Nuala Monaghan. De Rossa, Garland and others held responsible for Smullen's resignation from the WP were requested not to attend the funeral service in Glasnevin, but Goulding, Mac Giolla, Ó Cionnaith, Kathleen Lynch and Jim Sullivan were among the many WP members who gathered to hear Harris describe Smullen's political life as 'not the stuff of speeches but epic art', adding that 'to approach him in death, when it is safe, to offer him respect without rehabilitation, is only a hypocrisy or a hijack'.

Due to a lacklustre Fine Gael campaign it was Robinson who gained when Brian Lenihan became embroiled in a political controversy that had its origins in January 1982, when Garret FitzGerald asked President Hillery to dissolve the Dáil. Lenihan was one of a handful of senior Fianna Fáil members who phoned Hillery asking him to contravene his constitutional position above party politics and allow Charles Haughey to form a government without an election. Lenihan's public claims during the campaign not to have made any such phone call were directly contradicted by a taped interview he had given only five months earlier. Fianna

Fáil's attempts to defuse the controversy by citing Lenihan's ill health, and the party's personalized attacks on Robinson, only deepened the crisis. De Rossa stated that Lenihan's conduct was another case of Fianna Fáil's 'low standards in high places'. Lenihan's hopes were dealt a further blow when Haughey, cornered by his PD colleagues, dismissed him as Tánaiste just days before the election. Robinson's call for a new style of presidency, meanwhile, was resonating. Although the WP's campaign was limited in resources and manpower, it had an impact in areas of party strength, and the WP would later claim to have printed and distributed 600,000 pieces of literature supporting Robinson. Fianna Fáil and Fine Gael politicians began to stress that Robinson had the backing of the 'Marxist' WP, hoping this would weaken her appeal. When she appeared on television surrounded by WP supporters in Dun Laoghaire, Fianna Fáil pointedly referred to her 'Workers' Party minders', a label canvassers found repeated to them on the doorstep. De Rossa denounced the 'red scare', pointing out that Robinson was not a WP member but did represent a 'new and progressive strand in Irish politics'.

In the campaign's final week, with polls showing Robinson and Lenihan neck and neck, Fianna Fáil intensified their attacks. First came claims that the WP intended to use a Robinson presidency to access files on their political opponents. Then Robinson was tackled during a *Late Late Show* debate, as well as in Fianna Fáil statements, over claims she had declared herself a 'socialist' and was backed by a 'Marxist party'. In the final days Haughey weighed in personally, condemning Robinson's acceptance of 'Marxist' support, a line of attack that was repeated in newspaper ads. On television minister Seamus Brennan went further, claiming that due to WP influence a Robinson victory would severely damage Ireland's standing overseas and decrease foreign inward investment. He challenged De Rossa to deny his party was 'Marxist Leninist communist'. With a Robinson victory now looking likely, De Rossa's response was measured: he stated that Fianna Fáil was again attempting to create an 'atmosphere of intolerance and hysteria' as they had done during recent referendum campaigns. He added that it was 'never claimed that [Robinson] would support all of the policy positions adopted by the Workers' Party, nor would we ask her to do so'.

Robinson defeated Lenihan with the aid of Fine Gael transfers, becoming Ireland's first woman president. At the Dublin count De Rossa heralded the victory as a 'milestone' in a ten-year political process that had seen Ireland become an urban society 'willing to shake off rural values'. Robinson's support had been strongest among the urban middle classes, but she had also received substantial numbers of working-class votes and of those defined as rural. It was evident that her support was strongest in areas where Labour and the WP had TDs. Despite attempts by Spring to play down WP involvement in the campaign, De Rossa now talked of greater cooperation with Labour as a 'realistic option', a view echoed by left-wing Labour TD Emmet Stagg. De Rossa described this approach 'not as grabbing votes from the Labour Party but as broadening the constituency for the left'. Labour spokespeople also expressed a feeling that 'personal antagonisms' had been broken down in both parties.

Cooperation between the WP and Labour carried over into the Dáil. In December the WP TDs sponsored a bill seeking a referendum on redefining Articles Two and Three by inserting into the constitution the need for the 'consent of the majority of the people of Northern Ireland' before any change in that state's status. By the time of the vote on the bill Fine Gael and Labour support had been secured, despite Spring's 'misgivings' over its timing in the middle of another round of Anglo-Irish talks. Moving the bill, De Rossa called for an end to 'doublethink' on the North as well as greater understanding of unionist fears. He hoped the removal of the 'constitutional imperative' to take control of the whole 'national territory' would take away the 'mandate' claimed for Provo violence. The PDs opposed the bill, claiming they were seeking a wide-ranging reappraisal of the constitution, while Fianna Fáil opposition swung between nationalist dogma and the need to maintain leverage in Anglo-Irish negotiations. In the end the bill was comfortably defeated, with Tony Gregory among those opposing it, but the debate had seen the WP reaffirm its position as a radical anti-nationalist force and the party drew approving comment from unionist politicians.

As the WP's only representative on Belfast City Council Seamus Lynch was dismayed by the violent bickering between Sinn Féin and the DUP which marred many meetings. Following a council decision not to invite Mary Robinson to the city Lynch publicly expressed his frustration: 'We [Belfast City Council] are a disaster, we are a sham, we are a laughing stock. I find the behaviour of some of the people on this council embarrassing.' As the WP's most prominent public face in Northern Ireland, while still maintaining a position in Group B, Lynch was equally dismayed at the growing tension within the party and had to be dissuaded by De Rossa from quitting.

A deepening North–South divide within the party was most evident at party conferences, with Southern delegates complaining about the Northern members 'marching' in and inevitably voting for the 'revolutionary party' position. There was continued unease among the WP leadership over reports of OIRA activity and party financing. In early 1990 the WP's Northern Ireland Executive had issued a statement rejecting claims made in a Belfast court that a party member had asked a Turf Lodge woman to store guns and ammunition on behalf of the OIRA. The statement claimed the WP had 'no links to any armed organisations'. In the summer of 1990 the Belfast party was again denying any knowledge of the OIRA, following media reports concerning a confrontation in the Markets in which Group B members had beaten and shot two Provisionals. The armed wing would be back in the news later that year with further disturbances in Twinbrook, and more damagingly when Northern Ireland Office minister Brian Mawhinney told the House of Commons in December, 'I believe that the Official IRA still exists.' Unionist MP John Taylor confessed to being 'astounded' to hear that this was the case.

Group B's continued importance was evident in a financial report presented to the EPC in October 1990. From October 1989 until September 1990, costs covered by party head office had amounted to £360,500, of which WP funds provided £189,900 with the balance of £170,600 met by Repsol. It is unclear how widespread knowledge was among the WP leadership of Group B's continued role in funding Repsol. Two leading activists recall that in the period following the 1989 election De Rossa received from Garland a clear commitment to halt all Group B 'special activities', and some Group B activists were informed that a decision had been made to disband the organization. But Northern Group B operatives recall no significant decrease in their level of activity. The new impetus among a section of the leadership to sever the WP's reliance on Group B was not approved of by all party activists. Finglas councillor Lucia O'Neill recalls: 'There may have been some excesses in Belfast every now and then, but I imagine [Group B] was very controlled, very disciplined and that shows how political those who controlled it were.'

Internal criticism of the party's international stance centred on the relationship with North Korea. Knowledge of the true extent of Group B's link with the state was tightly guarded, but rumours of financial dealings were widespread. During 1990 Colm Breathnach had put forward a proposal to the International Affairs Committee that the party break relations with both China and North Korea ('a one-family dynastic state') and instead build links with democratic reform movements in the Far East. Breathnach, who had visited North Korea himself during 1989 and recalled conditions as 'Orwellian', was representing the views of a number of activists. There was also a proposal that the North Koreans no longer be invited as fraternal delegates to the Ard Fheis. But with Garland and others eager not to upset their Asian comrades, these motions were dispensed with before reaching the Ard Fheis floor.

As the stand-off following Saddam Hussein's 1990 invasion of Kuwait built towards a US invasion of Iraq in January 1991, the party demanded a Dáil recall to debate the matter and get assurances that Shannon airport would not be used to transport American troops to the region. De Rossa contrasted the measures being taken against Iraq with the lack of action against Israel, 'a habitual international criminal'. The WP supported the Campaign for

Peace in the Gulf, and Gilmore and others spoke on anti-war platforms. Beyond the parliamentary party activists helped organize protest marches. This protest campaign initially saw WP figures share platforms with members of the far left, but the declaration by some Trotskyists that they favoured an Iraqi victory caused unease for the WP TDs and brought cooperation to an end.

In early 1991 the party's Dublin city councillors led an attempt to deny the use of the Mansion House for the Sinn Féin Ard Fheis. This bid failed, but WP members were prominent in a New Consensus picket outside the venue, where Sinn Féin delegates harangued De Rossa with accusations of his party's involvement in the killing of Seamus Costello. Members also attended a smaller New Consensus demonstration outside the UDA's East Belfast headquarters.

There were divergent views within the party concerning commemoration of the seventy-fifth anniversary of the 1916 Rising. Some worried that the events could be used to legitimize the Provo campaign. In the Dáil the WP called for commemorations of the United Irishmen's 1791 foundation to be given equal billing with the 1916 events, an idea rebuffed by Haughey. The parliamentary group, and their supporters, used the 1916 debate to intensify opposition to republican ideology. In *Making Sense* Paul Bew argued that the Easter Rising had been an aberration that had allowed the ideas of 'marginal radicals' to hold sway for 40 years. With the Irish state's shedding of Sinn Féin's policies, he concluded, the 'Irish people had now moved on' from the 1916 Rising. In stark contrast, in the same issue, Mac Giolla wrote there should be no 'hang-ups' about celebrating 1916 – 'Tone and Pearse and Connolly helped to shape our destiny just as Billy McMillen or Joe McCann or Malachy McGurran did in more recent times.' He felt it 'ludicrous and childish' to draw comparisons between the 1916 leaders and the Provos, saying 'there is no more connection between them than there is between the Red Army Faction and the Red Army'. In the event the WP held its own commemorations, the Falls Road parade ending as usual at the Official plot in Milltown Cemetery and including a neatly dressed colour party.

A penetrating and influential critique of the party by former member Paddy Woodworth, published in the January/February 1991 issue of *Making Sense*, saw the WP's problems as deriving mainly 'from the deep, if not terminal crisis' of Soviet-style socialism, along with the 'subsidiary factor' of the rise of a 'new generation of TDs as an independent-minded grouping'. He argued that democratic centralism had been a stand-in for the hierarchical discipline of the party's military past: 'The leaders of the Official IRA were courageously dumping their guns, but most of them could not dump the attitudes with which they had held them. The cult of authoritarianism, the fetish for discipline, which are a necessary component of paramilitary organisations, was a psychological armoury which many were reluctant to relinquish.' Woodworth's concerns mirrored those prevalent within the parliamentary group. A draft design brief for a new party logo stated: 'The party is perceived, by those who have had no personal contact with its membership, as being unfriendly; rigid; hard; masculine; in short "Communist". We believe that this image acts as a restraint upon the Party's further progress.' The optimistic hopes of where this 'further progress' would lead was made clear in the brief eventually distributed to commercial design companies:

Over the next ten years, the Party will be seeking to increase its vote ten-fold, so as to form a Government by the year 2000. Present support is concentrated in local authority housing areas; i.e. predominantly amongst male, skilled and unskilled manual workers aged over 30. This strategy can only be achieved by extending Party support and vote into the white-collar, professional, female house-owning sector.

Such thinking was evident among the members of the commission that had been working on a new party programme for the previous six months. The group, whose members included Geraghty, Gilmore, John McManus and academic Proinsias Breathnach, produced a report entitled *Democracy, Freedom, Equality – a Draft Programme for Democratic Socialism* in late March 1991. The document articulated a desire to redefine the WP as an organization intent 'on the socialisation of the market mechanism' rather than seeking to establish a nationalized command economy.

The ascendency of the 'parliamentary group' seemed assured when it was announced just prior to the Ard Fheis that Garland was to stand down as general secretary. The decision was presented to the media as a personal one. Others within the leadership recalled the move as one to pre-empt a possible heave to oust the veteran leader, whose relationship with De Rossa was now strained, from his position of fourteen years. Garland would assume the role of party treasurer with Des Geraghty eventually replacing him as general secretary. Meanwhile, even as the parliamentary group seemed to be winning the internal leadership battle, in areas of traditional support, particularly in the North, those associated with 'the revolutionary party' were drawing lapsed members back to the organization and planning their response.

The first weekend of May 1991 saw another crucial party conference in Dublin's RDS. As he had done the preceding year, Garland opened the Ard Fheis with a call for calm debate during this 'critical time' for the party. He recalled that at the previous year's event a minority had attempted to 'hijack' proceedings, having a dig at Harris who had recently found employment as a media adviser with 'the Irish Tories of Fine Gael'. The days leading up to the Ard Fheis had seen the number of amendments whittled down from over 60 to a dozen that focused on what would be the WP's core definition and aims. The amendments called for a clear reference to the party's belief in 'class struggle', its definition as a 'revolutionary democratic socialist party' and the aim of establishing a 'secular socialist unitary Republic in Ireland'. The reform-minded members of the Ard Chomhairle were unsettled by a sizeable number of delegates' reaffirmation of traditional positions. From the podium Des O'Hagan led calls for the party to articulate a philosophy that sought the 'revolutionary transformation of capitalist society', and a majority voted in favour of the inclusion of references to 'class struggle' and 'the role of a revolutionary democratic socialist party' in the party's reform programme.

Even though the thorny issue of democratic centralism had been largely avoided and the newly amended party programme adopted, the Ard Fheis debates had exposed the fault lines between the parliamentary and revolutionary wings.

Despite initial misgivings WP trade unionists – including Des Geraghty, who was now SIPTU national group secretary – eventually supported a new social partnership deal, the Programme for Economic and Social Progress, as 'overall . . . a basis for progressive politics'. However, the party's TDs voted against the government on the issue in the Dáil. Rabbitte and Gilmore also jointly authored a pamphlet critiquing the new industrial relations laws enacted by Minister of Labour Bertie Ahern. In *Bertie's Bill* the TDs described the move as a 'subtle and decisive intervention on the side of the employer'.

WP influence in the unions had been affected by the party's internal turmoil. During 1990 Industrial Department protégé and teachers' union leader Kieran Mulvey had resigned, prompting wry comment from some that he had been such a 'secret member' that the first time many WP activists knew of his membership was when he left the party. By the early 1990s the flow of young members into the party had declined to a trickle, with WP Youth experiencing severe organizational and funding difficulties. Similarly WP influence in RTÉ had waned with the end of the Industrial Department, though allegations to the contrary remained common.

Activism was focused on the party's opposition to local charges. WP members protesting these levies had brought a Meath County Council meeting to an end by dumping bags of rubbish in the chamber, and in the run-up to the local elections Cork activist Ted Tynan was imprisoned for non-payment. However, many members felt that local agitation was now less well resourced and had a different emphasis; instead of saying, 'I'm here on behalf of the Workers' Party,' activists would say, 'I'm here on behalf of Eamon Gilmore.'

Despite the internal problems, and national poll ratings showing support stabilizing shy of 3.5 per cent, there was confidence within the WP that major gains would be made in the June 1991 local elections. The party ran 82 candidates in about a third of the country's 177 electoral areas; 21 of these were women, the highest proportion in any party that had Dáil representation.

The party's TDs had become increasingly identified with attempts to highlight corruption. Attention was focused on allegations of illegal activity by Larry Goodman's beef processing companies, which had been uncovered by a British TV investigation; Rabbitte disclosed further details of corrupt doings in the meat industry to the Dáil. The controversy led to the establishment of a tribunal of inquiry in May 1991, and the party demanded that a similar tribunal look into Dublin land dealings. A WP report, *The Rezoning Majority*, examined the activities of Fianna Fáil and Fine Gael members on Dublin County Council in rezoning land for the benefit of property developers. It estimated that over the previous six years select changes to the county plan had added £150 million to land values in the area and had been a 'licence to print money' for property developers. WP TDs also questioned the motivation behind government privatizations and called for the tighter regulation of politicians' gifts and personal interests. On occasion Fianna Fáil politicians retaliated with allegations of Official IRA activity. In May 1991 the organization was linked to the arrest in London of a Belfast man who had been trying to exchange 45 high-quality counterfeit $100 bills. The man was flown back to face charges in Belfast, and the RUC stated the case was connected to OIRA 'paramilitary fund-raising'. One Dublin Ard Chomhairle member recalls: 'The majority of active members in the Dun Laoghaire branch would not have been surprised [at the existence of the OIRA]. What would have bothered them? That it was making the papers.' Such fears were to the fore when the WP learned that BBC Northern Ireland planned to screen a documentary making allegations of WP–OIRA connections on the night of the Southern local elections. Despite attempts by Group B to intimidate the documentary makers, a torrent of damaging pre-broadcast publicity could not be prevented. De Rossa cancelled a scheduled interview with the programme makers and in the end it was John Lowry who recorded an interview countering the accusations.

Half an hour before polls closed on 27 June the *Spotlight* programme – *Sticking to Their Guns* – was broadcast. It claimed to uncover the 'murky world of one of Northern Ireland's least known paramilitaries'. Dredging through the Officials' violent past it included interviews with OIRA victim John Taylor, former member Tony Hayde and one-time Fine Gael Justice Minister Jim Mitchell, who said Gardaí had assured him the WP was 'merely the political expression of the Official IRA'. Drama rather than historical fact was to the fore, with a claim that eighteen people, 'eleven of them Provisionals', had died in the 1975 feud; in fact eleven people in all, seven of them Officials, had been killed in 1975. The programme showed greater accuracy in outlining the tax-exemption scam and naming some of those involved. It was also disclosed that a barman at the Twinbrook Social Club, recently convicted of an arms offence, had signed Lowry's election nomination papers. Similarly that VAT scam 'enforcer' Anthony McDonagh had signed nomination papers for Mary McMahon, and he along with others linked to the OIRA were photographed at WP events. There were also allegations of involvement in forgery and distributing counterfeit dollars. The programme included a claim by the SDLP's Brian Feeney that the Officials acted as a 'pseudo gang' in republican areas on behalf of the British. In a voiced-over interview (the British having introduced legislation banning the voices of 'terrorist supporters' from the airwaves) Markets Sinn Féin member Sean Montgomery described recent confrontations between the OIRA and the Provisionals in his area. John Lowry's interview claiming the WP had cut all links with paramilitarism after making the 'conscious decision' to become a fully democratic political party was interspersed among the more damning allegations.

Within minutes of the programme's conclusion the Belfast WP issued a statement likening it to a 'paramilitary kangaroo court' and dismissing its 'succession of totally spurious allegations'. Particular vitriol was reserved for Feeney, whose accusation was condemned as 'calculated incitement to murder'. The statement concluded: 'We can only hope that nobody is shot as a result of this broadcast.'

Things got worse the following day as the Southern local election results came in. The expected gains had not materialized, the WP vote nationally falling to 3.7 per cent from the 1989 high of 4.9 per cent, though the total number of WP councillors rose from 19 to 24, and the party did well in Cork and Waterford. The Dublin city WP councillors joined a 'civic alliance' with Labour, Fine Gael, Greens and Independents that elected a Labour Lord Mayor.

The election post-mortem began immediately. Publicly the result was portrayed as representing a 'slower . . . rate of progress . . . than expected'. Some blame was apportioned to the election's biggest gainer, Labour, which had refused repeated WP calls to enter a national vote-transfer pact and which was now ahead of the WP in Dublin. There was also grumbling about the role of the trade unions, 'who put a lot of money into the Labour campaign'. Others pointed to the fact that both the WP and Labour now espoused 'democratic socialism'. There was a view that Dick Spring was overshadowing De Rossa, in part because the WP president was dividing his time between the European Parliament and the Dáil, and there were rumours of a challenge to De Rossa's leadership.

Within the parliamentary group discussion centred on the *Spotlight* programme. Heffernan recalls: 'A lot of people said this sort of stuff is an albatross around our neck, this stuff just has to be sorted out once and for all.' An internal survey of local election candidates and directors of elections found that 56 per cent of respondents felt *Spotlight* had had a strong or very strong effect on the election. The survey also highlighted fears that 'idealist' voters were gravitating towards the Greens. The parliamentary group interpreted the findings as indicating a need for greater emphasis on electioneering and putting an end to allegations of OIRA activity.

The survey and the importance of the *Spotlight* allegations were keenly disputed. Lucia O'Neill, comfortably re-elected in North Dublin, recalls: 'In an area like Finglas [the *Spotlight* programme] would not have made one slight bit of difference.' Nonetheless, she shared other public representatives' doubts about the party's policy concerning Group B: 'You can't be doing that with the public, you can't lie to half your membership, have one half knowing one thing and another half thinking another . . . [it was] major deceit, not a little lie.' Within the Group B leadership the *Spotlight* programme caused division. Lynch could no longer tolerate what he saw as the intransigence of others in maintaining the paramilitary structure.

For De Rossa the OIRA allegations and the prospect of a general election within months, following Fianna Fáil's drubbing in the local poll, made it imperative that the 'revolutionary party' concept be finally discarded. He recalls: 'A revolutionary party needed at some point the use of quasi-legal or illegal methods and as far as I was concerned . . . that was no longer the case and that could no longer be the case in the Republic of Ireland or indeed in Northern Ireland.' De Rossa decided to tackle the problem head on by dealing conclusively with the party's critical financial situation. In this he felt he was representing the interests of ordinary party members against those of an 'elite group'. Debate at the Ard Chomhairle meeting on 7 September was dominated by a report drawn up by De Rossa, Seamus Harrison, Marie Brady and Gerry Doherty laying bare the reality of the WP's finances. In total the Southern party owed £296,000 in loans, with monthly repayments of over £10,000, while the further sum of £15,500 in bills was outstanding from the Ard Fheis and local elections. The cost of running head office was estimated at £29,345 per month. Southern party income was given as £18,592 per month, the vast majority of which was made up of European Parliament and Dáil subventions. The situation for the Northern party was little better. There £190,000 was owed in loans while monthly income was £9,000 compared to £9,750 in outgoings. According to the report, since 1989 over £200,000 claimed in subventions from the European Parliament had in large part kept the WP financially afloat. The report left Ard Chomhairle members in little doubt the party had been living well beyond its means:

Up to 1987 the vast bulk of expenses, party administration, general office expenses, rates, etc., elections, travel international and internal were covered by Repsol Ltd. Since 1987 the party has taken responsibility for election expenses through the development fund and bank borrowings. It is worth recalling that from 1977 when the party began its period of expansion as SFWP huge amounts of monies have been written off by Repsol for Election Printing and subsidies for party publications. These monies were seen as investment in the future of the party and this is an aspect of our deliberations we must continually keep in mind.

The report's proposals were stark. To pay off the debts the party's twelve property holdings should be sold off, to be replaced by smaller rented properties. The majority of party staff should be laid off and a system of contributions from party members based on income established. The Ard Chomhairle decided to accept the proposals 'in principle' but noted that more discussion was needed on their implementation. Concerns were expressed about the sensitivity of the information contained in the report, but a motion calling for all copies to be returned at the meeting's conclusion was defeated.

A battle over financial control of the WP had begun. In the following days De Rossa circulated a letter to WP members outlining the harsh financial measures proposed. This caused consternation, particularly among head office staff. Anger was also expressed over the fact that Mac Giolla and De Rossa were the only TDs contributing substantial amounts from their earnings to party coffers.

The following weekend the Ard Chomhairle reconvened for a two-day meeting in Wynn's Hotel off Dublin's O'Connell Street. The atmosphere was tense. Garland, Seamus Harrison and O'Hagan did not attend and Goulding stormed off complaining about the timing. The meeting commenced with the defeat of a motion, proposed by Gerry Doherty, that 'this meeting has not been reconvened in the spirit of the adjourned meeting and that any decisions arrived at; and there are some momentous decisions to be taken; will fall short in support and comradeship which has

been the hallmark of this Party's progress in past times'. The two
days were dominated by discussion of the proposed cutbacks and
the need to consolidate outstanding debts. Representing the head
office staff, Margaret O'Leary strongly objected to attempts to push
through job cuts, and agreement was reached that all premises
would be sold and other 'expenditure be cut to the bone' before
decisions on staff reductions. A Heffernan motion, seconded by
Mid-Ulster's Tom French, stated that the party 'will not be
involved in or benefit from any criminal activity'; the motion was
approved. It was also decided that a Dublin members' convention
would choose who should replace De Rossa as MEP so that he
could concentrate on his work as a TD.

The establishment of Families Against Intimidation and Terror, a
new Northern group campaigning against punishment attacks,
occasioned some controversy for the party. Sinn Féin was quick
to denounce FAIT as a 'recognised front of the Workers' Party
which itself has a paramilitary wing'. The fact that FAIT's
spokesperson, Henry Robinson, was a WP member and ex-OIRA
prisoner and that FAIT was in receipt of grants from the British
government led to questions about its independence; similar questions were asked about Peace Train, which also received British
funding. FAIT came to prominence in August 1991 when it
supported two youths who had taken sanctuary in Newry
Cathedral after being threatened with death by the Provisional
IRA. The incident coincided with tension in Newry as the Provos
attempted to enforce their writ in areas where Official influence
was still strong. The WP also supported the popular demonstrations
in Cooley, Co. Louth, after the brutal killing of local man Tom
Oliver by the Provisionals during August.

In Belfast the WP had made a small breakthrough in June
1991 when Seamus Lynch became the first non-unionist since the
Anglo-Irish Agreement to be elected chair of a council committee.
Among those who voted for him were DUP councillors and the
wife of assassinated hard-line loyalist George Seawright. But the
WP's inability to achieve its goals in Northern Ireland was now

publicly accepted by Henry Patterson, who told a cross-party think-in that he would welcome the British Labour Party establishing branches in the North because 'no existing organisation of the left in Northern Ireland has or is likely to have the credibility to persuade a substantial section of the population of the plausibility of a socialist alternative'. The days when Southern WP members were familiar with the day-to-day existence of their Northern comrades also seemed to be gone, Lynch noting that of 70 Dublin members he had recently addressed, only 16 had ever actually been in the North.

The autumn of 1991 saw the killing by a UFF gang of WP supporter Seamus Sullivan, the son of OIRA veteran Jim. Jim Sullivan appealed for no retaliation, and when his local MP, Gerry Adams, called to offer his condolences he dismissed him from his home. In the South, the party's Dáil contingent made headlines with a renewed onslaught on a government immersed in a spate of business scandals. The WP pressed the government hard on the controversies, fruitlessly calling for Garda investigations as well as publishing *Putting Our House in Order* – a document outlining ethical reform of parliament. Polls indicated that a majority of voters wanted Haughey to resign, and a new sense of unity of purpose was developing between the opposition parties. When De Rossa publicly revealed the contents of a letter from stockbroker Dermot Desmond to French company Pernod Ricard, in which Desmond sought a £2 million fee for work during the takeover of Irish Distillers and referred to having 'used up a large proportion of favours we can call upon from our political contacts' in securing 'a positive tax opinion from the Revenue Commissioners', Desmond accused De Rossa of 'KGB-style tactics' and questioned how he had obtained the letter. Fianna Fáil TDs adopted a similar line of defence in the Dáil, concentrating on allegations of WP–OIRA links during a three-day government confidence debate in October 1991. During the debate De Rossa emphasized the long-held WP view that corruption was endemic in the upper echelons of Irish society:

People have been stunned, shocked and sickened by the revelations of sharp practice, malpractice, downright dishonesty and corruption which have emerged. Day after day we have had more disclosures which have thrown new light on the operation of what has been referred to as the 'golden circle'. The operation of such a group had been well known. Certainly, the Workers' Party had pointed to it repeatedly. However, what has emerged for the first time in the past two months has revealed in all its ugliness the level of their greed and the ruthless nature of their activities ... Despite the high-sounding principles of the 1916 Proclamation and the fine aspirations of the democratic programme of the First Dáil we live in a Republic in which an individual's rank and status in society is determined by the amount of personal wealth he or she can accumulate. Indeed in Ireland the greatest prestige seems to attach to wealth accumulated in the least socially valuable way.

The WP president also dismissed an assertion by Haughey that he and Rabbitte had been meeting with the 'chief of staff of the Official IRA':

I want to state categorically that neither I nor Deputy Rabbitte have anything whatsoever to do with any group styling itself the Official IRA, the Provisional IRA, or any other paramilitary group. I have dedicated my time in politics to opposing para-militarism and will continue to oppose political violence with all the vigour at my disposal ... I do not know who the chief of staff of the Official IRA is, if indeed such a person exists, but then the Taoiseach has always seemed to know more about who is in the IRA than I ever have, and he seemed to have a particular interest in this area in 1969 and 1970 when the Provisional IRA was being established ... When he is on the subject of meetings, perhaps he could fill us in on some of the interesting persons, well known and not so well known, whom he met in 1969 and 1970.

Rabbitte dismissed the allegation of contact with the OIRA Chief of Staff as a 'base lie', adding 'it would suit the purposes of Fianna Fáil if the Workers' Party supporters were still painting letter boxes green or shooting at members of the security forces rather than making such a political nuisance of themselves in this House. The viciousness and sheer malice of the attacks on the Workers' Party by the Taoiseach, Deputy Haughey and Minister Burke must be some kind of barometer of the impact we are making on this Government.' In response to a Fianna Fáil TD's reference to WP Dáil employee Eugene Hickland's 1975 conviction, as a 16-year-old, for OIRA-related activities, Eric Byrne pointed out that Haughey had aided Hickland's Dáil security clearance.

The confidence vote was won by the government and left the WP parliamentary group rueing their inability to shake off the OIRA allegations. There was particular concern that Labour were now being identified as the leading force opposed to political corruption. Things got worse the following weekend with the publication by the London *Sunday Times* of an allegation that the WP had been among a number of parties that had received funds from the Soviet Union. The paper claimed that documentation uncovered following the August coup attempt in Moscow showed that a WP representative had received £28,206 from the KGB on 30 January 1989. There were also claims that money had been funnelled through 'friendly firms' linked to western communist parties. After an 'internal investigation' the WP dismissed the report as 'ridiculous', Heffernan stating that there was no evidence of 'Moscow gold' in the accounts of the party or of Repsol (possibly one of the 'friendly firms' referred to by the *Sunday Times*), which he described as 'separate from us' and 'not a funnel through which funds would come to the party'. By the end of the year De Rossa was claiming he was intent on travelling to Moscow to get to the bottom of the allegations and WP 'sources' were telling the *Irish Times* they believed 'money had changed hands'.

While the parliamentary group forswore Repsol subventions they had little concrete plans of where or how they would derive new long-term funding. Hope was placed in general political funding reform, which would include increased state aid and the full disclosure of private sector donations. In a November 1991 reply to a Beef Tribunal request for details of political donations

from the meat industry, Garland articulated the predicament that
Group B's activity had attempted to circumvent:

No, the Workers' Party got no money from anyone in the beef industry.
Our TDs led the way in exposing what was going on and turkeys
don't vote for Christmas. And if anyone in the beef industries or other
representatives of big business offered us money we wouldn't take it.
Business doesn't give money to political parties out of idealism or because
they like the colour of your eyes. They either want something pushed
or they want to buy silence. We're not for sale . . . What money we
get is through such things as development draws, raffles and national
collections. You'll get the full details of the Third Secret of Fatima before
you get the full details of who bankrolls Fianna Fáil and the rest.

Progress on selling party properties was slow and the Ard Chomhairle advised Northern branches, preparing for forthcoming
Westminster elections, that financial assistance from Dublin was
'unlikely'.

Meanwhile the leadership schism was worsening. Since the
beginning of the autumn De Rossa had been convening private
meetings of a small group of WP members in Des Geraghty's
house in Blackrock. Among those who attended were Geraghty,
Heffernan, Triona Dooney, Rosheen Callender, Gilmore, Rabbitte and Paddy Gillan. Around this time De Rossa was contacted
by a Southern party member and informed that 'revolutionary
party' meetings to discuss activity within the WP were still occurring. At the meetings in Geraghty's home plans were made for a
next stage of party development. Heffernan recalls: 'It was a very
difficult period for people who had in some cases put twenty years
or more into building this project to begin to think that the whole
thing might have to be abandoned and start again.' A similar
conclusion had also been reached by some leading Northern
members, among them Seamus Lynch, Patterson, McMahon and
Kevin Smyth. At 'revolutionary party' meetings, meanwhile, the
prevailing view was that the WP was now in the midst of a struggle
with elements that had forsaken the party's basic ideals. The

message was clear, as one OIRA veteran recalls: 'We were right and they were wrong, they were middle class, and all that rhetoric.' By December the numbers invited to meetings in Geraghty's house had grown, with on occasion over 30 TDs, councillors and other leading party members debating the course of action. Colm Breathnach recalls: 'Myself and Fearghal [Ross] were arguing for a split – only John McManus was backing us. The others were more cautious. They wanted to win the party . . . De Rossa wanted to win the party.' De Rossa was coming under increasing pressure, with polls showing party support declining and media reports of contact between WP TDs and Labour about a merger or defections. Rabbitte had been discussing the possibility of returning to Labour for several months. Division deepened when Garland argued with De Rossa over his decision to sack Hickland from his Dáil job; Eric Byrne recalls that there was a perception that Hickland had been sent to spy on the TDs.

While travelling the country collecting branch debts Gerry Doherty discovered a Group B operation had been undertaken in the Newry area during late 1991, despite assurances he had received that most 'special activities' had been ended. He confronted Garland and an emotional argument ended 27 years of comradeship. Other Group B members who had also been informed that a decision had been taken for the organization to be 'stood down' and cease functioning were angered to find out this was not the case. There was also conflict over which six out of thirteen head office employees were to be kept on, with De Rossa opposed to an EPC decision that his sister Marie Brady would be among those laid off. Unsure of gaining majorities for their policies, De Rossa and Geraghty stopped convening EPC meetings.

During the closing months of 1991 the wider WP membership had been prepared for major changes in the party. A Rules and Organization Commission, established by the 1991 Ard Fheis, had been holding regional meetings. Of the nine-person commission, headed by Gilmore, only two members, Lowry and Kane, were aligned with the 'revolutionary' wing.' On 4 January the deepening schism was exposed to public view with reports of a looming WP 'split' dominating the *Irish Times*. The paper quoted 'senior party sources' predicting the party would divide along modernist/old guard lines in March when a special conference on the Rules and Organization Commission's recommendations was scheduled. The paper's extensive reports were unashamedly supportive of the parliamentary group, and an editorial stated that it welcomed the WP's growth 'out of revolution' and its 'movement from the culture of the cabal, the self-styled army council and the politburo'. Journalists had been in discussions about the story with members of the parliamentary group since 26 December. The reports included an interview with De Rossa in which he stated that a 'kitchen cabinet', of which he was not a member, was attempting to exert control within the WP. He would not be drawn on the nature of this group but qualified his claim that the OIRA had been disbanded shortly after the 1972 ceasefire, saying:

I am talking about the organisation Official Sinn Féin was associated with in the early 70s. As far as I'm concerned that no longer exists. As I have said on numerous occasions, I have no control over nor would wish to have control over individuals who may style themselves the Official IRA.

He dismissed talk of a 'split' while accepting that some members might leave the organization. He was equally dismissive of any merger with Labour, claiming that that party had 'no real core values in terms of the kind of Ireland it wants to see evolve' and lacked 'intellectual energy'.

The public exposure of the party's internal debates caused confusion and anger among many members, but the parliamentary group were intent on pushing the pace, De Rossa and Geraghty citing the *Irish Times* reports in immediately calling a special meeting of Ard Chomhairle members and public representatives for 11 January. They were aware that before then Belfast Crown Court would hear the case of three men accused of robbing £13,000 from a drinks lorry on behalf of the OIRA in October 1990. Of the three men jailed, one was a WP member and another a supporter.

Among the first contributions at the extended Ard Chomhairle meeting was Garland's acceptance that he had asked for finance from Moscow, though he claimed that none had been forthcoming. A series of attacks followed on those, particularly Rabbitte, who were believed to be behind the media leaks. Others countered that it was the Official IRA and not the media that was the problem, McCartan boldly stating that some WP activists were also OIRA members. In the midst of these arguments Heffernan proposed a lengthy motion whose key clause was a condemnation of the OIRA and a statement that membership or support of the OIRA was incompatible with WP membership. The motion's final clause called for any remaining links with the CPSU and North Korea to be severed. Liz McManus stated that the OIRA 'shouldn't be graced with [the] name, it is a criminal gang'. Rabbitte held that 'time was running out' for a settlement of the 'profound political differences' between 'the vanguard party and democratic party'. He denied any role in the media leaks. In a move which may have confirmed fears that Group B would continue its hidden existence regardless of whether Heffernan's motion was carried, Goulding and Francie Donnelly claimed they did not believe the OIRA existed. Neither Gerry Doherty nor Seamus Lynch was willing to maintain such loyalty; Lynch stated that the nationalist community had been 'entitled to call us hypocrites on occasions'. Garland said he did not believe Rabbitte's denial of involvement in the *Irish Times* stories and that he had a problem with the Heffernan motion as he lacked confidence in the TDs. What he did have confidence in was revolutionary politics, believing Lenin's ideas were 'still to be followed'. Attempting to maintain a conciliatory position, Mac Giolla declared the leadership was 'lost' and called for a halt to the personal bitterness, an end to condemnations of the Dáil group and 'attempts to hound' Marxists and republicans out of the party. He conceded that the 'OIRA has got to be dealt with'.

After several hours of heated debate a vote on the motion was called. An amendment removing the reference to the CPSU and North Korea was carried. The substantive motion passed with

40 votes for, and the abstentions of Garland, Kane, O'Hagan and Brendan Burns. De Rossa now brought up the Belfast robbery, Hickland's role in the Dáil and information he had received about approaches to members to involve themselves in 'dangerous activity'. As well as these incidents he raised the issue of a 1991 Ard Fheis delegate, but not a party member, who had been charged with serious offences in July. Inquiries were ordered into these events, and it was decided to contact the Soviet Embassy about the allegations of financial aid. The meeting concluded with the passing of a motion, carried 22 to 7, expelling the Belfast member convicted of the drinks robbery. The specifics of the meeting were kept within the room, but De Rossa publicly stated that he was 'very pleased with the outcome' of the meeting and that a split was now 'extremely unlikely'. Heffernan was more cautious, stating that 'some voted for the motion who did not really agree with it. They are keeping their heads down and powder dry for another day.' Meanwhile Mike Jennings, the WP spokesman on crime, issued a statement calling for 'tougher action' against the OIRA to restore the party's credibility.

Des Geraghty was elected to replace De Rossa as MEP at a Dublin regional meeting on 20 January. Garland's decision not to put his name forward had surprised his opponents and dismayed comrades. Brian Whelan recalls: 'Sean gave up then, looked at what was happening and thought, "We're fucked."'

Charles Haughey finally resigned as Fianna Fáil leader in late January and the possibility of another Southern general election loomed. The parliamentary group did not intend to allow their opponents an opportunity to reorganize. At a special two-day Ard Chomhairle meeting on the last weekend of January, De Rossa unveiled a dramatic plan to 'reconstitute' the WP. It was clear, he said, that there were now 'two groups, almost two parties' within the WP whose views were fundamentally different. He described one group as 'representing the majority of members' who wanted 'an open democratic socialist party unambiguously controlled by the members'. The other group clung to the 'discredited Leninist concept of organisation where the principle of democratic centralism is used as a device by a small self-appointed political elite to manipulate the party and frustrate the democratic wishes of the majority of members'. Modelled on the actions of the Italian Communist Party twelve months previously, when the party had dissolved and then reconstituted itself on different lines and under a different name, his motion called for the convening of a special one-day Ard Fheis on 15 February to decide on a resolution to reconstitute the WP as an 'independent democratic socialist party' based on the 1991 party programme. It called for a repudiation of 'democratic centralism' and 'revolutionary tactics'. An eleven-member 'caretaker' Ard Chomhairle would be elected to oversee the 'standing down' and 're-registration' of all members, a move which would rid the party of the parliamentary group's opponents. Three trustees would be elected to take control of all the WP's property titles.

The proposal was furiously denounced by those aligned to the 'revolutionary party', and O'Hagan stormed out of the meeting before the proposal was passed by 35 votes to 5. The following day – breaking, ironically, with the principles of democratic centralism – O'Hagan publicly vented his anger, telling the *Irish Times* he expected the special Ard Fheis to be an 'intellectually bloody affair'. He dismissed the rival WP faction as 'middle-class liberals rather than socialists', adding: 'They should do the honest thing and quit the party rather than try to liquidate it. Their natural home is with the Progressive Democrats, Fine Gael or Labour . . . If you desert the centrality of the revolutionary class struggle, then you are deserting the possibility of achieving socialism.'

Both wings were now stating that it was unlikely their opponents could remain in the party. While it was known that the majority of Northern members would oppose the party's reconstitution, several, including Seamus Lynch and Gerry Cullen, publicly announced their support for the move. The Southern party was also clearly divided, a Waterford branch issuing a statement condemning De Rossa's 'witch hunt' against his internal opponents. The opposing positions were aired at fractious regional meetings. The OIRA's existence was a live issue among the Southern membership, particularly with the press linking the group to yet another Belfast robbery. Many members were shocked at what they were being told, Breathnach recalls: 'The majority of members, working-class people, [were] saying, "What the fuck is this?" And being told all the things that we had said were lies were true.' Brian Whelan remembers De Rossa making the case 'if we don't do this now we will lose the parliamentary party' and the WP would 'be left with perhaps Sherlock, and Mac Giolla' in the Dáil. Although loyal to the revolutionary party, Whelan understood the WP leader's predicament: 'We're criticizing corruption but here are we accused of robbing banks and you name it.' Garland, Lowry and O'Hagan were also canvassing, and in areas of traditional Official support they received a warmer reception than De Rossa. Their message was clear: the WP's 'fundamental principles' were under attack by 'opportunists' using the OIRA issue as a 'smokescreen'. In Belfast De Rossa addressed a crowded Cyprus Street meeting which included several OIRA veterans who had not been active in the party for years. He recalls being taken aback at the 'amount of people that came out . . . it was hot and heavy'. The atmosphere was not aided by a recent statement from De Rossa, in response to an upsurge in violence in the North, that in his 'personal view', internment should be considered as 'a very last resort'. Joe Quinn recalls him repeating this view at the Cyprus Street meeting: 'There was about 200 people and maybe 100 of them had been interned or their das or their wives or somebody.' As the main Northern supporter of De Rossa's approach, Lynch came under pressure from members fearful of attack if Group B was stood down, being told accusingly that 'it's alright for you, you have a fucking gun' in reference to his licensed sidearm.

The stage was set for a dramatic showdown as nearly 400 delegates, 120 of them Northerners, and many other WP members and supporters gathered in the Marine Hotel in Dun Laoghaire on 15 February for the special Ard Fheis. De Rossa began with a speech proposing the reconstitution motion:

At the outset of the Sixties . . . out of the shell of failed nationalism, typified by the Fifties Campaign, grew a movement committed to new thinking, new methods, and a new politics. Some of the architects of that New Departure are here today . . . The movement gravitated towards a socialist view of the world. It wasn't a perfectly formed view, nor was it fully formed. But it was honest and it attracted a generation of radicals who went on to build in the Seventies and Eighties what is now the Workers' Party.

The party had always been 'intelligently revisionist', and today it had arrived 'at another milestone' which would define 'whether the party has a future'. It was time to renounce old tactics and 'blinkered nostalgia' for a concept of working-class struggle based on the conditions of the 1930s. De Rossa highlighted the Beef Tribunal, foisted upon a 'reluctant administrative system', as an example of 'how the Workers' Party can keep the real enemies of the people in view'. He finished by imploring his comrades to 'adopt a New Departure here today . . . because the old destinations and destinies are gone'. The motion was seconded by Seamus Lynch. Garland then took to the podium to call for the motion's rejection. He confessed to 'being not only surprised but bitterly disappointed' that people he had once 'regarded as tough fighters in the class struggle' were 'succumbing to pessimism'. He traced the start of the WP's 'degeneration' to a 'poison' injected by Harris. The 'liquidators' had launched a 'vendetta' against the 'party's history . . . implemented with a ruthlessness that would do justice to Josef Stalin'. He would not 'follow the opportunists into the cul-de-sac of a social democratic parliamentary party', but he was 'totally and utterly opposed to any secret group or clique operating in this party to the detriment of the members and the party's aims and principles'.

Rumours had circulated about Tomás Mac Giolla's intentions, both groups claiming the former party president would side with them. He was initially dismissive of the De Rossa motion, saying he should have been walking his dog in Phoenix Park rather than taking part in this unnecessary exercise. He condemned De Rossa's 'extraordinary gaffe' in voicing support for internment. But then he surprised the hall by ending his speech with a call to support the motion. Saying, 'I want to stop the flow of blood. I want to heal the wounds,' the veteran blamed both sides for leaving little room for manoeuvre. His view was that compromise could still save his 'life's work'. Mac Giolla's conciliatory tone was not adhered to by the following speakers, one journalist present recalling that the atmosphere was 'electric . . . you could reach out and touch the anger'. Garland, for so long the party's central figure, was now subjected to attack, Joe Sherlock pointing an accusing finger at his comrade as he charged him with 'having a little secret army'. Neither side pretended that Group B did not exist. As some Northern delegates openly defended the 'Officials', Dun Laoghaire's Joe Ruddock stated 'the reality is that the dogs in the street know the Official IRA exists and that members of the Workers' Party are involved in it . . . We cannot point the finger at corruption in business when there are people in the party involved in this kind of gangsterism.' A Belfast delegate dismissed this definition of the OIRA, saying they were not 'thugs' and that their activities were necessary due to Northern Ireland's law and order being 'a joke'. Another claimed that 'London's men and Washington's men' were at work in the party. Supporting De Rossa, Mary McMahon announced that she had been 'part of the IRA' and that the organization had created the WP. She felt that the WP should do 'what they hadn't done in 1982: [be] straight with each other'. Fighting back tears, she said it was now time to move on, 'and I want each and every one of you to come with me'. Personal invective flowed, with Eric Byrne, who claimed to have believed the 'lies' about the non-existence of the OIRA, dismissed as a 'little guttie' by Cork's Kathleen Lynch. A Northern delegate asked fellow delegates pointedly, 'Where did you think the money was coming from?'

Despite the stern opposition De Rossa and his supporters were confident of achieving the two-thirds of votes necessary for the reconstitution motion to pass. After the secret ballot's first count, a worried huddle formed around the top table. After two recounts the result of 241 for and 133 votes against was announced: 9 short of the two-thirds required. De Rossa announced he would 'consider his position' before the following weekend's Ard Chomhairle meeting, telling delegates: 'You have made your decision. I honestly believe it is a bad decision, but you have made it.' As delegates left the hall, most knew that the party had been irrevocably damaged.

Despite the pleas of his Dáil colleagues to join them in a new organization Mac Giolla stayed loyal to the WP. This left De Rossa and the five other TDs one short of constituting a Dáil group, meaning they would miss out on some £100,000 in annual state funding. There was desperate lobbying of Emmet Stagg, who had resigned the Labour whip and was publicly pondering joining a different party. In Belfast, OIRA veterans attempted to broker a meeting between Lynch and Seamus Harrison to prevent a Northern split, but Lynch rebuffed their efforts, resigning from the WP on 21 February.

More than 60 leadership figures from both factions gathered at Wynn's Hotel the following day for an Ard Chomhairle meeting. De Rossa addressed them for less than five minutes, stating that 'fundamental and irreconcilable differences' now divided the party; he then adjourned the meeting, requesting that those who were leaving the WP follow him out the door, which the majority did. Among the roughly two dozen who remained were Garland, Goulding and Mac Giolla. Tears were shed and insults exchanged. Pat McCartan shook several people's hands as he left, though some refused to take his. Outside Mac Giolla, with May at his side, denounced those who, in pursuit of personal ambition, had 'betrayed' the WP. While his comrades defiantly talked of rebuilding, he was more downbeat: 'It took twenty-five years to build into a great and effective party and it has been smashed from within in a week.'

Epilogue

After the Ard Chomhairle meeting in Wynn's Hotel, most of those remaining with the WP headed to Club Uí Cadhain. Lucia O'Neill remembers that many 'got absolutely pissed and arrived home the next morning. It was such an anti-climax then because so much had been going on, those weeks were so intense, so much soul-searching, people genuinely upset, people crying.'

A majority of the WP members in the South signalled support for De Rossa, but in virtually every branch there were some who stayed loyal to the party. In De Rossa's own constituency of Finglas and in Waterford the majority strongly opposed the break-up of the WP. After a week pondering their next move, leading Cork city members Bernard and Kathleen Lynch opted for De Rossa's faction. In the North Seamus Lynch and Mary McMahon were in a minority in their support for De Rossa; Lynch received strong indications that both he and De Rossa were to be shot. Mac Giolla's decision to remain in the WP had immediate repercussions. The hopes that Labour TD Emmet Stagg would join the WP dissidents did not materialize, and the new group would no longer be entitled to Dáil funding or parliamentary speaking privileges.

De Rossa's supporters announced their intention of forming a new organization with a working title of 'New Agenda'. At their first press conference De Rossa pointedly suggested that questions about the OIRA should now be directed to those who remained with the WP. In turn Mac Giolla reflected that 'it is interesting to see the warm welcome that the new party is getting from all the newspapers, radio and TV as well as from the establishment parties. From day one the Workers' Party has been attacked and abused or ignored by all these people. They saw us as a great danger to the cosy political arrangement that existed here for decades.'

In late March 600 members of New Agenda met and narrowly voted to rename their party Democratic Left. Describing it as a 'party for those who have been excluded and marginalised from power in society', Pat Rabbitte declared that Democratic Left would be 'unashamedly socialist'. In the wake of the 'X case', which had seen thousands march for abortion law reform, DL announced that it would campaign for a new Southern constitution because of the 'scandalous' anti-woman clauses in the present one as well as the 'presumptuous, impractical and lethal territorial claims' of Articles Two and Three. In the *Irish Times* Dick Walsh felt that the party represented a new beginning for the Irish left, finally free of the last vestiges of Stalinism and republicanism. But DL was to remain an all-Ireland party, though Mary McMahon reckons the Northern branch had '50 people at most'. In contrast the WP had retained most of the Northern membership and had even grown a little because of the return of veterans for the factional battle.

Both of the post-split parties were soon made aware of the limitations of their appeal, North and South. In the April 1992 Westminster election Lynch and McMahon, running under the New Agenda label, polled just 2,133 votes between them (0.3 per cent) while the WP's 8 candidates took 4,359 votes (0.5 per cent). In November, after the fall of the Fianna Fáil/PD coalition, the parties also faced each other in a Dáil election. During the campaign Mac Giolla accused DL of not only embracing 'free market' politics but of abandoning republicanism, stating that the WP did 'not support the abolition of Articles Two and Three'. De Rossa made it clear that DL would support Labour's Dick Spring for Taoiseach and predicted that a left coalition of Labour, DL and Greens could take power. While Labour won a stunning 33 seats, its highest ever total, DL was among its victims, losing 3 of its 6 sitting TDs – Eric Byrne, Pat McCartan and Joe Sherlock. De Rossa saw his vote fall from 26.5 per cent to 12.2 per cent, in part reflecting the weakness of DL in a constituency where the WP maintained a strong organization. Pat Rabbitte's vote was also halved. One positive was that Liz McManus took a seat in Wicklow, succeeding where her husband had failed on several occasions. The election was no better for the WP, Tomás Mac Giolla losing his seat by just 59 votes. The party had run its newly elected President Marian Donnelly, a veteran activist from Co. Derry, against Pat McCartan in Dublin North-East, but she received only 239 votes. Overall the party received just 11,533 votes and all but 2 of its 18 candidates lost their deposits. The split had damaged the election prospects of both parties. The 3.5 per cent of the first-preference vote the two parties gained between them was a drop from the 5 per cent the WP had won in 1989; voter confusion and the fact that the parties had directly opposed each other in several areas were damaging. Labour, which held the balance of power in the new Dáil, negotiated with DL about a coalition deal involving themselves and Fine Gael. In the end, despite Labour's strong condemnation of Fianna Fáil throughout the election campaign, Dick Spring decided to go into government alongside new Fianna Fáil leader Albert Reynolds.

Further controversy over WP funding had emerged during the campaign. In late October the London *Independent* and the *Irish Times* published details of several letters found in the Communist Party archives in Moscow. Journalist Seamus Martin, himself a former WP member, described a letter bearing the signatures of Garland and De Rossa that had asked for a million pounds in aid for the WP. The 1986 letter had described the party's financial difficulties and how 'special activities' were no longer adequate to meet its needs. The WP immediately described the letter as a 'fabrication' and claimed that 'no requests were made by the Workers' Party for financial aid from the Soviet Union at any time'. De Rossa too denied any knowledge of the appeal, soon dubbed the 'Moscow Letter'. In the aftermath of the election the issue arose again. The *Irish Times* reported that a handwriting expert had asserted that the signatures were genuine. De Rossa argued that while it was possible that his signature had been forged, he knew nothing about Soviet aid. Indeed De Rossa claimed that while in the Workers' Party one of his DL colleagues had once been deceived into signing what he thought was a guarantee to pay rent on a premises, but turned out instead to be a guarantee for a loan.

In the midst of the speculation about DL being part of a new government, the influential and often controversial *Sunday Independent* columnist Eamon Dunphy wrote an article in which he referred to the London *Independent* and *Irish Times* articles about the 'Moscow Letter' and suggested there were links between pre-split WP fund-raising and criminality. Dunphy's views on Northern Ireland would have been close to those of Democratic Left and he had contributed to WP publications in the past. A week after the article appeared De Rossa initiated legal proceedings against the *Sunday Independent*, though it would be 1996 before the case would come to court.

In July 1993 Mac Giolla defeated a Fianna Fáil candidate in the election for Lord Mayor of Dublin, and his party colleagues Lucia O'Neill and Eamonn O'Brien became deputy lord mayors. Evidence of old enmities surfaced when Sinn Féin's Christy Burke and independent Tony Gregory abstained rather than vote for Mac Giolla, but he secured the support of Fine Gael, Labour and DL members. Nevertheless, the WP alleged that the 'grouping currently called Democratic Left' had tried to 'wreck' Mac Giolla's election.

In 1994 Democratic Left secured two morale-boosting Dáil by-election victories. Kathleen Lynch, who had failed to take a seat in Cork South Central in 1992, won a former Labour seat in Cork North Central, a constituency where the WP had polled poorly; while Eric Byrne, who had narrowly missed a seat in Dublin South Central, won a vacated Fianna Fáil seat there. The swing from the government parties to DL was seen as reflecting the electorate's anger at an unpopular Fianna Fáil-Labour government. The victories saw De Rossa declare that DL had overcome its 'teething problems' and now offered a serious alternative for voters.

In December 1994 the Fianna Fáil-Labour coalition fell in acrimonious circumstances over its handling of the Beef Tribunal and allegations of clerical sex abuse. Labour entered into negotiations with Fine Gael and Democratic Left to form a new government, without going to the electorate. Although some in DL opposed entering a governing coalition, the party's TDs were eager to exercise real power for the first time in their political careers and the talks produced a deal. In a new 'Rainbow Coalition' with Fine Gael leader John Bruton as Taoiseach, De Rossa became Minister for Social Welfare and Liz McManus, Pat Rabbitte and Eamon Gilmore became ministers of state.

In 1995 De Rossa described the coalition to a DL conference as a 'good, reforming and principled government'. His supporters credited De Rossa with ending discrimination against married women on social welfare, substantial increases in child benefit and helping formulate a National Anti-Poverty Strategy. The coalition also won a narrow victory in a referendum to legalize divorce. There was a close working relationship between De Rossa and Bruton, which caused some tension with Labour and within DL. Despite participation in government, DL continued to decline at local level as it struggled with funding and a feeling among some activists that it was merely a platform for a group of talented politicians rather than a distinct political party. The 1997 general election saw DL retain 4 seats with 2.5 per cent of the vote nationally. The WP won just 7,808 first-preference votes, or 0.44 per cent of the national total.

De Rossa put much personal energy into his libel case against the *Sunday Independent*, which came to court in November 1996. Explaining his reasons for taking the case, De Rossa claimed that Dunphy's 1992 article had accused him of 'being a crook and a criminal . . . not suitable to be a representative of the people of the country . . . not a decent person'. De Rossa maintained that the 'Moscow Letter' was a 'forgery'. The *Sunday Independent* did not contend that De Rossa had signed the letter but merely that he was not deliberately libelled by Dunphy's article. Questioned as to a lack of personal papers relating to his political career, De Rossa explained that at Christmas 1992 he had taken 'everything in the house connected with the WP' and put it into bags which he then burnt in his back garden. Combative exchanges between

the *Sunday Independent*'s counsel Patrick MacEntee and De Rossa
followed. In response to questions about his political history,
De Rossa argued that he had not been associated with anybody
in Sinn Féin during the 1960s who had 'advocated violence' and
that he thought the OIRA had ceased to exist after its ceasefire in 1972. Questioned further, he stated: 'I cannot tell you as a
fact that the Official IRA ceased to exist. I do not know because
I had no connection with it.' Asked to explain the nature of
'fraternal' links between the WP and the Soviet Communist Party,
an irritated De Rossa said he had 'no interest' in discussing
'mumbo-jumbo'. After only eight days the jury was discharged
because an article in the *Sunday Independent* by Gene Kerrigan,
reporting this and other exchanges, was held to have potentially
prejudiced the case.

When the case was heard again in March 1997 both sides produced handwriting experts who gave starkly differing assessments
of the 'Moscow Letter'. De Rossa's counsel argued that it was 'a
good forgery' while the *Sunday Independent*'s expert contended that
it was 'most likely' real. MacEntee accused De Rossa of having
told 'lies' about the length of time he spent in Moscow. When
MacEntee asked if the 'terms Group A and Group B' meant
anything to him, De Rossa replied that he 'thought they were
blood groups'. After two weeks the jury was once again discharged,
having failed to reach agreement on a verdict. By the third trial,
in July, the *Sunday Independent*'s new counsel Michael McDowell
was arguing that De Rossa could have been 'tricked' by Sean
Garland into signing the letter. De Rossa admitted that Garland
might have 'lied' to him about Soviet funding and again told the
court how after the 'traumatic' split of 1992 he had burnt all his
documentation relating to the party to 'be rid of the memories'.
Garda superintendent Joseph Egan gave evidence that the OIRA
had remained active throughout the 1980s and was linked to the
WP, but Egan's evidence was presented without the jury being
present and was not highlighted in press reports. To the surprise
of many observers, the jury agreed that De Rossa had been libelled
and awarded him £300,000, a record for an Irish libel case. In

1999 an appeal by the *Sunday Independent* against the award was rejected by the court. In June 2005 the European Court of Human Rights finally ruled against a *Sunday Independent* appeal against the size of the award.

The peace process that unfolded in Northern Ireland during the 1990s kept the Northern branch of the WP very much on the sidelines, and eventually precipitated another split. A group of internal dissidents set up the Campaign for Democracy in the WP, which demanded a re-evaluation of the party's role. They accused the WP leadership of corruption and thinking that

they could play with the State while at the same time still pretend to be socialists planning the overthrow of that state. After the Provo pogrom they adopted the dangerous premise that our obvious enemies were our friends. In short out of a noble endeavour we were pawns in a corrupt economic conspiracy. All who disagreed were traitors or trots.

As the dispute escalated the entire Newry branch was expelled after being accused of 'sectarian' and 'anti-social' activities. Other members were expelled in Dublin and Belfast, while secret courts martial of OIRA members were held. Several were warned that they 'would go down a hole' if they did not desist from criticizing the leadership. Those expelled labelled themselves the Official Republican Movement (ORM).

In July 1997 there was serious rioting in Newry after the Orange Order was allowed to march down the Garvaghy Road in Portadown. During several days of disorder, after protest marches led by Sinn Féin, the Buttercrane Shopping Centre was looted and much property destroyed. Sinn Féin blamed the looting on ex-WP members and claimed that SF members who had tried to stop the rioting had had guns pulled on them. The Official Republicans replied that the violence had shown that the Provisionals 'cannot bring mobs on to the streets and give them petrol and tell them to burn this but leave that'. The war of words soon escalated and two Officials were kneecapped by the Provos. The following day two

Newry Provisionals were shot. Peace talks soon followed and an uneasy calm was restored. The Official Republicans announced that there was 'a political opposition in Newry that will not be intimidated'.

Violent clashes resumed between the new group and their former WP comrades. The WP claimed that the group were gangsters who had links to the Newry criminal Paddy Farrell, who had recently been shot dead by his girlfriend. Loyalist paramilitaries were told that the group was a 'new INLA', while word reached the Provisionals that the ORM wanted to settle scores from the 1970s. The RUC raided the homes of several of the group's members, who claimed the raids occurred at the WP's prompting. In early 1998 the group adopted the title Republican Left. Mac Giolla's response was that he did 'not wish them well . . . they'll get no support from the people of Ireland, north or south'. Republican Left had a short existence. Most of its membership favoured returning to the Official Republican Movement title and remaining a 'pressure group' rather than a new political party. The ORM supported the Good Friday Agreement in 1998 and established An Eochair, an OIRA ex-prisoners' group. It also sponsored various cross-community initiatives and talks between republican and loyalist prisoners' groups. A few activists associated with Republican Left, who had wanted to form a new party, instead set up the Irish Socialist Network, a 'radical democratic socialist organisation'.

In late 1998, following a year and a half of internal discussion on foot of the disappointing 1997 general election, delegates to a special DL conference voted by 171 votes to 21 to merge with the Labour Party. Labour leader Ruairi Quinn, for his part, had worked to smooth previous tensions between his party and DL's TDs. Supporting the merger, Des Geraghty reassured delegates that 'we do not want a "New Labour", a wishy-washy thing in which we will have to walk away from our working-class roots'. He added that in the new party there would continue to be a place for those who identified themselves as 'socialists' or indeed 'Marxists'. Eamon Gilmore struck a suitably confident note that the party would complete 'the unfinished business of Connolly: to put the Left in power'. For Mary McMahon the merger was 'like turning off a life support machine' as 'DL was going nowhere'. It signalled the end of a political organization north of the border, as the Labour Party did not have a presence there.

The Workers' Party described the merger as a 'betrayal of the working class'. Des O'Hagan suggested that unity between Labour and Fine Gael was the next step and that De Rossa had been 'a failure in government. As Minister for Social Welfare under the Celtic Tiger, things didn't get any better for the unemployed and marginalised.' The continuing bitterness of the divide was brought back into public view when Cathal Goulding died, aged 76, on St Stephen's Day 1998. Goulding had been living in a cottage at Myshall, Co. Carlow, for several years. When asked once about the likelihood of the Northern Ireland peace process succeeding, he had quipped with characteristic humour that it proved that, 'We were right, but too soon, Gerry Adams is right, but too late – and Ruairí Ó Brádaigh will never be fucking right.' Goulding was cremated at Dublin's Glasnevin Cemetery, in a secular ceremony featuring music and poetry. Among the mourners were Jim and Peter Sheridan, former judge Mary Kotsonouris, Goulding's partner Moira Woods and his several children. Giving the main oration, Sean Garland claimed that Goulding's greatest achievement had been 'transforming . . . a narrow nationalist movement into a class-conscious party of the working class'. Throughout his life Goulding had opposed 'sectarian nationalist bigots, ultra-leftists [and] the opportunists of Democratic Left. He hated the hypocrisy with which these particular traitors, of the now dissolved DL, sought to hide their betrayal.' While other speakers denounced 'De Rossa and his circus', De Rossa himself stood outside the service listening to the orations; despite being verbally abused and told to leave, he refused to go. De Rossa argued that he wanted to show respect to a man who had 'greatly influenced' him.

Goulding's funeral had brought the Workers' Party briefly back into public view. Aside from a couple of councillors in Waterford, there was little indication of the party's existence as the twenty-first century began. By 2009, with just two elected representatives, the party had reverted to a republican standpoint reminiscent in some ways of its 1970s Official Sinn Féin incarnation. In contrast, former party members were to be found at high levels throughout society, North and South. There were many in prominent positions in trade unions as diverse as SIPTU, IFUT, CPSU, IMPACT and the Craft Butchers. Former OIRA prisoner Brendan Mackin had been president of the Irish Congress of Trade Unions in 2005 while ex-WP activist Sally Ann Kinahan was ICTU assistant general secretary in 2008. As the unions sought to defend their members with the onset of recession, the ICTU's Paul Sweeney and CPSU's Blair Horan, both ex-WP members, were prominent advocates. Kieran Mulvey took his role as chairman of the Labour Relations Commission to a new level in attempting to broker a settlement to a bitter dispute between Cork hurlers and their management. There were former members in the non-governmental sector and in advisory bodies to the Northern Ireland Assembly.

The party's alumni were also well represented in the media. Eoghan and Ann Harris were prominent at the *Sunday Independent*, as was Patricia Redlich. For a long period ex-WP members Liam Clarke and Henry McDonald interpreted Irish politics for the British *Sunday Times* and *The Observer* respectively, while Hugh Jordan was employed by the Belfast *Sunday World*. Artist Brian Maguire, novelist Ronan Bennett and playwright Martin Lynch are among ex-members prominent in the arts. Pat McCartan and Michael White became judges during the period of the 'Rainbow Coalition'.

The movement's legacy is most visible in the Irish Labour Party. Since 1999 De Rossa has served as party president and as an MEP. Pat Rabbitte was party leader from 2002 to 2007, when he was succeeded by Eamon Gilmore. There was some irony in the fact that both Labour's general election candidates in Wicklow during 2007, Liz McManus and Nicky Kelly, were former Official Sinn Féin members who had taken different sides in 1975.

Not all the ex-members remained on the left. Paul Bew was an adviser for a period to UUP leader David Trimble and was appointed as an independent peer to the House of Lords in 2006. After leaving the WP Eoghan Harris initially worked for Fine Gael, then for independent presidential candidate Derek Nally in 1997. He became a vocal supporter of US President George W. Bush and the war in Iraq. During the 2007 general election campaign he endorsed Bertie Ahern and Fianna Fáil. Harris was appointed to the Seanad by Fianna Fáil in 2007.

The reluctance of some former members of the movement to discuss their political past had seen young Democratic Left members brand the WP 'the Scottish party', in reference to actors' superstitious aversion to mentioning the title of *Macbeth*. The dynamic often worked the other way in Northern Ireland: Sinn Féin now commemorates the Falls Curfew without any mention that it was the Officials that bore the brunt of the fighting. John Pat Mullan and Hugh Herron, senior OIRA members in Tyrone when British soldiers killed them in 1972, are now listed on the Provisional roll of honour. When Ivan Barr died in 2008, *An Phoblacht*'s fulsome tribute failed to mention that he had been a leading member of the Officials in Strabane until the late 1970s.

The rewriting is understandable. When the Provisional IRA's armed struggle was ongoing, the Officials were demonized as 'reformists' for having a ceasefire and for demanding a locally elected assembly with a Bill of Rights and a community police service. In 2009 Sinn Féin were part of a coalition government with the DUP, running a local assembly with its purse strings controlled from London, and they demanded a Bill of Rights to protect citizens. When dissidents killed British soldiers, Sinn Féin ministers called for the public to help capture those responsible. The ironies implicit in Sinn Féin's political evolution were obvious to former Provisional prisoner Anthony McIntyre as long ago as 2002, when, referring to the bloodletting between his organization and the OIRA, he reflected that

the seeming losers in those feuds – the Officials – must be sitting wryly observing that, body counts apart, they ultimately came out on top. We, who wanted to kill them – because they argued to go into Stormont, to remain on ceasefire, support the reform of the RUC, uphold the consent principle and dismiss as rejectionist others who disagreed with them – are now forced to pretend that somehow we are really different from them; that they were incorrigible reformists while we were incorruptible revolutionaries; that killing them had some major strategic rationale. And all the while the truth 'sticks' in our throats. They beat us to it – and started the peace process first.

Sinn Féin's success in establishing their narrative of the Troubles rankles with many former WP members. John McManus maintains that the WP's opposition to the Provos is possibly their finest legacy: 'The Official movement, for all the mistakes they made, saw through Irish nationalism at a very early stage, before anybody else did, which was a remarkable achievement, given where they'd come from. They understood the blind alley of nationalism, of sectarianism, that it wasn't the road to liberation.' For activists in Belfast and elsewhere, where the 'bitterness felt as bad as anything in the Civil War', it is no surprise that many, even today, baulk at welcoming the Provisionals' involvement in constitutional politics.

But the Workers' Party also rewrote their own history. The activities of the IRA in 1969, and the fact that after 1970 the Official IRA killed British soldiers, policemen, loyalists and civilians, planted bombs and feuded with their rivals, were airbrushed from the party's view of itself. The WP's strident opposition to terrorism was expressed without reference to or apology for their own past. As Paddy Woodworth commented in 1991:

It is one thing to say, 'We did this, we won't do it any more and we don't think the Provos should either.' People can understand and respect it. It is another altogether to come on like a bunch of choirboys, when the dogs in the street know the WP's history . . . that pisses the hell out of most people, and they're right. Nobody expects rectitude from Fianna Fáil, because they don't really promise it. The WP does . . .

While some have railed against the duplicity that was excused by the adoption of a 'revolutionary morality' – where the ends justified the means – other veterans believe that such theorizing merely covered more basic motivations. Former leading Dublin OIRA activist Lar Malone asserts: 'I'm struggling for me, what I want and the type of society I want. That is the way it was with everybody. I don't believe in . . . fellas going around saying "We're fighting for the workers"; once you hear that you have a hypocrite in front of you.'

On 30 January 2009, as Sean Garland left the Workers' Party's new Dublin headquarters in Mountjoy Square, officers of the Garda Extradition Unit arrested him on foot of a new warrant issued by US Secretary of State Condoleezza Rice in the final days of the Bush administration. The warrant accused Garland of conspiring with others outside the United States, including agents of the North Korean government, in the counterfeiting and distribution of almost perfect copies of US dollars. He would spend the following two weeks in Dublin's Cloverhill Prison before his eventual release on bail of £100,000 with the condition he surrender the deeds of his family home and keep a mobile phone with him at all times to allow Gardaí to track his movements.

Somewhat surprisingly, the first former WP figure to publicly declare his opposition to the renewed threat of extradition was Senator Eoghan Harris, who asked why this 'old, sick republican, who led the Official IRA to ceasefire in 1972 and who is charged with a major, but bloodless, crime of alleged forgery' was being 'singled out for this unique persecution' while the Northern peace process had seen much worse offences effectively swept under the carpet. Fianna Fáil Senator Labhrás Ó Murchú called on US President Barack Obama to vanquish the ghosts of the Bush administration and extend the new 'regime of diplomacy [and] friendship' to 'this very small case of Mr Garland'. Garland's old comrade Mick Finnegan, who had replaced Garland as WP president in 2006, reconvened the Stop the Extradition of Sean Garland Committee. In the European Parliament a Greek communist MEP decried the 'political persecution' of Garland on the 'trumped up charges of a Communist conspiracy to undermine the American dollar'.

At the time of writing Garland awaits a judicial decision on his possible extradition to the US. Ironically, the former OIRA leader's arrest on allegations of 'economic sabotage' came as the global financial crisis had exposed the excesses of what was being widely described as Ireland's corrupt system of 'crony capitalism'. As the Republic faced into the worst economic crisis in the state's history, core WP demands, such as nationalizing the banking system and state ownership of property assets, had again entered mainstream political debate.

Postscript

On 19 October 2009, Official IRA weapons (believed to be under the control of the Official Republican Movement) were put beyond use in the presence of members of the Independent International Commission on Decommissioning (IICD), including General John de Chastelain. The weapons included rifles, sub-machine guns and handguns, among them a revolver used in the fighting in Belfast in August 1969. Decommissioning occurred after several years of contact between Official republicans and the IICD. The Official Republican Movement stated that 'the era of the defenders, the illegal funders, the back room boys is gone' and appealed to their 'comrades and former comrades whether they have three letters in their title or just the one' to disarm so that 'all energies' can be 'focused on the creation of a cross-community voice to energize those on the margins of society to demand their economic rights'.

Acknowledgements

The authors would like to thank the staffs of the National Library of Ireland (especially Gerry Kavanagh), the Dublin Public and Gilbert Library, University College Dublin Archives, the National Archives of Ireland and the National Archives, Kew; Yvonne Murphy, Ross Moore and Kris Brown of the Northern Ireland Political Collection at the Linenhall Library; Tony Ebbs and Padraig Mannion at the Workers' Party of Ireland head office; Alison Loughran and Tommy Hale of An Eochair and Laura Duffy of Expac. For documents, photographs or other assistance: Colm Breathnach, Sean Curry, Gerry Cushnahan, Richard Dunphy, Eamon Farrell, Mike Jennings, Tara Keenan Thompson, Jim Lane, Feargus Mac Aogáin, P. J. McClean, Mary McMillen, Seamus Martin, Ed Moloney, Jim Monaghan, Peter Mooney, Seamus Murphy, Dermot Nolan, Paul O'Brien, Aindrias Ó Cathasaigh, Fachtna Ó Drisceoil, Eunan O'Halpin, Jer O'Leary, Margaret O'Leary, Eamon Phoenix, Alan Power, Sean Prendiville, Bob Purdie, Kacper Rekawek, Peter Rigney, Geoff Roberts, Mick Ryan, Patrick Smylie, Malachy Steenson, Fergal Tobin, Matt Treacy, Brian Trench, Patrick Webb and Padraig Yeates. Thanks to Ciaran Swan for the maps and Peter Heathwood for visual sources.

Brian Hanley would like to thank the following colleagues and friends for their support, encouragement and friendship: Guy Beiner, Cathy Bergin, Aoife Bhreatnach, Pete Boyle, Anna Bryson, Marion Casey, Marie Coleman, R. V. Comerford, Finbar Cullen, Anne Dolan, Brendan Donohue, Terry Dooley, Richard English, Catherine Fahy, Diarmaid Ferriter, Grainne Fox, John Gibney, Mags Glennon, Tommy Graham, Dave Hann, Jason Harte, David and Deirdre Hayton, Roisin Higgins, Jacqui Hill, Stefanie Jones, Lar Joye, Jennifer Kelly, Fintan Lane, Charles Laverty, Damian Lawlor, Joseph Lee, Sean Lucey, Donal McAnallen, Conor McCabe, Tony and Mandy McEwan, Fearghal McGarry, Charlie Maguire, Filipe Meneses, Joe Mooney, Paddy Mulroe, Will Murphy, Bruce Nelson, Donal Ó Drisceoil, Kate O'Malley, Cathal Ó Murchú, Aodhan Perry, Cieran Perry, Glen and Mildred Philips, Niamh Puirséil, John M. Regan, Paul Rouse, John Paul Ryan, John and Lisa Samuelsen, Dave and Trazi Smyth, Ian Speller, Steve Tilzey, John P. Waters, Clair Wills. A special thanks to my father Paddy Hanley and to Kay, also to my brother Dara, my sisters Una and Patricia, my brothers-in-law (the two Dereks and Killian) and to my father-in-law and mother-in-law Shaun and Sandra Doherty. Finally, I cannot sum up how much I owe to my wife Orla. She has lived with this project for the past five years and she has supported me in every way, especially at times when I feared it would never be completed. Thank you, my love.

Scott Millar would like to thank the following colleagues, friends, family and others who assisted with this book over the years: Niall Donald, Paul Cleary, Cian O'Callaghan, Eithne O'Leary, Fionan Murphy, Deirdre Murphy, Philip Shanahan, John Burns, John Lee, Niamh Lyons, Juno McEnroe, Caroline O'Doherty, Killian Forde, Declan Forde, Jenny Jennings, Elizabeth Dunphy, Mark Grehan, Neil and Sorcha Collins, Patrick Scahill, Paul Butler, Richard Oakley, Peter Lahiff, Diane McDermott, Simon Chambers, Conor Emerson, John Lennon, David Mullen, Matthew Devaney, Philip Clifford, Caroline Quinn, Shaun Connolly, Paul O'Brien, Mary Regan, James Doyle, Andrew Ryan, Tom Lyons, Deaglán de Bréadún, Neil Delahaye, Douglas Dalby, Gerry Gable, John Carroll, Michelle O'Keefe, Dearbhail McDonald, John Donald, Senan Hogan, Tony Kelly, John O'Mahony, Tim Vaughan, Noeleen Rooney, Avril Cox, Sebastian Artigues Manresa, Rebecca, Victoria and Cristina Artigues Cox, Marguerita Manresa Soner, Emilio Gonzalez Perez, Marguerita Artigues Manresa, Juan Rios Montaniz, Lorenzo Adrover Artigues, Billy Higgins, Deidre Noonan, Gavin Farrell, Gene Lynch, John Doyle, Sara Burke, Malachy Steenson, Ruth Cleary, Jenny Butterly, Debra and Harry Furey, Ruby, Alf, Stephaine and Nicola Taylor, Harry Edwards, Mick Sherry (RIP), Ian and Florence Henderson, George and Fiona Millar. Most of all Scott would like to thank his parents, Ann and Eugene, for provoking a concern for politics, history and social justice, and the memory of Florence Millar, a committed Dundee socialist in her own way.

The authors wish especially to thank our editor, Brendan Barrington, for his support and assistance.

Several of those who assisted us have passed away during the writing of this book: Ivan Barr, Tony Gregory, Ann Heathwood, Harry McKeown, Billy Mitchell, Denis O'Leary and Johnnie White.

Bibliography

Interviews

Ivan Barr, Sandy Boyer, Colm Breathnach, Brian Brennan, John Burns, Eric Byrne, Larry Carragher, Liam Cassidy, Liam Clarke, Shay Cody, Seamus Collins, Anthony Coughlan, Fintan Cronin, Sean Curry, John Cushnahan, Máirín de Burca, Proinsias De Rossa, Harry Donaghy, Francie Donnelly, Marian Donnelly, Oliver Donohue, Brendan Dowling, Noel Dowling, Elizabeth Doyle, Roderick Dunbar, Sean Dunne, Tommy Fallon, Brian Feeney, Gerry Flynn, Gerry Foley, Paddy Gallagher, Sean Garland, Des Geraghty, Gerry Gregg, Tony Gregory, Tony Hayde, Peter Heathwood, Tony Heffernan, James Connolly Heron, Anne Holliday, Bernie Hughes, Mike Jennings, Roy Johnston, Jimmy Jordan, Frank Keane, John Keane, Pat John Kelly, Sean Kelly, Frank Keoghan, Patrick Kinsella, Jim Lane, Stephen Lewis, Bob Lowrey, John Lowry, Gerry Lynch, Seamus Lynch, Feargus Mac Aogáin, Eamonn McCann, Paddy Joe McClean, Sean McConnell, Ken McCue, Seamus McDonagh, Tomás Mac Giolla, Tommy McKearney, Harry McKeown, Joan McKiernan, Brendan Mackin, Bobby McKnight, Mary McMahon, Alec McManus, John McManus, Art McMillen, Leonard McNally, Lar Malone, Padraig Mannion, Seamus Martin, Eamon Melaugh, Billy Mitchell, Jim Monaghan, Tony Moriarty, Catherine Murphy, Seamus Murphy (Armagh), Seamus Murphy (Bray), John Nixon, Dermot Nolan, Michael Nugent, Ruairí Ó Brádaigh, Bill O'Brien, Cian O'Callaghan, Dave O'Grady, Des O'Hagan, Brendan O'Hare, Sean O'Hare, Jer O'Leary, Margaret O'Leary, Eoin Ó Murchú, John O'Neill, Lucia O'Neill, Paddy O'Regan, Seamus Ó Tuathail, Henry Patterson, Sean Prendiville, Joe Quinn, Terry Robson, Seamus Rodgers, Harry Rose, John Ryan, Mick Ryan, Helena Sheehan, Mary Shelley, Kevin Smyth, Margaret Smyth, Paul Sweeney, Brian Trench, Brian Whelan, Fergus Whelan, Johnnie White, Paddy Woodworth, Padraig Yeates.

We are also grateful to those who spoke to us but wish to remain anonymous.

Archival sources

Archives of Irish America, Tamiment Library, New York
National Archives of Ireland, Dublin
National Archives (United Kingdom), Kew
Northern Ireland Political Collection, Linen Hall Library, Belfast

Public Records Office of Northern Ireland, Belfast
University College Dublin Archives

Official reports

Government of Northern Ireland (Cameron), Disturbances in Northern Ireland
(Belfast, 1969).
Government of Northern Ireland (Scarman), Violence and Civil Disturbances in
Northern Ireland (Belfast, 1972).
Interim Report on the Report of the Independent Commission of Inquiry into the
Dublin and Monaghan Bombings (Dublin, 2003).

Newspapers and periodicals

Advance
Andersonstown News
An Eochair
An Fuinneog
An Phoblacht (Cork)
An Phoblacht (Dublin)
An Phoblacht/Republican News
An Solas (Belfast)
An Solas (London)
An t-Oglac
Ballyfermot Republican
Ballymurphy News
Barricade Bulletin (Belfast)
Barricade Bulletin (Derry)
Belfast Newsletter
Belfast Telegraph
Challenge
Civil Rights
Class Politics
Combat
Communist Comment
Connolly News
Contact
Derry Journal
Drithleog (Dublin)
Drithleog (New York)
Eolas

Finglas People
Focus
Foghlaim
Fortnight
Galway News
Galway People
Gralton
Guardian
Hibernia
Hot Press
In Dublin
Intercontinental Press
Ireland, Irlanda, Irelande, Irland
Irish American Review
Irish Communist
Irish Democrat
Irish Echo (New York)
Irish Independent
Irish Militant
Irish News
Irish People
Irish Press
Irish Rebel (Birmingham)
Irish Rebel (Boston)
Irish Socialist
Irish Times
Leeside People

Liberty News

Limerick Socialist

Local Voice (Dublin)

Lurgan Mail

Magill

Making Sense

Mid-Ulster Observer

New Hibernia

Newry Reporter

Northern People

Notes and Comments

Nuacht Náisiúnta

Nusight

Official Republican Bulletin

People's Hope (Belfast)

People's Press (Markets)

Phoenix

Pobal

Republican News (Belfast)

Republican News (Cork)

Republican News (Dublin)

Republican Worker (Cork)

Resistance

Rosc Catha

Saoirse

Saor Éire – People's Voice

Site Action Press

Southside News (Dublin)

Spearhead

Starry Plough (Derry)

Starry Plough (Dublin)

Starry Plough (Turf Lodge)

Strabane Chronicle

Sunday Independent

Sunday News

Sunday Press

Sunday Tribune

Sunday World

Teoiric

The Blanket

The Plough (south Down/south Armagh)

The Rising of the Moon

The Separatist

The Voice (Strabane)

This Week

Times (London)

Times Change

Tomorrow's People

Torch (Coalisland)

Torch (Lurgan)

Tyrone Democrat

Ulster

United Irishman

United Irishman (Belfast)

USI News

Vanguard

Village

Voice of the North

Waterford People

Wealth of the Nation

Women's View

Workers' Life

Workers' Party Report

Workers' Republic

Workers' Weekly

Articles, books and pamphlets

Adams, G., *Before the Dawn: An Autobiography* (London, 1996).

Alonso, R., *The IRA and Armed Struggle* (London, 2006).

Amnesty International, *Report of an Enquiry into Allegations of Ill-Treatment in Northern Ireland* (London, 1972).

Anderson, B., *Joe Cahill: A Life in the IRA* (Dublin, 2002).

Anderson, J. L., *Che Guevara: A Revolutionary Life* (London, 1997).

Andrew, C., & Gordievsky, O., *KGB: The Inside Story* (London, 1990).

Andrew, C., & Mitrokhin, V., *The Mitrokhin Archive: The KGB in Europe and the West* (London, 2000).

Anon., *Fianna Fáil and the IRA* (Dublin, N/D).

Anon., *Fianna Fáil – the IRA Connection* (Dublin, N/D).

Barzilay, D., *The British Army in Ulster*, Vol. 1 (Belfast, 1973).

Bean, K., *The New Politics of Sinn Féin* (Liverpool, 2007).

Bean, K., & Hayes, M., *Republican Voices* (Monaghan, 2001).

Behan, D., *Ireland Sings* (London, 1965).

—— *Teems of Times and Happy Returns* (Dublin, 1979).

—— *A Tribute to Malachy McGurran* (Dublin, 1985).

Bell, J. B., *The Secret Army: The IRA 1916–1979* (Dublin, 1979).

—— *IRA Tactics and Targets* (Dublin, 1990).

—— *The Gun in Politics: An Analysis of Irish Political Conflict, 1916–86* (New Brunswick, 1991).

—— *The Irish Troubles: A Generation of Violence, 1967–92* (Dublin, 1993).

Beresford, D., *Ten Men Dead* (London, 1987).

Bernard, M., *Daughter of Derry: The Story of Bridget Sheils Makowski* (London, 1989).

Bew, P., *Ireland: The Politics of Enmity* (London, 2007).

Bew, P., Gibbon, P., & Patterson, H., *The State in Northern Ireland* (Manchester, 1979).

—— *Northern Ireland 1921–1996: Political Forces and Social Classes* (London, 1996).

Bew, P., Hazelkorn, E., & Patterson, H., *The Dynamics of Irish Politics* (London, 1989).

Bew, P., & Patterson, H., *The British State and the Ulster Crisis: From Wilson to Thatcher* (London, 1985).

Bird, C., *This is Charlie Bird* (Dublin, 2006).

Bishop, P., & Mallie, E., *The Provisional IRA* (London, 1988).

Bourke, R., *Peace in Ireland: The War of Ideas* (London, 2003).

Boyne, S., *Gunrunners: The Covert Arms Trail to Ireland* (Dublin, 2006).

Brenner, L., *United States, Britain, Ireland: A Special Special Relationship* (Dublin, 1972).

Bric, M., & Coakley, J. (eds), *From Political Violence to Negotiated Settlement* (Dublin, 2004).

British and Irish Communist Organisation, *The Two Irish Nations* (Belfast, 1971).

—— *The Economics of Partition* (Belfast, 1972).

Browne, V., & Farrell, M., *Magill Book of Irish Politics* (Dublin, 1981).

Bruce, S., *The Red Hand: Protestant Paramilitaries in Northern Ireland* (Oxford, 1992).

Bryson, A. (ed), *The Insider: The Belfast Prison Diaries of Eamonn Boyce 1956–62* (Dublin, 2007).

Burton, F., *The Politics of Legitimacy: Struggles in a Belfast Community* (London, 1978).

Callaghan, J., *A House Divided: The Dilemma of Northern Ireland* (London, 1973).

Clann na hÉireann, *The Battle of Belfast* (London, 1972).

—— *Spies in Ireland* (London, 1974).

Clare, P. K., *Racketeering in Northern Ireland: The New Patriot Game* (Chicago, 1989).

—— 'Subcultural Obstacles to the Control of Racketeering in Northern Ireland' in *Conflict Quarterly*, 10/4 (1990).

Clarke, L., *Broadening the Battlefield: The H-Blocks and the Rise of Sinn Féin* (Dublin, 1987).

Clarke, L., & Johnston, K., *Martin McGuinness: From Guns to Government* (Edinburgh, 2002).

Clews, R., *To Dream of Freedom: The Story of the MAC and the Free Wales Army* (Ceredigion, 2001).

Cody, S., O'Dowd, J., & Rigney, P., *The Parliament of Labour: One Hundred Years of Dublin Council of Trade Unions* (Dublin, 1986).

Coleman, M., *IFUT: A History* (Dublin, 2000).

Collins, E., *Killing Rage* (London, 1997).

Connolly, L., *The Irish Women's Movement: From Revolution to Devolution* (London, 2002).

Connolly, L., & O'Toole, T., *Documenting Irish Feminisms – The Second Wave* (Dublin, 2005).

Coogan, T. P., *The IRA* (London, 1995).

—— *The Troubles: Ireland's Ordeal and the Search for Peace* (London, 1995).

Corcoran, M., & O'Brien, M., *Political Censorship and the Democratic State: The Irish Broadcasting Ban* (Dublin, 2004).

Coughlan, A., *C. Desmond Greaves, 1913–1988: An Obituary Essay* (Dublin, 1991).

Coulter, C., *Students, Student Unions and USI* (Dublin, 1983).

Crawford, C., *Inside the UDA: Volunteers and Violence* (London, 2003).

Cronin, S., *A Man of the People: Jemmy Hope* (Dublin, 1964).

—— *Irish Nationalism: A History of its Roots and Ideology* (Dublin, 1980).

Cumings, B., *North Korea: Another Country* (New York, 2004).

Currie, A., *All Hell Will Break Loose* (Dublin, 2004).

Cusack, J., & McDonald, H., *UDA: Inside the Heart of Loyalist Terror* (Dublin, 2004).

—— *UVF: The Endgame* (Dublin, 2008).

Daly, T., *The Rás: Ireland's Unique Bike Race, 1953–2003* (Dublin, 2003).

Davenport, M., & Sharrock, D., *Gerry Adams: Man of War, Man of Peace* (London, 1997).

Davidson, A. J., *Defamed! Famous Irish Libel Trials* (Dublin, 2008).

De Baroid, C., *Ballymurphy and the Irish War* (London, 1990).

Demet, C., *Desertion: Bloody Sunday* (Manchester, 2005).

Devlin, B., *The Price of My Soul* (London, 1969).

Devlin, P., *Straight Left: An Autobiography* (Belfast, 1993).

Dillon, M., *The Dirty War* (London, 1990).

Dillon, M., & Lehane, D., *Political Murder in Northern Ireland* (Middlesex, 1973).

Doherty, P., *Paddy Bogside* (Dublin, 2001).

Doolan, L., Dowling, J., & Quinn, B., *Sit Down and Be Counted – The Cultural Evolution of a Television Station* (Dublin, 1969).

Dooley, T., *'The Land for the People': The Land Question in Independent Ireland* (Dublin, 2004).

Dunne, D., & Kerrigan, G., *Round Up the Usual Suspects* (Dublin, 1984).

Dunphy, R., 'The Workers' Party and Europe: Trajectory of an Idea' in *Irish Political Studies*, 7, 1992.

——'The Contradictory Politics of the Official Republican Movement, 1969–1992' in R. Deutsch, *Les Républicanismes Irlandais* (Paris, 1997).

——'A Group of Individuals Trying to Do Their Best: The Dilemmas of Democratic Left' in *Irish Political Studies*, 13, 1998.

Dunphy, R., & Hopkins, S., 'The Organizational and Political Evolution of the Workers' Party of Ireland' in *Journal of Communist Studies*, Vol. 8, Issue 3, 1992.

Edwards, A., & Bloomer, S., *A Watching Brief? The Political Strategy of Progressive Loyalism Since 1994* (Belfast, 2004).

Elliot, S., & Flackes, W. D., *Northern Ireland: A Political Directory 1968–1999* (Belfast, 1999).

English, R., *Armed Struggle: A History of the IRA* (London, 2003).

Farrell, M., *Northern Ireland. The Orange State* (London, 1980).

Farrell, M. (ed), *Twenty Years On* (Dingle, 1998).

Feeney, B., *Sinn Féin: A Hundred Turbulent Years* (Dublin, 2002).

Ferriter, D., *The Transformation of Ireland, 1900–2000* (London, 2004).

Fisk, R., *The Point of No Return: The Strike which Broke the British in Ulster* (London, 1975).

Flynn, S., & Yeates, P., *Smack! The Criminal Drugs Racket in Ireland* (Dublin, 1985).

Foley, G., *Ireland in Rebellion* (New York, 1971).

——*Problems of the Irish Revolution – Can the IRA meet the challenge?* (New York, 1972).

Foster, R., *Modern Ireland, 1600–1972* (London, 1990).

Gallagher, M., *The Irish Labour Party in Transition, 1957–1982* (Dublin, 1982).

Garland, R., *Seeking a Political Accommodation: The Ulster Volunteer Force: Negotiating History* (Belfast, 1997).

——*Gusty Spence* (Belfast, 2001).

Garland, S., *Marxism: A General Introduction* (Dublin, 1972).

Geraghty, D., *Luke Kelly: A Memoir* (Dublin, 1994).

Geraghty, T., *The Irish War* (London, 1998).

Gertz, B., *The China Threat: How the People's Republic Targets America* (Washington, D.C., 2000).

Gilmore, G., *Labour and the Republican Movement* (Dublin, 1966).

Godson, D., *Himself Alone: David Trimble and the Ordeal of Unionism* (London, 2004).

Gogan, L., *Larry Gogan's Pop File* (Dublin, 1979).

Goldring, M., *Faith of Our Fathers: A Study of Irish Nationalism* (Dublin, 1987).

Greaves, C. D., *The Life and Times of James Connolly* (London, 1961).

——*Liam Mellows and the Irish Revolution* (London, 1971).

Hall, M., *Seeds of Hope: Ex-Prisoners Project* (Newtownabbey, 2000).

Hanley, B., *The IRA, 1926–1936* (Dublin, 2002).

—— ' "Agitate, Educate, Organise" the IRA's *An t-Oglac*, 1965–68' in *Saothar*, 32, 2007.

—— 'The IRA and Trade Unionism, 1922–72' in F. Devine, F. Lane & N. Puirséil (eds), *Essays in Irish Labour History* (Dublin, 2008).

Harnden, T., *Bandit Country: The IRA and South Armagh* (London, 1999).

Heaney, S., *John Hewitt: 1907–1988 – The Universal Poet* (Belfast, 1988).

Hennessey, T., *Northern Ireland: The Origins of the Troubles* (Dublin, 2005).

—— *The Evolution of the Troubles, 1970–72* (Dublin, 2007).

Hobsbawm, E., *Bandits* (London, 2001).

Holland, J., *Too Long a Sacrifice: Life and Death in Northern Ireland Since 1969* (New York, 1981).

—— *The American Connection: US Guns, Money and Influence in Northern Ireland* (Dublin, 1989).

—— *Phoenix: Policing the Shadows* (London, 1997).

—— *Hope Against History: The Ulster Conflict* (London, 1999).

Holland, J., & McDonald, H., *INLA: Deadly Divisions* (Dublin, 1994).

Holmes, M., 'The Establishment of Democratic Left' in *Irish Political Studies*, 9, 1994.

Horgan, J., *Broadcasting and Public Life: RTÉ News and Current Affairs 1926–1997* (Dublin, 2004).

Hyndman, M., *Further Afield: Journeys from a Protestant Past* (Belfast, 1996).

Ireland, J. de Courcy, *Revolutionary Movements of the Past* (Dublin, 1971).

Irish Republican Clubs, *Irish America 1776–1976* (New York, 1976).

Johnston, R., *The Lessons of the Irish Question* (Dublin, 1967).

—— *A Century of Endeavour: A Biographical and Autobiographical view of the Twentieth Century in Ireland* (Dublin, 2006).

Jordan, H., *Milestones in Murder: Defining Moments in Ulster's Terror War* (Edinburgh, 2001).

Joyce, J., & Murtagh, P., *The Boss: Charles J. Haughey in Government* (Dublin, 1983).

Kelleher, D., *Republicanism, Christianity and Marxism* (Greystones, 1972)

—— *On to the Republic!* (Dublin, 1982).

—— *Buried Alive in Ireland* (Greystones, 2001).

—— *Irish Republicanism: The Authentic Perspective* (Greystones, 2001).

Kenny, K., *The American Irish: A History* (Harlow, 2000).

Keogh, D., *Jack Lynch: A Biography* (Dublin, 2008).

Lane, J., *Miscellaneous Notes on Republicanism and Socialism in Cork City, 1954–69* (Cork, 2005).

Larkin, P., *A Very British Jihad: Collusion, Conspiracy and Cover-Up in Northern Ireland* (Belfast, 2004).

Lee, J. J., *Ireland: Politics and Society, 1912–1985* (Cambridge, 1989).

Liaison of the Left, *Go to Work Ireland!* (Dublin, 1977).

Long, D., *Awakening the Spirit of Freedom* (Limerick, 2006).

Lukas, G., *What is Orthodox Marxism?* (Dublin, 1993).

Lundy, P., & McGovern, M., *Ardoyne: The Untold Truth* (Belfast, 2002).

Lyder, A., *Pushers Out – The Inside Story of Dublin's Anti-Drugs Movement* (Victoria, 2005).

Mac Con Iomaire, L., *Breandán Ó hEithir: Iomramh Aonair* (Chonnachta, 2000).

McCann, E., *What Happened in Derry* (London, 1972).

—— *War and an Irish Town* (London, 1979).

—— *Bloody Sunday in Derry: What Really Happened* (Tralee, 1992).

McCarthy, C., *Decade of Upheaval: Irish Trade Unions in the 1960s* (Dublin, 1973).

McCarthy, K., *Republican Cobh and the East Cork Volunteers* (Dublin, 2008).

McDermott, J., *Northern Divisions. The Old IRA and the Belfast Pogroms 1920–22* (Belfast, 2001).

McDonald, F., & Sheridan, K., *The Builders* (Dublin, 2008).

McDonald, H., *Colours: Ireland from Bombs to Boom* (Edinburgh, 2004).

—— *Gunsmoke and Mirrors* (Dublin, 2008).

MacEoin, U., *The IRA in the Twilight Years 1923–1948* (Dublin, 1997).

—— *Harry: The Story of Harry White* (Dublin, 1984).

McGarry, F. (ed), *Republicanism in Modern Ireland* (Dublin, 2003).

McGarry, P., *First Citizen: Mary McAleese and the Irish Presidency* (Dublin, 2008).

McGuffin, J., *Internment!* (Tralee, 1973).

—— *The Guinea Pigs* (London, 1974).

McGuire, M., *To Take Arms: A Year in the Provisional IRA* (London, 1973).

McIntyre, A., 'Modern Irish Republicanism and the Belfast Agreement: Chickens Coming home to Roost, or Turkeys Celebrating Christmas?' in R. Wilford (ed), *Aspects of the Belfast Agreement* (Oxford, 2001).

McKay, S., *Northern Protestants: An Unsettled People* (Belfast, 2000).

McKittrick, D., Kelters, S., Feeney, B., & Thornton, C., *Lost Lives: The Stories of the Men, Women and Children who Died as a Result of the Northern Ireland Troubles* (Edinburgh, 1999).

McManus, J., *Health Care: The Case for Socialist Medical Care* (Dublin, 1977).

Mac Manus, R., *The Road from Ardoyne: The Making of a President* (Dingle, 2004).

Mac Stíofáin, S., *Memoirs of a Revolutionary* (London, 1975).

Maguire, L., *IRA Internments and the Irish Government: Subversives and the State, 1939–1962* (Dublin, 2008).

Maguire, M., *Servants of the Public: A History of the Local Government and Public Services Union 1901–1990* (Dublin, 1998).

Maillot, A., *New Sinn Féin: Irish Republicanism in the Twenty-First Century* (London, 2004).

Martin, S., *Good Times and Bad: From the Coombe to the Kremlin* (Dublin, 2008).

Milotte, M., *Communism in Modern Ireland: The Pursuit of the Workers' Republic Since 1916* (Dublin, 1984).

Moloney, E., *A Secret History of the IRA* (London, 2002).

Moore, C., *The Christy Moore Songbook* (Dingle, 1984).

Mulholland, M., *The Longest War: Northern Ireland's Troubled History* (Oxford, 2002).

Munck, R., & Rolston, B., *Belfast in the Thirties. An Oral History* (Belfast, 1987).

Murphy, B., & Kelters, S., *Eyewitness: Four Decades of Northern Life* (Dublin, 2003).

Murphy, M. A., *Gerry Fitt: A Political Chameleon* (Dublin, 2007).

Murray, R., *The SAS in Ireland* (Dublin, 1990).

Myers, K., *Watching the Door* (Dublin, 2006).

National Commemoration Committee, *Tírghra* (Dublin, 2002).

Nelson, S., *Ulster's Uncertain Defenders: Loyalists and the Northern Ireland Conflict* (Belfast, 1984).

Ni Dhonnchada, M., & Dorgan, T., *Revising the Rising* (Derry, 1991).

Northern Aid, *Torture: The Record of British Brutality in Ireland* (Bray, 1972).

Northern Ireland Civil Rights Association, *We Shall Overcome* (Belfast, 1978).

O'Brien, B., *The Long War: The IRA and Sinn Féin* (Dublin, 1999).

O'Brien, G., *An Garda Síochána and the Scott Medal* (Dublin, 2008).

O'Brien, J., *The Arms Trial* (Dublin, 2000).

—— *The Modern Prince: Charles J. Haughey and the Quest for Power* (Dublin, 2002).

O'Broin, E., *Sinn Féin and Left Republicanism* (London, 2009).

O'Callaghan, S., *The Informer* (London, 1998).

O'Connor, E., *A Labour History of Waterford* (Waterford, 1989).

—— *Reds and the Green: Ireland, Russia and the Communist Internationals, 1919–43* (Dublin, 2004).

O'Connor, F., *In Search of a State: Catholics in Northern Ireland* (Belfast, 1993).

Ó Corráin, D., *Rendering to God and Caesar: The Irish Churches and the Two States 1949–73* (Manchester, 2006).

Ó Dochartaigh, F., *Ulster's White Negroes: From Civil Rights to Insurrection* (Edinburgh, 1994).

Ó Dochartaigh, N., *From Civil Rights to Armalites: Derry and the Birth of the Northern Ireland Troubles* (Basingstoke, 2005).

O'Doherty, M., *The Telling Year* (Dublin, 2007).

Ó Drisceoil, D., *Peadar O'Donnell* (Cork, 2001).

Official IRA, *EEC is Ireland's Downfall* (Dublin, 1972).

—— *The Reporter's Guide to Ireland* (Dublin, 1974).

O'Hagan, D., *Irish Republicanism: Separatist, Secular, Socialist* (New York, 1975).

—— *The Concept of Republicanism* (Dublin, 1975).

—— *The Republican Tradition* (Dublin, 1975).

—— *Liam MacMaolain: Separatist, Socialist, Republican* (Belfast, 1976).

O'Halpin, E., *Defending Ireland. The Irish State and its Enemies Since 1922* (Oxford, 1999).

—— 'Intelligence and Anglo-Irish relations, 1922–73' in E. O'Halpin, R. Armstrong & J. Olhmeyer, *Intelligence, Security and International Power* (Dublin, 2006).

O'Hearn, D., *Bobby Sands: Nothing but an Unfinished Song* (London, 2006).

Ó hEithir, B., *The Begrudger's Guide to Irish Politics* (Dublin, 1986).

O'Malley, P., *The Uncivil Wars: Ireland Today* (Belfast, 1983).

Ó Murchú, E., *Culture and Revolution in Ireland* (Dublin, 1971).

—— *The Workers' Party: Its Evolution and its Future* (Dublin, 1982).

Ó Tuathail, S., *They Came in the Morning* (Dublin, 1971).

Patterson, H., *The Politics of Illusion: Socialism and Republicanism in Modern Ireland* (London, 1989).

—— *The Politics of Illusion: A Political History of the IRA* (London, 1997).

—— *Ireland Since 1939* (Dublin, 2007).

Porter, N. (ed), *The Republican Ideal: Current Perspectives* (Belfast, 1998).

Prince, S., *Northern Ireland's 68: Civil Rights, Global Revolt and the Origins of the Troubles* (Dublin, 2007).

Puirseil, N., *The Irish Labour Party, 1922–1973* (Dublin, 2007).

Purdie, B., *Politics in the Streets – The Origins of the Civil Rights Movement in Northern Ireland* (Dublin, 1990).

Quinn, R., *Straight Left: A Journey in Politics* (Dublin, 2005).

—— 'The Labour Party and the Trade Unions' in T. Hastings, *The State of the Unions* (Dublin, 2008).

Quinn, R. J., *A Rebel Voice: A History of Belfast Republicanism, 1925–1972* (Belfast, 1999).

Redmond, S., *Desmond Greaves and the Civil Rights Movement in Northern Ireland* (London, 2000).

Rekawek, K., 'How "Terrorism" Does Not End: The Case of the Official IRA' in *Critical Studies on Terrorism*, Vol. 1, No. 3, December 2008.

Republican Clubs, *Where We Stand: The Republican Position* (Dublin, 1972).

—— *Belfast Ring Road* (Belfast, 1973).

—— *Pogrom!* (Belfast, 1975).

—— *Policing and You* (Belfast, 1975).

—— *Torture: The Case of the Beechmount 3* (Belfast, 1976).

—— *No Pasaran! The Story of the Irish Volunteers for the Spanish Republic* (Belfast, 1977).

—— *The Framing of Councillor MacDonagh* (Belfast, 1977).

—— *The Case for Democratic Devolved Government in Northern Ireland* (Belfast, 1980).

—— *Being Young in West Belfast* (Belfast, 1981).

Republican Movement, *The Case Against the Common Market* (Dublin, 1967).

—— *Ireland Today and Some Questions on the Way Forward* (Dublin, 1969).

—— *Freedom Manifesto* (Dublin, 1970).

—— *The Lessons of History* (Dublin, 1970).

—— *Manifesto of the Workers' and Small Farmers' Republic* (Dublin, 1971).

—— *Ardboe Martyrs* (Tyrone, 1972).

—— *In the 70s: The IRA speaks* (Dublin, 1972).

—— *Republicanism Part 1: From 1790* (Dublin, 1972).

—— *Republicanism Part 2: From 1922 to 1966* (Dublin, 1972).

Resources Protection Campaign, *Ireland's Resources: The Case for State Control* (Dublin, 1975).

Resources Study Group, *Irish Mining: The Need for Action* (Dublin, 1972).

—— *Navan and Irish Mining* (Dublin, 1972).

Rooney, E., 'From Republican Movement to Workers' Party: An Ideological Analysis' in C. Curtin, M. Kelly, & L. O'Dowd, *Culture and Ideology in Ireland* (Galway, 1984).

Sands, T., *The Songman: A Journey in Irish Music* (Dublin, 2005).

Sassoon, D., *One Hundred Years of Socialism – The Western European Left in the Twentieth Century* (London, 1996).

Seamus Costello Commemoration Committee, *Seamus Costello: Irish Republican Socialist* (Dublin, 1978).

Sheehy, K., *More Questions than Answers: Reflections on a life in the RUC* (Dublin, 2008).

Shipley, P., *Revolutionaries in Modern Britain* (London, 1976).

Sinnerton, H., *David Ervine* (Dingle, 2002).

Sinn Féin, *Nation or Province?* (Dublin, 1963).

—— *Imperialism and the Irish Nation* (Dublin, 1969).

—— *Ground Rent is Robbery* (Dublin, 1970).

—— *Stolen Waters* (Dublin, 1970).

—— *The EEC – An Alternative* (Dublin, 1971).

—— *Writings of John Mitchel* (Dublin, 1972).

—— *Document on Irish Liberation* (Dublin, 1973).

—— *Handbook of Republican Relations* (Dublin, 1975).

—— *The Great Oil and Gas Robbery* (Dublin, 1975).

—— *The Public Sector and the Profit Makers* (Dublin, 1975).

—— *Women's Rights in Ireland* (Dublin, 1975).

—— *A Refinery for Dublin Bay* (Dublin, 1976).

—— *Handbook for New Members* (Dublin, 1976).

—— *The Banks* (Dublin, 1976).

—— *Tony O'Reilly's Last Game* (Dublin, 1976).

Sinn Féin The Workers' Party, *The Irish Industrial Revolution* (Dublin, 1977)

—— *Come On the Taxpayers!* (Dublin, 1978).

—— *From the Party to the Youth Movement* (Dublin, 1979).

—— *Nuclear Power and Ireland* (Dublin, 1979).

—— *Planning for a Better Future* (Dublin, 1979).

—— *Rapid Rail for a Greater Dublin* (Dublin, 1979).

—— *Those Who Leave: The Truth about Socialist Vietnam and the 'Boat People'* (Dublin, 1979).

—— *Against Terrorism* (Dublin, 1980).

—— *H-Block – The Socialist Perspective* (Dublin, 1980).

—— *The Land for the People* (Belfast, 1980).

—— *Women in Ireland* (Dublin, 1980).

—— *Peace, Work and Class Politics* (Dublin, 1981).

—— *Crisis in the Engineering Industry* (Belfast, 1982).

Skillen, C., 'Pravda's Provos: Russian and Soviet Manipulation of News from Ireland' in *Irish Political Studies*, 8, 1993.

Staunton, E., *The Nationalists of Northern Ireland, 1918–1973* (Dublin, 2001).

Stopper, A., *Mondays at Gaj's: The Story of the Irish Women's Liberation Movement* (Dublin, 2006).

Sunday Times Insight Team, *Ulster: A Penguin Special* (London, 1972).

Swan, S., *Official Irish Republicanism, 1962–1972* (Lulu, 2006).

Sweetman, R., *On Our Knees – Ireland 1972* (Dublin, 1972).

Taylor, P., *Provos: The IRA and Sinn Féin* (London, 1997).

—— *Loyalists* (London, 1999).

Teague, P. (ed), *Beyond the Rhetoric: Politics, the Economy and Social Policy in Northern Ireland* (London, 1987).

Tobin, F., *The Best of Decades: Ireland in the 1960s* (Dublin, 1996).

Treacy, M., 'Rethinking the Republic: The Republican Movement in 1966' in R. O'Donell (ed), *The Impact of the 1916 Rising* (Dublin, 2008).

Union of Students in Ireland, *What's Mined is Ours* (Dublin, 1973).

Van Voris, W. H., *Violence in Ulster: An Oral Documentary* (Massachusetts, 1975).

Walker, B. M. (ed.), *Parliamentary Election Results in Ireland, 1918–92* (Belfast, 1992).

Walsh, L., *The Final Beat: Gardaí Killed in the Line of Duty* (Dublin, 2001).

Walsh, P., *Irish Republicanism and Socialism: The Politics of the Irish Republican Movement 1905–1994* (Belfast, 1994).

Warner, G., 'The Falls Road Curfew Revisited' in *Irish Studies Review*, Vol. 14, No.3, August 2006.

Whalen, B., *Inside the IRA* (Philadelphia, 1975).

Whelan, K., 'The Revisionist Debate in Ireland' in *Boundary 2*, Vol. 1, No. 1, 2004.

White, R. W., *Provisional Irish Republicans: An Oral and Interpretative History* (Connecticut, 1993).

—— *Ruairí Ó Brádaigh: The Life and Times of an Irish Revolutionary* (Indiana, 2006).

Wilson, A. J., *Irish America and the Ulster Conflict, 1968–1994* (Belfast, 1995).

Wood, I. S., *Crimes of Loyalty: A History of the UDA* (Edinburgh, 2006).

Woodworth, P., *Dirty War, Clean Hands – ETA, the GAL and Spanish Democracy* (Cork, 2000).

Workers' Association, *One Island, Two Nations* (Belfast, 1973).

—— *Warmongering! The Irish Press and the Troubles in Northern Ireland* (Belfast, 1973).

—— *The Ulster General Strike* (Belfast, 1974).

—— *Why Articles 2 & 3 Must Go* (Dublin, 1974).

Workers' Party, *The Current Political Situation in Northern Ireland* (Belfast, 1983).

—— *The Case for Devolved Government in Northern Ireland* (Dublin, 1985).

—— *Ireland and the Socialist Countries* (Dublin, 1986).

—— *Media Attacks on the Party* (Dublin, 1986).

—— *The Workers' Party and the Anglo-Irish Agreement* (Dublin, 1986).

—— *Belfast: A City for Working People* (Belfast, 1987).

—— *Building Workers' Party Youth* (Dublin, 1987).

—— *Fight back with the Workers' Party* (Dublin, 1987).

—— *Public Health and Private Wealth* (Dublin, 1987).

—— *Bertie's Bill* (Dublin, 1990).

—— *A Draft Programme for Democratic Socialism* (Dublin, 1991).

—— *The Rezoning Majority: A Study of the Abuse of Planning* (Dublin, 1991).

—— *The Workers' Party in the Dáil: The First Ten Years* (Dublin, 1991).

—— *Patterns of Betrayal: The Flight from Socialism* (Dublin, 1992).

—— *Cathal Goulding, Thinker, Socialist, Republican, Revolutionary, 1923–1998* (Dublin, 1999).

——*A Celebration of Seán Ó Cionnaith* (Dublin, 2003).
——*Civil Rights: Reform or Revolution* (Dublin, 2008).
Yeltsin, B., *The View from the Kremlin* (London, 1994).

Theses

Berg, A., 'Did the SFWP influence the *Today Tonight* coverage of the Bobby Sands hunger strike and its aftermath in 1981? A study of bias in *Today Tonight*' (MA, DCU, 2003).
Meade, C. A., 'Success and Transformation: An Analysis of the Workers' Party in the Eighties' (MA, UCD, 1990).
Millar, S., '"The Risen People?" The Development of Sinn Fein in Dublin 1980–2002' (MA, DCU, 2002).
Ó hAdhmaill, F., 'The Function and Dynamics of a Ghetto: A Study of Nationalist West Belfast' (PhD, University of Ulster, 1990).
Rooney, E. P., 'From Opposition to Legitimacy? A Sociological Analysis of the Official republican movement' (PhD, QUB, 1985).

Unpublished memoirs

Ó Comain, L., *Towards Revolution: The Memoirs and Thoughts of an Irish Republican* (Derry, N/D).
Ó Seaghda, D., *Na Fianna Eireann: Historical Documents, 2–4* (Dublin, 2001).
Purdie, B., *Remembering the Official Republicans* (Oxford, 2006).

Visual sources

Brookeborough, RTÉ, January 1997.
Brother Where Art Thou? TG4, March 2006.
Cooke St, RTÉ, August 1977.
Gallery, BBC 1, May 1983.
No Go! The Free Derry Story, BBC NI, September 2006.
Peter Heathwood Collection of recordings relating to the Workers' Party and Official Republicanism (eight DVDs, 1982–95).
Seven Ages, Programmes 5 & 6 RTÉ, 2002.
Spotlight, BBC 1, 20 February 1992.
Sticking to Their Guns, BBC 1, *Spotlight*, 27 June 1991.
Sullivan's Story, UTV, 28 September 1989.
The History of the Troubles According to My Da, UTV, February 2007.
The Last Colony, Channel 4, August 1994.
The Member for West Belfast, UTV, *World in Action*, December 1983.

The Patriot Game, TG4, March 2007.
The Sparks that Lit the Bonfire, BBC 2, *Timewatch*, January 1992.
The Super Dollar Plot, BBC1, *Panorama*, 20 June 2004.
Today Tonight, RTÉ, 29 April 1984 and 5 March 1986.
Watchdog, BBC 1, 1 March 1984.
Workers' Party, Party Political Broadcast, RTÉ, November 1982.
Workers' Party Youth, *From Sinn Féin to the Workers' Party*, 1986.

Notes

Frequently cited sources are abbreviated as follows.

AC	Ard Chomhairle
AIA	Archives of Irish America
AP	In authors' possession
BAI	British Army Intelligence
Bel Tel	*Belfast Telegraph*
BSI	Bloody Sunday Inquiry
CEC	Central Executive Committee
CS	Coiste Seasta
EMC	Executive Management Committee
GAC	General Army Convention
IN	*Irish News*
IP	*Irish People*
Ir Ind	*Irish Independent*
Ir Pr	*Irish Press*
IRA vol.	IRA volunteer
IT	*Irish Times*
NAI	National Archives of Ireland
NAUK	National Archives United Kingdom
NP	*Northern People*
OIRA vol.	Official IRA volunteer
PIRA vol.	Provisional IRA volunteer
PRONI	Public Record Office of Northern Ireland
UCDA	University College Dublin Archives
UI	*United Irishman*

Sinn Féin, SFWP and Workers' Party AC, CEC, CS and EMC minutes are held by the Workers' Party of Ireland.

Prologue

Notes for pages ix to xiii

ix 'The clapping and cheering', authors present at this event; **x** 'We can do no better', text of speech, AP; 'Instead he declared', Sean Garland statement, 15 Nov. 2005; 'The US indictment', USA v. Sean Garland, 19 Oct. 2005, AP; **xi** 'remove the border and unite the country', Sean Garland interview.

1. The Patriot Game

Notes for pages 1 to 21

1 'In early September', R. W. White, *Ó Brádaigh*, p. 114; *Starry Plough*, No. 3, 1973; *IP* 10 Jan. 1974; **2** 'Goulding and most', Garda report, Sept. 1951 in Jus8/802, NAI; J. B. Bell, *Secret Army*, pp. 240–1; 'In early 1946', *IT*, 5 April 1946; **3** 'The "three Macs"', Garland; **4** 'In 1950', *UI*, May 1950; White, *Ó Brádaigh*, p. 354; 'The 1950s', Patterson, *Ireland*, pp. 78–97; **5** 'The deference', D. Ferriter, *Transformation* pp. 463–5; J. J. Lee, *Ireland*, p. 266; **6** 'Republicans', *UI*, Sept. 1950, Aug. 1951, Oct. 1952, Sept. & Oct. 1953; 'Dublin Fianna', Proinsias De Rossa; 'In the South', Garda reports, 22 June 1952, 20 June 1954 in Jus8/900, NAI; **7** 'According to', Garland, Mick Ryan, Tomás Mac Giolla; 'They even', IRA statement, Nov. 1954, AP; 'In 1951', Garda report, June 1952 in DFA A/12, NAI; **8** 'Mac Giolla', Mac Giolla; 'Cathal Goulding', Garda report, Sept. 1951 in Jus8/802/18, NAI; 'During their trial', *UI*, Nov. 1953; **9** 'Young IRA', Garland, *IT*, 18 June 1954; Bell, *Secret Army*, pp. 257–61; 'The Gardaí', Garda reports, 21 June & 27 Oct. 1954 in DFA A/12, NAI; *UI*, July 1954; **10** 'The Armagh', Ryan, Jim Lane, Seamus Collins, Máirín de Burca; 'The IRA men', Seamus Murphy; **11** 'Weapons', Garland, Murphy; 'The IRA revival', *Resurgent Ulster*, Jan., Sept., Oct., Dec. 1954; 'The introduction', Garda report, 19 March 1957 in John A. Costello Papers, P 190/708 (7), UCDA; **12** 'Garland and others', Garland, Ryan; 'Despite the criticism', Lane, Ryan; 'New recruits', De Rossa; 'During 1955', Garland; 'Outlining', *Notes on Guerrilla Warfare*, 1956; **13** 'He was influenced', captured IRA doc in Jus8/1061, NAI; 'But the IRA', Patterson, *Ireland*, pp. 134–7; **14** 'In December', Lane, Garland, Ryan; 'Operation Harvest', *UI*, 15 Dec. 1956; Garland in D. Long, *Awakening*; **15** 'Some veterans', Mac Giolla, Garland, captured IRA document in Jus8/1061, NAI; 'On New Year's', Garland, Paddy O'Regan; **16** 'With the deaths', *Irish Catholic*, 10 Jan. 1957; De Rossa; Garda report, 19 March 1957 in John A. Costello Papers, P 190/708 (7), UCDA; 'Cork Sinn Féin', Lane; **17** 'The new government', *UI*, June, July, Aug., Sept. 1957; 'Indeed certain', Collins; 'In 1959', Garda estimates in D/T 98/6/494, NAI; **18** 'A large number', Garland; 'By mid-1958', *UI*, Oct. 1958; 'After their release', Garland, Ryan; 'In November', Garland; A. Bryson, *The Insider*, pp. 49–52; 'Belfast volunteer', Art McMillen; **19** 'Teenage Fianna', Brendan Mackin; 'About 3,400', Garda report, 21 June 1959 in Jus8/900, NAI; 'With Mick Ryan',

Ryan; 'Internment', *UI*, June 1960; 'The Gardaí', Garda report, 20 Nov. 1961 in D/T 98/6/494, NAI; 'He promised', *Bel Tel*, 28 Nov. 1961; **20** 'The campaign', Garland; 'In November', E. O'Halpin, *Defending*, p. 300; Mac Giolla; 'There were also', *Ir Pr*, 15 & 19 Jan. 1962; 'The Department', P. Berry, 8 June 1970 in Jus2001/6/10, NAI; RUC report, 13 April 1962 HA/32/1/1349, PRONI; 'The decision', Ryan, *UI*, March 1962; Garland; de Burca; **21** 'Some Southern', Garland.

2. Army of the People: 1962–1968

Notes for pages 22 to 69

22 'The IRA', *UI*, April 1962; 'Minister for Justice', 30 March 1962 in D/T 98/6/494, NAI; **23** 'The Ireland', F. Tobin, *Best of*, pp. 4–8, 12–22; H. Patterson, *Ireland*, pp. 161–8; *IT*, 13 Feb. 1965; 'For the IRA', Garland; **24** 'Another dispute', Garland; *UI*, June 1962; **25** 'By all accounts', *Sunday Tribune*, 9 Sept. 1984; 'Seamus Costello', Sean Curry, Sean Dunne; 'Mick Ryan', Ryan; **26** 'Garland', Garland, Padraig Yeates; 'After his return', Ryan; **27** 'The Gardaí', Garda reports, 1 Dec. 1964–21 Nov. 1966 in Jus98/6/495, NAI; 'What next?', Ryan; IRA vols; 'The wider public', *IT*, 19 Jul. 1963; 'One source', *UI*, June 1965; *Guth na Bhfiann* Aug–Sept. 1966; **28** 'In Belfast', Belfast IRA vols; 'The failure', *Bel Tel*, 16 Feb. 1966; **30** 'The highlight', H. Patterson, *Illusion* (1989), p. 96; R. Johnston, *Century*, pp. 175–6; *An t-Oglac*, May 1965 in HA/32/2/13, PRONI; Mac Giolla; 'Goulding's increasing', B. Anderson, *Joe Cahill*, pp. 155–6; Seamus Murphy; **31** 'As Mac Giolla', Mac Giolla; 'The Soviets', C. Andrew & V. Mitrokhin, *Mitrokhin Archive*, pp. 236–7; **32** 'The dynamics', R. Foster, *Modern Ireland*, p. 584; 'The idea', Garland, *An t-Oglac*, June 1965; **33** 'In Belfast', Liam McMillen speech, June 1972, AP; Jim Sullivan memoir, AP; 'The two men', *IN*, 18 June 1963; Belfast IRA vols; **34** 'The Falls Road', Belfast IRA vols; Curry; 'There were', Seamus Lynch, Belfast IRA vols; **35** 'Public attention', *IN*, 29 Sept–5 Oct. 1964; McMillen, speech; *UI*, Nov. 1964; **36** 'Away from', *UI*, May 1963 & April 1964; 'There was little', Roy Johnston, Anthony Coughlan, *Tuairisc*, July 1965; **37** 'Greave's ambition', *Irish Democrat*, Sept. 1959, March & Dec. 1961; **38** Johnston, *UI*, Oct. & Nov. 1964; 'Coughlan was', Coughlan; **39** 'In British', Intelligence report, 6 July 1970 in FCO 33/1204, NAUK; 'Suspicion', U. MacEoin, *Twilight Years*, pp. 875–7; 'Another republican', *IT*, 21 March 1964, *UI*, April 1964; 'All units', *An t-Oglac*, May 1965; **40** 'One of the first', Garda reports, Jus98/6/495, NAI; 'The IRA's', Mac Giolla, *An t-Oglac*, May 1965; **41** 'Born in', *Oxford Dictionary of National Biography*, 2007; *Sunday Times*, 12 Sept. 1971; 'At his first', S. Mac Stíofáin, *Memoirs*, p. 93; Johnston; **42** 'The question', Ryan; 'While these', *Irish Democrat*, Jan. 1965; 'During February', IRA leaflet, 24 April 1965, AP; **43** 'IRA volunteers', *UI*, April & Aug. 1965; Dublin IRA vols; 'During the same', captured IRA reports in Jus98/6/495, NAI; *UI*, Nov. 1965–Jan. 1966; **44** 'Mindful of this', *UI*, Sept. 1965; 'Mac Giolla', *IN*, 19 April 1965; 'Eagerness', Dublin IRA vols; *UI*, April 1963; 'Several of', Lane, *An Phoblacht* (Cork), Sept. 1966; **45** 'Similar dissent', Frank Keane; *Ir Ind*, 6 May 1967; 'A visit',

UI, Feb. 1965; **46** 'Another vessel', Garland; Garda reports in Jus98/6/495, NAI; 'The same month', *IT*, 26 Oct. 1965; 'The 'five'', *Ir Pr*, 4 Dec. 1965; Belfast IRA vols; 'The Garda', Garda reports in Jus98/6/495, NAI; *An t-Oglac*, June 1965; British-based IRA vol.; **47** 'This pointed', Ryan; 'Irish America', FBI reports, 17 Oct. & 9 Nov. 1963, 13 Oct. 1964 in Prendiville collection, AIA; **48** 'Senior Clan', *UI*, March 1967; captured Army Council minutes in Jus98/6/495; Ryan, Garland; 'There was', Ryan, *Bel Tel*, 17 Feb. 1966; **49** 'It will', *An t-Oglac*, June 1965; 'Political developments', Yeates, Collins; 'The IRA', British-based IRA vols; **50** 'The FWA', IRA vols; *Bel Tel*, 21 Sept. 1968; 'Clann', report, 26 Oct. 1965 in DFA 305/14/263/23, NAI; Yeates, Collins; 'Other sections', Mackin, Yeates, British-based IRA vols; **51** 'The IRA saw', Army Council minutes, 1 Jan. 1966; McMillen speech; 'Popular nationalism', L. Gogan, *Pop File*; 'But the IRA', *Evening Herald*, 1–4 Nov. 1965; *Sunday Independent*, 21 Jan. 1966; **52** 'The Special Branch', *Bel Tel*, 15 Feb. 1966; JIC minutes, 21 April 1966 in CAB 159/45, NAUK; 'In Feburary', *Bel Tel*, 19–22 Feb. 1966; *IT*, 20 April 1966; **53** 'A raid', IRA vols; 'In May', *Ir Ind*, 10 May 1966; *IT*, 14 May 1966; *UI*, June 1966; **54** 'During March', *Evening Herald*, 20–24 April 1966; IRA vols; 'Easter brought', *IN*, 18 April 1966; **55** 'Betty Sinclair', *Irish Democrat*, May 1966; 'The numbers', Johnnie White; northern IRA vols; 'In Dublin', Bobby McKnight; **56** 'Seventeen', Tony Heffernan; 'The post-Easter', McMillen speech; 'The emergence', Billy Mitchell; Belfast IRA vols; **57** 'During 1965', *An t-Oglac*, June 1965; 'In June', *UI*, June 1966; IRA leaflet, AP; S. Swan, *Official Irish*, pp. 183–5; 'At Bodenstown', *UI*, July 1966; **58** 'Another opportunity', Ryan, *IT*, 22 Sept. 1966; 'The Military', Social and Military plan in Jus98/6/495, NAI; **60** 'Newer political', Johnston, *Tuairisc*, 31 Aug. 1966; *IN*, 15 Aug. 1966; 'The IRA convention', Garda report, 9 Dec. 1966 in Jus98/6/495, NAI; **62** 'Even as', *An Phoblacht* (Cork), May 1966; *Irish Militant*, May & Sept 1966, April 1968; **63** 'Beyond the political', *IT*, 10 Jan. 1967, 28 Feb. 1967; *UI*, Dec. 1967; Dublin IRA vols; 'Some military', *UI*, June 1967; **64** 'In Derry', *Hansard*, 13 June 1968; 'At Bodenstown', *UI*, July 1967; G. Adams *Before*, p. 82; 'During the summer', Ryan; 'The meeting heard', minutes of meeting, 29–30 Aug. 1967, AP; **65** 'But if', Mac Giolla; *An t-Oglac*, Dec. 1967, AP; 'In Dublin', Ryan; Dublin IRA vols; **66** 'Despite having', McMillen speech; *IN*, 15 Jan. 1968; 'Armed involvement', *UI*, July 1968; 'In July', Scarman Tribunal, 18.6; *UI*, Sept. 1968; Garda report, 18 March 1969 in DJ 2000/36/3, NAI; **67** 'the device', Dublin IRA vol.; 'Meanwhile', Dublin IRA vols; **68** 'Tensions', AC minutes, 20 July 1968; Margaret O'Leary; 'The stressing', Dublin IRA vols; 'By the', Garda reports in DJ2000/36/3, NAI; IRA vols; Mac Stíofáin, *Memoirs*, p. 110; **69** 'The implications', *IT*, 5 Aug. 1968; *Washington Post*, 8 Aug. 1968 in DFA 305/14/263/2G, NAI.

3. A New Revolution

Notes for pages 70 to 107

70 'The Sinn Féin', Garda report, 20 Nov. 1961 in D/T 98/6/494, NAI; 'Proinsias', T. Mitchell to P. De Rossa, 4 Aug. 1962, De Rossa; 'The tall', *IT*, 23 June 1969; 71 'He argued', *UI*, Dec. 1962; 'Mac Giolla', Mac Giolla; *UI*, Jan. 1966; 'Her father', *IT*, 23 Jan. 1987; 72 'Irish-Ireland', *UI*, June 1964, March 1965, Dec. 1965; 73 'A speaker', *UI*, Sept. & Oct. 1963; 'The movement's', *UI*, Jan–Dec 1964; 74 'During 1964', AC minutes, 4 July 1964; 'Sinn Féin', B. M. Walker, *Parliamentary Elections*, pp. 25–6; 75 'The first', *UI*, March, April & May 1965; 76 'By June's', Ruairí Ó Brádaigh, *UI*, July 1965; 77 'Some', de Burca, De Rossa; 'By the', *UI*, Nov. 1965; 78 'In April', *IN*, 21 March 1966; 'Fitt', *IN*, 30 May 1967; 79 'By the Ard', *Clár*, Ard Fheis, Nov. 1966, AP; 80 'Beyond the', RUC report, 10 Oct. 1966 in HA 32/2/13, PRONI; 81 'His reading', Dunne; 'Other', Heffernan; *IT*, 6 Jan. 2007; SF membership forms 1968–9; 82 'One marker', Lar Malone, Des Geraghty; 'The decade's', *Hibernia*, June 1966; Eoin Ó Murchú; 83 'The Republican', Dermot Nolan; 84 'Increased', *UI*, May 1966, Sept. 1969; 'Their often', Ó Murchú; 'Whereas', Tony Gregory; 'Dwyer's pub', Dublin IRA vol.; 'Increased republican', *UI*; 85 'A Wolfe Tone', NICRA, 1978; McMillen speech; Adams in M. Farrell (ed) *Twenty Years On*, pp. 39–53; 86 'Paddy Devlin', McMillen speech; Harry McKeown, Mackin; 'In early 1967', *IN*, 15 Nov. 1967; Mary McMahon; 87 'Derry', White, Eamon Melaugh, Eamonn McCann; 88 'The Derry', *UI*, Sept. 1968; 'Housing', *UI*, Feb. 1967; 89 'As with', Dunne, De Rossa; 90 'But', *UI*, July 1967; 'If Goulding's', Dunne; R. Johnston, *Century*, p. 125; S. Swan, *Official*, p. 227; 91 'In October', *Republican Educational Manual*, 1967; 92 'The November', *UI*, Dec. 1967; 93 'Costello', Ryan, Garland; 'Not everyone', De Rossa; AC minutes, 23 March 1968; CS minutes, 18 Feb. & 29 March 1967; 95 'Young', Heffernan; *UI*, June 1968; 'During', *UI*, May 1967, Oct. 1968; Johnston, *Century*, p. 234; 96 'Some new', Jer O'Leary; Dublin IRA vol.; 'This coincided', Ryan; 97 'It was', Republican movement to Clann na hÉireann, 1968, AP; 'By January', Ryan; *Evening Herald*, 15 Jan. 1968; 98 'Private security', Dublin IRA vol.; 'De Rossa', De Rossa; *IT*, 17 June 1968; 'In Belfast', *IN*, 4 & 14 March 1968; 99 'During 1967', Sean Kelly; 'Costello', Ryan, AC minutes, 23 March 1968; Costello speech, 23 Feb. 1969; 'One consequence', *Evening Herald*, 20 Jan. 1968; *Hansard*; 13 June 1968; *IN*, 5 June 1968; 101 'The civil rights', CS minutes, 29 July 1968; RUC report, 18 Aug. 1969 in Scarman, p. 53–4; *IN*, 20 June 1968, 5 July 1968; 102 'An internal', captured republican strategy document quoted in RUC report, 7 July 1969 in HA/32/2/28, PRONI; 103 'Old habits', Seamus Ó Tuathail, McKnight; McMillen speech; AC minutes, 21 Sept. 1968; Curry; 'In the aftermath', Melaugh, McCann; 104 'Goulding', UTV, 27 Sept. 1968 in HA 32/2/28, PRONI; 'At an IRA', McMillen speech; Belfast IRA vols; 'Across', Heffernan; McMillen speech; RTÉ, *Seven Ages*, 5, 2002; 105 'But the', Ó Tuathail; CS minutes, 28 Oct. & 23 Nov. 1968; 'The Derry', L. Ó Comain, *Towards Revolution*; John Nixon; 106 'While', *UI*,

Oct. 1968; *IT*, 18 Oct. 1968; 'Sinn Féin', *Clár*, Ard Fheis, Dec. 1968; *UI*, Jan. 1969; **107** 'In early', Kevin Smyth; *Fortnight*, 26 April 1974.

4. 1969: Backlash

Notes for pages 108 to 148

108 'In different', D/J, 18 March 1969 in Jus2000/36/3, NAI; 'The year', *IT*, *IN* 1–30 Jan. 1969; **109** 'Republicans', *UI*, Jan, Feb, March 1969; Cameron report, p. 86; Belfast, Derry and Dublin IRA vols; **110** 'IRA activity', Dublin IRA vols; *UI*, June & July 1969; *IT*, 12 June 1969; Garda reports in Jus2000/36/3, NAI; **111** 'Meanwhile', *IT*, 9 Aug. and 18 Nov. 1969; Dublin IRA vols; 'Eyes', B. M. Walker, *Parliamentary*, pp. 78–81; *IN*, 7 April 1969; *UI*, May 1969; **112** 'But', *Belfast Newsletter*, 18 April 1969; CS minutes, 2 Dec. 1968, 27 Jan. 1969; *UI*, April & June 1969; S. Swan, *Official*, p. 268; *Bel Tel*, 5–10 Feb. 1969; **113** 'A major', AC minutes, 22 Dec. 1968, 4 Jan. 1969; CS minutes, 27 Jan., 17 Feb., 11 March, 31 March 1969; **114** 'Devlin's', *IN*, 21 April 1969; McMillen speech; Belfast IRA vols; *IT*, 22 April 1969; JIC, 16 June 1969 in CAB 186/3, NAUK; 'The events', Clann activists; FBI reports, 1969–70 in Prendiville collection, AIA; **115** 'Back in', *Ireland Today*, March & June 1969; **117** 'During', CS minutes, 14 July 1969; 'Some', Lane *int*, S. Flynn & P. Yeates, *Smack!*, p. 25; *IN*, 7 March 1969; Dublin splinter group member; **118** 'The IRA', AC minutes, 23 March & 28 April 1969; IRA vols; *Ir Pr*, 15 May 1969; *IT*, 21 May 1969; **119** 'Attempts', *IT*, 26 Sept. 1969; 'The Sinn Féin', CS minutes, 9 June 1969; *UI*, Jan & Oct. 1969; 'In June', AC minutes, 24 May 1969; CS minutes, 19 May 1969; *IT*, 11 & 17 June 1969; **120** 'Much', *UI*, May & Nov 1968, May 1969; *Crisis*, March 1969; **121** 'The relationship', *UI*, March & May 1969; D. Geraghty, *Luke*, p. 106; Dublin IRA vol.; 'Republican activity', Dept. Justice, 18 March & 14 July 1969 in Jus2000/36/3, NAI; **123** 'Also', *IT*, 5 July 1969; R. W. White, *Ó Brádaigh*, pp. 144–5; Dublin IRA vol.; Ryan, McKnight; **124** 'While', P. Taylor, *Provos*, pp. 45–6; *Sunday Press*, 24 Aug. 1969; McMillen speech; Belfast IRA vols; 'Confidence', *IT*, 24 June 1969; N. Ó Dochartaigh, *Civil Rights*, p. 107; *IN*, July 1969; Ó Brádaigh, Ryan; *This Week*, 7 Aug. 1970; **125** 'Barricades', E. McCann, *War*, pp. 58–70; White; Belfast IRA vols; **126** 'On 13 August', McMillen speech; Belfast IRA vols; **127** 'On 14 August', *IN*, 12–19 Aug. 1969; Belfast IRA vols; **128** 'Those involved', Belfast IRA vols; *IN*, 5 Sept. 1969; G. Adams, *Dawn*, p. 105; **129** 'Elsewhere', *IT*, 16–23 Aug. 1969; *The Plough*, June 1974; Dublin IRA vols; **130** 'The units', *IT*, 18–19 Aug. 1969; *UI*, Sept. 1969; R. English, *Armed Struggle*, p. 104; **131** 'Sinn Féin', CS minutes, 11 Aug. 1969; *IT*, 13–16 Aug. 1969; Fergus Whelan, Paddy Woodworth; **132** 'The IRA', *UI*, Sept. & Oct. 1969; *Bel Tel*, 26 Aug. 1969; *Ir Pr*, 23 Aug 1969; 'Politically', *IN*, 5 Sept. 1969; *UI*, Sept. 1969; AC minutes, 23 Aug. 1969; CS minutes, 1 Sept. & 6 Oct. 1969; Dunne; **133** 'Some of', Ó Comain, *Towards*; Ivan Barr, Ryan, White, Lane; Belfast and Dublin IRA vols; *IT*, 19 April 1971; **134** 'Republicans', AC minutes, 23 Aug. & 20 Sept. 1969; CS minutes, 20 Sept. 1969; BBC, 6 Sept. 2006; 'In Belfast', NI

Command, 1 Sept. 1969 in WO 305/3758, NAUK; *Bel Tel*, 8 Sept. 1969; Belfast IRA vols; Adams, *Dawn*, p. 126; J. Sullivan, *Memoir* (Belfast, N/D); **136** 'Remembering', *IT*, 29 April 1970; Curry, Sean O'Hare; **137** 'Meanwhile', J. O'Brien, *Arms Trial*, p. 66; Anon., *Fianna Fáil – The IRA Connection*; White, McCann; Belfast IRA vols; **138** 'The Special', P. Berry to J. Lynch, 8 June 1970 in Jus2001/6/10, NAI; J. Kelly in *The Blanket*, 17 Aug. 2006; McKnight; **139** 'it was becoming', O'Brien, *Arms*, pp. 77–8; Garda report 3C/437/70 in D. Keogh, *Jack Lynch*, pp. 272–9; *Ir Pr*, 11 June 1970; *UI*, Nov. & Dec. 1969; *IT*, 9 Dec. 1969; Belfast IRA vols; **140** 'The promise', O' Brien, *Arms*, p. 77; Belfast IRA vols; **141** 'The race', *IT*, 19 Nov. 1969, 14 Dec. 1971; B. Yeltsin, *Kremlin*, pp. 311–14; C. Andrew & V. Mitrokhin, *Mitrokhin*, p. 493; Dublin IRA vols; **142** 'Local Clan', *UI*, Sept. 1969; American-based activists; Joan McKiernan; FBI report, 27 Oct. 1969 in Prendiville, AIA; 'small donations', Dublin IRA vols; **143** 'The Dublin', Saor Éire member, Lane; 'In November', CS minutes, 10 Nov. 1969; *UI*, Oct. & Nov. 1969, *Comhar Mean Fomhair*, 1969; **144** 'Preparation', Ó Murchú, Mac Giolla; *IN*, 31 Jan 1990; White, *Ó Brádaigh*, p. 150; **145** 'The convention', Ryan; Dublin IRA vols; *IT*, 29 Dec. 1969; B. Anderson, *Cahill*, p. 185; *IN*, 10 Jan. 1970; *UI*, Jan. 1970; **146** 'The Sinn Féin', *Nuacht Náisúnta*, 26 Jan. 1970; *UI*, Feb. 1970; Kevin Smyth, Ryan; *An Phoblacht* (Dublin), Feb. 1970; **147** 'The split', O'Leary, Gregory, de Burca, Garland, Ryan; Tyrone PIRA vol.

5. Defence and Retaliation

Notes for pages 149 to 199

149 'The Official', *IT*, 22 Sept 1971; *IN*, 30 April 1970; BAI, 22 Oct. 1970 in WO 305/3783, NAUK; *IN*, 18 May 1970; *Ir Pr*, 12 Feb. 1971; Dublin OIRA vols; **150** 'Some of', American-based OIRA vols; *This Week*, 7 Aug. 1970; BAI, 16 April 1970 in WO 305/3783, NAUK; 'at Easter', *IN*, 30 April & 15 May 1970; Devlin in Van Voris, *Violence in Ulster*, pp. 190–5; US Embassy, Dublin, 18 May 1971, AP; **151** 'In Derry', *IN*, 28–29 April 1970; Belfast OIRA vols; BAI, 30 April 1970 in WO 305/3783, NAUK; McMillen in R. Sweetman, *On Our*, p. 197; **152** 'The clandestine', J. O'Brien, *Arms*, pp. 115–25; *IT*, 11 May 1970; 'Outside', Belfast OIRA vols; **154** 'Away', Dublin OIRA vols; 'The political', *UI*, July 1971; *Nuacht Náisúnta*, No. 27, 7 April 1970; *Hibernia*, 17 April 1970; **155** 'The consequences', *Derry Journal*, 3 April 1970; *IT*, 6 April 1970; BAI, 16 April 1970 in WO 305/3783, NAUK; Belfast OIRA vols; **156** 'Street', *IN*, 19 May 1970; *UI*, July 1970; R. J. Quinn, *Rebel*, pp. 164–5; 'On 3 July', Belfast OIRA vols; BAI, 9–11/July 1970 in WO 305/3783, NAUK; G. Warner, 'The Falls'; D. Barzilay, *The British Army*, pp. 11–16; **159** 'For the', *This Week*, 17 July 1970; Belfast OIRA vols; 'The problem', Ó Comain; BSI, 2 Feb. 2001; BAI, 22 Oct. 1970 in WO 305/3783, NAUK; Dublin OIRA vol.; **160** 'To ensure', Belfast OIRA vols; *Times*, 30 July 1971; Liam McMillen notes; 'Following', Harry McKeown; **161** 'Most', Harry Donaghy; BAI, 8 Oct & 3 Dec. 1970 in WO 305/3783, NAUK; *This Week*,

Dec. 1970; **162** 'In Belfast', *IN*, 8 Dec. 1970; *Sunday News*, 13 Dec. 1970; 'Ironically', RTÉ, *Féach*, 8 Feb. 1971; *UI*, March 1971; Belfast OIRA vols; *IT*, 10 & 18 March 1971; **164** 'Street', *IT*, 23 April & 6 July 1971; Belfast OIRA vols; 'In early', *IT*, 5 July 1971; Belfast OIRA vols; *This Week*, 5 March 1971; **165** 'The Officials', Terry Robson; *IN*, 3 Aug. 1971; **166** 'Such slogans', *IN*, 9–13 Aug. 1971; *IT*, 21 Aug. 1971; OIRA vols; PIRA vol.; **167** 'In the', Belfast OIRA vols; *IN*, 26 Aug. 1971; *UI*, Sept & Oct 1971; *Newry Reporter*, 9 Sept. 1971; *Derry Journal*, 21 Sept. 1971; **168** 'On 22 September', Curry; *IN*, 23 Sept. 1971; **169** 'On 5 October', *UI*, Nov. 1971; Belfast and Dublin OIRA vols; *IT*, 8 Dec. 1970; **170** 'Life on', OIRA vols; *This Week*, 12 Nov. 1971; S. Boyne, *Gunrunners*, p. 36; McKnight; JIC, Dec. 1971 in CAB 1869, NAUK; **171** 'During the winter', *IT*, 14 Dec 1971; *Newry Reporter*, 9 Dec. 1971; *Mid Ulster Observer*, 23 Dec. 1971; *UI*, Jan & Feb 1972; **172** 'Unlike the', OIRA GHQ member; *Hibernia*, 4 Feb. 1972; quoted in JIC, Dec. 1971 in CAB 1869, NAUK; *Lurgan Mail*, 21 Jan. 1972; OIRA 9, BSI; OIRA vol.; PIRA vol.; **173** 'In Derry', Derry OIRA vol.; *Derry Journal*, 21 Jan. & 2 Feb. 1972; OIRA testimonies, BSI; **174** 'On the day', OIRA testimonies, BSI; OIRA vols; *IT*, 1–5 Feb. 1972; E. McCann, *What Happened*; **175** 'Not surprisingly', Belfast OIRA vols; *IN*, 20 March 1972; Newry OIRA vol.; 'The Official', *IN*, 2 Feb. 1972; OIRA vols; *IT*, 18 March 1975; *UI*, March 1972; OIRA GAC minutes, 20 Oct. 1972, AP; *Mid Ulster Observer*, 2 March 1972; **177** 'One response', *UI*, July 1972; PM, 13 March 1972 in HO & NIO CJ4/193, NAUK; 'In early April', Commanders Diary, NI Log Sheets, 15 April 1972 in WO 305/4199, NAUK; Belfast OIRA vols; *UI*, May 1972; **179** 'Despite Goulding's', *UI*, May 1972; *Derry Journal*, 23 May 1972; *Sunday Press*, 28 May 1972; BBC, 30 May 1972; McCann, *War*; OIRA 7, BSI; Dublin OIRA vol.; White; **180** 'A meeting', OIRA vols; Ó Murchú; *UI*, June 1972; **181** 'In Belfast', OIRA vols; D. Beresford, *Ten Men*, p. 152; **182** 'The Official Fianna', D. Ó Seaghda, *Na Fianna*; Belfast OIRA; 'In fact', Belfast OIRA vols; *Nuacht Náisiúnta*, 8 Aug. 1972; M. Dillon & D. Lehane, *Political Murder*, pp. 84–6; *Strabane Chronicle*, 22 July 1972; **183** 'But the', Belfast OIRA vols; *UI*, Aug. & Sept. 1972; *Newry Reporter*, 2 Dept. 1972; **184** 'Around this', OIRA vols; E. O'Halpin *Intelligence, Security*; **186** 'In late September', Hughes in *The Blanket*, 8 May 2003; Belfast OIRA vols; *UI*, Nov. 1972; E. P. Rooney, 'From Opposition', p. 149; **187** 'Opposition', Derry OIRA vol., minutes of OIRA GACs, 20 Oct. & 9 Dec. 1972, AP; **188** 'Eoin', Ó Murchú; *IT*, 1 Dec. 1972; American-based OIRA vols; **189** 'The British', PM, 29 Aug. 1972 in HO & NIO CJ4/195, NAUK; OIRA Director Intelligence to units, 4 Oct. 1972, AP; 'In December', OIRA GAC minutes, 9 Dec. 1972; *IT*, 22 Dec. 1972; **190** 'By 1973', Belfast OIRA vols; McKeown, Mitchell, McMahon; **191** 'For example', *Newry Reporter*, 8 March 1973, *UI*, May 1973; OIRA vols; 'The one thing', Belfast OIRA vols; Dillon & Lehane, *Political Murder*, p. 285; **192** 'One of the', *IN*, 7 July 1973; *IT*, 5 & 10 Sept 1973; Garland; Belfast OIRA vols; *Newry Reporter*, 23 Aug. 1973; **194** 'The OIRA', *A Reporter's Guide to Ireland*, AP; Report of *Independent* Commission of Inquiry into the Dublin and Monaghan Bombings, p. 34; Belfast OIRA vol.; **195** 'In Derry', Derry OIRA vol.; Belfast OIRA vols; *IN*, 16 Feb

1974; **196** 'In 1974', C. Andrew & V. Mitrokhin, *Mitrokhin*, p. 502; OIRA vols; 'Finance', OIRA vols; *IT*, *Newry Reporter*, 16 Jan. 1974, 10 April 1974, 11 July 1975; Rooney, 'From Opposition', p. 142; 'Unlike', Newry OIRA; *Newry Reporter*, 4 July & 24 Oct. 1974; **198** 'During August', *IT*, 3 Aug. 1974; *IN*, 8 Aug. 1974; *IT*, 28 Aug. 1974; OIRA vols; PIRA vol.; *Times*, 12 Nov. 1974.

6. Civil Rights not Civil War

Notes for pages 200 to 233
200 'Prior', *IN*, 12 Jan. & 3 March 1970; Smyth; *IN*, 17 Aug. 1970; *UI*, March 1970; McMahon; CS minutes, 19 April 1971; **201** 'The emergence', M. Lynch on *Gallery*, BBC 1, 11 May 1983; *IN*, 2 May 1970, 30 April 1971; *IP*, 11 Jan. 1974; McMahon; **202** 'The political', *IT*, 8 Dec. 1970; CS minutes, 13 July 1970; *Ir Pr*, 6 Feb. 1971, *International*, Sept. 1971, *IN*, 12 April 1971; *Mid Ulster Observer*, 15 April 1971; **203** 'Despite', CS minutes, 30 Aug. 1971; McMahon; **204** 'On his', Ó Murchú; *UI*, May, June, July 1971; 'The first', *This Week*, 17 Dec. 1970; *UI*, Aug. 1970; CS minutes, 16 Nov. 1970, 5 Dec. 1970, 1 March 1971; *Ir Pr*, 10 Aug. 1971; US Embassy to State Dept, 1 March 1971, AP; Des O'Hagan, Heffernan; **205** 'While the', *Freedom Manifesto*, 1970; Brian Brennan; **206** 'Unionism', John Nixon, Jim Monaghan, Robson, McCann; **207** 'Some Official', Ó Murchú, Bob Purdie, Yeates; *IT*, 18 June 1973; **208** 'The Catholic Church', *IT*, 5 Jan. 1972; Devlin in Van Voris, *Violence*, p. 191; BAI, 13 Aug. 1970 in WO 305/3783, NAUK; *IT*, 1 Nov. 1971; Mulready letter, 4 Nov. 1971, AP; 'Labour's', *IT*, 25 Oct. 1971; *Hibernia*, 20 Oct. 1972; **209** 'For most', Ó Tuathail, P. J. McClean; Republican Clubs leaflets, Aug. 1971; E. McCann, *War*, p. 103; *Derry Journal*, 2 May 1972; **210** 'Scores', Art McMillen, S. Lynch, Mackin; OIRA prisoners; **212** 'Prison life', Dublin OIRA prisoners; Tony Moriarty email, 1 Sept. 2004; *UI*, Feb. 1973; Mackin; *Nuacht Náisiúnta*, 9 Oct. 1973; *IP*, 23 Nov. 1973; *An Eochair*, 1973–4; **214** 'The Irish', Helena Sheehan; Belfast OIRA vols; Purdie; *IT*, 4 Feb. 1972; C. Demet, *Desertion*; **215** 'The Officials', *Nuacht Náisiúnta*, 23 Feb. 1971; memo in FCO 87/536–1, NAUK; Young Liberals to OSF, 29 Dec. 1971; *Irish Echo*, 12 June 1971, 25 Sept. 1971, 12 Feb. 1972, 4 March 1972; Sandy Boyer, Bob Lowery, Sheehan; Leadership republican movement to IRC, Sept. 1972; **216** 'In Britain', *IT*, 24 July 1970; Yeates, Collins, Seamus McDonagh; **218** 'One consequence', Margaret Smyth, Report on Belfast Republican Clubs, Aug. 1972, AP; 'On the role of violence', Belfast OIRA vols; 'The state of the movement in South Down/South Armagh', Aug. 1972, AP; **219** 'Many Northern', Nixon, Kelly, Jimmy Jordan, Moriarty, Frank Keoghan, Monaghan; *Hibernia*, 3 March 1972; **221** 'On both sides', Ó Murchú, Yeates; *UI*, Oct. 1970; **222** 'Although', Robson; *UI*, Sept. & Oct. 1972; OIRA Army Council minutes, 8 Oct. 1972, AP; OIRA executive election, Oct. 1972, AP; **223** 'After the', *International*, Sept. 1971; *Where We Stand*, Derry Republican Clubs report, 23 Aug. 1972; *IN*, 23 March 1973; memo, 31 Jan. 1973 in FCO 87/177, NAUK; **224** 'In response', *IN*, 10 May 1973; *Newry Reporter*, 7 June 1973;

Derry Journal, 8 June 1973; Republican Clubs meeting, Mornington 27–28 July 1973, AP; Belfast OIRA vols; **225** 'The Official', *UI*, June 1973; Republican Clubs meeting, Mornington 27–28 July 1973, AP; **226** 'Even more', *IT*, 9 Oct. 1972; McKeown, Mitchell, O'Hagan; K. Myers, *Watching the Door*, pp. 167–9; OIRA to UVF, 1974, AP; *Combat*, 8 April 1974; **228** 'A powerful', Belfast OIRA vols; Report Mornington meeting, 8 June 1974, AP; **229** 'In the US', reports on IRC, spring & Nov. 1974; Dublin OIRA vols; Collins; *Rosc Catha*, Feb., March, June, July, Nov., Dec. 1974; **230** 'During this', McKeown; Belfast OIRA vols; Liam McMillen notes; **232** 'In Long Kesh', *IN*, 14–16 Sept. 1974; Curry, Nixon, Mackin; *UI*, Nov. 1974; *IN*, 8 April 1974.

7. Towards the Revolutionary Party

Notes on pages 234 to 281

234 'Events', CS minutes, Jan. 1973, June 1971; Goulding in *Inside the IRA* (1974); CS minutes, 20 July 1970; Heffernan; Dublin OSF members; **235** 'An interested', reports from US Embassy to State Dept, 19 Jan. & 3 Feb. 1970, AP (courtesy Tara Keenan); 'The British', confidential report, 6 July 1970 in FCO 33/1204, NAUK; **236** 'The Officials', *UI*, Aug. & Sept. 1970; *Hibernia*, 25 Sept. 1970; *IT*, 11 Sept. 1971; *UI*, Oct. 1971; **238** 'The housing', Dunne; *UI*, June 1970; *IT*, 2 July 1970; F. Whelan, *Dublin Housing Action: An Analysis* (N/D); CS minutes, 30 Nov. 1970; **240** 'As the', *UI*, March, 1970, July 1971; *Nuacht Náisiúnta*, 30 May 1971; **241** 'Internal', *IT*, 21 Jan 1971; *Vanguard*, Oct. 1971; CS minutes, 13 July 1970; *Nuacht Náisiúnta*, Jan. 1970, 30 May 1971; CS minutes, 15 Nov. 1971; **242** 'At all', CS minutes, 9 Feb., 2 June, 30 Oct., 6 Dec. 1970, 1 & 8 March 1971; *UI*, Dec. 1970; Gregory; 'Despite', *UI*, April 1970; *IT*, 7 July 1971; CS minutes, 10 May 1971; *IT*, 14 April 1971; J. Horgan, *Broadcasting*, pp. 79, 104–5; Donohue; *Hibernia*, 16 July 1971; Dublin OIRA vols; *Ir Pr*, 13 May 1972; **244** 'In December', CS minutes, 29 Nov. 1971; Malone, Dunne, F. Whelan; **245** 'Despite the', *UI*, Oct 1971; CS minutes, 3 March 1972; de Burca; **246** 'One of those', Johnston, D. Blatherwick, 18 Jan. 1972 in FCO 87/531–1, NAUK; 'The Official', *IT*, 1 Jan. 1971; Malone; **247** 'Despite', *Sunday Independent*, 12 Dec. 1971; Heffernan to MacQuaid, 16 Dec. 1971, AP; *This Week*, 9 Aug. 1970; D. Ó Corráin, *Rendering*, pp. 163–4; State of Security Rep. of Ireland 1972, 19 May 1972 in CAB 134/3574 & Report, 10 Jan. 1972 in FCO 87/7, NAUK; **248** 'Jimmy', Jimmy Jordan, Liz Doyle, Ó Murchú; Dublin OSF members; **249** 'Disputes', North-West OSF report, 4 Nov. 1971; Dublin CC report, 19 May 1972; Arden letter, 22 Dec. 1972, AP; **250** 'The influx', Purdie; *UI*, May 1971; Bodenstown address, June 1972; **251** 'Key', Education Dept report 1972; Mornington report, 1973; Sheehan; **252** 'Maintaining', Mornington report, 1973; McMahon, Gerry Flynn; *Foghlaim*, summer 1973; 'Garland', Goulding in J. Holland & H. McDonald, *Deadly*, p. 23; *Intercontinental Press*, 31 Aug. 1978; Purdie; Gerry Foley email, 14 Sept. 2004; **254** 'Meanwhile', Des Geraghty, Sheehan, Malone, O'Hagan, Garland, Paul Sweeney, Dunne, Donohue; **255** 'The thinking', RIDD report, May 1972; CS minutes, 24 July, 9 & 23 Oct., 6 Nov., 4 Dec. 1972; **256** 'Alongside', Sheehan, O'Hagan, John McManus, Ó Murchú, Noel Dowling, Liz Doyle, F. Whelan, Ryan; **257** 'On the', OIRA officers; **259** 'A priority', Yeates, Garland; report on *Irish People*, 14 March 1974; 'With most', Heffernan, Gregory; Dublin OIRA vols; *UI*, April 1972; **260** 'Recruitment', Dublin OIRA vols; **261** 'In February', SF Election News, Feb. 1973; C. Bird, *This is*, p. 20; *UI*, March 1920; 'Some notes on the election and results', Aug. 1973; **262** 'Discussion', 'Discussion Documents on Organisation and Structure', 1973; *Bel Tel*, 13 Nov. 1973; **264** 'Meetings', OIRA vols; 'The Organisation of the Proletariat's Armed Forces', AP; H. Patterson, *Illusion*, p. 148; 'In Dublin', Ryan; OIRA vols; *IT*, 14 Sept. 1973; **265** 'With', CS minutes, 2 April, 3 Sept., 10 Oct. 1973; **266** 'Attempts', confidential telegrams, 26 Feb. & 1 March 1972 in PREM 15/1046, NAUK; 'In October', *UI*, Oct. 1973; Garland, O'Hagan, Yeates; **268** 'In sections', Ó Murchú, Yeates, Foley; *IT*, 26 Nov. 1973, *Hibernia*, 30 Nov. 1973; British Embassy, 28 Nov. 1973 in FCO 87/178, NAUK; Ard Fheis report, 1973; **270** 'Outside', North Munster CC, 6 Dec. 1973; CS minutes, 10 Dec. 1973; letters to CS, 3 Dec. 1973 & 21 Jan. 1974; Robson; **271** 'The first', OIRA courts martial report, 21 Feb. 1974; M. Bernard, *Daughter*, p. 116; Costello to AC, 7 April 1974; Report of Committee into Allegations of Irregularities at Ard Fheis, 23 March 1974; **273** 'In the June', *UI*, July 1974; Kelly; OIRA orders 14 & 17, July 1974; Woodworth; **274** 'Since not all', Keoghan, de Burca; Education Course, 1974; CS minutes, 3 Nov. 1974; Dublin AGM report, 1974, AP; **275** 'Ó Murchú's', OIRA GAC industrial report, Sept. 1974, AP; CS minutes, 21 Sept. 1974; *Magill*, May 1982; O'Leary, Eric Byrne; **278** 'For some', Small Farmers Defence Association report 1974; *UI*, Aug. 1974; *IT*, 23 July 1974; *Clár*, Anti-Imperialist Festival, 1974; McManus; **279** 'Republicanism', CS minutes, 14 May 1974; *IT*, 24 Oct. 1974; *Irish Independent*, 5 Nov. 1974; Bird, *This is*, p. 21; **280** 'As 1974', Ó Murchú; Ard Fheis report, 1974.

8. 'Brothers Fighting Brothers'

Notes for pages 282 to 314

282 'For over', *UI*, May 1975; *Intercontinental Press*, 9 June 1975; *IT*, 3 March, 9 April, 5 July 1975; American-based OIRA vols; *IT*, 7 Dec. 1974; *Starry Plough* (Dublin), April 1975; *IT*, 10 Dec. 1974; **283** 'About', Official SF report, 1975, AP; *IT*, 9 Dec. 1975; OIRA intelligence document, AP; *Starry Plough*, Jan. 1976; G. Lynch; Belfast OIRA vols; **284** 'Northern', Barr; Co. Derry OIRA vols; Belfast OIRA vols; *In Dublin*, 14 May 1987; OIRA intel. report, AP; **285** 'There was', McMahon, Flynn, S. Lynch; *UI*, March 1975; **286** 'The far left', Brian Trench, McCann; *IT*, 27 Feb. 1975; *IN*, 4 Jan & 30 April 1975; **287** 'The Officials', *Hibernia*, 7 March 1975; *Starry Plough*, April 1975; OIRA intel. Report, AP; 'Some in', Belfast OIRA vols; AC minutes, 15 Feb. 1975; McKeown; *Intercontinental Press*, 9 June 1975; *IT*, 28 Feb. 1975; **288** 'In his', *IT*, 28 Feb. & 1 March 1975; McMillen notes; **289** 'Tension', Sheehan, Gregory, Garland, Heffernan; OSF statement, 2 March 1975; **290** 'There were', McKeown; *IT*, 3, 5 & 7 March 1975; mediation notes, AP; *Andersonstown News*, 8 March 1975; *IT*, 31 March 1975; **291** 'The Official', *UI*, April & May 1975; **292** 'Even', Belfast OIRA vols; *UI*, March 1975; *Sunday News*, 16 Feb. 1975; *IT*, 5 March & 16 April 1975; **294** 'The Officials and UVF', *IT*, 21 May 1975; *Hibernia*, 1 July 1975; Mitchell; *Combat*, March 1975; **295** 'Pressure', *IT*, 13 Feb., 22 Feb., 22 April 1975; Newry OIRA vol.; *Strabane Chronicle*, 10 May 1975; **296** 'On Monday', *Andersonstown News*, 3 May 1975; J. Holland & H. McDonald, *Deadly*, p. 69; *IN*, 30 April 1975; *IT*, 1 May 1975; *UI*, May & June 1975; **297** 'In Belfast', Belfast OIRA vols; Dublin OIRA vol.; *IT*, 11 Dec. & 20 Dec. 1975; S. Lynch; **298** 'The political', AC minutes, 19 July, 20 Sept., 19 Oct., 1975; CS minutes, 16 June 1975; **299** 'Although', *UI*, June 1975; *IT*, 20 Dec. 1975; 'The People v. B. Madden', in Jus2006/145/26, NAI; OIRA vols; **300** 'On 22 June', *IT*, 26 June 1975; *An Eochair*, No. 11, 1975; OIRA vols; *IT*, 13 May and 23 June 1975; **301** 'In bringing', OIRA Operations Dept. report, 1975, AP; OIRA vols; CS minutes, 3 Feb. 1975; **302** 'The new', Ó Murchú; Dublin OIRA vols; Comhairle Ceanntair, 28 March 1975; **303** 'The internal', CS minutes, 10 March, 7 April, 14 April 1975; letters, 24 April 1975, AP; **304** 'As head', OIRA vols; *Teoiric*, 1975; Nolan; **305** 'While some', Mornington report, 28–29 June 1975, AP; RPC Annual Report, 1974–5; OSF membership forms, 1975; CS minutes, 3 Feb. & 6 Oct. 1975; Woodworth; **306** 'The feud', *Sunday World*, 12 Jan. 1975; *Sunday News*, 5 Jan. 1975; *Irish Echo*, 3 Oct. 1981, 29 March 2000; Pyle letter, 6 March 1975; 'Propaganda', 1975, AP; **308** 'The party's press', *UI*, Dec. & Jan. 1975; *IT*, 2 Dec. 1974; AC minutes, 20 Sept. 1975; CS minutes, 29 Sept. 1975; report, 18 Oct. 1975; OIRA vols; *IT*, 3 & 20 Oct. 1975; **309** 'In June', *UI*, April, May, June, July 1975; Dublin OSF members; **310** 'In the North', *Newry Reporter*, 24 Aug. 1975; *Andersonstown News*, 23 Aug. 1975; *UI*, Oct. 1975; Mornington report, 28–29 June 1975, AP; *Newry Reporter*, 29 May 1975; Newry OIRA vols; **312** 'In Belfast', *UI*, July 1975; *Derry Journal*, 30 May 1975; *Strabane Chronicle*, 9 Aug. 1975; *Sunday News*, 28 Sept. 1975; *Newry Reporter*, 9 Oct. 1975; *Andersonstown News*, 18 Oct. 1975; *Hibernia*, 16 May 1975; OSF *Handbook for New Members* (1975).

9. The 'Pogrom'

Notes for pages 315 to 335

315 'As darkness', *IT*, 30 Oct. 1975; *IN*, 30 Oct. 1975; O'Hare, Smyth, McKnight; Republican Clubs, *Pogrom!*; **316** 'When it', O'Hagan; Belfast OIRA vols; *IN*, 31 Oct. & 1–5 Nov. 1975; *IT*, 1–5 Nov. 1975; *Belfast Newsletter*, 1 Nov. 1975; *IT*, 8 Nov. 1975; **318** 'The main', *IN*, 1–5 Nov. 1975; Smyth, Ó Tuathail, McKeown; *IN*, 6–12 Nov. 1975; *Republican News*, 15 Nov. 1975; Belfast OIRA vols; **320** 'The Clonard', Belfast OIRA vols; O' Hagan; *IT*, 12 Nov. 1975; O'Hare; *IT*, 15 Nov. 1975; 'Confidential Mediators report on Truce 11 Feb. 1976', AP; Republican Clubs, *Pogrom!*; *IT*, 8 Nov. 1975; McKeown; **322** 'The events', Belfast OIRA vols;

McMahon; OIRA intelligence report, 12 Jan. 1976, AP; O'Hare, Smyth, Brennan; *Irish Echo*, 8 Nov. 1975; Ó Tuathail; Ard Fheis report, 1976; Dublin OIRA vols; *IT*, 31 Jan. 1976; Jordan; **324** 'The scars', Ard Fheis report; *IT*, 5–6 Jan. & 19 Jan. 1976; *Newry Reporter*, 8 Jan. 1976; *IT*, 7 Oct. 1976; Republican Clubs discussion document, Dec. 1977; **325** 'Sinn Féin', CS minutes, 23 Feb. 1976; AC minutes, 1 Jan. & 26 March 1976; *IT*, 12 June 1976; CS minutes, 17 May 1976; *IP*, 26 March 1976; Keoghan, De Rossa, B. Whelan, Bernie Hughes; CS minutes, 11 Oct. 1976; *Contact*, Oct/Nov 1976; *UI*, March 1976; **326** 'By 1976', USI congress report, 9–12 Jan. 1975; *IT*, 15 Jan. 1976; AC minutes, 26 March 1976; John Lowry; CS minutes, 23 Feb. 1976; *UI*, May & Sept 1976; *IP*, 20 Feb. 1976; AC minutes, 26 March 1976; L. McManus letter (1976); *UI*, July 1976; **328** 'The Industrial', *UI*, Jan. 1976; *IT*, 21 Nov. 1975, 11 Feb. 1976; J. Horgan, *Broadcasting*, p. 145; Dublin Industrial Dept members; Ó Murchú; Dublin OSF members; Woodworth; *UI*, Jan. 1976; AC minutes, 25 Sept. 1976; CS minutes, 12 July 1976; D. Kelleher, *Buried*, pp. 349–51; **329** 'The sixtieth', *IT*, 2 April 1976; CS minutes, 25 Oct. & 4 Dec. 1976; James Connolly Heron; IRSP *Framed* (1979); **331** 'The phasing', *UI*, Feb. 1976; *Newry Reporter*, 19 Feb. 1976; *IT*, 19 Jan. 1976; *UI*, March 1976; AC minutes, 26 March, 3 April, 29 May 1976; OIRA prisoners; *IN*, 25 May 1976; NIO 26 Oct. 1976 in PCC 1/5/28, PRONI; **332** 'A Stormont', *IT*, 2 Jan. 2007; State of Security Assessment, 28 Oct. 1976 in FCO 87/536, NAUK; OIRA vols; *IT*, 14 June 1976; *Newry Reporter*, 22 April 1976; *UI*, Sept. 1976; E. P. Rooney, 'From Opposition'; AC minutes, 3 April 1976; **334** 'By 1976', *UI*, Dec. 1976; CS minutes, 6 Sept. 1976; *UI*, Aug. & Oct. 1976; AC minutes, 26 March, 3 April, 27 Nov. 1976; *IT*, 16 & 24 July 1976; report, 28 Oct. 1976 in FCO 87/536, NAUK; *UI*, June & Nov. 1976.

10. A Historic Mission

Notes for pages 336 to 376

336 'There was', *UI*, Feb. 1977; Sweeney; *IT*, 24 Jan. 1977; **337** 'Although', CS minutes, 31 Jan. & 14 Feb. 1977; de Burca; AC minutes, 3 Dec. 1977; Sweeney; Sinn Féin The Workers' Party, *The Irish Industrial Revolution*; Brian Whelan; **340** 'An attraction', Shay Cody; *UI*, May 1977; Ó Murchú; Irish Socialist, *Which Way for Socialism?* (1977); CPI 'Memorandum to Fraternal Communist and Workers Parties', 30 March 1977, AP; CS minutes, 14 Feb. 1977; SFWP to international organizations, July 1977; **341** 'Smullen', Dowling, Woodworth, Heffernan to Coiste Seasta, 26 Oct. 1977; AC minutes, 3 Dec. 1977; CS minutes, 17 & 31 Jan., 14 & 21 Feb., 12 & 25 April, 11 & 16 July 1977; *Hibernia*, 3 Aug. 1977; **343** 'Nationally', SFWP, 7 June 1977; H. Patterson, *Ireland*, p. 269; *IT*, 18 June 1977; *IP*, 24 June 1977; Cork poster, 1977; **344** 'In the aftermath', *UI*, July 1977; SFWP election report, 1977; CS minutes, 28 June 1977; **345** 'During the', CS minutes, 1 & 4 July 1977; Woodworth; AC minutes, 16 July & 24 Sept. 1977; CS minutes, 8 & 15 Aug. 1977; **346** 'The Labour', Rep. of Irl. Dept report Socialist

Labour Party in FCO 87/602, NAUK; *IT*, 6 & 10 Oct. 1977; **348** 'The late 1970s',
C. Coulter, *Students*; *IT*, 20–21 Jan. 1980; IDYM minutes, 28–29 March 1980;
report 'IDYM-Students', 1981; AC minutes, 24 Sept. 1977; 'The Party and USI'
(1979), AP; **349** 'The recruitment', Dowling; *IT*, 9 Oct. 1978; Donohue; *IT*,
12 March 1997; *Starry Plough*, Dec. 1980; Cody; *Hibernia*, 12 & 26 Oct. 1978;
AC minutes, 26 Nov. 1977; **351** 'SFWP's', Byrne; *UI*, March 1978; CS minutes,
3 & 29 April, 5 May, 3 & 17 July, 12 Sept., 8 & 17 Oct., 7 Nov. 1977, 3 July, 6
Dec. 1978; Woodworth; *UI*, Feb. & Dec. 1978; *IT*, 5 Sept. 1978; *USI News*, April
1979; McMahon, Flynn; *Clár*, Ard Fheis, 1978–80; **353** 'Domestically', CS minutes,
13 Feb. & 8 Aug. 1978; *IP*, 7 Jan. 1977; *UI*, June 1978; *IP*, 3 March 1978; *UI*, Oct.
1979; CS minutes, 10 & 17 Dec. 1977, 6 Feb. & 11 Dec. 1978; **355** 'When Jack
Lynch's', F. Whelan, Cody; S. Cody, J. O'Dowd & P. Rigney, *Parliament*, p. 231;
Notes & Comments, April 1978; **356** 'The Irish People', CS minutes, 14 Jan. 1977;
IP, 4 March, 12 Aug., 7 Oct. 1977, 31 March 1978; Garland; *Notes & Comments*,
Dec. 1977; Yeates; *IP*, 5 Aug. 1977; Donohue, Cody, F. Whelan; **358** 'The influ-
ence', *Magill*, April 1979; *IT*, 3 March 1979; *UI*, March 1979; *IT*, 5 March 1979;
Hibernia, 15 March 1979; *IT*, 23 March 1979; *IP*, 23 March 1979; **360** 'The show',
IT, 21–22 March 1979; Patterson, *Ireland*, p. 274; CS minutes, 7 & 14 Nov. 1977;
UI, Dec. 1977; *IP*, 6 Jan. 1978; Yeates; *Workers' Life*, Nov. 1980; *Magill*, Feb. 1983;
361 'The gap', IDYM minutes, 29 March 1980, 11 April 1981; O'Hagan, Flynn;
Teoiric, summer 1979; **362** 'As the Soviets', CS minutes, 11 Nov. 1980; IDYM
minutes, 12 Oct. 1980; Sinn Féin The Workers' Party, *Those Who Leave*; *IT*, 23 June
1980; *IP*, 14 Dec. 1980; Yeates; **363** 'Despite', SFWP memo, 10 Aug. 1978; CPI,
8 Jan. 1979; SFWP, 14 Aug. 1979; CPI, 1 Oct. 1979, AP; **364** 'Despite these', CS
minutes, 3 Oct. 1977; Dowling, Yeates; *IT*, 8 March & 6 April 1980; J. Horgan,
Broadcasting, p. 167; **366** 'In total', *IP*, 11, 18, 25 May 1979; *Hibernia*, 24 May 1979;
Cody; *IP*, 15 June 1979, 22 Jan. 1980; *Workers' Life*, June 1980; **367** 'The party',
O'Leary script, AP; Liam Maguire letter, 21 Nov. 1979; regional party meetings
report, 1979; Paddy Gallagher; **368** 'The matter', *IT*, 23 Jan. 1980; *IP*, 22 Jan. 1980;
F. Whelan, Cody; *IT*, 20–22 & 24 Jan. 1980, 16–19 Jan. 1981; *Workers' Life*,
Feb. 1981; **369** 'The 1980', *UI*, March 1980; *IT*, 10 March 1980; **370** 'The Ard
Fheis', *Hibernia*, 13 March 1980; CS minutes, 20 Oct. & 11 Nov. 1980; **371** 'While
Garland', *USI News*, March 1979; Gerry Gregg, Fintan Cronin; *IT*, 23 June 1980;
Woodworth, Patrick Kinsella; **373** 'The input', Garland; *Irish Independent*, 10 Oct.
2000; *Ir Pr*, 2 Aug. 1980; *Magill*, June 2005; Gregg, Cronin; CS minutes, 14 & 21
Jan., 23 Jan., 29 April 1980, 2 Feb. 1981; *Hibernia*, 24 Jan. 1980; **374** 'Sales of', *IT*,
8 March 1979; Flynn; *Workers' Life*, Nov. 1980; **375** 'Although', John Ryan; CS
minutes, 14 Jan., 19 & 26 May, 21 July 1980; SFWP membership forms, 1980–1;
Jordan, Woodworth; **376** 'The problem', CS minutes, 26 Jan & 2 Feb 1981; General
Secretary's report, Ard Fheis, 1981; *IT*, 23 June 1980.

11. Peace, Work and Class Politics

Notes for pages 377 to 400

377 'After', E. P. Rooney, 'From Opposition', p. 256; *IN*, 2 Feb., 7 May & 4 Dec. 1977; *UI*, Feb & May 1977; **378** 'The Clubs', *Newry Reporter*, 28 April 1977; *IT*, 12 & 14 April 1977; *UI*, May & June 1977; *IN*, 19–21 May 1977; **379** 'Early summer', *Newry Reporter*, 30 June 1977; *IN*, 2 June 1977; M. Smyth; P. Lundy & M. McGovern, *Ardoyne*, p. 323; *IN*, 28–29 June 1977; G. Adams, *Dawn*, p. 255; Belfast OIRA vols; S. Lynch; **380** 'Despite', *UI*, Aug. 1977; Belfast OIRA vols; *IN*, 2 May 1977; *Ballymurphy News*, 16 April 1977; *IP*, 1 April 1977; *Workers' Life*, July 1980; *Ballymurphy News*, 23 March 1978; **381** 'The Clubs', *IP*, 9 Dec. 1977; *IN*, 25 Sept. 1977; *Ballymurphy News*, 12 Oct. 1978; Barr; *IN*, 2 Aug. & 24 Dec. 1977; **382** 'Controversies', *Fortnight*, March 1984; *IN*, 24 Dec. 1977; L. Clarke, *Broadening*, pp. 62–7; *IT* 23 Jan. 1978; **383** 'In Coalisland', *Notes & Comments*, Feb. 1978; AC minutes, 18 Feb. 1978; *UI*, Feb. 1978; *Clár*, Ard Fheis, 1978; *UI*, Dec. 1978; CS minutes, 19 Dec. 1977; **384** 'It was clear', *UI*, May 1978; *IN*, 3 March 1978; *Starry Plough*, 1977; *Ballymurphy News*, 1977–8; CS minutes, 6 June 1978; *Clár*, Ard Fheis, 1978; *IN*, 31 July 1978; Yeates, S. Lynch, McMahon, Smyth, O'Hare, Seamus Murphy; CS minutes, 17 Oct. 1977; Brennan; **386** 'Industrial Department', Mornington meeting, 8 June 1978, AP; AC minutes, 2 Sept. 1978; *Clár*, Ard Fheis, 1979; *UI*, Nov 1978; *IN*, 29 Nov. 1979; *UI*, May 1979; *Newry Reporter*, 19 April 1979; **387** 'The Republican Clubs', *IN*, 30 Jan. 1979; AC minutes, 1 July 1979; *Irish Socialist*, May 1979; *UI*, June 1979; Barr; *IN*, 11 March 1978; AC minutes, 13 Jan. 1979; *IN*, 12 Sept. 1979; **388** 'The one place', *UI*, July 1978, Jan. 1979; CS minutes, 29 April, 10 May 1980; *Irish Echo*, 10 May 1980; CS minutes, 8 Dec. 1980; *Workers' Life*, Dec. 1980; Clann letter, 26 March 1977; *Magill*, Sept. 1979; Clann documents, 1979, 1980, AP; CS minutes, 16 July 1979, 3 June 1980; **390** 'Amid', *UI*, Nov. 1978; AC minutes, 31 March 1979; *IP*, 27 April 1979; Henry Patterson, Liam Clarke, Smyth, O'Hare; **391** 'Despite', Belfast Central report (1979), AP; Smyth; Belfast RCWP members report, 29 July 1979, AP; Armagh & South Down RCWP members meeting, 29 July 1979, AP; Belfast AGM report, 14 April 1980, AP; Brian Feeney; **393** 'The hostility', *Ballymurphy News*, March 1979, 7 Oct 1979; Peter Heathwood, Murphy; CS minutes, 12 Dec. 1977, 14 Aug. 1978; *UI*, July 1978; *UI*, Oct. 1979; *Teoiric*, winter 1977/78; **394** 'At a RCWP', Northern members conference report, 27–28 Sept. 1980, AP; Clarke, K. Smyth, Patterson; RCWP NI regional meeting, 11 Sept. 1980; Belfast RCWP AGM, 14 April 1989, AP; Brennan, Smyth, McMahon; **396** 'The Clubs members', *Workers' Life*, May & June 1980; NI Executive RCWP, 31 Aug., 29 Sept. 1980; CS minutes, 11 Nov. 1980; *Hibernia*, 25 June 1980; *IT*, 25 June 1980; **397** 'Political life', *Clár*, Ard Fheis, 1979; *IN*, 13 June 1980; CS minutes, 1 Dec. 1980; 'H-Block: the Socialist Perspective' (1980); *Women's View*, winter 1980; *IN*, 28 Oct. 1980; *IT*, 18 Dec. 1980; *IT*, 25 June 1980; CS minutes, 1 Sept. 1980; Donaghy, O'Hare; *IN*, 21 Nov. 1980; **399** 'The party', *IP*, 6 Feb & March 1981; *Northern People*, 16 Jan., 6 & 27 Feb. 1981; *IP*, 13 March 1981; S. Lynch; *IT*, 1 March 1980.

12. Group B

Notes for pages 401 to 421

401 'Nobody', OIRA Army Council document, 1977, AP; 'On April', *IN*, 27 April
& 15 Dec. 1977; Belfast Group B members; **402** 'Group B', *IT*, 23 July, 25 Nov.,
6 Oct. 1977, 20 Nov. 1980; Group B members; 'The murder', *IT*, 6–7 Oct. 1977;
Garda source; *Starry Plough*, July 1982; OIRA intelligence report, 12 Jan. 1976,
AP; J. B. Bell, *Tactics*, pp. 77–81; Belfast Group B members; **403** 'Similarly', *IT*,
2 Aug. 1977; Group B members; Army Council member; J. B. Bell, *Troubles*,
p. 283; Group B members Belfast, Newry and Dublin; **404** 'Group B', Group B
and SFWP members Dublin, Newry, Wicklow; Irish Army Intelligence report,
15 Feb. 1977 in D/T 2008/79/31089, NAI; 'Northern Ireland: Future Terrorist
Trends' in S. Cronin, *Nationalism*, pp. 340–1; **405** 'Training', Group B members;
406 'Although', Group B members; Garda source; SFWP members; *IT*, 2 Nov.
1978; **407** 'Internally', Group B members; R. Dunphy 'The Contradictory Politics',
pp. 117–37; *Dundalk Democrat*, 17 May & 14 June 1980; Belfast OIRA documents,
1975, AP; Long Kesh OIRA prisoners communiqué to leadership, 25 April 1977,
AP; **409** 'Another view', *IT*, 23 June 1980; Trench; CS minutes, 17 Sept. 1980;
IT, 25 June 1980; 'What the party', *Notes & Comments*, Dec. 1981; *IT*, 26 Oct.
1991; financial report to WP Ard Chomhairle, 7 Sept. 1991, AP; SFWP member;
410 'In the North', RCWP member; *IN*, 15 & 28 April 1977, 10 June 1978, 14 July
1980; *Newry Reporter*, 21 July 1977; *IN*, 25 Oct. & 4 Nov. 1977, 6 & 15 June 1978,
4 Feb. 1981; *Starry Plough*, April 1978; *IN*, 22 April 1980; **411** 'The uneasy', *IN*,
1 & 4 Sept. 1980; Dublin Group B members; CS minutes, 27 Nov. 1978; CPI to
SFWP, 8 Jan. 1979, AP; **412** 'But the', *IT*, 23 Nov. 1981; *Hibernia*, Sept. 1980; *UI*,
Dec. 1978, Oct. 1979; *IT*, 26 June 1980; **413** 'Another function', 'Reaction in
Ireland', Group B intelligence report, 27 March 1977, AP; **414** 'Although', Group
B members; Army Council members; RCWP member; E. P. Rooney, 'From
Opposition', p. 143; Belfast Group B member; **415** 'The need', *IT*, 5 Sept. 1978;
G. O'Brien, *An Garda*, pp. 103–4; *IT*, 10 Oct. 1978; Group B members; **416** 'By
the early', Army Council members; Dublin Group B members; *IT*, 29 June 1983;
Workers' Life, 1981–2; S. Flynn & P. Yeates, *Smack*, pp. 43–6; **417** 'In the context',
Army Council member; McKeown, Barr; Group B members; **419** 'In Belfast', *IT*,
21 Jan. 1978; *Watchdog*, BBC 1, 1 Jan. 1984; *IT*, 25 June 1980; McKeown; *IN*,
27 Jan. 1984; J. Cusack & H. McDonald, *UDA*, pp. 400–1; *IN*, 12 March 1983;
Group B members.

13. Hunger Strikes, Haughey and Heroin

Notes on pages 422 to 449

422 'On 1 March', D. Beresford, *Ten Men*, pp. 30–62; *Northern People*, 10 & 20 April 1981; *IN*, 18 & 24 April, 9 May, 14 May, 18 July 1981; **423** 'Council', CS minutes, 11 May 1981; *IN*, 21 May 1981; **424** 'During the', McMahon; CS minutes, 6 July 1981; *IT*, 31 July 1971; Dowling, O'Hagan; *Newry Reporter*, 13 & 20 Aug. 1981; *IN*, 26 & 30 June 1981; **425** 'One Belfast', Belfast RCWP members; Woodworth, Yeates, McMahon, Garland; *An Phoblacht*, 21 March, 9 & 30 May, 8 Aug. 1981; D. O'Hearn, *Nothing*, pp. 30–1; **426** 'Sands', CS minutes, 6 Aug. 1981; AC minutes, August 1981; *IN*, 17 Aug. 1981; Moore notes, AP; 'During', *IN*, 22 July 1981; Jordan, Patterson; *Notes & Comments*, Aug. 1981; *IP*, 20 Nov. 1981; **427** 'The impact', *IT*, 16 March 1981; CS minutes, 26 Jan & 9 March 1981; *IT*, 7 March 1981; **428** 'Industrial', S. McDonagh, B. Whelan; OIRA vol.; B. Dowling, Byrne, Sweeney; *Workers' Life*, Sept. 1981; **429** 'RTÉ', Gregg, Cronin; J. Horgan, *Broadcasting*, p. 166; P. McGarry, *First Citizen*, pp. 84–92; *IT*, 19 Nov. 1981; Padraig Mannion, A. Berg; 'Did SFWP', *Magill*, June 2005; *IP*, 16 Sept. 1980, 20 March 1981; *IT*, 10 Dec. 1981; **431** 'Away', John O'Neill; *IT*, 22 Feb. 1982; Lucia O'Neill; *IP*, 30 Oct. 1981; B. Whelan, Mike Jennings; *IT*, 3 & 13 June 1981; SFWP membership forms, 1980–1; *Workers' Life*, July 1981; Gallagher; SFWP General Election report, 1981; *Notes & Comments*, Aug. & Sept. 1981; **432** 'Having', CS minutes, 16 June 1981; *IT*, 10 March 1982; *IT*, 30 June 1981; Yeates; *IP*, 24 July 1981; CS minutes, 27 July 1981; *IP*, 7 Aug. 1981; CS minutes, 21 Sept. 1981; *IP*, 4 Dec. 1981; **433** 'The coalition', *Notes & Comments*, Sept., Nov., Dec. 1981, Jan. 1982; **434** 'On 27 January', CS minutes, 28 Jan. 1982; *IT*, 4 & 13 Feb. 1982; *IP*, 5 & 12 March 1982; *IT*, 24 Feb. 1982; **435** 'The re-election', *IT*, 22 & 24 Feb. 1982; *IT*, 5–8 March 1982; J. Joyce & P. Murtagh, *The Boss*, p. 54; *IP*, 12 March 1982; Yeates; *IT*, 10–11 March 1982; *Workers' Life*, April 1982; *IP*, 12 March 1982; Mannion; **437** 'In the North', CS minutes, 18 & 22 March 1982; *Workers' Life*, April 1982; Flynn; *IT*, 10 Nov. 1982; CS minutes, 17 April 1982; Mac Giolla; *Workers' Life*, May 1982; **438** 'The only', CS minutes, 5 & 18 Jan. 1982; *Notes & Comments*, Jan. 1982, *Clár*, Ard Fheis, 1982; Jennings; *IP*, 14 May, 2 Oct., 4 Dec. 1981; E. Harris to Mac Giolla etc., May 1982, AP; **439** 'Despite', CS minutes, 13 & 17 April 1982, 12 June 1982; Woodworth; AC minutes, 29 May & 3 July 1982; **440** 'The Party's', *IT*, 9 March 1982; CS minutes, 13 April 1982; *Magill*, April & May 1982; *IT*, 22–23 April 1982; *Workers' Life*, May 1982; CS minutes, 28 April & 5 Aug. 1982; **441** 'In the', *Ir Pr*, 5 June 1982; R. Dunphy, 'The Contradictory', p. 137; Newry Group B members; *Newry Reporter*, 27 May 1982; Dublin Group B members; *Starry Plough*, July 1982; OIRA statement, 4 June 1982, AP; *Magill*, June 1982; **442** 'Garda', Garda source; *Ir Pr*, 7–8 June 1982; *IT*, 7 June 1982; *Magill*, June 1982; Belfast Group B members; Ed Moloney statement, 3 April 1992, AP; Dublin WP activists; **444** 'In June', Yeates; AC minutes, 29 May 1982; CS minutes, 18 March, 5 April & 6 July 1982; Heffernan; *IT*, 27 April 1982; E. Harris to SFWP,

May 1982, *AP*; *IT*, 22 April 1982; CS minutes, 13 April 1982; *IT*, 27 April 1982; WP report on TD's Dáil experience, AP, CS minutes, 18 April & 28 Sept. 1982; **445** 'Other party', CS minutes, 13 April 1981; H. McDonald, *Colours*, p. 82; 'Report on participation in FDJ Summer Work Camp July/Aug 1981', AP; *Workers; Life*, Aug., Oct. 1981, May 1982; *IP*, 15 Oct. 1981; **446** 'Another divisive', CS minutes, 17 April, 7 June, 17 July, 16 Aug. 1982; **447** 'Meanwhile', *IT*, 24 Feb. 1982; J. S. Bradshaw et al., 'Drug Misuse in Ireland' (Dublin, 1983); *Workers' Life*, Nov. 1981, Jan. 1982; Yeates; **448** 'De Rossa', CS minutes, 6 & 20 Sept., 18 Oct. 1982; *IT*, 24 April 1982; *Workers' Life*, Nov. 1982, Feb. 1983; 'In September', Heffernan; *Workers' Life*, Nov. 1982; Joyce & Murtagh, *The Boss*, p. 291; CS minutes, 11 & 18 Oct. 1982; *IP*, 5 Nov. 1982; *IT*, 4 Nov. 1982.

14. Fight Back!

Notes to pages 450 to 493
450 'In November', *IP*, 4 April 1986; WP election broadcast, Nov. 1982; CS minutes, 11 Dec. 1982; *IT*, 13 Nov. 1982; Gallagher; CS minutes, 2 & 11 Dec. 1982; **451** 'Fine Gael', CS minutes, 11 Dec. 1982; Heffernan; *IT*, 23 March 1982; *IP*, 15 April & 20 May 1983; CS Minutes, 6 Nov. 1982; **452** 'Despite', *Notes & Comments*, Dec. 1982; CS minutes, 2 & 11 Dec. 1982; *IN*, 22 May 1981; *Newry Reporter*, 22 July 1982; CS minutes, 18 Oct. 1982, 2 Dec. 1982; Breathnach; **453** 'Concerns', AC minutes, 9 Sept. 1984; CS minutes, 11 Dec. 1982; WP Organization Sub-Committee report, March 1983, AP; **455** 'Efforts', CS minutes, 11 April 1983; AC minutes, 7 June 1983; *IT*, 23 May 1983; CS minutes, 7 & 21 Feb. 1983; AC minutes, 7 May 1983; *IP*, 12 & 19 Aug. 1983; *Workers' Life*, March, June, Oct. 1983; Breathnach, Gallagher, Heffernan; *IP*, 16 Sept. 1983; **456** 'By-elections', *Workers' Life*, Jan. 1984; AC minutes, 26 Nov. 1983; reports, 30 Nov. 1983 in Fianna Fáil Archives P176/383 (18 & 67), UCDA; *IP*, 25 March 1983; Breathnach; **457** 'Rivalry', Cody, Mary Shelley; *Gralton*, Oct./Nov. 1983; *IP*, 19 Aug. 1981; *IT*, 4 March 1982; Geraghty, Dowling; **458** 'While the', *IT*, 12 & 14 April 1983; *IP*, 20 Feb. 1987; AC minutes, 24 Sept., 26 Nov. 1983; *IT*, 21 May 1983; Ken McCue, J. O'Neill; *Notes & Comments*, Dec. 1983; *IP*, 4 Nov. 1983; *Workers' Life*, April 1984; **460** 'The WP', *Dáil Debates*, 19 May 1983; *IN*, 23 May 1983; *IT*, 29 June 1983, 21 Jan. 1984; *Notes & Comments*, Dec. 1983; *IT*, 21 May 1983; *Workers' Life*, March 1983; *IT*, 29 Dec. 1983; **461** 'Despite', *Ireland*, spring 1983; *IP*, 16 Sept. 1983; *IT*, 10 Sept. 1983; E. O'Halpin, *Defending*, p. 322; *Gralton*, Oct./ Nov. 1983; *Workers' Life*, June 1983; S. Garland to Secretary, Central Committee CPSU, 20 Oct. 1983, AP; Garland; *Workers' Life*, Feb. & Aug. 1984; Woodworth; *Sunday Tribune*, 11 Nov. 1984; *Magill*, 15 Nov. 1984; **463** 'In February', *Notes & Comments*, Dec. 1983; *Class Politics*, autumn 1983; Conor McCabe, John Burns, S. Garland to M. Gordeev, 4 Feb. 1985, AP; *Workers' Life*, 1981–3; *Notes & Comments*, April 1984; **464** 'The need', Dave O'Grady; E. P. Rooney, 'From Opposition', p. 243; L. O'Neill, J. O'Neill; **465** 'In Leinster', Heffernan; EMC

minutes, 10 June 1984; CEC minutes, 28 Jan. & 9 Sept. 1984; **466** 'In the European',
CEC minutes, 23 June 1984; WP report on European elections, AP; *IP*, 27 May
1983; McCue; student report, July 1987; CEC minutes, 28 Jan. 1984; *IP*, 12 Oct.
1984; Jennings; **467** 'The growing tension', *IT*, 22 April 1984; EMC minutes,
21 Jan. & May 1985; **468** 'The WP', *Notes & Comments*, July 1985; *IP*, 8 March
1984, 10 April 1985; AGM report Cork SC, 27 April 1986; Catherine Murphy,
Feargus MacAogain, Stephen Lewis, Jordan; **469** 'The election', EMC minutes,
10 April 1985; CEC minutes, 1 Oct. 1985; **470** 'In most', CEC minutes, 7 Sept.
1985; *IP*, 20 July 1984; CEC minutes, 7 Sept. 1985; *Workers' Life*, Jan./Feb. 1985;
Jennings, J. O'Neill; WP 'Response to crime' (N/D); *IP*, 4 Nov. 1983, 1 Jan. 1985;
471 'In late', EMC minutes, 25 Nov. & 2 Dec. 1985; *IP* 3 & 10 Jan. 1986; *Making
Sense*, Nov. 1988; **472** 'So-called', *IP*, 22 Feb. 1985; *Bel Tel*, 16 Feb. 1983, *IP*, 3
Jan. 1986; Divorce Action Group to WP, 27 May 1995; *IT*, 26 July 1986; *Notes &
Comments*, May/June 1986; **473** 'The bifurcation', B. Whelan, Jennings, L. O'Neill,
Byrne, Shelley; CEC minutes, 30 March 1985; *Irish Independent*, 24 June 1987;
O'Grady, Murphy, MacAogain, Breathnach; **474** 'The most', *IT*, 19 Dec. 1985; *IP*,
20 Dec. 1985, *Today Tonight*, RTÉ, 5 March 1986; S. Lynch; *IT*, 5 March 1986; *Ir
Pr*, 14 April 1986; **475** 'An internal', 'Today Tonight of 5 March: Some Background
Notes' (1986), AP; 'Media Attacks on the Party' (1986), AP; *IP*, 18 April 1986;
Notes & Comments, June 1986; *IT*, 14 April & 12 Nov. 1986; Breathnach; **476** 'In
January 1987', *IP*, 3 Oct. 1986, 9, 23 & 30 Jan. 1987; Jennings; 'Text for Party
Political Broadcast' (1987), AP; *IP*, 2 Jan. 1987; C. A. Meade, 'Success and Transfor-
mation', pp. 24–7; **478** 'The left', WP 'Dáil election results', 27 Feb. 1987; *In
Dublin*, 5 March 1987; *IT*, 20 Feb. & 11 March 1987; *IP*, 20 March 1987; WP
election leaflet Dublin Central, 1987; **480** 'In a complete', *Irish Independent*, 1 April
1987; *IT*, 24 April 1987; *Liberty News*, summer 1987; *IP*, 12 June & 23 Oct. 1987,
18 March 1988; **481** 'Meanwhile', *IT*, 17 Oct. 1987; *IP*, 16 Oct. 1987; *IT*, 18–20
Nov. 1987; *Liberty News*, winter 1987; Geraghty; *Irish Socialist*, Nov. 1987; **482** 'The
WP', *IT*, 27 April 1987; *IP*, 6 Nov. 1987; Jennings, MacAogain; *IP*, 14 March
1986, 18 Sept. 1987; S. Garland to V. Minderov, 7 April 1987, AP; International
report to CEC meeting, 4–5 Dec. 1987, AP; **483** 'Relations', Garland to Secretary
International Dept CPSU, 7 Aug. 1986, AP; BBC World Service reports, 25 Sept.
1985 & 10 Sept. 1986; De Rossa; *IT*, 16 Dec. 1992; 'As violence', *IP*, 4 Sept. 1987;
T. Heffernan, 'Section 31', 14 Jan. 1988, AP; E. Harris, 'Television and Terrorism',
15 Nov. 1987; *Sunday Tribune*, 29 Nov. 1987; *IP*, 27 March 1987; *IT*, 21 Jan. 1987;
In Dublin Annual (1987); *In Dublin*, 7 Jan. 1988; *Magill*, June 2005; **486** 'Relations',
IT, 20 Nov. 1987; *Ir Pr*, 2 June 1988; J. O'Neill, McCue; *IP*, 23 Oct. 1987;
B. Whelan, McDonagh; **487** 'De Rossa', *IT*, 18 April 1988; E. Honecker to WP,
15 April 1988, AP; *IP*, 22 April 1988; *Making Sense*, summer 1988; *IP*, 29 April
1988; *Notes & Comments*, 1 Aug. 1988; *IP*, 13 May 1988; **488** 'The WP', *Making
Sense*, Nov. 1988; C. Murphy, MacAogain; *Notes & Comments*, 2 Dec. 1988; *Making
Sense*, Jan. 1989; **489** 'The discussions', J. O'Neill, McDonagh, Breathnach; International report to CEC meeting, 4–5 Dec. 1987, AP; *IP*, 1 & 15 July 1988; WKP
statement, 15 Nov. 1988, AP; BBC World Service report, 17 Sept. 1988; **490** 'In

January 1989', *IT*, 17 Dec. 1988, 13 March 1989; Sweeney, N. Dowling; *IP*, 14 April 1989; *IT*, 10 April 1989; **491** 'De Rossa's', Breathnach, J. O'Neill, Heffernan, De Rossa; *Making Sense*, May/June 1988; **492** 'The European', *IP*, 26 May 1989; *IT*, 2 & 9 June 1989; *Irish Independent*, 8 June 1989; *Cork Examiner*, 15 June 1989; *IT*, 17 June 1989; Financial report to WP CEC, 7 Sept. 1991, AP; *IT*, 13 July 1989; *IP*, 2 Jan. 1987; Lewis, F. Whelan, Breathnach, L. O'Neill; *Ir Pr*, 17 June 1989.

15. Workers Unite!

Notes for pages 494 to 518

494 'Northern', AC minutes, 29 May 1982; *Workers' Life*, Sept. 1980; *IN*, 4, 12, 13 & 14 Jan. 1982; *Northern People*, 5 March 1982; AC minutes, 28 Aug. 1982; **495** 'Overall', *Workers' Life*, Nov. 1982; John Cushnahan, McMahon; *IN*, 21 Oct. 1982; *Northern People*, 12 Nov. 1982; AC minutes, 16 Nov. 1982, 15 Jan. 1983, McMahon; *Fortnight*, Oct. 1983; *Ulster*, July/Aug. 1984; *Northern People*, 21 Jan. & 16 Sept. 1983; **496** 'In 1985', S. Lynch; I. S. Wood, *Crimes*, pp. 72–3, 91–2; *IN*, 17 Oct. 1986, 14 Feb. 1987; **497** 'The party', *Northern People*, 21 Jan. 1983, 25 May 1985; Feeney; *Northern People*, 6 May 1983; *IN*, 7 June 1983; AC minutes, 26 March 1983; *Workers' Life*, Oct. 1983; **498** 'violence', *IT*, 12 March 1983; *Northern People*, 15 April & 3 June 1983; *Belfast Newsletter*, 7 June 1983; *IN*, 4 June 1983; **499** 'Sinn Féin's', *IN*, 11 June 1983; McMahon; P. Bew & H. Patterson, *British State*, p. 146; 'The electoral', *Northern People*, 12 Aug. 1983, 29 June 1984; *Class Politics*, Aug. 1983; CEC minutes, 7 Sept. 1985; ITV, *World In Action*, 19 Dec. 1983; *IT*, 29 Dec. 1983; *Bel Tel*, 18 Jan. 1984; **501** 'Physical', *IN*, 14 June & 2 Nov. 1983; WP, *The Case* (1985); Smyth; **502** 'In 1984', CEC minutes, 10 March 1984; *IN*, 2 May 1985; EMC minutes, 4 March 1985; Smyth, S. Lynch; **503** 'Unionists', EMC minutes, 24 June, 29 July & 6 Aug. 1985; *Northern People*, 9 Aug. 1985; *Fortnight*, Oct. 1985; **504** 'In 1982', 'The British Labour Party and Ireland: a Strategy for Progress' (1982), AP; *Workers' Life*, Aug. & Dec. 1983; *Fortnight*, Feb. 1984; *Workers' Life*, Dec. 1983; Collins; *Andersonstown News*, 14 Nov. 1987; **505** 'By the', *IN*, 6 Dec. 1985; *Bel Tel*, 10 Jan. 1984; *IT*, 1 & 27 Jan. 1984; P. K. Clare, *Racketeering*, pp. 18–19; Smyth, McMahon; *Bel Tel*, 12 March 1985; **506** 'The WP's', *IN*, 8 & 20 May, 15 Aug. 1985; *Sunday News*, 19 May 1985; *An Phoblacht*, 25 July 1985; EMC minutes, 2 Sept. 1985; former OIRA prisoner; *Andersonstown News*, 10 Oct. 1987; *IN*, 9 Nov. 1987; McMahon; **507** 'The party', *Ir Pr*, 19 April 1985; *Fortnight*, Jan., Feb., March 1983; *Bel Tel*, 22 March 1984; former OIRA prisoner; P. J. Kelly; E. P. Rooney, 'From Opposition'; *Fortnight*, 2 June 1986; **508** 'Negotiations', *IT*, 15–20 Nov. 1985; EMC minutes, 18 & 25 Nov. 1985; *Dáil Debates*, 19 Nov. 1985; EMC minutes, 28 Jan. 1986; *IN*, 21 Aug. 1986; **509** 'As Unionist', *IT*, 14 & 16 April 1986; *Bel Tel*, 6 June 1986; **510** 'In November', Sinn Féin, *Politics of Revolution* (1986); *Irish Independent*, 29 Jan. 1986; J. O'Neill; Belfast WP members; 'The sympathy', C. Skillen, 'Pravda's Provos': O'Hagan: EMC minutes, 16 & 23 Sept. 1985; *IT*, 9 Nov. 1987; *IP*, 16 Oct. 1987; *IP*, 4 Sept. 1987; **512** 'Working class',

Women's View, Dec. 1987; *IN*, 3–4 June 1987; McMahon, K. Smyth, M. Smyth; 'Despite the', *Fortnight*, 1983–7; *Northern People*, 20 Dec. 1985; *Sunday World*, 20 May 1984; *Notes & Comments*, May/June 1986; **513** 'As rumours', *IN*, 4 June 1987; *Bel Tel*, 25 June 1987; *IT*, 29 June 1987; **514** 'In early 1988', *Ir Pr*, 4 April 1988; *IT*, 18 April 1988; *IP*, 22 April 1988; *IT*, 18 April 1988; McMahon; Belfast WP members; **515** 'In August', *Making Sense*, Jan. 1989; *IP*, 5 Aug. & 14 Oct. 1988; McClean; 'The Enniskillen', *IP*, 3 Feb. & 21 April 1989, 17 Feb., 17 March, 7 April 1989, 19 Jan. 1990; **516** 'In March', *IT*, 10 April 1989; *Bel Tel*, 21 Jan. 1989; *IT*, 12 April 1989; *IN*, 12 Sept. 1988; *IP*, 26 May 1989; *Making Sense*, Aug. 1989; **517** 'August 1989', *IP*, 3 Nov. 1989; UTV, *Sullivan's Story*, 28 Sept. 1989; Lowry, O'Hagan.

16. Special Activities

Notes for pages 519 to 545

519 'By the time', WP to CPSU, 15 Sept. 1986 in Archives of the Soviet Communist Party, Stanford University Fond 89. Op. 13. D. 11 (courtesy Geoff Roberts); *IT*, 26–7 Oct. 1992; RTÉ, *Today Tonight*, 5 March 1986; Group B member; **520** 'Local Gardaí', Garda source; *Sunday Tribune*, 24 Aug. 1997; *Village*, 22–8 Jan. 2005; F. Cronin; 'The US', Garda source; *IT*, 10 Sept. 1983, 24 Nov. 1986; Dublin WP member; **521** 'Flynn's killing', Dublin Group B members; *IT*, 29 & 30 June, 2 July 1983; **522** 'Some', *IT*, 18 Feb. 1983; Dublin WP members; **523** 'The Group', *Magill*, 18 April 1985; *IT*, 21 Jan. 1984, 1 March 1997; Belfast Group B members; **524** 'The movement's', Belfast Group B members; *Starry Plough*, Jan. 1982; *IN*, 18 & 28 Jan. 1982; *Sunday News*, 22 Jan. 1984; *IT*, 2–4 Feb. 1983, 12 March 1983; *IN*, 15 March 1983; **525** 'The OIRA', *Fortnight*, Sept. 1983; *IN*, Dec. 1984; Belfast Group B members; **526** 'The building', K. Sheehy (email, 1 Jan. 2009); *IT*, 27 Jan. 1984; BBC, *Watchdog*, 1 March 1984; **527** 'The success', *IT*, 27 Jan. 1984; Belfast Group B members; *Irish Independent*, 20 Aug. 1987; *Bel Tel*, 31 Jan. 1984; *IT*, 1 Feb. 1984; Armagh Group B members; *Newry Reporter*, 17 Nov. 1983, 28 June 1984; **528** 'In August', *IT*, 6 Aug. & 5 Oct. 1984; Dublin Group B members; *IT*, 11 & 13 June 1986; WP document (1987), AP; *IT*, 26–30 Jan. 1988, 17 May 1993; **530** 'During the', *IN*, 8 & 20 May 1985; *Irish Independent*, 20 Aug. 1987; *IN*, 15 Aug. 1985; Cronin; **531** 'The Today Tonight', 'The Workers' Party', AP; Cronin; Dublin WP members; RTÉ, *Today Tonight*, 5 March 1986; *IN*, 5 Dec. 1985; *Sunday Tribune*, 4 Jan. 1987; **532** 'That a public', Belfast Group B members; Armagh Group B members; **533** 'The party's', *IT*, 13 Nov. 1986, 16 Dec. 1992; Garland to Secretary International Dept, CPSU, 1 July 1986, 23 Oct. 1986, 19 March 1987, AP; Garland to Secretary, International Dept, CPSU, 7 Aug. 1986, AP; Garland; **534** 'A long letter', WP to CPSU, 15 Sept. 1986 in Archives of the Soviet Communist Party, Stanford University Fond 89. Op. 13. D. 11; Garland; *IT*, 14 Nov. 1996, 6 March 1997; **535** 'In February', V. Zagladin, 16 Feb. 1987 in Archives of the Soviet Communist Party Fond 89, Op. 13, D. 11; *Independent*, 25 Oct. 1992; WP financial report, Sept. 1991, AP; *IT*, 17 July 1997; *Sunday Business Post*, 1 Nov. 1992; Group B members; **536** 'Group B', *IT*, 30 May 1986; *Sunday Tribune*, 4 Jan. 1987; Belfast Group B members; *Sunday Tribune*, 23 Aug. 1987; *Phoenix*, 28 Aug. 1987; K. Sheehy, *More Questions*, pp. 88–9; **538** 'It was becoming', Belfast Group B members; Belfast WP members; **539** 'The growing', *IT*, 29 June 1987; *Sunday Tribune*, 28 June 1987; *IT*, 4 Jan. 1988; Belfast Group B members; **540** 'In late', Belfast and Dublin Group B members; Garda source; **542** 'While', V. Kruchkov, 21 Dec. 1988 and K. Brutents 6 Jan. 1989 in Archives of the Soviet Communist Party Fond 89, Op. 13, D. 34; C. Andrew & O. Gordievsky, *KGB*, p. 665; *Sunday Tribune*, 29 Dec. 1991; **543** 'Although', BBC 1, *Spotlight*, 20 Feb 1992; *IN*, 9 Nov. 1987; *IT*, 4 June 1989; *IN*, 24 Feb. 1992; PIRA intelligence document 'Workers Party Structures' (1990); **544** 'While there', Dublin WP members; Breathnach; Belfast Group B member.

17. The Flight from Socialism

Notes for pages 546 to 587

546 'On the night', *IP*, 17 Nov. 1989; **547** 'The WP's', *IT*, 28 June, 4, 10 & 19 July 1989; *IP*, 3 Nov. 1989; C. Murphy; **548** 'The party', McCue, Michael Nugent, Anne Holliday; *Notes & Comments*, 2 Aug. 1989; *IT*, 25 July 1989; R. Dunphy, 'The Workers' Party': Breathnach; *Sunday Business Post*, 15 July 1990; McMahon; **549** 'Harris', Harris, *The Necessity of Social Democracy* (1990); Lowry, Breathnach, McMahon; **550** 'Harris now', F. Whelan; *Magill*, April 1990; Breathnach, J. O'Neill, Donohue; 'The party', *Making Sense*, March/April 1990; Breathnach, 'The Story of the Struggle' (1990), AP; *Notes & Comments*, Feb./March 1990; **551** 'In the run', De Rossa, Breathnach; *Magill*, April 1990; **552** 'The first', *IT*, 8 March 1990; *Sunday Business Post*, 30 Sept. 1990; **553** 'The internal', *IP*, 16 March 1990; *Sunday Tribune*, 11 & 18 March, 4 April 1990; *IT*, 12 & 16 March 1990; *News & Views*, July 1990; *IT*, 24 April 1990; **554** 'The following', *IT*, 30 April 1990; R. Dunphy & S. Hopkins, 'The Organizational and Political Evolution of the Workers' Party'; *Irish Independent*, 30 April 1990; F. Whelan, Byrne; *IP*, 4 May 1990; **557** 'The parliamentary', *IT*, 1, 3, 4 & 5 May, 12 July 1990; Heffernan, Yeates; *Notes & Views*, July 1990; **558** 'Some WP', Byrne; *IT*, 2 & 24 May 1990; *News & Views*, July 1990; *IT*, 27 July 1990; J. O'Neill, Lewis, Breathnach, B. Whelan; **559** 'With Robinson', *IT*, 16 Oct. 1990; MacAogain; *IP*, June 1990; *IT*, 29 June 1990; **560** 'As Robinson's', *IT*, 17 July 1990; *Making Sense*, July/Aug. 1990; *IT*, 6 & 8 Oct. 1990, 1 Nov. 1990; *IT*, 17 Dec. 1990; MacAogain; *IT*, 16 Oct. 1990; **561** 'In the campaign's', *IT*, 2, 3, 10 & 25 Nov., 5, 6 & 12 Dec. 1990; *Making Sense*, March/April 1991; **563** 'As the WP's', *IT*, 3 Jan. 1991; S. Lynch, Byrne; *IT*, 23 Feb. 1990; *Parliamentary Debates*, 11 Dec. 1990; *IN*, 28 June 1991; 'Group B's', Financial report to WP AC/CEC, 7 Nov. 1991, AP; Dublin WP members; Belfast Group B members; L. O'Neill; **564** 'Internal', Breathnach, 'Document for WP International Committee' (1990); Seamus Martin, Shelley; *IT*, 8, 10, 15, 19 & 26 Jan., 4 Feb., 16 March 1991; **565** 'There were', *Making Sense*, March/April 1991; *IN*, 1 April 1991; BBC 1,

Spotlight, 27 June 1991; **566** 'A penetrating', *Making Sense*, Jan/Feb. 1991; WP 'Draft Brief to Designers', 17 & 19 Jan. 1991, AP; 'Such thinking', *IT*, 21 March, 3 May 1991; Lowry; **567** 'The first', *IT*, 4 & 6 May 1991; *Tomorrow's People*, 27 May 1991; *Irish Independent*, 6 May 1991; **568** 'Despite', *IP*, Feb. 1991; *IT*, 21 Feb. 1991; *Bertie's Bill* (1991); *IT*, 20 Oct. 1990, 24 Aug. 1991; WP Youth report to EMC, 13 Aug. 1990; *Notes & Comments*, Feb/March 1990; *Tomorrow's People*, 27 May 1991; Lewis; *IT*, 3 June 1991; **569** 'The party's', *IT*, 17 May 1991; *Tomorrow's People*, 1 May & 24 June 1991; *IT*, 4 June 1991; *IN*, 4 & 7 June 1991; MacAogain; AC/CEC minutes, 8 June 1991; P. Larkin, *A Very British*, pp. 77–89; *IT*, 25 June 1991; **570** 'Half an hour', BBC 1, *Spotlight*, 27 June 1991; *IT*, 29 June 1991; *Focus*, summer 1991; **571** 'Things got', Heffernan; *IT*, 1 July 1991; *Focus*, summer 1991; *IT*, 9 July 1991, 'Analysis of Post-Election Questionnaire for WP Candidates and Directors of Elections' (Sept. 1991), AP; L. O'Neill, Lynch; **572** 'For De Rossa', De Rossa; EMC reports for AC/CEC meeting of 7 Sept. 1991, AP; **573** 'The following', AC minutes, 13–14 Sept. 1991, AP; **574** 'The establishment', IT, 16 July & 5 Aug. 1991; *Parliamentary Debates*, 19 July 1991; *IT*, 1 & 14 Aug. 1991; *Tomorrow's People*, 23 Aug. & 9 Sept. 1991; **575** 'The autumn', *IT*, 4 & 7 Sept. 1991; Heffernan; *IT*, 13 Sept, 5, 14 & 15 Oct. 1991; *Tomorrow's People*, 2 Nov. 1991; *Dáil Debates*, 17 Oct. 1991; *IT*, 19 Oct. 1991; **577** 'The confidence', *IT*, 18 & 28 Oct., 29 & 31 Dec. 1991; *Tomorrow's People*, Dec. 1991; AC minutes, 23 Nov. 1991; **578** 'Meanwhile', De Rossa, Heffernan, Breathnach, McMahon, Smyth, Patterson, O'Hare, Byrne; *IT*, 16 & 30 Dec. 1991; EPC minutes, 16 Dec. 1991; *IT*, 4 Jan. 1992; **579** 'During the', *IT*, 4 Jan. 1992; Heffernan; **580** 'The public', L. O'Neill; *IT*, 9 Jan. 1992; Jennings, McMahon, Joe Quinn; 'Notes on AC meeting 11 Jan. 1992' (Colm Breathnach), AP; Jennings press release, 24 Jan. 1992, AP; *IT*, 13 Jan. 1992; Heffernan, B. Whelan; **582** 'Charles Haughey', *IT*, 27 Jan. 1992; *Tomorrow's People*, Feb. 1991; Reports of meetings Belfast Region WP, 3 Jan. 1992 & Cork/Limerick 1 Dec. 1991, AP; **583** 'Both wings', *Sunday Tribune*, 2 Feb. 1992; Breathnach, B. Whelan, Garland, Lowry, Quinn, De Rossa, Smyth, Lynch; *IT*, 2 Feb. 1992; **584** 'The stage', *IT*, 14 & 17 Feb. 1992; *Sunday Press*, 16 Feb. 1992; *Sunday Tribune*, 16 Feb. 1992; *Irish Independent*, 17 Feb. 1992; *Ir Pr*, 18 Feb. 1992; J. Burns, B. Whelan, Breathnach, L. O'Neill, McMahon, O'Hare, G. Lynch; Workers' Party, *Patterns of Betrayal*; *IT*, 24 Feb. 1992; *Irish Independent*, 24 Feb. 1992.

Epilogue

Notes for pages 588 to 601
588 'After', L. O'Neill, S. Lynch; Mac Giolla letter, 27 Feb. 1992, AP; *IT*, 30 Feb. 1992; 'In late', McMahon; WP *Update*, March/April 1992; **589** 'Both', *IT*, 12 Nov. 1992; R. Dunphy, 'A Group of Individuals'; M. Holmes, 'The Establishment of Democratic Left'; **590** 'Further', *Independent*, 25 Oct. 1992; *IT*, 26–27 Oct., 7 Dec. 1992; *Sunday Independent*, 13 Dec. 1992; **591** 'In July', *IT*, 6 July 1993; *IP*, Sept. 1993; *IT*, 12 Nov. 1994; Dunphy, Breathnach, Murphy; **592** 'De Rossa',

A. J. Davidson, *Defamed*, pp. 61–91; *IT*, 17 July, 6, 13, 14 & 20 Nov. 1996; *Sunday Independent*, 17 Nov. 1996; *IT*, 6–15 March, 1–31 July 1997; *Sunday Tribune*, 24 Aug. 1997; *IT*, 17 June 2005; **594** 'The peace', *IT*, 10 Feb. 1997; WP dissident document (1996), AP; ORM members; *Newry Reporter*, 10 July & 28 Aug. 1997; *IN*, 10 & 16 July, 7 Aug. 1997; *IT*, 17 July 1997; *Sunday Tribune*, 24 Aug. 1997 & 4 Jan. 1998; **595** 'In late 1998', *IT*, 14 Dec. 1998; S. Millar; McMahon; *Sunday Business Post*, 13 Dec. 1998; R. English, *Armed*, p. 315; *IT*, 25 Dec. 1998, 2 Jan. 1999; **598** 'The reluctance', Cian O'Callaghan; NCC, *Tirghra*; *The Blanket*, 29 Oct. 2002; **599** 'Sinn Féin's', McManus; Belfast OIRA; *Making Sense*, Jan./Feb. 1991; Malone; **600** 'On 30 January', *IT*, 31 Jan. & 19 Feb. 2009; WP press release, 26 March 2009.

Index